# MEDITERRANEAN DIET COOKBOOK FOR BEGINNERS

THE EASIEST WAY TO SUCCESSFULLY START A HEALTHY AND CAREFREE LIFESTYLE.

**1001+** FLAVORFUL, CREATIVE AND AFFORDABLE RECIPES THAT YOU CAN INSTANTLY REPLICATE

Kendall Anderson

# Table of Contents

## APPETIZERS AND SNACK .............. 13

1. Marinate Anchovies .............. 13
2. Baked Apples .............. 13
3. Beetroot Chips .............. 14
4. Bell Pepper Muffins .............. 14
5. Hot Pepper Dip with Cheese .............. 14
6. Artichoke Dip with Mozzarella .............. 14
7. Phyllo Bites with Cheddar .............. 15
8. Chili Chicken Wings .............. 15
9. Chunky Nuts Mix .............. 15
10. Artichoke Dip .............. 15
11. Eggplant Dip .............. 16
12. Potato Spread .............. 16
13. Cucumber Chunks with Avocado .............. 16
14. Cucumber Tomato Okra Salsa .............. 16
15. Date and Fig Smoothie .............. 17
16. Eggplant Caponata .............. 17
17. Mediterranean Nachos .............. 17
18. Eggplant Bites .............. 18
19. Endive Bites .............. 18
20. Fig-Pecan Bites .............. 18
21. Roasted Baby Potatoes .............. 18
22. Frozen Blueberry Yogurt .............. 19
23. Garlic Bean Dip .............. 19
24. Greek Style Nachos .............. 19
25. Grilled Tempeh Sticks .............. 19
26. Homemade Salsa .............. 20
27. Italian Style Potato Fries .............. 20
28. Jalapeno Chickpea Hummus .............. 20
29. Kale Wraps with Apple and Chicken .............. 21
30. Layered Dip .............. 21
31. Lemon Cauliflower Florets .............. 21
32. Light Garlic Hummus .............. 21
33. Potatoes with Parmesan .............. 22
34. Parsley Cheese Balls .............. 22
35. Peanut Butter Yogurt Dip .............. 22
36. Italian Potatoes .............. 22
37. Radish Bread Bites .............. 23
38. Rice Burgers .............. 23
39. Roasted Chickpeas .............. 23
40. Salty Almonds .............. 24
41. Strawberry Popsicle .............. 24
42. Sweet Potato Fries .............. 24
43. Tomato Finger Sandwich .............. 24
44. Traditional Mediterranean Hummus .............. 25
45. Tuna Salad in Lettuce Cups .............. 25
46. Tzatziki .............. 25
47. Wheat Berry Burgers .............. 25
48. Whole-Grain Lavash Chips .............. 26
49. Zucchini Chips .............. 26
50. Walnut and Freekeh Pilaf .............. 26
51. Italian Roasted Vegetables .............. 27
52. Mediterranean Crostini .............. 27
53. Bruschetta Hummus Platter .............. 27
54. Garlic-Lemon Hummus .............. 28
55. Mediterranean Trail Mix .............. 28
56. Savory Mediterranean Popcorn .............. 28
57. Turkish-Spiced Nuts .............. 28
58. Lemony Orzo .............. 29
59. Puff Pastry Roll with Roasted Vegetables .............. 29
60. Turmeric Crunchy Chickpeas .............. 29
61. Crispy Garlic Oven Potatoes .............. 30
62. Hummus .............. 30
63. Eggplant Caviar .............. 30
64. Walnut and Red Pepper Spread .............. 31
65. Green Olive Tapenade .............. 31
66. Skordalia .............. 31
67. Mint Labneh .............. 32
68. Marinated Olives .............. 32
69. Pickled Turnips .............. 32
70. Stuffed Celery .............. 32
71. Butternut Squash Fries .............. 33
72. Dried Fig Tapenade .............. 33
73. Sweet Potato Chips .............. 33
74. Mediterranean Nachos with Hummus .............. 33
75. Hummus and Olive Pita Bread .............. 34
76. Roast Asparagus .............. 34
77. Zaatar Fries .............. 34
78. Vegetable Chicken Wraps .............. 34
79. Roasted Baby Potatoes (2nd Version) .............. 35
80. Fig with Yogurt and Honey .............. 35
81. Greek Shrimp Saganaki .............. 35
82. Greek Fava .............. 35
83. Hummus, Feta & Bell Pepper Crackers .............. 36
84. Tomato & Basil Bruschetta .............. 36
85. Lemon-Pepper Cucumbers .............. 36
86. Falafel .............. 36
87. Walnut-Feta Yogurt Dip .............. 37
88. Date Wraps .............. 37
89. Clementine & Pistachio Ricotta .............. 37
90. Serrano-Wrapped Plums .............. 37
91. Greek Salad Wraps .............. 38
92. Dill Salmon Salad Wraps .............. 38
93. Chicken Parmesan Wraps .............. 38
94. Quinoa & Dried Apricots and Figs .............. 39
95. Classic Apple Oats .............. 39
96. Salted Anchovies .............. 39
97. Arancini with Ricotta .............. 40
98. Tuna Bottarga .............. 40
99. Seasoned Olives .............. 40
100. Potato Arancini .............. 40
101. Breaded Prickly Pears' Peels Cutlets .............. 41
102. Sword Fish Carpaccio .............. 41
103. Tuna Carpaccio .............. 41
104. Fried Ricotta .............. 42
105. Palermitana style Potato Croquettes .............. 42
106. Sicilian Style Mussels Au Gratin .............. 42
107. Cauliflower Croquettes .............. 42
108. Borage Fritters .............. 43
109. Fried Pumpkin Flowers .............. 43
110. Marinated Shrimp .............. 43
111. Fried Milk .............. 43
112. Battered Sea Anemones .............. 44
113. Ricotta Croquettes .............. 44
114. Olives with wild Fennel .............. 44
115. Fried Black Olives .............. 44
116. Green Olives with Garlic and Parsley .............. 45
117. Panelle .............. 45
118. Meat Dumplings .............. 45
119. Anchovy Dumplings .............. 45
120. Bell Pepper Roast .............. 46
121. Roasted Tomatoes .............. 46
122. Stuffed Dried Tomatoes .............. 46

| # | Item | Page |
|---|---|---|
| 123. | Sea Urchins | 46 |
| 124. | Fritters with Ham and Cheese | 47 |
| 125. | Fried Skewers | 47 |
| 126. | Vegetable Timbale | 47 |
| 127. | Beet and Ricotta Pie | 48 |
| 128. | Friselle | 48 |
| 129. | Marinated Eels | 48 |
| 130. | Chickpea Flat Bread | 49 |
| 131. | Sea Salad (2nd Version) | 49 |
| 132. | Zucchini Pie | 49 |
| 133. | Artichoke Tart | 49 |
| 134. | Eggplant Pie | 50 |
| 135. | Lettuce Fritters | 50 |
| 136. | Stuffed Tomatoes | 50 |
| 137. | Sweet-and-sour Crunchy Bites | 51 |
| 138. | Eggplant Rolls | 51 |
| 139. | Chicken Salad | 51 |
| 140. | Mortadella Mousse | 51 |
| 141. | Chicken Breast in Balsamic Vinegar | 52 |
| 142. | Stuffed Anchovies | 52 |
| 143. | Anchovies Au Gratin | 52 |
| 144. | Bruschetta with Sausage | 52 |
| 145. | Saffron Mussels | 53 |
| 146. | Au Gratin Mussels | 53 |
| 147. | Fried Veggie Starter | 53 |
| 148. | Sour Whitebait | 53 |
| 149. | Cappon Magro | 54 |
| 150. | Chickpea Fritters | 54 |
| 151. | Whitebait Flat Bread | 55 |
| 152. | Onion Focaccia | 55 |
| 153. | Focaccia with Sage | 55 |
| 154. | Rice Grenadine | 55 |
| 155. | Fish Stuffed Grenadine | 56 |
| 156. | Fried Paniccia | 56 |
| 157. | Paniccia | 56 |
| 158. | Pizza Genovese | 56 |
| 159. | Tomato Appetizer | 57 |
| 160. | Asparagus Pie | 57 |
| 161. | Beet Pie | 57 |
| 162. | Artichoke Pie | 58 |
| 163. | Thistle Pie | 58 |
| 164. | Onion Pie | 58 |
| 165. | Spelt Pie | 59 |
| 166. | Mushroom Pie | 59 |
| 167. | Pumpkin Pie | 59 |
| 168. | Scamorza Crunchy Bites | 60 |
| 169. | Hot Asparagus | 60 |
| 170. | Fried Pumpkin Flowers (2nd Version) | 60 |
| 171. | Sea Appetizer | 60 |
| 172. | Tuna Starter | 61 |
| 173. | Chicken Pastry Rolls | 61 |
| 174. | Au Gratin Scallops | 61 |
| 175. | Seasoned Bresaola | 61 |
| 176. | Veggie Fritters | 62 |
| 177. | Porcini Mushroom Mixed Starter | 62 |
| 178. | Black Olives with Orange | 62 |
| 179. | Anchovy and Zucchini Fritters | 62 |
| 180. | Zucchini and Eggplant Fritters | 63 |
| 181. | Tomatoes and Anchovy Fritters | 63 |
| 182. | Tuna Roll | 63 |
| 183. | Potato and Bacon Rolls | 63 |
| 184. | Chicken Rolls | 64 |
| 185. | Ham in Balsamic Vinegar | 64 |
| 186. | 5-Minute Tomato & Cucumber Toast | 64 |
| 187. | Avocado and Chickpea Sandwiches | 65 |
| 188. | Olive Paste and Avocado on Rye Bread | 65 |
| 189. | Cottage Cheese and Berries Omelet | 65 |
| 190. | Egg White Scramble with Cherry Tomatoes & Spinach | 65 |
| 191. | Feta - Avocado & Mashed Chickpea Toast | 66 |
| 192. | Feta & Quinoa Egg Muffins | 66 |
| 193. | Feta Cheese Baked in Foil | 66 |
| 194. | Feta Frittata | 67 |
| 195. | Chili Oregano Baked Cheese | 67 |
| 196. | Greek Style Quesadillas | 67 |
| 197. | Mediterranean Burrito | 67 |
| 198. | Egg Bake | 68 |
| 199. | Pumpkin Pie Parfait | 68 |
| 200. | Mediterranean Eggs | 68 |
| 201. | Baked Eggs in Avocado | 69 |
| 202. | Quinoa Buffalo Bites | 69 |
| 203. | Asparagus Frittata | 69 |
| 204. | Bacon and Lemon spiced Muffins | 69 |
| 205. | Cannellini Bean Lettuce Wraps | 70 |

BREADS, PIZZAS AND FOCACCIAS .......................... 71

| # | Item | Page |
|---|---|---|
| 206. | Focaccia Dough | 71 |
| 207. | Cauliflower Focaccia | 71 |
| 208. | Rolled Focaccia with Sausage and Ricotta | 72 |
| 209. | Small Focaccias with Anchovies | 72 |
| 210. | Broccoli Focaccia | 72 |
| 211. | Bread Balls | 73 |
| 212. | Tomato and Eggplant Focaccia | 73 |
| 213. | Panzanella | 73 |
| 214. | Rustic Pizza with Mozzarella | 73 |
| 215. | Bread with Walnuts | 74 |
| 216. | Bread with Potatoes | 74 |
| 217. | Pizza with Cheese | 74 |
| 218. | Red Hot Pepper Bruschetta | 74 |
| 219. | Corn Focaccia | 75 |
| 220. | Focaccia with Tuna and Black Olives | 75 |
| 221. | Rolled Pizza with Potatoes | 75 |
| 222. | Focaccia with Broccoli and Sausage | 75 |
| 223. | Focaccia with Onion, Tomatoes and Olives | 76 |
| 224. | Calzone with Ham and Cheese | 76 |
| 225. | Small Pizzas with Onion and Anchovy | 76 |
| 226. | Bread with Scamorza, Capers and Anchovies | 76 |
| 227. | Hot Focaccia with Fennel Seeds | 77 |
| 228. | Mushroom Pie (2nd Version) | 77 |
| 229. | Cheese Pie | 77 |
| 230. | Potato Pie | 78 |
| 231. | Olives and Mozzarella Pie | 78 |
| 232. | Chickpea Focaccia | 78 |
| 233. | Focaccia with Anchovies; Black Olives and Cheese | 78 |
| 234. | Pie with Liver and Onions | 79 |
| 235. | Focaccia with Olives and Oregano | 79 |
| 236. | Focaccia with Potatoes and Onion | 79 |
| 237. | Focaccia with Tomatoes, Peppers and Anchovies | 79 |
| 238. | Focaccia with Tuna and Peppers | 80 |
| 239. | 5 Minute Pizza | 80 |
| 240. | Family Pizza | 80 |
| 241. | Fig and Prosciutto Pita Bread Pizza | 81 |

BREAKFAST .......................... 82

| # | Recipe | Page |
|---|---|---|
| 242. | Eggs with Zucchini Noodles | 82 |
| 243. | Banana Oats | 82 |
| 244. | Slow-cooked Peppers Frittata | 83 |
| 245. | Avocado and Apple Smoothie | 83 |
| 246. | Avocado Toast | 83 |
| 247. | Mini Frittatas | 83 |
| 248. | Avocado Muffins | 84 |
| 249. | Berry Oats | 84 |
| 250. | Tomatoes Oatmeal | 84 |
| 251. | Quinoa Muffins | 84 |
| 252. | Quinoa and Eggs Pan | 85 |
| 253. | Stuffed Tomatoes (2nd Version) | 85 |
| 254. | Scrambled Eggs | 85 |
| 255. | Watermelon "Pizza" | 85 |
| 256. | Ham Muffins | 86 |
| 257. | Avocado Chickpea Pizza | 86 |
| 258. | Banana and Quinoa Casserole | 86 |
| 259. | Spiced Chickpeas Bowls | 86 |
| 260. | Avocado Spread | 87 |
| 261. | Cheesy Yogurt | 87 |
| 262. | Baked Omelet Mix | 87 |
| 263. | Stuffed Sweet Potato | 87 |
| 264. | Cauliflower Fritters | 88 |
| 265. | Tuna Salad | 88 |
| 266. | Veggie Quiche | 88 |
| 267. | Potato Hash | 89 |
| 268. | Leeks and Eggs Muffins | 89 |
| 269. | Artichokes and Cheese Omelet | 89 |
| 270. | Quinoa and Eggs Salad | 89 |
| 271. | Garbanzo Bean Salad | 90 |
| 272. | Hearty Pear and Mango Smoothie | 90 |
| 273. | Eggplant Salad | 90 |
| 274. | Artichoke Frittata | 90 |
| 275. | Eggs in a Squash | 91 |
| 276. | Barley Porridge | 91 |
| 277. | Cool Tomato and Dill Frittata | 91 |
| 278. | Strawberry and Rhubarb Smoothie | 92 |
| 279. | Bacon and Brie Omelet Wedges | 92 |
| 280. | Couscous Salad | 92 |
| 281. | Coconut Porridge | 93 |
| 282. | Crumbled Feta and Scallions | 93 |
| 283. | Quinoa Chicken Salad | 93 |
| 284. | Cheesy Olives Bread | 94 |
| 285. | Cheesy Yogurt | 94 |
| 286. | Corn and Shrimp Salad | 94 |
| 287. | Berry Oats (2nd version) | 94 |
| 288. | Blueberries Quinoa | 95 |
| 289. | Blueberry, Hazelnut, and Lemon Grain Salad | 95 |
| 290. | Brown Rice Salad | 95 |
| 291. | Endives, Fennel and Orange Salad | 95 |
| 292. | Greek Yogurt with Walnuts and Honey | 96 |
| 293. | Homemade Muesli | 96 |
| 294. | Hummus and Tomato Breakfast Pittas | 96 |
| 295. | Raisin Quinoa Breakfast | 97 |
| 296. | Raspberries and Yogurt Smoothie | 97 |
| 297. | Stuffed Pita Breads | 97 |
| 298. | Sun-dried Tomatoes Oatmeal | 97 |
| 299. | Sweet Potato Tart | 97 |
| 300. | Tahini Pine Nuts Toast | 98 |
| 301. | Tangerine and Pomegranate Fruit Salad | 98 |
| 302. | Walnuts Yogurt Mix | 99 |
| 303. | Fruit Bulgur Breakfast Bowls | 99 |
| 304. | Ricotta Toast with Strawberries | 99 |
| 305. | Cauliflower Breakfast Porridge | 99 |
| 306. | Spinach and Egg Breakfast Wraps | 100 |
| 307. | Oats with Raspberries | 100 |
| 308. | Scramble Eggs with Tomatoes | 100 |

## PASTA, RICE AND SOUPS ........................................ 101

| # | Recipe | Page |
|---|---|---|
| 309. | Truffle Cannelloni | 101 |
| 310. | Boscaiola Style Spelt | 101 |
| 311. | Ricotta Gnocchi | 102 |
| 312. | Spaghetti allo Scoglio | 102 |
| 313. | Penne with Ricotta and Cherry Tomatoes | 102 |
| 314. | Tagliatelle with Boar | 102 |
| 315. | Broth Passatelli | 103 |
| 316. | Pasta with Pumpkin | 103 |
| 317. | Pasta with Peas | 103 |
| 318. | Pasta with Chickpeas | 104 |
| 319. | Rigatoni with Peppers | 104 |
| 320. | Rice and Bean Soup | 104 |
| 321. | Risotto with Zucchini and Squid | 104 |
| 322. | Green Risotto with Porcini Mushrooms | 105 |
| 323. | Spaghetti with Squid Ink | 105 |
| 324. | Spaghetti with Tuna Sauce | 105 |
| 325. | Spaghetti with Walnuts and Asparagus | 105 |
| 326. | Cold Spaghetti | 106 |
| 327. | Spaghetti with Squid and Mushrooms | 106 |
| 328. | Stracciatella | 106 |
| 329. | Mushroom Tagliatelle | 106 |
| 330. | Spaghetti with Clams | 107 |
| 331. | Vermicelli with Clams | 107 |
| 332. | Meat Tortelloni with Parmesan and Truffle Sauce | 107 |
| 333. | Chestnut, Ricotta and Spelt Soup | 108 |
| 334. | Spelt and Mushroom Soup | 108 |
| 335. | Lentil Soup | 108 |
| 336. | Pasta and Potato Soup | 108 |
| 337. | Pumpkin and Beans Soup | 108 |
| 338. | Zucchini and Potato Soup | 109 |
| 339. | Chicory Soup | 109 |
| 340. | Green Beans Soup | 109 |
| 341. | Potato Soup | 110 |
| 342. | Zucchini and Egg Soup | 110 |
| 343. | Cabbage Stew | 110 |
| 344. | Legume Soup | 110 |
| 345. | Macaroni with Pork Ragù and Vegetables | 111 |
| 346. | Tagliatelle with Aged Ricotta | 111 |
| 347. | Almond Pesto Pasta | 111 |
| 348. | Pasta with Sword Fish Ragù | 111 |
| 349. | Pasta with Tomato and Eggplant | 112 |
| 350. | Pasta with Peppers and Tomatoes | 112 |
| 351. | Broccoli Soup | 112 |
| 352. | Spaghetti with Artichokes | 112 |
| 353. | Farfalle Pasta with Peas | 113 |
| 354. | Farfalle Pasta with Capers | 113 |
| 355. | Pesto Silk Blankets | 113 |
| 356. | Stuffed Macaroni | 114 |
| 357. | Cappelletti with Ricotta and Herbs | 114 |
| 358. | Pumpkin Cappelletti | 114 |
| 359. | Pasta with Mushrooms | 115 |
| 360. | Pasta with Royal Agaric Mushrooms, and Walnuts | 115 |
| 361. | Fettuccine with Eggplant and Green Beans | 115 |
| 362. | Tagliatelle with Pesto | 115 |

| # | Title | Page |
|---|---|---|
| 363. | Tagliatelle with 3 Flours | 116 |
| 364. | Ravioli with Artichoke Stuffing | 116 |
| 365. | Pesto Ravioli with Potatoes | 116 |
| 366. | Ravioli with Potato, Leek and Zucchini | 117 |
| 367. | Ravioli with Seafood | 117 |
| 368. | Linguine with Squid | 117 |
| 369. | Puttanesca Linguine | 118 |
| 370. | Spaghetti with Anchovies and Capers | 118 |
| 371. | Spaghetti with Squid | 118 |
| 372. | Tagliatelle au gratin with Asparagus | 118 |
| 373. | Tagliatelle with Chickpeas and Potatoes | 119 |
| 374. | Tortiglioni with Peppers and Guanciale | 119 |
| 375. | Spaghetti Flan | 119 |
| 376. | Chestnut Flour Trofie | 120 |
| 377. | Rice with Milk and Chestnuts | 120 |
| 378. | Pumpkin Rice | 120 |
| 379. | Rice with Dried Mushrooms and Anchovy Flavor | 121 |
| 380. | Rice with Pesto | 121 |
| 381. | Rice, Tomatoes and Porcini Mushrooms | 121 |
| 382. | Spaghetti with Bacon | 121 |
| 383. | Penne with Hot Salami | 122 |
| 384. | Penne with Basil | 122 |
| 385. | Baked Gnocchi with Ragù and Mozzarella | 122 |
| 386. | Saffron Risotto | 122 |
| 387. | Pasta with Fresh Pecorino and Ragù | 123 |
| 388. | Pasta with Eggplant and Ricotta | 123 |
| 389. | Risotto with Apples | 123 |
| 390. | Pasta with Olive Pesto | 124 |
| 391. | Risotto with Red Radish | 124 |
| 392. | Bucatini with Leaf Broccoli | 124 |
| 393. | Bucatini with Tomato and Ricotta | 124 |
| 394. | Bucatini with Hot Peppers | 125 |
| 395. | Bucatini with Eggs and Asparagus | 125 |
| 396. | Macaroni with Sausage and Ricotta | 125 |
| 397. | Macaroni with Sausage and Tomato Sauce | 125 |
| 398. | Chickpea and Broccoli Soup | 126 |
| 399. | Zucchini and Pumpkin Flowers Soup | 126 |
| 400. | Oven Backed Pasta with Cauliflower | 126 |
| 401. | Pasta with Sardines | 126 |
| 402. | Pasta with Cauliflowers | 127 |
| 403. | Pasta with Lentils | 127 |
| 404. | Pasta with Pecorino and Eggs | 127 |
| 405. | Pasta with Beans and Sausages | 127 |
| 406. | Spaghetti with Dried Tomatoes | 128 |
| 407. | Salad's Spaghetti | 128 |
| 408. | Spaghetti Primavera | 128 |
| 409. | Penne with Sausage and Olives | 128 |
| 410. | Penne with Potatoes and Eggs | 129 |
| 411. | Pasta with Potatoes and Zucchinis | 129 |
| 412. | Rice Balls in Broth | 129 |
| 413. | Rigatoni with Beans and Mushrooms | 129 |
| 414. | Rice with Fennel and Ricotta | 130 |
| 415. | Fusilli with Meatalls | 130 |
| 416. | Vegetable Tagliatelle | 130 |
| 417. | Tagliatelle with Chickpeas and Dried Peppers | 130 |
| 418. | Pasta with Onion Sauce | 131 |
| 419. | Pasta with Bacon and Vegetables | 131 |
| 420. | Asparagus Soup | 131 |
| 421. | Potato and Broccoli Soup | 131 |
| 422. | Beet Soup | 132 |
| 423. | Chicory and Potatoes Soup | 132 |
| 424. | Spicy Fettuccine | 132 |
| 425. | Spicy Gnocchi | 132 |
| 426. | Macaroni with Artichokes and Clams | 133 |
| 427. | Macaroni, Bacon and Mozzarella | 133 |
| 428. | Spaghetti with Crab Sauce | 133 |
| 429. | Tagliatelle with Frog Sauce | 133 |
| 430. | Tagliatelle with Mushroom Ragù | 134 |
| 431. | Baked Tagliatelle | 134 |
| 432. | Pasta with Scallion Sauce | 134 |
| 433. | Dogtooth Violet with Sausage | 134 |
| 434. | Tagliatelle Pie | 135 |
| 435. | Tagliatelle with Tomato and Parsley | 135 |
| 436. | Tagliatelle with Bean Cream | 135 |
| 437. | Tagliatelle with Walnut Sauce | 136 |
| 438. | Cannelloni | 136 |
| 439. | Cabbage Tortelli | 136 |
| 440. | Tortelli with Apple Filling | 137 |
| 441. | Tortelloni with Ricotta and Parsley | 137 |
| 442. | Onion Soup | 138 |
| 443. | Barley and Endive Soup | 138 |
| 444. | Pork Meat Soup | 138 |
| 445. | Peas Soup | 138 |
| 446. | Crab Soup | 139 |
| 447. | Maltagliati with Beans and Chestnuts | 139 |
| 448. | Polenta | 139 |
| 449. | Polenta with Cauliflower | 139 |
| 450. | Polenta with Figs | 140 |
| 451. | Balsamic Vinegar Risotto | 140 |
| 452. | Spaghetti with Eggplant | 140 |
| 453. | Spaghetti with Anchovies | 140 |
| 454. | Chickpeas Soup | 141 |
| 455. | Rice with Eggs | 141 |
| 456. | Garlic Soup | 141 |
| 457. | Mantis Shrimp Soup | 141 |
| 458. | Beans Soup | 142 |
| 459. | Spinach Soup | 142 |
| 460. | Avocado, Roasted Mushroom and Feta Spaghetti | 142 |
| 461. | Tomato, Arugula and Feta Spaghetti | 142 |
| 462. | Zucchini Noodles | 143 |
| 463. | Halibut Soup | 143 |
| 464. | Tuna Whole Wheat Pasta | 143 |
| 465. | Tuna Risotto | 143 |
| 466. | Barley and Chicken Soup | 144 |
| 467. | Broccoli Pesto Spaghetti | 144 |
| 468. | Chicken Breast Soup | 144 |
| 469. | Courgette Risotto | 144 |
| 470. | Creamy Chicken Soup | 145 |
| 471. | Creamy Penne | 145 |
| 472. | Fennel Wild Risotto | 145 |
| 473. | Homemade Chicken Broth | 146 |
| 474. | Homemade Vegetable Broth | 146 |
| 475. | Cauliflower Rice and Chipotle Chicken | 146 |
| 476. | Jalapeno Bacon Cheddar Soup | 146 |
| 477. | Chicken Pasta | 147 |
| 478. | Herb Risotto | 147 |
| 479. | Pasta with Vegetables | 147 |
| 480. | Roasted Pepper Pasta | 148 |
| 481. | Whole Wheat Pasta with Tuna | 148 |
| 482. | Vegan Olive Pasta | 148 |
| 483. | Italian Chicken Pasta | 149 |
| 484. | Greek Chicken Pasta | 149 |
| 485. | Pesto Chicken Pasta | 149 |

| # | Recipe | Page |
|---|---|---|
| 486. | Spinach Pesto Pasta | 149 |
| 487. | Herb Polenta | 150 |
| 488. | Pecorino Pasta with Sausage and Fresh Tomato | 150 |
| 489. | Pesto Pasta and Shrimps | 150 |
| 490. | Puttanesca Style Bucatini | 150 |
| 491. | Raw Tomato Sauce & Brie on Linguine | 151 |
| 492. | Red Wine Risotto | 151 |
| 493. | Bell Pepper Soup | 151 |
| 494. | Chicken Wild Rice Soup | 152 |
| 495. | Squash and Turmeric Soup | 152 |
| 496. | Leek, Potato, and Carrot Soup | 152 |
| 497. | Beef Sage Soup | 153 |
| 498. | Classic Minestrone | 153 |
| 499. | Cheesy Broccoli Soup | 153 |
| 500. | Mediterranean Lentil Soup | 154 |
| 501. | Turkey Meatball and Ditalini Soup | 154 |
| 502. | Potato Soup (2nd Version) | 154 |
| 503. | Mint Avocado Chilled Soup | 155 |
| 504. | Beetroot and Carrot Soup | 155 |
| 505. | Barley Risotto | 155 |
| 506. | Beef with Broccoli and Cauliflower Rice | 155 |
| 507. | Chicken and Rice Soup | 156 |
| 508. | Chickpeas Soup (2nd Version) | 156 |
| 509. | Farfalle with Fresh Tomatoes | 156 |
| 510. | Fish Soup | 157 |
| 511. | Fried Rice with Spinach, Peppers & Artichokes | 157 |
| 512. | Greek Lima Beans Soup | 157 |
| 513. | Gluten-Free Spanish Rice | 158 |
| 514. | Ground Pork and Tomatoes Soup | 158 |
| 515. | Herbed Wild Rice | 158 |
| 516. | Mushroom Soup | 158 |
| 517. | Flavorful Mac & Cheese | 159 |
| 518. | Mac & Cheese | 159 |
| 519. | Italian Mac & Cheese | 159 |
| 520. | Israeli Pasta | 160 |
| 521. | Spaghetti Squash | 160 |
| 522. | Garlic Prawn and Pea Risotto | 160 |
| 523. | Greek Pasta Salad | 161 |
| 524. | Lemon Mushroom Rice | 161 |
| 525. | Mediterranean Lentils and Rice | 161 |
| 526. | Spaghetti with Mustard and Capers Dressing | 162 |

FISH AND SEAFOOD ................................................................ 163

| # | Recipe | Page |
|---|---|---|
| 527. | Eel with Grapes | 163 |
| 528. | Eel Fritta | 163 |
| 529. | Parmigiana Cod | 164 |
| 530. | Cod with Potatoes | 164 |
| 531. | Baked Gray Mullet | 164 |
| 532. | Cod with Dressing | 164 |
| 533. | Sea Bream Baked in Foil | 165 |
| 534. | Fried Cod | 165 |
| 535. | Sauté Catfish | 165 |
| 536. | Fried Frogs | 166 |
| 537. | Frogs in Oil | 166 |
| 538. | Stuffed Sardines | 166 |
| 539. | Roasted Squid | 166 |
| 540. | Oven Sturgeon | 167 |
| 541. | Grilled Tuna | 167 |
| 542. | Marinated and Fried Anchovies | 167 |
| 543. | Grilled Lobster | 168 |
| 544. | Au gratin Lobster | 168 |
| 545. | Cod with Olives and Potatoes | 168 |
| 546. | Seasoned Squid | 168 |
| 547. | Breaded Grilled Squid | 169 |
| 548. | Squid in Dressing | 169 |
| 549. | Fried Squid | 169 |
| 550. | Stuffed Squid | 169 |
| 551. | Grouper in Dressing | 170 |
| 552. | Roasted Mantis Shrimp | 170 |
| 553. | Fried Sandeel Fish | 170 |
| 554. | Sword Fish Cutlets | 170 |
| 555. | Mussels with Pepper | 171 |
| 556. | Baked Dentex with Olives | 171 |
| 557. | Grilled Dentex | 171 |
| 558. | Herring in Oil | 171 |
| 559. | Au Gratin Mackerel | 172 |
| 560. | Fried Squid and Shrimp | 172 |
| 561. | Fried Damselfish | 172 |
| 562. | Shrimp with Mint | 172 |
| 563. | Fried Shrimp | 173 |
| 564. | Baked Shrimp | 173 |
| 565. | Grilled Shrimp | 173 |
| 566. | Crabs in Dressing | 173 |
| 567. | Mixed Grill | 174 |
| 568. | Sword Fish Rolls | 174 |
| 569. | Baked Bream Fish | 174 |
| 570. | Fried Cod (2nd version) | 174 |
| 571. | Menola Fish with Onion | 175 |
| 572. | Bream with Potatoes | 175 |
| 573. | Sweet and Sour Dogfish | 175 |
| 574. | Bream Fish in Salt Crust | 175 |
| 575. | Sword Fish in Dressing | 176 |
| 576. | Sword Fish with Oil | 176 |
| 577. | Sword Fish with Olives, Capers and Mint | 176 |
| 578. | Fried Sea Scallops | 176 |
| 579. | Cod Balls | 177 |
| 580. | Sardine Balls with Sauce | 177 |
| 581. | Mediterranean Baked Salmon | 177 |
| 582. | Salmon Frittata | 178 |
| 583. | Salmon Kebabs | 178 |
| 584. | Coconut Clam Chowder | 178 |
| 585. | Cod in Tomato Sauce | 178 |
| 586. | Creamy Fish Stew | 179 |
| 587. | Mediterranean Fish Tacos | 179 |
| 588. | Shrimp with Alfredo Sauce | 179 |
| 589. | Salmon Stew | 180 |
| 590. | Feta Tomato Sea Bass | 180 |
| 591. | Codfish with Shrimp | 180 |
| 592. | Garlicky Clams | 180 |
| 593. | Garlicky Shrimp | 181 |
| 594. | Healthy Carrot & Shrimp | 181 |
| 595. | Honey Garlic Shrimp | 181 |
| 596. | Mediterranean Fish Fillets | 181 |
| 597. | Mussels with Tomatoes & Wine | 182 |
| 598. | Salmon with Broccoli | 182 |
| 599. | Pesto Fish Fillet | 182 |
| 600. | Salmon with Potatoes | 183 |
| 601. | Salsa Fish Fillets | 183 |
| 602. | Seafood Stew | 183 |
| 603. | Shrimp Scampi | 183 |
| 604. | Shrimp Zoodles | 184 |
| 605. | Lemon Clams | 184 |
| 606. | Stewed Mussels & Scallops | 184 |

| 607. | Stuffed Swordfish | 184 |
|---|---|---|
| 608. | Tilapia in Herb Sauce | 185 |
| 609. | Tomato Olive Fish Fillets | 185 |
| 610. | Tuna with Olives | 185 |
| 611. | Butter Shrimp | 186 |
| 612. | Creamy Fish Gratin | 186 |
| 613. | Fish Stew | 186 |
| 614. | Greek Roasted Fish | 187 |
| 615. | Grilled Salmon with Pineapple Salsa | 187 |
| 616. | Seafood Corn Chowder | 187 |
| 617. | Tuna Tapas and Avocado | 187 |
| 618. | Avocados Stuffed with Salmon | 188 |
| 619. | Tuna Cobbler | 188 |
| 620. | Herbed Roasted Cod | 188 |
| 621. | Lemony Parmesan Salmon | 188 |
| 622. | Tuna Melts | 189 |

BEEF AND LAMB .................................................. 190

| 623. | Lamb with Egg | 190 |
|---|---|---|
| 624. | Veal Roast with Lemon | 190 |
| 625. | Flattened Meat Loaf | 191 |
| 626. | Sweet and Sour Meatballs with Almonds | 191 |
| 628. | Castrated Chops | 192 |
| 629. | Lamb Ribs | 192 |
| 630. | Veal Meatballs with Chocolate | 192 |
| 631. | Beef Filet with Ham | 192 |
| 632. | Lamb Mince | 193 |
| 633. | Beef Mince | 193 |
| 634. | Veal Mince with Peas | 193 |
| 635. | Stew with Milk | 194 |
| 636. | Stuffed Lamb Leg | 194 |
| 637. | Lamb with Potatoes | 194 |
| 638. | Baked Lamb | 194 |
| 639. | Lamb with Mint | 195 |
| 640. | Lamb with Eggs | 195 |
| 641. | Roasted Veal coated in Breadcrumbs | 195 |
| 642. | Veal Rolls with Sauce | 196 |
| 643. | Baked Castrate | 196 |
| 644. | Veal Cutlet with Pecorino | 196 |
| 645. | Veal Rolls with Raisins and Pine Nuts | 196 |
| 646. | Lard Meatballs | 197 |
| 647. | Veal with Capers | 197 |
| 648. | Baked Skewer Rolls | 197 |
| 649. | Silverside with Tomato | 198 |
| 650. | Ground Beef and Brussels Sprouts | 198 |
| 651. | Italian Mini Meatballs | 198 |
| 652. | Beef & Tapioca Stew | 198 |
| 653. | Beef, Artichoke & Mushroom Stew | 199 |
| 654. | Ground Lamb Koftas | 199 |
| 655. | Lamb Chops with Veggies | 200 |
| 656. | Lamb Shanks with Veggies | 200 |
| 657. | Leg of Lamb with Potatoes | 200 |
| 658. | Steak with Hummus | 201 |
| 659. | Steak with Yogurt Sauce | 201 |
| 660. | Bacon Cheeseburger Casserole | 202 |
| 661. | Balsamic Beef and Mushrooms Mix | 202 |
| 662. | Cheesy Bacon Burger | 202 |
| 663. | Sesame Beef | 203 |
| 664. | Stuffed Meatballs | 203 |
| 665. | Greek Style Mini Burger Pies | 203 |
| 666. | Lamb and Potatoes Stew | 204 |
| 667. | Mouth-watering Beef Pie | 204 |
| 668. | Lamb with Vegetables | 204 |
| 669. | Beef Tartar | 205 |

POULTRY ................................................................ 206

| 670. | Rabbit with Mushrooms | 206 |
|---|---|---|
| 671. | Baked Rabbit | 206 |
| 672. | Chicken with Peppers | 207 |
| 673. | Chicken with Vinegar | 207 |
| 674. | Snipe in a Pan | 207 |
| 675. | Cacciatora Chicken | 207 |
| 676. | Turkey with Ham and Cheese | 208 |
| 677. | Chicken Mince | 208 |
| 678. | Duck Ham | 208 |
| 679. | Goose with Salt | 208 |
| 680. | Guinea Fowl Hen with Bacon | 209 |
| 681. | Goose with Sauce | 209 |
| 682. | Rabbit with Sauce | 209 |
| 683. | Sweet and Sour Rabbit | 210 |
| 684. | Rabbit Stew | 210 |
| 685. | Portuguese Style Rabbit | 210 |
| 686. | Rabbit with Almonds | 210 |
| 687. | Broiled Chicken | 211 |
| 688. | Baked Chicken with Pecorino | 211 |
| 689. | Chicken with Potatoes | 211 |
| 690. | Chicken in Salt Crust | 212 |
| 691. | Chicken with Vinegar (2$^{nd}$ version) | 212 |
| 692. | Sweet and Sour Chicken | 212 |
| 693. | Chicken Pot Pie | 212 |
| 694. | Chicken Stew with Potatoes | 213 |
| 695. | Quail in a Pan | 213 |
| 696. | Chicken & Veggie Kabobs | 213 |
| 697. | Chicken with Caper Sauce | 213 |
| 698. | Chicken, Dried Fruit & Olives Casserole | 214 |
| 699. | Grilled Chicken Breasts | 214 |
| 700. | Bbq Chicken Pizza | 215 |
| 701. | Chicken Broccoli Salad with Avocado Dressing 215 | |
| 702. | Chicken Stew | 215 |
| 703. | Coconut Curry Chicken Tenders | 215 |
| 704. | Garlic Chicken Balls | 216 |
| 705. | Garlicky Tomato Chicken Casserole | 216 |
| 706. | Herbed Roasted Chicken Breasts | 216 |
| 707. | Glazed Chicken | 217 |
| 708. | Paprika Moussaka | 217 |
| 709. | Low-Carb Chicken Curry | 217 |
| 710. | Marinated Chicken Breasts | 218 |
| 711. | Roasted Turkey Legs | 218 |
| 712. | Bacon Wings | 218 |
| 713. | Buffalo Chicken Sliders | 219 |
| 714. | Chicken Omelet | 219 |
| 715. | Chicken Salad (2$^{nd}$ version) | 219 |
| 716. | Chicken Skillet | 220 |
| 717. | Turkish Marinated Chicken | 220 |
| 718. | Chicken Stuffed Peppers | 220 |
| 719. | High Protein Chicken Meatballs | 220 |
| 720. | Mediterranean Chicken Bites | 221 |

PORK ...................................................................... 222

| 721. | Baked Ham | 222 |
|---|---|---|
| 722. | Dried Sausage Stew | 222 |
| 723. | Chops in Balsamic Vinegar | 223 |
| 724. | Pork and Ricotta Meat Loaf | 223 |
| 725. | Pork Chop Stew | 223 |
| 726. | Stuffed Pork Ribs | 224 |

| # | Item | Page |
|---|---|---|
| 727. | Pork Ribs with Wine | 224 |
| 728. | Pork Cutlet | 224 |
| 729. | Homemade Pork Buns | 224 |
| 730. | Prosciutto e Faggioli | 225 |
| 731. | Oregano Pork Mix | 225 |
| 732. | Pork Chops with Capers | 225 |
| 733. | Pork Loins | 225 |
| 734. | Sausages with Tomato | 226 |
| 735. | Sausages in Pan | 226 |
| 736. | Pork Stew | 226 |
| 737. | Braised Sausage | 226 |
| 738. | Fried Sausage | 227 |
| 739. | Sausage Ragout | 227 |
| 740. | Grilled Pork Chops | 227 |
| 741. | Pork Cutlets | 227 |
| 742. | Brown Sugar Smokies | 228 |

**VEGETABLES AND SALADS** ............................................. 229

| # | Item | Page |
|---|---|---|
| 743. | Veggie Bowls | 229 |
| 744. | Eggplants with Balsamic Vinegar | 229 |
| 745. | Asparagus with Ham | 230 |
| 746. | Boiled Broccoli | 230 |
| 747. | Broccoli with Tomato | 230 |
| 748. | Asparagus au gratin | 230 |
| 749. | Onion and Bean Salad | 231 |
| 750. | Tomato and Onion Salad | 231 |
| 751. | Tomato and Cucumber Salad | 231 |
| 752. | Lettuce and Fennel Salad | 231 |
| 753. | Orange Salad | 232 |
| 754. | Baked Cardoon | 232 |
| 755. | Cardoons with Dressing | 232 |
| 756. | Fried Cauliflowers | 232 |
| 757. | Fried Onion | 233 |
| 758. | Sweet and Sour Onions | 233 |
| 759. | Fennels with Sauce | 233 |
| 760. | Fried Pumpkin Flowers (3rd Version) | 233 |
| 761. | Stuffed Mushrooms Porcini | 234 |
| 762. | Eggplants with Ham | 234 |
| 763. | Potatoes with Balsamic Vinegar | 234 |
| 764. | Potato Cream | 234 |
| 765. | Mixed Peppers | 235 |
| 766. | Mixed Fried Vegetables | 235 |
| 767. | Stuffed Tomatoes (3rd Version) | 235 |
| 768. | Potato Puree | 235 |
| 769. | Meat Stuffed Zucchini | 236 |
| 770. | Battered Cauliflowers | 236 |
| 771. | Battered Onion | 236 |
| 772. | Potato Croquettes | 236 |
| 773. | Cheesy Cauliflower Florets | 237 |
| 774. | Bean Salad | 237 |
| 775. | Mushroom and Olives Steaks | 237 |
| 776. | Veggie Casserole | 237 |
| 777. | Buffalo Cauliflower | 238 |
| 778. | Cauliflower Curry | 238 |
| 779. | Cucumber Bowl with Spices and Greek Yogurt | 238 |
| 780. | Mediterranean Chickpea Salad | 238 |
| 781. | Black Bean Stuffed Sweet Potatoes with Quinoa | 239 |
| 782. | Bok Choy with Tofu Stir Fry | 239 |
| 783. | Chickpeas and Millet Stew | 240 |
| 784. | Greek Baked Zucchini & Potatoes | 240 |
| 785. | Green Beans & Feta | 240 |
| 786. | Herbed Garlic Black Beans | 240 |
| 787. | Kale - Mediterranean-Style | 241 |
| 788. | Maple Lemon Tempeh Cubes | 241 |
| 789. | Mediterranean Endive Boats | 241 |
| 790. | Mediterranean Potatoes | 241 |
| 791. | Greek Eggplant Dish | 242 |
| 792. | Almond Kale | 242 |
| 793. | Apples and Pomegranate Salad | 242 |
| 794. | Arugula Salad | 243 |
| 795. | Balsamic Eggplant Mix | 243 |
| 796. | Bean Lettuce Wraps | 243 |
| 797. | Cheese Beet Salad | 243 |
| 798. | Chickpea Salad | 244 |
| 799. | Creamy Carrot Chowder | 244 |
| 800. | Creamy Chicken Salad | 244 |
| 801. | Feta Tomato Salad | 244 |
| 802. | Braised Kale with Cherry Tomatoes | 245 |
| 803. | Gorgonzola Sweet Potato Burgers | 245 |
| 804. | Greek Stuffed Collard Greens | 245 |
| 805. | Grilled Veggie and Hummus Wrap | 246 |
| 806. | Mediterranean Quiche | 246 |
| 807. | Mediterranean Sweet Potato | 246 |
| 808. | Mediterranean Veggie Bowl | 247 |
| 809. | Melon Salad | 247 |
| 810. | North African Peanut Stew over Cauliflower Rice | 247 |
| 811. | Orange Celery Salad | 248 |
| 812. | Passion Fruit and Spicy Couscous | 248 |
| 813. | Pistachio Arugula Salad | 248 |
| 814. | Pork and Greens Salad | 249 |
| 815. | Roasted Brussels Sprouts And Pecans | 249 |
| 816. | Rosemary Beets | 249 |
| 817. | Sautéed Garlic Spinach | 249 |
| 818. | Spanish Green Beans | 250 |
| 819. | Spicy Green Beans Mix | 250 |
| 820. | Quinoa Salad | 250 |
| 821. | Stewed Okra | 250 |
| 822. | Tomato Tabbouleh | 251 |
| 823. | Zucchini Lasagna | 251 |
| 824. | Zucchini-Eggplant Gratin | 252 |
| 825. | Wrapped Plums | 252 |
| 826. | Tomato Salad | 252 |
| 827. | Turkish Salad | 252 |
| 828. | Braised Artichokes | 253 |
| 829. | Fried Artichokes | 253 |
| 830. | Artichokes in a Pan | 253 |
| 831. | Artichokes in a Pan with Lemon | 253 |
| 832. | Fried Thistles | 254 |
| 833. | Thistles in Batter | 254 |
| 834. | Fried Cauliflower | 254 |
| 835. | Boiled Cauliflower | 254 |
| 836. | Baked Onions | 254 |
| 837. | Boiled Onions | 255 |
| 838. | Mint Beans | 255 |
| 839. | Stewed Beans | 255 |
| 840. | Broad Beans with Onion | 255 |
| 841. | Broad Beans and Bacon | 256 |
| 842. | Mint Broad Beans | 256 |
| 843. | Fresh Stewed Broad Beans | 256 |
| 844. | Battered Pumpkin Flowers | 256 |
| 845. | Cutlet Mushrooms | 256 |
| 846. | Grilled Mushrooms | 257 |

**SAUCES, SALSAS AND DRESSINGS** ............................................. 258

| # | Item | Page |
|---|---|---|
| 847. | Anchovy Sauce | 258 |
| 848. | Garlic Sauce | 258 |
| 849. | Garlic Sauce for Fish | 258 |
| 850. | Walnut Cream | 259 |
| 851. | Spinach Cream | 259 |
| 852. | Mushroom Sauce | 259 |
| 853. | Mushrooms Dressing | 259 |
| 854. | Genovese Pesto | 259 |
| 855. | Genovese Sauce | 260 |
| 856. | Dark Sauce | 260 |
| 857. | Béchamel Sauce | 260 |
| 858. | Tomato Sauce | 260 |
| 859. | Hot Sauce | 260 |
| 860. | Sauce for Boiled Dishes | 261 |
| 861. | Green Sauce with Pine Nuts | 261 |
| 862. | Green Sauce with Capers | 261 |
| 863. | Sweet and Sour Sauce | 261 |
| 864. | Red Sauce for Boiled Meat | 261 |
| 865. | Snail Sauce | 262 |
| 866. | Lean Sauce | 262 |
| 867. | Chicken Ragù | 262 |
| 868. | Herb Sauce | 262 |
| 869. | Apple Sauce | 263 |
| 870. | Pepper Sauce | 263 |
| 871. | Cod Sauce | 263 |
| 872. | Onion Sauce | 263 |
| 873. | Tomato and Guanciale Sauce | 263 |
| 874. | Parsley Sauce | 264 |
| 875. | Egg Sauce | 264 |
| 876. | Anchovy and Capers Sauce | 264 |
| 877. | Garlic Pesto | 264 |
| 878. | Tomato Salsa | 264 |
| 879. | Mayonnaise | 265 |
| 880. | Marinading | 265 |
| 881. | Beef Ragù | 265 |
| 882. | Raw Sauce | 265 |
| 883. | Carrot Sauce | 265 |
| 884. | Red Sauce with Balsamic Vinegar | 266 |
| 885. | Boar Sauce | 266 |
| 886. | Grape Sauce | 266 |

DESSERTS ............................................................. 267

| # | Item | Page |
|---|---|---|
| 887. | Apple Fritters | 267 |
| 888. | Amaretti (Cookies) | 267 |
| 889. | Long Dessert | 268 |
| 890. | Family Cookies | 268 |
| 891. | Ring Cookies | 268 |
| 892. | Baked Doughnuts | 268 |
| 893. | Lemon Pudding | 268 |
| 894. | Breadcrumbs Dessert | 269 |
| 895. | Batter Dessert | 269 |
| 896. | Milk Dessert | 269 |
| 897. | Ricotta and Coffee Dessert | 269 |
| 898. | Carnival Dessert | 270 |
| 899. | Doughnut | 270 |
| 900. | Crunchy Almond Bar | 270 |
| 901. | Easter Cake | 270 |
| 902. | Puff Pastry | 271 |
| 903. | Dried Fruit Cake | 271 |
| 904. | Sweet Salami | 271 |
| 905. | Almond and Liquor Cake | 271 |
| 906. | Raisin and Rum Cake | 272 |
| 907. | Almond Cake | 272 |
| 908. | Prune Cake | 272 |
| 909. | Italian Style Pumpkin Pie | 273 |
| 910. | Cherry Soup | 273 |
| 911. | Apple and Berries Ambrosia | 273 |
| 912. | Baked Ricotta & Pears | 273 |
| 913. | Banana Cinnamon Fritters | 274 |
| 914. | Caramel Popcorn | 274 |
| 915. | Creamy Peach Smoothie | 274 |
| 916. | Blueberry Smoothie | 275 |
| 917. | Red Quinoa Peach Porridge | 275 |
| 918. | Walnuts Yogurt Dip | 275 |
| 919. | Yogurt Dip | 275 |
| 920. | Apples and Plum Cake | 275 |
| 921. | Banana Shake Bowls | 276 |
| 922. | Blackberry and Apples Cobbler | 276 |
| 923. | Black Tea Cake | 276 |
| 924. | Cherry Cream | 276 |
| 925. | Cocoa Brownies | 277 |
| 926. | Cold Lemon Squares | 277 |
| 927. | Glazed Mediterranean Puffy Fig | 277 |
| 928. | Figs Pie | 277 |
| 929. | Greek Cheesecake | 278 |
| 930. | Almond Rice Dessert | 278 |
| 931. | Apple Couscous Pudding | 278 |
| 932. | Banana Cinnamon Cupcakes | 279 |
| 933. | Bananas Foster | 279 |
| 934. | Berries Stew | 279 |
| 935. | Cardamom Almond Cream | 279 |
| 936. | Chia and Berries Smoothie Bowl | 279 |
| 937. | Chocolate Covered Strawberries | 280 |
| 938. | Chocolate Ganache | 280 |
| 939. | Cinnamon Chickpeas Cookies | 280 |
| 940. | Cocoa Sweet Cherry Cream | 280 |
| 941. | Cranberries and Pears Pie | 281 |
| 942. | Creamy Mint Strawberry Mix | 281 |
| 943. | Dessert Cheese Pie | 281 |
| 944. | Frosty Strawberry Dessert | 281 |
| 945. | Greek Almond Rounds Shortbread | 282 |
| 946. | Ice Cream Sandwich Dessert | 282 |
| 947. | Green Tea and Vanilla Cream | 283 |
| 948. | Hazelnut-Orange Olive Oil Cookies | 283 |
| 949. | Mediterranean Stuffed Custard Pancakes | 283 |
| 950. | Orange-Glazed Apricots and Ouzo Whipped Cream | 284 |
| 951. | Poached Cherries | 284 |
| 952. | Strawberries Cream | 284 |
| 953. | Watermelon-Strawberry Rosewater Yogurt | 285 |
| 954. | Key Lime Pie | 285 |
| 955. | Lemon Cream | 285 |
| 956. | Mandarin Cream | 286 |
| 957. | Minty Coconut Cream | 286 |
| 958. | Orange Cake | 286 |
| 959. | Papaya Cream | 286 |
| 960. | Peach Sorbet | 287 |
| 961. | Strawberry Phyllo Cups | 287 |
| 962. | Pumpkin Cream | 288 |
| 963. | Apples and Rhubarb Cream | 288 |
| 964. | Strawberry Rhubarb Crunch | 288 |
| 965. | Ricotta Ramekins | 288 |
| 966. | Strawberry Angel Dessert | 288 |
| 967. | Vanilla Cake | 289 |
| 968. | Watermelon Cream | 289 |
| 969. | Lemon Curd Filled Almond-Lemon Cake | 289 |

| | | | |
|---|---|---|---|
| 970. | Mascarpone and Ricotta Stuffed Dates | 290 | |
| 971. | Mediterranean Biscuits | 290 | |
| 972. | Mediterranean Bread Pudding | 290 | |
| 973. | Mediterranean Cheesecake | 291 | |
| 974. | Grapes Stew | 291 | |
| 975. | Orange Cookies | 291 | |
| 976. | Pumpkin Cookies | 292 | |
| 977. | Favette | 292 | |
| 978. | Sweetened Almonds | 292 | |
| 979. | Pistachio Cookies | 292 | |
| 980. | Moscardini | 292 | |
| 981. | Almond Nibbles | 293 | |
| 982. | Chocolate Almond Balls | 293 | |
| 983. | Marsala's Balls | 293 | |
| 984. | Orange Almond Balls | 293 | |
| 985. | Easter Cake (2nd version) | 293 | |
| 986. | Ricotta Cheese Flan | 294 | |
| 987. | Almond Cake (2nd version) | 294 | |
| 988. | Hazelnut Cake | 294 | |
| 989. | Sponge Cake | 294 | |
| 990. | St. Joseph's Beard | 295 | |
| 991. | Creamy Cinnamon Milk | 295 | |
| 992. | Chickpeas with Honey | 295 | |
| 993. | Starch Cream | 295 | |
| 994. | Milk Cream | 295 | |
| 995. | Ricotta Cream | 296 | |
| 996. | Sweet Couscous | 296 | |
| 997. | Chocolate Rice | 296 | |
| 998. | Ricotta and Honey | 296 | |
| 999. | Battered Eggs in Marsala | 297 | |
| 1000. | Cream Cannoli | 297 | |
| 1001. | Angel Hair | 297 | |
| 1002. | Ricotta Fritters | 297 | |
| 1003. | Sweet Fried Ricotta | 298 | |
| 1004. | Coffee Granita | 298 | |
| 1005. | Yellow Melon Granita | 298 | |

Conversion Tables ..................................................................299

30-Day Meal Plan ................................................................. 302

INDEX: ........................................................................... 3024

# APPETIZERS AND SNACK

## 1. Marinate Anchovies

**Prep time: 1 hour**  **Servings: 4**

**Ingredients:**
- *18 oz of fresh anchovies*
- *extra virgin olive oil*
- *1 hot pepper*
- *1 sprig of parsley*
- *Juice of 1 lemon*
- *2 garlic cloves*
- *salt*

**Prep:** Clean the anchovies, open them down the middle and remove the bones. Then carefully wash and dry them.
Lay them on a large plate to form one layer. Verse the lemon juice until completely covered and let marinate for 24 hours covering them with surround wrap.
Drain the anchovies from the marinate liquid and move them on a serving plate
Season with a drizzle of oil, chopped parsley, a few garlic slices, hot pepper and a pinch of salt and let the taste develop for at least one hour before serving.

**Nutrition:** Calories 416 Kcal; Carbs 3 g; Protein 16.5 g; Fat 38 g

## 2. Baked Apples

**Prep Time: 10 minutes**  **Cook Time: 25 minutes**
**Servings: 4**

**Ingredients:**
- *½ lemon, squeezed*
- *1 ½ pounds of sliced apples*
- *¼ teaspoon cinnamon*

**Prep:** Set the temperature of your oven to 350 ° F to preheat.
Take a piece of parchment paper and lay on top of a baking pan.
Combine lemon juice, cinnamon, and apples into a bowl and mix well. Pour the apples onto the baking pan and arrange them so they are not doubled up. Place the pan in the oven and set timer to 2 minutes.

**Nutrition**: Calories: 91, Fats: 0.4 g, Carbs: 23 g, Protein: 0.6 g

### 3. Beetroot Chips

**Prep Time:** 10 minutes  
**Servings:** 4

**Cook Time:** 15 minutes

**Ingredients:**
- *1 beetroot, peeled*
- *1 tsp. salt*
- *1 tbsp. sunflower oil*

**Prep:** Slice the beetroot and sprinkle with salt.
Add the oil and stir with a spatula.
Arrange the beetroot in the tray one-by-one and bake for 12 minutes at 370 ° F.
Then flip chips on another side and cook for 3 minutes more.

**Nutrition:** Calories 41, Fat: 3.5 g, Carbs: 2.6 g, Protein: 0.5 g

### 4. Bell Pepper Muffins

**Prep Time:** 15 minutes  
**Servings:** 4

**Cook Time:** 15 minutes

**Ingredients:**
- *4 eggs, beaten*
- *4 tsps. butter, softened*
- *1 tsp. baking powder*
- *2 bell peppers, chopped*
- *4 tbsps. wheat flour, whole grain*
- *½ tsp. ground black pepper*
- *½ tsp. salt*

**Prep:** Mix up together wheat flour, eggs, butter, baking powder, ground black pepper, and salt.
When the batter is smooth, add the chopped bell pepper. Mix well.
Fill ½ part of each muffin mold with bell pepper batter.
Bake the muffins for fifteen minutes at 365 ° F.

**Nutrition:** Calories 145, Fat: 8.3 g, Carbs: 11.5 g, Protein: 7.2 g

### 5. Hot Pepper Dip with Cheese

**Prep Time:** 5 minutes  
**Servings:** 6

**Cook Time:** 10 minutes

**Ingredients:**
- *1 cup Cheddar cheese*
- *¼ cup cilantro, chopped*
- *1 chili pepper, chopped*
- *1 tsp. garlic powder*
- *¼ cup milk*

**Prep:** Bring the milk to boil. Add cheese in the milk and simmer the mixture for 2 minutes. Stir it constantly. Add chili pepper, cilantro, and garlic powder. Mix up the mixture well.
Serve the dip when it is at room temperature.

**Nutrition:** Calories 82, Fat: 6.4 g, Carbs: 1.3 g, Protein: 5 g

### 6. Artichoke Dip with Mozzarella

**Prep Time:** 10 minutes  
**Servings:** 6

**Cook Time:** 10 minutes

**Ingredients:**
- *1 cup sour cream*
- *1 cup fresh spinach*
- *4 oz. artichoke hearts, drained*
- *1 cup Mozzarella cheese, shredded*
- *1 tsp. chili flakes*

**Prep:** Chop the artichoke hearts into small pieces.
Put spinach in a blender and blend until smooth. Mix together artichokes with spinach. Add Mozzarella, sour cream, and chili flakes. Mix well.
Transfer the mixture in the pan and flatten it. Bake for 10 minutes at 360 ° F.

**Nutrition:** Calories 104, Fat: 8.8 g, Carbs: 4.2 g, Protein: 3.4 g

## 7. Phyllo Bites with Cheddar

**Prep Time:** 10 minutes  
**Servings:** 8  
**Cook Time:** 15 minutes

**Ingredients:**
- 3 Phyllo sheets
- ½ cup Cheddar cheese
- 2 eggs, beaten
- 1 tbsp. butter

**Prep:** Mix up together Cheddar cheese with eggs.
Spread the round spring form pan with butter. Place 2 Phyllo sheets inside the spring form pan.
Place Cheddar cheese mixture on top of Phyllo sheets and cover with remaining Phyllo dough sheet.
Preheat the oven to 365 ° F.
Cut the Phyllo dough pie onto eight pieces and bake for fifteen minutes.

**Nutrition:** Calories 112, Fat: 5.3 g, Carbs: 11.8 g, Protein: 6 g

## 8. Chili Chicken Wings

**Prep Time:** 10 minutes  
**Servings:** 4  
**Cook Time:** 20 minutes

**Ingredients:**
- 4 chicken wings, boneless
- 1 tsp. chili pepper, minced
- 1 tbsp. olive oil
- 1 tsp. minced garlic
- 2 tbsps. balsamic vinegar
- ½ tsp. salt

**Prep:** Whisk together minced chili pepper, oil, minced garlic, balsamic vinegar, and salt.
Preheat the oven to 360 ° F. Line the baking tray with parchment.
Rub the chicken wings with sauce and transfer in the tray. Bake for 20 minutes. Flip them onto other side after 10 minutes of cooking.

**Nutrition:** Calories 137, Fat: 10 g, Carbs: 3.7 g, Protein: 5.8 g

## 9. Chunky Nuts Mix

**Prep Time:** 10 minutes  
**Servings:** 6  
**Cook Time:** 1 hour 30 minutes

**Ingredients:**
- 1 cup cashews, halved
- 2 cups raw walnuts, chopped or halved
- 1/3 cup coconut sugar
- 1 cup coconut flakes, unsweetened
- 6 ounces dried banana slices
- 1 ½ teaspoons liquid coconut oil
- 1 teaspoon vanilla extract
- ½ cup of chocolate chips

**Prep:** Turn your crockpot to high and add the cashews, walnuts, vanilla, coconut oil, and sugar. Combine until the ingredients are well mixed and cook for 45 minutes. Reduce the temperature on your crockpot to low. Continue to cook for another 20 minutes.
Place a piece of parchment paper on your counter.
Once the mix is done cooking, remove it from the crockpot and set on top of the parchment paper.
Let the mixture sit and cool for 20 minutes.
Pour the contents into a bowl and add the bananas and chocolate chips. Mix the ingredients together.

**Nutrition:** Calories: 251, Fats: 6.2 g, Carbs: 1 g, Protein: 3 g

## 10. Artichoke Dip

**Prep Time:** 10 minutes  
**Servings:** 8  
**Cook Time:** 5 minutes

**Ingredients:**
- 28 oz. can artichoke hearts, quartered
- 1 1/2 cups parmesan cheese, shredded
- 1 cup sour cream
- 1 cup mayonnaise
- oz. can green chilies
- 1 cup of water
- Salt and pepper to taste

**Prep:** Add artichokes, water, and chilies into the instant pot.
Seal pot with the lid, select manual and set timer for 1 minute.
Once done, release pressure using quick release. Remove lid. Drain excess water.
Set instant pot on sauté mode. Add remaining ingredients and stir well and cook until cheese is melted.

**Nutrition**: Calories 262 Fat 7.6 g Carbs 14.4 g Sugars 2.8 g Protein 8.4 g

## 11. Eggplant Dip

**Prep Time: 10 minutes**  
**Servings: 4**

**Cook Time: 20 minutes**

**Ingredients:**
- 1 eggplant
- 1/2 tsp. paprika
- 1 tbsp. olive oil
- 1 tbsp. fresh lime juice
- 2 tbsp. tahini
- 1 garlic clove
- 1 cup of water
- Salt and pepper to taste

**Prep**: Add water and eggplant into the instant pot. Seal pot with the lid, select manual and set timer for 20 minutes.
Once done, release pressure using quick release. Remove lid.
Drain eggplant and let it cool. Remove eggplant skin and transfer eggplant flesh into the food processor.
Add remaining ingredients and process until smooth.

**Nutrition**: Calories 107, Fat 7.7 g, Carbs 9.6 g, Protein 2.4 g

## 12. Potato Spread

**Prep Time: 10 minutes**  
**Servings: 6**

**Cook Time: 15 minutes**

**Ingredients:**
- 1 lb sweet potatoes, peeled and chopped
- 3/4 tbsp. fresh chives, chopped
- 1/2 tsp. paprika
- 1 tbsp. garlic, minced
- 1 cup tomato puree
- Salt and pepper

**Prep**: Add all ingredients except chives into the inner pot of instant pot and stir well.
Seal pot with lid and cook for 15 minutes.
Once done, allow to release pressure naturally for ten minutes then release the rest using quick release. Remove lid.
Transfer instant pot potato mixture into the food processor and process until smooth.
Garnish with chives and serve.

**Nutrition**: Calories 107, Fat 0.2 g, Carbs 25.3 g, Protein 3 g

## 13. Cucumber Chunks with Avocado

**Prep Time: 10 minutes**

**Servings: 5**

**Ingredients:**
- 1 cucumber
- 5 cherry tomatoes
- 2 oz. avocado, pitted
- ¼ tsp. minced garlic
- ¼ tsp. dried basil
- ¾ tsp. sour cream
- ¾ tsp. lemon juice

**Prep**: Trim the cucumber and slice it on 5 thick slices.
After this, churn avocado until it become a creamy mass.
Add sour cream, minced garlic, dried basil, and lemon juice. Mix well.
Spread the avocado mass over the cucumber and top with the cherry tomatoes.

**Nutrition:** Calories 57, Fat: 2.8 g, Carbs: 8 g, Protein: 1.8 g

## 14. Cucumber Tomato Okra Salsa

**Prep Time: 10 minutes**  
**Servings: 4**

**Cook Time: 15 minutes**

**Ingredients:**
- 1 lb tomatoes, chopped
- 1/4 tsp. red pepper flakes
- 1/4 cup fresh lemon juice
- 1 cucumber, chopped
- 1 tbsp. oregano, chopped
- 1 tbsp. fresh basil, chopped
- 1 tbsp. olive oil
- 1 onion, chopped
- 1 tbsp. garlic, chopped
- 1 1/2 cups okra, chopped
- Salt and pepper

**Prep**: Add oil into the inner pot of instant pot and set the pot on sauté mode.
Add onion, garlic, pepper, and salt and sauté for 3 minutes. Add remaining ingredients except for cucumber and stir well. Seal pot with lid and cook on high for 12 minutes.
Allow to release pressure for 10 minutes then release remaining using quick release. Remove lid.
Then add cucumber and mix well.

**Nutrition**: Calories 98, Fat 4 g, Carbs 14 g, Protein 2.7 g

## 15. Date and Fig Smoothie

**Prep Time: 5 minutes**                                                                 **Servings: 2**

**Ingredients:**
- 2 date, pitted
- 2 fig, chopped
- 2 oz. Greek yogurt
- 1/2 cup almond milk
- 1/2 tsp. ground cardamom
- 2 tsp. honey

**Prep**: Place all ingredients in the food processor and blend the mixture until smooth.
Pour the cooked smoothie in the servings glass.

**Nutrition**: Calories 147, Fat: 3 g, Carbs: 27.3 g, Protein: 4 g

## 16. Eggplant Caponata

**Prep Time: 10 minutes**                                                                **Cook Time: 5 minutes**
**Servings: 8**

**Ingredients:**
- 1 eggplant, cut into 1/2-inch chunks
- 1 lb tomatoes, diced
- 1/2 cup tomato puree
- 1/4 cup dates, chopped
- 2 tbsp. vinegar
- 1/2 cup fresh parsley, chopped
- 2 celery stalks, chopped
- 1 onion, chopped
- 2 zucchini, cut into 1/2-inch chunks
- Salt and pepper

**Prep**: Add all ingredients into the inner pot of instant pot and stir well.
Seal pot with lid and cook on high for 5 minutes. Release pressure using quick release. Remove lid.
Stir well and serve.

**Nutrition**: Calories 61, Fat 0.5 g, Carbs 15 g, Protein 2.4 g

## 17. Mediterranean Nachos

**Prep Time: 10 minutes**                                                                **Cook Time: 10 minutes**
**Servings: 6**

**Ingredients**:
- 1 cup nachos
- 1/3 cup Monterey Jack cheese, shredded
- 2 oz. black olives, sliced
- 2 tomatoes, chopped

**Prep**: Crash the nachos and arrange them in the casserole mold in a layer.
Layer the black olives and tomatoes over the nachos. Flatten the ingredients.
Make the layer of cheese and cover mold with foil. Secure the edges.
Bake for 10 minutes at 365 ° F.
Remove the foil from the mold and serve.

**Nutrition**: Calories 134, Fat: 7 g, Carbs: 10 g, Protein: 5 g

## 18. Eggplant Bites

**Prep Time:** 15 minutes  
**Servings:** 8  
**Cook Time:** 30 minutes

**Ingredients:**
- 2 eggs, beaten
- 3 oz. Parmesan, grated
- 1 tbsp. coconut flakes
- ½ tsp. ground paprika
- 1 tsp. salt
- 2 eggplants, trimmed

**Prep:** Slice the eggplants into the thin circles.
Sprinkle the vegetables with salt and mix up. Leave them for 5-10 minutes.
Drain eggplant juice and sprinkle with ground paprika.
Mix together Parmesan and coconut flakes.
Dip each eggplant circle in the egg and then coat in the Parmesan mixture.
Line the baking tray with parchment and place eggplants on it. Bake the vegetables for 30 minutes at 360 º F.
Flip the eggplants into another side after 12 minutes of cooking.

**Nutrition:** Calories 77, Fat: 3.8 g, Carbs: 8.6 g, Protein: 6 g

## 19. Endive Bites

**Prep Time:** 10 minutes  
**Servings:** 10

**Ingredients:**
- 6 oz. endive
- 2 pears, chopped
- 4 oz. Blue cheese, crumbled
- 1 tsp. olive oil
- 1 tsp. lemon juice
- ¾ tsp. ground cinnamon

**Prep:** Separate endive into 10 spears.
In the bowl combine chopped pears, oil, lemon juice, ground cinnamon, and cheese.
Fill the endive spears with cheese mixture.

**Nutrition**: Calories 73, Fat: 3.7 g, Carbs: 7.2 g, Protein: 2.7 g

## 20. Fig-Pecan Bites

**Prep Time:** 10 minutes  
**Servings:** 6  
**Cook Time:** 20 minutes

**Ingredients:**
- ½ cup chopped pecans
- 2 tablespoons honey
- ¾ cup dried figs, about 6 to 8, diced
- 2 tablespoons wheat flaxseed
- ¼ cup quick oats
- 2 tablespoons regular or powdered peanut butter

**Prep:** Combine the figs, quick oats, pecans, peanut butter, and flaxseed into a bowl. Stir the ingredients well.
Drizzle honey and mix everything. Do your best to press all the ingredients into the honey as you are stirring.
Get your hands damp.
Divide the mixture into four sections. Divide each of the four sections into 3 separate sections.
Take one of the three sections and roll them up. Repeat with each section so you have a dozen bites once you are done.

**Nutrition**: Calories: 156, Fats: 5 g, Carbs: 25 g, Protein: 3.2 g

## 21. Roasted Baby Potatoes

**Prep Time:** 10 minutes  
**Servings:** 4  
**Cook Time:** 10 minutes

**Ingredients:**
- 2 lbs. baby potatoes, cut in half
- 1/2 cup vegetable stock
- 1 tsp. paprika
- 3/4 tsp. garlic powder
- 1 tsp. onion powder
- 2 tsp. Italian seasoning
- 1 tbsp. olive oil
- Salt and pepper

**Prep:** Add oil into the inner pot of instant pot and set on sauté mode.

Add potatoes and sauté for 5 minutes. Add remaining ingredients and stir well.
Seal pot with lid and cook on high for five minutes.
Release pressure using quick release. Remove lid. Stir well and serve.

**Nutrition**: Calories 176, Fat 4.6 g, Carbs 29 g, Protein 6 g

## 22. Frozen Blueberry Yogurt

**Prep Time: 10 minutes**  **Cook Time: 30 minutes**
**Servings: 6**

**Ingredients:**
- 2/3 cup honey
- 2 cups chilled yogurt
- 1 pint blueberries
- 1 juiced and zested lemon

**Prep:** With a saucepan on your burner set to medium heat, add the honey, juiced lemon, zest, and blueberries.
Stir the mixture as it begins to simmer for fifteen minutes.
When the liquid is nearly gone, pour the contents into a bowl and place in the fridge for 20 minutes.
Once the fruit is cooled, combine with the yogurt.
Mix until the ingredients are well incorporated.

**Nutrition**: Calories: 234, Fats: 2.5 g, Carbs: 51 g, Protein: 3.1 g

## 23. Garlic Bean Dip

**Prep Time: 10 minutes**  **Cook Time: 45 minutes**
**Servings: 6**

**Ingredients:**
- 1 cup dry beans, rinsed
- 1/2 tsp. cumin
- 1/2 cup salsa
- 2 garlic cloves
- 2 chipotle peppers in adobo sauce
- 5 cups vegetable stock
- Salt and pepper

**Prep**: Add beans, stock, garlic, and chipotle peppers into the instant pot.
Seal pot with lid and cook on high for 45 minutes.
Release pressure using quick release. Remove lid.
Drain beans and reserve 1/2 cup of stock.
Transfer beans, reserve stock, and remaining ingredients into the food processor and process until smooth.

**Nutrition**: Calories 128, Fat 1 g, Carbs 22 g, Protein 7.8 g

## 24. Greek Style Nachos

**Prep Time: 7 minutes**  **Servings: 3**

**Ingredients:**
- 3 oz. tortilla chips
- ¼ cup Greek yogurt
- 1 tbsp. fresh parsley, chopped
- ¼ tsp. minced garlic
- 2 kalamata olives, chopped
- 1 tsp. paprika
- ¼ tsp. ground thyme

**Prep**: In the mixing bowl mix up together Greek yogurt, parsley, minced garlic, olives, paprika, and thyme. Add tortilla chips and mix up gently.

**Nutrition**: Calories 80, Fat: 1.5 g, Carbs: 14 g, Protein: 3 g

## 25. Grilled Tempeh Sticks

**Prep Time: 5 minutes**  **Cook Time: 10 minutes**
**Servings: 6**

**Ingredients:**
- 3 and half cups soy tempeh
- 1 tsp. olive oil

- ½ tsp. ground black pepper
- ¼ tsp. garlic powder

**Prep**: Cut tempeh into the sticks.
Sprinkle each tempeh stick with garlic powder, ground black pepper, and olive oil.
Preheat the grill to 375 ° F.
Place tempeh sticks in the grill and cook them for five minutes from each side.

**Nutrition**: Calories 87, Fat: 2.4 g, Carbs: 10 g, Protein: 6 g

## 26. Homemade Salsa

**Prep Time**: 10 minutes  
**Servings**: 8  
**Cook Time**: 5 minutes

**Ingredients**:
- 12 oz. grape tomatoes, halved
- 1/4 cup fresh cilantro, chopped
- 1 lime juice
- 28 oz. tomatoes, crushed
- 1 tbsp. garlic, minced
- 1 green bell pepper, chopped
- 1 red bell pepper, chopped
- 2 onions, chopped
- 6 whole tomatoes
- Salt

**Prep**: Add whole tomatoes into the instant pot and smash the tomatoes.
Add garlic, grape tomatoes, bell peppers, and onions and stir well.
Seal pot with lid and cook on high for 5 minutes. Allow to release pressure naturally for 10 minutes then release remaining using quick release. Remove lid.
Add cilantro, lime juice, and salt and stir well.

**Nutrition**: Calories 14 g, Fat 1 g, Carbs 33 g, Protein 6.7 g

## 27. Italian Style Potato Fries

**Prep Time**: 10 minutes  
**Servings**: 4  
**Cook Time**: 40 minutes

**Ingredients**:
- 1/3 cup baby red potatoes
- 1 tbsp. Italian seasoning
- 3 tbsps. canola oil
- 1 tsp. turmeric
- ½ tsp. of salt
- ½ tsp. dried rosemary
- 1 tbsp. dried dill

**Prep**: Cut the potatoes into the wedges and transfer in a bowl.
Sprinkle the vegetables with turmeric, rosemary, Italian seasoning, canola oil, salt, and dill.
Shake the potato wedges carefully.
Line the baking tray with baking paper. Place the potatoes wedges in the tray. Flatten it well to make one layer.
Preheat the oven to 375 ° F.
Place the tray in the oven and bake for 40 minutes. Stir the potatoes from time to time.

**Nutrition**: Calories 120, Fat: 11.5 g, Carbs: 4 g, Protein: 0.5 g

## 28. Jalapeno Chickpea Hummus

**Prep Time**: 10 minutes  
**Servings**: 4  
**Cook Time**: 25 minutes

**Ingredients**:
- 1 cup dry chickpeas, soaked overnight and drained
- 1 tsp. ground cumin
- 1/4 cup jalapenos, diced
- 1/2 cup fresh cilantro
- 1 tbsp. tahini
- 1/2 cup olive oil
- Salt and pepper to taste

**Prep**: Add chickpeas into the instant pot and cover with vegetable stock.
Seal pot with lid and cook on high for 25 minutes.
Allow to release pressure naturally. Remove lid.
Drain chickpeas and transfer into the food processor along with remaining ingredients and process until smooth.

**Nutrition**: Calories 424, Fat 30.2 g, Carbs 31.5 g, Protein 10.4 g

## 29. Kale Wraps with Apple and Chicken

**Prep Time:** 10 minutes  
**Servings:** 4  
**Cook Time:** 10 minutes

**Ingredients:**
- 4 kale leaves
- 4 oz. chicken fillet
- ½ apple
- 1 tbsp. butter
- ¼ tsp. chili pepper
- ¾ tsp. salt
- 1 tbsp. lemon juice
- ¾ tsp. dried thyme

**Prep:** Chop the fillet into the cubes. Then mix up together chicken with salt and chili pepper.
Heat up butter in the skillet. Add chicken cubes and oast them for four minutes.
Meanwhile, chop the apple into cubes and add it in the chicken. Mix well.
Sprinkle the ingredients with dried thyme and lemon juice.
Cook for five minutes over the medium-high heat.
Fill the kale leaves with the chicken mixture and wrap.

**Nutrition:** Calories 105, Fat: 5 g, Carbs: 6 g, Protein: 10 g

## 30. Layered Dip

**Prep Time:** 10 minutes  
**Servings:** 12

**Ingredients:**
- ½ cup hummus
- 8 tbsps. Tzatziki
- 1 cup tomatoes, chopped
- 1 cup cucumbers, chopped
- 1 tsp. olive oil
- 1 tbsp. lemon juice
- 1/3 cup fresh parsley, chopped
- 1 jalapeno pepper, chopped

**Prep:** In the mixing bowl mix up together fresh parsley, lemon juice, olive oil, cucumbers, tomatoes, and jalapeno pepper.
Make layer of ½ part tomato mixture in a casserole mold.
Top it with the layer of hummus. Add the remaining tomato mixture and flatten well. Top it with Tzatziki.
Store the dip in the refrigerator for to 3 hours.

**Nutrition:** Calories 47, Fat: 3.7 g, Carbs: 3.2 g, Protein: 1 g

## 31. Lemon Cauliflower Florets

**Prep Time:** 15 minutes  
**Servings:** 6  
**Cook Time:** 12 minutes

**Ingredients:**
- 1-pound cauliflower head, trimmed
- 3 tbsps. lemon juice
- 3 eggs, beaten
- 1 tsp. salt
- 1 tsp. ground black pepper
- 2 cups water, for cooking
- 3 tbsps. almond butter
- 1 tsp. turmeric

**Prep:** Place the cauliflower head in the pan. Add water and boil the cauliflower for 8 minutes.
When the vegetable is cooled, separate it onto the florets.
Whisk together eggs, salt, turmeric, and ground black pepper.
Dip cauliflower florets into the egg mixture.
Place the almond butter in the skillet and heat it up.
Roast the cauliflower florets for 2 minutes on each side over the medium heat.
Sprinkle the cooked florets with lemon juice.

**Nutrition:** Calories 102, Fat: 6.7 g, Carbs: 6 g, Protein: 6 g

## 32. Light Garlic Hummus

**Prep Time:** 10 minutes  
**Servings:** 12  
**Cook Time:** 40 minutes

**Ingredients:**
- 1 1/2 cups dry chickpeas, rinsed
- 2 1/2 tbsp. fresh lemon juice
- 1 tbsp. garlic, minced
- 1/2 cup tahini
- 6 cups of water
- Salt and pepper

**Prep:** Add water and chickpeas into the instant pot. Seal pot with a lid, select manual and set timer for 40 minutes.
Allow to release pressure. Remove lid.
Drain chickpeas and reserved 1/2 cup liquid.
Transfer chickpeas, reserved liquid, tahini, pepper, lemon juice, garlic, and salt into the food processor and process until smooth.

**Nutrition**: Calories 150, Fat 7 g, Carbs 17.7 g, Protein 6.5 g

## 33. Potatoes with Parmesan

**Prep Time:** 10 minutes  
**Servings:** 4  
**Cook Time:** 6 minutes

**Ingredients:**
- 2 lb potatoes, rinsed and cut into chunks
- 2 tbsp. parmesan cheese, grated
- 2 tbsp. olive oil
- 1/2 tsp. parsley
- 1/2 tsp. Italian seasoning
- 1 tsp. garlic, minced
- 1 cup vegetable broth
- 1/2 tsp. salt

**Prep:** Add all ingredients except cheese into the instant pot and stir well.
Seal pot with lid and cook on high for 6 minutes.
Release pressure using quick release. Remove lid.
Add parmesan and stir until cheese is melted.

**Nutrition**: Calories 236, Fat 8 g. Carbs 36 g, Protein 5.8 g

## 34. Parsley Cheese Balls

**Prep Time:** 10 minutes  
**Servings:** 6  
**Cook Time:** 1 minute

**Ingredients:**
- 1/3 cup Cheddar cheese, shredded
- 1 tbsp. dried dill
- 1 egg, beaten
- ½ tsp. salt
- 2 tbsps. coconut flakes
- 3 tbsps. sunflower oil

**Prep**: Mix up together cheese with dill, salt, and coconut flakes. Add egg and stir carefully until homogenous.
Make balls from the cheese mixture.
Heat up oil in the skillet. Place cheese balls in the hot oil and roast for ten seconds from each side.

**Nutrition**: Calories 103, Fat: 10 g, Carbs: 0.6 g, Protein: 2.4 g

## 35. Peanut Butter Yogurt Dip

**Prep Time:** 10 minutes  
**Servings:** 4

**Ingredients:**
- 2 tbsps. peanut butter
- 1 oz. Greek Yogurt
- 1 tsp. sesame seeds
- ½ tsp. vanilla extract
- 1 tbsp. honey

**Prep:** Put peanut butter and Greek yogurt in the big bowl.
Mix up the mixture until fluffy. Add sesame seeds, vanilla extract, and honey. Stir it carefully.
Store the dip in the fridge.

**Nutrition**: Calories 75, Fat: 4.4 g, Carbs: 6.6 g, Protein: 3 g

## 36. Italian Potatoes

**Prep Time:** 10 minutes  
**Servings:** 6  
**Cook Time:** 7 minutes

**Ingredients:**
- 2 lbs. baby potatoes, cut in half
- 3/4 cup vegetable broth
- 6 oz. Italian dry dressing mix

**Prep**: Add all ingredients into the inner pot of instant pot and stir well.
Seal pot with lid and cook on high for 7 minutes.
Allow to release pressure naturally for 3 minutes then release remaining using quick release. Remove lid.
Stir well and serve.

**Nutrition**: Calories 147, Fat 0.5 g, Carbs 41.7 g, Protein 4.3 g

## 37. Radish Bread Bites

**Prep Time: 10 minutes**  
**Servings: 8**  
**Cook Time: 10 minutes**

**Ingredients:**
- 2 tbsps. butter
- 1/3 cup milk
- 1 ½ cup wheat flour, whole grain
- 1 tsp. salt
- 1 tsp. avocado oil
- 1 cup radish
- 1 tbsp. cream cheese

**Prep:** Melt butter and add it together with milk. Stir the liquid.
Then mix together butter mixture with flour.
Knead the dough until it becomes soft. Cut the dough into eight pieces. Roll up every piece into the circle.
Pour avocado oil in the skillet.
Roast the flatbreads for one minute on each side over the medium heat.
After this, slice the radish and mix it up with salt and cream cheese.
Top cooked flatbreads with radish.

**Nutrition:** Calories 123, Fat: 3.8 g, Carbs: 18.9 g, Protein: 3 g

## 38. Rice Burgers

**Prep Time: 10 minutes**  
**Servings: 4**  
**Cook Time: 30 minutes**

**Ingredients:**
- 1/3 cup rice
- 1 cup of water
- ½ tsp. Salt
- 2 tbsps. ricotta cheese
- 1 egg
- ¼ cup yellow onion, diced
- 1 tsp. sunflower oil
- ½ tsp. ground black pepper
- 1 tbsp. wheat flour, whole grain

**Prep:** Pour water in a pan, and add rice and salt.
Close the lid and boil rice for 15 minutes.
Meanwhile, heat up oil in the skillet. Add diced onion and roast it. Combine cooked rice with onion.
Add wheat flour, black pepper, and egg. Mix up the mixture.
Then make medium size burgers. Bake the burgers for 10 minutes at 355°F.
Top the cooked appetizer with ricotta cheese.

**Nutrition:** Calories 104, Fat: 3g, Carbs: 15.1g, Protein: 3.7g

## 39. Roasted Chickpeas

**Prep Time: 10 minutes**  
**Servings: 8**  
**Cook Time: 3 hours**

**Ingredients:**
- 1 cup chickpeas, canned
- 1 tsp. salt
- ½ tsp. ground coriander
- ½ tsp. ground paprika
- ½ tsp. dried thyme
- ¾ tsp. cayenne pepper
- 2 tbsps. olive oil

**Prep:** Drain the chickpeas and dry them carefully. Place them in the baking tray.
Mix up together ground paprika, dried thyme, salt, ground coriander, and cayenne pepper.
Sprinkle the chickpeas with spices and shake well. Drizzle with olive oil.
Preheat the oven to 375F.
Place the tray with chickpeas in the oven and cook them for 35 minutes.
Flip the chickpeas on another side occasionally.

**Nutrition:** Calories 122, Fat: 5.1 g, Carbs: 15.4 g, Protein: 4.9 g

## 40. Salty Almonds

**Prep Time:** 1 hour 10 minutes
**Servings:** 5

**Cook Time:** 15 minutes

**Ingredients:**
- 1 cup almonds
- 3 tbsps. salt
- 2 cups of water

**Prep:** Bring water to boil.
After this, add 2 tbsps. of salt in water and stir it.
Add almonds, and let them soak for 1 hour.
Meanwhile, line the the baking sheet with baking paper and preheat the oven to 350°F.
Arrange the almonds in one layer in the baking sheet, after drying them. Sprinkle them with the remaining salt.
Bake for 15 minutes. Mix it from time to time.

**Nutrition:** Calories 110, Fat: 9.5 g, Carbs: 4.1 g, Protein: 4 g

## 41. Strawberry Popsicle

**Prep Time:** 10 minutes
**Servings:** 5

**Cook Time:** 10 minutes

**Ingredients:**
- ½ cup almond milk
- 1 ½ cups fresh strawberries

**Prep:** Using a blender to combine the almond milk and strawberries thoroughly in a bowl.
Pour the mixture into the popsicle molds and combine the sticks into the mixture.
Place in the freezer for 4 hours.

**Nutrition:** Calories: 3, Fats: 0.5 g, Carbs: 7 g, Protein: 0.6 g

## 42. Sweet Potato Fries

**Prep Time:** 10 minutes
**Servings:** 5

**Cook Time:** 35 minutes

**Ingredients:**
- 1 tsp. Zaatar spices
- 3 sweet potatoes
- 1 tbsp. dried dill
- 1 tsp. salt
- 3 tsps. sunflower oil
- ½ tsp. paprika

**Prep:** Pour water into the crockpot. Peel the sweet potatoes and cut them into the fries.
Line the baking tray with parchment.
Place the layer of the sweet potato in the tray.
Sprinkle the vegetables with dried dill, salt, and paprika.
Then sprinkle sweet potatoes with Zaatar and mix up well with the help of the fingertips.
Sprinkle the sweet potato fries with sunflower oil.
Preheat the oven to 375F.
Bake the sweet potato fries for 35 minutes. Stir the fries every 10 minutes.

**Nutrition:** Calories 28, Fat: 2.9 g, Carbs: 0.6 g, Protein: 0.2 g

## 43. Tomato Finger Sandwich

**Prep Time:** 10 minutes

**Servings:** 6

**Ingredients:**
- 6 corn tortillas
- 1 tbsp. cream cheese
- 1 tbsp. ricotta cheese
- ½ tsp. minced garlic
- 1 tbsp. fresh dill, chopped
- 2 tomatoes, sliced

**Prep:** Cut each tortilla into 2 triangles.
Then mix up together ricotta cheese, cream cheese, minced garlic, and dill.

Spread 6 triangles with cream cheese mixture.
Then place sliced tomato and top with remaining tortilla triangles.

**Nutrition:** Calories 71, Fat: 1.6 g, Carbs: 12.8 g, Protein: 2.3 g

## 44. Traditional Mediterranean Hummus

**Prep Time:** 10 minutes  
**Servings:** 7

**Cook Time:** 45 minutes

**Ingredients:**
- 1 cup chickpeas, soaked
- 6 cups of water
- ½ cup lemon juice
- 3 tbsp. olive oil
- 1 tsp. salt
- 1/3 tsp. harissa

**Prep:** Put the water in a large pot and boil along with the chickpeas for 45 minutes.
Then transfer chickpeas in the food processor. Add 1 cup of the chickpeas water and the lemon juice. Add salt and harissa as well.
Blend the hummus until it is smooth. Add olive oil and pulse for 10 seconds.
Transfer the hummus in the bowl and store it in the fridge up to 2 days.

**Nutrition:** Calories 160, Fat: 7.9 g, Carbs: 17.8 g, Protein: 5.7 g

## 45. Tuna Salad in Lettuce Cups

**Prep Time:** 10 minutes  
**Servings:** 6

**Cook Time:** 10 minutes

**Ingredients:**
- 4 Romaine lettuce leaves
- 8 oz. tuna fillet
- 1 tsp. balsamic vinegar
- ½ tsp. olive oil
- 1 tbsp. fresh dill, chopped
- ¼ tsp. salt
- ¾ tsp. chili pepper
- 1 tomato, chopped
- ¾ cup Plain yogurt

**Prep:** Rub the tuna fillet with salt and chili pepper and drizzle with olive oil.
Cook the tuna for 10 minutes at 365°F.
Then cool it and chop it.
In the bowl combine chopped tuna, fresh dill, yogurt, tomato, and balsamic vinegar. Mix well.
Fill the lettuce leaves with the tuna mixture.

**Nutrition:** Calories 152, Fat: 11.2 g, Carbs: 3.4 g, Protein: 9 g

## 46. Tzatziki

**Prep Time:** 10 minutes

**Servings:** 4

**Ingredients:**
- 1 large cucumber, trimmed
- 3 oz. Greek yogurt
- 1 tsp. olive oil
- 3 tbsps. fresh dill, chopped
- 1 tbsp. lime juice
- ¾ tsp. salt
- 1 garlic clove, minced

**Prep:** Grate the cucumber and squeeze out the juice. Place it in the bowl.
Add Greek yogurt, salt, lime juice, olive oil, dill, and minced garlic. Mix up the mixture until smooth.
Store Tzatziki in the refrigerator for up to 2 days.

**Nutrition:** Calories 44, Fat: 1.8 g, Carbs: 5.1 g, Protein: 3.2 g

## 47. Wheat Berry Burgers

**Prep Time:** 25 minutes  
**Servings:** 6

**Cook Time:** 15 minutes

**Ingredients:**
- 1 cup wheat berry, cooked
- 2 eggs
- ¼ cup ground chicken

- *1 tbsp. wheat flour, whole grain*
- *1 tsp. Italian seasoning*
- *1 tbsp. olive oil*
- *1 tsp. salt*

**Prep:** In a mixing bowl mix up together ground chicken and wheat berry. Crack the eggs in the mixture.
Then add Italian seasoning, wheat flour, and salt. Mix the mixture until smooth.
Then make the burgers and freeze them in the freezer for 20 minutes.
Heat the olive oil in the pan. Place the frozen burgers in the hot oil and roast for 4 minutes on each side over the high heat.
Then cook burgers for another 10 minutes. Flip them onto another side occasionally.

**Nutrition:** Calories 97, Fat: 5.7 g, Carbs: 9.2 g, Protein: 5.2 g

### 48. Whole-Grain Lavash Chips

**Prep Time: 8 minutes**
**Servings: 4**

**Cook Time: 10 minutes**

**Ingredients:**
- *1 lavash sheet, whole grain*
- *1 tbsp. canola oil*
- *1 tsp. paprika*
- *½ tsp. chili pepper*
- *½ tsp. salt*

**Prep:** In a bowl whisk together paprika, canola oil, chili pepper, and salt.
Then cut lavash sheets roughly (in the shape of chips).
Sprinkle chips with oil mixture and arrange in the tray in a thin layer.
Bake the lavash chips for 10 minutes at 365°F. Turn them occasionally on another side to avoid burning.
Cool the cooked chips before serving.

**Nutrition:** Calories 73, Fat: 4 g, Carbs: 8.4 g, Protein: 1.6 g

### 49. Zucchini Chips

**Prep Time: 15 minutes**
**Servings: 4**

**Cook Time: 20 minutes**

**Ingredients:**
- *1 zucchini*
- *2 oz. Parmesan, grated*
- *½ tsp. paprika*
- *1 tsp. olive oil*

**Prep:** Slice the zucchini into the chips with a vegetable slices.
Then mix together paprika and Parmesan.
Drizzle the zucchini chips with olive oil. After this, dip every zucchini slice in the cheese mixture.
Place the zucchini in the lined baking dish and bake for 20 minutes at 375°F.
Flip the zucchini to the other side after 10 minutes of cooking.
Cool the chips well before serving.

**Nutrition:** Calories 64, Fat: 4.3 g, Carbs: 2.3 g, Protein: 5.2 g

### 50. Walnut and Freekeh Pilaf

**Prep Time: 15 minutes**
**Servings: 4**

**Cook Time: 15 minutes**

**Ingredients:**
- *2½ cups freekeh*
- *3 tablespoons extra-virgin olive oil, divided*
- *2 medium onions, diced*
- *¼ teaspoon ground cinnamon*
- *¼ teaspoon ground allspice*
- *5 cups chicken stock*
- *½ cup chopped walnuts*
- *Salt*
- *Freshly ground black pepper*
- *½ cup plain, unsweetened, full-fat Greek yogurt*
- *1½ teaspoons freshly squeezed lemon juice*
- *½ teaspoon garlic powder*

**Prep:** In a small bowl, soak the freekeh covered in cold water for 5 minutes. Drain and rinse the freekeh, then rinse one more time.
In a large sauté pan, heat 2 tablespoons oil, add the onions and cook until it is fragrant. Add the freekeh, cinnamon, and allspice.
Stir periodically for 1 minute.
Add the stock and walnuts and season with salt and pepper. Bring it to a simmer.

Cover and reduce the heat to low—Cook for 15 minutes. Once freekeh is tender, remove from the heat and allow to rest for 5 minutes.
In a bowl, combine the lemon juice, yogurt, and garlic powder. You may need to add salt to bring out the flavors. Add the yogurt mixture to the freekeh and serve.

**Nutrition:** Calories: 653 Protein: 23 g Carbs: 91 g Sugars: 4 g Fat: 25 g

## 51. Italian Roasted Vegetables

**Prep Time:** 15 minutes
**Servings:** 6

**Cook Time:** 45 minutes

**Ingredients:**
- Nonstick cooking spray
- 2 eggplants, peeled and sliced ⅛ inch thick
- 1 zucchini, sliced ¼ inch thick
- 1 yellow summer squash, sliced ¼ inch thick
- 2 Roma tomatoes, sliced ⅛ inch thick
- ¼ cup, plus 2 tablespoons olive oil, divided
- 1 tablespoon garlic powder
- ¼ teaspoon dried oregano
- ¼ teaspoon dried basil
- ¼ teaspoon salt
- Freshly ground black pepper

**Prep:** Preheat the oven to 400°F.
Spray a 9-by-13-inch baking dish with cooking spray. In the dish, toss the eggplant, zucchini, squash, and tomatoes with 2 tablespoons oil, garlic powder, oregano, basil, salt, and pepper.
Standing the vegetables up (like little soldiers), alternate layers of eggplant, zucchini, squash, and Roma tomato.
Drizzle the top with the remaining ¼ cup of olive oil.
Bake, uncovered, for 40 to 45 minutes, or until vegetables are golden brown.

**Nutrition:** Calories: 186g Protein: 3 g Carbs: 15 g Fat: 14 g

## 52. Mediterranean Crostini

**Prep Time:** 15 minutes
**Servings:** 6

**Cook Time:** 10 minutes

**Ingredients:**
- 1 baguette, sliced ¼ inch thick
- 5 tablespoons extra-virgin olive oil
- ¼ teaspoon salt
- ⅛ Teaspoon freshly ground black pepper
- ½ cup store-bought hummus or Garlic-Lemon Hummus
- 1 cup quartered grape tomatoes
- 1 cup diced cucumber
- 4 chopped pitted Kalamata olives
- ½ cup crumbled feta cheese
- ½ cup chopped flat-leaf parsley, for garnish
- ⅓ cup Pickled Turnips

**Prep:** Preheat the oven to 350°F.
On baking sheets, arrange the baguette slices and carefully brush the tops and sides with the oil. Sprinkle with salt and pepper.
Bake for 10 minutes or until the toasts become slightly crispy. Remove them from the oven and set aside.
Once the slices are cool, spread a thin layer of hummus on the toast.
Individually, spoon tomatoes, cucumber, olives, and feta cheese onto the toast. Garnish with fresh parsley and pickled turnips.

**Nutrition:** Calories: 436 Protein: 14 g Carbs: 55 g Fat: 19 g

## 53. Bruschetta Hummus Platter

**Prep Time:** 15 minutes

**Servings:** 6

**Ingredients:**
- ½ cup finely diced fresh tomato
- ⅓ Cup finely diced seedless English cucumber
- 1 teaspoon extra-virgin olive oil
- 1 (10-ounce) container plain hummus
- 2 tablespoons balsamic glaze
- 2 tablespoons crumbled feta cheese
- 1 tablespoon fresh chopped parsley
- ¼ cup Herbed Oil
- 4 warmed pitas, cut into wedges, for serving
- Carrot sticks, for serving
- Celery sticks, for serving
- Sliced bell peppers, for serving
- Broccoli, for serving
- Purple cauliflower, for serving

**Prep:** In a small bowl, mix the tomato and cucumber and toss with the olive oil. Pile the cucumber mixture over a fresh container of hummus. Drizzle the hummus and vegetables with the balsamic glaze. Top with crumbled feta and fresh parsley.

Put the hummus on a large cutting board. Pour the Herbed Oil in a small bowl and put it on the cutting board. Surround the bowls with the pita wedges and cut carrot sticks, celery sticks, sliced bell peppers, broccoli, and cauliflower.

**Nutrition:** Calories: 345 Protein: 9 g Carbs: 32 g Fat: 19 g

## 54. Garlic-Lemon Hummus

**Prep Time: 15 minutes**  **Servings: 6**

**Ingredients:**
- 1 (15-ounce) can chickpeas, drained and rinsed
- 4 to 5 tablespoons tahini (sesame seed paste)
- 4 tablespoons extra-virgin olive oil, divided
- 2 lemons juice
- 1 lemon, zested, divided
- 1 tablespoon minced garlic
- Pinch salt

**Prep:** In a food processor, combine the chickpeas, tahini, and 2 tablespoons of olive oil, lemon juice, half of the lemon zest, and garlic and blend for up to 1 minute. After 30 seconds of blending, stop and scrape the sides down with a spatula before blending for another 30 seconds. Add salt as desired. Add 1 teaspoon of water at a time to help thin the hummus to a better consistency. Scoop the hummus into a bowl, then drizzle with the remaining 2 tablespoons of olive oil and remaining lemon zest.

**Nutrition:** Calories: 216 Protein: 5 g Carbs: 17 g Fat: 15 g

## 55. Mediterranean Trail Mix

**Prep Time: 5 minutes**  **Servings: 6**

**Ingredients:**
- 1 cup roughly chopped unsalted walnuts
- ½ cup roughly chopped salted almonds
- ½ cup shelled salted pistachios
- ½ cup roughly chopped apricots
- ½ cup roughly chopped dates
- ⅓ Cup dried figs, sliced in half

**Prep:** In a large zip-top bag, combine the walnuts, almonds, pistachios, apricots, dates, and figs and mix well.

**Nutrition:** Calories: 348 Protein: 9 g Carbs: 33 g Total Fat: 24 g

## 56. Savory Mediterranean Popcorn

**Prep Time: 5 minutes**  **Cook Time: 2 minutes**
**Servings: 4 to 6**

**Ingredients:**
- 3 tablespoons extra-virgin olive oil
- ¼ teaspoon garlic powder
- ¼ teaspoon freshly ground black pepper
- ¼ teaspoon of sea salt
- ⅛ Teaspoon dried thyme
- ⅛ Teaspoon dried oregano
- 12 cups plain popped popcorn

**Prep:** In a large sauté pan or skillet, heat the oil over medium heat until shimmering. Then, add the garlic powder, pepper, salt, thyme, and oregano until fragrant.
In a large bowl, drizzle the oil over the popcorn, toss, and serve.

**Nutrition:** Calories: 183 Protein: 3 g Carbs: 19 g Fat: 12 g

## 57. Turkish-Spiced Nuts

**Prep Time: 10 minutes**  **Cook Time: 5 minutes**
**Servings: 4 to 6**

**Ingredients:**
- 1 tablespoon extra-virgin olive oil
- 1 cup mixed nuts (walnuts, almonds, cashews, peanuts)
- 2 tablespoons paprika
- 1 tablespoon dried mint
- ½ tablespoon ground cinnamon
- ½ tablespoon kosher salt
- ¼ tablespoon garlic powder
- ¼ teaspoon freshly ground black pepper
- ⅛ Tablespoon ground cumin

**Prep:** In a small to a medium saucepan, heat the oil on low heat.
Once the oil is warm, add the nuts, paprika, mint, cinnamon, salt, garlic powder, pepper, and cumin and stir continually until the spices are well incorporated with the nuts.

**Nutrition:** Calories: 204 Protein: 6 g Carbs: 10 g Sugars: 2 g Fat: 18 g

## 58. Lemony Orzo

**Prep Time: 5 minutes**  **Cook Time: 5 minutes**
**Servings: 2 Cups**

**Ingredients:**
- 1 cup dry orzo
- 1 cup halved grape tomatoes
- 1 (6-ounce) bag baby spinach
- 2 tablespoons extra-virgin olive oil
- ¼ teaspoon salt
- Freshly ground black pepper
- ¾ cup crumbled feta cheese
- 1 lemon, juiced and zested

**Prep:** Bring a medium pot of water to a boil. Stir in the orzo and cook uncovered for 8 minutes. Drain the water, then return the orzo to medium heat.
Add in the spinach and tomatoes and cook until the spinach is wilted. Add the oil, salt, and pepper and mix well. Top the dish with feta, lemon juice, and lemon zest, then toss one or two more times and enjoy!
Variation Tip: For additional fiber and protein, try whole-wheat orzo. You can even find gluten-free orzo for a gluten-free version of this dish.

**Nutrition:** Calories: 610 Protein: 21 g Carbs: 74 g Fat: 27 g

## 59. Puff Pastry Roll with Roasted Vegetables

**Prep Time: 10 minutes**  **Cook Time: 35 minutes**
**Servings: 4 to 6**

**Ingredients:**
- Nonstick cooking spray
- 1 zucchini, cut in ¼-inch-thick slices
- ½ bunch asparagus, cut into quarters
- 1 package (6-inch) whole-grain pastry discs, in the freezer section, at room temperature
- 1 large egg, beaten

**Prep:** Preheat the oven to 350°F.
Spray a baking sheet with cooking spray and arrange the zucchini and asparagus on it in a single layer. Roast for 15 to 20 minutes, until tender. Set aside to cool.
Allow the pastry dough to warm to room temperature. Place the discs on a floured surface.
Place a roasted zucchini slice on one half of each disc, then top with asparagus. Fold the empty side over the full side and pinch the turnover closed with a fork.
Once all discs are full and closed, brush the turnovers with the beaten egg and put them onto a baking sheet. Bake for 10 to 15 minutes, until golden brown. Let cool completely before eating.

**Nutrition:** Calories: 334 Protein: 9 g Carbs: 42 g Total Fat: 15 g

## 60. Turmeric Crunchy Chickpeas

**Prep Time: 15 minutes**  **Cook Time: 30 minutes**
**Servings: 4**

**Ingredients:**
- 2 (15-ounce) cans organic chickpeas, drained and rinsed
- 3 tablespoons extra-virgin olive oil
- 2 teaspoons Turkish or smoked paprika
- 2 teaspoons turmeric
- ½ teaspoon dried oregano
- ½ teaspoon salt
- ¼ teaspoon ground ginger
- ⅛ Teaspoon ground white pepper

**Prep:** Preheat the oven to 400°F. Line a baking sheet with parchment paper and set aside.
Completely dry the chickpeas. Lay the chickpeas out on a baking sheet, roll them around with paper towels, and allow them to air-dry. I usually let them dry for at least 2½ hours, but can also be left to dry overnight.
In a medium bowl, combine the olive oil, paprika, turmeric, oregano, salt, ginger, and white pepper (if using).

Add the dry chickpeas to the bowl and mix to combine.

Put the chickpeas on the prepared baking sheet and cook for 30 minutes, or until the chickpeas turn golden brown. At 15 minutes, move the chickpeas around on the baking sheet to avoid burning. Check every 10 minutes in case the chickpeas begin to crisp up before the full cooking time has elapsed.

Remove from the oven and set them aside to cool.

**Nutrition:** Calories: 308 Protein: 11 g Carbs: 40 g Fat: 13 g

## 61. Crispy Garlic Oven Potatoes

**Prep Time:** 30 minutes  
**Servings:** 2  
**Cook Time:** 30 minutes

**Ingredients:**
- 10 ounces golden mini potatoes, halved
- 4 tablespoons extra-virgin olive oil
- 2 teaspoons dried, minced garlic
- 1 teaspoon onion salt
- ½ teaspoon paprika
- ¼ teaspoon freshly ground black pepper
- ¼ teaspoon red pepper flakes
- ¼ teaspoon dried dill

**Prep:** Preheat the oven to 400°F.

Soak the potatoes and put in a bowl of ice water for 30 minutes. Change the water if you return, and the water is milky.

Rinse and dry the potatoes, then put them on a baking sheet.

Drizzle the potatoes with oil and sprinkle with the garlic, onion salt, paprika, pepper, red pepper flakes, and dill. Using tongs or your hands, toss well to coat.

Lower the heat to 375°F, add potatoes to the oven, and bake for 20 minutes.

At 20 minutes, check and flip potatoes. Bake for another 10 minutes, or until the potatoes are fork-tender.

**Nutrition:** Calories: 344 Protein: 3 g Carbs: 24 g Sugars: 1 g Fat: 28 g

## 62. Hummus

**Prep Time:** 20 Minutes  
**Servings:** 4

**Ingredients:**
- 1 (15-ounce) can chickpeas, drained and rinsed
- ½ cup plus 3 tablespoons cold water, divided
- 4 garlic cloves, peeled
- ½ teaspoon ground cumin
- ¼ cup tahini
- ½ cup freshly squeezed lemon juice
- Salt

**Prep:** In a food processor, combine the chickpeas, ½ cup of cold water, and garlic. Process for about 5 minutes or until well combined. Add tahini, cumin, and lemon juice and season with salt. Process into a smooth, spreadable paste, about 2 minutes more. If your hummus is a little thick, add more cold water, 1 tablespoon at a time, and process until it reaches the desired consistency.

**Nutrition:** Calories: 203 Carbs: 22 g Protein: 9 g Fat: 10 g

## 63. Eggplant Caviar

**Prep Time:** 10 Minutes  
**Servings:** 4  
**Cook Time:** 1 Hour

**Ingredients:**
- 2 (1-pound) eggplants
- 2 garlic cloves, mashed
- ½ cup finely chopped fresh parsley
- ½ cup finely diced red bell pepper
- ¼ cup freshly squeezed lemon juice, plus more as needed
- 2 tablespoons tahini
- ⅛ Teaspoon salt, plus more as needed

**Prep:** Preheat the broiler.

Pierce the eggplants with a fork in several places to prevent them from bursting in the oven, and place them on a rimmed baking sheet. Broil for about 3 minutes until the skin is charred on one side. Flip the eggplants and broil the other side for about 3 minutes more until charred. Remove and let cool.

Carefully remove the skin from the eggplants and scoop the pulp into a bowl. Using a fork or wooden pestle, mash the pulp into a smooth purée.

Add the garlic, parsley, red bell pepper, lemon juice, tahini, and salt. Stir until well combined. Taste and season with more salt, as needed.

Refrigerate for at least 1 hour before serving. Leftover "caviar" can be kept refrigerated in an airtight container for up to 5 days or frozen for up to 1 month—Thaw in the refrigerator overnight before using it.

**Nutrition:** Calories: 115 Carbs: 17 g Protein: 4 g Fat: 5 g

## 64. Walnut and Red Pepper Spread

**Prep Time: 20 minutes**  **Servings: 6**

**Ingredients:**
- 3 slices whole-wheat bread
- 1 red bell pepper, seeded and coarsely chopped
- ½ onion, chopped
- 1 cup walnuts
- 3 tablespoons Harissa, or store-bought
- 2 tablespoons pomegranate molasses or cranberry juice
- ½ teaspoon ground coriander
- ½ teaspoon ground cumin
- ¼ cup olive oil

**Prep:** In a food processor, combine the bread, red bell pepper, onion, and walnuts.

Process for a few seconds until combined but coarse. Do not over process. You want to retain some texture of the walnuts in this spread.

Add the harissa, molasses, coriander, cumin, and olive oil. Process for a few seconds until the mixture resembles an almost smooth paste.

Refrigerate any leftovers in an airtight container for up to 1 week, or freeze for 2 to 3 months.

**Nutrition:** Calories: 300 Carbs: 19 g Protein: 6 g Fat: 24g;

## 65. Green Olive Tapenade

**Prep Time: 20 minutes**  **Servings: 6**

**Ingredients:**
- 2 cups pitted green olives
- 1 cup coarsely chopped walnuts
- 1 onion, chopped
- ½ cup chopped fresh parsley
- ¼ cup freshly squeezed lemon juice
- ¼ cup olive oil
- 1 teaspoon dried oregano

**Prep:** In a food processor, combine the olives, walnuts, onion, and parsley. Pulse about 5 times until the mixture is coarsely chopped.

Add the lemon juice, olive oil, and oregano—process for a few seconds more. The spread should be finely chopped but not puréed.

**Nutrition:** Calories: 259 g Carbs: 8 g Protein: 4 g Fat: 26 g

## 66. Skordalia

**Prep Time: 30 minutes**  **Servings: 6**

**Ingredients:**
- 1 cup water
- 5 large slices Italian bread, crusts removed
- 8 garlic cloves, peeled
- ⅛ Teaspoon salt, plus more as needed
- 4 potatoes, peeled and boiled
- ½ cup apple cider vinegar, plus more as needed
- ½ cup olive oil

**Prep:** Pour the water onto a rimmed baking sheet and put the bread slices into the water. Soak the bread for 5 minutes. Remove the bread and squeeze out the excess water. Set aside.

In a medium bowl, using a fork or wooden pestle, mash the garlic and salt into a smooth paste. Add the boiled potatoes and soaked bread and gently mash and mix to combine.

Add the vinegar and olive oil and continue to mix until you have no lumps. Slowly mix in more vinegar if the skordalia is too thick to spread.

Cover and refrigerate until serving. Spoon any leftovers into an airtight container and freeze for up to 1 month.

**Nutrition:** Calories: 320 Fat: 18 g Carbs: 36 g Protein: 5 g

## 67. Mint Labneh

**Prep Time:** 10 minutes

**Servings:** 6

**Ingredients:**
- 32 ounces Plain Yogurt, or store-bought
- ½ teaspoon salt
- ¼ cup olive oil
- ¼ cup finely chopped fresh mint

**Prep:** In a large bowl, stir together the yogurt and salt.
Line a colander with several layers of cheesecloth. Spoon the yogurt mixture into the lined colander. Place the colander over a sink or a bowl and let the mixture sit for 2 hours or until most water is drained.
Spoon the labneh into a bowl and stir in the olive oil and mint until well combined. The labneh can be refrigerated in an airtight container for 1 to 2 weeks.

**Nutrition:** Calories: 173 Fat: 14 g Carbs: 8 g Protein: 5 g

## 68. Marinated Olives

**Prep Time:** 10 minutes

**Servings:** 4

**Ingredients:**
- ¼ cup olive oil
- ¼ cup red wine vinegar
- Grated zest of 1 lemon
- 1 teaspoon chopped fresh rosemary
- 2 cups jarred olives, drained

**Prep:** In a medium bowl, whisk the olive oil, vinegar, lemon zest, and rosemary until blended.
Add the olives and gently stir to coat. Toss well and let marinate for at least 3 hours before serving.

**Nutrition:** Calories: 209 Fat: 21 g Carbs: 7 g Protein: 1 g

## 69. Pickled Turnips

**Prep Time:** 15 minutes

**Servings:** 12

**Ingredients:**
- 4 cups water
- ¼ cup salt
- 1 cup white distilled vinegar
- 1 small beet, peeled and quartered
- 1 garlic clove, peeled
- 2 pounds turnips, peeled, halved, and cut into ¼-inch half-moons

**Prep:** In a medium bowl, whisk the water and salt until the salt dissolves. Whisk in the vinegar.
Place the beet and garlic in a clean 2-quart glass jar with a tight-sealing lid. Layer the turnips on top.
Pour the vinegar mixture over the turnips to cover them. Seal the lid tightly and let the jar sit at room temperature for 1 week.

**Nutrition:** Calories: 26 Fat: 0 g Carbs: 6 g Protein: 1 g

## 70. Stuffed Celery

**Prep Time:** 15 Minutes
**Servings:** 3

**Cook Time:** 20 Minutes

**Ingredients:**
- Olive oil
- 1 clove garlic, minced
- 2 tbsp Pine nuts
- 2 tbsp dry-roasted sunflower seeds
- ¼ cup Italian cheese blend, shredded
- 8 stalks celery leaves
- 1 (8-ounce) fat-free cream cheese
- Cooking spray

**Prep:** Sauté garlic and pine nuts over a medium setting for the heat until the nuts are golden brown. Cut off the wide base and tops from celery.
Remove two thin strips from the round side of the celery to create a flat surface.
Mix Italian cheese and cream cheese in a bowl and spread into cut celery stalks.
Sprinkle half of the celery pieces with sunflower seeds and a half with the pine nut mixture. Cover mixture and let stand for at least 4 hours before eating.

**Nutrition:** Calories: 64 Carbs: 2 g Fat: 6 g Protein: 1 g

## 71. Butternut Squash Fries

**Prep Time:** 5 Minutes  **Cook Time:** 10 Minutes
**Servings:** 2

**Ingredients:**
- 1 Butternut squash
- 1 tbsp Extra virgin olive oil
- ½ tbsp Grapeseed oil
- 1/8 tsp Sea salt

**Prep:** Remove seeds from the squash and cut into thin slices. Coat with extra virgin olive oil and grapeseed oil. Add a sprinkle of salt and toss to coat well.
Arrange the squash slices onto three baking sheets and bake for 10 minutes until crispy.

**Nutrition:** Calories: 40 Carbs: 10 g Fat: 0 g Protein: 1 g

## 72. Dried Fig Tapenade

**Prep Time:** 5 Minutes  **Servings:** 1

**Ingredients:**
- 1 cup Dried figs
- 1 cup Kalamata olives
- ½ cup Water
- 1 tbsp Chopped fresh thyme
- 1 tbsp extra virgin olive oil
- ½ tsp Balsamic vinegar

**Prep:** Prepare figs in a food processor until well chopped, add water, and continue processing to form a paste.
Add olives and pulse until well blended. Add thyme, vinegar, and extra virgin olive oil and pulse until very smooth. Best served with crackers of your choice.

**Nutrition:** Calories: 249 Carbs: 64 g Fat: 1 g Protein: 3 g

## 73. Sweet Potato Chips

**Prep Time:** 15 Minutes  **Servings:** 4

**Ingredients:**
- 1 large Sweet potato
- 1 tbsp Extra virgin olive oil
- Salt

**Prep:** Preheated oven at 300°F. Slice your potato into nice, thin slices that resemble fries.
Toss the potato slices with salt and extra virgin olive oil in a bowl. Bake for about one hour, flipping every 15 minutes until crispy and browned.

**Nutrition:** Calories: 150 Carbs: 16 g Fat: 9 g Protein: 1 g

## 74. Mediterranean Nachos with Hummus

**Prep Time:** 15 Minutes  **Cook Time:** 20 Minutes
**Servings:** 4

**Ingredients:**
- 4 cups salted pita chips
- 1 (8 oz.) red pepper (roasted)
- Hummus
- 1 tsp Finely shredded lemon peel
- ¼ cup Chopped pitted Kalamata olives
- ¼ cup crumbled feta cheese
- 1 plum (Roma) tomato, seeded, chopped
- ½ cup chopped cucumber
- 1 tsp Chopped fresh oregano leaves

**Prep:** Preheated oven 400°F. Arrange the pita chips on a heatproof platter and drizzle with hummus.
Top with olives, tomato, cucumber, and cheese and bake until warmed through. Sprinkle lemon zest and oregano and enjoy while it's hot.

**Nutrition:** Calories: 130 Carbs: 18 g Fat: 5 g Protein: 4 g

### 75. Hummus and Olive Pita Bread

**Prep Time:** 5 Minutes

**Servings:** 3

**Ingredients:**
- 7 pita bread cut into 6 wedges each
- 1 (7 ounces) container plain hummus
- 1 tbsp Greek vinaigrette
- ½ cup Chopped pitted Kalamata olives

**Prep:** Spread the hummus on a serving plate.
Mix vinaigrette and olives in a bowl and spoon over the hummus. Enjoy with wedges of pita bread.

**Nutrition:** Calories: 225 Carbs: 40 g Fat: 5 g Protein: 9 g

### 76. Roast Asparagus

**Prep Time:** 15 Minutes

**Cook Time:** 5 Minutes

**Servings:** 4

**Ingredients:**
- 1 tbsp Extra virgin olive oil (1 tablespoon)
- 1 medium lemon
- ½ tsp Freshly grated nutmeg
- ½ tsp black pepper
- ½ tsp Kosher salt

**Prep:** Warm the oven to 500°F. Put the asparagus on an aluminum foil and drizzle with extra virgin olive oil, and toss until well coated. Roast the asparagus in the oven for five minutes; toss and continue roasting until browned. Sprinkle the asparagus with zest, nutmeg, salt, and pepper.

**Nutrition:** Calories: 123 Carbs: 5 g Fat: 11 g Protein: 3 g

### 77. Zaatar Fries

**Prep Time:** 10 Minutes

**Cook Time:** 35 Minutes

**Servings:** 5

**Ingredients:**
- 1 teaspoon Zaatar spices
- 3 sweet potatoes
- 1 tablespoon dried dill
- 1 teaspoon salt
- 3 teaspoons sunflower oil
- ½ teaspoon paprika

**Prep:** Pour water into the crockpot. Cut the sweet potatoes into fries.
Line the baking sheet with baking paper. Put on it the sweet potato layer.
Sprinkle the vegetables with salt, dried dill, and paprika. Then sprinkle potatoes with Za'atar and mix up well with the help of the fingertips. Sprinkle the sweet potato fries with sunflower oil—Preheat the oven to 375F.
Bake the sweet potato fries within 35 minutes. Stir the fries every 10 minutes.

**Nutrition:** Calories 28 Fat 2.9 g Fiber 0.2 g Carbs 0.6 g Protein 0.2 g

### 78. Vegetable Chicken Wraps

**Prep Time:** 15 Minutes

**Servings:** 4

**Ingredients:**
- 2 cups cooked chicken, chopped
- ½ English cucumbers, diced
- ½ red bell pepper, diced
- ½ cup carrot, shredded
- 1 scallion, white and green parts, chopped
- ¼ cup plain Greek yogurt
- 1 tablespoon freshly squeezed lemon juice
- ½ teaspoon fresh thyme, chopped
- Pinch of salt
- Pinch of ground black pepper
- 4 multigrain tortillas

**Prep:** Take a medium bowl and mix in chicken, red bell pepper, cucumber, carrot, yogurt, scallion, lemon juice, thyme, sea salt and pepper. Mix well.
Spoon one quarter of chicken mix into the middle of the tortilla and fold the opposite ends of the tortilla over the filling.
Roll the tortilla from the side to create a snug pocket.
Repeat with the remaining ingredients and serve.

**Nutrition:** Calories: 278 Fat: 4 g Carbs: 28 g Protein: 27 g

## 79. Roasted Baby Potatoes (2nd Version)

**Prep Time:** 10 Minutes  
**Servings:** 4  
**Cook Time:** 35 Minutes

### Ingredients:
- 2 pounds new yellow potatoes, scrubbed and cut into wedges
- 2 teaspoons rosemary, chopped
- 1 teaspoon garlic powder
- 1 teaspoon sweet paprika
- ½ teaspoon sea salt
- ½ teaspoon freshly ground black pepper
- 2 tablespoons olive oil

**Prep:** Pre-heat your oven to 400 degrees Fahrenheit.
Take a large bowl and add potatoes, garlic, paprika, olive oil, rosemary, sea salt and pepper.
Spread potatoes in single layer on baking sheet and cook for 35 minutes.

**Nutrition:** Calories: 225 Fat: 7 g Carbs: 37 g Protein: 5 g

## 80. Fig with Yogurt and Honey

**Prep time:** 5 minutes  
**Servings:** 2

### Ingredients:
- 6 dried figs, sliced
- 4 teaspoons honey
- 1 1/3 cups low-fat plain Greek style yogurt

**Prep:** Divide the figs into 2 bowls. Add honey and yogurt into a bowl and stir. Pour over the figs and serve.

**Nutrition:** Calories 208 Fat 3 g Carbs 39 g Protein 9 g

## 81. Greek Shrimp Saganaki

**Prep time:** 5 minutes  
**Servings:** 4  
**Cook time:** 35 minutes

### Ingredients:
- 2 pounds medium sized shrimps, peeled, deveined, with tails
- ½ cup olive oil
- 2 cups chopped onion
- 2 teaspoons crushed red pepper flakes
- 8 cloves garlic, chopped
- 4 cups chopped tomatoes
- 4 ounces proof (40% alcohol)
- 2 teaspoons chopped oregano leaves
- 4 cups, crumbled Greek feta cheese
- 8 sprigs parsley

**Prep:** Place shrimp in a bowl. Season with salt. Add half the lemon juice. Toss. Place a large saganaki (It is a skillet with 2 handles that is available in Greece) over medium heat.
Add oil. When oil is heated, add onion. Sauté for about 3 minutes or until light brown. Stir in garlic and red pepper flakes and sauté until aromatic. Stir in tomatoes, proof and oregano and sauté until thick and the tomatoes are softened.
Mix well. Lay shrimp on top, over the scallion mixture, all over the saganaki. Cover and cook until shrimp is pink and tender. When done, remove from heat. Transfer shrimp to a serving platter. Sprinkle feta cheese on top and serve.

**Nutrition:** Calories 976 Fat 62 g Carbs 37 g Protein 55 g

## 82. Greek Fava

**Prep time:** 10 minutes  
**Servings:** 4  
**Cook time:** 30 minutes

### Ingredients:
- 2 cups Santorini fava (yellow split peas), rinsed
- 2 medium onions, chopped
- 2 ½ cups water
- 2 cups +2 tablespoons vegetable broth
- 1 teaspoon salt or Himalayan pink salt

### To garnish:
- Lemon juice as required
- Chopped parsley

**Prep:** Place fava in a large pot. Add onions, broth, water and salt and stir. Place over medium heat. When it begins to boil, reduce the heat and cook until fava is tender.
Remove from heat and cool. Blend until creamy. Ladle into small plates. Add lemon juice and stir. Garnish with parsley and serve.

**Nutrition:** Calories 405 Fat 1 g Carbs 75 g Protein 25 g

## 83. Hummus, Feta & Bell Pepper Crackers

**Prep time:** 10 minutes     Servings: 2

**Ingredients:**
- 4 tablespoons hummus
- 2 large whole grain crisp bread
- 4 tablespoons crumbled feta
- 1 small bell pepper, diced

**Prep:** Top the pieces of crisp bread with hummus. Sprinkle feta cheese and bell peppers and serve.

**Nutrition:** Calories 136 Fat 7 g Carbs 13 g Protein 6 g

## 84. Tomato & Basil Bruschetta

**Prep time:** 10 minutes     **Cook time:** 10 minutes
**Servings:** 3

**Ingredients:**
- 3 tomatoes, finely chopped
- 1 clove garlic, minced
- ¼ teaspoon garlic powder
- A handful basil leaves, coarsely chopped
- Salt to taste
- Pepper to taste
- ½ teaspoon olive oil
- ½ tablespoon balsamic vinegar
- ½ tablespoon butter
- ½ baguette French bread or Italian bread, cut into ½ inch thick slices

**Prep:** Add tomatoes, garlic and basil in a bowl and toss well. Add salt and pepper. Drizzle oil and vinegar and toss well. Set aside for an hour.
Melt the butter and brush it over the baguette slices. Place in an oven and toast the slices. Sprinkle the tomato mixture on top and serve right away.

**Nutrition:** Calories 162 Fat 4 g Carbs 29 g Protein 4 g

## 85. Lemon-Pepper Cucumbers

**Prep time:** 5 minutes     Servings: 2

**Ingredients:**
- 1 large cucumber, sliced
- Lemon juice
- ground pepper to taste

**Prep:** Place cucumber slices on a serving platter. Trickle lemon juice over it. Garnish with pepper and serve.

**Nutrition:** Calories 24 Fat 0 g Carbs 6 g Protein 1 g

## 86. Falafel

**Prep time:** 30 minutes     **Cook time:** 15 minutes
**Servings:** 2

**Ingredients:**
- 1 cup dried chickpeas (do not use cooked or canned)
- ½ cup fresh parsley leaves, discard stems
- ¼ cup fresh dill leaves, discard stems
- ½ cup fresh cilantro leaves
- 4 cloves garlic, peeled
- ½ tablespoon ground black pepper
- ½ tablespoon ground coriander
- ½ tablespoon ground cumin
- ½ teaspoon cayenne pepper (optional)
- ½ teaspoon baking powder
- ¼ teaspoon baking soda
- Salt to taste
- 1 tablespoon toasted sesame seeds
- Oil, as required

**Prep:** Rinse chickpeas and soak in water overnight. Cover with at least 3 inches of water. Drain and dry by patting with a kitchen towel.
Add all the fresh herbs into a food processor. Process until finely chopped. Add chickpeas, spices and garlic and pulse for not more than 40 seconds each time until smooth.
Transfer into a container. Cover and chill for at least 1 hour or until use. Divide the mixture into 12 equal portions and shape into patties.
Place a deep pan over medium heat. Pour enough oil to cover at least 3 inches from the bottom of the pan.
When the oil is well heated, but not smoking, drop falafel, a few at a time and fry until medium brown.
Remove and place on a plate.

**Nutrition:** Calories 93 Fat 3.8 g Carbs 1.3 g Protein 3.9 g

## 87. Walnut-Feta Yogurt Dip

**Prep time: 15 minutes**                                                                     **Servings: 8**

**Ingredients:**
- 2 cups plain low-fat yogurt
- ¼ cup crumbled feta cheese
- 3 tablespoons chopped walnuts or pine nuts
- 1 teaspoon chopped fresh oregano or marjoram or ½ teaspoon dried oregano or marjoram, crushed
- Freshly ground pepper to taste
- Salt to taste
- 1 tablespoon snipped dried tomatoes (not oil packed)
- Salt to taste
- Walnut halves to garnish
- Assorted vegetable sticks to serve

**Prep:** For yogurt dip, place 3 layers of cotton cheesecloth over a strainer. Place strainer over a bowl. Add yogurt into the strainer. Cover the strainer with cling wrap. Refrigerate for 24-48 hours.
Discard the strained liquid and add yogurt into a bowl. Add feta cheese, walnuts, seasoning, and herbs and mix well. Cover and chill for an hour.
Garnish with walnut halves. Serve with vegetable sticks.

**Nutrition:** Calories 68 Fat 4 g Carbs 5 g Protein 4 g

## 88. Date Wraps

**Prep time: 10 minutes**                                                                     **Servings: 8**

**Ingredients:**
- 8 whole dates, pitted
- 8 thin slices prosciutto
- Freshly ground pepper to taste

**Prep:** Take one date and one slice prosciutto. Wrap the prosciutto around the dates and place on a serving platter. Garnish with pepper and serve.

**Nutrition:** Calories 35 Fat 1 g Carbs 6 g Protein 2 g

## 89. Clementine & Pistachio Ricotta

**Prep time: 5 minutes**                                                                     **Servings: 2**

**Ingredients:**
- 2/3 cup part-skim ricotta
- 2 clementine's, peeled, separated into segments, deseeded
- 4 teaspoons chopped pistachio nuts

**Prep:** Place 1/3 cup ricotta in each of 2 bowls. Divide the clementine segments equally and place over the ricotta. Sprinkle pistachio nuts on top and serve.

**Nutrition:** Calories 178 Fat 9 g Carbs 15 g Protein 11 g

## 90. Serrano-Wrapped Plums

**Prep time: 10 minutes**                                                                     **Servings: 4**

**Ingredients:**
- 2 firm ripe plums or peaches or nectarines, quartered
- 1 ounce thinly sliced Serrano ham or prosciutto, cut into 8 pieces

**Prep:** Take one piece of ham and one piece of fruit. Wrap the ham around the fruit and place on a serving platter.

**Nutrition:** Calories 30 Fat 1 g Carbs 4 g Protein 2 g

## 91. Greek Salad Wraps

**Prep Time:** 15 minutes  
**Servings:** 2

**Cook Time:** 10 minutes

**Ingredients:**

- 1½ cups seedless cucumber, peeled and chopped (about 1 large cucumber)
- 1 cup chopped tomato (about 1 large tomato)
- ½ cup finely chopped fresh mint
- 1 (2.25-ounce) can sliced black olives (about ½ cup), drained
- ¼ cup diced red onion (about ¼ onion)
- 2 tablespoons extra-virgin olive oil
- 1 tablespoon red wine vinegar
- ¼ teaspoon freshly ground black pepper
- ¼ teaspoon kosher or sea salt
- ½ cup crumbled goat cheese (about 2 ounces)
- 4 whole-wheat flatbread wraps or soft whole-wheat tortillas

**Prep:** In a large bowl, mix together the cucumber, tomato, mint, olives, and onion until well combined.
In a small bowl, whisk together pepper, oil, vinegar, and salt. Drizzle the dressing over the salad, and mix gently.
With a knife, spread the goat cheese evenly over the four wraps. Spoon a quarter of the salad filling down the middle of each wrap. Fold up each wrap: Start by folding up the bottom, then fold one side over and fold the other side over the top. Repeat with the remaining wraps and serve.

**Nutrition:** Calories: 262; Fat: 15 g; Carbs: 23 g; Protein: 7 g

## 92. Dill Salmon Salad Wraps

**Prep Time:** 20 minutes  
**Servings:** 2

**Cook Time:** 60 minutes

**Ingredients:**

- 1-pound salmon filet, cooked and flaked, or 3 (5-ounce) cans salmon
- ½ cup diced carrots (about 1 carrot)
- ½ cup diced celery (about 1 celery stalk)
- 3 tablespoons chopped fresh dill
- 3 tablespoons diced red onion (a little less than 1/8 onion)
- 2 tablespoons capers
- 1½ tablespoons extra-virgin olive oil
- 1 tablespoon aged balsamic vinegar
- ½ teaspoon freshly ground black pepper
- ¼ teaspoon kosher or sea salt
- 4 whole-wheat flatbread wraps or soft whole-wheat tortillas

**Prep:** In a large bowl, mix together the salmon, carrots, celery, dill, red onion, capers, oil, vinegar, pepper, and salt.
Divide the salmon salad among the flatbreads. Fold up the bottom of the flatbread, roll up the wrap and serve.

**Nutrition:** Calories: 336; Fat: 16 g; Carbs: 23 g; Protein: 32 g

## 93. Chicken Parmesan Wraps

**Prep Time:** 10 minutes  
**Servings:** 2

**Cook Time:** 20 minutes

**Ingredients:**

- Nonstick cooking spray
- 1-pound boneless, skinless chicken breasts
- 1 large egg
- ¼ cup buttermilk
- 2/3 cup whole-wheat panko or whole-wheat bread crumbs
- ½ cup grated Parmesan cheese (about 1½ ounces)
- ¾ teaspoon garlic powder, divided
- 1 cup canned low-sodium or no-salt-added crushed tomatoes
- 1 teaspoon dried oregano
- 6 (8-inch) whole-wheat tortillas, or whole-grain spinach wraps
- 1 cup fresh mozzarella cheese (about 4 ounces), sliced
- 1½ cups loosely packed fresh flat-leaf (Italian) parsley, chopped

**Prep:** Preheat the oven to 425°F. Line a rimmed baking sheet with aluminum foil. Place a wire rack on the aluminum foil, and spray the rack with nonstick cooking spray. Set aside.
Put the chicken breasts in a large, zip top plastic bag. With a rolling pin, pound the chicken so it is evenly flattened, about ¼ inch thick.

Slice the chicken into six portions. (It's fine if you have to place 2 smaller pieces together to form six equal portions.)
In a wide bowl, whisk together buttermilk and the egg. In another wide, shallow bowl, mix together the panko crumbs, Parmesan cheese, and ½ teaspoon of garlic powder.
Dip each portion of chicken breast into the egg mixture and then into the Parmesan crumb mixture. Place the chicken on the prepared wire rack. Bake the chicken for 15 minutes.
Transfer the chicken to a cutting board, and slice each portion diagonally into ½-inch pieces.
In a small, microwave-safe bowl, mix together oregano, tomatoes, and the remaining ¼ teaspoon of garlic powder.
Cover the bowl with a paper towel and microwave for about 1 minute on high, until very hot. Set aside.
Wrap the tortillas in a damp paper towel or dishcloth and microwave for 30 to 45 seconds on high, until warmed.
To assemble the wraps, divide the chicken slices evenly among the six tortillas and top with the cheese.
Spread 1 tablespoon of the warm tomato sauce over the cheese on each tortilla, and top each with about ¼ cup of parsley.
To wrap each tortilla, fold in the bottom of the tortilla, and fold one side over and fold the other side over the top. Serve the wraps immediately, with the remaining sauce for dipping.

**Nutrition:** Calories: 373; Fat: 10 g; Carbs: 33 g; Protein: 30 g

## 94. Quinoa & Dried Apricots and Figs

**Prep Time:** 10 minutes
**Servings:** 2

**Cook Time:** 17 minutes

**Ingredients:**
- 3 c. water
- ¼ c. cashew nut
- 8 dried apricots
- 4 dried figs
- 1 tsp. cinnamon

**Prep:** In a pot, mix water and quinoa.
Let simmer for 15 minutes, until the water evaporates.
Chop dried fruit.
When quinoa is cooked, stir in all other ingredients.

**Nutrition:** 65 Calories, 44 g Carbs, 7 g Fat, 13 g Protein, 28 g

## 95. Classic Apple Oats

**Prep Time:** 10 minutes
**Servings:** 2

**Cook Time:** 15 minutes

**Ingredients:**
- ½ tsp. cinnamon
- ¼ tsp. ginger
- 2 apples make half-inch chunks
- ½ c. oats, steel cut
- 1½ c. water
- Maple syrup
- ¼ tsp. salt
- Clove
- ¼ tsp. nutmeg

**Prep:** Take Instant Pot and carefully arrange it over a clean, dry kitchen platform.
Turn on the appliance.
In the cooking pot area, add the water, oats, cinnamon, ginger, clove, nutmeg, apple, and salt. Stir the ingredients gently.
Close the pot lid and seal the valve to avoid any leakage. Find and press the "Manual" cooking setting and set cooking time to 5 minutes.
Allow the recipe ingredients to cook for the set time, and after that, the timer reads "zero."
Press "Cancel" and press "NPR" setting for natural pressure release. It takes 8-10 times for all inside pressure to release.
Open the pot and arrange the cooked recipe in serving plates.
Sweeten as needed with maple or agave syrup and serve immediately.
Top with some chopped nuts, optional.

**Nutrition:** Calories: 232, Fat: 5.7 g, Carbs: 48.1 g, Protein: 5.2 g

## 96. Salted Anchovies

**Prep time:** 40 minutes

**Servings:** 4

**Ingredients:**
- 350g of salted anchovies
- extra virgin olive oil
- 1 hot pepper
- Chopped parsley

**Prep:** Scrape off the salt from the anchovies using a knife; open them in half and remove the bones. Lay them on a serving plate and sprinkle them with the chopped parsley and hot pepper. Pour generously the oil and let the flavor develop for some hours before serving.

**Nutrition:** Calories 400 Kcal; Carbs 3 g; Protein 12.5 g; Fat 35 g

## 97. Arancini with Ricotta

**Prep time: 45 minutes**      **Cook time: 25 minutes**
**Servings: 4**

**Ingredients:**
- 4 ½ cups of rice
- 10 oz of cow ricotta cheese
- 8 oz of primosale cheese
- ¾ cup of grated caciocavallo cheese
- 5 eggs
- flour
- breadcrumbs
- extra virgin olive oil
- salt and pepper

**Prep:** Boil the rice in plenty of salted water; drain it and move it into a bowl. Add the ricotta cheese and the caciocavallo cheese and carefully combine. When rice is warm add 2 beaten eggs and a crack of pepper.
Take a spoon of rice and press it the palm of your hand. Fill it with some primosale cheese cube and cover it with another spoon of pressed rice.
Shape the mixture to form a round ball and roll it in flour, in the remaining eggs (that have previously been beaten with a pinch of salt) and as a last step in the breadcrumbs. Fry the Arancini in hot oil until golden-brown.

**Nutrition:** Calories 600; Carbs 50 g; Protein 13.5 g; Fat 38 g

## 98. Tuna Bottarga

**Prep time: 10 minutes**      **Servings: 4**

**Ingredients:**
- 1 1/2 cup of tuna bottarga
- 1 lemon
- Pepper
- Extra virgin olive oil

**Prep:** Slice the tuna bottarga into thin slices and lay them on a serving plate.
Cover them with a drizzle of olive oil and let them rest for some hours. When you are ready to serve, remove the excess oil and combine some olive oil and a crack of pepper.

**Nutrition:** Calories 420; Carbs 3 g; Protein 12.1 g; Fat 15 g

## 99. Seasoned Olives

**Prep time: 1 hour**      **Servings: 6**

**Ingredients:**
- 5 cups of pickled green olives
- 3 carrots
- 4 garlic cloves
- 1 stick of celery
- 1 sprig of parsley
- oregano
- ½ cup of white wine vinegar
- Pepper
- Extra virgin olive oil

**Prep:** Wash and dry the olives. Lightly beat them with a meat beater until slightly opened but without breaking the pit.
After pitting them, move them to a bowl and season with vinegar, chopped garlic and parsley, pepper and oregano to taste.
Add the oil generously and mix carefully.
Cut the carrots and celery into round pieces and then add them to the olives.
Stir repeatedly until the ingredients are well distributed and let the flavor develop for at least 24 hours before serving.

**Nutrition:** Calories 189; Carbs 1.2 g; Protein 0.8 g; Fat 20 g

## 100. Potato Arancini

**Prep time: 1 hour**      **Cook time: 5-6 minutes**
**Servings: 4**

**Ingredients:**
- 35 oz of potatoes
- Breadcrumbs
- 3 eggs

- extra virgin olive oil
- 2 yolks
- 2 1/2 tbsp of butter
- 1/4 cup brewer's yeast
- Flour
- Salt and pepper
- 9 oz of ground beef ragù and peas

**Prep:** Wash the potatoes and boil them leaving the skin on in plenty of salted water. Peel and mash them while still hot. Let the mashed potatoes cool down and knead them with 2 yolks, butter and 2 tablespoons of flour and yeast melted in a little warm water. Season with a crack of salt and pepper and form into 2.5-inch balls. Make a well in each ball to fill it with the ground beef ragù (you can use a pastry syringe to help). Close the well and let rest for one hour.
After the needed time roll the arancini in the flour and then into the beaten eggs with a pinch of salt and lastly in the breadcrumbs. Fry them in hot oil and serve.

**Nutrition:** Calories 420; Carbs 18.7 g; Protein 10.8 g; Fat 35.2 g

## 101. Breaded Prickly Pears' Peels Cutlets

**Prep time:** 40 minutes  
**Servings:** 4  
**Cook time:** 3-4 minutes

**Ingredients:**
- 35 oz prickly pear's peels
- 3 eggs
- Flour to taste
- Breadcrumbs to taste
- extra virgin olive oil
- a pinch of salt

**Prep:** Carefully wash the peels and gently remove the outermost part with thorns. Cut them and turn them in flour.
Coat in beaten eggs with a pinch of salt and then into the breadcrumbs.
Fry them in abundant hot oil; drain and serve.

**Nutrition:** Calories 400; Carbs 3 g; Protein 0.8 g; Fat 32 g

## 102. Sword Fish Carpaccio

**Prep time:** 15 minutes  
**Servings:** 4

**Ingredients:**
- 550 g of sword fish in thin slices
- Lemon juice
- Extra virgin olive oil
- parsley
- Salt
- pepper

**Prep:** Lay the fish onto a try to form one layer, season with 1 cup of lemon juice. Let marinate for some hours; drain and move onto a serving plate.
sprinkle with oil, chopped parsley, salt and pepper and let the flavor develop for about ten minutes before serving.

**Nutrition:** Calories 240; Carbs 4.6 g; Protein 17 g; Fat 18 g

## 103. Tuna Carpaccio

**Prep time:** 20 minutes  
**Servings:** 4

**Ingredients:**
- 450 g fresh tuna sliced into thin slices
- 1 sprig of parsley
- 1 sprig of basil
- 1 sprig of mint
- Extra virgin olive oil
- Salt and pepper to taste
- 5 lemons
- oregano

**Prep:** Carefully wash and dry the tuna. Lay the slices onto a plate to form one layer; cover in lemon juice and let marinate for 6 hours.
Drain the fish and transfer onto a serving plate.
Sprinkle on top chopped herbs, drizzle some olive oil and a pinch of salt and pepper.
Let the flavor develop for 10 minutes before serving.

**Nutrition:** Calories 245 Kcal; Carbs 12 g; Protein 11 g; Fat 16.7 g

## 104. Fried Ricotta

**Prep time:** 5 minutes  
**Servings:** 6  
**Cook time:** 10 minutes

**Ingredients:**
- 2 eggs
- 17 oz of ricotta cheese
- 3/4 cup of grated cheese
- Lard
- 1 1/4 cup of breadcrumbs

**Prep:** Mix the eggs, ricotta, cheese, and breadcrumbs in a big mixing bowl.
Pour a spoon of the mixture in the pan with the lard.
Drain the fritters and dry with a paper towel, then serve.

**Nutrition:** Calories 510.1, Carbs 4.2 g, Protein 12.4 g, Fat 42.2 g

## 105. Palermitana style Potato Croquettes

**Prep time:** 50 minutes  
**Servings:** 4  
**Cook time:** 35 minutes

**Ingredients:**
- 35 oz of potatoes
- 3 garlic cloves
- 1 sprig of parsley
- 2 spoons of grated pecorino cheese
- 1 egg
- Flour to taste
- Salt and Pepper
- Olive oil

**Prep:** Wash the potatoes and boil them in plenty of hot water with the skin still on. Once they are cooked, peel them and press them with a potato masher.
Combine the mixture with the pecorino cheese, the beaten egg, a crack salt and pepper, garlic and chopped parsley.
Shape into 2 inch fingers. Pass them into the flour and fry in plenty of hot oil.

**Nutrition:** Calories 423; Carbs 18 g; Protein 11 g; Fat 35.4 g

## 106. Sicilian Style Mussels Au Gratin

**Prep time:** 1 hour  
**Servings:** 4  
**Cook time:** 20 minutes

**Ingredients:**
- 35 oz of mussels
- 1 1/4 cup of breadcrumbs
- 4 tbsp of grated pecorino cheese
- 2 garlic cloves
- 1 sprig of parsley
- Salt and pepper
- 2 spoon of extra virgin olive oil

**Prep:** Brush and carefully wash the mussels. Transfer them in a pan, cover with a lid at high heat until thy open.
Remove the empty half of the shell. In a bowl combine the breadcrumbs (previously toasted in a greased pan), the pecorino cheese, chopped garlic and parsley, salt and pepper.
Combine well all the ingredients and distribute the mixture over the mussels until they are fully coated.
Lay the mussels on an oven tray lined with parchment paper; season with some oil and cook in the oven at 350°F for 20 minutes.

**Nutrition:** Calories 290; Carbs 17.5 g; Protein 17 g; Fat 16.5 g

## 107. Cauliflower Croquettes

**Prep time:** 1 hour  
**Servings:** 4  
**Cook time:** 35 minutes

**Ingredients:**
- 1 cauliflower of 52 oz
- Flour
- 1 egg
- 2 spoons of grated pecorino cheese
- Olive oil
- Salt and pepper

**Prep:** Cut the cauliflower into smaller heads and boil them in hot salted water. Once they are cooked, drain and move them to a clay pot. Mash them with a fork and add the beaten egg, the pecorino cheese and pepper. Combine well until you reach a smooth mixture; add enough flour to reach the consistency of a dough easy to manipulate.

Take a spoonful of dough at a time and form slightly elongated balls with the aid of another spoon.
Roll in the flour and fry in hot oil.

**Nutrition:** Calories 110 Kcal; Carbs 5 g; Protein 2.6 g; Fat 9 g

### 108. Borage Fritters

**Prep time: 30 minutes**  
**Servings: 4**

**Cook time: 30-35 minutes**

**Ingredients:**
- 28 oz di borage
- 2 eggs
- extra virgin olive oil to taste
- Flour to taste
- Salt to taste

**Prep:** Carefully wash the borage and boil it I plenty of salted water. When it is cooked drain and mince it.
Peel the eggs and move to a bowl, beat them and add 2 spoons of flour, the borage and a handful of salt. Gently combine and if the mixture is not thick enough, add some more flour.
Shape the balls with the help of a spoon, fry in plenty of hot oil until golden-brown.

**Nutrition:** Calories 70 Kcal; Carbs 8.5 g; Protein 8.7 g; Fat 3.3 g

### 109. Fried Pumpkin Flowers

**Prep time: 20 minutes**  
**Servings: 4**

**Cook time: 5 minutes**

**Ingredients:**
- 16 pumpkin flowers
- 2 eggs
- 1 spoonful of grated pecorino cheese
- Flour to taste
- Salt and pepper
- 1 cup of olive oil

**Prep:** Remove the stem from the pumpkin flowers; wash and dry them carefully and then roughly chop them.
Beat the eggs in a bowl with a dash of salt and pepper, the pecorino cheese and 2 spoon of flour. Let the mixture rest for 10 minutes.
Shape into balls with a spoon.
Warm up the oil in pan and fry the balls turning them on each side.

**Nutrition:** Calories 68; Carbs 8 g; Protein 1.1 g; Fat 3 g

### 110. Marinated Shrimp

**Prep time: 1 hour**

**Servings: 4**

**Ingredients:**
- 35 oz of shrimp
- 3 lemons
- 1 garlic clove
- 1 sprig of parsley
- Salt
- 4 spoons of extra virgin olive oil

**Prep:** Wash the shrimp in plenty of water. Gently remove the head and the skin and with a toothpick the black string on the back.
Move the shrimp in a bowl laying them forming one layer. Add the pressed garlic and cover with the lemon juice. Let marinate for a couple of hours.
Drain the shrimp and move them onto a serving plate. Season with oil, salt and chopped parsley.
Let the taste develop for a few minutes before serving.

**Nutrition:** Calories 280; Carbs 5.5 g; Protein 15 g; Fat 15 g

### 111. Fried Milk

**Prep time: 20 minutes**  
**Servings: 4**

**Cook time: 30 minutes**

**Ingredients:**
- 1 liter of milk
- 1 1/2 cup of cornstarch
- 65 g of butter
- 110 g of grated parmesan cheese
- 2 yolks
- Flour to taste
- Extra virgin olive oil
- A pinch of salt

**Prep:** Let the cornstarch melt in some milk; add the remaining melted butter and milk.
Season with a crack of salt, simmer on low heat until the mixture thickens. When the consistency is very dense turn off the heat and let cool down.
Add the yolks and the parmesan cheese.
Spread the cream on a greased tray and let cool down completely. Then, slice into pieces, cover them in flour and fry them in plenty of hot oil.

**Nutrition:** Calories 600; Carbs 69 g; Protein 9.5 g; Fat 31 g

### 112. Battered Sea Anemones

**Prep time: 20 minutes**      **Cook time: 10 minutes**
**Servings: 4**

**Ingredients:**
- *21 oz of sea anemones*
- *Flour to taste*
- *Extra virgin olive oil*
- *A pinch of salt*

**Prep:** Rinse thoroughly the sea anemones and boil them 5-6 minutes.
Accurately dry them and dip them into the batter made by water, flour and salt. Fry in plenty of hot oil.

### 113. Ricotta Croquettes

**Prep time: 25 minutes**      **Cook time: 25 minutes**
**Servings: 6**

**Ingredients:**
- *2 eggs*
- *24 oz of ricotta cheese*
- *Breadcrumbs*
- *Salt and pepper*
- *10 oz of grated parmesan cheese*
- *Butter and oil to fry*

**Prep:** Mix the breadcrumbs with the ricotta in a bowl; combine the mixed eggs, add salt and pepper. Accurately mix until you reach a firm and soft dough. Form many balls and slightly flatten them, then coat them in breadcrumbs.
Fry in a pan with butter and oil. Flip on both sides and lay them on a paper towel them once golden-brown.

**Nutrition:** Calories 291, Carbs 21.2 g, Protein 12.3 g, Fat 18.4 g

### 114. Olives with wild Fennel

**Prep time: 20 minutes**      **Servings: 4**

**Ingredients:**
- *550 g of pickled green olives*
- *Oregano*
- *1 hot pepper*
- *Fennel seeds*
- *extra virgin olive oil*
- *white vinegar*

**Prep:** Soak the olives in water for 3 days, changing the water every 24 hours.
Drain and press them with a meat beater to take off the pit. Move to a bowl and season with the chopped pepper, a handful of fennel seeds and a pinch of oregano.
Add a drizzle of oil and vinegar to taste and let the taste develop for some hours before serving.

**Nutrition:** Calories 189; Carbs 1.2 g; Protein 0.8 g; Fat 20 g

### 115. Fried Black Olives

**Prep time: 5 minutes**      **Cook time: 15 minutes**
**Servings: 4**

**Ingredients:**
- *17 oz of big black olives*
- *oregano*
- *1 garlic clove*
- *extra virgin olive oil*

**Prep:** Press the garlic and let it sizzle in a pan with 6 tablespoons of oil. Remove the garlic and add the olives.

Combine a pinch of oregano, keep cooking the olives on medium heat and flip them regularly to let the flavor develop. Once they start to crease, turn off the heat and serve hot.

**Nutrition:** Calories 389; Carbs 1.2 g; Protein 0.8 g; Fat 30 g

## 116. Green Olives with Garlic and Parsley

**Prep time:** 30 minutes  **Servings:** 4

**Ingredients:**
- 320 g of pickled green olives
- 1 celery stick
- 6 garlic cloves
- 1 sprig of parsley
- extra virgin olive oil
- pepper

**Prep:** Wash the olives and let them soak in water for 24 hours. Then drain and press them to remove the pit. Transfer to a clay pot and add chopped garlic and parsley and celery cut in circles. Cover in a sprinkle of pepper and season generously with oil. Gently mix and let the flavor develop for 12 hours before serving.

**Nutrition:** Calories 189 Kcal; Carbs 1.2 g; Protein 0.8 g; Fat 20 g

## 117. Panelle

**Prep time:** 30 minutes  **Cook time:** 35 minutes
**Servings:** 8

**Ingredients:**
- 17 oz of chickpea flour
- 1 sprig of parsley
- 1,5 liters of water
- Peanut oil
- salt

**Prep:** Sift the flour in a pan and slowly add 1,5 liters of water, mix until there are no lumps. Add a pinch of salt.
Put the pan over low heat to let the mixture thicken, stir with a wooden spoon in the same direction. After about 30 minutes, the mixture should not stick to the pan.
Add the chopped parsley and pour everything in a rectangular non-stick tray damped with some cold water. Flatten the surface and let it firm. When the mixture will have cooled down completely, flip it on a chopping board and cut into slices.
Heat up some oil and fry few panelle at a time until golden.

**Nutrition:** Calories 409; Carbs 42 g; Protein 0.8 g; Fat 30 g

## 118. Meat Dumplings

**Prep time:** 70 minutes  **Cook time:** 20 minutes
**Servings:** 4

**Ingredients:**
- 550 g of flour
- 3 eggs
- 10 oz ground veal meat
- ½ cup of béchamel sauce
- 50 g of salami
- 1 cup of primosale cheese
- 2 1/2 tbsp of butter
- extra virgin olive oil
- salt and pepper

**Prep:** Vigorously knead the sifted flour with 2 tablespoons of oil, the eggs, a handful of salt, warm water as needed to achieve a soft and elastic dough. Let the dough rest under a napkin.
In the meantime, sizzle the ground meat in a pan with butter. When it is cooked let it cool down together with the béchamel, sliced salami and cut cheese.
Roll out the dough in thin sheets and cut out disks of 4 inch diameter. Distribute on each disk the cooked ground meat, close every disk in a half moon shape sealing the edges firmly after damping the rims with some water
Fry the dumplings in plenty of hot oil and serve while still.

**Nutrition:** Calories 560; Carbs 52.2 g; Protein 15 g; Fat 32 g

## 119. Anchovy Dumplings

**Prep time:** 1 hour  **Cook time:** 20 minutes
**Servings:** 4

**Ingredients:**
- 17 oz flour
- 1 1/2 cup of primosale cheese
- 1 cup of anchovy fillets in oil

- extra virgin olive oil
- salt
- 2 eggs

**Prep:** Sift the flour, pile it on the counter and make a well. Peel the eggs and add 2 tablespoons of oil and some warm water with a pinch of salt. Combine well all ingredients and knead the dough for a long time until it becomes soft. Roll it out and cut out disks. Fill the disks with chopped anchovies and pieces of primosale cheese. Fold the disks on top of the filling and shape them into half moons, seal the edges by slightly dampening them with some water.
Fry the dumplings in plenty of hot oil.

**Nutrition:** Calories 520; Carbs 52 g; Protein 15 g; Fat 32.9 g

### 120. Bell Pepper Roast

**Prep time:** 20 minutes  
**Servings:** 4  
**Cook time:** 30 minutes

**Ingredients:**
- ½ Kg of red bell peppers
- ½ Kg of yellow bell peppers
- 1 sprig of basil
- 2 garlic cloves
- ½ cup of olive oil
- Salt and pepper

**Prep:** Wash the peppers, then dry and oven roast them. When the peel darkens move them in a paper bag, close it and let them inside for a few minutes, then peel them.
Discard the seeds and the guts; cut them into slices and lay them on a serving plate.
Cover the peppers with sliced garlic, chopped basil and some olive oil, salt and pepper. Let the flavor develop for some hours before serving.

**Nutrition:** Calories 141; Carbs 1.8 g; Protein 2.7 g; Fat 8.3 g

### 121. Roasted Tomatoes

**Prep time:** 20 minutes  
**Servings:** 4  
**Cook time:** 5 minutes

**Ingredients:**
- 4 big red
- 2 garlic cloves
- 1 cup of breadcrumbs
- Oregano
- extra virgin olive oil
- salt and pepper

**Prep:** Wash the tomatoes and slice them in a quarter inch slices. Move them onto a clay pot sprinkle salt and pepper, chopped garlic and oregano. Combine 1 cup of oil and let the flavor develop for about 1 hour, turning the tomatoes ever so often.
Drain the tomatoes and cover breadcrumbs seasoned with a pinch of salt and oregano.
Roast the tomatoes on high heat flipping them halfway through.

**Nutrition:** Calories 210; Carbs 32.2 g; Protein 11 g; Fat 22 g

### 122. Stuffed Dried Tomatoes

**Prep time:** 20 minutes  
**Servings:** 4

**Ingredients:**
- 9 oz of dried tomatoes in oil
- 180 g of breadcrumbs
- 4 tbsp of grated pecorino cheese
- ½ tablespoon of capers
- 1 garlic clove
- 5 tablespoons of olive oil
- 1 sprig of parsley
- 1 pickled anchovy
- pepper

**Prep:** Scrape off the salt from the anchovy, remove the bones and chop it. Then melt it in the oil.
Mix the breadcrumbs with the pecorino cheese, chopped garlic and parsley and a pinch of pepper. Add the anchovy, washed and minced capers and combine well everything.
Drain the tomatoes and dry them onto a paper towel. Distribute half onto to the prepares mixture and cover them with the remaining half.

**Nutrition:** Calories 401; Carbs 52.2 g; Protein 16 g; Fat 12 g

### 123. Sea Urchins

**Prep time:** 1 hour  
**Servings:** 4

**Ingredients:**
- 40 sea urchins
- 2 lemons
- Bread slices

**Prep:** Cut the sea urchins with the special scissors and divide them in two. Discard the empty half and clear any spike from the other half.
Consume the sea urchins scooping the eggs with a slice of bread and some lemon drops.

**Nutrition:** Calories 140 Kcal; Carbs 1.4 g; Protein 17 g; Fat 3.4 g

## 124. Fritters with Ham and Cheese

**Prep time:** 1 hour  
**Servings:** 5  
**Cook time:** 20 minutes

**Ingredients:**
- 1 spoon of butter
- ½ a package of yeast
- 1 1/2 cup of baked ham
- 1 1/2 cup of fresh caciocavallo cheese
- Extra virgin olive oil
- Salt
- 1,5 liters of water
- 4 eggs
- Flour to taste

**Prep:** Pour the water in a pan, add the butter and a pinch of salt and bring to a boil on low heat. Then pour the needed flour to achieve a thick mixture, stirring with a wooden spoon. Once the mixture will stop sticking to the sides of the pan, turn off the heat and let cool down. Incorporate the eggs one at the time, the sifted yeast and let it rise for 1 hour. Then, combine the sliced ham and cheese, shape the mixture into balls and fry in plenty of hot oil, turning the fritters ever so often to allow them to golden evenly. Remove the fritters from the oil, put them onto some paper towels to let them dry. Sprinkle some salt before serving.

**Nutrition:** Calories 560; Carbs 52.2 g; Protein 15 g; Fat 32 g

## 125. Fried Skewers

**Prep time:** 40 minutes  
**Servings:** 4  
**Cook time:** 6-7 minutes

**Ingredients:**
- 6 slices of hardened bread
- 10 oz of primosale cheese
- 4 eggs
- 1 sprig of parsley
- breadcrumbs
- 1 spoon of grated pecorino cheese
- Milk
- Extra virgin olive oil
- Salt and pepper
- 1 1/2 cup of ground veal meat
- flour

**Prep:** Mix the meat with the grated pecorino cheese, 1 spoonful of breadcrumbs, chopped parsley and a pinch of salt and pepper. Shape into balls and put them aside.
Cut the bread into 1-inch squares and dampen them into the milk. Cut the primosale into squares the same size as the bread. Assemble the skewers alternating 3 pieces of cheese, 3 meatballs and 4 slices of bread, making sure to start and finish with the bread.
Roll the skewers into flour, then into the beaten eggs with a pinch of salt, and then into the breadcrumbs.
Fry them in plenty of oil and serve them while still hot.

**Nutrition:** Calories 470; Carbs 11.1 g; Protein 18.8 g; Fat 39 g

## 126. Vegetable Timbale

**Prep time:** 1 hour  
**Servings:** 6  
**Cook time:** 70 minutes

**Ingredients:**
- 14 oz of flour
- 9 eggs
- 1 yolk
- 1 1/2 cup of butter
- 1 spoon of sugar
- 10 oz of peas
- 17 oz of asparagus
- 3 artichokes
- 50 g of dried sausage
- 50 g of grated pecorino
- 1 cup of primosale cheese
- 17 oz of fresh mushrooms
- Extra virgin olive oil
- butter to grease the mold
- salt and pepper

**Prep:** Sift the flour, pour on the counter and make a well in the middle. Pour in the well 1 egg, 1 yolk, a pinch of salt, 2-3 spoons of water and gently knead until you reach a thick mixture (add some water if needed). Wrap the dough in surround wrap and let it rest in the fridge for 1 hour.

Clean and chop the asparagus then boil them in salted water. Clean and cut into wedges the mushrooms and the artichokes.
Warm up 3 spoons of oil in a pan and cook the mushroom and artichokes. Season with salt and put aside.
Cook in boiling water the peas, drain them and pour into a bowl.
Add the mushroom, artichokes, asparagus, chopped sausage and the diced primosale cheese. Pour the beaten eggs, pecorino cheese, a crack of salt and pepper and gently mix.
Take out the dough from the fridge and divide it into two pieces, one slightly bigger than the other. Roll it out and cover the greased mold with the bigger half making sure to cover the sides as well.
Fill with the eggs, vegetables and cover all with the smaller half of the dough.
Seal the edges and bake in the oven at 350° for 45 minutes.

**Nutrition:** Calories 207 Kcal; Carbs 15.2 g; Protein 15 g; Fat 32 g

## 127. Beet and Ricotta Pie

**Prep time: 30 minutes**  **Cook time: 40 minutes**
**Servings: 4**

**Ingredients:**
- *35 oz of beets*
- *17 oz of ricotta cheese*
- *Extra virgin olive oil*
- *3 eggs*
- *Salt and pepper to taste*

**Prep:** Wash the beets then cook them into salted boiling water. Drain and chop them up. Transfer into a pan with 2 spoons of oil, then move into a bowl and let them cool down.
In the meantime, sift the ricotta cheese and mix it with the beaten eggs. Season with salt and pepper and add everything to the beets.
Pour the mixture in greased tray and bake in the oven at 350° F for 20 minutes.

**Nutrition:** Calories 610; Carbs 52.6 g; Protein 16 g; Fat 30 g

## 128. Friselle

**Prep time: 30 minutes**  **Cook time: 80 minutes**
**Servings: 4**

**Ingredients:**
- *14 oz of flour*
- *Salt to taste*
- *20 g of brewer's yeast*

**Prep:** Dissolve the yeast in a little warm water and mix it with the flour and a pinch of salt.
Shape the dough into big doughnuts and join them 2 by 2.
Let them rise for half an hour and then oven bake at 320° F for 80 minutes. Remove them from the oven and cut horizontally halfway through.

**Nutrition:** Calories 130; Carbs 10.2 g; Protein 1.5 g; Fat 8.7 g

## 129. Marinated Eels

**Prep time: 40 minutes**  **Cook time: 20 minutes**
**Servings: 4**

**Ingredients:**
- *35 oz of eels*
- *extra virgin olive oil*
- *1 onion*
- *3 garlic cloves*
- *1,5 liters of wine vinegar*
- *3 basil leaves*
- *2 bay twigs*
- *1 twig of mint*
- *salt*

**Prep:** Wash the eels and remove the guts then cut into 4 inch long stripes.
In a casserole, warm up plenty of oil, the finely chopped onion and pressed garlic cloves sizzle. When they become golden pour the vinegar, mint, bay and basil and let them boil for 5 minutes.
Put the eels in a glass bowl and coat them with the marinading.
Cover with a thin towel and let it marinate for 3 or 4 days.

**Nutrition:** Calories 460; Carbs 11.2 g; Protein 22 g; Fat 33.5 g

## 130. Chickpea Flat Bread

**Prep time:** 5 minutes  
**Servings:** 4  
**Cook time:** 30 minutes

**Ingredients:**
- 17 oz of chickpea flour
- ½ cup of extra virgin olive oil
- Salt and pepper

**Prep:** In a big mixing bowl pour 1.5 liters of water and add the chickpea flour, keep mixing with a wooden spoon to avoid any clumps from forming. Add salt to taste and let the cream rest for 3 hours.
Grease a baking tray with olive oil and pour the mixture, mixing to incorporate the oil.
Put the tray into a preheated oven at 350°F and let it bake for 30 minutes, or until the flat bread is fully baked.
Serve while still warm and cut it into triangles adding a dash of pepper.

**Nutrition:** Calories 187; Carbs 20.2 g; Protein 8.2 g; Fat 8.1 g

## 131. Sea Salad (2nd Version)

**Prep time:** 50 minutes  
**Servings:** 4  
**Cook time:** 50 minutes

**Ingredients:**
- 35 oz of mussels
- 17 oz of shrimp
- 24 oz of octopus
- 14 oz of squid
- vinegar
- Parsley
- Olive oil
- Salt and pepper

**Prep:** Let the mussels purge in cold water for one night. The following day boil them in a pot and allow to open. Take the mussels of and move them into a bowl.
Meanwhile separately boil the shrimp, octopus and squid. Clean the shrimp and chop the octopus and squid.
Combine everything with the mussels in a bowl, season with oil, a dash of vinegar, salt, pepper and chopped parsley. Give everything a stir and let the flavor develop for a couple of hours.

**Nutrition:** Calories 390; Carbs 10.4 g; Protein 52 g; Fat 17 g

## 132. Zucchini Pie

**Prep time:** 30 minutes  
**Servings:** 6  
**Cook time:** 30 minutes

**Ingredients:**
- 21 oz of zucchini
- 1 1/4 cup of breadcrumbs
- Zest of 1 lemon
- 1 1/4 cup of grated parmesan
- 3 eggs
- Salt and pepper
- 1 cup of milk

**Prep:** Wash the zucchini and remove the extremities. Grate them and put them in a bowl. Add
100g of breadcrumbs wetted with the milk, the lemon zest, salt and pepper and mix it all up. Then, add the eggs and parmesan and gently mix it.
Grease a pan with butter, sprinkle some breadcrumbs and add the zucchini mixture, lay everything smooth. Sprinkle some more breadcrumbs on top and lay some butter curls here and there.
Bake at 390°F for about 30 minutes.

**Nutrition:** Calories 472; Carbs 33.2 g; Protein 23 g; Fat 27 g

## 133. Artichoke Tart

**Prep time:** 15 minutes  
**Servings:** 4  
**Cook time:** 50 minutes

**Ingredients:**
- 10 artichokes
- Juice of 1 lemon
- 2 garlic cloves
- 1 sprig of parsley
- 3 eggs
- extra virgin olive oil
- 4 spoons of grated pecorino cheese
- butter (to grease the tray)
- Salt and pepper

**Prep:** Clean the artichokes from the outer layer of leaves and the tips. Cut them into thin wedges and let them soak in water with the added lemon juice.
In a pan let sauté the pressed garlic cloves and the chopped parsley. Add the artichokes, a cup of water, salt and pepper. Stir the mixture and cook with a lid on for about 40 minutes on a low heat.
In the meantime, beat the eggs in a bowl, season with some salt and pepper and then add the grated pecorino cheese. Once the artichokes are ready, remove them from the heat, add the eggs and mix some more. Then, pour the whole mixture to a greased tray and bake at 350°F for 10 minutes.

**Nutrition:** Calories 377 Kcal; Carbs 23.2 g; Protein 15.4 g; Fat 22.5 g

## 134. Eggplant Pie

**Prep time:** 25 minutes  **Cook time:** 30 minutes
**Servings:** 4

**Ingredients:**
- 5 eggplants
- 1 liter of ragù
- 4 chopped basil leaves
- 9 oz of grated pecorino cheese
- Salt and pepper
- extra virgin olive oil

**Prep:** Remove the stem from the eggplants, wash them and slice them into very thin slices of about ½ cm. Lay them in a colander and cover completely with salt to remove all the water and let them rest for 2 hours.
Heat up some oil in a pan. Fry the eggplant slices flipping them every occasionally. Dry them onto some paper towel.
Grease a tray with a drizzle of oil, add the eggplants forming one layer and season with salt and pepper.
Then, add a thin layer of ragù, the chopped basil and the grated pecorino cheese. Lay another layer of eggplants and keep alternating the layers until the top of the tray, finishing with the ragù.
Put the tray in a preheated oven at 375°F and let it cook for 20 minutes.

**Nutrition:** Calories 474 Kcal; Carbs 22.2 g; Protein 19 g; Fat 34 g

## 135. Lettuce Fritters

**Prep time:** 25 minutes  **Servings:** 6

**Ingredients:**
- 17 oz of flour
- 4 eggs
- 1/4 cup of brewer's yeast
- 1 lettuce head
- extra virgin olive oil
- salt

**Prep:** Pout the flour in a bowl with the yeast (previously melted into some warm water), the eggs and a pinch of salt. Gently mix and let the batter rest for at least 3 hours.
Wash thoroughly the lettuce, slice it into thin strips and incorporate them into the batter. Heat the oil into the pan and fry the batter one spoonful at a time until the fritters golden.

**Nutrition:** Calories 111; Carbs 7.2 g; Protein 1.9 g; Fat 8.2 g

## 136. Stuffed Tomatoes

**Prep time:** 30 minutes  **Cook time:** 70 minutes
**Servings:** 6

**Ingredients:**
- 12 ripe tomatoes
- 1 chopped onion
- 1 sprig of parsley
- 1 chopped celery stick
- 70 g of fresh mushrooms
- 70 g of parmesan cheese
- 4 eggs
- oregano
- Extra virgin olive oil
- Salt and pepper
- 70 g of breadcrumbs (30 g dry and 2 1/2 tbsp dampened in milk)
- 4 tbsp of butter

**Prep:** Cut the tomatoes horizontally to form a sort of lid with the top part and the stem. Wash out the seeds into some water.
In a pan heat up the butter and the onion, the celery, the mushrooms and the chopped parsley, then pound everything in a mortar.
Combine the mixture with the breadcrumbs dampened into the milk, the parmesan cheese, the eggs a dash of oregano, salt and pepper.
Stuff the tomatoes with the mixture and cover them with the lid. Drizzle some olive oil on top and sprinkle the breadcrumbs.
Bake in a greased pan for 30 minutes at 350°F.

**Nutrition:** Calories 401; Carbs 52.2 g; Protein 16 g; Fat 12 g

## 137. Sweet-and-sour Crunchy Bites

**Prep time:** 40 minutes  **Servings:** 6

**Ingredients:**
- 14 tbsp of butter
- 110 g of sugar
- 1 cup of raw ham
- 6 spoons of white wine vinegar
- 2 teaspoons of flour
- 70 g of raisins
- 70 g of pine nuts
- Pepper
- 10 slices of sandwich bread

**Prep:** Soak the raisins into the vinegar and let them marinate for about half an hour.
Meanwhile, sauté the pine nuts into butter and sugar until they are lightly caramelized. Add the vinegar, marinated raisin and flour. Mix until everything thickens without any lumps.
Add the ham finely chopped and some pepper. Remove from the heat.
Drizzle some vinegar onto the sandwich bread.
Melt 60 g of butter in a pan and fry the bread slices until golden. Take the pan off the heat and move the bread onto a paper towel to dry off the excess grease.
Spread the slices with the mixture and serve them warm.

**Nutrition:** Calories 211; Carbs 17.2 g; Protein 7.6 g; Fat 12 g

## 138. Eggplant Rolls

**Prep time:** 15 minutes  **Cook time:** 30 minutes
**Servings:** 6

**Ingredients:**
- 3 eggplants
- 1 liter of sunflower oil
- 8 oz of breadcrumbs
- 8 oz of grated parmesan cheese
- 3 cloves
- 2 onions
- Butter
- Olive oil
- vegetable broth
- Salt and pepper
- Tomato sauce

**Prep:** Cut the eggplants into vertical stripes and lay them on a colander covering them with salt. After about 30 minutes rinse them off with cold water and dry them. Fry the eggplants in hot sunflower oil in a pan and then lay them onto some paper towel.
Sauté the chopped onion with some oil, then add the cloves to develop the taste (remove later) and add some broth at a time. Keep frying the onion until it softens.
Add the breadcrumbs, parmesan cheese and a handful of salt and pepper.
Stuff the eggplant slices with the tomato sauce, roll them and bake in the oven for few minutes.

**Nutrition:** Calories 28; Carbs 0.5 g; Protein 3.1 g; Fat 1.9 g

## 139. Chicken Salad

**Prep time:** 15 minutes  **Servings:** 6

**Ingredients:**
- 21 oz of boiled chicken breast
- Salt and pepper
- 1 1/2 cup of baked ham cut into strips
- 1 celery stick cut into strips
- Half a lemon
- 1 cup of Emmenthal cheese cut into strips
- Extra virgin olive oil
- 1 teaspoon of mustard
- 3 teaspoons of mayonnaise
- 1 lettuce

**Prep:** In a bowl mix the mayonnaise with the mustard, add some oil, lemon and a pinch of salt and pepper.
Cut the lettuce into strips. Mix the chicken, ham and cheese and season with the mayonnaise and mustard seasoning.

**Nutrition:** Calories 691; Carbs 7.2 g; Protein 44 g; Fat 52.2 g

## 140. Mortadella Mousse

**Prep time:** 10 minutes  **Servings:** 6

**Ingredients:**
- 450 g of mortadella
- 1 teaspoon of grated parmesan
- 8 oz of whipped cream

**Prep:** Pulse the mortadella with the parmesan cheese to form a paste. Gently fold from top to bottom the whipped cream using a spatula.

**Nutrition:** Calories 245; Carbs 12.2 g; Protein 6 g; Fat 19 g

## 141. Chicken Breast in Balsamic Vinegar

**Prep time:** 20 minutes  **Cook time:** 10 minutes
**Servings:** 6

**Ingredients:**
- 2 chicken breasts
- extra virgin olive oil
- parmesan scales
- balsamic vinegar
- 20 g of arugola
- 28 oz of tomatoes
- Tabasco sauce
- 1 small diced onion
- Salt and pepper

**Prep:** For the marinated seasoning, cut the tomatoes into cubes, add some salt and lay them into a strainer for 15 minutes to allow the water to drain. Move the tomatoes in a bowl and add the onion, tabasco sauce, a drizzle of oil and a pinch of pepper, let everything marinate for 30 minutes.
Meanwhile, cook the chicken breasts into a pan on a low heat with some olive oil and cover with a lid. Turn the breasts after about 10 minutes and when they are fully cooked add some salt and pepper. Let them cool and then cut into strips.
In a serving plate, lay a handful of arugola, arrange the chicken breasts and season with a drizzle of oil, balsamic vinegar, salt and pepper. Spread some spoons of the marinated sauce, parmesan scales and again a drizzle of balsamic vinegar.

**Nutrition:** Calories 331; Carbs 3.2 g; Protein 26.9 g; Fat 21 g

## 142. Stuffed Anchovies

**Prep time:** 30 minutes  **Cook time:** 5 minutes
**Servings:** 6

**Ingredients:**
- 35 oz of boneless anchovies
- 1 chopped garlic clove
- 1 1/4 cup of small squid
- 1 cup of shelled mussels
- 1 cup of shelled shrimp
- 1 hot pepper
- extra virgin olive oil
- 2 beaten eggs
- breadcrumbs

**Prep:** Fry into some oil the roughly chopped squid, shrimp, mussels and chopped garlic and hot pepper. Let it cool.
Pour some of the mixture in every anchovy and close the sides with a toothpick, coat them into the eggs and then into the breadcrumbs. Fry the anchovies into plenty of hot oil until golden.

## 143. Anchovies Au Gratin

**Prep time:** 15 minutes  **Cook time:** 10 minutes
**Servings:** 6

**Ingredients:**
- 35 oz of boneless anchovies
- Breadcrumbs to taste
- 1 spoon of chopped garlic
- Extra virgin olive oil to season
- 2 spoons of parsley

**Prep:** Lay the anchovies on a greased tray with some oil and cover them with chopped garlic and parsley, a dust breadcrumbs and a drizzle of oil.
Put into a preheat oven at 350°F for 10 minutes.

**Nutrition:** Calories 416; Carbs 12.2 g; Protein 16 g; Fat 37 g

## 144. Bruschetta with Sausage

**Prep time:** 20 minutes  **Servings:** 4

**Ingredients:**
- 14 oz of sausage
- 8 slices of bread
- 1 garlic clove
- Extra virgin olive oil

**Prep:** Lay the bread slices on the preheated oven grill at 350°F. remove them once they have become golden and then rub some garlic on. Spread the sausage and a drizzle of oil and serve.

**Nutrition:** Calories 205; Carbs 8.2 g; Protein 6 g; Fat 9 g

## 145. Saffron Mussels

**Prep time: 20 minutes**  **Cook time: 20 minutes**
**Servings: 6**

**Ingredients:**
- 2 Kg of mussels
- 1 chopped onion
- 1 sprig of parsley
- 1 bay leaf
- 1 cup of dry white wine
- 50 ml of extra virgin olive oil
- 1 pack of saffron dust

**Prep:** Clean the mussels and wash them in water several times.
In a pot deglaze with the wine the mussels, onion, parsley. When the wine has evaporated open the mussels with a closed shell. Separate the mussels from the shells and move them onto a serving plate.
Save the cooking water of the mussels and boil it, add some oil and the saffron and give it a mix. Pour the water on the mussels and serve.

**Nutrition:** Calories 205; Carbs 5.2 g; Protein 10.9 g; Fat 13.5 g

## 146. Au Gratin Mussels

**Prep time: 30 minutes**  **Cook time: 15 minutes**
**Servings: 6**

**Ingredients:**
- 2 Kg of mussels
- 1 1/2 cup of breadcrumbs
- 2 cloves of chopped garlic
- 2 spoons of chopped parsley
- Juice of 1 lemon
- 50 ml of extra virgin olive oil

**Prep:** Mix the breadcrumbs with the chopped parsley and garlic in a bowl; season with the lemon juice and oil and mix the mussels in. Lay the mussels on a tray and bake in a preheated oven at 390°F for 15 minutes.

**Nutrition:** Calories 295; Carbs 17.5 g; Protein 17 g; Fat 16.5 g

## 147. Fried Veggie Starter

**Prep time: 20 minutes**  **Cook time: 10 minutes**
**Servings: 6**

**Ingredients:**
- 6 artichoke hearts
- 1 lemon
- 4 carrots
- 2 zucchini
- 1 leek
- 3 eggs
- 60g of flour
- 0,2l of latte
- 0,2l of extra virgin olive oil
- 0,3l of peanut oil
- 2 spoons of chopped parsley
- salt

**Prep:** In a bowl add some lemon juice to some water make it acidulous, soak the artichoke hearts cut into wedges.
Boil the artichoke hearts leaving them a little hard, do the same with the carrots and leeks. Then cut into pieces the leeks and carrots.
Mix well the flour, eggs, milk and a pinch of salt in a bowl.
In a pan pour the two kinds of oil, fry the vegetables covered in the batter previously made. Let the vegetables drain onto a paper towel.

**Nutrition:** Calories 550; Carbs 21.5 g; Protein 4.6 g; Fat 50.5 g

## 148. Sour Whitebait

**Prep time: 5 minutes**  **Cook time: 2 minutes**
**Servings: 6**

**Ingredients:**
- 35 oz of fresh whitebait
- extra virgin olive oil
- 2 lemons

- *Salt and pepper*
- *1 spoon of chopped parsley*

**Prep:** Clean the whitebait and put it into boiling water. Prepare the sauce by putting the oil, lemon juice, chopped parsley, salt and pepper into a bowl.
After cooking for 2 minutes, drain the whitebait and serve it covered in the prepared sauce.

## 149. Cappon Magro

**Prep time: 55 minutes**  **Cook time: 50 minutes**
**Servings: 10-12**

**Ingredients:**
- *1 big Capone fish or dogfish*
- *36 shrimp or scampi*
- *36 oysters*
- *6 salted anchovies cut into fillets and rinsed*
- *4 tbsp of thin slices of mosciame of fish*
- *1 cauliflower cut into clumps*
- *1 celery stick cut into pieces*
- *10 oz of green beans*
- *3 sprigs of salsify*
- *8 oz of diced potatoes*
- *1 big red beet diced*
- *3 carrots julienne style cut*
- *6 cleaned artichokes and soaked into acidulated water*
- *Extra virgin olive oil*
- *4 garlic cloves*
- *vinegar*
- *75 g of pine nuts*
- *4 tbsp of capers*
- *Pulp of 12 green olives*
- *Breadcrumbs wet into vinegar*
- *4 anchovies*
- *3 hard boiled egg yolks*
- *ground parsley*
- *Coarse salt*
- *24 pickled mushrooms*
- *6 hardboiled eggs cut into quarters*
- *12 pickles*
- *10 oz sailor's crackers*
- *3 garlic cloves*
- *12 black olives*
- *12 green olives*
- *1 1/2 cup of pickled vegetables*
- *Ground salt*
- *pepper*
- *white wine vinegar*
- *1 lemon*
- *1 big lettuce*

**Prep:** Thoroughly clean the fish in boil it into some water with salt and onion, celery, carrots to add flavor, white wine vinegar, pepper grains and parsley sprigs. Drain the boiled fish and clean it by removing the head, the skin and bones. Boil the lobster in the same water of the previously cooked fish for about 20 minutes. Boil the scampi or shrimp for 5 minutes and then clean them. Season everything with oil, lemon, salt and pepper. Open the mollusks. Cook separately the vegetables in boiling water. Keep all the vegetables crunchy apart from the potatoes which will have to be fully cooked. Season with oil, salt and vinegar even if the ingredients are still warm.
Mash together the coarse salt, parsley, garlic, pine nuts, capers, egg yolks, anchovies, olive pulp and the wet breadcrumbs. Add oil and vinegar when the soup is ready.
Wet the crackers with water and vinegar, rub the garlic on and let them rest between two plates.
Create the decoration by laying on a large plate the lettuce leaves and then the crackers. Put the slices of mosciame of fish and cover with the vegetables and white fish. Cover each layer with sauce and keep layering all the ingredients to form a pyramid. Garnish the base of the pyramid with the green sauce. Place the as desired hardboiled egg wedges, mushrooms, capers, pickles, anchovy fillets and olives. Add the lobster shell on top and sprinkle the pulp. Finish by garnish the base by laying some more skewered slices of fish mosciame, the mollusks, shrimp or scampi.

**Nutrition:** Calories 940Kcal; Carbs 17.5 g; Protein 63 g; Fat 50.8 g

## 150. Chickpea Fritters

**Prep time: 1 night + 10 minutes**  **Cook time: 10 minutes**
**Servings: 6**

**Ingredients:**
- *700g chickpea flour*
- *50g of brewer's yeast*
- *1 spoon of fresh marjoram*
- *Extra virgin olive oil*
- *salt*

**Prep:** Melt the yeast into some warm water. Mix the flour with water to make a liquid batter.
Combine the batter with the melted yeast and let it rest overnight.
Add the minced marjoram and salt. Heat up the oil in a pan and add the batter one spoon at a time. Remove the fritters from the pan when they swell up and are golden, let them drain onto a plate lined with a paper towel.

**Nutrition:** Calories 154; Carbs 6.5 g; Protein 4.2 g; Fat 11.5 g

## 151. Whitebait Flat Bread

**Prep time:** 5 hours e 10 minutes
**Servings:** 6

**Cook time:** 10 minutes

**Ingredients:**
- 17 oz of chickpea flour
- Extra virgin olive oil
- 200g of whitebait

**Prep:** Beat with a whip the flour with 1,5 liters of water to achieve a dense cream with no clumps. Add the salt and let it rest for 4-5 hours, then scrape off the foam that had formed on top.
Add the whitebait to the cream and then pour everything in a tray lined with parchment paper and mix the cream to the oil. Bake in the oven at 370°F until a golden crust forms.
Serve warm.

## 152. Onion Focaccia

**Prep time:** 2 hours e 30 minutes
**Servings:** 6

**Cook time:** 20 minutes

**Ingredients:**
- 35 oz of flour
- 30g of brewer's yeast
- 1 big onion sliced
- Ground salt
- Extra virgin olive oil

**Prep:** Pour the flour on a chopping board, making a well in the middle, pour in it 6 spoons of oil, the yeast melted into some warm water, 3 pinches of salt, 1 cup of water. Knead the dough for 10 minutes. Cover it with a cloth for 2 hours.
Grease a tray and sprinkle some salt, roll out the dough and bake in a preheat oven at 375°FC. The focaccia is ready when it turns golden.

**Nutrition:** Calories 461; Carbs 65.5 g; Protein 5.8 g; Fat 13.5 g

## 153. Focaccia with Sage

**Prep time:** 4 hours e 10 minutes
**Servings:** 6

**Cook time:** 35 minutes

**Ingredients:**
- 35 oz of flour
- 3/4 cup of brewer's yeast
- ½ cup of white vinegar
- Ground salt
- Olive oil
- 1 sprig of sage
- Coarse salt

**Prep:** Melt the yeast in some cold water and mix it with half of the flour. Cover with the remaining of the flour and layer a cloth on top. Let it rest for 2 hours.
Take the dough and make a hole in the center to put the minced sage leaves, 5 spoons of oil and white vinegar. Knead well the dough, add the ground salt and let it rest for another 2 hours.
Grease the bottom of a casserole and sprinkle some salt, spread the dough about 1 cm thick by using your hands. Pinch the dough in various spots to forms small dimples, grease the top with some oil and sprinkle the coarse salt. Preheat the oven at 375°F and bake.

**Nutrition:** Calories 420; Carbs 62 g; Protein 4.7 g; Fat 16.5 g

## 154. Rice Grenadine

**Prep time:** 10 minutes
**Servings:** 6

**Cook time:** 8 minutes

**Ingredients:**
- 17 oz risotto
- 5 spoons of grated parmesan cheese
- 4 eggs
- 1 minced garlic clove
- 1 spoon of minced parsley
- 50 g of breadcrumbs
- Salt and pepper
- Sunflower seed oil

**Prep:** In a large mixing bowl add the rice, parmesan cheese, 3 eggs, the minced garlic and parsley, salt and pepper.
With the mixture form some balls and take them to a beaten egg and then into the breadcrumbs. Heat up the oil in a pan and then fry the balls. Serve warm.

**Nutrition:** Calories 480 Kcal; Carbs 66.5 g; Protein 25.2 g; Fat 13.5 g

### 155. Fish Stuffed Grenadine

**Prep time:** 30 minutes  
**Servings:** 6  
**Cook time:** 1 hour

**Ingredients:**
- *17 oz of rise*
- *2 monkfish*
- *20 g of dried mushrooms*
- *4 canned tomatoes with no seeds*
- *1 sliced artichoke heart*
- *2 1/2 tbsp of butter*
- *1 chopped onion*
- *1 chopped celery stick*
- *1 spoon of minced parsley*
- *1 cup of breadcrumbs*
- *5 eggs*
- *4 spoons of grated parmesan cheese*
- *nutmeg*
- *salt*
- *pepper*

**Prep:** Chop the celery, onion and parsley. Soak the dried mushrooms into some warm water and roughly chop them. Take the bones off the monkfish. Fry the minced celery, onion and parsley in the butter. When they are ready, add the monkfish pieces and the dried mushrooms.
Mix everything and leave it on a low heat for 30 minutes. Cut into dices the tomatoes and add them in. dust on some nutmeg and salt, put a lid on and let it cook. If the broth dries up, add some water.
Once it is ready, put away one cup of cooking broth.
Put the rice in a big mixing bowl and add the broth, 3 eggs, parmesan cheese and give it a good mix.
Beat the egg and roll the balls in it, then into the breadcrumbs and fry them into hot oil.

**Nutrition:** Calories 482; Carbs 68.5 g; Protein 25.2 g; Fat 13.5 g

### 156. Fried Paniccia

**Prep time:** 15 minutes  
**Servings:** 6  
**Cook time:** 1 hour e 30 minutes

**Ingredients:**
- *450g chickpea flour*
- *salt*
- *33 oz of olive oil*

**Prep:** Warm the 33 oz of water into a pot. Pour some flour at a time and mix to avoid forming any lumps. Put the pot back on the stove and let cook for 1 hour and 20 minutes and keep stirring. Cool down the paniccia on a counter top. Slice into thin slices. Heat up the oil and fry the slices of paniccia. Drain the slices onto some paper towel and add the salt.

**Nutrition:** Calories 780 Kcal; Carbs 46.5 g; Protein 15.2 g; Fat 53.5 g

### 157. Paniccia

**Prep time:** 15 minutes  
**Servings:** 6  
**Cook time:** 1 hour e 20 minutes

**Ingredients:**
- *17 oz of chickpea flour*
- *Extra virgin olive oil*
- *Lime juice*
- *salt*
- *black pepper*

**Prep:** heat up 33 oz of water in a pot. Pour some flour at a time and mix to avoid forming any lumps. Put the pot back on the stove and let cook for 1 hour and 20 minutes and keep stirring. Serve the paniccia warm with a drizzle of oil, some lemon drops and ground black pepper.

**Nutrition:** Calories 711; Carbs 40.5 g; Protein 16.2 g; Fat 50.5 g

### 158. Pizza Genovese

**Prep time:** 2 hours e 30 minutes  
**Servings:** 6  
**Cook time:** 30 minutes

**Ingredients:**
- *4 ½ cups of 00 flour*
- *3tbsp brewer's yeast*
- *5 spoons of extra virgin olive oil*
- *4 spoons of grated parmesan*
- *10 minced basil leaves*
- *salt*
- *pepper*
- *½ cup of ricotta cheese*
- *5 eggs*

**Prep:** Melt the yeast into one cup of warm water. Pour the flour onto a counter and add in the middle 3 spoons of oil, the yeast, a pinch of salt and one cup of water. Knead for at least 10 minutes, then cover it with a cloth and let rest for 2 hours. Take a bowl and beat the eggs adding the parmesan cheese, basil and sifted ricotta. Add salt and pepper and mix.
Divide the mixture in two and roll them into thin sheets. Take one sheet onto an oiled tray, cover it with the beaten egg mixture. Then layer on the second sheet and stick the edges of the two sheets and press them down with the help of a fork. Preheat the oven at 390°F and bake for 25/30 minutes, until the top layer is golden.

**Nutrition:** Calories 476; Carbs 91.5 g; Protein 21.2 g; Fat 13.5 g

### 159. Tomato Appetizer

**Prep time: 20 minutes**  **Servings: 6**

**Ingredients:**
- 6 tomatoes
- 2 spoons of fresh chopped parsley
- 1 porcini mushroom
- 3 tbsp of pine nuts
- 1 spoon of capers
- 4 basil leaves
- Salt
- Olive oil
- 1 cup of mayonnaise

**Prep:** Cut the tomatoes in half and remove the seeds. In a mixing bowl with mayonnaise, a pinch of salt and ground pepper diluted into the lemon juice. Add an egg yolk and whip in the same direction. Then add 33 oz of oil and keep mixing. Grind in a mortar the capers, pine nuts, basil, parsley and the mushroom. Add the salt and dilute with the oil.
Add the mayonnaise and stuff everything in the tomatoes.

**Nutrition:** Calories 420; Carbs 1.5 g; Protein 1.2 g; Fat 22.7 g

### 160. Asparagus Pie

**Prep time: 20 minutes**  **Cook time: 1 hour**
**Servings: 6**

**Ingredients:**
- 4 ½ cups of 0 flour
- 5 tbsp of extra virgin olive oil
- 5,5 oz of asparagus
- 2 ¼ cups of grated parmesan cheese
- 6 eggs
- 5 ¾ tbsp of butter
- salt

**Prep:** Pour the flour and make a well in it on a counter. Add in the well some oil, pinch of salt, some warm water and knead for about 10 minutes. Divide the dough into 27 balls and let them rest covered by a cloth. Wash the asparagus and boil them into salted water for 5 minutes. When they are cooked, divide the tureen from the pulp of the stems. Broil the asparagus into the butter. Add the eggs, parmesan cheese and oil to the asparagus.
Take 12 balls and roll them with a rolling pin, then lay them onto a greased tray one on top of the other, greasing each layer until the second last. Roll the remaining balls of dough. Put the stuffing of eggs and asparagus on the last layer and cover with an oiled pastry. Finish by adding the remaining pastries well greased on both sides. Oven bake at 350°F in a preheat oven for one hour.

**Nutrition:** Calories 448; Carbs 44 g; Protein 22.2 g; Fat 20.5 g

### 161. Beet Pie

**Prep time: 30 minutes**  **Cook time: 20 minutes**
**Servings: 6**

**Ingredients:**
- 4 ½ cups of flour
- 5 tbsp of extra virgin olive oil
- 3.3 oz of beets
- 1 onion
- 4 cups of curd
- salt

**Prep:** Let the curd drain on a cloth tied on the sink.
Put the flower on the counter and make a well, add in it the oil, two pinches of salt and warm water. Knead for at least 10 minutes and then divide it into two equal parts. Let the dough rest covered by a cloth. Cut the sticks of the beets, wash and cut the beets into stripes and let them drain in a colander. Then dry with a cloth. Chop the onion and broil it in some oil. Add the beets and some salt. Mix and let cook. Roll out the two parts of the dough with a rolling pin. Cover the bottom of a greased tray with one half of the dough with the broiled beets and the salted curd. Cover with the other half of the dough and seal the edges.
Brush the top with some oil and punch some holes with a fork. Bake at 350°F for 20 minutes.

**Nutrition:** Calories 560; Carbs 35.5 g; Protein 14.6 g; Fat 39.5 g

## 162. Artichoke Pie

**Prep time:** 2 hours 30 minutes  
**Servings:** 6

**Cook time:** 40 minutes

**Ingredients:**
- 4 ½ cups of flour
- ½ cup of white wine
- 12 tender artichokes
- 4 cups of extra virgin olive oil
- 1 lemon
- 1 cup of cagliata
- 10 eggs
- 1 white chopped onion
- 1 tbsp of fresh parsley
- 3 ¾ of grated parmesan cheese
- salt
- pepper

**Prep:** Clean the artichokes and finely chop them. Soak them in water with lemon juice. Lay the flower on the counter and knead for 10 minutes with the white wine, salt, half a cup of water, then let the dough rest for 2 hours covered by a cloth.
Broil the onion in some oil, butter and parsley. Add into the pan the artichoke slices and let cook for 10 minutes at high heat. Put the mixture in a bowl and let it cool off. Then add 5 eggs, the curd, grated cheese, salt and pepper.
Divide the dough into three parts and roll it, then cover the bottom of a greased tray with the first layer and make 5 dimples to rest the 5 eggs and oil. Cover everything with some oil and bake at 350°F in a preheated oven for half an hour.

**Nutrition:** Calories 376; Carbs 26.5 g; Protein 15.2 g; Fat 22.5 g

## 163. Thistle Pie

**Prep time:** 1 hours 20 minutes  
**Servings:** 6

**Cook time:** 30 minutes

**Ingredients:**
- 4 ½ cups of 00 flour
- ½ cup of white wine
- 2 midsized thistles
- 1 lemon
- 4 tsp di butter
- 4 tbsp of extra virgin olive oil
- ½ chopped onion
- 1 tbsp of fresh chopped parsley
- ¾ cup of grated parmesan cheese
- 1 cup of curd
- salt
- pepper

**Prep:** Knead the flour with the wine, some salt and half a cup of water. Let it rest for one hour covering it with a cloth, then divide the dough in two parts and roll them with a rolling pin.
Wash the thistles, cut the leaves into pieces and discard the strings. Put everything into some water with lemon juice. Boil the thistles twice, drain them and mash them in a mortar.
In a pan put the oil and butter and fry the onion and chopped parsley. Combine the mixture of thistles, grated cheese, salt and pepper.
Cover the bottom of a greased tray with one rolled out dough, spread the thistles mix on and the salted curd. Cover everything with the second half of the dough, close the sides and grease the top. Punch some holes with a fork and bake at 350° F in a preheated oven.

**Nutrition:** Calories 265; Carbs 26.5 g; Protein 7.9 g; Fat 19.5 g

## 164. Onion Pie

**Prep time:** 1 hour e 30 minutes  
**Servings:** 6

**Cook time:** 1 hour

**Ingredients:**
- 4 ½ cups of flour
- 3 tbsp of extra virgin olive oil
- 2 lbs. of red sweet onions
- 5 ½ of butter
- 2 ¼ tbsp of grated parmesan cheese
- 2 ¼ tbsp of dried mushrooms
- salt
- pepper

**Prep:** let the mushroom soak in some warm water. Clean the onions and roughly chop them. Wash the onions and boil them in salted water for 5 minutes. Fry the boiled onions and the mushrooms in a pan with some butter. Mix and combine the grated cheese, salt and pepper.
Knead the flour with oil and a cup of warm water for 10 minutes, then divide the dough in 33 pieces, dust some flour and cover with a cloth. Let it rest for about one hour.
Roll with a rolling pin the 33 pieces of dough, place 13 of them on a greased tray, greased between one layer and the other. On the last layer put the prepared onion stuffing. Continue covering the other 20 layers greasing each one of them. Grease also the last layer and oven bake at 390°F for 50 minutes.

**Nutrition:** Calories 377; Carbs 26.5 g; Protein 11.2 g; Fat 19.1 g

### 165. Spelt Pie

**Prep time:** 1 hours e 30 minutes  
**Servings:** 6  
**Cook time:** 30 minutes

**Ingredients:**
- 4 ½ cups of 00 flour
- 5 tbsp of extra virgin olive oil
- 1 ¾ cup of spelt
- 2 potatoes
- 4 eggs
- ½ cup of ricotta
- 1 garlic clove
- 4 tbsp of grated parmesan cheese
- nutmeg
- salt
- pepper

**Prep:** Soak the spelt overnight. Boil the spelt for 3 hours, drain it and pour into a bowl.
Knead the four with oil, half a cup of water for 10 minutes, then divide the dough in two parts and roll it out with a rolling pin. Roll the pastry in some surround wrap and let it rest for one hour. Boil and peel the potatoes, then sift the potatoes and add the spelt. Add the minced garlic, cheese, nutmeg, pepper and eggs and mix everything well. Add some salt if needed.
Cover the bottom of a greased tray with the first pastry, spread the inside with the filling and cover with the second pastry. Grease the surface and punch some holes with a fork. Bake in a preheated oven at 350°F until the top is golden brown.

**Nutrition:** Calories 529 Kcal; Carbs 79.5 g; Protein 8.2 g; Fat 18.5 g

### 166. Mushroom Pie

**Prep time:** 1 hour and 30 minutes  
**Servings:** 6  
**Cook time:** 30 minutes

**Ingredients:**
- 4 ½ cups of 00 flour
- 7 tbsp of olive oil
- 2 lbs. of fresh mushrooms or ½ cup of dried mushrooms
- salt
- pepper

**Prep:** Knead the flour with the oil for at least 10 minutes, put some salt in some warm water and then split the dough in two and roll it out with a rolling pin. Roll the pastry on parchment paper and let it rest. Clean and cut into slices the mushrooms, both the stem and top and fry everything with two whole garlic cloves and some salt. Drain the water released by the mushrooms and add some ground pepper, oil and minced catmint and let it all cook on a low heat for 20 minutes.
Cover the bottom of a greased tray with the first dough layer and add the mushroom stuffing. Cover then with the second layer, join the edges and stab some holes by using a fork. On a preheated oven bake at 350°F until the top is golden.

**Nutrition:** Calories 441; Carbs 23.5 g; Protein 16.2 g; Fat 31.5 g

### 167. Pumpkin Pie

**Prep time:** 3 hours and 30 minutes  
**Servings:** 6  
**Cook time:** 30 minutes

**Ingredients:**
- 4 ½ cups of 00 flour
- Extra virgin olive oil
- 3 lbs. of pumpkin
- 2 tbsp of dried mushrooms
- 1 cup of grated parmesan cheese
- 5 eggs
- 5 tbsp of butter
- Nutmeg
- Salt and pepper
- 1 chopped onion

**Prep:** Knead the flour with oil, salt and warm water for at least 10 minutes, then divide the dough in two pieces, cover them with a cloth and leave to rest. Soak the mushrooms in some warm water.
Chop the pumpkin and gut it by removing the skin and seeds, then cover the pieces in salt and cover with a cloth. Let the pumpkin drain by tying it on top of the sink for about three hours. Chop the pumpkin and move it into a bowl.
In a casserole, fry the chopped pumpkin and mushrooms with butter for 5 minutes. Add the mushrooms to the pumpkin mixture and then add the cheese, eggs, lots of pepper, nutmeg and mix it for 10 minutes.
Roll out the dough with a rolling pin and form 2 thin layers. Put one of the layers on a greased pan and pour in the pumpkin and mushroom stuffing.
Cover with the other layer of dough, join the sides and poke some holes on the top with a fork. Bake at 350°F in a preheated oven until the top is golden.

**Nutrition:** Calories 518; Carbs 23.9 g; Protein 18.3 g; Fat 38.8 g

### 168. Scamorza Crunchy Bites

**Prep time:** 5 minutes  
**Servings:** 4  
**Cook time:** 5 minutes

**Ingredients:**
- 8 slices of bread
- Milk to taste
- 2 tbsp of extra virgin olive oil
- 1 ¾ cups of sweet scamorza
- Salt and pepper

**Prep:** Grease the bottom and sides of an oven tray with some oil and lay the bread slices. Brush on little with some milk to dampen them.
Cut the scamorza cheese into thin sliced and lay them over the bread. Add a pinch of salt, pepper and drizzle some oil. Bake at 350°F for 5 minutes, or until the bread will be golden and the cheese has melted.

**Nutrition:** Calories 230; Carbs 1.9 g; Protein 22.1 g; Fat 26 g

### 169. Hot Asparagus

**Prep time:** 15 minutes  
**Servings:** 4

**Ingredients:**
- 2 ¾ cups of asparagus
- Hot pepper
- Extra virgin olive oil
- Salt
- Lemon juice

**Prep:** clean the asparagus, chop them and boil them into plenty of salted water. Layer them on a serving plate. Season with a drizzle of oil, salt, hot pepper and lemon juice.

**Nutrition:** Calories 87; Carbs 5.7 g; Protein 12.8 g; Fat 1.8 g

### 170. Fried Pumpkin Flowers (2nd version)

**Prep time:** 10 minutes  
**Servings:** 4  
**Cook time:** 10 minutes

**Ingredients:**
- 2 cups of pumpkin flowers
- 2 eggs
- 2 ½ cups of flour
- 2 ¾ cups of grated parmesan cheese
- 2 basil leaves
- A pinch of salt and pepper
- Extra virgin olive oil to taste

**Prep:** Clean the pumpkin flowers, put them into a bowl and add some salt. Beat the eggs with 4 tbsp of parmesan cheese, add the flour, and the remaining cheese. Add the water released by the pumpkin flower a little at a time and mix. Add salt, pepper, minced basil and keep mixing. Squeeze well the flowers, cut them into big chunks and add them to the batter. Heat up some oil in a pan, fry the flowers for 2 minutes on each side.

**Nutrition:** Calories 550; Carbs 39.8 g; Protein 6.1 g; Fat 38.9 g

### 171. Sea Appetizer

**Prep time:** 30 minutes  
**Servings:** 4  
**Cook time:** 60 minutes

**Ingredients:**
- 1 ¼ cup of clams
- 2 cups of octopus
- 2 cups of squid
- 1 ¼ cup of mussels
- 3 ¼ cups of dentex
- 1 ¼ cup of shelled shrimp
- 1 lemon
- 5 pickles
- 1 sprig of parsley
- Extra virgin olive oil
- Salt and pepper

**Prep:** Boil the fish in plenty of hot water, then drain it.
Remove the bones from the dentex and cut into pieces the squid and octopus. Move all the fish to a bowl and add the pickles, chopped parsley, some oil, lemon juice, salt and pepper, then mix.

**Nutrition:** Calories 390; Carbs 9.8 g; Protein 49.1 g; Fat 18 g

## 172. Tuna Starter

**Prep time:** 45 minutes  **Servings:** 4

**Ingredients:**
- 5 salted anchovies
- 1 ½ cup of tuna in oil
- ¼ cup of butter
- The juice of 1 lemon
- 1 tbsp of extra virgin olive oil
- ¾ cup of radish
- 1 pickle
- Salt and pepper

**Prep:** Carefully wash the anchovies to remove the salt; cut the head and the tail. Pulse them with the butter cut into pieces, tuna, lemon juice and pepper. Roll the mixture and leave it into some parchment paper to rest in the fridge for at least 3 hours. Chop the pickle and the radish and sprinkle them onto the tuna mixture, then serve.

**Nutrition:** Calories 329; Carbs 8.9 g; Protein 16.1 g; Fat 16 g

## 173. Chicken Pastry Rolls

**Prep time:** 1 hour and 30 minutes  **Cook time:** 40 minutes
**Servings:** 6

**Ingredients:**

**For the stuffing:**
- 2 chopped onions
- 2 ¼ cups of minced chicken
- 3 tsp of olive oil
- 2 eggs
- ½ cup of water
- Premade Pastry
- Salt and pepper
- 3 tbsp of grated bread

**For the pastry:**
- ½ cup of butter
- ½ cup of sugar
- Salt
- 2 cups of flour
- 4 egg yolks

**Prep:** Chop the onion, brown it in a pan with a little oil, salt and pepper.
Soften the breadcrumbs with some water, then add the eggs and mix.
To prepare the pastry, pour the flour and make a well, add the butter cut into pieces. Knead the flour and butter until you reach a granulated mixture.
Pour in the sugar, a pinch of salt, the egg yolks and knead vigorously. Roll out the dough with a rolling pin, fold it and roll it out again. Knead the dough forming a ball, the wrap it in some surround wrap and rest it in the fridge for 3 hours.
Take out the dough, roll it out and add the stuffing, then roll it.
Bake it in a preheated oven at 375°F for 30 minutes. Wait for it to cool down, then cut into slices and serve.

**Nutrition:** Calories 349, Carbs 49.4 g, Protein 22 g, Fat 21.1 g

## 174. Au Gratin Scallops

**Prep time:** 15 minutes  **Cook time:** 15 minutes
**Servings:** 4

**Ingredients:**
- 8 scallops
- ¼ cup of extra virgin olive oil
- Parsley
- Marjoram
- ½ cup of bread chunks
- Lemon zest
- Salt and pepper

**Prep:** Chop the bread chunks and pulse it with salt, pepper and oil. Coat the scallops into the crumbs and lay them onto an oven tray. Bake in a ventilated oven at 375°F for 15 minutes.

**Nutrition:** Calories 260; Carbs 21 g; Protein 9.1 g; Fat 14.6 g

## 175. Seasoned Bresaola

**Prep time:** 30 minutes  **Servings:** 4

**Ingredients:**
- 1 ¼ cup of bresaola
- The juice of 2 lemons
- Extra virgin olive oil
- Thyme
- Marjoram
- pepper

**Prep:** Lay the slices of bresaola in a plate, sprinkle on the minced thyme, marjoram, lemon juice, pepper and a drizzle of oil. Cover with some surround wrap and marinate for 30 minutes.

**Nutrition:** Calories 121; Carbs 4.4 g; Protein 22.1 g; Fat 8.6 g

## 176. Veggie Fritters

**Prep time:** 15 minutes  
**Cook time:** 10 minutes  
**Servings:** 4

**Ingredients:**
- 1 ¾ cup of zucchini
- 1 ¾ cup of potatoes
- 2 sprigs of thyme
- 3/4 cup of flour
- 1 tsp of sweet paprika
- Salt and pepper
- Extra virgin olive oil
- 1 ½ cup of carrots

**Prep:** Wash the zucchini and remove the extremities. Peel the carrots and potatoes and grate them on a large hole setting grater. Add the paprika and flour and mix. Add the salt, pepper and thyme leaves. Mix everything, form some balls and fry them into hot oil for 5 minutes.

**Nutrition:** Calories 140; Carbs 7.7 g; Protein 2.1 g; Fat 7.6 g

## 177. Porcini Mushroom Mixed Starter

**Prep time:** 90 minutes  
**Servings:** 4

**Ingredients:**
- ½ stick of celeriac
- ½ stick of celery
- 2 ¼ cups of porcini mushrooms in oil
- 2 slices of baked ham of 1/8 inch thick
- Juice of 1 lemon
- 2 potatoes
- Mayonnaise
- Parsley
- 1 green apple
- 2 heads of endive

**Prep:** Wash all the vegetables and cut them into strips. Cut the baked ham and the green apple in the same manner. Drain the oil from the mushrooms and slice them. Pour everything in a bowl and season with mayonnaise and lemon juice. Add the minced parsley mix it in and serve.

**Nutrition:** Calories 242; Carbs 3.1 g; Protein 12.1 g; Fat 13.6 g

## 178. Black Olives with Orange

**Prep time:** 5 minutes  
**Servings:** 4

**Ingredients:**
- ¾ cup of black olives
- 1 garlic clove
- Extra virgin olive oil
- Zest of ½ an orange
- salt

**Prep:** Season the olives with chopped garlic, diced orange peel and olive oil. Add the salt and mix well. Let it rest for 24 hours before serving.

**Nutrition:** Calories 122; Carbs 0.2 g; Protein 0.4 g; Fat 13.5 g

## 179. Anchovy and Zucchini Fritters

**Prep time:** 10 minutes  
**Cook time:** 5 minutes  
**Servings:** 4

**Ingredients:**
- 14 oz of bread dough
- Extra virgin olive oil
- 8 salted anchovy fillets
- ½ onion

**Prep:** Wash and slice the zucchini. Fry them in a pan with some oil, chopped onion and a pinch of salt. Pour some flower in your hands, take some dough and add the zucchini and some anchovy pieces. Fry the dough into hot oil and serve hot.

**Nutrition:** Calories 151; Carbs 7.4 g; Protein 12.1 g; Fat 8.4 g

## 180. Zucchini and Eggplant Fritters

**Prep time:** 10 minutes  
**Servings:** 4  
**Cook time:** 5 minutes

**Ingredients:**
- 21 oz of bread dough
- 1 cup of eggplant
- 1 cup of zucchini
- ½ chopped onion
- Oregano
- Extra virgin olive oil
- salt

**Prep:** Wash and slice the zucchini and eggplant. Fry the vegetables into a pan with some oil and chopped onion, minced oregano and salt.
Pour some flower in your hands, take some dough and add the zucchini and eggplant.
Fry the dough into hot oil and serve hot.

**Nutrition:** Calories 111; Carbs 7.9 g; Protein 1.8 g; Fat 8.1 g

## 181. Tomatoes and Anchovy Fritters

**Prep time:** 20 minutes  
**Servings:** 4  
**Cook time:** 15 minutes

**Ingredients:**
- 2 cups of flour
- 1 pack of pizza yeast
- 4 ripe tomatoes
- 8 salted anchovies
- Extra virgin olive oil
- water
- salt

**Prep:** Peel the tomatoes after boiling them. Gut them and chop them up.
Prepare the batter in a bowl with flour, water, salt, yeast and then add the tomatoes and anchovies.
Gently mix.
Take the mixture with a spoon and pour it into the hot oil to fry it.

**Nutrition:** Calories 156; Carbs 7.3 g; Protein 12.8 g; Fat 8.8 g

## 182. Tuna Roll

**Prep time:** 30 minutes  
**Servings:** 6

**Ingredients:**
- 2 ½ cups of tuna in oil
- ½ cup of butter
- 1 lemon
- 6 salted anchovies
- 3 hardboiled eggs
- 12 pickled artichokes
- 12 green olives without the pit
- Pepper
- Olive oil
- 1 shot of Brandy
- vegetable paper

**Prep:** Wash the anchovies under current water to remove the salt. Open them and remove the bones and tail, then pat dry them.
Sift the tuna and anchovies; pour the cream in a bowl, juice the lemon and add it in, 1 shot of Brandy and some ground pepper. Melt the butter and beat it with a whisk and then add it to the bowl, mix all well.
Grease the vegetable paper with olive oil and butter; pour the mixture and roll it tightly.
Tie the ends and rest in the fridge for some hours.
Meanwhile hard-boil 3 eggs.
Unravel and cut into slices the roll to prepare it for serving. Prepare a side dish with pickled artichokes, olives and hardboiled eggs.

**Nutrition:** Calories 207, Carbs 3.7 g, Protein 10.5 g, Fat 16.5 g

## 183. Potato and Bacon Rolls

**Prep time:** 1 hour  
**Servings:** 6  
**Cook time:** 40 minutes

**Ingredients:**
- 2 ¼ cups of potatoes
- ¾ cup of bacon
- 21 oz of premade pastry dough
- ¾ cup of grated parmesan cheese
- Black pepper

**Prep:** Boil the potatoes in salted water; drain, peel and mash them with a potato masher to reach a creamy consistency. Cut the bacon into cubes and fry them in a separate pan. Then, add the potato cream and add in the parmesan cheese and pepper. Combine the mixture.

Take the pastry dough, stuff it and make it into a roll. Preheat the oven at 375°F and bake for 30 minutes. Let it cool, slice it and serve.

**Nutrition:** Calories 350, Carbs 45 g, Protein 8 g, Fat 12 g

### 184. Chicken Rolls

**Prep time: 1 hour**            **Cook time: 40 minutes**
**Servings: 6**

**Ingredients:**
- 2 chopped onions
- 12 oz Ground chicken meat
- 3 tsp of olive oil
- 2 eggs
- Salt and pepper
- Premade pastry dough
- ½ cup of water
- 3 tbsp of breadcrumbs

**Prep:** Chop the onion and let it sizzle in a pan with a little oil, salt and pepper.
Soften the breadcrumbs with water and then add the eggs. Give it a good mix.
Take the pastry, stuff it and roll it. Preheat the oven at 375°F for 30 minutes. Let it cool, slice it and serve.

**Nutrition:** Calories 340, Carbs 47.4 g, Protein 22 g, Fat 10.1 g

### 185. Ham in Balsamic Vinegar

**Prep time: 15 minutes**            **Cook time: 15 minutes**
**Servings: 6**

**Ingredients:**
- 14 oz of sweet raw ham
- 3 tbsp of pine nuts
- 8 tbsp of balsamic vinegar
- 1 cup of milk cream
- 2-3 tbsp of grated parmesan cheese
- 2 tbsp of butter
- 1 tsp of sugar
- Salt and white pepper

**Prep:** Melt the butter in a pan on medium heat. Pour in the balsamic vinegar and let evaporate some of it; combine in the sugar.
Pour the milk cream and let it reduce for a few minutes but don't let it get to a boil.
When it is cooked, pour in the parmesan cheese and adjust the taste of salt and pepper.
Lay the ham onto a plate, add the pine nuts and pour on the seasoning.
Serve immediately to prevent the sauce from cooling down.

**Nutrition:** Calories 330, Carbs 3.4 g, Protein 29.4 g, Fat 20.1 g

### 186. 5-Minute Tomato & Cucumber Toast

**Prep Time: 10 minutes**            **Cook Time: 6-10 minutes**
**Servings: 1**

**Ingredients:**
- 1 small Heirloom tomato
- 1 Persian cucumber
- 1 tsp. Olive oil
- 1 pinch Oregano
- Kosher salt and pepper as desired
- 2 tsp. Low-fat whipped cream cheese
- 2 pieces Trader Joe's Whole Grain Crisp bread or your choice
- 1 tsp. Balsamic glaze

**Prep:** Dice the cucumber and tomato. Combine all the fixings except for the cream cheese.
Smear the cheese on the bread and add the mixture.
Top it off with the balsamic glaze and serve.

**Nutrition:** Calories: 177, Protein: 3 g, Fat: 8 g

### 187. Avocado and Chickpea Sandwiches

**Prep Time:** 4 minutes  **Serving:** 4

**Ingredients:**
- 1/2 cup canned chickpeas
- 1 small avocado
- 2 green onions, finely chopped
- 1 egg, hard boiled
- 1/2 tomato, cucumber

**Prep:** Mash the avocado and chickpeas with a fork until smooth. Add in salt and green onions and combine well. Spread the mixture on the four slices of bread. Top each slice with cucumber tomato, and egg.

**Nutrition:** 309 Calories, 9 g Fat, 2 g Protein

### 188. Olive Paste and Avocado on Rye Bread

**Prep Time:** 5 minutes  **Serving:** 4

**Ingredients:**
- 1 avocado, halved, peeled and finely chopped
- 1 tbsp. green onions, finely chopped
- 2 tbsp. green olive paste
- 4 lettuce leaves
- 1 tbsp. lemon juice

**Prep:** Crush avocados with a fork or potato masher until almost smooth. Add the onions, green olive paste and lemon juice. Season with salt and pepper to taste. Stir to combine.
Toast 4 slices of bread until golden brown. Spread 1/4 of the avocado mixture on each slice of bread, top with a lettuce leaf and serve.

**Nutrition:** 291 Calories, 13 g Fat, 3 g Protein

### 189. Cottage Cheese and Berries Omelet

**Prep Time:** 5 minutes  **Cook Time:** 4 minutes
**Servings:** 1

**Ingredients:**
- 1 egg, whisked
- 1 teaspoon cinnamon powder
- 1 tablespoon almond milk
- 3 ounces cottage cheese
- 4 ounces blueberries

**Prep:** Scourge egg with the rest of the ingredients except the oil and toss.
Preheat pan with the oil over medium heat, add the eggs mix, spread, cook for 2 minutes on each side, transfer to a plate and serve.

**Nutrition:** 190 Calories, 8 g Fat, 2 g Protein

### 190. Egg White Scramble with Cherry Tomatoes & Spinach

**Prep Time:** 5 minutes  **Cook Time:** 8-10 minutes
**Servings:** 4

**Ingredients:**
- 1 tbsp. Olive oil
- 1 whole Egg
- 10 Egg whites
- ¼ tsp. Black pepper
- ½ tsp. Salt
- 1 garlic clove, minced
- 2 cups cherry tomatoes, halved
- 2 cups packed fresh baby spinach
- ½ cup Light cream or Half & Half
- ¼ cup finely grated parmesan cheese

**Prep:** Whisk the eggs, pepper, salt, and milk.
Prepare a skillet using the med-high temperature setting. Toss in the garlic when the pan is hot to sauté for approximately 30 seconds.
Pour in the tomatoes and spinach and continue to sauté it for one additional minute. The tomatoes should be softened, and the spinach wilted.
Add the egg mixture into the pan using the medium heat setting. Fold the egg gently as it cooks for about two to three minutes. Remove from the burner, and sprinkle with a sprinkle of cheese.

**Nutrition:** Calories 142, Protein: 15 g, Fat: 2 g

## 191. Feta - Avocado & Mashed Chickpea Toast

**Prep Time:** 10 minutes  
**Servings:** 4  
**Cook Time:** 15 minutes

**Ingredients:**
- 15 oz. can Chickpeas
- 2 oz. - ½ cup Diced feta cheese
- 1 Pitted avocado

**Fresh juice:**
- 2 tsp. Lemon (or 1 tbsp. orange)
- 2 tsp. Honey
- ½ tsp. Black pepper
- 4 slices Multigrain toast

**Prep:** Toast the bread. Drain the chickpeas in a colander. Scoop the avocado flesh into the bowl.
Use a large fork/potato masher to mash them until the mix is spreadable.
Pour in the lemon juice, pepper, and feta.
Combine and divide onto the four slices of toast.
Drizzle using the honey and serve.

**Nutrition:** Calories: 337, Protein: 13 g, Fat: 13 g

## 192. Feta & Quinoa Egg Muffins

**Prep Time:** 20 minutes  
**Servings:** 12  
**Cook Time:** 50 minutes

**Ingredients:**
- 1 cup cooked quinoa
- ½ cup white onion
- 8 eggs
- 2 cups baby spinach, chopped
- 1 tbsp. fresh oregano
- 1 cup crumbled feta cheese
- ½ cup Kalamata olives
- ½ tsp. salt
- Also Needed: 12-cup muffin tin
- 1 cup tomatoes
- 2 tsp.+ more for coating pans olive oil

**Prep:** Heat the oven to reach 350° F.
Lightly grease the muffin tray cups with a spritz of cooking oil.
Prepare a skillet using the medium temperature setting and add the oil. When it's hot, toss in the onions to sauté for two minutes.
Dump the tomatoes into the skillet and sauté for one minute. Fold in the spinach and continue cooking until the leaves have wilted (1 min.).
Transfer the pot to the countertop and add the oregano and olives. Set aside.
Crack the eggs into a mixing bowl, using an immersion stick blender to mix them thoroughly. Add the cooked veggies in with the rest of the fixings.
Stir until it's combined and scoop the mixture into the greased muffin cups.
Set the timer to bake the muffins for 30 minutes until browned, and the muffins are set.
Cool for about ten minutes.

**Nutrition:** Calories 113, Protein: 7 g, Fat: 7 g

## 193. Feta Cheese Baked in Foil

**Prep Time:** 15 minutes  
**Serving:** 5  
**Cook Time:** 16 minutes

**Ingredients:**
- 14 oz. feta cheese, cut in slices
- 1 tbsp. paprika
- 4 oz. butter
- 1 tsp. dried oregano

**Prep:** Cut the cheese into four medium-thick slices and place on sheets of butter lined aluminum foil.
Place a little bit of butter on top each feta cheese piece, sprinkle with paprika and dried oregano and wrap. Place on a tray and bake in a preheated to 350 F oven for 15 minutes.

**Nutrition:** 279 Calories, 9 g Fat, 2 g Protein

### 194. Feta Frittata

**Prep Time:** 15 minutes  
**Servings:** 2  
**Cook Time:** 25 minutes

**Ingredients:**
- 1 small clove Garlic
- 1 Green onion
- 2 Large eggs
- ½ cup Egg substitute
- 4 tbsp. Crumbled feta cheese - divided
- 1/3 cup Plum tomato
- 4 thin Avocado slices
- 2 tbsp. Reduced-fat sour cream
- Also Needed: 6-inch skillet

**Prep:** Thinly slice/mince the onion, garlic, and tomato. Peel the avocado before slicing.
Heat the pan using the medium temperature setting and spritz it with cooking oil.
Whisk the egg substitute, eggs, and the feta cheese. Add the egg mixture into the pan. Cover and simmer for four to six minutes. Sprinkle it using the rest of the feta cheese and tomato. Cover and continue cooking until the eggs are set or about two to three more minutes. Wait for about five minutes before cutting it into halves.
Serve with the avocado and sour cream.

**Nutrition:** Calories: 203, Fat: 12 g, Protein: 17 g

### 195. Chili Oregano Baked Cheese

**Prep Time:** 5 minutes  
**Servings:** 4  
**Cook Time:** 35 minutes

**Ingredients:**
- 8 oz. feta cheese
- 4 oz. mozzarella, crumbled
- chili pepper, sliced
- 1 tsp. dried oregano
- tbsps. olive oil

**Prep:** Place the feta cheese in a small deep-dish baking pan. Top with the mozzarella then season with pepper slices and oregano.
Cover the pan with aluminum foil and cook in the preheated oven at 350F for 20 minutes.
Serve the cheese right away.

**Nutrition:** Calories 292, Fat: 24.2 g, Carbs: 3.7 g, Protein: 16.2 g

### 196. Greek Style Quesadillas

**Prep Time:** 10 minutes  
**Servings:** 4  
**Cook Time:** 10 minutes

**Ingredients:**
- 4 whole wheat tortillas
- cup Mozzarella cheese, shredded
- 1 cup fresh spinach, chopped
- tablespoon Greek yogurt
- 1 egg, beaten
- ¼ cup green olives, sliced
- 1 tablespoon olive oil
- 1/3 cup fresh cilantro, chopped

**Prep:** In the bowl, combine together Mozzarella cheese, spinach, yogurt, egg, olives, and cilantro.
Then pour olive oil in the skillet.
Place one tortilla in the skillet and coat it with Mozzarella mixture.
Place the second tortilla and spread it with cheese mixture again.
Then place the third tortilla and coat it with remaining cheese mixture.
Cover it with the last tortilla and fry it for 5 minutes on each side over medium heat.

**Nutrition:** Calories 193; Fat 7.7 g; Carbs 23.6 g; Protein 8.3 g

### 197. Mediterranean Burrito

**Prep Time:** 10 minutes  
**Servings:** 2

**Ingredients:**
- 2 wheat tortillas
- 2 oz. red kidney beans, canned, drained
- 2 tablespoons hummus
- 2 teaspoons tahini sauce
- cucumber
- lettuce leaves
- 1 tablespoon lime juice
- 1 teaspoon olive oil
- ½ teaspoon dried oregano

**Prep:** Mash the red beans until pureed. Then spread the tortillas with the bean puree on one side. Add hummus and tahini sauce.
Cut the cucumber into the wedges and place on top of the tahini sauce. Then add lettuce leaves.
Make the dressing: mix together dried oregano, olive oil, and lime juice.
Sprinkle the lettuce leaves with the dressing and wrap the wheat tortillas.

**Nutrition:** Calories 288; Fat 10.2 g; Carbs 38.2 g; Protein 12.5 g

## 198. Egg Bake

**Prep Time:** 10 minutes  
**Servings:** 2  
**Cook Time:** 30 minutes

**Ingredients:**
- 1 tablespoon olive oil
- 1 slice whole-grain bread
- 4 large eggs
- 3 tablespoons unsweetened almond milk
- ½ teaspoon onion powder
- ¼ teaspoon garlic powder
- ¾ cup chopped cherry tomatoes
- ¼ teaspoon salt
- Pinch freshly ground black pepper

**Prep:** Preheat the oven to 375°F.
Coat two ramekins with the olive oil and transfer to a baking sheet. Line the bottom of each ramekin with ½ of bread slice.
In a medium bowl, whisk together the eggs, almond milk, onion powder, garlic powder, tomatoes, salt, and pepper until well combined. Pour the mixture evenly into two ramekins. Bake in the preheated oven for 30 minutes, or until the eggs are completely set. Cool for 5 minutes before serving.

**Nutrition:** Calories: 240 Fat: 17.4 g Protein: 9 g Carbs: 12.2 g

## 199. Pumpkin Pie Parfait

**Prep Time:** 5 minutes  
**Servings:** 4

**Ingredients:**
- 1 (15-ounce / 425-g) can pure pumpkin purée
- 4 teaspoons honey
- 1 teaspoon pumpkin pie spice
- ¼ teaspoon ground cinnamon
- 2 cups plain Greek yogurt
- 1 cup honey granola

**Prep:** Combine the pumpkin purée, honey, pumpkin pie spice, and cinnamon in a large bowl and stir to mix well. Cover the bowl with plastic wrap and chill in the refrigerator for at least 2 hours.
Make the parfaits: Layer each parfait glass with ¼ cup pumpkin mixture in the bottom. Top with ¼ cup of yogurt and scatter each top with ¼ cup of honey granola. Repeat the layers until the glasses are full.

**Nutrition:** Calories: 263 Fat: 8.9 g Protein: 15.3 g Carbs: 34.6 g

## 200. Mediterranean Eggs

**Prep Time:** 5 minutes  
**Servings:** 4  
**Cook Time:** 20 minutes

**Ingredients:**
- 2 tablespoons extra-virgin olive oil
- 1 cup chopped shallots
- 1 teaspoon garlic powder
- 1 cup finely diced potato
- 1 cup chopped red bell peppers
- 1 (14.5-ounce/ 411-g) can diced tomatoes, drained
- ¼ teaspoon ground cardamom
- ¼ teaspoon paprika
- ¼ teaspoon turmeric
- 4 large eggs
- ¼ cup chopped fresh cilantro

**Prep:** Preheat the oven to 350°F.
Heat the olive oil in an ovenproof skillet over medium-high heat until it shimmers.
Add the shallots and sauté for about 3 minutes, occasionally stirring, until fragrant.
Fold in the garlic powder, potato, and bell peppers and stir to combine.
Cover and cook for 10 minutes, stirring frequently. Add the tomatoes, cardamom, paprika, and turmeric and mix well.
When the mixture begins to bubble, remove from the heat, and crack the eggs into the skillet.
Transfer the skillet to the preheated oven and bake for 5 to 10 minutes.
Remove from the oven and garnish with the cilantro before serving.

**Nutrition:** Calories: 223 g Fat: 11.8 g Protein: 9.1 g Carbs: 19.5 g

## 201. Baked Eggs in Avocado

**Prep Time:** 5 minutes
**Servings:** 2

**Cook Time:** 15 minutes

**Ingredients:**
- 1 large ripe avocado
- 2 large eggs
- Salt and ground black pepper, to taste
- 4 tablespoons jarred pesto, for serving
- 2 tablespoons chopped tomato, for serving
- 2 tablespoons crumbled feta cheese, for serving

**Prep:** Preheat the oven to 425°F.
Cut the avocado in half, remove the core, and scoop out a tablespoon of flesh from each half to create a hole enough to fit an egg.
Transfer the avocado halves (cut-side up) to a baking sheet.
Crack 1 egg into each avocado half and sprinkle with pepper and salt.
Bake in the preheated oven for 10 to 15 minutes, or until the eggs are cooked to your preferred doneness.
Remove the avocado halves from the oven. Scatter each avocado half evenly with the jarred pesto, chopped tomato, and crumbled feta cheese (if desired). Serve immediately.

**Nutrition:** Calories: 301 Fat: 25.9 g Protein: 8.1 g Carbs: 9.8 g

## 202. Quinoa Buffalo Bites

**Prep Time:** 10 minutes
**Servings:** 4

**Cook Time:** 15 minutes

**Ingredients:**
- 2 cups cooked quinoa
- 1 cup shredded mozzarella
- 1/2 cup buffalo sauce
- 1/4 cup +1 Tbsp flour
- 1 egg
- 1/4 cup chopped cilantro
- 1 small onion, diced

**Prep:** Preheat oven to 350 °F.
Mix all ingredients in large bowl.
Press mixture into greased mini muffin tins.
Bake for approximately 15 minutes or until bites are golden.
Enjoy on its own or with blue cheese or ranch dip.

**Nutrition:** Calories: 212; Carbs: 30.6 g; Protein: 15.9 g; Fat: 3.0 g

## 203. Asparagus Frittata

**Prep Time:** 20 minutes
**Servings:** 4

**Cook Time:** 20 minutes

**Ingredients:**
- Bacon slices, chopped: 4
- Salt and black pepper
- Eggs (whisked): 8
- Asparagus (trimmed and chopped): 1 bunch

**Prep:** Heat a pan, add bacon, stir and cook for 5 minutes. Add asparagus, pepper, and salt, stir and cook for another 5 minutes. Add the chilled eggs, spread them in the pan, let them stand in the oven and bake for 20 minutes at 350° F.
Share and divide between plates and serve.

**Nutrition:** Calories 251; Carbs 16 g; Fat 6 g; Protein 7 g

## 204. Bacon and Lemon spiced Muffins

**Prep Time:** 10 minutes
**Servings:** 12

**Cook Time:** 20 minutes

**Ingredients:**
- Lemon thyme, 2 tsps.
- Salt
- Almond flour, 3 cup.
- Melted butter, ½ cup.
- Baking soda, 1 tsp.
- Black pepper
- Medium eggs, 4
- Diced bacon, 1 cup.

**Prep:** Set a mixing bowl in place and stir in the eggs and baking soda to incorporate well.
Whisk in the seasonings, butter, bacon, and lemon thyme.
Set the mixture in a well-lined muffin pan.
Set the oven for 20 minutes at 350 °F, allow to bake.
Allow the muffins to cool before serving.

### 205. Cannellini Bean Lettuce Wraps

**Prep Time: 10 minutes**  **Cook Time: 15 minutes**
**Servings: 4**

**Ingredients:**
- 1 tbsp. Olive oil
- ½ cup Red onion
- 1 medium/ ¾ cup Tomatoes
- ¼ tsp. Freshly cracked black pepper
- ¼ cup Fresh curly parsley
- 15 oz. can cannellini beans
- ½ cup Prepared hummus
- 8 Romaine lettuce leaves

**Prep:** Drain and rinse the vegetables and beans. Chop the tomatoes and onion into fine pieces. Add the oil into a skillet to heat using the medium heat temperature setting. Chop and toss in the onions, tomatoes, and pepper to sauté for six. Stir occasionally. Pour in the drained beans and simmer them for three additional minutes.
Mix in the parsley after removing it from the burner.
Spread the hummus over each of the leaves of lettuce. Spread the bean mixture to the center of each leaf. Fold it over to make a wrap to serve.

**Nutrition:** Calories 235, Fat: 20 g, Protein: 4 g

# BREADS, PIZZAS AND FOCACCIAS

## 206. Focaccia Dough

**Prep time: 40 minutes**  **Servings: 4**

**Ingredients:**
- 4 ½ cups of wheat flour
- 1 ¾ tbsp brewer's yeast
- A pinch of sugar
- A pinch of salt
- 3 ½ tbsp of lard
- 1 cup of water

**Prep:** Melt the yeast into ¾ cup of warm water and mix in a pinch of sugar.
On a side, combine the lard with a handful of salt, sifted flour and knead for a long time. While kneading, add some more water (about ¼ cup) and keep mixing by hand.
After about 20 minutes, gather the dough in a ball and place it in a bowl with some flour on the bottom. carve a cross shape on the top and let it rest with a cloth on top for some hours in a warm place.

**Nutrition:** Calories 646; Carbs 96.5 g; Protein 14.7 g; Fat 22.4 g

## 207. Cauliflower Focaccia

**Prep time: 50 minutes**  **Cook time: 70 minutes**
**Servings: 6**

**Ingredients:**
- 21 oz of focaccia dough (see recipe n. 206)
- 1 medium sized cauliflower
- ¾ cup of black olives
- ¾ cup of sardines
- 1 ¼ cup of fresh caciocavallo cheese
- 1 onion
- Salt
- 1 tsp of capers
- 8 tbsp of olive oil

**Prep:** Wash the cauliflowers and let it boil in plenty of salted water.
Thinly slice the onion and make it sizzle in a pan with 4 tbsp of olive oil. Add the drained cauliflower and let the taste develop for a few minutes.
Knead the dough and roll it out into a thin layer. Cut out 2 disks and make one bigger than the other.

Place the biggest disk on a greased tray, add the cauliflower, the caciocavallo cheese in cubes, chopped pit less olives, capers and chopped sardines.
Cover everything with the smaller disk and seal the edges. Brush on top the remaining oil and let it rest in a warm place for 1 hour. Oven bake at 430°F for 45-50 minutes.

**Nutrition:** Calories 334; Carbs 52.7 g; Protein 25.2 g; Fat 9.5 g

### 208. Rolled Focaccia with Sausage and Ricotta

**Prep time: 45 minutes**  
**Servings: 4**  
**Cook time: 40 minutes**

**Ingredients:**
- 21 oz of focaccia dough (see recipe n. 206)
- ¾ cup of ricotta cheese
- 1 egg
- 5 oz of sausage
- 3 tbsp of extra virgin olive oil
- Salt and pepper

**Prep:** In a bowl combine the ricotta with chopped sausage, a beaten egg and a pinch of salt and pepper.
Roll the dough into a ½ inch layer and lay it on some parchment paper.
Spread on top the ricotta and sausage filling and roll the dough on itself. Seal the edges and brush on some olive oil.
Put the focaccia with the parchment paper on an oven tray and bake at 430°F for 35-40 minutes.

**Nutrition:** Calories 657; Carbs 57.5 g; Protein 36.3 g; Fat 32.5 g

### 209. Small Focaccias with Anchovies

**Prep time: 1 hour**  
**Servings: 4**  
**Cook time: 25 minutes**

**Ingredients:**
- 4 ½ cups of 0 flour
- 1 ¾ tbsp brewer's yeast
- 1 ¾ tbsp of lard
- 3 ¼ cups of primosale cheese
- 4 salted anchovies
- 4 tbsp of olive oil
- Oregano
- Salt
- pepper

**Prep:** Sift the flour and put 1 ½ cup in a bowl, combine in the yeast melted into half a cup of warm water. Let it rise for about 1 hour.
Put the remaining flour onto the counter, knead it with the lard and a pinch of salt, add some water to reach a firm dough consistency. Combine the risen dough and knead for a long time until it becomes soft and elastic. Move the dough onto a casserole with some floured dashed in and let it rest for 1 hour in a warm and dry place, covered by a cloth.
When the rising time has finished, divide the dough in two round loaves and oven bake for 20-25 minutes at 430°F.
Cut the loaves in half while they are still hot and stuff them with the saltless chopped anchovies, sliced cheese, a pinch of oregano, oil and a dash of pepper.

**Nutrition:** Calories 480; Carbs 56.5 g; Protein 21.2 g; Fat 13.5 g

### 210. Broccoli Focaccia

**Prep time: 30 minutes**  
**Servings: 4**  
**Cook time: 50 minutes**

**Ingredients:**
- 4 ½ cups of focaccia dough (see recipe n. 206)
- 5 ½ cups of broccoli
- 2 cups of sausage
- 2 ¾ cups of caciocavallo cheese
- Extra virgin olive oil
- Salt
- Hot pepper

**Prep:** Boil the broccoli sprouts into salted water. Drain them while still crunchy in consistency and move them to a pot. Add the chopped sausage, the caciocavallo cheese in cubes and a pinch of hot pepper.
Knead the dough for a few minutes then roll it into a half inch layer and cut out 2 disks. Layer one disk on a greased tray and cover the bottom and sides with it. Pour in the stuffing and cover it with the second disk, seal well the edges. Brush the top with 1 tbsp of oil and let it rest for 30 minutes.
Bake at 375°F for 45-50 minutes.

**Nutrition:** Calories 340; Carbs 56.5 g; Protein 25.2 g; Fat 9.5 g

## 211. Bread Balls

**Prep time:** 15 minutes  
**Servings:** 4  
**Cook time:** 20 minutes

**Ingredients:**
- 3 ¼ cups of breadcrumbs
- ½ cup of grated pecorino cheese
- 1 sprig of parsley
- 1 garlic clove
- 2 eggs
- ¼ cup of tomato sauce
- 4 basil leaves
- 5 tbsp of olive oil
- Salt and pepper

**Prep:** take the breadcrumbs to a bowl, add the pecorino cheese, minced garlic and parsley and a dash of salt and pepper. Add the beaten eggs and gently mix.
Shape the balls the size of a walnut and let them sizzle in a pan with hot oil. When they are golden, drain the excess oil and place them into the tomato sauce, previously brought to a boil in a pot. Add the basil leaved to enhance the taste and let it simmer for 15 minutes.

**Nutrition:** Calories 182; Carbs 13.8 g; Protein 3.2 g; Fat 12.6 g

## 212. Tomato and Eggplant Focaccia

**Prep time:** 50 minutes  
**Servings:** 4  
**Cook time:** 1 hour

**Ingredients:**
- 4 ½ cups of focaccia dough (see recipe n. 206)
- 2 eggplants
- 1 onion
- 35 oz of ripe tomatoes
- 1 cup of primosale cheese
- 2 basil leaves
- Extra virgin olive oil
- Salt and pepper

**Prep:** Wash the eggplants, dice it and cut off the stem. Cover them in salt inside a colander to let out the water. Rinse, dry and fry the eggplants in plenty of hot oil.
Wash the tomatoes, peel, gut and dice them.
Slice the onion and let it shrink in a pan with 3 tbsp of oil. Add the tomatoes, a pinch of salt and pepper and let it cook for about 10 minutes.
Knead the dough and roll it into a ¼ inch thick layer and divide it into 2 disks. Take one disk and cover the bottom and sides of a greased tray. Pout the eggplants, tomatoes and cubed primosale cheese. Mixt it all up and cover with the second dough disk. Seal the edges and brush the top with 1 tbsp of oil. Let the dish rest for 1 hour in a warm place.
Then oven bake at 430°F for 40-45 minutes.

**Nutrition:** Calories 512; Carbs 74.1 g; Protein 15.2 g; Fat 19.1 g

## 213. Panzanella

**Prep time:** 15 minutes  
**Servings:** 6

**Ingredients:**
- 7 ¼ cups of sliced hard bread
- 6 sliced ripe tomatoes
- 4 minced basil leaves
- 1 minced hot pepper
- White wine vinegar
- Salt
- Olive oil
- 1 chopped onion

**Prep:** After moving the bread slices into a bowl, soften them with some water. Add the onion, tomatoes, basil and hot pepper. Season with salt, vinegar, oil and mix several times.

**Nutrition:** Calories 180; Carbs 23.4 g; Protein 1.8 g; Fat 10.6 g

## 214. Rustic Pizza with Mozzarella

**Prep time:** 30 minutes  
**Servings:** 6  
**Cook time:** 80 minutes

**Ingredients:**
- 4 ½ of bread dough
- 7 oz of diced mozzarella
- 2 beaten eggs
- 1 cup of parmesan cheese
- Lard to grease the pan

**Prep:** Stretch out the dough with a rolling pin ad divide in two pieces. Take one and cover the bottom and sides of a greased tray. Pour in the beaten eggs, spread the mozzarella dices and parmesan cheese, then cover with the second layer of dough. Fold the sides and bake in the oven at 350°F for 80 minutes.

**Nutrition:** Calories 413; Carbs 53.8 g; Protein 18.3 g; Fat 13.9 g

## 215. Bread with Walnuts

**Prep time:** 30 minutes  
**Cook time:** 40 minutes  
**Servings:** 6

**Ingredients:**
- 35 oz of bread dough
- 1 ½ cup of shelled walnuts
- ½ cup of sunflower seed oil

**Prep:** Add the previously toasted and chopped walnuts and oil to the dough. Knead to combine well the ingredients. Make several small round loaves and bake them at 464°F for 40 minutes.

**Nutrition:** Calories 403 Kcal; Carbs 61.6 g; Protein 11.5 g; Fat 12.3 g

## 216. Bread with Potatoes

**Prep time:** 25 minutes  
**Cook time:** 35 minutes  
**Servings:** 8

**Ingredients:**
- 2 ½ cups of Manitoba flour
- 2 ¼ cups of potatoes
- 1 ½ tbsp of brewer's yeast
- Extra virgin olive oil
- salt

**Prep:** Cook the potatoes with the peel on in plenty of boiling water. Drain, peel and mash them with a potato masher. Let them cool in a bowl.
Meanwhile, prepare the sifted flour onto a counter, add the yeast, salt and cooled potato mash. Add a drizzle of oil and knead vigorously. Shape the dough into a round loaf and let it rest for 30 minutes covered by surround wrap.
Preheat the oven and bake at 375 ° for 20 minutes.

**Nutrition:** Calories 185; Carbs 29.5 g; Protein 5.5 g; Fat 5.1 g

## 217. Pizza with Cheese

**Prep time:** 20 minutes  
**Cook time:** 70 minutes  
**Servings:** 8

**Ingredients:**
- 4 whole eggs
- 2 yolks
- ½ cup of yeast
- 1 cup of grated pecorino cheese
- 1 cup of fresh pecorino cubes
- ½ cup of parmesan cheese
- 1 cup of warm milk
- 1/2 cup of seed oil
- 4 ½ cups of 0 flour
- 1 tbsp of salt
- 1 tbsp of pepper

**Prep:** Mix the eggs with the grated pecorino and parmesan. Add the flour, oil, melted yeast in some warm milk, salt and pepper. Combine the pecorino cubes in the dough and make a ball (or 2 as preferred) and put it over a high-top tray greased with butter (the dough should reach half of the tray as it will double in size after rising). Cover it with a cloth, let it rise for at least one hour in a warm place.
Preheat the oven at 480°F, brush the top of the dough with the beaten egg yolks.
Lower the temperature of the oven to 350°F when you are ready to bake. Bake for 70 minutes.

**Nutrition:** Calories 484; Carbs 50.2 g; Protein 21.9 g; Fat 21.8 g

## 218. Red Hot Pepper Bruschetta

**Prep time:** 5 minutes  
**Cook time:** 5 minutes  
**Servings:** 4

**Ingredients:**
- 8 bread slices
- Extra virgin olive oil
- Hot red pepper

**Prep:** Preheat the oven at 350°F and put the bread on the grill. When the slices tur golden, remove them from the grill, lay them on a plate and season them with a drizzle of oil and hot pepper to taste.

### 219. Corn Focaccia

**Prep time:** 15 minutes  
**Servings:** 4  
**Cook time:** 20 minutes

**Ingredients:**
- 2 cups of corn flour
- ¾ cup of flour
- 1 tbsp of yeast
- 5 salted anchovies
- 1 cup of green olives

**Prep:** Combine the two types of flour in a mixing bowl and add the yeast melted into some warm water. Knead until you reach a soft and elastic dough, let it to rest for about one hour covered by a cloth. Roll out the dough on a tray and place on top the anchovies and olives. Bake at 430°F for about 20 minutes.

**Nutrition:** Calories 439; Carbs 65.5 g; Protein 15.5 g; Fat 15.1 g

### 220. Focaccia with Tuna and Black Olives

**Prep time:** 25 minutes  
**Servings:** 4  
**Cook time:** 40 minutes

**Ingredients:**
- 21 oz of premade bread dough
- ½ cup of lard
- 1 ¾ of canned tomatoes
- ¼ cup of capers
- 5 oz of tuna in oil
- ¼ cup of salted anchovies
- ¼ cups of pit less black olives
- Salt and pepper
- Extra virgin olive oil

**Prep:** Cook in a pot the tomatoes with oil, tuna, boneless chopped anchovies, olives and capers. Combine the dough with 2 tbsp lard, pepper, salt and divide it into 2 parts. Lay one half on a greased tray with a drizzle of oil. Add the olive and tuna filling. Cover the other half dough and fold the edges. Brush the top with the remaining lard. Preheat the oven and bake at 430°F for 30 minutes or until the top has a golden crust.

**Nutrition:** Calories 461; Carbs 65.7 g; Protein 18.5 g; Fat 13.1 g

### 221. Rolled Pizza with Potatoes

**Prep time:** 40 minutes  
**Servings:** 4  
**Cook time:** 60 minutes

**Ingredients:**
- 1 ¼ cup of boiled potatoes
- 1 tbsp of yeast
- 3 tbsp of olive oil
- 3 eggs
- 5 slices of sweet bacon
- 1 cup of caciocavallo cheese
- 2 hardboiled eggs
- 4 cups of flour

**Prep:** Prepare the dough with the flour, boiled and mashed potatoes, yeast, oil, eggs and salt. Let the dough rise for 1 hour with a cloth on top, then roll it out. Cover it with the bacon slices, caciocavallo and hardboiled eggs. Roll it and bake in a preheated oven at 320°F for 40 minutes.

**Nutrition:** Calories 499; Carbs 51.5 g; Protein 22.7 g; Fat 20.1 g

### 222. Focaccia with Broccoli and Sausage

**Prep time:** 20 minutes  
**Servings:** 4  
**Cook time:** 30 minutes

**Ingredients:**
- 4 ½ cups of flour
- 4 tbsp of lard
- 1 cup of milk
- 2 eggs
- 1 tbsp of yeast
- 1 cup of broccoli
- ¾ cup of hot sausage
- salt

**Prep:** In a pan fry the broccoli and sausage with a drizzle of oil.
Prepare the dough with the flour, milk, eggs and salt, let it rise for one hour.
Divide it into 2 pieces and roll them out. Lay one on the bottom of a tray. Pour over the broccoli and sausage and cover with the remaining dough.
Bake in a preheated oven at 375°F for 30 minutes.

**Nutrition:** Calories 520 Kcal; Carbs 44.5 g; Protein 17.7 g; Fat 30.1 g

## 223. Focaccia with Onion, Tomatoes and Olives

**Prep time:** 20 minutes  **Cook time:** 40 minutes
**Servings:** 4

**Ingredients:**
- 4 ½ cups of flour
- 1 tbsp of yeast
- 1 tbsp of lard
- 2 onions
- ¼ cup of capers
- ¼ cup of black olives
- 1 cup of canned tomatoes
- 3 tbsp of extra virgin olive oil
- Salt
- 8 anchovies

**Prep:** Chop the onions and fry them in a pan with oil, tomatoes, tomatoes, capers, anchovies and olives.
Prepare the dough with the flour, yeast, lard and let it rest for one hour. Divide it in two and roll it out, lay one layer on the bottom of a tray. Pour on top the tomato filling and cover it with the other rolled out dough, drizzle some oil on top.
Preheat the oven and bake at 275°F for at least 40 minutes.

**Nutrition:** Calories 534; Carbs 52.5 g; Protein 19.7 g; Fat 20.1 g

## 224. Calzone with Ham and Cheese

**Prep time:** 10 minutes  **Cook time:** 10 minutes
**Servings:** 4

**Ingredients:**
- 28 oz of bread dough
- ½ cup of ricotta
- ½ cup of raw ham
- ½ cup of provolone cheese
- 2 yolks
- Nutmeg
- Salt and pepper
- Olive oil

**Prep:** Combine the ricotta with the yolks, provolone and the chopped ham. Add a pinch of salt and pepper and grated nutmeg. Roll out the dough, cut into 15 inch length pieces per side, stuff it with the filling. Fold over the dough and pinch the sides, fry it into hot oil.

**Nutrition:** Calories 442; Carbs 43.3 g; Protein 18.6 g; Fat 21.6 g

## 225. Small Pizzas with Onion and Anchovy

**Prep time:** 10 minutes  **Cook time:** 15 minutes
**Servings:** 4

**Ingredients:**
- 28 oz of bread dough
- ½ cup of salted anchovies
- 2 onions
- Olive oil
- Oregano
- salt

**Prep:** Cut out of the dough 7 inch in diameter disks. Cut the onion into thin slices and cook them in oil. Distribute the onion into the dough disks, add the anchovy fillets, dust on some oregano. Preheat the oven and bake at 350°F for 10 minutes, serve hot.

**Nutrition:** Calories 460; Carbs 64.7 g; Protein 18.3 g; Fat 12.4 g

## 226. Bread with Scamorza, Capers and Anchovies

**Prep time:** 5 minutes  **Cook time:** 15 minutes
**Servings:** 4

**Ingredients:**
- 8 bread slices
- 8 scamorza slices
- Handful of pickled capers

- 2 eggs
- ½ cup of milk
- 2tbsp of grated parmesan cheese
- Extra virgin olive oil
- Salt and pepper

**Prep:** Soak the bread slices into the milk and lay them on tray greased with some oil. Place on top the scamorza, capers and minced capers. Add a pinch of salt and drizzle some oil.
Beat the eggs with the parmesan and then pour them in the tray.
Bake in a preheated oven at 350°F until the top is golden.

**Nutrition:** Calories 442; Carbs 35.2 g; Protein 16.3 g; Fat 27 g

### 227. Hot Focaccia with Fennel Seeds

**Prep time:** 25 minutes  
**Cook time:** 30 minutes  
**Servings:** 4

**Ingredients:**
- 4 ½ cups of flour
- 1 hot pepper
- ½ cup of fennel seeds
- Hot water
- Extra virgin olive oil
- salt

**Prep:** Pour the flour on the counter, add the water, oil, salt and knead. Add the fennel seeds and minced hot pepper. Knead again until the ingredients are combined and roll out the dough.
Move the dough in a greased tray and bake in a preheated oven at 375°F for 30 minutes.

**Nutrition:** Calories 461; Carbs 95 g; Protein 12.3 g; Fat 22 g

### 228. Mushroom Pie (2nd Version)

**Prep time:** 20 minutes  
**Cook time:** 45 minutes  
**Servings:** 6

**Ingredients:**
- 2 ¼ cups of flour
- 2 eggs
- ½ cup of lard
- Salt
- 3 cups of mixed mushrooms
- Parsley
- 1 lemon
- Olive oil
- Salt and pepper

**Prep:** Pour the flour on a surface and make a well in it, pour in the melted lard and a little salt. Knead the dough and later add 1 egg and some hot water. Keep kneading and let the dough rest for some hours.
Meanwhile, wash the mushrooms, chop them and cook them in a pan with little oil and chopped parsley.
Remove them from the heat and when they are cooked combine them with the other egg and lemon juice.
Divide the dough in half, roll it, take one half and cover a tray. With the other half cover the pie after adding the mushroom filling.
Bake in a preheated oven at 350°F for 45 minutes circa.

**Nutrition:** Calories 442; Carbs 24 g; Protein 17.6 g; Fat 31.2 g

### 229. Cheese Pie

**Prep time:** 20 minutes  
**Cook time:** 30 minutes  
**Servings:** 6

**Ingredients:**
- Premade pastry dough
- 2 ¾ cups of sweet grated provolone
- 1 onion
- 1 egg
- 3 tbsp of milk
- Nutmeg
- Salt and pepper

**Prep:** Slice the onion and cook it into a pan with some water. Add salt and pepper.
Put half of the dough on a greased tray and place on 1 ¾ cup of provolone, the egg beaten with milk, salt, pepper, nutmeg and onion. Layer on top the other part of dough and fold in the edges. Sprinkle on top the remaining cheese and bake in a preheated oven at 350°F for 20-30 minutes.

**Nutrition:** Calories 510; Carbs 19.7 g; Protein 25.3 g; Fat 12.4 g

## 230. Potato Pie

**Prep time: 20 minutes**  
**Servings: 4**

**Cook time: 40 minutes**

**Ingredients:**
- 35 oz of potatoes
- 3 eggs
- 1 ¾ cup of scamorza cheese
- 3 sausages
- 2 tbsp of grated pecorino cheese
- Breadcrumbs
- lard
- Salt and pepper

**Prep:** Boil the potatoes in salted water, drain them when they are cooked. Peel and mash them to achieve a puree. Combine the potatoes to the eggs, pecorino, salt and pepper. Grease a tray with some lard, sprinkle some breadcrumbs and place on the potato puree. Lay it gently with a spatula and distribute on top the sliced scamorza and the roughly chopped sausage. Cover with the other half of the dough, lay it gently and cover it with another layer of breadcrumbs and lard.
Bake in the oven at 375°F per 30-40 minutes.

**Nutrition:** Calories 492; Carbs 44.2 g; Protein 19.7 g; Fat 26.9 g

## 231. Olives and Mozzarella Pie

**Prep time: 20 minutes**  
**Servings: 6**

**Cook time: 45 minutes**

**Ingredients:**
- 35 oz of bread dough
- 1 mozzarella
- 1 onion
- 2 ripe tomatoes
- ½ cup of picked artichokes
- ½ cup of mushrooms in oil
- ¼ cup of black pit less olives
- 1 hot pepper
- ¼ of grated pecorino cheese
- Olive oil
- salt

**Prep:** Slice the onion and cook it in a pan with some oil.
Divide the dough in two parts and roll it out on a greased tray. Stuff the dough with the diced mozzarella, sliced tomatoes, onion, olives, artichokes, mushrooms and minced hot pepper.
Sprinkle some pecorino and cover everything with the other half of the dough. Seal the edges and bake at 350°F for about 45 minutes.

**Nutrition:** Calories 422 Kcal; Carbs 23.1 g; Protein 7.8 g; Fat 36.3 g

## 232. Chickpea Focaccia

**Prep time: 30 minutes**  
**Servings: 6**

**Cook time: 30 minutes**

**Ingredients:**
- 3 ¼ cups of chickpea flour
- 3 ¼ cups of wheat flour
- Yeast
- Olive oil
- Salt and pepper

**Prep:** Mix the two kinds of flour and pour them on a surface making a well in the middle. Pour in the warm water, salt, yeast, oil and gently mix. Season the dough with black pepper, keep kneading and let rest for about 30 minutes.
Lay it on a tray and bake in a preheated oven at 450°F for 30 minutes.

**Nutrition:** Calories 438; Carbs 66.2 g; Protein 9.7 g; Fat 16 g

## 233. Focaccia with Anchovies; Black Olives and Cheese

**Prep time: 5 minutes**  
**Servings: 6**

**Cook time: 30 minutes**

**Ingredients:**
- 24 oz of bread dough
- salt
- 1 cup of pit less black olives
- Olive oil
- 1 cup of salted anchovies
- 2 cups of diced caciocavallo cheese

**Prep:** Roll the dough over a greased tray and spread on the caciocavallo, olives and chopped anchovies. Season with a drizzle of oil and bake in a preheated oven at 375°F for 30 minutes.

**Nutrition:** Calories 389; Carbs 59.1 g; Protein 11.8 g; Fat 32.3 g

### 234. Pie with Liver and Onions

**Prep time:** 15 minutes  **Cook time:** 45 minutes
**Servings:** 6

**Ingredients:**
- *24 oz of bread dough*
- *2 chicken livers*
- *2 onions*
- *Oregano*
- *Olive oil*
- *salt*

**Prep:** Soften the onions with a little oil and water in a pan, then chop the liver and combine it in. add some salt and season with the oregano.
Divide the dough in 2 parts and roll out one half on a slightly greased tray. Stuff it with the liver mixture, put on the other half and seal well the edges.
Bake in a preheated oven at 350°F for 40-45 minutes.

**Nutrition:** Calories 287; Carbs 61 g; Protein 19.7 g; Fat 22 g

### 235. Focaccia with Olives and Oregano

**Prep time:** 5 minutes  **Cook time:** 20 minutes
**Servings:** 6

**Ingredients:**
- *24 oz of bread dough*
- *1 ¼ cup of black lives with no pits*
- *Oregano*
- *Olive oil*
- *salt*

**Prep:** Roll out the dough on a greased tray, spread on the olives. Drizzle some oil and a handful of salt. Bake in a preheated oven 375°F for 20-30 minutes.

**Nutrition:** Calories 336; Carbs 50.2 g; Protein 7.1 g; Fat 8.4 g

### 236. Focaccia with Potatoes and Onion

**Prep time:** 10 minutes  **Cook time:** 20 minutes
**Servings:** 6

**Ingredients:**
- *24 oz of bread dough*
- *4 potatoes*
- *1 onion*
- *Olive oil*
- *salt*

**Prep:** Peel the potatoes, slice and cook them in a pan with some oil, salt and chopped onion. Roll out the dough in a greased tray, spread on top the potato and onion filling.
Bake in a preheated oven 375°F for 20-30 minutes.

**Nutrition:** Calories 186; Carbs 49.7 g; Protein 5.9 g; Fat 6.6 g

### 237. Focaccia with Tomatoes, Peppers and Anchovies

**Prep time:** 10 minutes  **Cook time:** 20 minutes
**Servings:** 6

**Ingredients:**
- *24 oz of bread dough*
- *1 ¼ cup of tomatoes*
- *1 ¼ cup of sweet bell pepper*
- *¾ cup of salted anchovies*
- *Olive oil*
- *salt*

**Prep:** Pan fry the tomatoes, chopped peppers and drizzle some oil and a pinch of salt.
Meanwhile, roll out the dough in a greased tray and spread on the vegetable spread and chopped anchovies.
Bake in a preheated oven 375°F for 20-30 minutes.

**Nutrition:** Calories 386; Carbs 59.2 g; Protein 10.6 g; Fat 11.1 g

## 238. Focaccia with Tuna and Peppers

**Prep time: 5 minutes**                                           **Cook time: 20 minutes**
**Servings: 6**

**Ingredients:**
- 24 oz of bread dough
- Olive oil
- 1 cup of tuna in oil
- salt
- 1 ½ cup of grilled peppers
- Ground garlic

**Prep:** Roll out the dough in a greased tray, spread on the crumbled tuna, peppers, ground garlic and a drizzle of oil. Bake in a preheated oven 375°F for 20-30 minutes.

**Nutrition:** Calories 465; Carbs 69 g; Protein 15.3 g; Fat 16.7 g

## 239. 5 Minute Pizza

**Prep Time: 10 minutes**                                          **Cook Time: 20 minutes**
**Servings: 2**

**Ingredients:**

**Pizza Crust**
- 2 large Eggs
- 2 tbsp. Parmesan Cheese

**Toppings**
- 5 oz. Mozzarella Cheese
- 3 tbsp. Rao's Tomato Sauce
- 1 tbsp. Psyllium Husk Powder
- 1/2 tsp. Italian Seasoning
- 1 tbsp. Freshly Chopped
- Basil
- Salt to Taste
- 2 tsp. Frying Oil

**Prep:** Measure out all dry ingredients into a bowl or container that can fit your immersion blender.
Add the eggs and blend everything using an immersion blender.
Be sure to continue blending for about 30-40 seconds, allowing the Psyllium husk to absorb some of the liquid.
Heat frying oil in a pan over medium-high heat.
Once very hot, pour the mixture into the pan and spread out in a circle shape.
Once the edges have started to look slightly brown, flip the pizza crust.
Turn the broiler on high in the oven.
Bake on the opposite side for another 30-40 seconds, then turn the oven off. Spoon Rao's tomato sauce over the pizza and spread.
Add cheese, and then put the pizza into the oven. Leave a slit open in the oven. Once it's bubbling, remove it from the oven.
Serve with fresh chopped basil over the top.

**Nutrition:** 459 Calories, 3 5g Fat, 5g Carbs, 27 g Protein

## 240. Family Pizza

**Prep Time: 30 minutes**                                          **Cook Time: 25 minutes**
**Servings: 16**

**Ingredients:**

**Pizza crust:**
- Water, warm (1 cup)
- Salt (1/2 teaspoon)
- Flour, whole wheat (1 cup)
- Olive oil (2 tablespoons)
- Dry yeast, quick active (1 package)
- Flour, all purpose (1 ½ cups)
- Cornmeal
- Olive oil

**Filling:**
- Onion, chopped (1 cup)
- Mushrooms, sliced, drained (4 ounces)
- Garlic cloves, chopped finely (2 pieces)

- *Parmesan cheese, grated (1/4 cup)*
- *Ground lamb, 80% lean (1 pound)*
- *Italian seasoning (1 teaspoon)*
- *Pizza sauce (8 ounces)*
- *Mozzarella cheese, shredded (2 cups)*

**Prep:** Mix yeast with warm water. Combine with flours, oil (2 tablespoons), and salt by stirring and then beating vigorously for half a minute. Let the dough sit for twenty minutes.
Preheat oven at 350 degrees F.
Prep 2 square pans (8-inch) by greasing with oil before sprinkling with cornmeal.
Cut the rested dough in half; place each half inside each pan. Set aside, covered, for thirty to forty-five minutes. Cook in the air fryer for twenty to twenty-two minutes.
Sauté the onion, beef, garlic, and Italian seasoning until beef is completely cooked. Drain and set aside.
Cover the air-fried crusts with pizza sauce before topping with beef mixture, cheeses, and mushrooms.
Return to oven and cook for twenty minutes.

**Nutrition:** Calories 215; Protein 10 g; Carbs 20 g

## 241. Fig and Prosciutto Pita Bread Pizza

**Prep Time: 5 minutes**
**Servings: 6**

**Cook Time: 20 minutes**

**Ingredients:**
- *4 pita breads*
- *8 figs, quartered*
- *8 slices prosciutto*
- *8 oz. mozzarella, crumbled*

**Prep:** Place the pita breads on a baking tray.
Top with crumbled cheese then figs and prosciutto.
Bake in the preheated oven at 350F for 8 minutes.

**Nutrition:** Calories 445, Fat: 13.7 g, Carbs: 41.5 g, Protein: 39 g

# BREAKFAST

### 242. Eggs with Zucchini Noodles

**Prep time:** 10 minutes  **Cook time:** 11 minutes

**Servings:** 2

**Ingredients:**
- 2 tablespoons extra-virgin olive oil
- 3 zucchinis, cut with a spiralizer
- 4 eggs
- Salt and black pepper to the taste
- A pinch of red pepper flakes
- Cooking spray
- 1 tablespoon basil, chopped

**Prep:** In a bowl, combine the zucchini noodles with olive oil, salt, and pepper and mix well.
Grease a tray with cooking spray and divide the zucchini noodles into four nests.
Crack an egg onto each nest, sprinkle with pepper, salt, and red pepper flakes and bake at 350 degrees F for 11 minutes.
Divide between plates, sprinkle the fresh basil on top and serve.

**Nutrition:** Calories 296, Fat 23.6 g, Carbs 10.6 g, Protein 14.7 g

### 243. Banana Oats

**Prep time:** 10 minutes  **Servings:** 2

**Ingredients:**
- 1 banana, peeled and sliced
- ¾ cup almond milk
- ½ cup cold brewed coffee
- 2 dates, pitted
- 2 tablespoons cocoa powder
- 1 cup rolled oats
- 1 and ½ tablespoons chia seeds

**Prep:** In a blender, combine the banana with milk and the rest of the ingredients. Pulse, divide into bowls and serve.

**Nutrition:** Calories 451, Fat 25.1 g, Carbs 55.4 g, Protein 9.3 g

## 244. Slow-cooked Peppers Frittata

**Prep time:** 10 minutes  
**Servings:** 6  
**Cook time:** 3 hours

**Ingredients:**
- ½ cup almond milk
- 8 eggs, whisked
- Salt and black pepper to the taste
- 1 teaspoon oregano, dried
- 1 and ½ cups roasted peppers, chopped
- ½ cup red onion, chopped
- 4 cups baby arugula
- 1 cup goat cheese, crumbled
- Cooking spray

**Prep:** In a bowl, combine the eggs with salt, pepper and the oregano. Whisk well.
Grease the slow cooker with cooking spray, put the peppers and the remaining ingredients inside, and pour the eggs mixture over them.
Put the lid on and cook on Low for 3 hours.

**Nutrition:** Calories 259, Fat 20.2 g, Carbs 4.4 g, Protein 16.3 g

## 245. Avocado and Apple Smoothie

**Prep time:** 5 minutes  
**Servings:** 2

**Ingredients:**
- 3 cups spinach
- 1 green apple, cored and chopped
- 1 avocado, peeled, pitted and chopped
- 3 tablespoons chia seeds
- 1 teaspoon honey
- 1 banana, frozen and peeled
- 2 cups coconut water

**Prep:** In your blender, combine the spinach with the apple and the rest of the ingredients, pulse, divide into glasses and serve.

**Nutrition:** Calories 168, Fat 10.1 g, Carbs 21 g, Protein 2.1 g

## 246. Avocado Toast

**Prep time:** 10 minutes  
**Servings:** 2

**Ingredients:**
- 1 tablespoon goat cheese, crumbled
- 1 avocado, peeled, pitted and mashed
- A pinch of salt and black pepper
- 2 whole wheat bread slices, toasted
- ½ teaspoon lime juice
- 1 persimmon, thinly sliced
- 1 fennel bulb, thinly sliced
- 2 teaspoons honey
- 2 tablespoons pomegranate seeds

**Prep:** In a bowl, combine the avocado pulp with pepper, salt, lime juice and cheese. Whisk.
Spread onto toasted bread slices, top with the remaining ingredients and serve.

**Nutrition:** Calories 348, Fat 20.8 g, Carbs 38.7 g, Protein 7.1 g

## 247. Mini Frittatas

**Prep time:** 5 minutes  
**Servings:** 12  
**Cook time:** 15 minutes

**Ingredients:**
- 1 yellow onion, chopped
- 1 cup parmesan, grated
- 1 yellow bell pepper, chopped
- 1 red bell pepper, chopped
- 1 zucchini, chopped
- Salt and black pepper to the taste
- 8 eggs, whisked
- A drizzle of olive oil
- 2 tablespoons chives, chopped

**Prep:** Heat a skillet with the oil over medium-high heat, add the zucchini, the onion, and the rest of the ingredients except the chives and eggs and sauté for 5 minutes stirring often.
Divide the mixture on the bottom of a muffin pan, pour the eggs mixture on top, sprinkle pepper, salt, and the chives and bake at 350 degrees F for 10 minutes.

**Nutrition:** Calories 55, Fat 3 g, Carbs 3.2 g, Protein 4.2 g

### 248. Avocado Muffins

**Prep Time:** 10 minutes  
**Servings:** 12  
**Cook Time:** 20 minutes

**Ingredients:**
- 6 bacon slices; chopped.
- 1 yellow onion; chopped.
- 1/2 teaspoon baking soda
- 1/2 cup coconut flour
- 1 cup coconut milk
- 2 cups avocado; pitted, peeled and chopped
- 4 eggs
- Salt and black pepper to the taste

**Prep:** Heat up a pan, add onion and bacon; stir and brown for a few minutes.
In a bowl, mash avocado pieces with a fork and whisk well with the eggs. Add milk, salt, pepper, baking soda and coconut flour and stir everything. Add bacon mix and stir again. Add coconut oil to muffin tray, divide eggs and avocado mix into the tray, heat oven at 350 degrees F and bake for 20 minutes.
Divide muffins between plates and serve.

**Nutrition:** Calories: 200; Fat: 7; Carbs: 7; Protein: 5

### 249. Berry Oats

**Prep time:** 5 minutes  
**Servings:** 2

**Ingredients:**
- ½ cup rolled oats
- 1 cup almond milk
- ¼ cup chia seeds
- A pinch of cinnamon powder
- 2 teaspoons honey
- 1 cup berries, pureed
- 1 tablespoon yogurt

**Prep:** In a bowl, combine oats with milk and the rest of the ingredients except yogurt.
Mix, divide into bowls, top with yogurt and serve cold.

**Nutrition:** Calories 420, Fat 30.3 g, Carbs 35.3 g, Protein 6.4 g

### 250. Tomatoes Oatmeal

**Prep time:** 10 minutes  
**Servings:** 4  
**Cook time:** 25 minutes

**Ingredients:**
- 3 cups water
- 1 cup almond milk
- 1 tablespoon olive oil
- 1 cup steel-cut oats
- ¼ cup sun-dried tomatoes, chopped
- A pinch of red pepper flakes

**Prep:** In a pan, mix the milk with water, bring to a boil over medium heat.
Meanwhile, heat a skillet with the oil over medium-high heat, add the oats, cook them for 2 minutes and transfer to the skillet with the milk.
Stir the oats, add the tomatoes and simmer over medium heat for 23 minutes.
Divide the mixture into bowls, sprinkle the red pepper flakes on top and serve.

**Nutrition:** Calories 170, Fat 17.8 g, Carbs 3.8 g, Protein 1.5 g

### 251. Quinoa Muffins

**Prep time:** 10 minutes  
**Servings:** 12  
**Cook time:** 30 minutes

**Ingredients:**
- 1 cup quinoa, cooked
- 6 eggs, whisked
- Salt and pepper to the taste
- 1 cup Swiss cheese, grated
- 1 small yellow onion, chopped
- 1 cup white mushrooms, sliced
- ½ cup sun-dried tomatoes, chopped

**Prep:** In a bowl, combine all ingredients and whisk well.
Divide the mixture into a silicone muffin pan, bake at 350 degrees F for 30 minutes and serve.

**Nutrition:** Calories 123, Fat 5.6 g, Carbs 10.8 g, Protein 7.5 g

## 252. Quinoa and Eggs Pan

**Prep time:** 10 minutes
**Servings:** 4
**Cook time:** 23 minutes

**Ingredients:**
- 4 bacon slices, cooked and crumbled
- A drizzle of olive oil
- 1 small red onion, chopped
- 1 red bell pepper, chopped
- 1 sweet potato, grated
- 1 green bell pepper, chopped
- 2 garlic cloves, minced
- 1 cup white mushrooms, sliced
- ½ cup quinoa
- 1 cup chicken stock
- 4 eggs, fried
- Salt and black pepper to the taste

**Prep:** Heat a skillet with the oil over medium-low heat, add the bell peppers, onion, garlic, sweet potato and the mushrooms, toss and sauté for 5 minutes.
Add quinoa, toss and cook for 1 more minute.
Add the broth, salt and pepper, stir and cook for 15 minutes.
Divide the mix between plates, top each serving with a fried egg, sprinkle with salt, pepper and crumbled bacon.

**Nutrition:** Calories 304, Fat 14 g, Carbs 27.5 g, Protein 17.8 g

## 253. Stuffed Tomatoes (2nd Version)

**Prep time:** 10 minutes
**Servings:** 4
**Cook time:** 15 minutes

**Ingredients:**
- 2 tablespoons olive oil
- 8 tomatoes, insides scooped
- ¼ cup almond milk
- 8 eggs
- ¼ cup parmesan, grated
- Salt and black pepper to the taste
- 4 tablespoons rosemary, chopped

**Prep:** Grease a baking dish with the oil and arrange the tomatoes inside.
Crack an egg into each tomato, add milk and the rest of the ingredients.
Place the baking dish in the oven and bake at 375 degrees F for 15 minutes.

**Nutrition:** Calories 276, Fat 20.3 g, Carbs 13.2 g, Protein 13.7 g

## 254. Scrambled Eggs

**Prep time:** 10 minutes
**Servings:** 2
**Cook time:** 10 minutes

**Ingredients:**
- 1 yellow bell pepper, chopped
- 8 cherry tomatoes, cubed
- 2 spring onions, chopped
- 1 tablespoon olive oil
- 1 tablespoon capers, drained
- 2 tablespoons black olives, pitted and sliced
- 4 eggs
- A pinch of salt and black pepper
- ¼ teaspoon oregano, dried
- 1 tablespoon parsley, chopped

**Prep:** Heat a skillet with the oil over medium-high heat, add the bell pepper and spring onions. Sauté for 3 minutes.
Add the capers, tomatoes, and olives and sauté for another 2 minutes.
Crack the eggs into the pan, add pepper, salt, and the oregano and scramble for 5 minutes.
Divide between plates, sprinkle the parsley and serve.

**Nutrition:** Calories 249, Fat 17 g, Carbs 13.3 g, Protein 13.5 g

## 255. Watermelon "Pizza"

**Prep time:** 10 minutes
**Servings:** 4

**Ingredients:**
- 1 slice of watermelon cut 1-inch thick and then from the center cut into 4 wedges similar to pizza slices
- 6 kalamata olives, pitted and sliced
- 1 ounce feta cheese, crumbled
- ½ tablespoon balsamic vinegar
- 1 teaspoon mint, chopped

**Prep:** Arrange the watermelon "pizza" on a plate, sprinkle the olives and the rest of the ingredients on each slice and serve.

**Nutrition:** Calories 91, Fat 2.9 g, Carbs 14 g, Protein 2 g

### 256. Ham Muffins

**Prep time:** 10 minutes  
**Servings:** 6  

**Cook time:** 15 minutes

**Ingredients:**
- 9 ham slices
- 5 eggs, whisked
- 1/3 cup spinach, chopped
- ¼ cup feta cheese, crumbled
- ½ cup roasted red peppers, chopped
- A pinch of salt and black pepper
- 1 and ½ tablespoons basil pesto
- Cooking spray

**Prep:** Grease a muffin tin with cooking spray and line each muffin mould with 1 and ½ slices of ham. Divide into the moulds the peppers and the rest of the ingredients except the eggs, pesto, salt and pepper.
In a bowl, mix the eggs with salt and pepper, and pesto. Whisk and pour over the peppers mixture.
Bake the muffins in the oven at 400 degrees F for 15 minutes and serve.

**Nutrition:** Calories 108, Fat 6.7 g, Carbs 1.8 g, Protein 9.3 g

### 257. Avocado Chickpea Pizza

**Prep time:** 20 minutes  
**Servings:** 2  

**Cook time:** 20 minutes

**Ingredients:**
- 1 and ¼ cups chickpea flour
- A pinch of salt and black pepper
- 1 and ¼ cups water
- 2 tablespoons olive oil
- 1 teaspoon onion powder
- 1 teaspoon garlic, minced
- 1 tomato, sliced
- 1 avocado, peeled, pitted and sliced
- 2 ounces gouda, sliced
- ¼ cup tomato sauce
- 2 tablespoons green onions, chopped

**Prep:** In a bowl, mix the chickpea flour with water, salt, pepper, oil, onion powder and the garlic. Mix well until combined, knead a bit, put in a bowl, cover and set aside for 20 minutes.
Transfer the dough to a work surface, form a small circle, transfer it to a baking sheet lined with baking paper and bake at 425 degrees F for 10 minutes.
Spread the tomato sauce over the pizza, also spread the rest of the ingredients and bake at 400 degrees F for another 10 minutes.

**Nutrition:** Calories 416, Fat 24.5 g, Carbs 36.6 g, Protein 15.4 g

### 258. Banana and Quinoa Casserole

**Prep time:** 10 minutes  
**Servings:** 8  

**Cook time:** 1 hour and 20 minutes

**Ingredients:**
- 3 cups bananas, peeled and mashed
- ¼ cup pure maple syrup
- ¼ cup molasses
- 1 tablespoon cinnamon powder
- 2 teaspoons vanilla extract
- 1 teaspoon cloves, ground
- 1 teaspoon ginger, ground
- ½ teaspoon allspice, ground
- 1 cup quinoa
- ¼ cup almonds, chopped
- 2 and ½ cups almond milk

**Prep:** In a baking dish, combine the bananas with the rest of the ingredients, toss and bake at 350 degrees F for 1 hour and 20 minutes.

**Nutrition:** Calories 213, Fat 4.1 g, Carbs 41 g, Protein 4.5 g

### 259. Spiced Chickpeas Bowls

**Prep time:** 10 minutes  
**Servings:** 4  

**Cook time:** 30 minutes

**Ingredients:**
- 15 ounces canned chickpeas, drained and rinsed
- ¼ teaspoon cardamom, ground
- ½ teaspoon cinnamon powder
- 1 and ½ teaspoons turmeric powder
- 1 teaspoon coriander, ground
- 1 tablespoon olive oil
- A pinch of salt and black pepper
- ¾ cup Greek yogurt
- ½ cup green olives, pitted and halved
- ½ cup cherry tomatoes, halved
- 1 cucumber, sliced

**Prep:** Spread the chickpeas on a lined baking sheet, add the cinnamon, turmeric, oil, cardamom, coriander, salt and pepper. Stir and bake at 375 degrees F for 30 minutes.
In a bowl, combine the roasted chickpeas with the rest of the ingredients, toss and serve.

**Nutrition:** Calories 519, Fat 34.5 g, Carbs 49.8 g, Protein 12 g

## 260. Avocado Spread

**Prep time:** 5 minutes  **Servings:** 8

**Ingredients:**
- 2 avocados, peeled, pitted and roughly chopped
- 1 tablespoon sun-dried tomatoes, chopped
- 2 tablespoons lemon juice
- 3 tablespoons cherry tomatoes, chopped
- ¼ cup red onion, chopped
- 1 teaspoon oregano, dried
- 2 tablespoons parsley, chopped
- 4 kalamata olives, pitted and chopped
- A pinch of salt and black pepper

**Prep:** Put the avocados in a bowl and mash.
Add the rest of the ingredients, stir to combine and serve as a spread.

**Nutrition:** Calories 110, Fat 10 g, Carbs 5.7 g, Protein 1.2 g

## 261. Cheesy Yogurt

**Prep time:** 4 hours and 5 minutes  **Servings:** 4

**Ingredients:**
- 1 cup Greek yogurt
- 1 tablespoon honey
- ½ cup feta cheese, crumbled

**Prep:** In a blender, combine the yogurt with honey and cheese and pulse well.
Divide into bowls and freeze for four hours before serving.

**Nutrition:** Calories 161, Fat 10 g, Carbs 11.8 g, Protein 6.6 g

## 262. Baked Omelet Mix

**Prep time:** 10 minutes  **Cook time:** 45 minutes
**Servings:** 12

**Ingredients:**
- 12 eggs, whisked
- 8 ounces spinach, chopped
- 2 cups almond milk
- 12 ounces canned artichokes, chopped
- 2 garlic cloves, minced
- 5 ounces feta cheese, crumbled
- 1 tablespoon dill, chopped
- 1 teaspoon oregano, dried
- 1 teaspoon lemon pepper
- A pinch of salt
- 4 teaspoons olive oil

**Prep:** Heat a skillet with the oil over medium-high heat, add the garlic and spinach and sauté for 3 minutes.
In a baking dish, combine the eggs with the artichokes and the rest of the ingredients, including the spinach mix as well.
Bake at 375 degrees F for 40 minutes, divide between plates and serve.

**Nutrition:** Calories 187, Fat 12 g, Carbs 5 g, Protein 10 g

## 263. Stuffed Sweet Potato

**Prep time:** 10 minutes  **Cook time:** 40 minutes
**Servings:** 8

**Ingredients:**
- 8 sweet potatoes, pierced with a fork
- 14 ounces canned chickpeas, drained and rinsed
- 1 small red bell pepper, chopped
- 1 tablespoon lemon zest, grated
- 2 tablespoons lemon juice
- 3 tablespoons olive oil
- 1 teaspoon garlic, minced
- 1 tablespoon oregano, chopped
- 2 tablespoons parsley, chopped
- A pinch of salt and black pepper
- 1 avocado, peeled, pitted and mashed
- ¼ cup water
- ¼ cup tahini paste

**Prep:** Place the potatoes on a baking sheet lined with parchment paper and bake at 400 degrees F for 40 minutes. Cool them and make a slit in the middle of each.
In a bowl, combine the chickpeas with the lemon zest, half of the oil, bell pepper, half of the lemon juice, oregano, half of the garlic, half of the parsley, salt and pepper, mix and stuff the potatoes with this mixture.
In another bowl, mix the avocado with tahini, water, the rest of the lemon juice, oil, garlic and parsley, whisk well and spread over the potatoes.

**Nutrition:** Calories 308, Fat 2 g, Carbs 38 g, Protein 7 g

## 264. Cauliflower Fritters

**Prep time:** 10 minutes  
**Servings:** 4  
**Cook time:** 50 minutes

**Ingredients:**
- 30 ounces canned chickpeas, drained and rinsed
- 2 and ½ tablespoons olive oil
- 1 small yellow onion, chopped
- 2 cups cauliflower florets chopped
- 2 tablespoons garlic, minced
- A pinch of salt and black pepper

**Prep:** Spread half of the chickpeas on a baking sheet lined with parchment paper. Season with 1 tablespoon oil, salt and pepper. Toss and bake at 400 degrees F for 30 minutes.
Transfer the chickpeas to a food processor, pulse and place the mix in a bowl.
Heat up a pan with the ½ tablespoon oil over medium-high heat, add the onion and the garlic and sauté for 3 minutes.
Add cauliflower, and cook for another six minutes. Transfer to a blender, add the rest of the chickpeas, pulse, stir and shape fritters out of this mix.
Heat up a pan with the rest of the oil over medium-high heat, add the fritters, cook them for 3 minutes on each side and serve.

**Nutrition:** Calories 331, Fat 13 g, Carbs 44.7 g, Protein 13.6 g

## 265. Tuna Salad

**Prep time:** 10 minutes  
**Servings:** 2

**Ingredients:**
- 12 ounces canned tuna in water, drained and flaked
- ¼ cup roasted red peppers, chopped
- 2 tablespoons capers, drained
- 8 kalamata olives, pitted and sliced
- 2 tablespoons olive oil
- 1 tablespoon parsley, chopped
- 1 tablespoon lemon juice
- A pinch of salt and black pepper

**Prep:** In a bowl, combine the tuna with roasted peppers and the rest of the ingredients, toss, divide between plates and serve.

**Nutrition:** Calories 250, Fat 17.3 g, Carbs 2.7 g, Protein 10.1 g

## 266. Veggie Quiche

**Prep time:** 6 minutes  
**Servings:** 8  
**Cook time:** 55 minutes

**Ingredients:**
- ½ cup sun-dried tomatoes, chopped
- 1 prepared pie crust
- 2 tablespoons avocado oil
- 1 yellow onion, chopped
- 2 garlic cloves, minced
- 2 cups spinach, chopped
- 1 red bell pepper, chopped
- ¼ cup kalamata olives, pitted and sliced
- 1 teaspoon parsley flakes
- 1 teaspoon oregano, dried
- 1/3 cup feta cheese, crumbled
- 4 eggs, whisked
- 1 and ½ cups almond milk
- 1 cup cheddar cheese, shredded
- Salt and black pepper to the taste

**Prep:** Heat up a pan with the oil over medium-high heat, add the garlic and onion and sauté for 3 minutes.
Add the bell pepper and sauté for 3 minutes more. Add the olives, parsley, spinach, oregano, salt and pepper and cook everything for 5 minutes. Add tomatoes and the cheese, toss and take off the heat.
Arrange the pie crust in a plate, pour the spinach and tomatoes mix inside and spread.
In a bowl, mix the eggs with salt, pepper, the milk and half of the cheese, whisk and pour over the mixture in the pie crust.
Sprinkle the remaining cheese on top and bake at 375 degrees F for 40 minutes.
Cool the quiche down, slice and serve for breakfast.

**Nutrition:** Calories 211, Fat 14.4 g, Carbs 12.5 g, Protein 8.6 g

## 267. Potato Hash

**Prep time:** 10 minutes  
**Servings:** 4

**Cook time:** 15 minutes

**Ingredients:**
- A drizzle of olive oil
- 2 gold potatoes, cubed
- 2 garlic cloves, minced
- 1 yellow onion, chopped
- 1 cup canned chickpeas, drained
- Salt and black pepper to the taste
- 1 and ½ teaspoon allspice, ground
- 1 pound baby asparagus, trimmed and chopped
- 1 teaspoon sweet paprika
- 1 teaspoon oregano, dried
- 1 teaspoon coriander, ground
- 2 tomatoes, cubed
- 1 cup parsley, chopped
- ½ cup feta cheese, crumbled

**Prep:** Heat up a pan with a drizzle of oil over medium-high heat, add the potatoes, onion, garlic, salt and pepper and cook for 7 minutes.
Add the rest of the ingredients except the tomatoes, parsley and the cheese, toss, cook for 7 more minutes and transfer to a bowl. Add the remaining ingredients, toss and serve for breakfast.

**Nutrition:** Calories 535, Fat 20.8 g, Carbs 34.5 g, Protein 26.6 g

## 268. Leeks and Eggs Muffins

**Prep time:** 10 minutes  
**Servings:** 2

**Cook time:** 20 minutes

**Ingredients:**
- 3 eggs, whisked
- ¼ cup baby spinach
- 2 tablespoons leeks, chopped
- 4 tablespoons parmesan, grated
- 2 tablespoons almond milk
- Cooking spray
- 1 small red bell pepper, chopped
- Salt and black pepper to the taste
- 1 tomato, cubed
- 2 tablespoons cheddar cheese, grated

**Prep:** In a bowl, combine the eggs with the milk, salt, pepper and the rest of the ingredients (except the cooking spray) and whisk well.
Grease a muffin tin with the cooking spray and divide the eggs mixture in each muffin mould.
Bake at 380 degrees F for 20 minutes and serve them for breakfast.

**Nutrition:** Calories 308, Fat 19.4 g, Carbs 8.7 g, Protein 24.4 g

## 269. Artichokes and Cheese Omelet

**Prep time:** 10 minutes  
**Servings:** 1

**Cook time:** 8 minutes

**Ingredients:**
- 1 teaspoon avocado oil
- 1 tablespoon almond milk
- 2 eggs, whisked
- A pinch of salt and black pepper
- 2 tablespoons tomato, cubed
- 2 tablespoons kalamata olives, pitted and sliced
- 1 artichoke heart, chopped
- 1 tablespoon tomato sauce
- 1 tablespoon feta cheese, crumbled

**Prep:** In a bowl, combine the eggs with the milk, salt, pepper and the rest of the ingredients except the avocado oil and whisk well.
Heat up a pan with the avocado oil over medium-high heat, add the omelet mix, spread into the pan, cook for four minutes, flip, cook for 4 minutes more, transfer to a plate and serve.

**Nutrition:** Calories 303, Fat 17.7 g, Carbs 21.9 g, Protein 18.2 g

## 270. Quinoa and Eggs Salad

**Prep time:** 5 minutes

**Servings:** 4

**Ingredients:**
- 4 eggs, soft boiled, peeled and cut into wedges
- 2 cups baby arugula
- 2 cups cherry tomatoes, halved
- 1 cucumber, sliced
- 1 cup quinoa, cooked
- 1 cup almonds, chopped
- 1 avocado, peeled, pitted and sliced
- 1 tablespoon olive oil
- ½ cup mixed dill and mint, chopped
- A pinch of salt and black pepper
- Juice of 1 lemon

**Prep:** In a large salad bowl, combine the eggs with the arugula and the rest of the ingredients, toss, divide between plates and serve for breakfast.

**Nutrition:** Calories 519, Fat 32.4 g, Carbs 43.3 g, Protein 19 g

## 271. Garbanzo Bean Salad

**Prep time: 10 minutes**  **Servings: 4**

**Ingredients:**
- 1 and ½ cups cucumber, cubed
- 15 ounces canned garbanzo beans, drained and rinsed
- 3 ounces black olives, pitted and sliced
- 1 tomato, chopped
- ¼ cup red onion, chopped
- 5 cups salad greens
- A pinch of salt and black pepper
- ½ cup feta cheese, crumbled
- 3 tablespoons olive oil
- 1 tablespoon lemon juice
- ¼ cup parsley, chopped

**Prep:** In a salad bowl, combine the garbanzo beans with the cucumber, tomato and the rest of the ingredients except the cheese and toss.
Divide the mix into small bowls, sprinkle the cheese on top and serve for breakfast.

**Nutrition:** Calories 268, Fat 16 g, Carbs 24 g, Protein 9 g

## 272. Hearty Pear and Mango Smoothie

**Prep Time: 10 minutes**  **Servings: 1**

**Ingredients:**
- 1 ripe mango, cored and chopped
- ½ mango, peeled, pitted and chopped
- 1 cup kale, chopped
- ½ cup plain Greek yogurt
- 2 ice cubes

**Prep:** Add pear, mango, yogurt, kale, and mango to a blender and puree.
Add ice and blend until smooth.

**Nutrition:** Calories: 293 Fat: 8 g Carbs: 53 g Protein: 8 g

## 273. Eggplant Salad

**Prep Time: 20 minutes**  **Cook Time: 15 minutes**
**Servings: 8**

**Ingredients:**
- 1 large eggplant, washed and cubed
- 1 tomato, seeded and chopped
- 1 small onion, diced
- 2 tablespoons parsley, chopped
- 2 tablespoons extra virgin olive oil
- 2 tablespoons distilled white vinegar
- ½ cup feta cheese, crumbled
- Salt as needed

**Prep:** Preheat a grill to medium-high.
Pierce the eggplant a few times using a knife/fork.
Cook the eggplants on the grill for about 15 minutes until charred. Keep them aside and let them cool.
Remove the skin from the eggplant and dice the pulp.
Transfer the pulp to a mixing bowl and add onion, parsley, feta cheese, tomato, olive oil, and vinegar. Mix well and chill for 1 hour.
Season with salt and serve.

**Nutrition**: Calories: 99 Fat: 7 g Carbs: 7 g Protein: 3.4 g

## 274. Artichoke Frittata

**Prep Time: 5 minutes**  **Cook Time: 10 minutes**
**Servings: 4**

**Ingredients:**
- 8 large eggs
- ¼ cup Asiago cheese, grated
- 1 tablespoon fresh basil, chopped
- 1 teaspoon fresh oregano, chopped
- Pinch of salt
- 1 teaspoon extra virgin olive oil

- 1 teaspoon garlic, minced
- 1 cup canned artichoke
- pepper
- 1 tomato, chopped

**Prep:** Pre-heat your oven to broil.
Take a medium bowl and whisk in eggs, Asiago cheese, oregano, basil, salt and pepper.
Blend in a bowl.
Place an ovenproof skillet over medium-high heat and add olive oil. Add garlic and sauté for 1 minute.
Remove skillet from heat and pour in egg mixture.
Return skillet to heat and sprinkle artichoke and tomato over eggs. Cook frittata without stirring for 8 minutes.
Place skillet under the broiler for 1 minute until the top is lightly browned.
Cut frittata into 4 pieces and serve.

**Nutrition:** Calories: 199 Fat: 13 g Carbs: 5 g Protein: 16 g

## 275. Eggs in a Squash

**Prep Time:** 10 minutes  
**Servings:** 5  
**Cook Time:** 20 minutes

**Ingredients:**
- 2 acorn squash
- 6 whole eggs
- 2 tablespoons extra virgin olive oil
- Salt and pepper as needed
- 5-6 pitted dates
- 8 walnut halves
- A fresh bunch of parsley

**Prep:** Preheat your oven to 375 º Fahrenheit.
Slice squash crosswise and prepare 3 slices with holes.
While slicing the squash, make sure that each slice has a measurement of ¾ inch thickness. Remove the seeds from the slices.
Take a baking sheet and line it with baking paper. Transfer the slices to your baking sheet and season them with salt and pepper.
Bake in your oven for 20 minutes.
Chop the walnuts and dates on your cutting board.
Take the baking dish out of the oven and drizzle slices with olive oil.
Crack an egg into each of the holes in the slices and season with pepper and salt. Sprinkle the chopped walnuts on top.
Bake for 10 minutes more.
Garnish with parsley and add maple syrup.

**Nutrition:** Calories: 198 Fat: 12 g Carbs: 17 g Protein: 8 g

## 276. Barley Porridge

**Prep Time:** 5 minutes  
**Servings:** 4  
**Cook Time:** 25 minutes

**Ingredients:**
- 1 cup barley
- 1 cup wheat berries
- 2 cups unsweetened almond milk
- 2 cups water
- ½ cup blueberries
- ½ cup pomegranate seeds
- ½ cup hazelnuts, toasted and chopped
- ¼ cup honey

**Prep:** Take a saucepan and place it over medium-high heat.
Add barley, wheat berries, almond milk, water and bring to a boil. Reduce the heat to low and simmer for 25 minutes.
Divide between serving bowls and top each serving with 2 tablespoons blueberries, 2 tablespoons pomegranate seeds, 2 tablespoons hazelnuts, 1 tablespoon honey.

**Nutrition:** Calories: 295 Fat: 8 g Carbs: 56 g Protein: 6 g

## 277. Cool Tomato and Dill Frittata

**Prep Time:** 5 minutes  
**Servings:** 4  
**Cook Time:** 10 minutes

**Ingredients:**
- 2 tablespoons olive oil
- 1 medium onion, chopped
- 1 teaspoon garlic, minced
- 2 medium tomatoes, chopped
- 6 large eggs
- ½ cup half and half
- ½ cup feta cheese, crumbled
- ¼ cup dill weed
- Salt as needed
- Ground black pepper

**Prep:** Preheat your oven to a temperature of 400 º Fahrenheit.
Take a large-sized ovenproof pan and heat up your olive oil over medium-high heat. Toss in the onion, garlic, tomatoes, and stir fry them for 4 minutes.
While they are being cooked, take a bowl and beat together your eggs, half and half cream and season the mix with some pepper and salt. Pour the mixture into the pan with your vegetables and top it with crumbled feta cheese and dill weed. Cover with the lid and let it cook for 3 minutes.
Place the pan inside your oven and let it bake for 10 minutes.

**Nutrition:** Calories: 191 Fat: 15 g Carbs: 6 g Protein: 9 g

## 278. Strawberry and Rhubarb Smoothie

**Prep Time: 5 minutes**  **Cook Time: 3 minutes**
**Servings: 1**

**Ingredients:**
- 1 rhubarb stalk, chopped
- 1 cup fresh strawberries, sliced
- ½ cup plain Greek strawberries
- Pinch of ground cinnamon
- 3 ice cubes

**Prep:** Take a small saucepan and fill with water over high heat.
Bring to boil and add rhubarb; cook for 3 minutes. Drain and transfer to a blender.
Add strawberries, honey, yogurt, and cinnamon and pulse mixture until smooth. Add ice cubes and blend until thick with no lumps. Pour into a glass and enjoy chilled.

**Nutrition:** Calories: 295 Fat: 8 g Carbs: 56 g Protein: 6 g

## 279. Bacon and Brie Omelet Wedges

**Prep Time: 10 minutes**  **Cook Time: 10 minutes**
**Servings: 6**

**Ingredients:**
- 2 tablespoons olive oil
- 7 ounces smoked bacon
- 6 beaten eggs
- Small bunch chives, snipped
- 3 ½ ounces brie, sliced
- 1 teaspoon red wine vinegar
- 1 teaspoon Dijon mustard
- 1 cucumber, halved, deseeded, and sliced diagonally
- 7 ounces radish, quartered

**Prep:** Turn your grill on and set it to high.
Take a small-sized pan and add 1 teaspoon of oil; allow the oil to heat up. Add bacon and fry until crisp. Drain it on kitchen paper.
Take another non-stick cast iron frying pan and place it over grill, heat 2 teaspoons of oil.
Add bacon, eggs, chives, ground pepper to the frying pan. Cook on LOW until they are semi-set.
Carefully lay brie on top and grill until the brie sets and is a golden texture. Remove it from the pan and cut up into wedges.
Take a small bowl and create dressing by mixing olive oil, mustard, vinegar and seasoning.
Add cucumber to the bowl and mix, serve alongside the omelet wedges.

**Nutrition:** Calories: 35 Fat: 31 g Carbs: 3g Protein: 25 g

## 280. Couscous Salad

**Prep Time: 15 minutes**

**Ingredients:**

**For Lemon Dill Vinaigrette:**
- Juice of 1 large sized lemon
- 1/3 cup of extra virgin olive oil
- 1 teaspoon of dill weed
- 1 teaspoon of garlic powder
- Salt as needed
- Pepper

**For Israeli Couscous:**
- 2 cups of Pearl Couscous
- Extra virgin olive oil
- 2 cups of halved grape tomatoes
- Water as needed
- 1/3 cup of finely chopped red onions
- ½ of a finely chopped English cucumber
- 15 ounces of chickpeas

- 14 ounce can of artichoke hearts (roughly chopped up)
- ½ cup of pitted Kalamata olives
- 15-20 pieces of fresh basil leaves, roughly torn and chopped up
- 3 ounces of fresh baby mozzarella

**Prep:** Prepare the vinaigrette by taking a bowl and add the ingredients listed under vinaigrette.
Mix them well and keep aside.

Take a medium-sized heavy pot and place it over medium heat.
Add 2 tablespoons of olive oil and allow it to heat up. Add couscous and keep cooking until golden brown. Add 3 cups of boiling water and cook the couscous according to the package prep. Once done, drain in a colander and keep aside.
Take another large-sized mixing bowl and add the remaining ingredients except the cheese and basil.
Add the cooked couscous and basil to the mix and mix everything well.
Give the vinaigrette a nice stir and whisk it into the couscous salad. Mix well.
Adjust the seasoning as required. Add mozzarella cheese. Garnish with some basil.

**Nutrition:** Calories: 393 Fat: 13 g Carbs: 57 g Protein: 13 g

## 281. Coconut Porridge

**Prep Time:** 15 minutes

**Servings:** 6

**Ingredients:**
- Powdered erythritol as needed
- 1 ½ cups almond milk, unsweetened
- 2 tablespoons protein powder
- 3 tablespoons Golden Flaxseed meal
- 2 tablespoons coconut flour

**Prep:** Take a bowl and mix in flaxseed meal, protein powder, coconut flour and mix well.
Add mix to saucepan over medium heat. Add almond milk and stir, let the mixture thicken.
Add powdere erythritol (as needed) and serve.

**Nutrition:** Calories: 259 g Fat: 13 g Carbs: 5 g Protein: 16 g

## 282. Crumbled Feta and Scallions

**Prep Time:** 5 minutes
**Servings:** 12

**Cook Time:** 15 minutes

**Ingredients:**
- 2 tablespoons of unsalted butter (replace with canola oil for full effect)
- ½ cup of chopped up scallions
- 1 cup of crumbled feta cheese
- 8 large sized eggs
- 2/3 cup of milk
- ½ teaspoon of dried Italian seasoning
- Salt as needed
- Freshly ground black pepper as needed
- Cooking oil spray

**Prep:** Preheat your oven to 400 º Fahrenheit.
Take a 3-4 ounce muffin pan and grease with cooking oil.
Take a non-stick pan and place it over medium heat. Add butter and allow the butter to melt. Add half of the scallions and stir fry. Keep them to the side.
Take a medium-sized bowl and add eggs, Italian seasoning and milk and whisk well. Add the stir fried scallions and feta cheese and mix. Season with pepper and salt.
Pour the mix into the muffin tin. Transfer the muffin tin to your oven and bake for 15 minutes.
Serve with a sprinkle of scallions.

**Nutrition:** Calories: 106 Fat: 8 g Carbs: 2 g Protein: 7 g

## 283. Quinoa Chicken Salad

**Prep Time:** 15 minutes
**Servings:** 8

**Cook Time:** 20 minutes

**Ingredients:**
- 2 cups of water
- 2 cubes of chicken bouillon
- 1 smashed garlic clove
- 1 cup of uncooked quinoa
- 2 large sized chicken breast cut up into bite-sized portions and cooked
- 1 large sized diced red onion
- 1 large sized green bell pepper
- ½ cup of Kalamata olives
- ½ cup of crumbled feta cheese
- ¼ cup of chopped up parsley
- ¼ cup of chopped up fresh chives
- ½ teaspoon of salt
- 1 tablespoon of balsamic vinegar
- ¼ cup of olive oil

**Prep:** Take a saucepan and bring your water, garlic, and bouillon cubes to a boil.
Stir in quinoa and reduce the heat to medium-low.
Simmer for about 15-20 minutes until the quinoa has absorbed all the water and is tender.

Discard your garlic cloves and scrape the quinoa into a large-sized bowl.
Gently stir in the cooked chicken breast, bell pepper, onion, feta cheese, chives, salt and parsley into your quinoa.
Drizzle some lemon juice, olive oil, and balsamic vinegar. Stir everything until mixed well.

**Nutrition:** Calories: 99 g Fat: 7 g Carbs: 7 g Protein: 3.4 g

## 284. Cheesy Olives Bread

**Prep Time:** 1 hour and 40 minutes  **Cook Time:** 30 minutes
**Servings:** 10

**Ingredients:**
- 4 cups whole-wheat flour
- 3 tbsps. oregano, chopped
- 2 tsps. dry yeast
- ¼ cup olive oil
- 1 ½ cups black olives, pitted and sliced
- 1 cup of water
- ½ cup feta cheese, crumbled

**Prep:** In a bowl, mix the flour with the water, the yeast, and the oil. Stir and knead your dough very well.
Put the dough in a bowl, cover with plastic wrap, and keep in a warm place for 1 hour.
Divide the dough into 2 bowls and stretch each ball well. Add the rest of the ingredients to each ball and tuck them inside. Knead the dough well again. Flatten the balls a bit and leave them aside for 40 minutes more.
Transfer the balls to a baking sheet lined with parchment paper, make a small slit in each, and bake at 425F for 30 minutes.
Serve the bread as a Mediterranean breakfast.

**Nutrition:** Calories 251, Fat: 7.3 g, Carbs: 39.7 g, Protein: 6.7 g

## 285. Cheesy Yogurt

**Prep Time:** 4 hours and 5 minutes  **Servings:** 4

**Ingredients:**
- 1 cup Greek yogurt
- 1 tablespoon honey
- ½ cup feta cheese, crumbled

**Prep:** In a blender, combine the yogurt with honey and cheese and pulse well.
Divide into bowls and freeze for 4 hours before serving.

**Nutrition:** 161 Calories, 10 g Fat, 6.6 g Protein

## 286. Corn and Shrimp Salad

**Prep Time:** 10 minutes  **Cook Time:** 10 minutes
**Servings:** 4

**Ingredients:**
- 4 ears of sweet corn, husked
- 1 avocado, peeled, pitted and chopped
- ½ cup basil, chopped
- 1-pound shrimp, peeled and deveined
- 1 and ½ cups cherry tomatoes, halved

**Prep:** Put the corn in a pot, boil water and cover, over medium heat for 6 minutes.
Drain, cool down, cut corn from the cob and put it in a bowl.
Thread the shrimp onto skewers and brush with some of the oil.
Place the skewers on the preheated grill, cook over medium heat for 2 minutes on each side, remove from skewers and add over the corn.
Place the rest of the ingredients to the bowl, toss, divide between plates and serve.

**Nutrition:** 371 Calories, 22 g Fat, 23 g Protein

## 287. Berry Oats (2nd version)

**Prep Time:** 5 minutes  **Servings:** 2

**Ingredients:**
- ½ cup rolled oats
- 1 cup almond milk
- ¼ cup chia seeds
- 2 teaspoons honey
- 1 cup berries, pureed

**Prep:** In a bowl, combine the oats with the milk and the rest of the ingredients except 1 tbsp. of yogurt, toss, divide into bowls, top with the yogurt and serve cold.

**Nutrition:** 420 Calories, 30 g Fat, 6.4 g Protein

### 288. Blueberries Quinoa

**Prep Time:** 5 minutes  **Servings:** 4

**Ingredients:**
- 2 cups quinoa, almond milk
- ½ teaspoon cinnamon powder
- 1 tablespoon honey
- 1 cup blueberries
- ¼ cup walnuts, chopped

**Prep:** In a bowl, scourge quinoa with the milk and the rest of the ingredients, toss, divide into smaller bowls.

**Nutrition:** 284 Calories, 14.3 g Fat, 4.4 g Protein

### 289. Blueberry, Hazelnut, and Lemon Grain Salad

**Prep Time:** 5 minutes  **Cook Time:** 10 minutes
**Servings:** 8

**Ingredients:**
- 1 cup steel-cut oats
- 1 cup dry golden quinoa
- ½ cup dry millet
- 3 tbsps. olive oil, divided
- ¾ tsp. salt
- 1 x 1" piece fresh ginger, peeled and cut into coins
- 2 large lemons, zest and juice
- ½ cup maple syrup
- 1 cup Greek yogurt
- ¼ tsp. nutmeg
- 2 cups hazelnuts, roughly chopped and toasted
- 2 cups blueberries or mixed berries
- 4 ½ cups water

**Prep:** Grab a mesh strainer and add the oats, quinoa, and millet. Wash well then pop to one side.
Find a 3-quart saucepan, add a tbsp. of the oil, and pop over medium heat. Add the grains and cook for 2-3 minutes to toast. Pour in the water, salt, ginger coins, and lemon zest. Bring to the boil then cover with lid and lower heat. Allow to simmer for 20 minutes. Turn off the heat and let stand for five minutes. Fluff with a fork, remove the ginger then leave to cool for at least an hour. Grab a large bowl and add the grains.
Take a medium bowl and add the remaining olive oil, lemon juice, maple syrup, yogurt, and nutmeg. Whisk well to combine. Pour this over the grains and stir well.
Add the hazelnuts and blueberries, stir again then pop into the fridge overnight.

**Nutrition:** Calories 363, Fat: 11 g, Carbs: 60 g, Protein: 7 g

### 290. Brown Rice Salad

**Prep Time:** 10 minutes  **Servings:** 4

**Ingredients:**
- 9 oz. brown rice, cooked
- 7 cups baby arugula
- 15 oz. canned garbanzo beans, drained and rinsed
- 4 oz. feta cheese, crumbled
- ¾ cup basil, chopped
- A pinch of salt and black pepper
- 2 tbsps. lemon juice
- ¼ tsp. lemon zest, grated
- ¼ cup olive oil

**Prep:** In a salad bowl, combine the brown rice with the arugula, the beans, and the rest of the ingredients, toss and serve cold.

**Nutrition:** Calories 473, Fat: 22 g, Carbs: 53 g, Protein: 13 g

### 291. Endives, Fennel and Orange Salad

**Prep Time:** 5 minutes  **Servings:** 4

**Ingredients:**
- 1 tbsp. balsamic vinegar
- 2 garlic cloves, minced
- 1 tsp. Dijon mustard
- 2 tbsps. olive oil
- 1 tbsp. lemon juice
- Sea salt and black pepper to taste
- ½ cup black olives, pitted and chopped
- 1 tbsp. parsley, chopped
- 7 cups baby spinach
- 2 endives, shredded
- 3 medium navel oranges, peeled and cut into segments
- 2 bulbs fennel, shredded

**Prep:** In a salad bowl, combine the spinach with the endives, oranges, fennel, and the rest of the ingredients, toss and serve.

**Nutrition:** Calories 97, Fat: 9.1 g, Carbs: 3.7 g, Protein: 1.9 g

## 292. Greek Yogurt with Walnuts and Honey

**Prep Time:** 5 Minutes                                           **Servings:** 4

**Ingredients:**
- 4 cups Greek yogurt, fat-free, plain or vanilla
- ½ cup California walnuts, toasted, chopped
- 3 tbsps. honey or agave nectar
- Fresh fruit, chopped or granola, low-fat

**Prep:** Spoon yogurt into 4 individual cups. Sprinkle 2 tbsps. of walnuts over each and drizzle 2 tsps. of honey over each. Top with fruit or granola, whichever is preferred.

**Nutrition:** Calories 300, Fat: 10 g, Carbs: 25 g, Protein: 29 g

## 293. Homemade Muesli

**Prep Time:** 15 minutes                                          **Cook Time:** 20 minutes
**Servings:** 8

**Ingredients:**
- 3 ½ cups rolled oats
- ½ cup wheat bran
- ½ tsp. kosher salt
- ½ tsp. ground cinnamon
- ½ cup sliced almonds
- ¼ cup raw pecans, coarsely chopped
- ¼ cup raw pepitas (shelled pumpkin seeds)
- ½ cup unsweetened coconut flakes
- ¼ cup dried apricots, coarsely chopped
- ¼ cup dried cherries

**Prep:** Take a medium bowl and combine the oats, wheat bran, salt, and cinnamon. Stir well.
Place the mixture onto a baking sheet.
Next place the almonds, pecans, and pepitas onto another baking sheet and toss. Pop both trays into the oven and heat to 350°F. Bake for 10-12 minutes. Remove from the oven and pop to one side.
Leave the nuts to cool but take the one with the oats, sprinkle with the coconut, and pop back into the oven for 5 minutes more. Remove and leave to cool.
Find a large bowl and combine the contents of both trays then stir well to combine. Throw in the apricots and cherries and stir well. Pop into an airtight container until required.

**Nutrition:** Calories 250, Fat: 10 g, Carbs: 36 g, Protein: 7 g

## 294. Hummus and Tomato Breakfast Pittas

**Prep Time:** 5 minutes                                           **Cook Time:** 10 minutes
**Servings:** 4

**Ingredients:**
- 4 large eggs, at room temperature
- Salt, to taste
- 2 whole-wheat pita bread with pockets, cut in half
- ½ cup hummus
- 1 medium cucumber, thinly sliced into rounds
- 2 medium tomatoes, large dice
- A pinch of fresh parsley leaves, coarsely chopped
- Freshly ground black pepper

**Prep**: Grab a large saucepan, fill with water, and pop over medium heat until it boils.
Add the eggs and cook for 7 minutes.
Immediately drain the water and place the eggs under cool water until they cool down. Pop to one side until you can handle them comfortably.
Peel the eggs and cut them into ¼" slices, sprinkle with salt, and pop to one side.
Grab a pitta pocket and spread with hummus, fill with cucumber and tomato, season well then add an egg. Sprinkle with parsley and hot sauce then serve.

**Nutrition:** Calories 377, Fat: 31 g, Carbs: 17 g, Protein: 11 g

### 295. Raisin Quinoa Breakfast

**Prep Time:** 15 minutes  **Serving:** 4

**Ingredients:**
- 1 cup quinoa
- 2 cups milk
- 2 tbsp. walnuts, crushed
- 2 tbsp. raisins, cranberries
- 1 tbsp. chia seeds

**Prep:** Rinse quinoa with cold water and drain. Place milk and quinoa into a saucepan and bring to a boil. Add ½ tsp. of vanilla. Reduce heat to low and simmer for about 15 minutes stirring from time to time.
Set aside to cool then serve in a bowl, topped with honey, chia seeds, raisins, cranberries and crushed walnuts.

**Nutrition:** 299 Calories, 7 g Fat, 1 g Protein

### 296. Raspberries and Yogurt Smoothie

**Prep Time:** 5 minutes  **Servings:** 2

**Ingredients:**
- 2 cups raspberries
- ½ cup Greek yogurt
- ½ cup almond milk
- ½ tsp. vanilla extract

**Prep:** In your blender, combine the raspberries with the milk, vanilla, and the yogurt, pulse well, divide into 2 glasses and serve.

**Nutrition:** Calories 245, Fat: 9.5 g, Carbs: 5.6 g, Protein: 1.6 g

### 297. Stuffed Pita Breads

**Prep Time:** 5 minutes  **Cook Time:** 15 minutes
**Servings:** 4

**Ingredients:**
- 1 ½ tbsp. olive oil
- 1 tomato, cubed
- 1 garlic clove, minced
- 1 red onion, chopped
- ¼ cup parsley, chopped
- 15 oz. canned fava beans, drained and rinsed
- ¼ cup lemon juice
- Salt and black pepper to the taste
- 4 whole-wheat pita bread pockets

**Prep:** Heat a pan with the oil over medium heat, add the onion, stir, and sauté for 5 minutes.
Add the rest of the ingredients, stir and cook for 10 minutes more.
Stuff the pita pockets with this mix.

**Nutrition:** Calories 382, Fat: 1.8 g, Carbs: 66 g, Protein: 28.5 g

### 298. Sun-dried Tomatoes Oatmeal

**Prep Time:** 10 minutes  **Cook Time:** 25 minutes
**Servings:** 4

**Ingredients:**
- 3 cups water
- 1 cup almond milk
- 1 tablespoon olive oil
- 1 cup steel-cut oats
- ¼ cup sun-dried tomatoes, chopped

**Prep:** In a pan, scourge water with the milk, bring to a boil over medium heat.
Meanwhile, pre-heat skillet with the oil over medium-high heat, add the oats, cook for about 2 minutes and transfer to the pan with milk.
Stir the oats, add the tomatoes and simmer over medium heat for 23 minutes.
Divide the mixture into bowls, sprinkle the red pepper flakes on top and serve.

**Nutrition:** 170 Calories, 17.8 g Fat, 1.5 g Protein

### 299. Sweet Potato Tart

**Prep Time:** 10 minutes  **Cook Time:** 1 hour and 10 minutes
**Servings:** 8

**Ingredients:**
- 2 pounds sweet potatoes, peeled and cubed
- ¼ cup olive oil + a drizzle
- 7 oz. feta cheese, crumbled
- 1 yellow onion, chopped
- 2 eggs, whisked
- ¼ cup almond milk
- 1 tbsp. herbs de Provence
- A pinch of salt and black pepper
- 6 phyllo sheets
- 1 tbsp. parmesan, grated

**Prep:** In a bowl, combine the potatoes with half of the oil, salt, and pepper, toss, spread on a baking sheet lined with parchment paper, and roast at 400F for 25 minutes.
Meanwhile, heat a pan with half of the remaining oil over medium heat, add the onion, and sauté for 5 minutes.
In a bowl, combine the eggs with the milk, feta, herbs, salt, pepper, onion, sweet potatoes, and the rest of the oil and toss.
Arrange the phyllo sheets in a tart pan and brush them with a drizzle of oil.
Add the sweet potato mix and spread it well into the pan.
Sprinkle the parmesan on top and bake covered with tin foil at 350F for 20 minutes.
Remove the tin foil, bake the tart for 20 minutes more, cool it down, slice, and serve for breakfast.

**Nutrition:** Calories 476, Fat: 16.8 g, Carbs: 68.8 g, Protein: 13.9 g

## 300. Tahini Pine Nuts Toast

**Prep Time:** 5 minutes          **Servings:** 2

**Ingredients:**
- 2 whole wheat bread slices, toasted
- 1 tablespoon tahini paste
- 2 teaspoons feta cheese, crumbled
- Juice of ½ lemon
- 2 teaspoons pine nuts

**Prep:** Whisk tahini with the 1 tsp. of water and the lemon juice well and spread over the toasted bread slices.
Top each serving with the remaining ingredients and serve.

**Nutrition:** 142 Calories, 7.6 g Fat, 5.8 g Protein

## 301. Tangerine and Pomegranate Fruit Salad

**Prep Time:** 15 minutes          **Cook Time:** 20 minutes
**Servings:** 5

**Ingredients:**

**For the grains:**
- 1 cup pearl or hulled barley
- 3 cups of water
- 3 tbsps. olive oil, divided
- ½ tsp. kosher salt

**For the fruit:**
- ½ large pineapple, peeled and cut into 1 ½" chunks
- 6 tangerines
- 1 ¼ cups pomegranate seeds
- 1 small bunch of fresh mint

**For the dressing:**
- 1/3 cup honey
- Juice and finely grated zest of 1 lemon
- Juice and finely grated zest of 2 limes
- ½ tsp. kosher salt
- ¼ cup olive oil
- ¼ cup toasted hazelnut oil

**Prep:** Place the grain into a strainer and rinse well.
Grab 2 baking sheets, line with paper, and add the grain. Spread well to cover then leave to dry.
Next, place the water into a saucepan and pop over medium heat.
Place a skillet over medium heat, add 2 tbsps. of the oil then add the barley. Toast for 2 minutes.
Add the water and salt and bring to a boil.
Reduce to simmer and cook for 40 minutes until most of the liquid has been absorbed.
Turn off the heat and leave to stand for 10 minutes to steam cook the rest.
Meanwhile, grab a medium bowl and add the honey, juices, zest, and salt, and stir well.
Add the olive oil then nut oil and stir again. Pop until the fridge until needed.
Remove the lid from the barley then place it onto another prepared baking sheet and leave to cool.
Drizzle with oil and leave to cool completely then pop into the fridge.
When ready to serve, divide the grains, pineapple, orange, pomegranate, and mint between the bowls.
Drizzle with the dressing then serve and enjoy.

**Nutrition:** Calories 400, Fat: 23 g, Carbs: 50 g, Protein: 3 g

## 302. Walnuts Yogurt Mix

**Prep Time:** 10 minutes  
**Servings:** 6

**Ingredients:**
- 2 and ½ cups Greek yogurt
- 1 and ½ cups walnuts, chopped
- 1 teaspoon vanilla extract
- ¾ cup honey
- 2 teaspoons cinnamon powder

**Prep:** In a bowl, incorporate yogurt with the walnuts and the rest of the ingredients, toss, divide into smaller bowls and keep in the fridge for 10 minutes before serving for breakfast.

**Nutrition:** 388 Calories, 24.6 g Fat, 10.2 g Protein

## 303. Fruit Bulgur Breakfast Bowls

**Prep Time:** 15 minutes  
**Cook Time:** 20 minutes  
**Servings:** 6

**Ingredients:**
- 2 cups 2% milk
- 1½ cups Uncooked bulgur
- 1 cup Water
- ½ tsp. Cinnamon
- 2 cups Frozen/fresh pitted dark sweet cherries
- 8 Dried/fresh chopped figs
- ½ cup Chopped almonds

**Prep:** Combine the cinnamon, water, milk, and bulgur.
Stir once and bring to a boil. Put a top on the pot. Reduce the temperature setting to medium low.
Continue cooking until the liquid is absorbed (10 min.).
Extinguish the flame, but leave the pan on the stove and stir in the cherries, almonds, and figs.
Stir well to thaw the cherries and hydrate the figs. Stir in the mint, and scoop into Servings bowls.
Serve with warm milk or serve it chilled to your liking.

**Nutrition:** Calories: 301, Fat: 6 g, Protein: 9 g

## 304. Ricotta Toast with Strawberries

**Prep Time:** 10 minutes  
**Servings:** 2

**Ingredients:**
- ½ cup crumbled ricotta cheese
- 1 tablespoon honey, plus additional as needed
- Pinch of sea salt, plus additional as needed
- 4 slices of whole-grain bread, toasted
- 1 cup sliced fresh strawberries
- 4 fresh basil leaves, cut into thin shreds

**Prep:** Mix the cheese, honey, and salt in a small bowl until well incorporated.
Spoon 2 tablespoons of the cheese mixture onto each slice of bread and spread it all over.
Sprinkle the sliced strawberry and basil leaves on top before serving.

**Nutrition:** Calories: 274 Fat: 7.9 g Protein: 15.1 g Carbs: 39.8 g

## 305. Cauliflower Breakfast Porridge

**Prep Time:** 5 minutes  
**Cook Time:** 5 minutes  
**Servings:** 2

**Ingredients:**
- 2 cups riced cauliflower
- ¾ cup unsweetened almond milk
- 4 tablespoons extra-virgin olive oil, divided
- 2 teaspoons grated fresh orange peel (from ½ orange)
- ½ teaspoon almond extract or extract
- ½ teaspoon ground cinnamon
- ⅛ Teaspoon salt
- 4 tablespoons chopped walnuts, divided
- 1 to 2 teaspoons maple syrup

**Prep:** Place the riced cauliflower, almond milk, 2 tablespoons of olive oil, orange peel, almond extract, cinnamon, and salt in a medium saucepan.
Stir to combine and bring the mixture to a boil over medium-high heat, stirring often.
Remove from the heat and add 2 tablespoons of chopped walnuts and maple syrup.

Stir again and divide the porridge into bowls. To serve, sprinkle each bowl evenly with the remaining 2 tablespoons of walnuts and olive oil.

**Nutrition:** Calories: 381 Fat: 37.8 g Protein: 5.2 g Carbs: 10.9 g

## 306. Spinach and Egg Breakfast Wraps

**Prep Time:** 10 minutes  
**Servings:** 2

**Cook Time:** 7 minutes

**Ingredients:**
- 1 tablespoon olive oil
- ¼ cup minced onion
- 3 to 4 tablespoons minced sun-dried tomatoes in olive oil and herbs
- 3 large eggs, whisked
- 1½ cups packed baby spinach
- 1 ounce (28 g) crumbled feta cheese
- Salt, to taste
- 2 (8-inch) whole-wheat tortillas

**Prep:** Heat the olive oil in a large skillet over medium-high heat.
Sauté the onion and tomatoes for about 3 minutes, occasionally stirring, until softened.
Reduce the heat to medium. Add the whisked eggs and stir-fry for 1 to 2 minutes.
Stir in the baby spinach and scatter with the crumbled feta cheese—season as needed with salt.
Remove the egg mixture from the heat to a plate. Set aside.
Working in batches, place 2 tortillas on a microwave-safe dish and microwave for about 20 seconds to make them warm.
Spoon half of the egg mixture into each tortilla. Fold in half and roll up, then serve.

**Nutrition:** Calories: 434 Fat: 28.1 g Protein: 17.2 g Carbs: 30.8 g

## 307. Oats with Raspberries

**Prep Time:** 5 minutes

**Servings:** 2

**Ingredients:**
- ⅔ cup unsweetened almond milk
- ¼ cup raspberries
- ⅓ cup rolled oats
- 1 teaspoon honey
- ¼ teaspoon turmeric
- ⅛ Teaspoon ground cinnamon
- Pinch ground cloves

**Prep:** Place the almond milk, raspberries, rolled oats, honey, turmeric, cinnamon, and cloves in a mason jar. Cover and shake to combine.
Transfer to the refrigerator for at least 8 hours, preferably 24 hours.

**Nutrition:** Calories: 81 g Fat: 1.9 g Protein: 2.1 g Carbs: 13.8 g

## 308. Scramble Eggs with Tomatoes

**Prep Time:** 10 minutes  
**Servings:** 4

**Cook Time:** 20 minutes

**Ingredients:**
- 2 tablespoons extra-virgin olive oil
- ¼ cup finely minced red onion
- 1½ cups chopped fresh tomatoes
- 2 garlic cloves, minced
- ½ teaspoon dried thyme
- ½ teaspoon dried oregano
- 8 large eggs
- ½ teaspoon salt
- ¼ teaspoon freshly ground black pepper
- ¾ cup crumbled feta cheese
- ¼ cup chopped fresh mint leaves

**Prep:** Heat the olive oil in a large skillet over medium heat.
Sauté the red onion and tomatoes in the hot skillet for 10 to 12 minutes, or until the tomatoes are softened.
Stir in the garlic, thyme, and oregano and sauté for 2 to 4 minutes, or until the garlic is fragrant.
Meanwhile, beat the eggs with the salt and pepper in a medium bowl until frothy.
Pour the beaten eggs into the skillet and reduce the heat to low—scramble for 3 to 4 minutes, stirring frequently, or until the eggs are set.
Remove from the heat and scatter with the feta cheese and mint. Serve warm.

**Nutrition:** Calories: 260 g Fat: 21.9 g Protein: 10.2 g Carbs: 5.8 g

# PASTA, RICE AND SOUPS

## 309. Truffle Cannelloni

**Prep time:** 40 minutes  
**Servings:** 4  
**Cook time:** 30 minutes

**Ingredients for the dough:**
- 4 eggs
- 1 ¾ cup of flour
- 2 cups of milk
- Salt and pepper

**Ingredients for the filling:**
- ¾ cup of ricotta
- 1 egg white
- ½ cup of grated parmesan
- ½ cup of grated pecorino
- Salt and pepper

**Ingredients for the topping:**
- ¼ cup of black truffle
- 2 cups of béchamel sauce
- 2 ¼ cups of parmesan cheese

**Prep:** Prepare the dough by mixing all the ingredients. Cook the dough with a crepe maker and then add in the filling made beforehand. Roll the dough and lay it on a tray brushed with 1 cup of béchamel.
Cover the dough with the remaining béchamel, grated parmesan and truffle cut into scales.
Bake in the oven 3750° for 20-30 minutes.

**Nutrition:** Calories 930; Carbs 76.9 g; Protein 42.4 g; Fat 55.1 g

## 310. Boscaiola Style Spelt

**Prep time:** 15 minutes  
**Servings:** 4  
**Cook time:** 30 minutes

**Ingredients:**
- 1 ¾ cup of spelt
- Olive oil
- 4 porcini mushrooms
- 2 tbsp of grated pecorino
- Red whine
- Meat broth
- Salt
- 2 sausages
- 1 onion

**Prep:** Place the finely chopped onion in a casserole with oil and let it brown for a few minutes, add the washed spelt, deglaze with the wine, and while mixing add the sliced mushrooms. Cook on a low heat pouring in some meat broth at a time. Serve with grated fresh pecorino on top.

**Nutrition:** Calories 609; Carbs 61 g; Protein 35.5 g; Fat 24.7 g

### 311. Ricotta Gnocchi

**Prep time: 30 minutes**  **Cook time: 60 minutes**
**Servings: 4**

**Ingredients:**
- 2 cups of ricotta
- ½ cup of cooked beets
- 3/4 cup of flour
- 2 eggs
- 1 ¼ tbsp of butter
- 1 cup of grated pecorino
- Nutmeg
- salt

**Prep:** Knead the flour with the ricotta and eggs, proceed to add the beets broke in half and half of the grated pecorino. Season with some nutmeg and a pinch of salt.
Shape the gnocchi and cook them in a pot full of water with some salt.
Meanwhile, prepare the sauce by melting the butter in a pan and adding the leftover pecorino.

**Nutrition:** Calories 418; Carbs 32 g; Protein 22.2 g; Fat 22.3 g

### 312. Spaghetti allo Scoglio

**Prep time: 40 minutes**  **Cook time: 20 minutes**
**Servings: 4**

**Ingredients:**
- 10 oz of spaghetti
- 5 oz of mussels
- 3 oz of clams
- 8 scampi
- 8 mantis shrimp
- 1 cup of cherry tomatoes
- Hot pepper
- Parsley
- Garlic
- Extra virgin olive oil
- Salt and pepper

**Prep:** In a pan let the garlic and hot pepper sizzle into some oil. Pour int the mussels and clams. Once the have opened, add the scampi, mantis shrimp and cherry tomatoes. Add salt and pepper to taste.
Meanwhile, cook the spaghetti *al dente* in a pot full of boiling salted water. Drain the pasta and sauté it in the pan with the fish seasoning. Sprinkle on some parsley and serve.

**Nutrition:** Calories 631; Carbs 85.9 g; Protein 32.1 g; Fat 15.9 g

### 313. Penne with Ricotta and Cherry Tomatoes

**Prep time: 20 minutes**  **Cook time: 10 minutes**
**Servings: 6**

**Ingredients:**
- 17 oz of penne pasta
- 17 oz of ripe tomatoes
- 2 cups of ricotta
- Extra virgin olive oil
- Garlic
- 4 basil leaves
- Salt and pepper

**Prep:** Peel the tomatoes and mash them in the sieve.
In a pan, let the garlic sizzle in some oil and then add the tomatoes. Add salt and pepper.
Cook the penne pasta in a pot full of salted water. When it is ready, drain the pasta and pour it into the pan adding the ricotta and basil leaves. Mix well and serve.

**Nutrition:** Calories 467; Carbs 71.3 g; Protein 15.2 g; Fat 13.5 g

### 314. Tagliatelle with Boar

**Prep time: 30 minutes**  **Cook time: 4 hours e 20 minutes**
**Servings: 4**

**Ingredients:**
- 14 oz of tagliatelle
- 10 oz of boar meat
- Red wine

- Cherry tomatoes
- 1 onion
- 5 garlic cloves
- Extra virgin olive oil
- Salt and pepper

**Prep:** Chop the meat into small pieces and marinate them with 3 garlic cloves, half chopped onion and red wine for at least 12 hours.
Sizzle the garlic and onion in a pan with some oil. Add the marinated meat, salt and pepper and then filter and add the wine previously used to marinate the mixture.
Cook on a low heat for at least 2 hours, then add the cherry tomatoes.
Cook the tagliatelle in a pot full of salted water and add the boar seasoning.

**Nutrition:** Calories 535; Carbs 55 g; Protein 36 g; Fat 18.1 g

## 315. Broth Passatelli

**Prep time: 10 minutes**
**Cook time; 5 minutes**
**Servings: 4**

**Ingredients:**
- 33 oz of meat broth
- 2 eggs
- 1 tbsp of flour
- 4 tbsp of breadcrumbs
- ½ cup of grated parmesan cheese
- Nutmeg

**Prep:** In a bowl, beat the eggs and add the flour, breadcrumbs, parmesan and a pinch of ground nutmeg and mix well. Press the mixture with a potato masher to shape small pipes.
Pour the passatelli in the boiling broth and cook for 5 minutes.

## 316. Pasta with Pumpkin

**Prep time: 30 minutes**                                  **Cook time: 30 minutes**
**Servings: 4**

**Ingredients:**
- 17 oz of short pasta
- 21 oz of pumpkin
- ½ onion
- 2 tbsp of olive oil
- ½ cup of grated parmesan
- Salt and pepper
- Ginger
- Rosemary

**Prep:** Brown the chopped onion and add most of the pumpkin cut in dices. Add salt and pepper and some water with 5-6 slices of ginger. Let it cook for about 15 minutes. When the pumpkin is cooked, blend it until it becomes creamy. Slice the remaining pumpkin and sauté it with oil and rosemary in a pan for 5 minutes.
Cook the pasta in a pot full of boiling salted water. Drain it and add it in the pan with the pumpkin cream.
Serve with some parmesan grated on top and some pumpkin slices.

**Nutrition:** Calories 508; Carbs 72.9 g; Protein 13.9 g; Fat 17.5 g

## 317. Pasta with Peas

**Prep time: 20 minutes**                                  **Cook time: 30 minutes**
**Servings: 4**

**Ingredients:**
- 14 oz of short penne pasta
- 1 ¼ cup of peas
- 6 tbsp of extra virgin olive oil
- 1 celery stick
- 1 carrot
- 1 ½ cup of tomato sauce
- 1 cup of white wine
- ½ cup of grated parmesan
- Salt and pepper

**Prep:** In a pan, brown in the oil the onion, celery and chopped carrot. When they will have reduced, add the peas and let them cook on a low heat for 10 minutes. Add the tomato sauce, wine and a pinch of salt and pepper. Let it simmer for about one hour.
Cook the pasta in a pot full of boiling salted water. Drain it and add the sauce in a serving plate.
Sprinkle some grated parmesan on top and then serve.

**Nutrition:** Calories 467; Carbs 77.3 g; Protein 16.9 g; Fat 10 g

### 318. Pasta with Chickpeas

**Prep time:** 20 minutes  
**Servings:** 6  
**Cook time:** 40 minutes

**Ingredients:**
- 17 oz of short pasta
- 10 oz of cooked chickpeas
- Extra virgin olive oil
- Grated parmesan
- Salt and pepper

**Prep:** Cook the pasta in a pot full of boiling salted water. Two minutes before the end of the cook time add the chickpeas, then drain the pasta and pour it into a casserole and season it with oil, pepper and parmesan.

**Nutrition:** Calories 567; Carbs 79.3 g; Protein 19.3 g; Fat 18.2 g

### 319. Rigatoni with Peppers

**Prep time:** 20 minutes  
**Servings:** 4  
**Cook time:** 35 minutes

**Ingredients:**
- 14 oz of rigatoni
- 2 green bell peppers
- 2 yellow bell peppers
- 4 basil leaves
- 1 garlic clove
- 2 ¼ tbsp of grated pecorino
- 4 tbsp of extra virgin olive oil
- Salt and pepper

**Prep:** Wash the peppers and remove the seeds and soul. Slice them and cook in some oil in a large pan. Lower the heat and cook with a lid on for 20 minutes. Add salt and pepper, giving it an occasional stir. Cook the pasta in a pot full of boiling salted water. Serve with grated parmesan on top.

**Nutrition:** Calories 430; Carbs 75.3 g; Protein 11.3 g; Fat 9 g

### 320. Rice and Bean Soup

**Prep time:** 10 minutes  
**Servings:** 4  
**Cook time:** 25 minutes

**Ingredients:**
- 10 oz of rice
- 10 oz of kidney beans
- ½ cup of tomato pulp
- ½ onion
- 1 celery stick
- Extra virgin olive oil
- Salt to taste

**Prep:** Soak the beans in water overnight. Boil them in a large pot with the celery and a handful of salt. If needed drain some water while the soup is boiling to prevent the cooking from stopping. Meanwhile in a pot, brown the onion in some oil and when it has reduced, add the tomato pulp and adjust the salt to taste. Let it cook for few minutes then pour the sauce in the bean pot and then add the rice. Let everything cook for some minutes. Keep the pot on a low heat until the rice has cooked.
Serve the soup with a drizzle of oil.

**Nutrition:** Calories 151; Carbs 24 g; Protein 4.6 g; Fat 3.9 g

### 321. Risotto with Zucchini and Squid

**Prep time:** 20 minutes  
**Servings:** 4  
**Cook time:** 80 minutes

**Ingredients:**
- 14 oz of rice
- 2 zucchinis
- 4 squid
- Vegetable broth
- Extra virgin olive oil
- 1 garlic clove
- Parsley
- salt

**Prep:** Cut the zucchini in cubes. Clean the squid and chop them into fine pieces.
Ina pan, let the onion brown in oil with a garlic clove. Add the zucchinis and a cup of hot vegetable broth and let it boil for some minutes. Add squid and cook for 2 minutes. Combine the rice and add some hot broth until the rice is fully cooked. Adjust the salt to taste and serve the soup hot with some chopped parsley on top.

**Nutrition:** Calories 522; Carbs 76.3 g; Protein 19.3 g; Fat 14.4 g

## 322. Green Risotto with Porcini Mushrooms

**Prep time:** 30 minutes  
**Servings:** 6  
**Cook time:** 35 minutes

**Ingredients:**
- 15 oz of rice
- 3 oz of spinach
- 1 onion
- Extra virgin olive oil
- 2 tbsp of butter
- 2 tbsp of guanciale
- ½ cup of white wine
- 1 ¾ cup of porcini mushrooms
- Filtered meat broth
- nutmeg
- 1 garlic clove

**Prep:** Boil the spinach in a pot full of salted water then drain them.
In a pan, fry the chopped garlic clove and the onion in some oil. Add the spinach and after few minutes add the rice. Let it toast for 1 minute, then deglaze it with wine. Pour two cups of hot broth and the mushrooms. Let the rice simmer until it is cooked by adding some broth when needed.
When the rice is cooked, add the butter and a pinch of nutmeg and let it melt.

**Nutrition:** Calories 540; Carbs 72.6 g; Protein 14.1 g; Fat 21.5 g

## 323. Spaghetti with Squid Ink

**Prep time:** 40 minutes  
**Servings:** 4  
**Cook time:** 15 minutes

**Ingredients:**
- 14 oz of squid with ink
- 14 oz of tomato pulp
- 14 oz of spaghetti
- 1 garlic clove
- Extra virgin olive oil
- 1 onion
- 1 hot pepper
- Parsley
- Salt and pepper

**Prep:** Slit the back of the squid to remove the bone. Open them in half and carefully remove the ink sack and put it aside. Fry the chopped garlic, onion and hot pepper. Add the squid cut into small pieces and let them fully cook. When they are ready, add the tomato, salt and one cup of water. Cook for about one hour. In the end add the ink and let it boil again for few minutes.
Separately cook the spaghetti in a pot full of salted water, drain them and add them to the pan with the squid and ink, add some pepper and chopped parsley.

**Nutrition:** Calories 474; Carbs 67.5 g; Protein 21.6 g; Fat 11.7 g

## 324. Spaghetti with Tuna Sauce

**Prep time:** 5 minutes  
**Servings:** 4  
**Cook time:** 10 minutes

**Ingredients:**
- 7 oz of canned tuna
- 14 oz of spaghetti
- ½ cup of pit less olives
- 2 ½ cups of tomato sauce
- 1 tsp of capers
- 1 salted anchovy
- Extra virgin olive oil
- 1 garlic clove
- Chopped Parsley
- Salt and pepper

**Prep:** In a pan fry the chopped garlic with the anchovy. Add the cut tuna, capers and olives. Let the taste develop for few minutes and then add the tomato and ½ cup of water. Add salt and pepper and let it boil for 10 minutes.
Cook the spaghetti in a pot full of salted water. Drain them, season with the tuna sauce and sprinkle on top some minced parsley.

**Nutrition:** Calories 398; Carbs 69.5 g; Protein 19.6 g; Fat 4.7 g

## 325. Spaghetti with Walnuts and Asparagus

**Prep time:** 40 minutes  
**Servings:** 4  
**Cook time:** 15 minutes

**Ingredients:**
- 11 oz of spaghetti
- 2 tbsp of grated pecorino
- 17 oz of asparagus
- ½ cup of shell less walnuts
- Extra virgin olive oil
- 1 sprig of parsley
- Pepper grains

**Prep:** Clean the asparagus and cut them in pieces, let them boil for 5 minutes. Move them to a pan and fry them in some oil. Meanwhile, cook the spaghetti in a pot full of salted water. Add the spaghetti to the asparagus in the pan, add the walnuts, pepper, pecorino and a dash of minced parsley.

**Nutrition:** Calories 823; Carbs 76.4 g; Protein 20.2 g; Fat 48.5 g

### 326. Cold Spaghetti

**Prep time:** 30 minutes  
**Servings:** 4  
**Cook time:** 15 minutes

**Ingredients:**
- 17 oz of spaghetti
- 11 oz of shrimp
- 12 oz of arugula
- 11 oz of cherry tomatoes
- extra virgin olive oil
- white wine vinegar
- Salt and pepper

**Prep:** Cook the shrimp in boiling water; clean the tomatoes and cut then into fine pieces. Mince the arugula.
Cook the spaghetti in a pot full of salted water. Drain them and wash under cold water.
In a bowl add the tomatoes, shrimp, arugula, some oil and vinegar, a handful of salt and pepper. Pour in the spaghetti and add some more oil. Let everything cool down to room temperature (not in the fridge) and serve after 2-3 hours.

**Nutrition:** Calories 520; Carbs 79.5 g; Protein 19.6 g; Fat 14.7 g

### 327. Spaghetti with Squid and Mushrooms

**Prep time:** 15 minutes  
**Servings:** 6  
**Cook time:** 15 minutes

**Ingredients:**
- 17 oz of spaghetti
- 14 oz of squid
- 17 oz of cherry tomatoes
- 11 oz of champignon mushrooms
- Extra virgin olive oil
- 1 garlic clove
- Parsley
- Salt and pepper

**Prep:** In a pan fry the minced garlic, mushrooms and chopped squid with some oil. After few minutes add the tomatoes and a dash of salt and pepper.
Meanwhile, cook the spaghetti in a pot full of salted water. When they are ready, drain them and move them into the pan with the seasoning and a pinch of minced parsley.

**Nutrition:** Calories 434; Carbs 68.1 g; Protein 16.2 g; Fat 9.6 g

### 328. Stracciatella

**Prep time:** 10 minutes  
**Servings:** 2  
**Cook time:** 4 minutes

**Ingredients:**
- 2 eggs
- 3 tbsp of grated parmesan cheese
- Nutmeg
- Zest of half a lemon
- 33 oz of meat broth

**Prep:** In a bowl beat the eggs and add the parmesan, lemon zest and a pinch of ground nutmeg. Add a cup of broth so the mixture softens up.
On the side, boil the remaining broth in a pot and then pour in all the mixture. Stir vigorously for 3-4 minutes.

**Nutrition:** Calories 179; Carbs 0.2 g; Protein 17.4 g; Fat 12.1 g

### 329. Mushroom Tagliatelle

**Prep time:** 40 minutes  
**Servings:** 6  
**Cook time:** 40 minutes

**Ingredients:**
- 21 oz of tagliatelle
- 7 oz of porcini mushrooms
- 7 oz of champignon mushrooms
- Extra virgin olive oil
- 1 garlic clove
- 1 hot pepper
- 3 oz of raw ham
- 17 oz of chicken broth
- salt

**Prep:** In a pan, fry into some oil the garlic and hot pepper. Add the diced ham and chopped up mushrooms. after 10 minutes add the hot chicken broth, adjust the salt to taste and keep cooking for 30 minutes.
Cook the tagliatelle in a pot full of salted water. Drain and season with the sauce.

**Nutrition:** Calories 426; Carbs 40.9 g; Protein 14 g; Fat 23 g

## 330. Spaghetti with Clams

**Prep time:** 15 minutes  
**Cook time:** 10 minutes  
**Servings:** 4

**Ingredients:**
- *17 oz of spaghetti*
- *½ cup of white wine*
- *Parsley*
- *Salt and pepper*
- *1 garlic clove*
- *11 oz of ripe cherry tomatoes*
- *17 oz of clams*

**Prep:** Let the clams soak in cold water and a handful of salt for 2-3 hours. Drain and rinse them.
In a pan fry into some oil the garlic, clams and tomatoes. Deglaze with the wine and when it has evaporated, cook with a lid on until the shells open. In the meantime, cook the spaghetti in a pot full of salted water. Add the pasta to the pan with the clams, dash some pepper and minced parsley and serve.

**Nutrition:** Calories 420; Carbs 67.8 g; Protein 15 g; Fat 9.3 g

## 331. Vermicelli with Clams

**Prep time:** 15 minutes  
**Cook time:** 25 minutes  
**Servings:** 6

**Ingredients:**
- *21 oz of vermicelli*
- *4 lb of mussels*
- *Chopped Parsley*
- *2 garlic cloves*
- *salt*
- *Pepper*

**Prep:** Wash and drain the mussels.
Pour in a pan the oil, mussels once the shells have opened. Take out the pulp and put it aside. Filter the broth through a cloth to remove the impurities. In a separate pan fry the remaining garlic into the oil. When the garlic is browned, remove it, pour the broth and let it thicken for few minutes. Season the vermicelli, cook them *al dente* in a pot of salted water with the clams and the water they released, stir for few minutes on a low heat and drain most of the broth, lastly add plenty of parsley.
Serve the vermicelli with the clams steaming hot.

## 332. Meat Tortelloni with Parmesan and Truffle Sauce

**Prep time:** 30 minutes  
**Cook time:** 10 minutes  
**Servings:** 4

**Ingredients for the dough:**
- *4 eggs*
- *14 oz of flour*

**Ingredients for the stuffing:**
- *11 oz of ground beef*
- *1 tbsp of grated parmesan*
- *1 egg*
- *Pinch of salt*

**Ingredients for the seasoning:**
- *¾ cup of black truffle*
- *½ cup of grated parmesan*
- *¾ cups of milk cream*
- *salt*

**Prep:** Knead the flour and eggs and let the dough to rest for about half an hour, with a cloth on top. Meanwhile, prepare the filling by mixing the cooked meat, egg, salt and parmesan.
Then roll out the dough and prepare the tortelloni with the filling.
In a pan, melt the parmesan with the cream and a pinch of salt.
Cook the tortelloni for 3-4 minutes in a pot full of salted water. Drain them and move them in the pan with the parmesan cream.
Serve in a plate with truffle scales on top.

**Nutrition:** Calories 594; Carbs 70.2 g; Protein 11.4 g; Fat 23 g

### 333. Chestnut, Ricotta and Spelt Soup

**Prep time:** 30 minutes  
**Servings:** 2  
**Cook time:** 40 minutes

**Ingredients:**
- ¾ cup of chopped chestnuts
- ½ cup of spelt
- 1 tsp of fennel seeds
- ½ cup of ricotta
- ½ onion
- 2 minced rosemary sprigs
- 4 tbsp of extra virgin olive oil
- 50 oz of vegetable broth
- 1 ½ of grated parmesan
- Salt and pepper

**Prep:** Let the onion and rosemary sizzle in a pan with some oil. Add the chestnuts, fennel seeds and spelt. When all the ingredients are combined, add the ricotta and boiling broth.
Cook for about 30-40 minutes. Serve with a dash of pepper and parmesan.

**Nutrition:** Calories 297; Carbs 61 g; Protein 11.4 g; Fat 24.7 g

### 334. Spelt and Mushroom Soup

**Prep time:** 15 minutes  
**Servings:** 4  
**Cook time:** 40 minutes

**Ingredients:**
- ¾ cup of champignon mushrooms
- 1 cup of spelt
- Extra virgin olive oil
- Salt and pepper
- 1 garlic clove

**Prep:** Boil the spelt and drain it once it is cooked. Meanwhile, fry the garlic into some oil and add the mushrooms to let them cook for few minutes. Combine everything and serve.

**Nutrition:** Calories 609; Carbs 71 g; Protein 15.4 g; Fat 14.7 g

### 335. Lentil Soup

**Prep time:** 20 minutes  
**Servings:** 6  
**Cook time:** 80 minutes

**Ingredients:**
- 14 oz of lentils
- 33 oz of water
- Extra virgin olive oil
- 2 garlic cloves
- 1 celery stick
- salt

**Prep:** Boil the lentils with the celery and garlic for 70-80 minutes. Adjust the salt to taste and serve with a drizzle of oil.

**Nutrition:** Calories 298; Carbs 43 g; Protein 18 g; Fat 6 g

### 336. Pasta and Potato Soup

**Prep time:** 15 minutes  
**Servings:** 4  
**Cook time:** 1 hour

**Ingredients:**
- 33 oz of potatoes
- 7 oz of short pasta (like ditali)
- 66 oz of chicken broth
- 1 onion
- 1 sprig of parsley
- Extra virgin olive oil
- Salt and pepper

**Prep:** Let the chopped onion and parsley reduce in a pan with 3 tbsp of oil. Add the peeled and diced potatoes and cook on medium heat for about 40 minutes.
Add salt and pepper to taste, pour the pasta in and let it cook.

**Nutrition:** Calories 532; Carbs 104 g; Protein 13.9 g; Fat 6.5 g

### 337. Pumpkin and Beans Soup

**Prep time:** 10 minutes  
**Servings:** 4  
**Cook time:** 2 hours

**Ingredients:**
- *14 oz of kidney beans*
- *7 oz of ditali pasta*
- *1 cup of diced bacon*
- *10 oz of yellow pumpkin pulp*
- *4 ripe tomatoes*
- *1 sprigs of wild fennel*
- *1 onion*
- *1 celery stick*
- *6 tbsp of extra virgin olive oil*
- *Salt and pepper*

**Prep:** Soak the beans in water overnight. Rinse and move them in a pot full of cold water. Add ½ chopped onion, celery, chopped pumpkin and minced fennel. Cook for 1 hour and 45 minutes.
Chop the remaining onion and let it reduce in a pan with oil and bacon. Add the canned tomatoes and cut them. Combine everything in the pot with the beans. Add salt and pepper.
Boil the water and cook the pasta. Serve by adding a drizzle of oil.

**Nutrition:** Calories 150; Carbs 14 g; Protein 6.2 g; Fat 7.7 g

## 338. Zucchini and Potato Soup

**Prep time: 20 minutes**  
**Servings: 4**  
**Cook time: 1 hour**

**Ingredients:**
- *1 zucchini*
- *17 oz of potatoes*
- *4 ripe tomatoes*
- *Salt and pepper*
- *7 oz of short pasta*
- *1 onion*
- *50 oz of vegetable broth*
- *1 celery stick*
- *1 sprig of parsley*
- *Extra virgin olive oil*

**Prep:** Peel the zucchini and potatoes and then dice them.
Thinly slice the onion, celery and parsley, let them reduce in a pan with 5 tbsp of oil. Add the peeled and chopped tomatoes and let the flavor develop for few minutes while occasionally stirring.
Add the zucchini and potatoes, the hot broth and cook for about 40 minutes.
Taste the salt ratio and drain the pasta. At the end, dust on some pepper and drizzle some oil.

**Nutrition:** Calories 538; Carbs 104 g; Protein 12.1 g; Fat 7.5 g

## 339. Chicory Soup

**Prep time: 5 minutes**  
**Servings: 6**  
**Cook time: 15 minutes**

**Ingredients:**
- *4 lbs of chicory*
- *2 garlic cloves*
- *2 lbs of vegetable broth*
- *Salt*
- *Hot Pepper*
- *Grated parmesan*
- *Extra virgin olive oil*
- *Grated Pecorino*

**Prep:** Wash chicory, drop them in boiling and remove from the heat when the water starts bubbling again. Drain them in a colander. Cook them in a pan with oil and garlic. Season the vegetables with hot pepper and salt. Let them cook on a medium heat for about 10 minutes and add some broth if needed. Let everything cook with a cheese crust. Turn off the heat and pour the grated cheese. Serve the soup while it is still steaming.

## 340. Green Beans Soup

**Prep time: 5 minutes**  
**Servings: 6**  
**Cook time: 15 minutes**

**Ingredients:**
- *28 oz of green beans*
- *2 garlic cloves*
- *2 lbs of vegetable broth*
- *Salt*
- *Hot Pepper*
- *Marjoram*
- *Extra virgin olive oil*
- *Parsley*
- *8 canned tomatoes*

**Prep:** Snip the edges from the green beans and boil them in the vegetable broth, leave them still crunchy. Drain and keep the excess broth aside. In a pan let the garlic sizzle in some oil, pour in the canned tomatoes and wait until the sauce is cooked and shiny, then add the green beans, a little hot pepper and the herbs. Let the flavor develop for about 10 minutes.
Add the extra broth in to water down the soup. Serve the soup while it is still steaming.

### 341. Potato Soup

**Prep time:** 5 minutes  
**Servings:** 4  
**Cook time:** 20 minutes

**Ingredients:**
- 4 oz of onions
- 2 canned tomatoes
- Basil
- Vegetable broth
- Salt and pepper
- Marjoram
- Parsley
- 2 lbs of potatoes
- ¼ cup of raw ham
- 1 ¾ cup of butter

**Prep:** Combine the sliced onion, diced ham and butter in a casserole and let it cook on low heat with some broth or water. When the onion softens up, add the potatoes chopped into fine pieces and a sprig of marjoram, parsley, salt, pepper, tomato and basil, cover in water or broth. Let the soup simmer until the potatoes are cooked.
Serve the soup, slightly runny, steamy and hot.

### 342. Zucchini and Egg Soup

**Prep time:** 5 minutes  
**Servings:** 6  
**Cook time:** 20 minutes

**Ingredients:**
- 3 lbs of zucchini
- Extra virgin olive oil
- Grated parmesan
- Salt and pepper
- 3 eggs
- 1 cup of lard
- 1 onion
- ¼ cup of raw ham

**Prep:** Wash the zucchini, dry and dice them.
Sizzle the onion with lard and oil in a pan then, add the zucchini, salt and cover with a lid. Let it cook on a low heat.
when the zucchini are cooked and well mixed, on a low heat, add the beaten the eggs with basil, parmesan, pepper and a pinch of salt, cook until the eggs start to slightly cook.
Serve the soup while steamy and hot.

### 343. Cabbage Stew

**Prep time:** 10 minutes  
**Servings:** 6  
**Cook time:** 1 hour

**Ingredients:**
- 4 lbs of cleaned savoy cabbage
- 1 hot pepper cut in half
- 2 garlic cloves
- Salt
- extra virgin olive oil

**Prep:** Remove the leaves from the cabbage, wash and dry them, then slice them.
Sizzle some garlic in hot oil in a large pan, when it starts to golden, add the cabbage and hot pepper. Let cook for about one hour on a low heat in a pot with a lid. When the cabbage is cooked add some salt.
Serve while hot.

### 344. Legume Soup

**Prep time:** 5 minutes  
**Servings:** 6  
**Cook time:** 40 minutes

**Ingredients:**
- 13 oz of cooked beans
- ¼ cup of minced lard
- 13 oz of raw lentils
- 1 savoy cabbage
- 1 chopped onion
- 1 endive
- Extra virgin olive oil
- Parsley
- 13 oz of cooked chickpeas

**Prep:** Boil the lentils in a pot full of water and one meat broth cube. Wash the lentils, drain and cook them, cook the beans and chickpeas as well for 20 minutes, then add again the lentils to the broth.
Let the onions, celery and carrots reduce in a pan with oil and lard; then add the cleaned endive the sliced cabbage and legumes with the broth. Let the flavor develop for about 15 minutes.

### 345. Macaroni with Pork Ragù and Vegetables

**Prep time:** 30 minutes  
**Servings:** 4  
**Cook time:** 1 hour e 20 minutes

**Ingredients:**
- 14 oz of macaroni
- 11 oz of ground pork meat
- 19 oz of tomato sauce
- 1 onion
- 1 bay leaf
- 4 basil leaves
- ½ cup of red wine
- ½ cup of grated pecorino cheese
- 1 garlic clove
- 5 tbsp of olive oil
- Salt and pepper
- Wild fennel
- 1 cup of breadcrumbs

**Prep:** Cook the fennel in a pan with some oil, bay and finely chopped onion. Add the pork meat and let it sizzle. Add the ½ cup of wine and let it evaporate. Add the tomato sauce and basil; adjust the salt and pepper to taste and let simmer on a low heat for about 1 hour.
Cook the pasta *al dente* in a pot full of salted water, drain it and add the sauce.
Sprinkle on top the breadcrumbs, some oil, the pecorino and minced garlic and parsley.

**Nutrition:** Calories 368; Carbs 61 g; Protein 15.1 g; Fat 26.4 g

### 346. Tagliatelle with Aged Ricotta

**Prep time:** 1 hour  
**Servings:** 4  
**Cook time:** 1 hour

**Ingredients:**
- 11 oz of flour
- 1 cup of aged ricotta
- 3,3 lbs of ripe tomatoes
- 1 onion
- 4 basil leaves
- 4 tbsp of olive oil
- Sugar
- Durum wheat semolina
- Salt and pepper

**Prep:** Sift the flour and pour in onto a counter, knead it with water and salt until you reach a firm and elastic consistency. Roll into a thin layer and cut the tagliatelle stripes about ¼ inch large. Spread on a handful of semolina so the stripes won't stick to each other.
Wash and cut the tomatoes, move them to a casserole and let them cook for about 10 minutes. Mash them with a vegetable mincer, pour the mixture into a pan with oil and the chopped onion. Add the basil, salt and pepper and a pinch of sugar. Allow to thicken on low heat.
Cook the tagliatelle *al dente* in a pot full of salted water. Strain them and season with the sauce.
Sprinkle with the grated ricotta and serve.

**Nutrition:** Calories 467; Carbs 71.3 g; Protein 15.2 g; Fat 13.5 g

### 347. Almond Pesto Pasta

**Prep time:** 15 minutes  
**Servings:** 4  
**Cook time:** 10 minutes

**Ingredients:**
- 13 oz of fusilli
- 12 oz of skinless almonds
- 4 basil leaves
- 1 cup of extra virgin olive oil
- 1 garlic clove
- 2 tbsp of grated parmesan
- salt

**Prep:** Blitz the almonds with a pinch of salt in a blender.
Wash and dry the basil; mash it in a mortar with a garlic clove. Add the parmesan and keep mashing.
Pour all the ingredients in a bowl and slowly add the oil.
Cook the fusilli in a pot full of salted water. Strain the pasta and add the seasoning, incorporate few spoonful of cooking water.

**Nutrition:** Calories 540; Carbs 84.4 g; Protein 13.2 g; Fat 16.7 g

### 348. Pasta with Sword Fish Ragù

**Prep time:** 15 minutes  
**Servings:** 4  
**Cook time:** 45 minutes

**Ingredients:**
- 14 oz of tagliatelle
- 2 lbs of sword fish slices
- 1 tbsp of salted capers

- 1 ¾ cup of pit less black olives
- 2 garlic cloves
- ½ cup of white wine
- 1 cup of tomato sauce
- ½ onion
- ½ cup of extra virgin olive oil
- 1 sprig of parsley
- Salt and pepper

**Prep:** Finely chop the onion, garlic and a sprig of parsley and sizzle them in a pan with some oil. When they have reduces, add the capers and the tomato sauce. Season with a pinch of salt and pepper. Add the diced fish and deglaze with the wine. Then cook with the lid on for 20 minutes. Halfway through the cooking add the olives.
Cook *al dente* the tagliatelle in a pot full of salted boiling water. Strain it and season with the sauce.
Serve with a handful of chopped parsley.

**Nutrition:** Calories 502; Carbs 68.5 g; Protein 20.2 g; Fat 16.1 g

## 349. Pasta with Tomato and Eggplant

**Prep time: 30 minutes**  
**Servings: 4**  
**Cook time: 20 minutes**

**Ingredients:**
- 13 oz of spaghetti
- 17 oz of tomato sauce
- 1 eggplant
- extra virgin olive oil
- 4 basil leaves
- ½ cup of grated parmesan
- Salt and pepper

**Prep:** Wash and thinly slice the eggplant. Cover it in salt and keep it in a colander to drain the excess water. Wash it out, pat dry and fry it in hot oil.
Cook the spaghetti in a pot full of salted boiling water. Add the eggplant slices and basil leaves, add on the side the grated parmesan.

**Nutrition:** Calories 534; Carbs 71.8 g; Protein 15.9 g; Fat 20.3 g

## 350. Pasta with Peppers and Tomatoes

**Prep time: 20 minutes**  
**Servings: 4**  
**Cook time: 1 hour**

**Ingredients:**
- 13 oz of spaghetti
- 2 lbs of peppers
- ½ cup tomato sauce
- 1 onion
- extra virgin olive oil
- 1 garlic clove
- 4 basil leaves
- Salt and pepper

**Prep:** Finely chop the onion and sizzle it in oil in a pan. Add the pepper stripes and let it cook for 5 minutes. Add the tomato sauce, basil leaves and a pinch of salt and pepper, keep cooking for about 40 minutes, with a lid on.
Cook the spaghetti in a pot full of salted boiling water, strain and season with the sauce.

**Nutrition:** Calories 397; Carbs 73.5 g; Protein 10 g; Fat 7.1 g

## 351. Broccoli Soup

**Prep time: 15 minutes**  
**Servings: 4**  
**Cook time: 35 minutes**

**Ingredients:**
- 2lbs of broccoli
- 13 oz of ditali pasta
- Salt and pepper
- 4 tbsp of olive oil

**Prep:** Cook the chopped broccoli in a pot full of salted boiling water for 20-25 minutes. Add the pasta in and cook it.
Distribute the soup in the plates and garnish with abundant pepper and 1 tbsp of oil.

**Nutrition:** Calories 369 Kcal; Carbs69.1 g; Protein 10.8 g; Fat 5.5 g

## 352. Spaghetti with Artichokes

**Prep time: 20 minutes**  
**Servings: 4**  
**Cook time: 30 minutes**

**Ingredients:**
- 13 oz of spaghetti
- 1 onion
- 6 artichokes
- 1 lemon
- 1 sprig of parsley
- ½ cup of olive oil
- Salt and pepper

**Prep:** Cut the artichokes and soak them in water with some lemon juice.
Sizzle the chopped onion in a pan with some oil, add the artichokes and let it marinate for few minutes. Sprinkle on the minced parsley, salt and pepper. Dampen the mixture with ½ cup of water and cook on medium heat for 20 minutes.
Cook the spaghetti in a pot full of salted boiling water, strain and season with the sauce.

**Nutrition:** Calories 402; Carbs 66.4 g; Protein 12.5 g; Fat 9.4 g

## 353. Farfalle Pasta with Peas

**Prep time:** 50 minutes
**Servings:** 6

**Cook time:** 30 minutes

**Ingredients:**
- 17 oz of farfalle pasta
- 8 oz of cleaned peas
- 1 cup of diced ham
- 1 onion
- 2 tbsp of extra virgin olive oil
- 2 ladles of broth
- 4 tbsp of butter
- ¾ cup of grated parmesan
- salt

**Prep:** In a pan with oil, 1 tbsp of butter, let them head and then add the diced ham and chopped onion, sizzle for 5 minutes. Add the peas and leave the pan on the heat for 10 minutes. Pour the broth and add the salt, cover and let it finish cooking.
Boil some water, add salt and pour in the farfalle pasta. Once the pasta is ready, strain it and add it into the pan with the sauce. Season with the remaining melted butter and grated parmesan.

**Nutrition:** Calories 358; Carbs 65 g; Protein 14.3 g; Fat 9 g

## 354. Farfalle Pasta with Capers

**Prep time:** 20 minutes
**Servings:** 4

**Cook time:** 1h 10 min

**Ingredients:**
- 13 oz of farfalle pasta
- 11 oz of capers
- Hot Pepper
- ¾ cup of olive oil
- 6 minced garlic cloves
- Parsley
- Salt

**Prep:** Rinse the capers in water for about 2 hours, frequently change the water; drain the capers and mince half of them. Sizzle the garlic into a pan with some oil, remove it when it starts to brown. Pour in the pan the capers and let them cook on a low heat for few minutes. Cook the pasta in a pot full of boiling salted water, strain it and move it to a casserole. Add the hot caper sauce and let cook on a low heat for few minutes.
Serve the pasta still hot and steamy.

## 355. Pesto Silk Blankets

**Prep time:** 30 minutes
**Servings:** 6

**Cook time:** 5 minutes

**Ingredients:**
- 17 oz of flour
- 2 tbsp of bran
- 4 eggs
- salt
- 1 garlic clove
- 2 basil bunches
- ¼ cup of grated parmesan
- ¼ cup of grated pecorino
- 1 tbsp of pine nuts
- 7 tbsp of extra virgin olive oil
- Coarse marine salt

**Prep:** Slowly knead the flour with the bran, eggs, salt then roll out the dough into thin layers and cut out 10 inch squares. Wash and dry the basil leaves. Put the garlic and salt in a mortar and start mashing. Add the basil leaves then the pine nuts and cheese. Lastly, add the oil one drop at a time to complete the pesto sauce.
Cook the pasta with salt and some oil. Strain it and season with the pesto.

**Nutrition:** Calories 684; Carbs 56.4 g; Protein 20.6 g; Fat 42.8 g

### 356. Stuffed Macaroni

**Prep time:** 60 minutes  
**Servings:** 6  

**Cook time:** 1 hour e 15 minutes

**Ingredients:**
- 17 oz of flour
- water
- 10 oz of veal pulp
- ¼ cup of butter
- 1 onion
- 1 tbsp of parsley
- ¾ cup of grated parmesan
- 1 tbsp of breadcrumbs
- 2 cups of meat broth
- Salt
- 3 eggs

**Prep:** Mince the onion and wet the breadcrumbs with meat broth or milk. Knead the flour with water until you reach a smooth dough, then let it rest.
Clean the veal pulp and sizzle it with butter, onion and rosemary for 15 minutes.
Mince the sizzled ingredients, add 3 yolks, 1 egg white, 1 tbsp of cheese and wet breadcrumbs, keep mixing and lastly add the salt. Take small servings of pasta and roll them with the stuffing inside. Seal the edges of the macaroni.
Place the macaroni on a tray, cover the bottom with the broth and leftover grated cheese, bake at 350°F for 1 hour.

**Nutrition:** Calories 790; Carbs 62.3 g; Protein 33.5 g; Fat 44.6 g

### 357. Cappelletti with Ricotta and Herbs

**Prep time:** 30 minutes  
**Servings:** 6  

**Cook time:** 10 minutes

**Ingredients:**
- 16 oz of flour
- 1 cup of dry white wine
- 3 eggs
- 8 oz borage
- 8 oz of beets
- 8 oz of ricotta
- 1 tbsp of butter
- ½ cup of grated parmesan cheese
- nutmeg
- salt
- 17 oz of walnuts
- 1 tbsp of pine nuts
- 6 tbsp of extra virgin olive oil
- ½ garlic clove
- 1 tbsp of chopped parsley
- marjoram

**Prep:** Knead the flour with the wine, 1 egg, pinch of salt and some water. Roll out the dough to form a 3 mm layer and let it rest covered by a cloth.
Wash the borage and beets, boil and cut them. Mix well adding eggs, sifted ricotta, melted butter and grated butter. Add some nutmeg and salt, then the filling is ready.
Boil the kernel of the walnuts to peel them. Mash together the walnuts, pine nuts, parsley, garlic and marjoram. Add salt and pepper and a drizzle of oil to complete the seasoning.
Cut the dough into 2 inch squared and put some stuffing in the center, then close them in a triangle and seal the edges. Boil the dough in salted water until they float and then drain and season them with the walnut dressing.

**Nutrition:** Calories 257; Carbs 7.5 g; Protein 19.3 g; Fat 16.5 g

### 358. Pumpkin Cappelletti

**Prep time:** 30 minutes  
**Servings:** 6  

**Cook time:** 30 minutes

**Ingredients:**
- 4 cups of flour
- 1 cup of dry white wine
- 4 eggs
- 2.6 lbs of yellow pumpkin
- pepper
- ground and coarse salt
- 1 3/4 cup of ricotta
- 1 3/4 cup grated parmesan
- 1 tbsp of breadcrumbs
- 1 garlic clove
- 3 tbsp of butter
- 18 sage leaves
- 2 tbsp of extra virgin olive oil
- 3 leaves of marjoram

**Prep:** Knead the flour with wine, 1 egg, a pinch of salt and some water. Roll out the dough to a 3 mm thick layer and let it rest covered by a cloth. Bake the pumpkin in the oven, covering it with aluminum foil. Peel the pumpkin, gut it and finely chop it.
Mash the garlic with the marjoram and a pinch of coarse salt, beat the remaining eggs and mix everything together. Add to the mixture the chopped pumpkin, ricotta, parmesan, 2 tbsp of oil and the breadcrumbs, mix well.
Take the dough and cut it into 2 inch squares, place the pumpkin filling in the middle and close them in triangles sealing the edges. Boil the pasta in hot water, strain it and season with melted butter and the sage leaves.

**Nutrition:** Calories 527; Carbs 65 g; Protein 14.3 g; Fat 9 g

### 359. Pasta with Mushrooms

**Prep time:** 30 minutes  
**Servings:** 6  
**Cook time:** 60 minutes

**Ingredients:**
- 21 oz of lasagne
- 8 oz of porcini mushrooms
- 4 tomatoes
- 2 tbsp of tomato sauce
- 2 garlic cloves
- 1 tbsp of minced parsley
- 1 tbsp of minced rosemary
- 2 tbsp of olive oil
- salt
- pepper
- 1 cup of broth
- 2 tbsp of butter

**Prep:** Mince the garlic and clean the mushrooms, then slice them. Peel and gut the tomatoes, move them in a pan with butter and oil, let it sizzle and add the minced garlic, rosemary and parsley.
Cut the tomato pulp and add it to the other ingredients in the pan.
Add some broth and cook for 30 minutes.
soften the lasagne into boiling water with salt then season them with the sauce.

**Nutrition:** Calories 327; Carbs 54.9 g; Protein 12.6 g; Fat 6.3 g

### 360. Pasta with Royal Agaric Mushrooms, and Walnuts

**Prep time:** 30 minutes  
**Servings:** 6  
**Cook time:** 20 minutes

**Ingredients:**
- 17 oz of raw pasta
- 10 oz of royal agaric mushrooms
- ½ cup of walnut kernels
- 1 garlic clove
- 2 tbsp of grated parmesan
- 2 tbsp of extra virgin olive oil
- Coarse Salt

**Prep:** Crush the walnut kernels with garlic and some coarse salt, then add the parmesan and keep crushing. Wash and clean the mushrooms then boil them into salted water and add in it the pasta 10 minutes later. Take some cooking water, some oil and add them to the crushed walnuts to finish preparing the cream.
Strain the pasta and mushrooms and season with the walnut cream.

**Nutrition:** Calories 823; Carbs 76.4 g; Protein 20.2 g; Fat 48.5 g

### 361. Fettuccine with Eggplant and Green Beans

**Prep time:** 20 minutes  
**Servings:** 6  
**Cook time:** 25 minutes

**Ingredients:**
- 17 oz of fettuccine
- 2 eggplants
- 1 ¼ cup of fresh green beans
- Genovese pesto (see recipe n. 854)

**Prep:** Discard the eggplant stems and the end, cut in half and then in slices, let soak into cold water. Snap in half the green beans and remove the tips.
Boil the eggplants and green beans for 15 minutes then drain them.
In a separate pot of salted water, add the pasta and the cooked vegetables.
When the pasta is ready, strain it and season with Genovese pesto.

**Nutrition:** Calories 559; Carbs 74.9 g; Protein 15.6 g; Fat 22.2 g

### 362. Tagliatelle with Pesto

**Prep time:** 1 hour 30 minutes  
**Servings:** 6  
**Cook time:** 10 minutes

**Ingredients:**
- 17 oz of flour
- 2 eggs
- ½ cup of white wine
- salt
- Genovese pesto (see recipe n. 854)

**Prep:** Knead the flour with the wine, eggs, water and some salt, then roll it out with a rolling pin into a 3 mm layer on a surface with some flour sprinkled on, then let it rest with a cloth on top.

Roll the dough and cut the tagliatelle not more than ¼ inch large and let them dry out.
Cook the tagliatelle in salted boiling water, strain and season with Genovese pesto.

**Nutrition:** Calories 648; Carbs 67 g; Protein 18.2 g; Fat 34.1 g

### 363. Tagliatelle with 3 Flours

**Prep time:** 30 minutes  
**Servings:** 6

**Cook time:** 10 minutes

**Ingredients:**
- 10 oz of chestnut flour
- 10 oz of wheat flour
- 10 oz of Manitoba flour
- 1 egg
- 2 potatoes
- ½ cup of green beans
- salt
- Genovese pesto (see recipe n.854)

**Prep:** Boil the potatoes and wedge them, snap the green beans and remove the tips. Cook the green beans into hot water.
On a surface, mix the flour types and knead in the egg, salt, water a little at a time to reach a soft and smooth dough. Roll out the dough to reach a thin layer and let it rest by covering it with a cloth. Roll the dough on itself and cut out the tagliatelle not more than ¼ inch wide and leave them on the counter.
Cook the tagliatelle in salted boiling water, strain and season with Genovese pesto, green beans and potatoes.

**Nutrition:** Calories 621; Carb s53 g; Protein 17.9 g; Fat 32.1 g

### 364. Ravioli with Artichoke Stuffing

**Prep time:** 4 hours  
**Servings:** 6

**Cook time:** 40 minutes

**Ingredients:**
- 21 oz of flour
- 5 eggs
- 8 artichokes
- 1 sprig of marjoram
- 1 ½ cup of ricotta
- 1 cup of broth
- 1 tbsp of parsley
- 1 lemon
- 6 tbsp of extra virgin olive oil
- ½ onion
- ½ garlic clove
- 5 tbsp of grated parmesan
- salt

**Prep:** Knead the flour with 2 eggs, a pinch of salt and water a little at a time. Roll out the dough into a thin layer and let it rest for 30 minutes. Clean the artichokes and use the hearts and sliced stems, soak them into water with lemon juice.
Mince the garlic and sizzle it in a pan with oil, artichokes and some broth. Add the minced parsley, stir and let it cook for 30 minutes covering with a lid. Take the mixture and add the ricotta, marjoram, grated cheese and 3 eggs.
Divide the dough in half, lay one on a surface and spoon the filling at ¾ inch apart and then cover with the other layer. Cut out squares around the filling with a rolling dough cutter and let rest for 2/3 hours.
Cook the ravioli a little at a time in boiling salted water. Strain them when they start to float.
Serve with grated parmesan.

**Nutrition:** Calories 631; Carbs 45.7 g; Protein 23.2 g; Fat 38.9 g

### 365. Pesto Ravioli with Potatoes

**Prep time:** 50 minutes  
**Servings:** 6

**Cook time:** 10 minutes

**Ingredients:**
- 21 oz of flour
- 4 eggs
- 14 oz of potatoes
- ¾ cup of ricotta
- 6 tbsp of grated parmesan
- 1 sprig of marjoram
- salt
- pepper
- Genovese pesto (see recipe n.854)

**Prep:** Knead the flour with 2 eggs, a pinch of salt and slowly adding water. Roll out the dough into a thin layer, cover it with a cloth and let it rest with a cloth for 30 minutes.
Boil the potatoes, peel and mash them with a potato masher to reach a creamy consistency. Mince the marjoram and add it to the mashed potatoes, add 2 eggs, grated cheese and ricotta. Give it a good mix, adjust salt and pepper to taste, then the filling will be ready.
Divide the dough in half, lay one on a surface and spoon the filling at ¾ inch apart, then cover with the other layer. Cut out squares around the filling with a rolling dough cutter and let rest for 2/3 hours.
Cook the ravioli a little at a time in boiling water and season with Genovese pesto.

**Nutrition:** Calories 549; Carbs 52.3 g; Protein 20.5 g; Fat 28.6 g

## 366. Ravioli with Potato, Leek and Zucchini

**Prep time:** 3 hours  
**Servings:** 6  
**Cook time:** 30 minutes

**Ingredients:**
- 24 oz of flour
- 4 eggs
- 14 oz of potatoes
- ¾ cup of ricotta
- 6 tbsp of grated parmesan
- 1 sprig of marjoram
- 2 leeks
- 2 zucchinis
- 5 tbsp of extra virgin olive oil
- ½ onion
- ½ cup of white wine
- 1 tbsp of fresh minced parsley
- 1 tbsp of butter
- Grated pecorino
- salt
- pepper

**Prep:** Knead the flour with 2 eggs, a pinch of salt and slowly add in water. Roll out the dough into a thin layer, cover it with a cloth and let it rest with a cloth for 30 minutes. Boil the potatoes, peel and mash them with a potato masher to reach a creamy consistency. Mince the marjoram and combine it to the potato mash, add 2 eggs, grated cheese and ricotta. Give it a good mix, adjust salt and pepper to taste, then the filling will be ready.
Divide the dough in half, lay one on a surface and spoon the filling at ¾ inch apart, then cover with the other layer. Cut out squares around the filling with a rolling dough cutter and let it rest for 2/3 hours.
Chop the onion and sizzle it in a pan with some oil. Boil the white part of the leeks and zucchinis. Cut the vegetables in circles and add them to the pan. Let them cook for 10 minutes. Add a tbsp of minced parsley, mix and let on the heat for another 2 minutes.
Cook the ravioli a little at a time and add the seasoning with some butter.

**Nutrition:** Calories 432; Carbs 52.3 g; Protein 11 g; Fat 16 g

## 367. Ravioli with Seafood

**Prep time:** 2 hours e 30 minutes  
**Servings:** 6  
**Cook time:** 50 minutes

**Ingredients:**
- 21 oz of flour
- 4 eggs
- 21 oz of gurnard
- 4 tbsp of grated parmesan
- ½ onion
- ½ celery stick
- 1 sprig of marjoram
- 17 oz of mussels
- 17 oz of clams
- 1 garlic clove
- 1 tbsp of minced parsley
- 1 tomato
- ½ cup of white wine
- 4 tbsp of extra virgin olive oil
- salt
- pepper
- 1 carrot
- 1 bay leaf

**Prep:** Knead the flour with 2 eggs, a pinch of salt and slowly add in water. Roll out the dough into a thin layer, cover it with a cloth and let it rest with a cloth for 30 minutes.
Chop the onion, garlic, celery, carrot and marjoram. Peel the tomato and gut it and add the bay leaf; add in the fish and let it cook for 10 minutes. Take the fish pulp and chop it with the marjoram, 2 eggs, parmesan and then add a pinch of salt and pepper. Keep the cooking broth.
Divide the dough in half, lay one on a surface and spoon the filling at ¾ inch apart, then cover with the other layer. Cut out squares around the filling with a rolling dough cutter and let rest for 2/3 hours.
In a pan on high heat, put in the shellfish and allow it to open, when they are ready finely chop them.
Sizzle in some oil the minced garlic, mussels, clams and ½ cup of white wine. Add some broth if needed. Dice the tomato and add it in. adjust salt and pepper to taste.
Cook the ravioli a little at a time in boiling salted water. Strain them when they start to float and season with the fish sauce.

**Nutrition:** Calories 360; Carbs 42.1 g; Protein 18.9 g; Fat 12.7 g

## 368. Linguine with Squid

**Prep time:** 10 minutes  
**Servings:** 6  
**Cook time:** 10 minutes

**Ingredients:**
- 17 oz of linguine
- 2,6 lbs of squid
- Parsley
- Pepper
- Salt
- 3 tbsp of dry white wine
- 2 garlic cloves
- 6 oz of oil

**Prep:** Clean, wash and dice the squid.
Sizzle the garlic in some oil, when it starts to brown add the squid, pepper, wine and some of the parsley. Cover the pot and let it cook, stirring at times. Add the remaining parsley and after few minutes turn off the heat. Cook the linguine *al dente*, season in a

casserole with some of the squid sauce and stir it on the heat for few minutes. Serve the pasta still hot and steamy, with a side of the remaining sauce.

### 369. Puttanesca Linguine

**Prep time: 20 minutes**  
**Servings: 6**

**Cook time: 20 minutes**

**Ingredients:**
- 21 oz of linguine
- 17 oz of can tomatoes
- Oregano
- Pepper
- Salt
- ½ cup of capers
- Minced hot pepper
- 3 garlic cloves
- Olive oil
- 5 tbsp of anchovies in oil
- 1 cup of black olives

**Prep:** Sizzle the garlic in a pot with some oil, when it browns remove it, add the tomatoes, the olives with no pit, oregano, hot pepper and washed capers. When the cooking is done, add the minced anchovies and parsley; let the heat on for a few minutes and then add salt to taste.
Cook the linguine in boiling salted water, strain them *al dente* and season with the sauce. Serve the pasta while still hot.

**Nutrition:** Calories 470.1; Carbs 75.4 g; Protein 14.6 g; Fat 12.6 g

### 370. Spaghetti with Anchovies and Capers

**Prep time: 30 minutes**  
**Servings: 6**

**Cook time: 15 minutes**

**Ingredients:**
- 17 oz of spaghetti
- 8 anchovies
- 1 tbsp of capers
- ½ garlic clove
- 1 tbsp of fresh parsley
- 4 tbsp of extra virgin olive oil
- 2 tbsp of butter
- 3 tomatoes
- salt
- pepper

**Prep:** Peel and gut the tomatoes. Remove the bones from the anchovies and wash them under running water, then let them dry. Chop the anchovies, capers, the garlic clove and parsley. Sizzle on a medium heat the crushed tomato pulp. Do not let the sauce get to a boil but let it thicken. Cook the spaghetti in boiling salted water. Drain it when it is ready (better *al dente*) and season with the sauce.

**Nutrition:** Calories 540; Carbs 89.4 g; Protein 14.1 g; Fat 11.7 g

### 371. Spaghetti with Squid

**Prep time: 20 minutes**  
**Servings: 6**

**Cook time: 1 hour**

**Ingredients:**
- 17 oz spaghetti
- 14 oz of squid
- 5 tomatoes
- 5 tbsp of olive oil
- 1 tbsp of minced parsley
- 1 garlic clove
- ½ onion
- ½ cup of white wine
- salt
- pepper

**Prep:** Peel and gut the tomatoes. Mince the garlic and onion. Clean the quid by removing the skin, ink blatter, eyes, the bone and wash under running water. Slice it in strips.
Sizzle the garlic and onion in oil, add the squid, tomato pulp and mix. Let it cook with a lid on for 45 minutes. Add some wine and salt and pepper.
Boil the water for the pasta and add in the spaghetti. Cook them *al dente*, then strain them and season with the sauce.

**Nutrition:** Calories 583; Carbs 73.3 g; Protein 24.5 g; Fat 21.3 g

### 372. Tagliatelle au gratin with Asparagus

**Prep time: 30 minutes**  
**Servings: 6**

**Cook time: 30 minutes**

**Ingredients:**
- 17 oz of flour
- 2 eggs
- 21 oz of asparagus

- 6 tbsp of extra virgin olive oil
- ½ celery stick
- 1 onion
- 1 tbsp of parsley
- 1 cup of white wine
- 33 oz of milk
- ½ cup of grated pecorino
- Vegetable broth
- salt
- pepper

**Prep:** Knead the flour with eggs and a pinch of salt. Add some water if needed to reach a soft and smooth dough., then roll it out with a rolling pin and let it rest for 30 minutes covered by a cloth. Roll the dough and start slicing the tagliatelle not wider then ¼ inch. Let them dry out.
Mince the onion and celery stick then sizzle them in a pan with the oil.
Cook the asparagus for 3 minutes in boiling water and divide the tips from the stems. Add the tips to the pan and deglaze with the wine. Add the milk and salt and pepper.
Cook the tagliatelle with the seasoning. Pour everything in a tray and add plenty of grated pecorino. Bake in the oven at 375° F per 5 minutes.

**Nutrition:** Calories 365; Carbs 71.4 g; Protein 15.3 g; Fat 9.8 g

## 373. Tagliatelle with Chickpeas and Potatoes

**Prep time: 1 night and 30 minutes**
**Servings: 6**

**Cook time: 25 minutes**

**Ingredients:**
- 17 oz of tagliatelle
- 17 oz of chickpeas
- 1 bay leaf
- 2 sage leaves
- 2 potatoes
- 6 tbsp of extra virgin olive oil
- 1 minced garlic clove
- Chopped celery, carrot and onion
- 1 tbs of minced rosemary
- 1 tbsp of minced parsley
- salt
- pepper

**Prep:** Soak the chickpeas in water and some baking soda overnight. The next day rinse them and boil them with the sage and bay leaves. Later add in the potatoes. Drain the chickpeas, peel and dice the potatoes. Season the remaining chickpeas in a pan with the minced celery, carrot and onion and let cook for 5 minutes. Add everything to the chickpea cream, the potatoes and add salt and pepper. Cook the tagliatelle al dente, strain and pour them into the pan with the sauce. Complete the seasoning with a drizzle of oil.

**Nutrition:** Calories 262; Carbs 41.3 g; Protein 18.8 g; Fat 2.3 g

## 374. Tortiglioni with Peppers and Guanciale

**Prep time: 20 minutes**
**Servings: 6**

**Cook time: 25 minutes**

**Ingredients:**
- 17 oz of tortiglioni
- 14 oz of yellow pepper
- 3 tbsp of pork guanciale
- 2 tbsp of butter
- 3 tbsp of olive oil
- 4 basil leaves
- 2 garlic cloves
- pepper
- salt

**Prep:** Mince the basil leaves and garlic cloves. Cut the pepper into 3 pieces and remove the stem and seeds, roast it in a pan until it is easy to remove the skin. Cut it in strips and dice the guanciale. Sizzle the garlic, basil and guanciale into oil and butter, then add the pepper and mix. Add salt and pepper and leave on the heat for 10 minutes.
Cook the tortiglioni in boiling water with salt, strain and season with the sauce.

**Nutrition:** Calories 397; Carbs 73.5 g; Protein 10.3 g; Fat 6.9 g

## 375. Spaghetti Flan

**Prep time: 30 minutes**
**Servings: 6**

**Cook time: 50 minutes**

**Ingredients:**
- 17 oz of spaghetti
- 14 oz of ripe tomatoes
- 1 anchovy
- butter
- 1 cup of canned tuna
- 4 tbsp of olive oil
- 6 tbsp of grated parmesan
- breadcrumbs
- 20 green olives
- salt and pepper

**Prep:** Mince the olives and fillet the anchovy. Peel and gut the tomatoes.

Cook the spaghetti al dente in boiling water with salt, strain and move them into a bowl. In a pan heat up the oil and add the chopped tomatoes, olives, tuna and the anchovy. Adjust salt and pepper to taste and let it all boil for 20 minutes on a low heat. Add the grated parmesan and ground pepper. Keep mixing and let it on the heat for another 10 minutes.
Grease a tray and sprinkle some breadcrumbs in. lay in the tray the seasoned spaghetti and bake at 375°F. Wait until a crust forms on top, then serve hot.

**Nutrition:** Calories 471; Carbs 72.7 g; Protein 13.4 g; Fat 14.1 g

### 376. Chestnut Flour Trofie

**Prep time:** 90 minutes  
**Cook time:** 10 minutes  
**Servings:** 6

**Ingredients:**
- 8 oz of wheat flour
- 10 oz of chestnut flour
- 1 ball of brewer's yeast
- salt

**Prep:** Combine the two types of flour and on the side melt the yeast. Knead the flour with the yeast, a pinch of salt and warm water. Let the dough rest for one hour covered by a cloth. Take some pieces in your hands, roll them and brush them against a surface to achieve small spirals of dough. Cook the pasta in boiling water with salt. Once it starts floating, strain and season as preferred.

**Nutrition:** Calories 567; Carbs 41.2 g; Protein 20.7 g; Fat 35.3 g

### 377. Rice with Milk and Chestnuts

**Prep time:** 1 night and 10 minutes  
**Cook time:** 3 hours  
**Servings:** 6 people

**Ingredients:**
- 17 oz of rice
- 1 ½ cup of dried chestnuts
- 33 oz of milk
- 1 tbsp of butter
- 3 tbsp of extra virgin olive oil
- ½ onion
- 1 sprig of parsley
- salt

**Prep:** Soak the chestnuts overnight.
Mince the onion and parsley. Drain the chestnuts and remove any leftover peel. In a pot pour 33 oz of milk and 17 oz of water, then add butter, some salt and the chestnuts. Cook for 2.5 hours and then add the rice, mix and let cook.
Sizzle the onion and parsley in the oil and pour them in the pot with the chestnuts when they are almost done cooking.
Mix well and serve while hot.

**Nutrition:** Calories 430 Kcal; Carbs 64.4 g; Protein 14.2 g; Fat 12.8 g

### 378. Pumpkin Rice

**Prep time:** 20 minutes  
**Cook time:** 60 minutes  
**Servings:** 6

**Ingredients:**
- 10 oz of rice
- 9 oz of fresh pumpkin
- 3 tomatoes
- 1 onion
- ¼ cup of butter
- 3 tbsp of extra virgin olive oil
- 33 oz of vegetable broth
- grated parmesan
- salt
- pepper

**Prep:** Peel and gut the tomatoes and chop the onion. Skin and gut the pumpkin and dice it. Sizzle the onion in some oil, then add the pumpkin cubes and mix. Let it cook for 10 minutes. Cut the tomatoes into cubes, add to the pan and adjust salt and pepper to taste. Let cook for 10 minutes, then add the broth. Wait 20 minutes, combine the rice, mix well and cook for 20 minutes.
Before serving, let some grated parmesan melt in.

**Nutrition:** Calories 543; Carbs 67.8 g; Protein 13 g; Fat 21.1 g

## 379. Rice with Dried Mushrooms and Anchovy Flavor

**Prep time:** 15 minutes  
**Servings:** 6  
**Cook time:** 30 minutes

**Ingredients:**
- 17 oz of rice
- 2 tbsp of butter
- 3 tbsp of extra virgin olive oil
- ½ onion
- 1 sprig of parsley
- ½ celery stick
- 1 carrot
- ¼ cup of dried mushrooms
- 1 anchovy
- 2 tbsp of grated parmesan
- pepper
- salt

**Prep:** mince half onion, a sprig of parsley, half celery stick, one carrot and rehydrate the mushrooms with water; fillet 1 anchovy. Sizzle in the oil and butter the onion, celery, carrot and parsley. Add the mushrooms, mix and let cook for few minutes. Add the anchovy fillet mashed with a fork. Mix and keep on a low heat. Boil the rice in water, halfway through the cook time, strain it and add it to the pan with the other ingredients. If the mixture is too dry, add some broth and keep mixing. Serve with some grated parmesan on top.

**Nutrition:** Calories 485; Carbs 48.4 g; Protein 11.1 g; Fat 21.8 g

## 380. Rice with Pesto

**Prep time:** 10 minutes  
**Servings:** 6  
**Cook time:** 30 minutes

**Ingredients:**
- 17 oz of rice
- 6 tbsp of Genovese pesto
- 2 tbsp of extra virgin olive oil
- 4 tbsp of grated parmesan
- salt

**Prep:** Cook the rice in hot water with salt. Strain it and while it is not completely cooked pour it into a bowl. Add plenty of pesto and grated cheese. Mix well and season before serving.

**Nutrition:** Calories 502 Kcal; Carbs 72.9 g; Protein 14.1 g; Fat 13.2 g

## 381. Rice, Tomatoes and Porcini Mushrooms

**Prep time:** 30 minutes  
**Servings:** 6  
**Cook time:** 1 hour

**Ingredients:**
- 17 oz of rice
- 4 fresh tomatoes
- 9 oz of porcini mushrooms
- 1 onion
- 1 garlic clove
- 3 basil leaves
- 1 tbsp of minced parsley
- 3 tbsp of extra virgin olive oil
- 3 tbsp of grated parmesan
- salt
- pepper
- ¾ cup of butter

**Prep:** Mine the onion and garlic and sizzle them in a pan with oil and 2 tbsp of butter. Mince the tomato pulp and add it to the other ingredients, add the basil leaves, salt and pepper. Let it all cook with a lid on for about 20 minutes on medium heat. Clean the mushrooms, slice them and add them to the pan with the minced parsley. Mix and let cook for one hour with a lid on. Cook the rice in hot water with salt, strain it and season with half of the sauce and 2 tbsp of butter and grated parmesan. Mix well and before serving, pour on top the remaining sauce.

**Nutrition:** Calories 551; Carbs 91.7 g; Protein 14.7 g; Fat 13.4 g

## 382. Spaghetti with Bacon

**Prep time:** 30 minutes  
**Servings:** 4  
**Cook time:** 10 minutes

**Ingredients:**
- 17 oz of spaghetti
- ½ cup of grated parmesan
- 1 ½ cup of sliced bacon
- 4 tbsp of olive oil
- Parsley
- 5 small onions
- Salt
- 3 garlic cloves

**Prep:** In a pan drizzle some oil and sizzle the chopped garlic and onions. Add the bacon and cook on a low heat. In a pot, cook the spaghetti in hot water with salt. Strain and add the bacon sauce. Serve by adding parmesan, some oil and parsley.

**Nutrition:** Calories 555; Carbs 72.1 g; Protein 20.3 g; Fat 19 g

## 383. Penne with Hot Salami

**Prep time:** 20 minutes  
**Servings:** 4  
**Cook time:** 30 minutes

**Ingredients:**
- 5 tbsp of olive oil
- 1 ¼ cup of hot salami
- 9 oz of potatoes
- 8 oz of spicy sausage
- ½ tbsp of paprika
- 1 garlic clove
- 4 sage leaves
- 10 oz of penne
- Salt
- 1 sprig of rosemary
- Fennel seeds

**Prep:** Peel, wash and cut the potatoes. Put them in a pot with cold water, bring to a boil and let it cook for 6 minutes. Put some salt in water and add the pasta, cooking it almost completely.
In a pan add 3 tbsp of oil, pressed garlic, fennel seeds, sage and rosemary.
Scramble the sausage and add it to the pan.
Add the strained cooked pasta in with the sausage. add salami, ½ tbsp of paprika and some cooking water. Add a drizzle of oil before serving.

**Nutrition:** Calories 679; Carbs 72.9 g; Protein 28.1 g; Fat 30.6 g

## 384. Penne with Basil

**Prep time:** 10 minutes  
**Servings:** 4  
**Cook time:** 15 minutes

**Ingredients:**
- 14 oz of penne
- ¾ cup of parmesan
- ¼ cup of basil
- 1 ½ cup of oil
- Pepper
- ½ cup of grated pecorino
- Salt
- 1 garlic clove

**Prep:** Mince the basil leaves after cleaning them with a dry cloth. Add them to an oven dish with cheese, garlic and oil while whisking with a fork, then let the mixture rest for one hour.
In a pot cook al dente the penne in boiling water with salt, strain and season with the sauce, mix well on very low heat for few minutes, bearing in mind not to let the cheese string too much.
Serve still hot and steaming.

## 385. Baked Gnocchi with Ragù and Mozzarella

**Prep time:** 20 minutes  
**Servings:** 4  
**Cook time:** 40 minutes

**Ingredients:**
- 2 lbs of gnocchi
- 2 lbs of canned tomatoes
- 7 oz of ground beef meat
- 7 oz mozzarella
- ½ cup of grated parmesan
- 1 basil leaf
- 4 tbsp of extra virgin olive oil
- Salt
- ½ onion

**Prep:** Heat up the oil in a pan, add the chopped onion, meat and cook until it becomes golden. Add the tomatoes and basil. Cook on a low heat for 30 minutes.
Cook the gnocchi in a pot full of water, strain them when they start floating. Dice the mozzarella.
Grease the oven dish with butter and layer alternating the gnocchi to the mozzarella. Cover the last layer with the sauce and sprinkle some parmesan. Cook for 5 minutes in the oven at 375°F.

**Nutrition:** Calories 780; Carbs 100.1 g; Protein 33.9 g; Fat 26.6 g

## 386. Saffron Risotto

**Prep time:** 5 minutes  
**Servings:** 4  
**Cook time:** 25 minutes

**Ingredients:**
- 1 tsp of saffron in pistils
- 1 ¼ cup of butter
- ¾ cup of grated parmesan
- Water
- Salt
- 10 oz of rice
- 1 onion
- ½ cup of white wine
- 33 oz of vegetable broth

**Prep:** Soak the saffron pistils overnight. Chop the onion and move it to a pan with ½ cup of melted butter on a low heat. Add the broth and cook for 10-15 minutes. Pour and toast the rice for 3-4 minutes and deglaze it with the wine. Cook the rice by adding the broth and closing the lid again.
Pour the water with saffron 5 minutes before the end of the cook time. When it is all cooked, add the salt and melt in the butter and parmesan.

**Nutrition:** Calories 620; Carbs 67.9 g; Protein 14.1 g; Fat 31.6 g

### 387. Pasta with Fresh Pecorino and Ragù

**Prep time:** 10 minutes  **Cook time:** 70 minutes
**Servings:** 4

**Ingredients:**
- 14 oz of penne pasta
- ½ pack of saffron
- 9 oz of fresh pecorino
- 8 oz of sausage
- 1 cup of minced beef meat
- 1 onion
- 2 tbsp of olive oil
- 10 oz of tomato sauce
- Salt

**Prep:** Mince the onion and sizzle it for 10 minutes with some oil, the sausage and ground meat. Add the tomato sauce and mix. Cook the sauce for around 1 hour, and adjust salt to taste.
Cook the pasta in a pot full of water with salt, strain it and keep aside 2 cups of cooking water in a bowl. Add to it the grated pecorino and add the sauce to the pasta.
Mix and serve.

**Nutrition:** Calories 728; Carbs 86 g; Protein 35.5 g; Fat 39.6 g

### 388. Pasta with Eggplant and Ricotta

**Prep time:** 20 minutes  **Cook time:** 60 minutes
**Servings:** 4

**Ingredients:**
- 11 oz of pennette pasta
- 17 oz of eggplant
- 2 garlic cloves
- 1 fresh basil leaf
- 8 oz of aged ricotta
- Extra virgin olive oil
- 29 oz of rice red tomatoes
- salt

**Prep:** Wash the tomatoes and cut them into quarters.
In a pan sizzle the garlic with some oil, add the tomatoes and cook for 20 minutes on a low heat, covering it with a lid. Move the ingredients to a vegetable grinder to achieve a pulp. Pour the pulp in a casserole and keep cooking for 10-15 minutes.
Cook the pasta in a pot full of water with salt.
Meanwhile, wash and remove the tips of the eggplants, slice them and fry in hot oil a 340°F.
Serve the pasta onto a serving plate, add on the eggplants, grated ricotta and basil.

**Nutrition:** Calories 593; Carbs 64 g; Protein 21.2 g; Fat 34.6 g

### 389. Risotto with Apples

**Prep time:** 15 minutes  **Cook time:** 30 minutes
**Servings:** 4

**Ingredients:**
- 8 oz of rice
- 3 tbsp of butter
- vegetable broth
- Extra virgin olive oil
- 3 apples
- 2 cups of white wine
- 3 tbsp of grated parmesan
- 1 lemon
- salt

**Prep:** Peel 2 apples, dice them and boil in water with the peel of 1 lemon for 5-6 minutes. Strain and collect the cooking water. Heat up some olive oil in a pan, add the rice and toast it for few minutes. Deglaze with wine, add the salt, pour the broth and let cook for 20 minutes.
Add the apples 10 minutes before the end of the cook time and slowly pour in the cooking water from the apples.
Add the butter and grated cheese; mix and serve with some dices of raw apple and lemon slices.

**Nutrition:** Calories 563; Carbs 82 g; Protein 12.2 g; Fat 14.6 g

### 390. Pasta with Olive Pesto

**Prep time:** 20 minutes  
**Servings:** 4  

**Cook time:** 10 minutes

**Ingredients:**
- 14 oz of short pasta
- 10 oz of green olives
- 1 garlic clove
- 1 sprig of basil
- 1 sprig of parsley
- 1 cup of grated parmesan
- 4 tbsp of extra virgin olive oil
- Salt and pepper

**Prep:** Remove the pits from the olives and blitz them with the basil, parsley, garlic, parmesan and oil.
Cook the pasta in a pot full of water with salt. Strain the pasta and add the olive pesto.

**Nutrition:** Calories 564; Carbs 68.7 g; Protein 15.9 g; Fat 25 g

### 391. Risotto with Red Radish

**Prep time:** 10 minutes  
**Servings:** 4  

**Cook time:** 30 minutes

**Ingredients:**
- 10 oz of rice
- 8 oz di radicchio rosso
- 1 onion
- 1 cup of walnuts
- 33 oz of vegetable broth
- Extra virgin olive oil
- 3 tbsp of grated parmesan

**Prep:** Heat up the broth and leave it on the stove.
In a pan, sizzle the onion with some oil. Cut the radish into small pieces and add it to the onion. Let it cook for 15 minutes. Add the rice and broth and mix. Let the rice cook and occasionally add the broth. When it has finished cooking, add the grated cheese.

**Nutrition:** Calories 488; Carbs 49.5 g; Protein 12.2 g; Fat 25.6 g

### 392. Bucatini with Leaf Broccoli

**Prep time:** 15 minutes  
**Servings:** 6  

**Cook time:** 15 minutes

**Ingredients:**
- 17 oz of bucatini
- 2 garlic cloves
- Salt
- 1 piece of hot pepper
- 24 oz of cleaned leaf broccoli
- 1 cup of olive oil
- 3 tbsp of grated pecorino
- 3 tbsp of grated parmesan

**Prep:** Cook the broccoli for 5 minutes in a pot of boiling water; strain without pressing them.
Sizzle the onion and garlic together, remove the latter once it is browned, add the cooked broccoli with salt and hot pepper, let the cooking finish on a medium heat.
Bring the cooking water from the broccoli to a boiling again, cook the bucatini in it, strain and move them to the pan with the vegetables, let the flavor develop and keep stirring for few minutes on low heat.
Turn off the heat and add cheese. Carefully mix.
Serve the bucatini while hot and steaming.

### 393. Bucatini with Tomato and Ricotta

**Prep time:** 10 minutes  
**Servings:** 6  

**Cook time:** 15 minutes

**Ingredients:**
- 21 oz of bucatini
- 2 lbs of canned tomatoes
- 16 oz of ricotta
- ½ cup of lard
- Salt and pepper
- 1 piece of onion
- 3 tbsp of oil
- 5 basil leaves
- 2 tbsp of grated parmesan

**Prep:** Brown the onion into the oil, pour in the tomatoes, pepper, salt and lard. add the basil at the end.
Cook the bucatini al dente in a pot of water with salt, strain and season with the remaining sauce, ricotta cream and grated parmesan.
Serve and provide a side of grated parmesan.

### 394. Bucatini with Hot Peppers

**Prep time:** 10 minutes  
**Servings:** 6  
**Cook time:** 25 minutes

**Ingredients:**
- 17 oz of bucatini
- Sweet green peppers
- 26 oz of canned tomatoes
- 1 ½ cup of olive oil
- Salt and pepper
- Basil
- 2 garlic cloves

**Prep:** Wash and drain the peppers, then sizzle them in a pan with some oil. Strain them once they are cooked and put them aside. Sizzle the garlic into the same pan and remove it when it becomes golden, pout salt, pepper, strained tomatoes and cook on a high heat for 20 minutes.
Add the peppers and basil and leave on the heat for few minutes.
Cook the bucatini and move them to the pan to absorb the flavor for few minutes on a low heat.
Serve still hot and steamy.

### 395. Bucatini with Eggs and Asparagus

**Prep time:** 15 minutes  
**Servings:** 4  
**Cook time:** 15 minutes

**Ingredients:**
- 14 oz of bucatini
- 17 oz of asparagus
- 2 eggs
- ½ cup of grated parmesan
- Extra virgin olive oil
- Salt and pepper

**Prep:** Cook the asparagus in a pan with how water and some oil.
Meanwhile cook the pasta in a pot full of water with salt. Strain in and season with the asparagus and a cup of cooking water. Add the beaten eggs, sprinkle the cheese and pepper. Combine well and serve.

**Nutrition:** Calories 540; Carbs 69.5 g; Protein 18.2 g; Fat 20.6 g

### 396. Macaroni with Sausage and Ricotta

**Prep time:** 10 minutes  
**Servings:** 4  
**Cook time:** 15 minutes

**Ingredients:**
- 10 oz of macaroni
- 1 ½ cup of sausage
- 1 ½ cup of ricotta
- salt

**Prep:** Scramble the sausage and let it cook into a pan with some water. Put the sausage in a bowl and mix it with the ricotta.
Cook the pasta in a pot full of water with salt. Strain and season with the sauce.

**Nutrition:** Calories 742; Carbs 65.7 g; Protein 28.2 g; Fat 40.4 g

### 397. Macaroni with Sausage and Tomato Sauce

**Prep time:** 5 minutes  
**Servings:** 6  
**Cook time:** 40 minutes

**Ingredients:**
- 21 oz of bucatini
- ½ cup of lard
- 2 lbs of sausage
- 1 cup of white wine
- 1 cup of oil
- 1 1/2 cup of tomato concentrate
- ½ cup of lard
- Pepper or hot pepper
- Grated parmesan
- Salt

**Prep:** Cook the bucatini and season them with the sausage sauce (see recipe of sausages with tomatoes), sprinkle on plenty of grated cheese.
In a pot full of water, cook the bucatini, strain and pour them in the sauce. Carefully mix for few minutes on a low heat.
Serve the pasta still hot and steamy.

### 398. Chickpea and Broccoli Soup

**Prep time:** 10 minutes  
**Servings:** 4  
**Cook time:** 40 minutes

**Ingredients:**
- 8 oz of chickpeas
- 17 oz of broccoli
- Extra virgin olive oil
- salt

**Prep:** Soak tithe chickpeas overnight. Then cook then in salted water for 40 minutes until you reach a cream consistency. Meanwhile cook the broccoli in a pan with some water. Add the chickpeas and season with a drizzle of oil.

**Nutrition:** Calories 224; Carbs 28.7 g; Protein 17.9 g; Fat 8.5 g

### 399. Zucchini and Pumpkin Flowers Soup

**Prep time:** 15 minutes  
**Servings:** 4  
**Cook time:** 30 minutes

**Ingredients:**
- 8 oz of zucchini and its flowers
- 1 onion
- 1 1/2 cup of canned tomatoes
- 1 1/2 cup of grated pecorino
- 2 potatoes
- Extra virgin olive oil
- salt

**Prep:** Peel the potatoes and dice them. Cut into chunks the zucchini and pumpkin flowers, mince the onion. Cook everything in a pan with tomatoes, oil, some water and a pinch of salt. Halfway through add the pecorino.

**Nutrition:** Calories 235; Carbs 18.1 g; Protein 8.9 g; Fat 4.5 g

### 400. Oven Backed Pasta with Cauliflower

**Prep time:** 30 minutes  
**Servings:** 4  
**Cook time:** 25 minutes

**Ingredients:**
- 11 oz of penne
- 14 oz of cauliflowers
- Breadcrumbs
- 1 garlic clove
- Extra virgin olive oil
- ½ cup of grated pecorino
- Salt and pepper

**Prep:** Cut the cauliflower in chunks and cook them into hot water. Drain them and in the same water cook the pasta *al dente*. In a pan, add the cauliflowers with some oil, a garlic clove and then the breadcrumbs.
Combine well the pasta with the vegetables and place everything in an oven dish with a dash of pecorino.
Preheat the oven at 375°F and let cook au gratin for 15 minutes before serving.

**Nutrition:** Calories 524; Carbs 72.1 g; Protein 20.9 g; Fat 24.5 g

### 401. Pasta with Sardines

**Prep time:** 15 minutes  
**Servings:** 4  
**Cook time:** 20 minutes

**Ingredients:**
- 14 oz of bucatini
- 8 oz of canned tomatoes
- 1 garlic clove
- 1 onion
- 10 oz sardine fillet
- Extra virgin olive oil
- parsley
- Salt and pepper

**Prep:** Brown the garlic in a pan with some oil. Remove it and add the onion finely chopped. Combine the sardines and minced tomatoes. Add salt and pepper.
Cook the pasta in a pot full of water. Strain and season it with the sauce.

**Nutrition:** Calories 571; Carbs 58.7 g; Protein 37.9 g; Fat 21.7 g

### 402. Pasta with Cauliflowers

**Prep time:** 5 minutes  
**Servings:** 6  
**Cook time:** 30 minutes

**Ingredients:**
- 14 oz of mixed pasta
- 28 oz of cleaned cauliflower
- 1 cup of oil
- 2 garlic cloves
- Salt
- 1 sprig of parsley
- 1 tsp of tomato concentrate
- ½ cup of minced lard
- Hot red Pepper
- Pepper

**Prep:** Sizzle the garlic, lard with oil in a pan.
Remove the browned garlic, then add the wash cauliflower into chunks, salt, pepper, tomato concentrate and a piece of hot pepper.
Cover the casserole and let simmer on medium heat occasionally stirring until the cauliflower has soften up.
Cook the pasta halfway through and then move it int the cauliflower mixture with some hot water if needed, then add the parsley.
Serve the thickened soup and the pasta still hot.

### 403. Pasta with Lentils

**Prep time:** 20 minutes  
**Servings:** 6  
**Cook time:** 50 minutes

**Ingredients:**
- 17 oz of small tubetti pasta
- 10 oz of lentils
- 3 garlic cloves
- Parsley
- Salt
- Pepper
- 4 canned tomatoes
- 1 cup of olive oil
- 1 tsp of tomato concentrate

**Prep:** cook the lentils in water on a low heat.
Without removing the lentils, take as much water out as possible once they have softened up.
Cover immediately with new boiling water.
Add the oil, garlic, tomato concentrate, pepper and canned tomatoes; let it slowly cook on a low heat for about half an hour.
Separately cook the pasta; strain it and move into the lentils to let them finish cooking, add the parsley.
Serve very hot with no broth.

**Nutrition:** Calories 552.6; Carbs 81.6 g; Protein 22.5 g; Fat 16.4 g

### 404. Pasta with Pecorino and Eggs

**Prep time:** 15 minutes  
**Servings:** 6  
**Cook time:** 15 minutes

**Ingredients:**
- 21 oz of small pasta
- 1 1/2 cup of lard or butter
- Basil
- 1 tbsp of grated pecorino
- Salt
- Pepper
- 4 tbsp of grated parmesan
- 3 eggs

**Prep:** In a pot cook the pasta in water with salt.
Meanwhile, beat the eggs with some salt and melt the lard in a casserole on low heat.
Strain pasta *al dente*, move them in the lard and add the grated cheese, pepper, basil and eggs. Gently mix everything.
Move on low heat again for about 1 minute, let the eggs start to cook and then serve.

### 405. Pasta with Beans and Sausages

**Prep time:** 25 minutes  
**Servings:** 6  
**Cook time:** 2 hours

**Ingredients:**
- 14 oz of mixed pasta
- 10 oz of beans
- 2 sausages
- Parsley
- Salt
- Pepper
- 67 oz of water
- ¾ cup of lard

**Prep:** Cook the beans in a pot full of water, covered with a lid on low heat. Crush the garlic cloves, parsley and lard until they make a thick cream; move to an oven dish and grill for 5 minutes.
Add the tomatoes, emptied from the seeds and cut in pieces, the scrambled sausage; cook for about

15 minutes on low heat.
When the beans are ready, pour the sauce in the pot with the cooking water and let simmer for another
30 minutes. Pour the pasta in the beans, raise the heat again to bring to a boil and add some water to keep the cooking going if needed.

### 406. Spaghetti with Dried Tomatoes

**Prep time:** 15 minutes  
**Servings:** 4  

**Cook time:** 10 minutes

**Ingredients:**
- 14 oz of spaghetti
- 1 cup of pickled dried tomatoes
- 2 garlic cloves
- Basil
- Oregano
- 1 hot pepper
- Parsley
- salt

**Prep:** Roughly chop the tomatoes and heat them in a pan with some of the oil, the garlic cloves, basil, hot pepper minced and a pinch of salt.
Cook the pasta in a pot full of water with salt. Strain it and season with the prepared sauce, add the minced oregano and parsley.

**Nutrition:** Calories 579; Carbs 84.7 g; Protein 17.9 g; Fat 17.1 g

### 407. Salad's Spaghetti

**Prep time:** 10 minutes  
**Servings:** 4  

**Cook time:** 15 minutes

**Ingredients:**
- 14 oz of spaghetti
- 21 oz of tomatoes
- 1 garlic clove
- Basil
- Oregano
- Parsley
- Olive oil
- Pepper
- Salt

**Prep:** Peel and gut the tomatoes, cut them in quarters and let them drip of half an hour.
Place them in a bowl, season with garlic, salt, herbs, pepper and oil, cover and let rest.
Cook the pasta *al dente* in a pot full of water with salt. Strain and pour immediately in the bowl with the tomatoes and gently mix.
Serve still hot and steamy.

### 408. Spaghetti Primavera

**Prep time:** 20 minutes  
**Servings:** 12  

**Cook time:** 30 minutes

**Ingredients:**
- 2lbs of spaghetti
- 3 ripe tomatoes
- 10 green peppers
- 3 big peppers
- 1 garlic clove
- 8 oz of grated parmesan.
- Basil
- Olive oil
- Pepper
- Salt

**Prep:** dice the peppers, slice the tomatoes and peppers. Mince with your fingers the basil. Pour everything in a bowl with pepper, salt, grated parmesan and oil. Let it rest for at least 3 hours.
Cook the pasta *al dente* in a pot full of water with salt, strain and add the sauce on top.
Serve still hot and steamy.

### 409. Penne with Sausage and Olives

**Prep time:** 15 minutes  
**Servings:** 4  

**Cook time:** 20 minutes

**Ingredients:**
- 14 oz of penne
- 1 1/2 cup of sausage
- 8 oz black olives
- 8 oz of canned tomatoes
- Oregano
- Extra virgin olive oil
- salt

**Prep:** cut the sausage into chunks and let it sizzle in a pan with some oil. Add the chopped tomatoes and olives, add salt, a pinch of oregano and mix.
Cook the pasta in a pot full of water with salt, strain and add the sauce on top.

**Nutrition:** Calories 635; Carbs 69.7 g; Protein 23.8 g; Fat 27.1 g

### 410. Penne with Potatoes and Eggs

**Prep time:** 15 minutes  
**Servings:** 4  

**Cook time:** 30 minutes

**Ingredients:**
- 10 oz of penne
- 9 oz of potatoes
- 4 eggs
- ½ cup of grated pecorino
- Extra virgin olive oil
- salt

**Prep:** Peel the potatoes, cut them in pieces and fry into hot oil. Add some salt and let them dry on some paper towel.
On the side, cook the pasta in a pot full of water with salt, strain it and put it in a casserole with hot oil. Combine the beaten eggs flavored with salt, pepper and pecorino. Add the potatoes and serve.

**Nutrition:** Calories 440; Carbs 78.1 g; Protein 10.9 g; Fat 9.1 g

### 411. Pasta with Potatoes and Zucchinis

**Prep time:** 15 minutes  
**Servings:** 4  

**Cook time:** 25 minutes

**Ingredients:**
- 10 oz of penne
- 2 potatoes
- 8 oz of zucchinis
- ½ of pecorino
- 8 oz of canned tomatoes
- 2 basil leaves
- Oregano
- Extra virgin olive oil
- salt

**Prep:** Peel the potatoes and slice them as well as the zucchinis. Peel the tomatoes and cut them in pieces. Cook the pasta in a pot full of water with salt, strain and put in an oven dish. Keep layering the potatoes, zucchini, tomatoes, minced basil and oregano, salt and pepper.
Drizzle some water on and bake in a preheated oven at 350°F for 25 minutes.

**Nutrition:** Calories 651; Carbs 79.1 g; Protein 29 g; Fat 18.1 g

### 412. Rice Balls in Broth

**Prep time:** 30 minutes  
**Servings:** 4  

**Cook time:** 40 minutes

**Ingredients:**
- 8 oz of rice
- 3 eggs
- ½ cup of grated pecorino
- Parsley
- Chicken broth
- Salt and pepper

**Prep:** cook the rice in a pot full of water, strain it and blend in the eggs, pecorino, parsley, salt and pepper. Shape some balls, put them in the broth and cook for about 10 minutes, serve immediately after.

**Nutrition:** Calories 451; Carbs 25.1 g; Protein 21 g; Fat 18.1 g

### 413. Rigatoni with Beans and Mushrooms

**Prep time:** 15 minutes  
**Servings:** 4  

**Cook time:** 15 minutes

**Ingredients:**
- 10 oz of rigatoni
- 1 cup of kidney beans
- 1 1/2 cup of porcini mushrooms
- Parsley
- 1 garlic clove
- Olive oil
- salt

**Prep:** Soak the beans overnight. Cook them into hot water with salt, stir often.

Wash the mushrooms, cut them in pieces and cook in a pan with garlic and oil for 5-10 minutes, then add the beans. Cook the pasta in a pot full of water with salt, strain and add it to the mushrooms and beans. Season with some oil and minced parsley.

**Nutrition:** Calories 710; Carbs 61.6 g; Protein 21.9 g; Fat 31.1 g

### 414. Rice with Fennel and Ricotta

**Prep time: 10 minutes**  **Cook time: 20 minutes**
**Servings: 4**

**Ingredients:**
- 11 oz of rice
- salt
- 1 1/2 cup of sheep ricotta
- 17 oz of fennel

**Prep:** wash mince and cook the fennel in plenty of hot water with salt. Strain and put aside saving the cooking water in which the rice will be cooked. When it is ready, add it to the ricotta and fennel and serve.

**Nutrition:** Calories 471; Carbs 66.6 g; Protein 9.9 g; Fat 27.1 g

### 415. Fusilli with Meatalls

**Prep time: 30 minutes**  **Cook time: 40 minutes**
**Servings: 4**

**Ingredients:**
- 11 oz of fusilli
- 9 oz of ground pork meat
- 1 basil leaf
- 8 oz of tomato sauce
- 1 cup of breadcrumbs
- ½ cup of grated parmesan
- garlic
- Parsley
- Olive oil
- Salt pepper

**Prep:** In a bowl mix the meat, breadcrumbs, parmesan, minced garlic and parsley, salt and pepper, and roll some balls to fry into hot oil.
In a pan, prepare the tomato sauce with a pinch of salt and basil. Add the meatballs and keep cooking for 20 minutes.
On a side, cook the pasta in a pot full of water with salt, strain and season with the meatball sauce.

**Nutrition:** Calories 720; Carbs 79.6 g; Protein 28.8 g; Fat 32.8 g

### 416. Vegetable Tagliatelle

**Prep time: 20 minutes**  **Cook time: 20 minutes**
**Servings: 4**

**Ingredients:**
- 11 oz of tagliatelle
- 1 cup of grilled peppers
- 1 cup zucchini
- 8 oz of tomatoes
- 2 onions
- 2 garlic cloves
- Oregano
- Olive oil
- Salt and pepper

**Prep:** Slice the onion and let it sizzle in a pan with a drizzle of oil and garlic. Wash and slice the zucchini and tomatoes, add them to the pan with the peppers. Add salt and pepper and cook for 15 minutes.
On the side, cook the pasta in a pot full of water with salt, strain and season with the vegetables and oregano.

**Nutrition:** Calories 542; Carbs 82 g; Protein 17 g; Fat 18 g

### 417. Tagliatelle with Chickpeas and Dried Peppers

**Prep time: 10 minutes**  **Cook time: 10 minutes**
**Servings: 4**

**Ingredients:**
- 9 oz of chickpeas
- 10 oz of tagliatelle
- 2 bay leaves
- 5 dried peppers
- Olive oil
- salt

**Prep:** Cook the chickpeas in a pot with water and bay leaves.

On the side, cook the pasta in a pot full of water with salt, strain and add the chickpeas.
Meanwhile, sizzle the tomatoes in a pan with some oil for 5 minutes. Pour them on the tagliatelle and chickpeas and serve immediately.

**Nutrition:** Calories 539; Carbs 71 g; Protein 18 g; Fat 19.2 g

### 418. Pasta with Onion Sauce

**Prep time:** 15 minutes  
**Servings:** 4

**Cook time:** 20 minutes

**Ingredients:**
- 10 oz of red onions
- 8 oz of canned tomatoes
- 1 cup of aged ricotta
- 11 oz of penne
- Red Pepper
- Salt
- Extra virgin olive oil

**Prep:** Slice the onions and cook them into the olive oil add in some water occasionally.
On the side prepare the tomato sauce and add the onions when they are ready. Add the red pepper.
Cook the pasta in a pot full of water with salt, strain it and season with the onion sauce and grated ricotta.

**Nutrition:** Calories 702; Carbs 82 g; Protein 29.2 g; Fat 28.9 g

### 419. Pasta with Bacon and Vegetables

**Prep time:** 15 minutes  
**Servings:** 4

**Cook time:** 20 minutes

**Ingredients:**
- 11 oz of short
- 8 oz of canned tomatoes
- 1 1/2 cup of bacon
- 1 eggplant
- 2 green peppers
- 1 basil leaf
- Extra virgin olive oil
- salt

**Prep**: Cook the chopped tomatoes and peppers into the oil, add the diced eggplants.
After 15 minutes, add bacon in chunks and basil.
Meanwhile, cook the pasta in a pot full of water with salt, strain it and season with the sauce.

**Nutrition:** Calories 418; Carbs 68 g; Protein 17.6 g; Fat 8.9 g

### 420. Asparagus Soup

**Prep time:** 15 minutes  
**Servings:** 4

**Cook time:** 15 minutes

**Ingredients:**
- 17 oz of asparagus
- 8 slices of toasted bread
- Meat broth
- 4 eggs
- 2 garlic cloves
- ½ cup of grated pecorino
- Parsley minced
- Olive oil
- Salt and pepper

**Prep:** Clean the asparagus, cut them into pieces and cook in a pan with some oil and garlic. After few minutes, add the broth and keep cooking for 10 minutes.
When they are ready, add the eggs, pecorino, parsley, salt and pepper. Mix carefully and portion into the plates where you have previously laid the bread.

**Nutrition:** Calories 451; Carbs 34 g; Protein 13.1 g; Fat 21.9 g

### 421. Potato and Broccoli Soup

**Prep time:** 15 minutes  
**Servings:** 5

**Cook time:** 15 minutes

**Ingredients:**
- 2 lbs of potatoes
- Pepper
- Olive oil
- 3.3 lbs of broccoli not cleaned yet
- 2 garlic cloves
- Hot pepper
- Parsley

**Prep:** dice the potatoes and cover them in water with salt.
Clean and boil the broccoli halfway through.
In a pan, sizzle the oil and garlic, add the potatoes with water and let cook until the potatoes are soft.
Combine the strained broccoli, parsley, hot pepper and the other herbs. Mix and let cook for 10 minutes, adding a little water if needed.
Serve the soup still hot but with little broth.

## 422. Beet Soup

**Prep time:** 10 minutes  
**Servings:** 4  
**Cook time:** 10 minutes

**Ingredients:**
- 4 precooked beets
- 2 onions
- 4 eggs
- Minced Parsley
- 8 toasted bred slices
- ½ cup of grated pecorino
- Olive oil
- Salt and pepper

**Prep:** Peel and slice the beets and cooked onions. Blend them, put them in a casserole, add some hot water, parsley and beaten eggs.
Season with some oil, pepper and pecorino.
Serve in the plates where you previously laid the bread.

**Nutrition:** Calories 155; Carbs 12.9 g; Protein 4 g; Fat 9.2 g

## 423. Chicory and Potatoes Soup

**Prep time:** 15 minutes  
**Servings:** 4  
**Cook time:** 30 minutes

**Ingredients:**
- 11 oz of chicory
- 2 potatoes
- 1 1/2 cup of pork guanciale
- Olive oil
- salt

**Prep:** Wash the chicory, peel the potatoes and dice them. Pour everything in a pot where the guanciale has been sizzled with some oil.
Once it is cooked, add salt and serve.

**Nutrition:** Calories 515; Carbs 52.9 g; Protein 19.1 g; Fat 31.2 g

## 424. Spicy Fettuccine

**Prep time:** 5 minutes  
**Servings:** 6  
**Cook time:** 10 minutes

**Ingredients:**
- 17 oz of fettuccine
- Red hot peppers
- extra virgin olive oil
- Salt
- 2 garlic cloves

**Prep:** Cook the pasta in a pot full of water with salt and strain it. Meanwhile, sizzle the garlic and hot peppers with some oil in a pan. Pour the mixture in a blender and blitz to reach a creamy consistency. Season the fettuccine with the cream.

**Nutrition:** Calories 462; Carbs 66 g; Protein 8.2 g; Fat 17 g

## 425. Spicy Gnocchi

**Prep time:** 5 minutes  
**Servings:** 6  
**Cook time:** 5 minutes

**Ingredients:**
- 2lbs of gnocchi
- 6 oz of bacon cubes
- ½ cup of olive oil
- 1 hot pepper
- 1 tbsp of parsley
- salt

**Prep:** In a pan, sizzle the bacon with oil, add the hot pepper and minced parsley.
Meanwhile, cook the gnocchi in a pot full of water with salt. Strain and pour into the pan, mix with the sauce and serve hot.

**Nutrition:** Calories 895; Carbs 72.9 g; Protein 43 g; Fat 27.3 g

### 426. Macaroni with Artichokes and Clams

**Prep time:** 25 minutes  
**Servings:** 6  
**Cook time:** 30 minutes

**Ingredients:**
- 17 oz of macaroni
- Olive oil
- 2 minced garlic cloves
- 2 cook artichokes sliced
- 6 peeled and chopped tomatoes
- 17 oz of clams
- 2 tbsp of minced parsley
- 2 basil leaves
- Black Pepper

**Prep:** In a pan, sizzle the garlic with the oil. Add the artichokes, tomatoes and mix well while leaving them to cook. After 10 minutes, add the clams (previously soaked in water for a few hours), basil, parsley and pepper. Cook until the clams open. Meanwhile, cook the pasta in a pot full of water with salt, strain it and pour it in the pan with the sauce.
Combine and serve.

**Nutrition:** Calories 390; Carbs 16.3 g; Protein 17 g; Fat 9.2 g

### 427. Macaroni, Bacon and Mozzarella

**Prep time:** 15 minutes  
**Servings:** 6  
**Cook time:** 15 minutes

**Ingredients:**
- 17 oz of macaroni
- 3/4 cup of bacon in cubes
- ½ hot pepper
- 6 minced canned tomatoes
- 1 ¼ cup of mozzarella cubes
- Salt and pepper

**Prep:** In a pan, sizzle the minced hot pepper with the oil. Add the bacon, tomatoes, salt and pepper and let them cook for 15 minutes.
Meanwhile, cook the pasta in a pot full of water with salt, strain and season with the mozzarella and sauce.

**Nutrition:** Calories 570; Carbs 66.3 g; Protein 25 g; Fat 22.2 g

### 428. Spaghetti with Crab Sauce

**Prep time:** 20 minutes  
**Servings:** 6  
**Cook time:** 55 minutes

**Ingredients:**
- 17 oz of spaghetti
- 14 oz of peeled minced tomatoes
- 6 crabs
- 3 pressed garlic cloves
- extra virgin olive oil
- ½ of white wine
- Hot pepper
- Salt and pepper

**Prep:** In a pan sizzle the garlic in some oil. Add the tomatoes, crabs and wine; add salt and pepper, mix and carry on with the cooking until the sauce thickens.
Meanwhile, cook the pasta in a pot full of water with salt, strain and season with the sauce and minced hot peppers.

**Nutrition:** Calories 822; Carbs 96.8 g; Protein 20.2 g; Fat 27.5 g

### 429. Tagliatelle with Frog Sauce

**Prep time:** 20 minutes  
**Servings:** 6  
**Cook time:** 25 minutes

**Ingredients:**
- 21 oz of tagliatelle
- 30 of cleaned frogs
- 1 ½ cups of boiled potatoes
- Olive oil
- 4 tomatoes
- ½ cup of white wine
- 2 tbsp of minced parsley
- 2 garlic cloves
- Salt and pepper
- Hot pepper

**Prep:** Marinate the frogs with salt and pepper.

In a pan sizzle the minced garlic and parsley with some oil, then add the hot peppers and tomatoes. After 5 minutes, combine the diced potatoes and frogs. Add salt and pepper, cover with a lid and let cook on a low heat.
Cook the pasta in a pot full of water with salt, strain and season with the sauce.

### 430. Tagliatelle with Mushroom Ragù

**Prep time:** 20 minutes   **Cook time:** 20 minutes
**Servings:** 6

**Ingredients:**
- 17 oz of tagliatelle
- 1 onion
- 1 carrot
- 1 celery stick
- 9 oz of minced beef meat
- 8 oz chopped sausage
- 2 cloves
- ½ cup of dried mushrooms
- 3 tbsp of grated pecorino
- salt

**Prep:** In a pan, sizzle the carrot, onion and celery with the minced meat and sausage. add the cloved, mix and let the flavor develop. Add the mushrooms, previously soaked, and keep cooking.
Cook the pasta in a pot full of water with salt, strain and season with the sauce with grated pecorino.

**Nutrition:** Calories 504; Carbs 51.8 g; Protein 24.3 g; Fat 22.5 g

### 431. Baked Tagliatelle

**Prep time:** 20 minutes   **Cook time:** 20 minutes
**Servings:** 6

**Ingredients:**
- 17 oz of tagliatelle
- Grated parmesan
- 3 tbsp of butter
- 1 cup of ragù

**Prep:** Cook the pasta in a pot full of water with salt, strain and season with butter and freshly grated cheese.
Pour the tagliatelle in a doughnut stamp, cover with half cup of ragù, add more grated cheese and punt in the oven (preheated at 350°F) let cook for 20 minutes. Serve hot.

**Nutrition:** Calories 827; Carbs 56 g; Protein 26.8 g; Fat 47.5 g

### 432. Pasta with Scallion Sauce

**Prep time:** 30 minutes   **Cook time:** 5 minutes
**Servings:** 6

**Ingredients:**
- 17 oz of short pasta
- 1 1/2 cup of peas
- 4 minced scallions
- 1 tsp of tomato concentrate
- 8 oz of raw ham
- 1 cup cup of white wine
- Butter and oil
- ½ fresh lettuce
- 1 tbsp of grated parmesan
- Salt and pepper

**Prep:** Sizzle the minced scallions in oil and butter, add salt and then wine. Let the wine evaporate, then add the tomato concentrate and boiled peas, previously cooked and cooled down.
Add the sliced lettuce, when the peas are almost cooked add salt and pepper.
On the side sauté the ham with some butter and oil.
Cook the pasta *al dente* and combine it to the pan with the sauce, add the ham and grated parmesan.

**Nutrition:** Calories 554; Carbs 76 g; Protein 21.9 g; Fat 19 g

### 433. Dogtooth Violet with Sausage

**Prep time:** 20 minutes   **Cook time:** 1 hour
**Servings:** 6

**Ingredients:**
- 17 oz of sausage
- 17 oz dogtooth violet
- 1 cup of white wine
- 2 tbsp of tomato concentrate
- 1 cup of fresh milk
- Butter and oil

- *Grated parmesan*
- *Salt and pepper*

**Prep:** Sizzle the onion in butter and oil in a pan. Add the sausage in pieces and let it cook. Pour the wine when the sausage is cooked and crispy and let deglaze. Add the milk, tomato concentrate, cook on low heat at add salt and pepper.
Cook the pasta in a pot full of water with salt, move to the pan with parmesan, the sausage sauce and a cup of cooking water.

**Nutrition:** Calories 804; Carbs 87 g; Protein 34 g; Fat 62.1 g

## 434. Tagliatelle Pie

**Prep time: 30 minutes**  **Cook time: 20 minutes**
**Servings: 6**

**Ingredients:**
- *10 oz of tagliatelle*
- *1 cup of meat ragù*
- *2 tbsp of butter*
- *1 egg*

**For the pastry:**
- *¾ cup of butter*
- *½ pack of yeast*
- *14 oz of flour*
- *½ cup of white wine*
- *Salt*
- *3 eggs*
- *¾ cup of sugar*

**Prep:** In a big mixing bowl, combine the flour, eggs and sugar with butter (already melted), and mix; add the yeast, white wine and a little salt, stir until you reach a smooth and soft dough.
Cook the pasta *al dente* in a pot full of water with salt, strain it, pour in a bowl with the ragù and grated cheese. Add one egg and mix.
In a tray greased with butter, roll about half of the pastry; stuff with the cooked and seasoned tagliatelle, cover with the other half of the pastry layer, seal the edges and put in the oven (preheated at 350°F) for few minutes. Serve as soon as it is out of the oven.

**Nutrition:** Calories 845; Carbs 84.1 g; Protein 63 g; Fat 56.3 g

## 435. Tagliatelle with Tomato and Parsley

**Prep time: 15 minutes**  **Cook time: 10 minutes**
**Servings: 6**

**Ingredients:**
- *2 tbsp of minced parsley*
- *Olive oil*
- *6 tomatoes*
- *2 garlic cloves*
- *Salt and pepper*

**Prep:** In a pan, sizzle the garlic and parsley; when the garlic had browned add the tomato pulp, salt and pepper. Let it cook on low heat.
Cook the pasta in a pot full of water with salt, strain *al dente* and pour in the pan, then mix.
Sautè in the pan to let the flavor sink in and serve still hot.

**Nutrition:** Calories 415; Carbs 72 g; Protein 11.1 g; Fat 8.3 g

## 436. Tagliatelle with Bean Cream

**Prep time: 35 minutes**  **Cook time: 25 minutes**
**Servings: 6**

**Ingredients:**
- *9 oz of tagliatelle*
- *21 oz of kidney beans*
- *¼ cup of butter*
- *17 oz canned tomatoes*
- *1 chopped onion*
- *½ cup of broth*

**Prep:** Cook the beans in a pot full of water with salt.
In a pan sizzle the onion in butter; add the tomatoes and broth and mix with a wooden spoon. Pour in 2/3 of the beans; blend the remaining amount, add the cream to the sauce and keep mixing for 5 minutes, add the salt.
Cook the pasta in a pot full of water with salt, strain *al dente* and season with the bean sauce. Serve hot.

**Nutrition:** Calories 392; Carbs 88 g; Protein 14.4 g; Fat 62.1 g

### 437. Tagliatelle with Walnut Sauce

**Prep time:** 10 minutes  
**Cook time:** 20 minutes  
**Servings:** 6

**Ingredients:**
- 3 tbs of butter
- 12 walnuts
- Salt
- 1 garlic clove

**Prep:** Boil the walnuts for few minutes.
Dry with a cloth, mash in a mortar with the garlic and create a cream, add butter in.
Cook the pasta in a pot full of water with salt, strain al dente and season with the walnut sauce previously made. Serve hot.

**Nutrition:** Calories 821; Carbs 75.4 g; Protein 20.3 g; Fat 42 g

### 438. Cannelloni

**Prep time:** 1h 30min  
**Cook time:** 50 minutes  
**Servings:** 6

**Ingredients:**

For the dough:
- 5 eggs
- 17 oz of flour

For the seasoning:
- ¼ cup of butter
- 1 egg
- 1 ¼ cup of ground veal meat
- nutmeg
- 8 oz of ground pork meat
- Tomato sauce
- ¾ cup of grated parmesan

For the béchamel:
- 33 oz of milk
- 1 cup of butter
- Salt
- 1 cup of flour
- nutmeg

For cooking:
- 8 oz of grated parmesan
- Butter

**Prep:** On a chopping board, lay the flout and make a well, add the eggs. Knead to achieve a smooth and firm dough; cover and let rest for at least one hour.
Prepare the seasoning: warm up the butter in a casserole, add the two meat types and cook for few minutes; turn down the heat and add the egg, grated cheese, nutmeg and salt.
For the béchamel: melt the butter in a casserole on a low heat, add the flour and mix with a wooden spoon; pour in the warm milk; add flavor with the nutmeg, add salt and cook for few minutes.
Take out the dough, roll it into a thin pastry with a rolling pin and cut into rectangular shapes.
Boil one piece at the time in salted water, strain and lay on a cloth to dry out. Fill each pastry with some meat filling, then roll them and lay onto a tray with some pieces of butter, one next to another; pour the tomato sauce, then some of the besciamella, sprinkle some grated cheese and bake in the oven at 350°F for 40 minutes. Serve while hot.

**Nutrition:** Calories 864; Carbs 58.1 g; Protein 38.2 g; Fat 54.3 g

### 439. Cabbage Tortelli

**Prep time:** 60 minutes  
**Cook time:** 5 minutes  
**Servings:** 6

**Ingredients:**

For the dough:
- 5 eggs
- Salt
- 17 oz di flour

For the filling:
- 1 ¼ cup of bacon
- 2 eggs
- Salt
- Nutmeg
- 3 tbsp of butter
- 3 lbs of savoy cabbage
- 1 ½ cup of parmesan

**For the seasoning:**
- *Grated parmesan*
- *4 tbsp of butter*

**Prep:** Wash the cabbage, boil it in salted water, strain, squeeze the excess water and chop.
On a chopping board, place the flour and make a well; add the eggs, salt and knead until the dough is smooth and firm. Let rest for few hours and cover with a bowl.
For the filling: mix the cabbage with the eggs, grated cheese, salt and nutmeg; mix with a wooden spoon.
Take out the dough, roll it in a thin pastry with a rolling pin. Cut out some squares; place a tbsp of filling in and cover with another layer, seal the edges. Let them dry on a chopping board with flour on the bottom.
Cook the tortelli in a pot full of water with salt, strain when they start to float and season with melted butter and grated cheese.

**Nutrition:** Calories 658; Carbs 68.7 g; Protein 28.2 g; Fat 34.2 g

## 440. Tortelli with Apple Filling

**Prep time: 1 hour**
**Servings: 6**

**Cook time: 10 minutes**

**Ingredients:**
**For the dough:**
- *4 eggs*
- *14 oz of flour*

**For the filling:**
- *8 oz of ricotta*
- *1 egg*
- *4 tbsp of grated parmesan*
- *24 oz of apple*
- *4 crushed amaretti*

**For the seasoning:**
- *Grated parmesan*
- *Butter*

**Prep:** On a chopping board place the flour and make a well, add the eggs and knead to reach a smooth and firm dough. Let rest for some hours. Roll out the dough with a rolling pin and cut out some squares.
Wash the apples, dry them and bake for 15-20 minutes. Let cool down. Mix in a bowl the pulp with the ricotta, egg, crushed amaretti and grated cheese.
Fill the pastries with the filling, scoop it into the pastry squares, fold and seal the edges.
Cook the tortelli in a pot full of water with salt, strain when they start floating. Season with melted butter and grated parmesan. Serve hot.

**Nutrition:** Calories 614; Carbs 69 g; Protein 18.2 g; Fat 21.3 g

## 441. Tortelloni with Ricotta and Parsley

**Prep time: 20 minutes**
**Servings: 6**

**Cook time: 20 minutes**

**Ingredients:**
**For the dough:**
- *4 eggs*
- *14 oz of flour*

**For the filling:**
- *2 eggs*
- *Salt*
- *14 oz of fresh ricotta*
- *1 tbsp of parsley*
- *4 tbsp of grated parmesan*

**For the seasoning:**
- *Grated parmesan*
- *Black truffle*
- *Melted butter*

**Prep:** In a bowl, combine the ricotta, parmesan, eggs and minced parsley. Mix with a wooden spoon. Let the mixture rest.
Meanwhile, pour the flour on a surface and make a well, add the eggs, knead carefully to reach a smooth and firm dough. Let rest for one hour, roll with a rolling pin to make a thin pastry. Cut into squares, add some filling in the middle, fold and seal the edges.
Cook the tortelloni al dente, strain when they start to float. Season with cheese and melted butter, cover with thin truffle scales.

**Nutrition:** Calories 627; Carbs 70 g; Protein 20.2 g; Fat 17.3 g

### 442. Onion Soup

**Prep time:** 5 minutes  
**Servings:** 4  

**Cook time:** 20 minutes

**Ingredients:**
- 2 onions
- Olive oil
- 8 bread slices
- Grated pecorino to taste (optional)

**Prep:** Cut the onions into very thin slices and place them in a casserole, add the oil, water and salt. Cover with a lid and cook on low heat for 20-30 minutes.

**Nutrition:** Calories 157; Carbs 10 g; Protein 3.2 g; Fat 9.3 g

### 443. Barley and Endive Soup

**Prep time:** 5 minutes  
**Servings:** 4  

**Cook time:** 2 hours

**Ingredients:**
- ¾ cup of barley
- 3 endive stems
- 1 egg
- ½ cup of milk
- 33 oz of water
- nutmeg
- ½ cup of butter

**Prep:** Cook the barley in a casserole with water and some salt. Mix and let cook on low heat for at least 2 hours. Then add the endive making sure it is well cleaned. Remove from the heat and add 1 beaten egg, water down with milk, a pinch of nutmeg and butter. Combine well and serve.

**Nutrition:** Calories 386; Carbs 33 g; Protein 13 g; Fat 20.6 g

### 444. Pork Meat Soup

**Prep time:** 5 minutes  
**Servings:** 4  

**Cook time:** 2 hours

**Ingredients:**
- 10 oz pork loin
- 2 sausages
- 8 oz of broccoli
- 8 slices of toasted bread
- 1 tbsp of grated parmesan
- pepper

**Prep:** In a large casserole, boil the pork meat and sausages on low heat for about one hour so make some broth. Remove the meat, cut it in pieces and put it back into the broth.
In another casserole, boil the broccoli in salted water and add them to the meat when they are cooked. Pour into the plates with bread slices on the bottom, sprinkle some parmesan and serve.

**Nutrition:** Calories 648; Carbs 11 g; Protein 59.6 g; Fat 38 g

### 445. Peas Soup

**Prep time:** 10 minutes  
**Servings:** 4  

**Cook time:** 30 minutes

**Ingredients:**
- 8 oz of peas
- 8 oz of pasta for soups (like quadrucci)
- 1 onion
- Extra virgin olive oil
- 1 carrot
- 1 celery stick
- Parsley
- 2 tbsp of tomato sauce
- Grated parmesan
- Salt and pepper

**Prep:** Finely chop and sizzle the onion in some oil together with the carrot, celery and parsley. Let brown and add the tomato sauce, salt and pepper. Let cook on low heat for 10-15 minutes and then pour in the peas, keep cooking for another 10 minutes. Add the pasta, carefully mix and add some hot water if needed. Finish cooking and serve with grated parmesan.

**Nutrition:** Calories 351; Carbs 41 g; Protein 19.8 g; Fat 15 g

## 446. Crab Soup

**Prep time:** 40 minutes  
**Servings:** 6  
**Cook time:** 30 minutes

**Ingredients:**
- 4 tbsp of olive oil
- 4 lbs of crab
- ¼ cup of tomato sauce
- Salt and pepper
- 6 garlic cloves
- 1 cup of red wine

**Prep:** Clean the crab, remove the legs, gills and top shell. Wash them carefully. Put them in a pot, sprinkle some salt and pepper, pour the oil and add the tomato sauce and red wine. Let boil for few minutes. Pour one cup of water and let it evaporate. Serve the crab aside the sauce.

**Nutrition:** Calories 221; Carbs 10.2 g; Protein 24 g; Fat 5.1 g

## 447. Maltagliati with Beans and Chestnuts

**Prep time:** 10 minutes  
**Servings:** 6  
**Cook time:** 25 minutes

**Ingredients:**
- 21 oz of yellow flour
- 9 oz di wheat flour
- 8 oz of beans
- 2 lbs of chestnuts
- salt

**Prep:** Combine the two types of flour add boiling water and a pinch of salt. Roll the pastry with a rolling pin, cut out in squares and let dry out on a cloth with flour on the bottom.
Bake the chestnuts, shell and peel them.
Pour 1 gallon of water in a pot. Add the cooked chestnuts and beans. Let them boil to reach an even mixture (frequently mix a wooden spoon). Dip the dough squares in the hot water and let them cook for 15 minutes.

**Nutrition:** Calories 650, Carbs 75.4 g, Protein 24.6 g, Fat 33.4 g

## 448. Polenta

**Prep time:** 20 minutes  
**Servings:** 6  
**Cook time:** 40 minutes

**Ingredients:**
- 750 g of corn flour
- Salt
- 118 oz of water

**Prep:** Boil the water in a pot add salt and dust the flour. Vigorously mix with a wooden spoon. Cook for 40 minutes and keep mixing.

**Nutrition:** Calories 483.4, Carbs 101.7 g, Protein 12.2 g, Fat 3.1 g

## 449. Polenta with Cauliflower

**Prep time:** 15 minutes  
**Servings:** 6  
**Cook time:** 40 minutes

**Ingredients:**
- Polenta (see recipe n. 420)
- 17 oz of savoy cabbage

**Prep:** Prepare the polenta. Meanwhile, cook the cabbage in a pan with garlic, salt and oil. Season the polenta with the cabbage and serve still hot and steamy.

**Nutrition:** Calories 580, Carbs 101 g, Protein 14.1 g, Fat 3.4 g

## 450. Polenta with Figs

**Prep time:** 10 minutes  
**Servings:** 6  

**Cook time:** 40 minutes

**Ingredients:**

- Polenta (see recipe n. 420)
- 1 ¾ cup of dried figs

**Prep:** Prepare the polenta. When there are 15 minutes left to the cook time, add the figs in chunks. Mix for the remaining 15 minutes to complete cooking.
Serve hot and steamy.

**Nutrition:** Calories 634, Carbs 104 g, Protein 15.1 g, Fat 10.7 g

## 451. Balsamic Vinegar Risotto

**Prep time:** 5 minutes  
**Servings:** 6  

**Cook time:** 15 minutes

**Ingredients:**
- 15 oz of rice
- 1 chopped onion
- ¾ cup of butter
- 4 tbsp of grated parmesan
- 1 cup of red wine
- 2 tbsp of balsamic vinegar
- ½ cup of hot broth

**Prep:** in a pan sizzle the onion in the butter. Pour in the rice and cover with broth. Bring to a boil and stir frequently with a wooden spoon. After 10 minutes pour the red wine and let deglaze. Add the grated cheese. Before serving pour some balsamic vinegar then enjoy.

**Nutrition:** Calories 586, Carbs 68 g, Protein 13.2 g, Fat 31.9 g

## 452. Spaghetti with Eggplant

**Prep time:** 20 minutes  
**Servings:** 6  

**Cook time:** 20 minutes

**Ingredients:**
- 14 oz of spaghetti
- 14 oz of eggplants
- Salt and pepper
- ½ cup of broth
- 2 tbsp of olive oil
- ¾ cup of butter
- 1 cup of white wine

**Prep:** Remove the stem and the tip from the eggplant and peel it.
Dice, add the salt and let rest for about one hour.
In a pan sizzle the eggplants with oil and butter; add the wine and let deglaze. Add the broth, adjust salt and pepper to taste and let cook on low heat.
Cook the penne in boiling water with salt, strain and season with the sauce.

**Nutrition:** Calories 382, Carbs 69.7 g, Protein 9 g, Fat 7.1 g

## 453. Spaghetti with Anchovies

**Prep time:** 20 minutes  
**Servings:** 6  

**Cook time:** 10 minutes

**Ingredients:**
- 17 oz of spaghetti
- 18 anchovies
- Salt and pepper
- 4 tbsp of butter

**Prep:** Rinse the anchovies under running water, remove the spine, head and tail. Mince and season with soften butter.
Cook the spaghetti in boiling water with salt, strain *al dente* and season with the anchovies. Sprinkle some pepper and serve.

**Nutrition:** Calories 442, Carbs 67.7 g, Protein 24 g, Fat 12.3 g

## 454. Chickpeas Soup

**Prep time:** 5 minutes  
**Servings:** 6  
**Cook time:** 1 hour e 20 minutes

**Ingredients:**
- 2 minced garlic cloves
- Salt
- 42 oz chickpeas
- 1 tbsp of dried mushrooms
- 3 tbsp of olive oil

**Prep:** Soak the mushrooms in warm water. Drain them after few hours.
In a pan sizzle the minced garlic with the oil. Pour 88 oz of water with salt, add the chickpeas and let simmer on low heat. After 1 hour add the mushrooms, mix and allow to finish cooking. Serve the soup still hot and steamy.

**Nutrition:** Calories 354, Carbs 47 g, Protein 19.2 g, Fat 11.5 g

## 455. Rice with Eggs

**Prep time:** 5 minutes  
**Servings:** 4  
**Cook time:** 1 hour

**Ingredients:**
- 9 oz of rice
- Peel of 1 lemon
- 67 oz of broth
- 3 eggs
- Grated parmesan

**Prep:** Pour the broth in a pot; when it is boiling add the rice. Let cook. Meanwhile, in a bowl whip the eggs with the lemon zest and then add the rice. Mix and finish cooking. Serve with a dust of grated parmesan.

**Nutrition:** Calories 482, Carbs 66 g, Protein 28.1 g, Fat 13.2 g

## 456. Garlic Soup

**Prep time:** 10 minutes  
**Servings:** 4  
**Cook time:** 30 minutes

**Ingredients:**
- ½ onion
- extra virgin olive oil
- 2 garlic cloves
- 1 1/2 cup of broth
- Salt and pepper
- 6 slices of toasted bread
- Grated parmesan

**Prep:** In a pan add the chopped garlic and onion in some oil. Cover in broth and let it boil. After 15 minutes turn off the heat and sift. Adjust salt and pepper to taste.
Pour the soup in some bowls to serve, add as a side the toasted bread. Sprinkle grated parmesan and enjoy.

**Nutrition:** Calories 152 kcal, Carbs 6.8 g, Protein 2.1 g, Fat 10.1 g

## 457. Mantis Shrimp Soup

**Prep time:** 30 minutes  
**Servings:** 6  
**Cook time:** 40 minutes

**Ingredients:**
- 42 oz of mantis shrimp
- Olive oil
- 1 chopped onion
- 6 tomatoes
- Salt and pepper
- 2 garlic cloves
- 2 tbsp of parsley

**Prep:** pour some oil in a pan. Slice the garlic and place in the pan with the onion when the oil has heated up. Dry and gut the tomatoes and place them into the pan. Adjust salt and pepper to taste and cook on a low heat.
Clean the mantis shrimp, remove the legs, head and shell. Add them to the pan, finish cooking with a lid on. Sprinkle some chopped parsley.

**Nutrition:** Calories 225 kcal, Carbs 11.3 g, Protein 24.2 g, Fat 4.5 g

### 458. Beans Soup

**Prep time:** 10 minutes  
**Servings:** 6  
**Cook time:** 40 minutes

**Ingredients:**
- 1 1/4 cup of mashed lard
- 1 tbsp of parsley
- Olive oil
- Bread slices
- 28 oz of peeled beans
- Salt and pepper
- 2 garlic cloves

**Prep:** In a pot sizzle the chopped garlic parsley and lard. pour in 100 oz of water, add the beans cover with a lid and let cook on a low heat. Adjust salt and pepper to taste, mix and serve.

**Nutrition:** Calories 46.5, Carbs 7.4 g, Protein 2.2 g, Fat 0.5 g

### 459. Spinach Soup

**Prep time:** 20 minutes  
**Servings:** 6  
**Cook time:** 30 minutes

**Ingredients:**
- 28 oz of spinach
- 2 tbsp of butter
- 50 oz of broth
- Salt
- Toasted bread
- Nutmeg

**Prep:** Wash the spinach and cook in boiling water with salt; strain, squeeze and mince.
Melt the butter in a pan, sizzle the spinach for few minutes.
In a pot, heat up the broth, add the spinach and nutmeg. Let boil for about half an hour.
Serve the soup still hot and steamy.

**Nutrition:** Calories 205, Carbs 10.5 g, Protein 4.2 g, Fat 16.2 g

### 460. Avocado, Roasted Mushroom and Feta Spaghetti

**Prep Time:** 20 minutes  
**Serving:** 5  
**Cook Time:** 17 minutes

**Ingredients:**
- 12 oz. spaghetti
- 2 avocados, peeled and diced
- 10-15 white mushrooms, halved
- 1 cup feta, crumbled
- 2 tbsp. green olive paste

**Prep:** Wrap baking tray with baking paper and place mushrooms on it. Spray with olive oil and season with salt and black pepper to taste. Roast in a prepared oven to 375 F for 15 minutes.
In a big pot of boiling salted water, cook spaghetti following package's prep. Drain and set aside.
In a blender, combine lemon juice, 2 garlic cloves, olive paste and avocados and blend until smooth.
Combine pasta, mushrooms and avocado sauce. Sprinkle with feta cheese and serve immediately.

**Nutrition:** 278 Calories, 10 g Fat, 4 g Protein

### 461. Tomato, Arugula and Feta Spaghetti

**Prep Time:** 20 minutes  
**Serving:** 6  
**Cook Time:** 3 minutes

**Ingredients:**
- 12 oz. spaghetti
- 2 cups grape tomatoes, halved
- 1 cup fresh basil leaves, roughly torn
- 1 cup baby arugula leaves
- 1 cup feta, crumbled

**Prep:** In a huge saucepan with salted boiling water, cook spaghetti according to package prep. Drain and keep aside.
Return saucepan to medium heat. Add olive oil, 2 garlic cloves and tomatoes. Season with pepper and cook, tossing, for 1-2 minutes or until tomatoes are hot. Add spaghetti, basil and feta. Toss lightly for 1 minute. Sprinkle with arugula and serve.

**Nutrition:** 278 Calories, 15 g Fat, 3 g Protein

### 462. Zucchini Noodles

**Prep Time:** 10 minutes  
**Servings:** 2  

**Cook Time:** 11 minutes

**Ingredients:**
- 2 tablespoons extra-virgin olive oil
- 3 zucchinis, cut with a spiralizer
- 4 eggs
- A pinch of red pepper flakes
- 1 tablespoon basil, chopped

**Prep:** In a bowl, combine the zucchini noodles with the salt, pepper and the olive oil and toss well.
Grease a baking sheet with cooking spray and divide zucchini noodles into 4 nests on it.
Crack an egg onto each nest, sprinkle with salt, pepper and the pepper flakes on top and bake at 350 degrees F for 11 minutes.
Divide the mix between plates, sprinkle with basil and serve.

**Nutrition:** 296 Calories, 23 g Fat, 3.3 g Fiber

### 463. Halibut Soup

**Prep Time:** 10 minutes  
**Servings:** 4  

**Cook Time:** 13 minutes

**Ingredients:**
- 1 lb halibut, skinless, boneless, & cut into chunks
- 2 tbsp ginger, minced
- 2 celery stalks, chopped
- 1 carrot, sliced
- 1 onion, chopped
- 1 cup of water
- 2 cups fish stock
- 1 tbsp olive oil
- Pepper
- Salt

**Prep:** Add oil into the inner pot of instant pot and set the pot on sauté mode. Add onion and sauté for 3-4 minutes. Add ginger, water, celery, carrot, and broth and stir well.
Seal pot with lid and cook on high for 5 minutes. Once done, release pressure using quick release. Remove lid.
Add fish and stir well. Seal pot again and cook on high for 4 minutes.
Once done, release pressure using quick release. Remove lid.
Stir and serve.

**Nutrition:** Calories 458, Fat 99.6 g, Carbs 6.3 g, Protein 86,1 g

### 464. Tuna Whole Wheat Pasta

**Prep Time:** 10 minutes  
**Servings:** 6  

**Cook Time:** 5 minutes

**Ingredients:**
- 15 oz whole wheat pasta
- 2 tbsp capers
- 3 oz tuna
- 2 cups can tomatoes, crushed
- 2 anchovies
- 1 tsp garlic, minced
- 1 tbsp olive oil
- Salt

**Prep:** Add oil into the inner pot of instant pot and set the pot on sauté mode. Add anchovies and garlic and sauté for 1 minute. Add remaining ingredients and stir well. Pour enough water into the pot to cover the pasta. Seal pot with a lid and select manual and cook on low for 4 minutes.
Once done, release pressure using quick release. Remove lid.
Stir and serve.

**Nutrition:** Calories 339, Fat 6 g, Carbs 56.5 g, Protein 15.2 g

### 465. Tuna Risotto

**Prep Time:** 10 minutes  
**Servings:** 6  

**Cook Time:** 23 minutes

**Ingredients:**
- 1 cup of rice
- 1/3 cup parmesan cheese, grated
- 1 1/2 cups fish broth
- 1 lemon juice
- 1 tbsp garlic, minced
- 1 onion, chopped
- 2 tbsp olive oil
- 2 cups can tuna, cut into chunks
- Pepper
- Salt

**Prep:** Add oil into the inner pot of instant pot and set the pot on sauté mode. Add garlic, onion, and tuna and cook for 3 minutes. Add remaining ingredients except for parmesan cheese and stir well.
Seal pot with lid and cook on high for 20 minutes.
Once done, release pressure using quick release. Remove lid.
Stir in parmesan cheese and serve.

## 466. Barley and Chicken Soup

**Prep Time:** 10 minutes  
**Servings:** 6  
**Cook Time:** 50 minutes

**Ingredients:**
- 1 lb. chicken breasts, skinless, boneless and cubed
- 1 tbsp. olive oil
- Salt and pepper to the taste
- celery stalks, chopped
- carrots, chopped
- 1 red onion, chopped
- 6 cups chicken stock
- ½ cup parsley, chopped
- ½ cup barley
- 1 tsp. lime juice

**Prep:** Heat up a pot with the oil over medium high heat, add the chicken, season with salt and pepper, and brown for cook for 8 minutes.
Add carrots, onion, and the celery, stir and cook for 3 minutes more. Add the rest of the ingredients (except parsley), bring to a boil and cook over medium heat for 40 minutes.
Add the parsley, stir and divide the soup into bowls to serve.

**Nutrition:** Calories 311, Fat: 8.4 g, Carbs: 17.4 g, Protein: 22.3 g

## 467. Broccoli Pesto Spaghetti

**Prep Time:** 5 minutes  
**Servings:** 4  
**Cook Time:** 35 minutes

**Ingredients:**
- 8 oz. spaghetti
- 1-pound broccoli, cut into florets
- 2 tbsps. olive oil
- 4 garlic cloves, chopped
- 4 basil leaves
- 2 tbsps. blanched almonds
- lemon, juiced
- Salt and pepper to taste

**Prep:** For the pesto, combine the broccoli, oil, garlic, basil, lemon juice and almonds in a blender and pulse until well mixed.
Cook the spaghetti in a large pot of salty water for 8 minutes or until al dente. Drain well.
Mix the warm spaghetti with the broccoli pesto and serve right away.

## 468. Chicken Breast Soup

**Prep Time:** 5 minutes  
**Servings:** 4  
**Cook Time:** 4 hours

**Ingredients:**
- 3 chicken breasts, skinless, boneless, cubed
- 2 celery stalks, chopped
- 2 carrots, chopped
- 2 tablespoons olive oil
- red onion, chopped
- garlic cloves, minced
- cups chicken stock
- 1 tablespoon parsley, chopped

**Prep:** In your slow cooker, mix all the ingredients except the parsley, cover and cook on High for 4 hours.
Add the parsley, stir and ladle the soup into bowls.

**Nutrition:** Calories 445, Fat 21.1 g, Carbs 7.4 g, Protein 54,3 g

## 469. Courgette Risotto

**Prep Time:** 10 minutes  
**Servings:** 8  
**Cook Time:** 5 minutes

**Ingredients:**
- 2 tablespoons olive oil
- 4 cloves garlic, finely chopped
- pounds Arborio rice
- 6 tomatoes, chopped
- 2 teaspoons chopped rosemary
- 6 courgettes, finely diced
- ¼ cups peas, fresh or frozen
- 12 cups hot vegetable stock
- Salt to taste

- *Freshly ground pepper*

**Prep:** Place a large, heavy-bottomed pan over medium heat and add the oil to heated it. Add onion and sauté until translucent. Add the tomatoes and cook until soft. Add rosemary and rice and stir well. Add half of the broth and cook until dry.
Add remaining stock and cook for 3-4 minutes.
Add courgette and peas, salt and pepper to taste, and cook until rice is tender. Add also the basil.
Let it sit for 5 minutes.

**Nutrition:** Calories 406; Fat 5 g; Carbs 82 g; Protein 14 g

### 470. Creamy Chicken Soup

**Prep Time:** 10 minutes
**Servings:** 8

**Cook Time:** 1 hour

**Ingredients:**
- 2 cups eggplant, cubed
- Salt and pepper to the taste
- ¼ cup olive oil
- yellow onion, chopped
- tbsps. garlic, minced
- red bell pepper, chopped
- tbsps. hot paprika
- ¼ cup parsley, chopped
- 1 and ½ tbsps. oregano, chopped
- cups chicken stock
- 1 lb. chicken breast, skinless, boneless and cubed
- 1 cup half and half
- egg yolks
- ¼ cup lime juice

**Prep:** Heat up a pot with the oil over medium heat, add the chicken, garlic and onion, and brown for 10 minutes. Add the bell pepper and the rest of the ingredients except the half and half, egg, yolks, and the lime juice, bring to a simmer and cook over medium heat for 40 minutes.
In a bowl, combine the egg yolks with the remaining ingredients with 1 cup of soup, whisk well and pour into the pot.
Whisk the soup, cook for 5 minutes more, divide into bowls and serve.

**Nutrition:** Calories 312, Fat: 17.4 g, Carbs: 20.2 g, Protein: 15.3 g

### 471. Creamy Penne

**Prep Time:** 10 minutes
**Servings:** 4

**Cook Time:** 25 minutes

**Ingredients:**
- ½ cup penne, dried
- 9 oz. chicken fillet
- teaspoon Italian seasoning
- 1 tablespoon olive oil
- 1 tomato, chopped
- 1 cup heavy cream
- 1 tablespoon fresh basil, chopped
- ½ teaspoon salt
- oz. Parmesan, grated
- 1 cup water, for cooking

**Prep:** Pour water in the pan, add penne, and boil it for 15 minutes. Then drain water.
Pour olive oil in the skillet and heat it up.
Slice the chicken fillet and put it in the hot oil. Sprinkle chicken with Italian seasoning and roast for 2 minutes from each side. Then add fresh basil, salt, tomato, and grated cheese. Stir well.
Add heavy cream and cooked penne.
Cook the meal for 5 minutes more over the medium heat. Stir it from time to time.

**Nutrition:** Calories 388; Fat 23.4 g; Carbs 17.6 g; Protein 17.6 g

### 472. Fennel Wild Risotto

**Prep Time:** 5 minutes
**Servings:** 6

**Cook Time:** 35 minutes

**Ingredients:**
- 2 tablespoons extra virgin olive oil
- shallot, chopped
- garlic cloves, minced
- 1 fennel bulb, chopped
- 1 cup wild rice
- ¼ cup dry white wine
- cups chicken stock
- 1 teaspoon grated orange zest
- Salt and pepper to taste

**Prep:** Heat the oil in a heavy saucepan.
Add the shallot, garlic, and fennel and cook for a few minutes until softened. Add the rice and cook for another 2 minutes. Then add the wine, broth and orange zest, with salt and pepper to taste. Cook on low heat for 20 minutes.

**Nutrition**: Calories: 162; Fat: 2g; Protein: 8g; Carbs: 20g

### 473. Homemade Chicken Broth

**Prep Time:** 5 minutes  
**Servings:** 4  
**Cook Time:** 30 minutes

**Ingredients:**
- tablespoon olive oil
- 1 chopped onion
- chopped stalks celery
- chopped carrots
- 1 whole chicken
- 2+ quarts of water
- 1 tablespoon salt
- ½ teaspoon pepper
- 1 teaspoon fresh sage

**Prep:** Sauté vegetables in oil.
Add chicken and water and simmer for 2+ hours until the chicken falls off the bone. Keep adding water as needed.
Remove the chicken carcass from the broth, place on a platter, and let it cool. Pull chicken off the carcass and put it into the broth.
Pour broth mixture into pint and quart mason jars. Be sure to add meat to each jar.
Leave one full inch of space from the top of the jar or it will crack when it freezes as liquids expand. Place jars in freezer for up to a year.
Take out and use whenever you make a soup.

**Nutrition:** Calories: 213; Fat: 6 g; Carbs: 16 g; Protein: 22 g

### 474. Homemade Vegetable Broth

**Prep Time:** 5 minutes  
**Servings:** 4  
**Cook Time:** 30 minutes

**Ingredients:**
- tablespoon olive oil
- 1 chopped onion
- chopped stalks celery
- chopped carrots
- 1 head bok Choy
- 6 cups or 1 package fresh spinach
- 2+ quarts of water
- 1 tablespoon salt
- ½ teaspoon pepper
- 1 teaspoon fresh sage

**Prep:** Sauté vegetables in oil. Add water and simmer for 1 hour.
Keep adding water as needed.
Pour broth mixture into pint and quart mason jars.
Leave one full inch of space from the top of the jar or it will crack when it freezes as liquids expand. Place jars in freezer for up to a year.
Take out and use whenever you make a soup.

**Nutrition:** Calories: 140; Fat: 2 g; Carbs: 22 g; Protein: 47 g

### 475. Cauliflower Rice and Chipotle Chicken

**Prep Time:** 10 minutes  
**Servings:** 4  
**Cook Time:** 20 minutes

**Ingredients:**
- 1/3 cup of salsa
- quantity of 14.5 oz. of can fire-roasted diced tomatoes
- 1 canned chipotle pepper + 1 teaspoon sauce
- ½ teaspoon of dried oregano
- 1 teaspoon of cumin
- 1 ½ lb. of boneless, skinless chicken breast
- ¼ teaspoon of salt
- 1 cup of reduced-fat shredded Mexican cheese blend
- 4 cups of frozen riced cauliflower
- ½ medium-sized avocado, sliced

**Prep:** Combine the first ingredients in a blender and blend until they become smooth.
Place chicken inside your instant pot, and pour the sauce over it. Cover the lid and close the pressure valve.
Set it to 20 minutes at high temperature. Let the pressure release on its own before opening.
Remove the piece and the chicken and then add it back to the sauce.
Microwave the riced cauliflower according to the prep on the package.
Before you serve, divide the riced cauliflower, cheese, avocado, and chicken equally among the four bowls.

**Nutrition:** Calories: 287; Protein: 35 g; Carbs: 19 g; Fat: 12 g

### 476. Jalapeno Bacon Cheddar Soup

**Prep Time:** 10 minutes  
**Servings:** 5  
**Cook Time:** 50 minutes

**Ingredients:**
- 1/2 lb. Bacon (About 8 slices)
- 4 medium Jalapeno Peppers, diced
- 4 tbsp. Butter
- 3 cups Chicken Broth
- 1 tsp. Dried Thyme
- 1 tsp. Garlic Powder
- 1 tsp. Onion Powder
- 1/2 tsp. Celery Seed
- 1/2 tsp. Cumin
- 3/4 cup Heavy Cream
- 8 oz. Cheddar Cheese
- Salt and Pepper to Taste

**Prep:** Slice or cut bacon into 1-inch pieces. Place in a skillet and cook until all pieces are crispy.
Remove bacon, reserving as much bacon fat as possible in the skillet. Place bacon on paper towels to dry and crisp up.
Dice four jalapeno peppers. Cut them in half, then slice the half into half and dice. Season and sauté the jalapenos in the bacon grease until lightly browned. Remove jalapenos and preserve as much bacon grease as you can in the pan.
Place jalapenos on bacon to dry off.
In a food processor, process 8 ounces of cheddar cheese using the grating attachment. Set aside.
In a new pot, add bacon fat, stock, butter, and spices. Bring to a boil and reduce heat to simmer for 15 minutes.
Using an immersion blender, blend all ingredients. Add cream and cheese and season again with salt and pepper.
Add bacon and jalapeno to the soup and mix well. Let simmer for 5 minutes before serving.

## 477. Chicken Pasta

**Prep Time:** 10 minutes  
**Servings:** 4  
**Cook Time:** 17 minutes

**Ingredients:**
- 9 oz whole-grain pasta
- 3 chicken breasts, skinless, boneless, cut into pieces
- 1/2 cup olives, sliced
- 1/2 cup sun-dried tomatoes
- 1 tbsp roasted red peppers, chopped
- 14 oz can tomatoes, diced
- 2 cups marinara sauce
- 1 cup chicken broth
- Pepper
- Salt

**Prep:** Add all ingredients except whole-grain pasta into the instant pot and mix well.
Seal the pot with lid and cook on high for 12 minutes. Once done, allow the pressure to release naturally. Remove the lid.
Add pasta and stir well. Seal pot again and select manual with timer for 5 minutes.
Once done, allow to release pressure naturally for 5 minutes then release remaining using quick release. Remove lid.
Stir well and serve.

**Nutrition:** Calories 615 Fat 15.4 g Carbs 71 g Protein 48 g

## 478. Herb Risotto

**Prep Time:** 10 minutes  
**Servings:** 4  
**Cook Time:** 15 minutes

**Ingredients:**
- 2 cups of rice
- 2 tbsp parmesan cheese, grated
- 3.5 oz heavy cream
- 1 tbsp fresh oregano, chopped
- 1 tbsp fresh basil, chopped
- 1/2 tbsp sage, chopped
- 1 onion, chopped
- 2 tbsp olive oil
- 1 tsp garlic, minced
- 4 cups vegetable stock
- Pepper
- Salt

**Prep:** Add oil into the inner pot of instant pot and set the pot on sauté mode. Add onion and garlic and sauté for 2-3 minutes. Add remaining ingredients (except parmesan cheese and heavy cream) and stir well. Seal pot with lid and cook on high for 12 minutes.
Once done, allow to release pressure naturally for 10 minutes then release remaining using quick release. Remove lid.
Stir in cream and cheese and serve.

**Nutrition:** Calories 514 Fat 17.6 g Carbs 79.4 g Protein 8.8 g

## 479. Pasta with Vegetables

**Prep Time:** 10 minutes  
**Servings:** 4  
**Cook Time:** 4 minutes

**Ingredients:**
- 8 oz whole wheat penne pasta
- 1 tbsp fresh lemon juice
- 2 tbsp fresh parsley, chopped
- 1/4 cup parmesan cheese, grated
- 14 oz can tomatoes, diced
- 1/4 cup almonds slivered
- 1/2 cup prunes
- 1/2 cup zucchini, chopped
- 1/2 cup asparagus, cut into 1-inch pieces
- 1/2 cup carrots, chopped
- 1/2 cup broccoli, chopped
- 1 3/4 cups vegetable stock
- Salt and pepper

**Prep:** Add stock, pars, tomatoes, prunes, zucchini, asparagus, carrots, and broccoli into the instant pot and stir well.
Seal pot with lid and cook on high for 4 minutes.
Once done, release pressure using quick release. Remove lid.
Add remaining ingredients and stir well.

**Nutrition:** Calories 303 Fat 2.6 g Carbs 63.5 g Protein 12.8 g

### 480. Roasted Pepper Pasta

**Prep Time:** 10 minutes  
**Servings:** 6  

**Cook Time:** 13 minutes

**Ingredients:**
- 1 lb whole wheat penne pasta
- 1 tbsp Italian seasoning
- 4 cups vegetable broth
- 1 tbsp garlic, minced
- 1/2 onion, chopped
- 14 oz jar roasted red peppers
- 1 cup feta cheese, crumbled
- 1 tbsp olive oil
- Pepper
- Salt

**Prep:** Add roasted pepper into the blender and blend until smooth. Add oil into the inner pot of instant pot and set the pot on sauté mode. Add garlic and onion and sauté for 2 minutes. Add blended roasted pepper and sauté for 2 minutes. Add remaining ingredients except feta cheese and stir well. Seal pot with lid and cook on high for 8 minutes.
Then allow to release pressure naturally for 5 minutes then release remaining using quick release. Remove lid.
Top with feta cheese and serve.

**Nutrition:** Calories 459 Fat 10.6 g Carbs 68.1 g Protein 21.3 g

### 481. Whole Wheat Pasta with Tuna

**Prep Time:** 10 minutes  
**Servings:** 6  

**Cook Time:** 8 minutes

**Ingredients:**
- 10 oz can tuna, drained
- 15 oz whole wheat rotini pasta
- 4 oz mozzarella cheese, cubed
- 1/2 cup parmesan cheese, grated
- 1 tsp dried basil
- 14 oz can tomatoes, diced
- 4 cups vegetable broth
- 1 tbsp garlic, minced
- 8 oz mushrooms, sliced
- 2 zucchini, sliced
- 1 onion, chopped
- 2 tbsp olive oil
- Pepper
- Salt

**Prep:** Add oil into the inner pot of instant pot and set the pot on sauté mode. Add zucchini, mushrooms, and onion and sauté until onion is softened. Add garlic and sauté for a minute. Add pasta, tuna, tomatoes, basil, and broth and stir well.
Seal pot with lid and cook on high for 4 minutes.
Then allow to release pressure naturally for 5 minutes then release remaining using quick release. Remove lid.
Add remaining ingredients and stir well.

**Nutrition:** Calories 346 Fat 11.9 g Carbs 31.3 g Protein 6.3 g

### 482. Vegan Olive Pasta

**Prep Time:** 10 minutes  
**Servings:** 4  

**Cook Time:** 5 minutes

**Ingredients:**
- 4 cups whole grain penne pasta
- 1/2 cup olives, sliced
- 1 tbsp capers
- 1/4 tsp red pepper flakes
- 3 cups of water
- 4 cups pasta sauce, homemade
- 1 tbsp garlic, minced
- Pepper
- Salt

**Prep:** Add all ingredients into the inner pot of instant pot and stir well. Seal pot with lid and cook on high for 5 minutes.
Once done, release pressure using quick release. Remove lid.
Stir and serve.

**Nutrition:** Calories 441 Fat 10.1 g Carbs 77.3 g Protein 11.8 g

### 483. Italian Chicken Pasta

**Prep Time:** 10 minutes  
**Servings:** 8  
**Cook Time:** 9 minutes

**Ingredients:**
- 1 lb chicken breast, skinless, boneless, and cut into chunks
- 1 cup mozzarella cheese, shredded
- 1 1/2 tsp Italian seasoning
- 1 tsp garlic, minced
- 1/2 cup cream cheese
- 1 cup mushrooms, diced
- 1/2 onion, diced
- 2 tomatoes, diced
- 2 cups of water
- 16 oz whole wheat penne pasta
- Pepper
- Salt

**Prep:** Add all ingredients (except cheeses) into the inner pot of instant pot and stir well.
Seal pot with lid and cook on high for 9 minutes.
Then allow to release pressure naturally for 5 minutes then release remaining using quick release. Remove lid.
Add cheeses and stir well.

**Nutrition:** Calories 328 Fat 8.5 g Carbs 42.7 g Protein 23.7 g

### 484. Greek Chicken Pasta

**Prep Time:** 10 minutes  
**Servings:** 6  
**Cook Time:** 10 minutes

**Ingredients:**
- 2 chicken breasts, skinless, boneless, and cut into chunks
- 1/2 cup olives, sliced
- 2 cups vegetable stock
- 1 lb whole grain pasta
- 12 oz Greek vinaigrette dressing
- Salt and pepper

**Prep:** Add all ingredients into the inner pot of instant pot and stir well. Seal pot with lid and cook on high for 10 minutes.
Once done, release pressure using quick release. Remove lid.
Stir well and serve.

**Nutrition:** Calories 325 Fat 25.8 g Carbs 10.5 g Protein 15.6 g

### 485. Pesto Chicken Pasta

**Prep Time:** 10 minutes  
**Servings:** 6  
**Cook Time:** 10 minutes

**Ingredients:**
- 16 oz whole wheat pasta
- 1 lb chicken breast, skinless, boneless, and diced
- 3 tbsp olive oil
- 1/2 cup parmesan cheese, shredded
- 1 tsp Italian seasoning
- 1/4 cup heavy cream
- 6 oz basil pesto
- 3 1/2 cups water
- Pepper
- Salt

**Prep:** Season chicken with Italian seasoning, pepper, and salt. Add oil into the inner pot of instant pot and set the pot on sauté mode. Add chicken to the pot and sauté until golden brown. Add remaining ingredients except for parmesan cheese, heavy cream, and pesto and stir well. Seal pot with lid and cook on high for 5 minutes.
Once done, release pressure using quick release. Remove lid.
Stir in heavy cream, parmesan cheese, and pesto and serve.

**Nutrition:** Calories 476 Fat 13 g Carbs 57 g Protein 28.7 g

### 486. Spinach Pesto Pasta

**Prep Time:** 10 minutes  
**Servings:** 4  
**Cook Time:** 10 minutes

**Ingredients:**
- 8 oz whole-grain pasta
- 1/3 cup mozzarella cheese, grated
- 1/2 cup pesto
- 5 oz fresh spinach
- 1 3/4 cup water
- 8 oz mushrooms, chopped
- 1 tbsp olive oil
- Pepper
- Salt

**Prep:** Add oil into the inner pot of instant pot and set the pot on sauté mode. Add mushrooms and sauté for 5 minutes. Add water and pasta and stir well. Seal pot with lid and cook on high for 5 minutes.
Once done, release pressure using quick release. Remove lid.
Stir in remaining ingredients and serve.

**Nutrition:** Calories 213 Fat 17.3 g Carbs 9.5 g Protein 7.4 g

### 487. Herb Polenta

**Prep Time:** 10 minutes  
**Servings:** 6  
**Cook Time:** 12 minutes

**Ingredients:**
- 1 cup polenta
- 1/4 tsp nutmeg
- 3 tbsp fresh parsley, chopped
- 1/4 cup milk
- 1/2 cup parmesan cheese, grated
- 4 cups vegetable broth
- 2 tsp thyme, chopped
- 2 tsp rosemary, chopped
- 2 tsp sage, chopped
- 1 small onion, chopped
- 2 tbsp olive oil
- Salt

**Prep:** Add oil into the inner pot of instant pot and set the pot on sauté mode. Add onion and herbs and sauté for 4 minutes. Add polenta, broth, and salt and stir well. Seal pot with lid and cook on high for 8 minutes.
Once done, allow to release pressure naturally. Remove lid.
Stir in remaining ingredients and serve.

**Nutrition:** Calories 196 Fat 7.8 g Carbs 23.5 g Protein 8.2 g

### 488. Pecorino Pasta with Sausage and Fresh Tomato

**Prep Time:** 10 minutes  
**Servings:** 4  
**Cook Time:** 20 minutes

**Ingredients:**
- ¼ cup torn fresh basil leaves
- 1/8 tsp black pepper
- ¼ tsp salt
- 6 tbsp grated fresh pecorino Romano cheese, divided
- 1 ¼ lbs. tomatoes, chopped
- 2 tsp minced garlic
- 1 cup vertically sliced onions
- 2 tsp olive oil
- 8 oz sweet Italian sausage
- 8 oz uncooked penne, cooked and drained

**Prep:** On medium high fire, place a nonstick fry pan with oil and cook for five minutes onion and sausage. Stir constantly to break sausage into pieces. Stir in garlic and continue cooking for two minutes more. Add tomatoes and cook for another two minutes. Remove pan from fire, season with pepper and salt. Mix well. Stir in 2 tbsp cheese and pasta. Toss well.
Transfer to a dish, garnish with basil and remaining cheese before serving.

**Nutrition:** Calories: 376; Carbs: 50.8 g; Protein: 17.8 g; Fat: 11.6 g

### 489. Pesto Pasta and Shrimps

**Prep Time:** 10 minutes  
**Servings:** 4  
**Cook Time:** 15 minutes

**Ingredients:**
- ¼ cup pesto, divided
- ¼ cup shaved Parmesan Cheese
- 1 ¼ lbs. large shrimp, peeled and deveined
- 1 cup halved grape tomatoes
- 4-oz angel hair pasta, cooked, rinsed and drained

**Prep:** On medium high fire, place a nonstick large fry pan and grease with cooking spray.
Add tomatoes, pesto and shrimp. Cook for 15 minutes or until shrimps are opaque, while covered.
Stir in cooked pasta and cook until heated through.
Transfer to a plate and garnish with Parmesan cheese.

**Nutrition:** Calories: 319; Carbs: 23.6 g; Protein: 31.4 g; Fat: 11 g

### 490. Puttanesca Style Bucatini

**Prep Time:** 20 minutes  
**Servings:** 4  
**Cook Time:** 40 minutes

### Ingredients:
- 1 tbsp capers, rinsed
- 1 tsp coarsely chopped fresh oregano
- 1 tsp finely chopped garlic
- 1/8 tsp salt
- 12-oz bucatini pasta
- 2 cups coarsely chopped canned no-salt-added whole peeled tomatoes with their juice
- 3 tbsp extra virgin olive oil, divided
- 4 anchovy fillets, chopped
- 8 black Kalamata olives, pitted and sliced into slivers

**Prep:** Cook bucatini pasta according to package prep. Drain, keep warm, and set aside.
On medium fire, place a large nonstick saucepan and heat 2 tbsp oil.
Sauté anchovies until it starts to disintegrate. Add garlic and sauté for 15 seconds. Add tomatoes, sauté for 15 to 20 minutes or until no longer watery. Season with 1/8 tsp salt. Add oregano, capers, and olives. Add pasta, sautéing until heated through.
To serve, drizzle pasta with remaining olive oil.

**Nutrition:** Calories: 207.4; Carbs: 31 g; Protein: 5.1 g; Fat: 7 g

## 491. Raw Tomato Sauce & Brie on Linguine

**Prep Time:** 10 minutes
**Servings:** 4

**Cook Time:** 12 minutes

### Ingredients:
- ¼ cup grated low-fat Parmesan cheese
- ½ cup loosely packed fresh basil leaves, torn
- 12 oz whole wheat linguine
- 2 cups loosely packed baby arugula
- 2 green onions, green parts only, sliced thinly
- 2 tbsp balsamic vinegar
- 2 tbsp extra virgin olive oil
- 3 large vine-ripened tomatoes
- 3 oz low-fat Brie cheese, cubed, rind removed and discarded
- 3 tbsp toasted pine nuts
- Pepper and salt to taste

**Prep:** Toss together pepper, salt, vinegar, oil, onions, Parmesan, basil, arugula, Brie and tomatoes in a large bowl and set aside.
Cook linguine following package prep. Reserve 1 cup of pasta cooking water after linguine is cooked. Drain and discard the rest of the pasta. Do not run under cold water, instead immediately add into bowl of salad. Let it stand for a minute without mixing.
Add ¼ cup of reserved pasta water into bowl to make a creamy sauce. Add more pasta water if desired. Toss to mix well.

**Nutrition:** Calories: 274.7; Carbs: 30.9 g; Protein: 14.6 g; Fat: 10.3 g

## 492. Red Wine Risotto

**Prep Time:** 10 minutes
**Servings:** 8

**Cook Time:** 25 minutes

### Ingredients:
- Pepper to taste
- 1 cup finely shredded Parmigian-Reggiano cheese, divided
- 2 tsp tomato paste
- 1 ¾ cups dry red wine
- ¼ tsp salt
- 1 ½ cups Italian 'risotto' rice
- 2 cloves garlic, minced
- 1 medium onion, freshly chopped
- 2 tbsp extra-virgin olive oil
- 4 ½ cups reduced sodium beef broth

**Prep:** On medium high fire, bring to a simmer broth in a medium fry pan. Lower fire so broth is steaming but not simmering.
On medium low heat, place a Dutch oven and heat oil.
Sauté onions for 5 minutes. Add garlic and cook for 2 minutes. Add rice, mix well, and season with salt.
Into rice, add a generous splash of wine and ½ cup of broth.
Lower fire to a gentle simmer, cook until liquid is fully absorbed while stirring rice every once in a while. Add another splash of wine and ½ cup of broth. Stirring once in a while. Add tomato paste and stir to mix well.
Continue cooking and adding wine and broth until broth is used up.
Once done cooking, turn off fire and stir in pepper and ¾ cup cheese.
To serve, sprinkle with remaining cheese.

**Nutrition:** Calories: 231; Carbs: 33.9 g; Protein: 7.9 g; Fat: 5.7 g

## 493. Bell Pepper Soup

**Prep Time:** 30 minutes
**Servings:** 4

**Cook Time:** 35 minutes

### Ingredients:
- 4 - cups low-sodium chicken broth
- 3 - red peppers
- 2 - medium onions

- 3 - tablespoon lemon juice
- 1 - tablespoon finely minced lemon zest
- A pinch cayenne peppers
- ¼ - teaspoon cinnamon
- ½ - cup finely minced fresh cilantro

**Prep:** In a stockpot, consolidate each one of the fixings except for the cilantro and warmth to the point of boiling over excessive warm temperature.
Diminish the warmth and stew, ordinarily secured, for around 30 minutes, till thickened. Cool marginally.
Utilizing a hand blender or nourishment processor, puree the soup.
Include the cilantro and tenderly heat.

**Nutrition:** 265 Calories, 8 g Fat, 5 g Protein

## 494. Chicken Wild Rice Soup

**Prep Time:** 10 minutes
**Servings:** 6
**Cook Time:** 15 minutes

**Ingredients:**
- 2/3 cup wild rice, uncooked
- 1 tablespoon onion, chopped finely
- 1 tablespoon fresh parsley, chopped
- 1 cup carrots, chopped
- 8-ounces chicken breast, cooked
- 2 tablespoon butter
- 1/4 cup all-purpose white flour
- 5 cups low-sodium chicken broth
- 1 tablespoon slivered almonds

**Prep:** Start by adding rice and 2 cups broth along with ½ cup water to a cooking pot. Cook the chicken until the rice is "Al dente" and set it aside.
Add butter to a saucepan and melt it. Stir in onion and sauté until soft then add the flour and the remaining broth.
Stir it and then cook for it 1 minute then add the chicken, cooked rice, and carrots. Cook for 5 minutes on simmer.
Garnish with almonds.

**Nutrition:** 287 Calories, 21 g Protein, 35 g Fat

## 495. Squash and Turmeric Soup

**Prep Time:** 10 minutes
**Servings:** 4
**Cook Time:** 30 minutes

**Ingredients:**
- 4 cups low-sodium vegetable broth
- 2 medium zucchini squash
- 2 medium yellow crookneck squash
- 1 small onion
- 1/2 cup frozen green peas
- 2 tablespoons olive oil
- 1/2 cup plain nonfat Greek yogurt
- 2 teaspoon turmeric

**Prep:** Warm the broth in a saucepan on medium heat. Toss in onion, squash, and zucchini.
Let it simmer for approximately 25 minutes then add oil and green peas.
Cook for another 5 minutes then allow it to cool.
Puree the soup using a handheld blender then add Greek yogurt and turmeric.
Refrigerate it overnight.

## 496. Leek, Potato, and Carrot Soup

**Prep Time:** 15 minutes
**Servings:** 4
**Cook Time:** 25 minutes

**Ingredients:**
- 1 - leek
- ¾ - cup diced and boiled potatoes
- ¾ - cup diced and boiled carrots
- 1 - garlic clove
- 1 - tablespoon oil
- Crushed pepper to taste
- 3 - cups low sodium chicken stock
- Chopped parsley for garnish
- 1 - bay leaf
- ¼ - teaspoon ground cumin

**Prep:** Trim off and take away a portion of the coarse inexperienced portions of the leek, reduce daintily, and flush altogether in virus water.
Warmth the oil in an extensively based pot. Include the leek and garlic, and sear over low warmth, for two-3 minutes, till sensitive.
Include, inlet leaf, cumin, and pepper.
Heat the mixture, mix constantly. Include the bubbled potatoes and carrots and stew for 10-15 minutes.
Modify the flavoring, eliminate the inlet leaf, and serve sprinkled generously with slashed parsley.

To make a pureed soup, manner the soup in a blender or nourishment processor till smooth come again to the pan. Include ½ field milk.
Bring to bubble and stew for 2-3 minutes.

**Nutrition:** 315 Calories, 8 g Fat, 15 g Protein

## 497. Beef Sage Soup

**Prep Time:** 10 minutes  
**Servings:** 4  
**Cook Time:** 20 minutes

**Ingredients:**
- ½ pound ground beef
- ½ teaspoon ground sage
- ½ teaspoon black pepper
- ½ teaspoon dried basil
- ½ teaspoon garlic powder
- 4 slices bread, cubed
- 2 tablespoons olive oil
- 1 tablespoon herb seasoning blend
- 2 garlic cloves, minced
- 3 cups chicken broth
- 1 ½ cups water
- 4 tablespoons fresh parsley
- 2 tablespoons parmesan cheese

**Prep:** Preheat your oven to 375°F.
Mix beef with sage, basil, black pepper, and garlic powder in a bowl, then set it aside.
Toss the bread cubes with olive oil in a baking sheet and bake them for 8 minutes.
Meanwhile, sauté the beef mixture in a greased cooking pot until it is browned. Stir in garlic and sauté for 2 minutes, then add parsley, water, and broth. Cover the beef soup and cook for 10 minutes on a simmer.
Garnish the soup with parmesan cheese and baked bread.

**Nutrition:** 336 Calories, 26 g Protein, 16 g Fat

## 498. Classic Minestrone

**Prep Time:** 12 minutes  
**Servings** 6  
**Cook Time:** 25 minutes

**Ingredients:**
- 2 tablespoons olive oil
- 3 cloves garlic
- 1 onion, diced
- 2 carrots
- 2 stalks celery
- 1 1/2 teaspoons dried basil
- 1 teaspoon dried oregano
- 1/2 teaspoon fennel seed
- 6 cups low sodium chicken broth
- 1 (28-ounce) can tomatoes
- 1 (16-ounce) can kidney beans
- 1 zucchini
- 1 Parmesan rind
- 1 bay leaf
- 1 bunch kale leaves, chopped
- 2 teaspoons red wine vinegar
- 1/3 cup freshly grated Parmesan
- 2 tablespoons chopped fresh parsley leaves

**Prep:** Preheat olive oil in the insert of the Instant Pot on Sauté mode. Add carrots, celery, and onion, sauté for 3 minutes. Stir in fennel seeds, oregano, and basil. Stir cook for 1 minute. Add stock, beans, tomatoes, parmesan, bay leaf, and zucchini.
Secure and seal the Instant Pot lid then select Manual mode to cook for minutes at high pressure.
Once done, release the pressure completely then remove the lid. Add kale and let it sit for 2 minutes in the hot soup. Stir in red wine, vinegar, pepper, and salt.
Garnish with parsley and parmesan.

**Nutrition:** 805 Calories, 124 g Protein, 34 g Fat

## 499. Cheesy Broccoli Soup

**Prep Time:** 11 minutes  
**Servings** 4  
**Cook Time:** 30 minutes

**Ingredients:**
- ½ cup heavy whipping cream
- 1 cup broccoli
- 1 cup cheddar cheese
- Salt, to taste
- 1½ cups chicken broth

**Prep:** Cook chicken broth in a large pot and add broccoli. Boil and stir in the rest of the ingredients.
Allow the soup to simmer on low heat for about 20 minutes.
Ladle out into a bowl and serve hot.

**Nutrition:** 188 Calories, 15 g Fat, 9.8 g Protein

### 500. Mediterranean Lentil Soup

**Prep Time:** 9 minutes  
**Servings** 4  
**Cook Time:** 20 minutes

**Ingredients:**
- 1 tablespoon olive oil
- 1/2 cup red lentils
- 1 medium yellow or red onion
- 2 garlic cloves
- 1/2 teaspoon ground cumin
- 1/2 teaspoon ground coriander
- 1/2 teaspoon ground sumac
- 1/2 teaspoon red chili flakes
- 1/2 teaspoon dried parsley
- 3/4 teaspoons dried mint flakes
- 2.5 cups water
- juice of 1/2 lime

**Prep:** Preheat oil in the insert of your Instant Pot on Sauté mode. Add onion and sauté until it turns golden brown. Toss in the garlic, parsley sugar, mint flakes, red chili flakes, sumac, coriander, and cumin.
Stir cook this mixture for 2 minutes. Add water, lentils, salt, and pepper. Stir gently.
Seal and lock the Instant Pot lid and select Manual mode for 8 minutes at high pressure.
Once done, release the pressure completely then remove the lid.
Stir well then add lime juice.

**Nutrition:** 525 Calories, 30 g Protein, 19.3 g Fat

### 501. Turkey Meatball and Ditalini Soup

**Prep Time:** 15 minutes  
**Servings** 4  
**Cook Time:** 40 minutes

**Ingredients:**

**Meatballs:**
- 1 pound 93% lean ground turkey
- 1/3 cup seasoned breadcrumbs
- 3 tablespoons grated Pecorino Romano cheese
- 1 large egg, beaten
- 1 clove crushed garlic
- 1 tablespoon fresh minced parsley
- 1/2 teaspoon kosher salt

**Soup:**
- 1 teaspoon olive oil
- 1/2 cup onion
- 1/2 cup celery
- 1/2 cup carrot
- 3 cloves garlic
- 1 can San Marzano tomatoes
- 4 cups reduced sodium chicken broth
- 4 torn basil leaves
- 2 bay leaves
- 1 cup ditalini pasta
- 1 cup zucchini, diced small
- Parmesan rind, optional
- Grated parmesan cheese, optional for serving

**Prep:** Thoroughly combine turkey with egg, garlic, parsley, salt, pecorino and breadcrumbs in a bowl.
Make 30 equal sized meatballs out of this mixture.
Preheat olive oil in the insert of the Instant Pot on Sauté mode.
Sear the meatballs in the heated oil in batches, until brown. Set the meatballs aside in a plate.
Add more oil to the insert of the Instant Pot. Stir in carrots, garlic, celery, and onion. Sauté for 4 minutes. Add basil, bay leaves, tomatoes, and Parmesan rind.
Return the seared meatballs to the pot along with the broth.
Secure and sear the Instant Pot lid and select Manual mode for 15 minutes at high pressure.
Once done, release the pressure completely then remove the lid.
Add zucchini and pasta, cook it for 4 minutes on Sauté mode.
Garnish with cheese and basil.

**Nutrition:** 261 Calories, 37 g Protein, 7 g Fat

### 502. Potato Soup (2nd Version)

**Prep Time:** 6 minutes  
**Servings** 4  
**Cook Time:** 30 minutes

**Ingredients:**
- 1 tablespoon butter
- 1 medium onion, diced
- 3 cloves garlic, minced
- 3 cups chicken broth
- 1 can/box cream of chicken soup
- 7-8 medium-sized russet potatoes
- 1 1/2 teaspoons salt
- 1 cup milk
- 1 tablespoon flour
- 2 cups shredded cheddar cheese

**Garnish:**
- 5-6 slices bacon, chopped
- Sliced green onions
- Shredded cheddar cheese

**Prep:** Heat butter in the insert of the Instant Pot on sauté mode. Add onions and sauté for 4 minutes until soft. Stir in garlic and sauté it for 1 minute. Add potatoes, cream of chicken, broth, salt, and pepper to the insert. Mix well then seal and lock the lid. Cook this mixture for 10 minutes at Manual Mode with high pressure.
Meanwhile, mix flour with milk in a bowl and set it aside.
Once the Instant Pot beeps, release the pressure completely. Remove the Instant Pot lid and switch the instant pot to Sauté mode. Pour in flour slurry and stir cook the mixture for 5 minutes until it thickens.
Add 2 cups of cheddar cheese and let it melt.
Garnish it as desired.

**Nutrition:** 784 Calories, 34 g Protein; 46.5 g Fat

### 503. Mint Avocado Chilled Soup

**Prep Time:** 6 minutes                                                    **Servings** 2

**Ingredients:**
- 1 cup coconut milk, chilled
- 1 medium ripe avocado
- 1 tablespoon lime juice
- Salt, to taste
- 20 fresh mint leaves

**Prep:** Put all the ingredients into an immersion blender and blend until a thick mixture is formed.
Allow to cool in the fridge for about 10 minutes.

**Nutrition:** 286 Calories, 27 g Fat, 4.2 g Protein

### 504. Beetroot and Carrot Soup

**Prep Time:** 12 minutes                                                   **Cook Time:** 32 minutes
**Servings** 6

**Ingredients:**
- 4 beets
- 2 carrots
- 2 potatoes
- 1 medium onion
- 4 cups vegetable broth
- 2 cups water
- 2 tbsp yogurt
- 2 tbsp olive oil

**Prep:** Peel and chop the beets.
Heat olive oil in a saucepan over medium high heat and sauté the onion and carrot until onion is tender. Add beets, potatoes, broth and water and bring to the boil. Reduce heat to medium and simmer, partially covered, for 30-40 minutes, or until beets are tender. Cool slightly. Blend the soup in batches until smooth.
Return it to pan over low heat and cook, stirring, for 4 to 5 minutes or until heated through. Season with salt and pepper.
Serve soup topped with yogurt and sprinkled with spring onions.

**Nutrition:** 301 Calories, 21 g Fat, 11 g Protein

### 505. Barley Risotto

**Prep Time:** 15 Minutes                                                   **Cook Time:** 8 Hours
**Servings:** 8

**Ingredients:**
- 2¼ cups hulled barley, rinsed
- 1 onion, finely chopped
- 4 garlic cloves, minced
- 1 (8-ounce) package button mushrooms, chopped
- 6 cups low-sodium vegetable broth
- ½ teaspoon dried marjoram leaves
- 1/8 teaspoon freshly ground black pepper
- 2/3 cup grated Parmesan cheese

**Prep:** In a 6-quart slow cooker, mix the barley, onion, garlic, mushrooms, broth, marjoram, and pepper. Cover and cook on low for 7 hours, or until the barley and the vegetables are tender.
Stir in the Parmesan cheese and serve.

**Nutrition:** Calories: 288; Carbs: 45 g; Fat: 6 g; Protein: 13 g

### 506. Beef with Broccoli and Cauliflower Rice

**Prep Time:** 10 minutes                                                   **Cook Time:** 30 minutes
**Servings:** 2

**Ingredients:**
- 1 lb. raw beef round steak, cut into strips.
- 1 Tbsp + 2 tsp. low sodium soy sauce
- 1 Splenda packet
- 1/2 C water
- 1 1/2 C broccoli florets
- 1 tsp. sesame or olive oil
- 2 Cups cooked, frozen riced cauliflower

**Prep:** Stir steak with soy sauce and let sit about 15 minutes.
Heat oil over medium-high heat and stir fry beef for 3-5 minutes or until browned. Remove from pan.
Place broccoli, Splenda and water.
Cover and cook 5 minutes, stirring sometimes. Add beef back in and heat up thoroughly.
Serve the dish with cauliflower rice.

**Nutrition:** Fats 16 g; Carbs: 9 g

## 507. Chicken and Rice Soup

**Prep Time:** 10 minutes
**Servings:** 4

**Cook Time:** 35 minutes

**Ingredients:**
- 6 cups chicken stock
- 1 and ½ cups chicken meat, cooked and shredded
- 1 bay leaf
- 1 yellow onion, chopped
- 2 tbsps. olive oil
- 1/3 cup white rice
- 1 egg, whisked
- Juice of ½ lemon
- 1 cup asparagus, trimmed and halved
- 1 cup carrots, chopped
- ½ cup dill, chopped
- Salt and black pepper

**Prep:** Heat up a pot with the oil over medium heat, add the onions and sauté for 5 minutes. Add the stock, dill, the rice, and the bay leaf, and stir. Bring to a boil over medium heat and cook for 10 minutes. Add the rest of the ingredients (except the egg) and the lemon juice, stir and cook for 15 minutes more. Add the egg whisked with the lemon juice gradually. Whisk the soup and cook for 2 minutes more. Divide into bowls and serve.

**Nutrition:** Calories 263, Fat: 18.5 g, Carbs: 19.8 g, Protein: 14.5 g

## 508. Chickpeas Soup (2nd Version)

**Prep Time:** 10 minutes
**Servings:** 4

**Cook Time:** 1 hour

**Ingredients:**
- 3 tomatoes, cubed
- 2 yellow onions, chopped
- 2 tbsps. olive oil
- 4 celery stalks, chopped
- ½ cup parsley, chopped
- 2 garlic cloves, minced
- 16 oz. canned chickpeas, drained and rinsed
- 6 cups water
- 1 tsp. cumin, ground
- Juice of ½ lemon
- 1 tsp. turmeric powder
- ½ tsp. cinnamon powder
- ½ tsp. ginger, grated
- Salt and pepper to the taste

**Prep:** Heat up a pot with the oil over medium heat, add the onion and the garlic and sauté for 5 minutes.
Add the tomatoes, celery, cumin, turmeric, cinnamon, and the ginger, stir and sauté for 5 minutes more. Add the remaining ingredients, bring the soup to a boil over medium heat and simmer for 50 minutes.
Ladle the soup into bowls and serve.

**Nutrition:** Calories 300, Fat: 15.4 g, Carbs: 29.5 g, Protein: 15.4 g

## 509. Farfalle with Fresh Tomatoes

**Prep Time:** 15 minutes
**Servings:** 4

**Cook Time:** 30 minutes

**Ingredients:**
- 4/2 lb. total weight Tomatoes
- ½ cup Fresh basil
- 3 tbsp. Red onion
- 1 clove Garlic ()
- 3 tbsp. Olive oil
- 1 tbsp. Red wine vinegar
- ¼ tsp. Black pepper
- ¾ tsp. Salt
- ½ lb. Farfalle pasta

**Prep:** Peel and remove the seeds from the tomatoes and dice them into ½-inch pieces. Cut the basil into slender ribbons, using the whole leaves for garnishing. Chop/mince the garlic and onion.
Prepare the sauce in a large mixing container using the tomatoes, onion, basil oil, garlic, vinegar, pepper, and salt. Toss to mix.
Prepare a large pot of water (about ¾ full) and wait for it to boil. Toss in the farfalle and simmer until it's al dente (10 min.) Pour it into a colander to drain.
Divide the pasta and sauce between the bowls and serve.

**Nutrition:** Calories 212.5, Fat: 11.2 g, Protein: 4.2 g

### 510.   Fish Soup

**Prep Time: 10 minutes**  
**Servings: 4**

**Cook Time: 20 minutes**

**Ingredients:**
- 2 tbsps. olive oil
- 1 tbsp. garlic, minced
- ½ cup tomatoes, crushed
- 1 yellow onion, chopped
- 1 quart of veggie stock
- 1 lb. cod, skinless, boneless and cubed
- ¼ tsp. rosemary, dried
- A pinch of salt and black pepper

**Prep:** Heat up a pot with the oil over medium heat, add the onion and the garlic and sauté for 5 minutes.
Add the rest of the ingredients, toss, simmer over medium heat for 15 minutes more, divide into bowls and serve for lunch.

**Nutrition:** Calories 198, Fat: 8.1 g, Carbs: 4.2 g, Protein: 26.4 g

### 511.   Fried Rice with Spinach, Peppers & Artichokes

**Prep Time: 10 minutes**  
**Servings: 4**

**Cook Time: 15-20 minutes**

**Ingredients:**
- 1 ½ cups Cooked rice
- 10 oz. Frozen chopped spinach
- 6 oz. Marinated artichoke hearts
- 4 oz. Roasted red peppers
- ½ tsp. Minced garlic
- ½ cup Crumbled feta cheese with herbs
- 2 tbsp. Olive oil

**Prep:** Prepare the vegetables. Mince the garlic. Thaw and drain the frozen spinach. Drain and quarter the artichoke hearts. Drain and chop the roasted red peppers.
Heat a skillet on the stovetop to warm the oil using the medium heat setting. Toss in the garlic to sauté for two minutes. Toss in the rice and continue cooking for about two minutes until well heated.
Fold in the spinach and continue cooking for three more minutes. Add the red peppers and artichoke hearts. Simmer for two minutes. Stir in the feta cheese and serve.

**Nutrition:** Calories 244, Fat: 12.9 g, Protein: 9.3 g

### 512.   Greek Lima Beans Soup

**Prep Time: 1 hour**  
**Servings: 8**

**Cook Time: 10 hours**

**Ingredients:**
- 16 oz. pkg. Dried lima beans
- 2 - 16 oz. cans Chopped tomatoes with juice
- 1 cup Olive oil
- 3 cloves Minced garlic
- Sea salt as desired
- 1 tsp. Freshly chopped dill
- Also Needed: 9 x 13 baking dish

**Prep:** Pour the beans into a large saucepan with water to fill two inches over the top of the beans. Set them aside to soak overnight. Set the oven at 375°F.
Place the saucepan over medium heat and let it to boil. When it boils, lower the heat to medium-low and simmer for 20 minutes. Dump the water and drain the beans in a colander.
Pour and fold the beans into the baking dish with the dill, salt, oil, garlic, and tomatoes.
Bake the beans for 1.5 to 2 hours. Add water as needed, stirring occasionally.

**Nutrition:** Calories 449, Fat: 27.5 g, Protein: 13 g

### 513. Gluten-Free Spanish Rice

**Prep Time:** 15 minutes  
**Servings:** 6

**Cook Time:** 40 minutes

**Ingredients:**
- 1 tbsp. Olive oil
- 2 cloves Garlic
- ½ cup Medium onion
- ½ cup green bell pepper
- 1 cup Long-grain rice - regular/uncooked
- ¼ tsp. Sea salt
- ¼ tsp. Crushed red pepper
- 1 ¾ cups Chicken broth
- 1 14.5 oz. can Undrained - Diced fire-roasted tomatoes

**Prep:** Heat the oil in the saucepan using the medium temperature setting.  
Chop/dice the onion, garlic, and bell pepper and toss them into the skillet for about five minutes, stirring constantly.  
Add in the red pepper, salt, broth (reduced sodium is best), rice, and tomatoes. Wait for it to boil. Reduce the temperature setting and cook until the rice is tender before Servings (20-25 min.).

**Nutrition:** Calories 170, Fat: 2.5 g, Protein: 4 g

### 514. Ground Pork and Tomatoes Soup

**Prep Time:** 10 minutes  
**Servings:** 4

**Cook Time:** 40 minutes

**Ingredients:**
- 1 lb. pork meat, ground
- Salt and black pepper to the taste
- 2 garlic cloves, minced
- 2 tsps. thyme, dried
- 2 tbsps. olive oil
- 4 cups beef stock
- A pinch of saffron powder
- 15 oz. canned tomatoes, crushed
- 1 tbsp. parsley, chopped

**Prep:** Heat up a pot with the oil over medium heat, add the meat and the garlic and brown for 5 minutes.  
Add the rest of the ingredients (except the parsley), bring to a simmer and cook for 25 minutes.  
Divide the soup into bowls, sprinkle the parsley on top and serve.

**Nutrition:** Calories 372, Fat: 17.3 g, Carbs: 28.4 g, Protein: 17.4 g

### 515. Herbed Wild Rice

**Prep Time:** 10 Minutes  
**Servings:** 8

**Cook Time:** 4 Hours

**Ingredients:**
- 3 cups wild rice, rinsed and drained
- 6 cups Roasted Vegetable Broth (here)
- 1 onion, chopped
- ½ teaspoon salt
- ½ teaspoon dried thyme leaves
- ½ teaspoon dried basil leaves
- 1 bay leaf
- 1/3 cup chopped fresh flat-leaf parsley

**Prep:** In a 6-quart slow cooker, mix the wild rice, vegetable broth, onion, salt, thyme, basil, and bay leaf. Cover and cook on low for 4 hours, or until the wild rice is tender but still firm. Cook this dish longer until the wild rice pops; that will take about 7 hours.  
Remove and discard the bay leaf.  
Stir in the parsley and serve.

**Nutrition:** Calories: 258; Carbs: 54g; Fat: 2g; Protein: 6g

### 516. Mushroom Soup

**Prep Time:** 10 Minutes  
**Servings:** 2

**Cook Time:** 20 minutes

**Ingredients:**
- 1 cup Cremini mushrooms, chopped
- 1 cup Cheddar cheese, shredded
- 2 cups of water
- ½ teaspoon salt
- 1 teaspoon dried thyme
- ½ teaspoon dried oregano
- 1 tablespoon fresh parsley, chopped
- 1 tablespoon olive oil
- 1 bell pepper, chopped

**Prep:** Pour the oil into the skillet. Add bell pepper and mushrooms, and roast for 5 minutes over the medium heat. Then sprinkle them with thyme, salt, and dried oregano. Add parsley and water. Stir and cook the soup for 10 minutes.  
After this, blend the soup until smooth and simmer for 5 minutes more.

Add cheese and continue to stir until melted.

**Nutrition:** Calories 320, Fat 26 g, Carbs 7.4 g, Protein 15.7 g

## 517. Flavorful Mac & Cheese

**Prep Time: 10 minutes**
**Servings: 6**

**Cook Time: 10 minutes**

**Ingredients:**
- 16 oz whole-grain elbow pasta
- 4 cups of water
- 1 cup can tomatoes, diced
- 1 tsp garlic, chopped
- 2 tbsp olive oil
- 1/4 cup green onions, chopped
- 1/2 cup parmesan cheese, grated
- 1/2 cup mozzarella cheese, grated
- 1 cup cheddar cheese, grated
- 1/4 cup passata
- 1 cup unsweetened almond milk
- 1 cup marinated artichoke, diced
- 1/2 cup sun-dried tomatoes, sliced
- 1/2 cup olives, sliced
- 1 tsp salt

**Prep:** Add pasta, water, tomatoes, garlic, oil, and salt into the instant pot and stir well.
Seal pot with lid and cook on high for four minutes.
Then allow to release pressure naturally for five minutes then release remaining using quick release. Remove lid.
Set pot on sauté mode. Add parmesan cheese, green onion, passata, mozzarella cheese, cheddar cheese, milk, artichoke, sun-dried tomatoes, and olive. Mix well.
Stir and cook until cheese is melted.

**Nutrition:** Calories 519 Fat 17.1 g Carbs 66.5 g Protein 25 g

## 518. Mac & Cheese

**Prep Time: 10 minutes**
**Servings: 8**

**Cook Time: 4 minutes**

**Ingredients:**
- 1 lb whole grain pasta
- 1/2 cup parmesan cheese, grated
- 4 cups cheddar cheese, shredded
- 1 cup milk
- 1/4 tsp garlic powder
- 1/2 tsp ground mustard
- 2 tbsp olive oil
- 4 cups of water
- Pepper
- Salt

**Prep:** Add pasta, garlic powder, mustard, oil, water, pepper, and salt into the instant pot.
Seal pot with lid and cook on high for 4 minutes.
Once done, release pressure using quick release. Remove lid.
Add remaining ingredients and stir well.

**Nutrition:** Calories 509 Fat 25.7 g Carbs 43.8 g Protein 27.3 g

## 519. Italian Mac & Cheese

**Prep Time: 10 minutes**
**Servings: 4**

**Cook Time: 6 minutes**

**Ingredients:**
- 1 lb whole grain pasta
- 2 tsp Italian seasoning
- 1 1/2 tsp garlic powder
- 1 1/2 tsp onion powder
- 1 cup sour cream
- 4 cups of water
- 4 oz parmesan cheese, shredded
- 12 oz ricotta cheese
- Salt and pepper

**Prep:** Add all ingredients except ricotta cheese into the inner pot of instant pot and stir well.
Seal pot with lid and cook on high for 6 minutes.
Once done, allow to release pressure naturally for 5 minutes then release remaining using quick release. Remove lid.
Add ricotta cheese and stir well.

**Nutrition:** Calories 388 Fat 25.8 g Carbs 18.1 g Protein 22.8 g

## 520. Israeli Pasta

**Prep Time:** 15 minutes  
**Servings:** 8  

**Cook Time:** 2 minutes

### Ingredients:
- Small bow tie or other small pasta (.5 lb.)
- 1/3 cup Cucumber
- 1/3 cup Radish
- 1/3 cup Tomato
- 1/3 cup Yellow bell pepper
- 1/3 cup Orange bell pepper
- 1/3 cup Black olives
- 1/3 cup Green olives
- 1/3 cup Red onions
- 1/3 cup Pepperoncini
- 1/3 cup Feta cheese
- 1/3 cup Fresh thyme leaves
- Dried oregano (1 tsp.)

### Dressing:
- 0.25 cup + more, olive oil
- juice of 1 lemon

**Prep:** Slice the green olives into halves.
Dice the feta and pepperoncini and finely dice the remainder of the veggies.
Prepare a pot of water with the salt, and simmer the pasta until it's "Al dente" (checking at two minutes under the listed time).
Rinse and drain in cold water.
Combine a small amount of oil with the pasta. Add the salt, pepper, oregano, thyme, and veggies.
Pour in the rest of the oil, lemon juice, mix and fold in the grated feta.
Pop it into the fridge within two hours, best if overnight.
Taste test and adjust the seasonings to your liking.
Add fresh thyme.

**Nutrition:** 65 Calories; 5.6 g Fats; 0.8 g Protein

## 521. Spaghetti Squash

**Prep Time:** 13 minutes  
**Servings** 6  

**Cooking Time:** 45 minutes

### Ingredients:
- 2 spring onions, chopped fine
- 3 cloves garlic, minced
- 1 zucchini, diced
- 1 red bell pepper, diced
- 1 tablespoon Italian seasoning
- 1 tomato, small & chopped fine
- 1 tablespoons parsley, fresh & chopped
- pinch lemon pepper
- dash sea salt, fine
- 4 ounces feta cheese, crumbled
- 3 Italian sausage links, casing removed
- 2 tablespoons olive oil
- 1 spaghetti sauce, halved lengthwise

**Prep:** Prep oven to 350°F (180°C), and get out a large baking sheet.
Coat it with cooking spray, and then put your squash on it with the cut side down.
Bake at 350°F (180°C) for 45 minutes. It should be tender.
Turn the squash over, and bake for 5 more minutes.
Scrape the strands into a larger bowl.
Cook tablespoon of olive oil in a skillet, and then add in your Italian sausage.
Cook at 8 minutes before removing it and placing it in a bowl.
Add another tablespoon of olive oil to the skillet and cook your garlic and onions until softened. This will take 5 minutes.
Throw in your Italian seasoning, red peppers and zucchini and cook for another 5 minutes. Your vegetables should be softened.
Mix in your feta cheese and squash, cooking until the cheese has melted.
Stir in your sausage, and then season with lemon pepper and salt.
Serve with parsley and tomato.

**Nutrition:** 423 Calories; 18g Protein; 30g Fat

## 522. Garlic Prawn and Pea Risotto

**Prep Time:** 15 minutes  
**Servings** 4  

**Cooking Time:** 30 minutes

### Ingredients:
- 1 pinch of salt
- 1 pinch of black pepper
- 1 red chili
- 3 tablespoons of extra-virgin olive oil
- 1 oz. of butter
- Juice of 1 lemon
- Zest of 1 lemon
- 50 Fl oz. of fish stock

- 1 cup of white wine
- 1 clove of garlic, finely diced
- 1 onion, diced
- 7 oz. of frozen peas
- 14 oz. of raw prawns
- 1 cup of Arborio rice

**Prep:** Rinse the prawns under running water and then remove their heads and shells. Keep these aside and keep the prawn meat aside.
Situate saucepan over medium heat, add one tablespoon of olive oil, garlic, half of the finely diced chili, prawn heads, and shells. Cook until the shells change color. Boil stock, then turn the heat down to a simmer.
In a separate medium saucepan over medium heat, add half the butter and the onions. Cook until the onions have softened. Add the risotto into the pan and stir continuously until you notice that the rice has become transparent in appearance.
Stir wine to the rice and cook.
Begin to ladle the broth over the rice, one spoonful at a time. Stir in the peas and prawns.
Continue adding broth until the rice has reached an "Al dente" texture, soft with a starchy center, around 20 to 30 minutes.
Continue to cook until the prawn meat has changed color.
Remove the risotto from the heat, then add the remaining chili, olive oil, and lemon juice.
Top with salt, pepper, and lemon zest.

**Nutrition:** 341 Calories; 16g Fat; 7g Protein

## 523. Greek Pasta Salad

**Prep Time:** 5 minutes  
**Servings:** 4  
**Cooking Time:** 11 minutes

**Ingredients:**
- Penne pasta (1 cup)
- Lemon juice (1.5 tsp.)
- Red wine vinegar (2 tbsp.)
- Garlic (1 clove)
- Dried oregano (1 tsp.)
- Black pepper and sea salt (as desired)
- Olive oil (.33 cup)
- Halved cherry tomatoes (5)
- Red onion (half of 1 small)
- Green & red bell pepper (half of 1 - each)
- Cucumber (¼ of 1)
- Black olives (.25 cup)
- Crumbled feta cheese (.25 cup)

**Prep:** Slice the cucumber and olives.
Chop/dice the onion, peppers, and garlic, and slice the tomatoes into halves.
Arrange a large pot with water and salt using the high-temperature setting. Once it's boiling, add the pasta and cook for 11 minutes.
Rinse it using cold water and drain in a colander.
Whisk the oil, juice, salt, pepper, vinegar, oregano, and garlic.
Combine the cucumber, cheese, olives, peppers, pasta, onions, and tomatoes in a large salad dish.
Add the vinaigrette over the pasta and toss.
Chill in the fridge (covered) for about 3 hours and serve as desired.

**Nutrition:** 307 Calories; 23.6g Fat; 5.4g Protein

## 524. Lemon Mushroom Rice

**Preparation Time:** 10 minutes  
**Servings:** 4  
**Cooking Time:** 30 minutes

**Ingredients:**
- 2 cups chicken stock
- 1 yellow onion, chopped
- ½ pound white mushrooms
- 2 garlic cloves, minced
- 8 ounces wild rice
- Juice and zest of 1 lemon
- 1 tablespoon chives, chopped
- 6 tablespoons goat cheese

**Prep:** Heat up a pot with the stock over medium heat, add the rice, onion and the rest of the ingredients (except the chives) and the cheese, bring to a simmer and cook for 25 minutes.
Add the remaining ingredients, cook everything for 5 minutes, divide between plates.

**Nutrition:** 222 Calories; 5.5g Fat; 5.6g Protein

## 525. Mediterranean Lentils and Rice

**Preparation Time:** 5 minutes  
**Servings** 4  
**Cooking Time:** 25 minutes

**Ingredients:**

- 2¼ cups low-sodium vegetable broth
- ½ cup lentils
- ½ cup uncooked instant brown rice
- ½ cup diced carrots
- ½ cup diced celery
- 1 (2.25-ounce) can sliced olives
- ¼ cup diced red onion
- ¼ cup chopped fresh curly-leaf parsley
- 1½ tablespoons extra-virgin olive oil
- 1 tablespoon freshly squeezed lemon juice
- 1 garlic clove
- ¼ teaspoon kosher or sea salt
- ¼ teaspoon black pepper

**Prep:** Position saucepan over high heat, bring the broth and lentils to a boil, cover, and lower the heat to medium-low. Cook for 8 minutes.
Raise the heat to medium, and stir in the rice. Cover the pot and cook the mixture for 15 minutes. Take away pot from the heat and let it sit, covered, for 1 minute, then stir.
While the lentils and rice are cooking, stir together the carrots, celery, olives, onion, and parsley in a large serving bowl.
In a small bowl, whisk together the lemon juice, oil, garlic, salt, and pepper. Set aside.
When cooked, place them in the serving bowl. Pour the dressing on top, and toss to combine.

**Nutrition:** 230 Calories; 8g Fat; 8g Protein

## 526. Spaghetti with Mustard and Capers Dressing

**Preparation Time:** 15 minutes
**Servings 4**

**Cooking Time:** 20 minutes

### Ingredients

**For pasta:**
- 1 pinch of salt
- 1 pinch of black pepper
- ½ teaspoon of chili flakes
- 8 oz. of spaghetti

**For dressing:**
- 1 pinch of salt
- 1 pinch of black pepper
- 2 tablespoons of extra-virgin olive oil
- 14 oz. of canned tuna chunks in oil
- 1/3 cup of kalamata olives
- 8 oz. of cherry tomatoes
- 1 tablespoon of Dijon mustard
- ¼ cup of lemon juice
- 1 tablespoon of lemon zest
- 1 clove of garlic, minced
- 3 oz. of arugula
- ½ cup of pine nuts
- 1 tablespoon of capers

**Prep:** Stir all the ingredients for the dressing.
Cook the pasta according the package prep.
Boil the eggs, deshell and cut them in half. Set this aside.
Rinse and drain cooked pasta.
Add the remaining ingredients, give it a toss, top with the eggs, and then drizzle with the mustard dressing.
Serve.

**Nutrition:** 287 Calories; 14g Fat; 4g Protein

# FISH AND SEAFOOD

### 527. Eel with Grapes

**Prep time:** 15 minutes  
**Servings:** 6  

**Cook time:** 40 minutes

**Ingredients:**
- 1 eel
- Olive oil
- Salt
- 9 oz of black grapes
- 2 garlic cloves

**Prep:** Gut, skin and cut the eel. Cook in a pan with oil and garlic. Cook evenly and add the grapes, let them boil for about half an hour on low heat. Add salt to taste and enjoy.

**Nutrition:** Calories 465, Carbs 11.4 g, Protein 22.8 g, Fat 33.5 g

### 528. Eel Fritta

**Prep time:** 40 minutes  
**Servings:** 6  

**Cook time:** 15 minutes

**Ingredients:**
- 52 oz of peeled eel
- 2 bay leaves
- 1 celery stick
- 1 carrot
- Juniper berry
- ½ onion
- 1 garlic clove
- Flour
- Salt and pepper
- ½ cup of vinegar
- 1 cup white wine
- 10 black pepper grains
- Olive oil

**Prep:** Marinate the eel in vinegar, chopped vegetables, herbs, and white wine for 2 hours. Drain, dry and cut the eel. Then roll them in flour.
In a pan, heat up the oil, when it is very hot, fry the fish pieces previously rolled into the flour. Drain them on some paper towel, dry and add salt and pepper, then they are ready to serve.

**Nutrition:** Calories 583, Carbs 17.1 g, Protein 22.8 g, Fat 47.7

### 529. Parmigiana Cod

**Prep time:** 35 minutes  
**Cook time:** 1h 10min  
**Servings:** 6

**Ingredients:**
- 52 oz of salted cod
- Flour
- ¼ cup of butter
- 3 tbsp of olive oil

**For Salsa:**
- Salt and pepper
- ½ cup of tomato sauce
- 2 tbsp di butter
- 1 tbsp of parsley

**Prep:** Carefully clean the cod, cut it in squares, roll them into the flour and fry in a pan with hot oil and butter. Remove the fish when it goldens, move it to a casserole with the simmering tomato sauce and butter. Let it cook for about 20 minutes to absorb all the flavor. Adjust salt and pepper to taste. Sprinkle some minced parsley and serve hot.

**Nutrition:** Calories 365, Carbs 28.1 g, Protein 33.4 g, Fat 14.9 g

### 530. Cod with Potatoes

**Prep time:** 15 minutes  
**Cook time:** 40 minutes  
**Servings:** 6

**Ingredients:**
- 35 oz of wet salted cod
- 2 tbsp of oil
- 2 garlic cloves
- Flour
- 3/4 cup of lard
- 6 ripe tomatoes
- 9 oz of potatoes
- Salt and pepper

**Prep:** cut the cod, roll it in flour and sizzle in hot oil, frying it evenly.
Mash the lard and put it in a separate pan, add the garlic and chopped potatoes. Pour in the tomato pulp cut into pieces. Add salt and pepper to taste, let cook for about 20 minutes with a lid on.

**Nutrition:** Calories 569, Carbs 48.1 g, Protein 43.8 g, Fat 24 g

### 531. Baked Gray Mullet

**Prep time:** 10 minutes  
**Cook time:** 25 minutes  
**Servings:** 6

**Ingredients:**
- 6 gray mullets
- 1 sprig of parsley
- 1 sprig of basil
- Juice of 1 lemon
- Pinch of hot pepper
- Salt and pepper
- White wine vinegar
- 2 garlic cloves
- Olive oil

**Prep:** Skin the fish, open them cutting vertically the belly and gut it. Wash and dry. Let the mullet fish marinate in a bowl with half a cup of oil, pepper, salt, lemon juice for about one hour.
Move the mullet fish to an oven tray and cook in a preheated oven at 350° -375° F for about 20 minutes. Occasionally pour on top some marinate liquid.
Prepare the sauce with garlic, basil, hot pepper, minced parsley, salt, pepper and 3 tbsp of vinegar. Whip everything and slowly add 6 tbsp of oil. Remove from the oven and bone the fish, then season with the dressing.

**Nutrition:** Calories 237, Carbs 12.3 g, Protein 20.5 g, Fat 13.7 g

### 532. Cod with Dressing

**Prep time:** 10 minutes  
**Cook time:** 15 minutes  
**Servings:** 6

**Ingredients:**
- 52 oz of cod
- 2 tbsp of butter
- 2 tbsp of raisins
- 1 chopped onion
- 3 tbsp of olive oil
- 1 tbsp of parsley

- *Salt and pepper*
- *1 garlic clove*
- *1tbsp of tomato concentrate watered down in 1 cup of warm water*

**Prep:** Soak the raisins into some water. After some hours, drain and squeeze them.
Cut into medium size pieces the cod. In a large pan sizzle oil, butter, minced onion, parsley and garlic (remove it when it browns). Put in the cod pieces, pour the tomato concentrate, add the raisins and a dash of salt and pepper.
Cover with a lid and let cook on low heat for about 1 hour. Add in some water if the mixture gets too dry.

**Nutrition:** Calories 385, Carbs 10.2 g, Protein 23.4 g, Fat 23.2 g

### 533. Sea Bream Baked in Foil

**Prep time:** 15 minutes  
**Servings:** 6  
**Cook time:** 40 minutes

**Ingredients:**
- *52 oz of sea bream*
- *4 tbsp of black olives*
- *1 tsp of pepper*
- *Salt*
- *1 sprig of parsley*
- *6 oz of olive oil*
- *1 tbsp of capes*
- *1 garlic clove*
- *6 sliced lemons*
- *Pepper grains*

**Prep:** Clean the sea bream, gut it and remove the fins, tail and scales.
Wash it again and stuff with olives and capers, then leave it to marinate in an oven tray with the lemon slices, minced garlic, oil, salt, pepper grains, minced parsley.
After marinating, move the fish on some vegetable paper. Pour the marinate liquid, add some lemon slices, close the foil and place onto a tray and in the preheated oven at 350°F and cook.
The seam bream will be ready in 30 minutes. Unwrap and enjoy.

**Nutrition:** Calories 198.4, Carbs 2.2 g, Protein 32.5 g, Fat 6.4 g

### 534. Fried Cod

**Prep time:** 40 minutes  
**Servings:** 6  
**Cook time:** 10 minutes

**Ingredients:**
- *28 oz of wet cod*
- *2 eggs*
- *2 lemons cut in wedges*
- *Salt*
- *Olive oil*
- *¼ cup of flour*
- *½ cup of milk*

**Prep:** Wash and coat the fish in the batter (milk, eggs, salt, flour).
Heat up the oil in a pan; put in the fish when the oil is hot, fry it until it goldens. Strain and dry in some paper towel. Serve still hot with a dash of salt.
Side the fish with the lemon wedges.

**Nutrition:** Calories 637, Carbs 7 g, Protein 35.8 g, Fat 53.3 g

### 535. Sauté Catfish

**Prep time:** 2 hours e 15 minutes  
**Servings:** 6  
**Cook time:** 40 minutes

**Ingredients:**
- *6 catfish*
- *1 celery stick*
- *1 onion*
- *1 carrot*
- *1 cup of vinegar*
- *3 basil leaves*
- *½ cup of olive oil*
- *Salt and pepper*
- *½ cup of tomato sauce*
- *parsley*

**Prep:** Clean, gut and remove the whiskers of the catfish. Remove the tail and fins. Chop the onion, carrot and basil and sizzle them in a pan with oil. Add the fish when the other ingredients have been sizzled. Let them absorb the flavors and let cook. Add the vinegar and a half cup of hot water and let evaporate. Add the tomato sauce, salt and pepper. Allow to finish cooking. Sprinkle some minced parsley and serve.

### 536. Fried Frogs

**Prep time:** 10 minutes  
**Servings:** 6  
**Cook time:** 10 minutes

**Ingredients:**
- 52 oz of cleaned frogs
- 2 tbsp of parsley
- 1 cup of butter
- Flour
- ½ cup of extra virgin olive oil
- 1 lemon cut in wedges
- Salt and pepper

**Prep:** Remove the legs form the body of the frogs, wash them and season with salt and pepper. Roll them into the flour. Heat up the oil and butter in a pan and then fry the frogs. Allow to drain on some paper towel, sprinkle on some minced parsley and enjoy. Side with the lemon wedges.

### 537. Frogs in Oil

**Prep time:** 10 minutes

**Ingredients:**
- Vinegar
- Frogs
- Olive oil
- water

**Prep:** In a bowl put in the frogs and cover in vinegar and water, allow to marinate for 4 days (occasionally stir them). Dry them with a cloth and move into a jar full of oil. Tighten the lid and save in a dark and fresh spot.

### 538. Stuffed Sardines

**Prep time:** 30 minutes  
**Servings:** 6  
**Cook time:** 30 minutes

**Ingredients:**
- 35 oz of sardines
- 12 tbsp of breadcrumbs
- Butter
- Pepper
- ¾ cup of salted anchovies
- 2 tbsp of pine nuts
- Olive oil
- 3 tbsp of parsley
- Juice of 2 lemons

**Prep:** Fillet the anchovies by opening them and wash under running water. Lay them on a cloth do dry. Mince the anchovies as well as the pine nuts and parsley.
Pour some oil in a bowl, add the minced ingredients and breadcrumbs. Season with pepper and gently mix. Clean the sardines and stuff with the filling.
Grease a pan with butter, lay the stuffed sardines and add some butter pieces. Bake in a preheated oven at
350°F for half an hour.
Juice the lemon and enjoy.

**Nutrition:** Calories 649, Carbs 27.9 g, Protein 33.8 g, Fat 46.2 g

### 539. Roasted Squid

**Prep time:** 10 minutes  
**Servings:** 4  
**Cook time:** 15 minutes

**Ingredients:**
- Olive oil
- 21 oz of squid
- Salt and pepper
- 8 oz of breadcrumbs
- Juice of 1 lemon

**Prep:** Clean the squid.
In a bowl add the breadcrumbs, salt, oil and pepper. Stuff the squid with the mixture.
Put the squid in the oven at 350°F and bake for 15 minutes. Season with lemon and salt.

**Nutrition:** Calories 310, Carbs 42.6 g, Protein 20.2 g, Fat 8.3 g

### 540. Oven Sturgeon

**Prep time:** 20 minutes  
**Servings:** 6  

**Cook time:** 40 minutes

**Ingredients:**
- 52 oz of sturgeon
- 3 sprigs of rosemary
- 1 sprig of sage leaves
- 4 pressed garlic cloves
- 2 lemons, of which 1 sliced
- Salt
- ½ bottle of white wine
- 3 tbsp of olive oil

**Prep:** remove the fins and tail of the sturgeon, then gut it.
Stuff with 2 garlic cloves, a pinch of salt, lemon slices and a sprig of rosemary.
Lay the fish onto a tray, turn on the heat and sizzle with garlic, sage and rosemary. Pour the white wine and bake in a preheated oven at 350°F, to finish cooking the fish. Squeeze on the lemon juice.

**Nutrition:** Calories 447, Carbs 6.6 g, Protein 50.9 g, Fat 22.5 g

### 541. Grilled Tuna

**Prep time:** 20 minutes  
**Servings:** 6  

**Cook time:** 10 minutes

**Ingredients:**
- 28 oz of tuna
- Extra virgin olive oil
- Juice of 2 lemons
- Salt and pepper
- 2 tbsp of parsley
- 2 garlic cloves
- 1 tbsp of vinegar
- 1 cup of white wine
- 1 onion

**Prep:** skin the tuna pieces. Lay them in a bowl and add vinegar, oil and the other ingredients (minced garlic, parsley and onion) and let marinate for at least one night.
Remove the pieces from the bowl and lay them on the grill.
Roast, occasionally flip the pieces and pour on some marinading.

**Nutrition:** Calories 403, Carbs 3.1 g, Protein 31.6 g, Fat 21.4 g

### 542. Marinated and Fried Anchovies

**Prep time:** 20 minutes  
**Servings:** 6  

**Cook time:** 10 minutes

**Ingredients:**
- 35 oz of anchovies
- 3 garlic cloves
- Mint leaves
- Hot Peppers
- Flour
- Vinegar
- Olive oil
- salt

**Prep:** Gut the fish and chop off the heads. Rinse out the salt and roll them into flour, then fry into hot oil.
Let them drip on some paper towel and in the meantime prepare the dressing. In a pan add the garlic, hot pepper and mint with very little water.
Layer the anchovies onto a plate and pour the dressing on top. Allow to marinate for 12 hours.

**Nutrition:** Calories 491, Carbs 7.1 g, Protein 10.5 g, Fat 38.7 g

## 543. Grilled Lobster

**Prep time:** 15 minutes  
**Servings:** 4  
**Cook time:** 25 minutes

**Ingredients:**
- 4 small lobsters
- 8 tbsp of extra virgin olive oil
- 4 tbsp of lemon juice
- Salt and pepper

**Prep:** Cut the lobsters vertically and put them on the hot grill. Let them cook for 15 minutes, brush on some oil, lemon juice, salt and pepper. Turn the lobsters and allow to finish cooking.

**Nutrition:** Calories 114, Carbs 3.9 g, Protein 21.1 g, Fat 2.5 g

## 544. Au gratin Lobster

**Prep time:** 15 minutes  
**Servings:** 4  
**Cook time:** 30 minutes

**Ingredients:**
- 2 lobsters of 35 oz each
- ½ cup of breadcrumbs
- 1 sprig of parsley
- ½ garlic clove
- Oregano
- Extra virgin olive oil
- Salt and pepper

**Prep:** Cut the lobsters vertically and cover in salt. Put them on a tray and add some water.
On the side, mix the breadcrumbs with minced garlic, parsley, a pinch of oregano, salt and pepper. Add 5 tbsp of oil and drizzle the dressing on the lobsters.
Oven bake at 350°F for 30 minutes.

**Nutrition:** Calories 197, Carbs 15.8 g, Protein 21.1 g, Fat 12.3 g

## 545. Cod with Olives and Potatoes

**Prep time:** 30 minutes  
**Servings:** 4  
**Cook time:** 50 minutes

**Ingredients:**
- 35 oz salted cod
- 24 oz of potatoes
- 1 onion
- 9 oz of canned tomatoes
- 1 1/2 cup of black olives
- 1 sprig of parsley
- 5 tbsp of extra virgin olive oil
- Salt and pepper

**Prep:** Soak the cod in water for 2 days, changing the water every 12 hours. Rinse it and gently dry it. Remove the skin and cut into pieces.
Slice the onion, let it reduce in a pan with some oil. Add the diced potatoes, minced tomatoes and keep cooking for 15 minutes. Then add in the fish.
Cover in minced parsley and cook for about 20 minutes.

**Nutrition:** Calories 578, Carbs 48.2 g, Protein 43.4 g, Fat 22 g

## 546. Seasoned Squid

**Prep time:** 10 minutes  
**Servings:** 4  
**Cook time:** 7 minutes

**Ingredients:**
- 35 oz of cleaned squid
- ½ cup of olive oil
- 1 sprig of parsley
- 1 lemon
- Salt and pepper

**Prep:** wash and cook the squid for 7-8 minutes in boiling water. Strain and cut in half. Move them onto a serving plate and dress with an emulsion of oil, lemon juice, salt and pepper. Sprinkle a handful of minced parsley and serve.

**Nutrition:** Calories 326, Carbs 2.2 g, Protein 24.2 g, Fat 21.2 g

## 547. Breaded Grilled Squid

**Prep time: 20 minutes**  **Cook time: 10 minutes**
**Servings: 4**

**Ingredients:**
- 4 midsized squid
- 2 cups of breadcrumbs
- *Extra virgin olive oil*
- *Salt and pepper*

**Prep:** Clean and gently wash the squid. Dry and cover them in salt. Brush on some olive oil, roll in the breadcrumbs seasoned with a pinch of pepper. Roast on a hot grill.

**Nutrition:** Calories 307, Carbs 39.6 g, Protein 17.2 g, Fat 9.3 g

## 548. Squid in Dressing

**Prep time: 20 minutes**  **Cook time: 1 hour**
**Servings: 4**

**Ingredients:**
- 28 oz of cleaned squid
- 1 sprig of parsley
- ½ cup of white wine
- 2 garlic cloves
- ½ cup of olive oil
- Salt and pepper

**Prep:** Carefully wash the squid, cut them into rings and chop the tentacles.
Brown the minced garlic and parsley in a pan with a little oil. Add the squid and flip them for a few minutes in the seasoning. Deglaze with the wine. Add salt and pepper, cover with a lid and cook on low heat for about 45 minutes.

**Nutrition:** Calories 327, Carbs 2.1 g, Protein 34 g, Fat 11.9 g

## 549. Fried Squid

**Prep time: 15 minutes**  **Cook time: 7 minutes**
**Servings: 4**

**Ingredients:**
- 28 oz of cleaned squid
- Flour
- *Extra virgin olive oil*
- 2 lemons
- salt

**Prep:** Carefully wash the squid, cut into rings the heads and leave whole the tentacles.
Roll the pieces in flour and fry in plenty of hot oil. When they become golden, move them onto some paper towel to absorb the excess oil. Sprinkle on some salt and side with lemon wedges.

**Nutrition:** Calories 914, Carbs 31.9 g, Protein 24.1 g, Fat 71.8 g

## 550. Stuffed Squid

**Prep time: 20 minutes**  **Cook time: 30 minutes**
**Servings: 4**

**Ingredients:**
- 8 squid
- 2 garlic cloves
- 1 sprig of parsley
- 1 cup di breadcrumbs
- 2 tbsp of grated pecorino
- 1 tbsp of capers
- *Extra virgin olive oil*
- *Salt and pepper*

**Prep:** Clean the squid, remove the heads and carefully empty them. Mince the tentacles, cook them in a pan with 2 tbsp of oil and move them to a bowl. Lightly toast the breadcrumbs. Add the minced pecorino, parsley, garlic, capers. Drizzle some oil and combine everything together, then stuff the squid. Close the opening with a toothpick and place the squid onto a greased tray. Oven bake at 350°F for about 20 minutes.

**Nutrition:** Calories 266, Carbs 16.2 g, Protein 19.4 g, Fat 12 g

### 551. Grouper in Dressing

**Prep time:** 20 minutes  
**Servings:** 4  
**Cook time:** 30 minutes

**Ingredients:**
- 35 oz of grouper
- 1 celery stick
- 1 carrot
- 1 onion
- 1 bay leaf
- 1 sprig of parsley
- ½ cup of olive oil
- 1 lemon
- Salt and pepper

**Prep:** Boil a pot full of water the carrot, bay leaf, celery, onion and parsley in. Dip the cleaned grouper and let it cook. Drain the fish, remove the skin and bones and place it onto a serving dish. Dress with an emulsion of oil, lemon, minced parsley and pepper.

**Nutrition:** Calories 223, Carbs 0.2 g, Protein 43.1 g, Fat 34.9 g

### 552. Roasted Mantis Shrimp

**Prep time:** 10 minutes  
**Servings:** 4  
**Cook time:** 25 minutes

**Ingredients:**
- 4 mantis shrimp
- 4 tbsp of olive oil
- 1 lemon
- Salt and pepper

**Prep:** Vertically cut in half the mantis shrimp, place them on the grill. Let it roast for 15 minutes, then flip them and allow to finish cooking.
Serve the shellfish still hot, dressed with an emulsion of oil, lemon juice, salt and pepper.

**Nutrition:** Calories 297, Carbs 5.9 g, Protein 53.7 g, Fat 4.8 g

### 553. Fried Sandeel Fish

**Prep time:** 15 minutes  
**Servings:** 4  
**Cook time:** 5 minutes

**Ingredients:**
- 28 oz sandeel fish
- Olive oil
- Flour
- salt

**Prep:** Gently wash the fish, roll them in flour and fry in plenty of hot oil. When they become golden, strain on a paper towel and serve.

**Nutrition:** Calories 882, Carbs 31.5 g, Protein 34.2 g, Fat 70.7 g

### 554. Sword Fish Cutlets

**Prep time:** 15 minutes  
**Servings:** 4  
**Cook time:** 5 minutes

**Ingredients:**
- 4 slices of sword fish
- 2 eggs
- Flour
- 1 sprig of parsley
- 1 lemon
- Extra virgin olive oil
- Salt
- Breadcrumbs
- 1 garlic clove

**Prep:** Wash and skin the sword fish then roll it in flour. Move the slices into the beaten eggs, move to a bowl with breadcrumbs and minced parsley garlic.
Fry the fish in plenty of hot oil. Side with some lemon wedges.

**Nutrition:** Calories 182, Carbs 14.4 g, Protein 14.1 g, Fat 41.7 g

### 555. Mussels with Pepper

**Prep time:** 1 hour  
**Servings:** 4  
**Cook time:** 15 minutes

**Ingredients:**
- 4 lbs of mussels
- 2 garlic cloves
- 1 sprig of parsley
- pepper

**Prep:** Brush and clean well the mussels. Move them in a tray with garlic, a dash of pepper and minced e parsley. Cook until the shells open and serve.

**Nutrition:** Calories 192, Carbs 6.9 g, Protein 11.8 g, Fat 13.4 g

### 556. Baked Dentex with Olives

**Prep time:** 15 minutes  
**Servings:** 4  
**Cook time:** 35 minutes

**Ingredients:**
- 35 oz of dentex steak
- 17 oz of canned tomatoes
- 1 onion
- 1 cup of black olives
- 2 garlic cloves
- Oregano
- 1 sprig of parsley
- 6 tbsp of olive oil
- Salt and pepper

**Prep:** let the minced onion reduce in a pot with some oil. Add the chopped tomatoes, olives. A pinch of oregano, minced parsley, salt and pepper, and let the sauce thicken.
Place the steaks of fish on a tray with a pinch of salt, the sauce and bake at 350°F for 20-25 minutes, flip the fish halfway through.

**Nutrition:** Calories 572 kcal, Carbs6.8 g, Protein 41.2 g, Fat 19.8 g

### 557. Grilled Dentex

**Prep time:** 15 minutes  
**Servings:** 4  
**Cook time:** 10 minutes

**Ingredients:**
- 28 oz of dentex steaks
- 1 sprig of parsley
- Mint
- 1 lemon
- 1 ½ cup of olive oil
- Salt and pepper

**Prep:** Gently wash and dry the dentex, cover in salt and roast on a hot grill. Finely mince the mint and parsley, add the oil, lemon juice and pepper. Combine well the ingredients. Season the fish with the sauce and serve.

**Nutrition:** Calories 461, Carbs 6 g, Protein 42.1 g, Fat 10.1 g

### 558. Herring in Oil

**Prep time:** 20 minutes  
**Servings:** 4  
**Cook time:** 10 minutes

**Ingredients:**
- 2 salted herrings
- Olive oil
- pepper

**Prep:** Wrap the herring in aluminum foil, crumple the edges and put a hot grill for 6-7 minutes, flip them and allow to finish cooking.

Open the foil and skin the fish. Remove the bones and spikes, move the fish to a bowl and dress with plenty of oil and pepper. Let marinate for few hours, then enjoy.

**Nutrition:** Calories 258 kcal, Carbs 16.5 g, Protein 20.2 g, Fat 11.6 g

### 559. Au Gratin Mackerel

**Prep time: 30 minutes**  
**Servings: 4**  
**Cook time: 20 minutes**

**Ingredients:**
- 4 cleaned mackerels
- 1 cup of breadcrumbs
- 1 lemon
- Extra virgin olive oil
- Capers
- Oregano
- Salt and pepper

**Prep:** Divide each mackerel into 2 filets, remove the bones, add salt and dip them into the oil. Roll the fish into a mixture of breadcrumbs, oregano, salt and pepper, and move them in a greased tray. Cover the filets with a handful of capers, 2 tbsp of oil and lemon juice.
Bake at 350°F for 20 minutes.

**Nutrition:** Calories 265, Carbs 23.6 g, Protein 10.1 g, Fat 15.7 g

### 560. Fried Squid and Shrimp

**Prep time: 20 minutes**  
**Servings: 4**  
**Cook time: 5 minutes**

**Ingredients:**
- 21 oz of squid
- 10 oz of shelled shrimp
- 2 eggs
- 1 cup of milk
- Flour
- Extra virgin olive oil
- salt

**Prep:** Clean, wash and dry the squid. Cut them into rings and move to the beaten eggs with milk. Let them soak for 20 minutes. Drain and move to the flour. Roll also the shrimp into the flour. Fry the fish into plenty of hot oil, cover in salt and serve.

**Nutrition:** Calories 988, Carbs 51 g, Protein 66.1 g, Fat 58.6 g

### 561. Fried Damselfish

**Prep time: 20 minutes**  
**Servings: 4**  
**Cook time: 5 minutes**

**Ingredients:**
- 28 oz damselfish
- Flour
- Extra virgin olive oil
- salt

**Prep:** Carefully wash and dry the fish. Roll into the flour and fry in a pan with plenty of hot oil. Rest onto some paper towel, add salt and serve.

**Nutrition:** Calories 674, Carbs 20.7 g, Protein 33.5 g, Fat 50.8 g

### 562. Shrimp with Mint

**Prep time: 30 minutes**  
**Servings: 4**  
**Cook time: 7 minutes**

**Ingredients:**
- 52 oz of shrimp
- ½ cup of white wine
- 1 sprig of mint
- 1 lemon
- ½ cup of olive oil
- Salt and pepper

**Prep:** Cook the shrimp per 7 minutes in plenty of hot water with the added wine. Let them cool down a little, shell and move them onto a serving dish. Cover with an emulsion of oil, lemon juice, pepper, minced mint and let marinate a few minutes before serving.

**Nutrition:** Calories 236, Carbs 9.2 g, Protein 14.6 g, Fat 15.7 g

## 563. Fried Shrimp

**Prep time:** 15 minutes     **Cook time:** 2 minutes
**Servings:** 4

**Ingredients:**
- *28 oz shelled shrimp*
- *Extra virgin olive oil*
- *Flour*
- *salt*

**Prep:** Roll in flour the shrimp tails and fry for 2 minutes in plenty of hot oil a few at a time. Put them onto paper towel to absorb the excess oil, cover in salt and serve.

**Nutrition:** Calories 972, Carbs 48 g, Protein 67.3 g, Fat 58.6 g

## 564. Baked Shrimp

**Prep time:** 15 minutes     **Cook time:** 25 minutes
**Servings:** 4

**Ingredients:**
- *52 oz of big shrimp*
- *3 tbsp of olive oil*
- *2 bay leaves*
- *Coarse Salt and pepper*

**Prep:** Cover the shrimp with coarse salt and lay them into one layer on a tray with the broken bay leaves. Bake a at 375°F for 10 minutes.
Remove the tray from the oven, add a drizzle of oil and a dash of pepper. Put back into the oven and complete baking at 350°F for 15 minutes.

**Nutrition:** Calories 237, Carbs 4.8 g, Protein 17.7 g, Fat 14.8 g

## 565. Grilled Shrimp

**Prep time:** 10 minutes     **Cook time:** 15 minutes
**Servings:** 4

**Ingredients:**
- *52 oz of big shrimp*
- *Extra virgin olive oil*
- *Coarse Salt*

**Prep:** Cover the shrimp in salt and place them on the grill. Cook for 15 minutes, occasionally brush on some oil and flip them a few times.

**Nutrition:** Calories 216, Carbs 4.1 g, Protein 17.7 g, Fat 7.9 g

## 566. Crabs in Dressing

**Prep time:** 20 minutes     **Cook time:** 15 minutes
**Servings:** 4

**Ingredients:**
- *35 oz of crabs*
- *1 lemon*
- *Extra virgin olive oil*
- *Salt and pepper*

**Prep:** Clean and rinse the crab. Move them in a casserole with plenty of water with salt and bring to a boil. Let cook for 10-15 minutes, then strain and let cool down a little.

Remove the claws and the bottom shell, season the pulp with an emulsion of oil, lemon juice and pepper.

**Nutrition:** Calories 321, Carbs 2.1 g, Protein 33 g, Fat 11.8 g

### 567. Mixed Grill

**Prep time: 1 hour**  
**Servings: 4**

**Cook time: 30 minutes**

**Ingredients:**
- *4 slices of sword fish*
- *4 squid*
- *4 small breams*
- *8 big shrimp*
- *1 sprig of parsley*
- *2 lemons*
- *1 cup of olive oil*
- *Salt and pepper*

**Prep:** Carefully clean all the fish, cover with salt and place them on the hot grill.
Prepare an emulsion of oil, lemon juice and pepper and minced parsley, serve and add on the side a bowl of dressing for each serving.

**Nutrition:** Calories 341, Carbs 6.8 g, Protein 37.6 g, Fat 17.5 g

### 568. Sword Fish Rolls

**Prep time: 15 minutes**  
**Servings: 4**

**Cook time: 25 minutes**

**Ingredients:**
- *12 slices of sword fish*
- *1 1/2 cup of breadcrumbs*
- *2 tbsp of pine nuts*
- *2 tbsp of raisins*
- *2 tbsp of grated pecorino*
- *1 sprig of parsley*
- *2 salted anchovies*
- *2 lemons*
- *Bay leaves*
- *Extra virgin olive oil*
- *Salt and pepper*

**Prep:** Lightly toast 1 cup di breadcrumbs with 2 tbsp of oil in a pan, combine the pecorino, minced parsley, pine nuts, raisins, rinsed anchovies, some tbsp of lemon juice, salt and pepper.
Distribute the mixture on the slices of fish and roll them. Place the rolls in some oil and then into the leftover breadcrumbs. Skew the rolls into wooden skewers alternating them with the bay leaves and place them into a greased tray. Season with a drizzle of oil, bake in a preheated oven at 375°F for 20 minutes.

**Nutrition:** Calories 177, Carbs 11.7 g, Protein 8.8 g, Fat 11.4 g

### 569. Baked Bream Fish

**Prep time: 20 minutes**  
**Servings: 4**

**Cook time: 40 minutes**

**Ingredients:**
- *1 bream of about 35 oz*
- *2 lemons*
- *Oregano*
- *5 tbsp of olive oil*
- *Salt and pepper*

**Prep:** Clean the fish and cover it completely in salt, pepper and oregano.
Grease the oven tray and place the fish in it, dress in an emulsion of oil, lemon juice, salt and pepper and bake at 350°F for 40 minutes. While baking, gently turn it a few times.

**Nutrition:** Calories 249, Carbs 3.9 g, Protein 21.8 g, Fat 14.9 g

### 570. Fried Cod (2nd Version)

**Prep time: 30 minutes**  
**Servings: 4**

**Cook time: 5 minutes**

**Ingredients:**

- *35 oz of small cod*
- *Flour*
- *Extra virgin olive oil*
- *salt*

**Prep:** Clean the cod and fold them so that the tail fits into the mouth. Roll them in flour and fry into plenty of hot oil. Place on a paper towel to absorb the excess oil, sprinkle some salt and serve.

**Nutrition:** Calories 639, Carbs 23.4 g, Protein 27.8 g, Fat 23.2 g

## 571. Menola Fish with Onion

**Prep time:** 20 minutes  
**Cook time:** 25 minutes  
**Servings:** 4

**Ingredients:**
- *35 oz of menolas*
- *4 red onions*
- *1 cup of vinegar*
- *Extra virgin olive oil*
- *Salt and pepper*

**Prep:** Wash and add salt to the fish. Fry in plenty of hot oil. When they are golden, strain and place them onto a serving dish. Finely chop the onions and let them reduce on low heat with ½ cup of oil and 2 tbsp of water. Add the vinegar and let it evaporate for few minutes. Turn off the heat and pour immediately on the fish. Let it marinate for 3 hours before serving.

**Nutrition:** Calories 591, Carbs 6.4 g, Protein 27.1 g, Fat 27.8 g

## 572. Bream with Potatoes

**Prep time:** 20 minutes  
**Cook time:** 30 minutes  
**Servings:** 4

**Ingredients:**
- *1 bream of c.a. 35 oz*
- *24 oz of potatoes*
- *½ cup of white wine*
- *Oregano*
- *4 tbsp of olive oil*
- *Salt and pepper*

**Prep:** Clean well the bream, cover in salt, lay it onto a greased tray. Distribute around it the peeled potato chunks. Season with oil and salt, oregano and wine mixed with 1 cup of water. Bake at 375°F for 30 minutes.

**Nutrition:** Calories 435, Carbs 5.5 g, Protein 51 g, Fat 24.5 g

## 573. Sweet and Sour Dogfish

**Prep time:** 20 minutes  
**Cook time:** 15 minutes  
**Servings:** 4

**Ingredients:**
- *35 oz of dogfish slices*
- *Flour*
- *1 onion*
- *½ cup of vinegar*
- *1 tbsp of sugar*
- *Extra virgin olive oil*
- *Salt and pepper*

**Prep:** Wash the fish and roll it in flour. Fry it in plenty of hot oil and cover in salt.
Thinly slice the onion, let it reduce in a pan with the oil and 2 tbsp of water. Pour the vinegar, sugar and cook for 2 minutes. Place the fish in a bowl, season with the dressing and let cool down completely before serving.

## 574. Bream Fish in Salt Crust

**Prep time:** 30 minutes  
**Cook time:** 40 minutes  
**Servings:** 4

**Ingredients:**
- *1 bream of about 35 oz*
- *1 thyme sprig*
- *6,6 oz of salt*
- *pepper*

**Prep:** Clean the fish and season it with some pepper. Place inside the belly the thyme. Pour the salt in a bowl and add 11 oz of water and carefully mix. Pour half of the salt in the tray to form a thick layer. Place the fish on it and cover completely in the remaining salt. Put in the oven at 375°F for about 40 minutes. Break the salt crust and serve.

**Nutrition:** Calories 159, Carbs 3.2 g, Protein 30.5 g, Fat 2.8 g

## 575. Sword Fish in Dressing

**Prep time:** 15 minutes  **Cook time:** 40 minutes
**Servings:** 4

**Ingredients:**
- 4 slices of sword fish
- 1 onion
- 1 garlic clove
- 9 oz of tomato sauce
- 1 1/2 cup of green olives with no pit
- 1 tbsp of capers
- Extra virgin olive oil
- 1 celery stick
- Flour
- Salt and pepper

**Prep:** Finely slice the onion and let it reduce in a pan with ½ cup of oil and minced garlic, celery and parsley. Add the tomato sauce, capers, olives, a pinch of salt and pepper and let it cook on a low heat for about ten minutes. Pour ½ cup of water and bring to a boil. Remove the fish and skin it, strain it and put it into a casserole, let cook on low heat for 20 minutes.

**Nutrition:** Calories 370, Carbs 5.4 g, Protein 20.3 g, Fat 24.1 g

## 576. Sword Fish with Oil

**Prep time:** 15 minutes  **Cook time:** 6 minutes
**Servings:** 4

**Ingredients:**
- 4 slices of sword fish
- ½ cup of olive oil
- 2 lemons
- Oregano
- Salt and pepper

**Prep:** Pour the oil in a bowl, add the lemon juice, a handful of salt, pepper and oregano. Whisk everything with a fork to reach an even creamy consistency.
Salt the slices and roast them on a hot grill. Then move onto a serving dish and season with the sauce.

**Nutrition:** Calories 441, Carbs 1.5 g, Protein 16.6 g, Fat 44 g

## 577. Sword Fish with Olives, Capers and Mint

**Prep time:** 15 minutes  **Cook time:** 30 minutes
**Servings:** 4

**Ingredients:**
- 4 slices of sword fish
- 1 1/2 cup green olives
- 1 carrot
- 1 celery stick
- 1 tbsp of capers
- 1 onion
- Mint leaves
- 1 cup of olive oil
- ½ cup of vinegar
- 1 tbsp of sugar
- Salt and pepper

**Prep:** Heat up 3 tbsp of oil in a pan and sizzle the fish slices, turn them to golden on each side.
In a separate pan, reduce the onion with the remaining oil. Add the chopped carrot, capers, olives with no pit, minced parsley, mint and let them cook. Pour in ½ cup of water and leave on the heat for few minutes.
Add the fish, salt and pepper, pour the vinegar with the sugar and let deglaze.

**Nutrition:** Calories 431, Carbs 5.5 g, Protein 31.7 g, Fat 21.6 g

## 578. Fried Sea Scallops

**Prep time:** 30 minutes  **Cook time:** 5 minutes
**Servings:** 4

**Ingredients:**
- *35 oz of sea scallops*
- *Flour*
- *Extra virgin olive oil*
- *salt*

**Prep:** Clean and shell the scallops. Roll in flour and fry in plenty of hot oil. When they are golden, strain and sprinkle with salt.

**Nutrition:** Calories 629, Carbs 23.1 g, Protein 28.9 g, Fat 23.1 g

## 579. Cod Balls

**Prep time:** 40 minutes
**Servings:** 4

**Cook time:** 20 minutes

**Ingredients:**
- *35 oz of salted cod filet*
- *1 cup of breadcrumbs*
- *1 sprig of parsley*
- *3 tbsp of grated pecorino*
- *1 garlic clove*
- *1 egg*
- *Milk*
- *Flour*
- *Extra virgin olive oil*
- *Salt and pepper*

**Prep:** Soak the cod for 2 days, change the water every 12 hours.
Boil the fish in a pot full of water, strain it, skin and remove the bones. Mince the fish pulp and mix it with the breadcrumbs, some milk, salt, pepper, the egg and minced garlic, parsley and pecorino. Roll into balls, coat them with the flour and fry in plenty of hot oil.

**Nutrition:** Calories 163, Carbs 8.7 g, Protein 8.5 g, Fat 11.8 g

## 580. Sardine Balls with Sauce

**Prep time:** 30 minutes
**Servings:** 4

**Cook time:** 50 minutes

**Ingredients:**
- *35 oz of sardines*
- *1 cup of breadcrumbs*
- *1 tbsp of pine nuts*
- *2 tbsp grated pecorino*
- *1 tbsp of raisins*
- *1 egg*
- *1 sprig of parsley*
- *16 oz of tomato sauce*
- *Flour*
- *1 bay leaf*
- *White wine*
- *Extra virgin olive oil*
- *Salt and pepper*

**Prep:** Clean the sardines, mince them and move them into a bowl. Add the breadcrumbs a little at a time, some water, minced parsley, pecorino, raisins, pine nuts, egg and a pinch of salt and pepper. Combine well everything.
Roll the mixture into balls, coat them in flour, sizzle in a pan with 1 cup of hot oil and bay leaves. Deglaze with wine. Add the tomato sauce, cover with a lid and keep cooking for 40 minutes, on medium heat.

**Nutrition:** Calories 261, Carbs 8.7 g, Protein 9.7 g, Fat 9.6 g

## 581. Mediterranean Baked Salmon

**Prep Time:** 35 minutes
**Serving:** 5

**Cook Time:** 11 minutes

**Ingredients:**
- *2 (6 oz.) boneless salmon fillets*
- *1 onion, tomato*
- *1 tbsp. capers*
- *1 tsp. dry oregano*
- *3 tbsp. Parmesan cheese*

**Prep:** Set oven to 350 F. Place the salmon fillets in a baking dish, sprinkle with oregano, top with onion and tomato slices, drizzle with olive oil, and sprinkle with capers and Parmesan cheese.
Wrap the dish with foil and bake for 30 minutes.

**Nutrition:** 291 Calories, 14 g Fat, 2 g Protein

## 582. Salmon Frittata

**Prep Time:** 5 minutes  
**Servings:** 4  
**Cook Time:** 27 minutes

**Ingredients:**
- 1-pound gold potatoes, roughly cubed
- 1 tablespoon olive oil
- 2 salmon fillets, skinless and boneless
- 8 eggs, whisked
- 1 teaspoon mint, chopped

**Prep:** Put the potatoes in a boiling water at medium heat, then cook for 12 minutes, drain and transfer to a bowl.
Arrange the salmon on a baking sheet lined with baking paper, grease with cooking spray, and broil over medium-high heat for 5 minutes on each side, cool down, flake and put in a separate bowl.
Warm up a pan with the oil over medium heat, add the potatoes, salmon, and the rest of the ingredients except the eggs and toss. Add the eggs on top, put the lid on and cook over medium heat for 10 minutes.
Divide the salmon between plates and serve.

**Nutrition:** 289 Calories, 11 g Fat, 4 g Protein

## 583. Salmon Kebabs

**Prep Time:** 30 minutes  
**Serving:** 5  
**Cook Time:** 6 minutes

**Ingredients:**
- 2 shallots, ends trimmed, halved
- 2 zucchinis, cut in 2-inch cubes
- 1 cup cherry tomatoes
- 6 skinless salmon fillets, cut into 1-inch pieces
- 3 limes, cut into thin wedges

**Prep:** Preheat barbecue or char grill on medium-high. Thread fish cubes onto skewers, then zucchinis, shallots and tomatoes. Repeat to make 12 kebabs. Bake the kebabs for about 3 minutes each side for medium cooked.
Situate to a plate, wrap with foil and set aside for 5 minutes to rest.

**Nutrition:** 268 Calories, 9 g Fat, 3 g Protein

## 584. Coconut Clam Chowder

**Prep Time:** 10 minutes  
**Servings:** 6  
**Cook Time:** 7 minutes

**Ingredients:**
- 6 oz clams, chopped
- 1 cup heavy cream
- 1/4 onion, sliced
- 1 cup celery, chopped
- 1 lb cauliflower, chopped
- 1 cup fish broth
- 1 bay leaf
- 2 cups of coconut milk
- Salt

**Prep:** Add all ingredients except clams and heavy cream and stir well. Seal pot with lid and cook on high for 5 minutes. Once done, release pressure using quick release. Remove lid. Add heavy cream and clams and stir well and cook on sauté mode for 2 minutes. Stir well and serve.

**Nutrition:** Calories 301, Fat 27.2 g, Carbs 13.6 g, Sugar 6 g, Protein 4.9 g

## 585. Cod in Tomato Sauce

**Prep Time:** 20 minutes  
**Servings:** 5  
**Cook Time:** 35 minutes

**Ingredients:**
- 1 teaspoon dried dill weed
- 2 teaspoons sumac
- 2 teaspoons ground coriander
- 1½ teaspoons ground cumin
- 1 teaspoon ground turmeric
- 2 tablespoons olive oil
- 1 large sweet onion, chopped
- 8 garlic cloves, chopped
- 2 jalapeño peppers, chopped
- 5 medium tomatoes, chopped
- 3 tablespoons tomato paste
- 2 tablespoons fresh lime juice
- ½ cup water
- Salt and ground black pepper, as required
- 5 (6-ounce) cod fillets
- ½ cup fresh parsley, chopped

**Prep:** For spice mixture: in a small bowl, add the dill weed and spices and mix well.

In a large skillet, heat the oil over medium-high heat and sauté the onion for about 2 minutes.
Add the garlic and jalapeno and sauté for about 2 minutes.
Stir in the tomatoes, tomato paste, lime juice, water, half of the spice mixture, salt and pepper and bring to a boil.
Reduce the heat to medium-low and cook, covered for about 10 minutes, stirring occasionally.
Meanwhile, season the cod fillets with the remaining spice mixture, salt and pepper evenly.
Place the fish fillets into the skillet and gently, press into the tomato mixture.
Increase the heat to medium-high and cook for about 2 minutes.
Reduce the heat to medium and cook, covered for about 10-15 minutes or until desired doneness of the fish.
Serve hot with the garnishing of the parsley.

**Nutrition:** Calories 285, Fat 7.7 g, Carbs 12.5 g, Protein 41.4 g

### 586. Creamy Fish Stew

**Prep Time:** 10 minutes  
**Servings:** 6  
**Cook Time:** 8 minutes

**Ingredients:**
- 1 lb white fish fillets, cut into chunks
- 2 tbsp olive oil
- 1 cup kale, chopped
- 1 cup cauliflower, chopped
- 1 cup broccoli, chopped
- 3 cups fish broth
- 1 cup heavy cream
- 2 celery stalks, diced
- 1 carrot, sliced
- 1 onion, diced
- Pepper
- Salt

**Prep:** Add oil into the inner pot of instant pot and set the pot on sauté mode. Add onion and sauté for 3 minutes. Add remaining ingredients except for heavy cream and stir well.
Seal pot with lid and cook on high for 5 minutes.
Once done, allow to release pressure naturally. Remove lid.
Stir in heavy cream and serve.

**Nutrition:** Calories 296, Fat 19.3 g, Carbs 7.5 g, Sugar 2.6 g, Protein 22.8 g

### 587. Mediterranean Fish Tacos

**Prep Time:** 10 minutes  
**Servings:** 8  
**Cook Time:** 8 minutes

**Ingredients:**
- 4 tilapia fillets
- 1/4 cup fresh cilantro, chopped
- 1/4 cup fresh lime juice
- 2 tbsp paprika
- 1 tbsp olive oil
- Pepper
- Salt

**Prep:** Pour 2 cups of water into the instant pot then place steamer rack in the pot.
Place fish fillets on parchment paper. Season fish fillets with paprika, pepper, and salt and drizzle with oil and lime juice.
Fold parchment paper around the fish fillets and place them on a steamer rack in the pot.
Seal pot with lid and cook on high for 8 minutes.
Once done, release pressure using quick release. Remove lid.
Remove fish packet from pot and open it. Shred the fish with a fork and serve.

### 588. Shrimp with Alfredo Sauce

**Prep Time:** 10 minutes  
**Servings:** 4  
**Cook Time:** 3 minutes

**Ingredients:**
- 12 shrimp, remove shells
- 1 tbsp garlic, minced
- 1/4 cup parmesan cheese
- 2 cups whole wheat rotini noodles
- 1 cup fish broth
- 15 oz alfredo sauce
- 1 onion, chopped
- Salt

**Prep:** Add all ingredients except parmesan cheese into the instant pot and stir well. Seal pot with lid and cook on high for 3 minutes.
Once done, release pressure using quick release. Remove lid.
Stir in cheese and serve.

**Nutrition:** Calories 669, Fat 23.1 g, Carbs 76 g, Protein 37.8 g

## 589. Salmon Stew

**Prep Time:** 10 minutes  
**Servings:** 6  
**Cook Time:** 8 minutes

**Ingredients:**
- 2 lbs salmon fillet, cubed
- 1 onion, chopped
- 2 cups fish broth
- 1 tbsp olive oil
- Pepper
- salt

**Prep:** Add oil into the inner pot of instant pot and set the pot on sauté mode. Add onion and sauté for 2 minutes. Add remaining ingredients and stir well. Seal pot with lid and cook on high for 6 minutes.
Once done, release pressure using quick release. Remove lid.
Stir and serve.

**Nutrition:** Calories 243, Fat 12.6 g, Carbs 0.8 g, Protein 31 g

## 590. Feta Tomato Sea Bass

**Prep Time:** 10 minutes  
**Servings:** 4  
**Cook Time:** 8 minutes

**Ingredients:**
- 4 sea bass fillets
- 1 1/2 cups water
- 1 tbsp olive oil
- 1 tsp garlic, minced
- 1 tsp basil, chopped
- 1 tsp parsley, chopped
- 1/2 cup feta cheese, crumbled
- 1 cup can tomatoes, diced
- Pepper
- Salt

**Prep:** Season fish fillets with pepper and salt.
Pour 2 cups of water into the instant pot then place steamer rack in the pot.
Place fish fillets on steamer rack in the pot. Seal pot with lid and cook on high for 5 minutes.
Once done, release pressure using quick release. Remove lid.
Remove fish fillets from the pot and clean the pot.
Add oil into the inner pot of instant pot and set the pot on sauté mode. Add garlic and sauté for 1 minute. Add tomatoes, parsley, and basil and stir well and cook for 1 minute. Add fish fillets and top with crumbled cheese and cook for a minute.

**Nutrition:** Calories 219, Fat 10.1 g, Carbs 4 g, Protein 27.1 g

## 591. Codfish with Shrimp

**Prep Time:** 10 minutes  
**Servings:** 6  
**Cook Time:** 5 minutes

**Ingredients:**
- 1 lb codfish, cut into chunks
- 1 1/2 lbs shrimp
- 28 oz can tomatoes, diced
- 1 cup dry white wine
- 1 bay leaf
- 1 tsp cayenne
- 1 tsp oregano
- 1 shallot, chopped
- 1 tsp garlic, minced
- 1 tbsp olive oil
- 1/2 tsp salt

**Prep:** Add oil into the inner pot of instant pot and set the pot on sauté mode. Add shallot and garlic and sauté for 2 minutes. Add wine, bay leaf, cayenne, oregano, and salt and cook for 3 minutes. Add remaining ingredients and stir well.
Seal pot with a lid and select manual and cook on low for 0 minutes.
Once done, release pressure using quick release. Remove lid.

**Nutrition:** Calories 281, Fat 5 g, Carbs 10.5 g, Protein 40.7 g

## 592. Garlicky Clams

**Prep Time:** 10 minutes  
**Servings:** 4  
**Cook Time:** 5 minutes

**Ingredients:**
- 3 lbs clams, clean
- 4 garlic cloves
- 1/4 cup olive oil
- 1/2 cup fresh lemon juice
- 1 cup white wine
- Pepper
- Salt

**Prep:** Add oil into the inner pot of instant pot and set the pot on sauté mode. Add garlic and sauté for 1 minute. Add wine and cook for 2 minutes. Add remaining ingredients and stir well. Seal pot with lid and cook on high for 2 minutes.
Once done, allow to release pressure naturally. Remove lid.

**Nutrition:** Calories 332, Fat 13.5 g, Carbs 40.5 g, Protein 2.5 g

## 593. Garlicky Shrimp

**Prep Time:** 15 minutes  
**Servings:** 4  
**Cook Time:** 6 minutes

**Ingredients:**
- 2 tablespoons olive oil
- 3 garlic cloves, sliced
- 1-pound shrimp, peeled and deveined
- 1 tablespoon fresh rosemary, chopped
- ½ teaspoon red pepper flakes, crushed
- Salt and ground black pepper, as required
- 1 tablespoon fresh lemon juice

**Prep:** In a large skillet, heat the oil over medium heat and sauté the garlic slices or about 2 minutes or until golden brown. With a slotted spoon, transfer the garlic slices into a bowl.
In the same skillet, add the shrimp, rosemary, red pepper flakes, salt and black pepper and cook for about 3-4 minutes, stirring frequently. Stir in the lemon juice and remove from the heat.
Serve hot with a topping of the garlic slices.

**Nutrition:** Calories 202, Fat 9.1 g, Carbs 3.2 g

## 594. Healthy Carrot & Shrimp

**Prep Time:** 10 minutes  
**Servings:** 4  
**Cook Time:** 6 minutes

**Ingredients:**
- 1 lb shrimp, peeled and deveined
- 1 tbsp chives, chopped
- 1 onion, chopped
- 1 tbsp olive oil
- 1 cup fish stock
- 1 cup carrots, sliced
- Pepper
- Salt

**Prep:** Add oil into the inner pot of instant pot and set the pot on sauté mode. Add onion and sauté for 2 minutes. Add remaining ingredients and stir well. Seal pot with lid and cook on high for 4 minutes.
Once done, release pressure using quick release. Remove lid.

**Nutrition:** Calories 197, Fat 5.9 g, Carbs 7 g, Protein 27.7 g

## 595. Honey Garlic Shrimp

**Prep Time:** 10 minutes  
**Servings:** 4  
**Cook Time:** 5 minutes

**Ingredients:**
- 1 lb shrimp, peeled and deveined
- 1/4 cup honey
- 1 tbsp garlic, minced
- 1 tbsp ginger, minced
- 1 tbsp olive oil
- 1/4 cup fish stock
- Pepper
- Salt

**Prep:** Add shrimp into the large bowl. Add remaining ingredients over shrimp and toss well.
Transfer shrimp into the instant pot and stir well. Seal pot with lid and cook on high for 5 minutes.
Once done, release pressure using quick release. Remove lid.

**Nutrition:** Calories 240, Fat 5.6 g, Carbs 20.9 g, Protein 26.5 g

## 596. Mediterranean Fish Fillets

**Prep Time:** 10 minutes  
**Servings:** 4  
**Cook Time:** 3 minutes

**Ingredients:**
- 4 cod fillets
- 1 lb grape tomatoes, halved
- 1 cup olives, pitted and sliced

- 2 tbsp capers
- 1 tsp dried thyme
- 2 tbsp olive oil
- 1 tsp garlic, minced
- Pepper
- Salt

**Prep:** Pour 1 cup water into the instant pot then place steamer rack in the pot.
Spray heat-safe baking dish with cooking spray. Add half grape tomatoes into the dish and season with pepper and salt.
Arrange fish fillets on top of cherry tomatoes. Drizzle with oil and season with garlic, thyme, capers, pepper, and salt. Spread olives and remaining grape tomatoes on top of fish fillets.
Place dish on top of steamer rack in the pot. Seal pot with a lid and select manual and cook on high for 3 minutes.
Once done, release pressure using quick release. Remove lid.

**Nutrition:** Calories 212, Fat 11.9 g, Carbs 7.1 g, Protein 21.4 g

## 597. Mussels with Tomatoes & Wine

**Prep Time:** 15 minutes
**Servings:** 6

**Cook Time:** 15 minutes

**Ingredients:**
- 1 tablespoon olive oil
- 2 celery stalks, chopped
- 1 onion, chopped
- 4 garlic cloves, minced
- ½ teaspoon dried oregano, crushed
- 1 (15-ounce) can diced tomatoes
- 1 teaspoon honey
- 1 teaspoon red pepper flakes, crushed
- 2 pounds mussels, cleaned
- 2 cups white wine
- Salt and ground black pepper, as required
- ¼ cup fresh basil, chopped

**Prep:** In a large skillet, heat the oil over medium heat and sauté the celery, onion and garlic for about 5 minutes. Add the tomato, honey and red pepper flakes and cook for about 10 minutes.
Meanwhile, in a large pan, add mussels and wine and bring to a boil. Simmer, covered for about 10 minutes. Transfer the mussel mixture into tomato mixture and stir to combine. Season with salt and black pepper and remove from the heat.
Serve hot with the garnishing of basil.

**Nutrition:** Calories 244, Fat 6 g, Carbs 14.3 g, Protein 19.1 g

## 598. Salmon with Broccoli

**Prep Time:** 10 minutes
**Servings:** 4

**Cook Time:** 4 minutes

**Ingredients:**
- 4 salmon fillets
- 10 oz broccoli florets
- 1 1/2 cups water
- 1 tbsp olive oil
- Pepper
- Salt

**Prep:** Pour water into the instant pot then place steamer basket in the pot.
Place salmon in the steamer basket and season with pepper and salt and drizzle with oil.
Add broccoli on top of salmon in the steamer basket. Seal pot with lid and cook on high for 4 minutes.
Once done, release pressure using quick release. Remove lid.

**Nutrition:** Calories 290, Fat 14.7 g, Carbs 4.7 g, Protein 36.5 g

## 599. Pesto Fish Fillet

**Prep Time:** 10 minutes
**Servings:** 4

**Cook Time:** 8 minutes

**Ingredients:**
- 4 halibut fillets
- 1/2 cup water
- 1 tbsp lemon zest, grated
- 1 tbsp capers
- 1/2 cup basil, chopped
- 1 tbsp garlic, chopped
- 1 avocado, peeled and chopped
- Pepper
- Salt

**Prep:** Add lemon zest, capers, basil, garlic, avocado, pepper, and salt into the blender blend until smooth.
Place fish fillets on aluminum foil and spread a blended mixture on fish fillets. Fold foil around the fish fillets.
Pour water into the instant pot and place trivet in the pot.
Place foil fish packet on the trivet. Seal pot with lid and cook on high for 8 minutes.
Once done, allow to release pressure naturally. Remove lid.

**Nutrition:** Calories 426, Fat 16.6 g, Carbs 5.5 g, Protein 61.8 g

### 600. Salmon with Potatoes

**Prep Time:** 10 minutes  
**Servings:** 4  
**Cook Time:** 15 minutes

**Ingredients:**
- 1 1/2 lbs Salmon fillets, boneless and cubed
- 2 tbsp olive oil
- 1 cup fish stock
- 2 tbsp parsley, chopped
- 1 tsp garlic, minced
- 1 lb baby potatoes, halved
- Pepper
- Salt

**Prep:** Add oil into the inner pot of instant pot and set the pot on sauté mode. Add garlic and sauté for 2 minutes. Add remaining ingredients and stir well. Seal pot with lid and cook on high for 13 minutes.
Once done, release pressure using quick release. Remove lid.

**Nutrition:** Calories 362, Fat 18.1 g, Carbs 14.5 g, Protein 37.3 g

### 601. Salsa Fish Fillets

**Prep Time:** 10 minutes  
**Servings:** 4  
**Cook Time:** 2 minutes

**Ingredients:**
- 1 lb tilapia fillets
- 1/2 cup salsa
- 1 cup of water
- Pepper
- Salt

**Prep:** Place fish fillets on aluminum foil and top with salsa and season with pepper and salt. Fold foil around the fish fillets. Pour water into the instant pot and place trivet in the pot. Place foil fish packet on the trivet.
Seal pot with lid and cook on high for 2 minutes.
Once done, release pressure using quick release. Remove lid.

**Nutrition:** Calories 342, Fat 10.5 g, Carbs 41.5 g, Protein 18.9 g

### 602. Seafood Stew

**Prep Time:** 20 minutes  
**Servings:** 6  
**Cook Time:** 25 minutes

**Ingredients:**
- 2 tablespoons olive oil
- 1 medium onion, chopped finely
- 2 garlic cloves, minced
- 1/4 teaspoon red pepper flakes, crushed
- 1/2 pound plum tomatoes, seeded and chopped
- 1/3 cup white wine
- 1 cup clam juice
- 1 tablespoon tomato paste
- Salt, as required
- 1-pound snapper fillets, cubed into 1-inch size
- 1-pound large shrimp, peeled and deveined
- 1/2 pound sea scallops
- 1/3 cup fresh parsley, minced
- 1 teaspoon fresh lemon zest, grated finely

**Prep:** In a large Dutch oven, heat oil over medium heat and sauté the onion for about 3-4 minutes. Add red pepper flakes and the garlic and sauté for about 1 minute. Add the tomatoes and cook for about 2 minutes. Stir in the wine, clam juice, tomato paste and salt and bring to a boil. Reduce the heat to low and simmer with lid for about 10 minutes. Stir in the seafood and simmer, covered for about 6-8 minutes. Stir in the parsley and remove from heat.
Serve hot with the garnishing of lemon zest.

**Nutrition:** Calories 313, Fat 7.8 g, Carbs 11.6 g, Protein 44.3 g

### 603. Shrimp Scampi

**Prep Time:** 10 minutes  
**Servings:** 6  
**Cook Time:** 8 minutes

**Ingredients:**
- 1 lb whole wheat penne pasta
- 1 lb frozen shrimp
- 2 tbsp garlic, minced
- 1/4 tsp cayenne
- 1/2 tbsp Italian seasoning
- 1/4 cup olive oil
- 3 1/2 cups fish stock
- Pepper
- Salt

**Prep:** Add all ingredients into the inner pot of instant pot and stir well. Seal pot with lid and cook on high for 6 minutes. Once done, release pressure using quick release. Remove lid.
Stir well and serve.

**Nutrition:** Calories 435, Fat 12.6 g, Carbs 54.9 g, Protein 30.6 g

## 604. Shrimp Zoodles

**Prep Time:** 10 minutes  
**Servings:** 4  
**Cook Time:** 5 minutes

**Ingredients:**
- 2 zucchini, spiralized
- 1 lb shrimp, peeled and deveined
- 1/2 tsp paprika
- 1 tbsp basil, chopped
- 1/2 lemon juice
- 1 tsp garlic, minced
- 2 tbsp olive oil
- 1 cup vegetable stock
- Pepper
- Salt

**Prep:** Add oil into the inner pot of instant pot and set the pot on sauté mode. Add garlic and sauté for a minute. Add shrimp and lemon juice and stir well and cook for 1 minute. Add remaining ingredients and stir well. Seal pot with lid and cook on high for 3 minutes.
Once done, release pressure using quick release. Remove lid.

**Nutrition:** Calories 215, Fat 9.2 g, Carbs 5.8 g, Protein 27.3 g

## 605. Lemon Clams

**Prep Time:** 10 minutes  
**Servings:** 4  
**Cook Time:** 10 minutes

**Ingredients:**
- 1 lb clams, clean
- 1 tbsp fresh lemon juice
- 1 lemon zest, grated
- 1 onion, chopped
- 1/2 cup fish stock
- Pepper
- Salt

**Prep:** Add all ingredients into the inner pot of instant pot and stir well. Seal pot with lid and cook on high for 10 minutes. Once done, release pressure using quick release. Remove lid.

**Nutrition:** Calories 76, Fat 0.6 g, Carbs 16.4 g, Protein 1.8 g

## 606. Stewed Mussels & Scallops

**Prep Time:** 10 minutes  
**Servings:** 4  
**Cook Time:** 11 minutes

**Ingredients:**
- 2 cups mussels
- 1 cup scallops
- 2 cups fish stock
- 2 bell peppers, diced
- 2 cups cauliflower rice
- 1 onion, chopped
- 1 tbsp olive oil
- Pepper
- Salt

**Prep:** Add oil into the inner pot of instant pot and set the pot on sauté mode. Add onion and peppers and sauté for 3 minutes. Add scallops and cook for 2 minutes. Add remaining ingredients and stir well. Seal pot with lid and cook on high for 6 minutes.
Once done, allow to release pressure naturally. Remove lid.
Stir and serve.

## 607. Stuffed Swordfish

**Prep Time:** 15 minutes  
**Servings:** 2  
**Cook Time:** 14 minutes

**Ingredients:**
- 1 (8-ounce) (2-inch thick) swordfish steak
- 1½ tablespoons olive oil, divided
- 1 tablespoon fresh lemon juice
- 2 cups fresh spinach, torn into bite size pieces
- 1 garlic clove, minced
- ¼ cup feta cheese, crumbled

**Prep:** Preheat the outdoor grill to high heat. Lightly, grease the grill grate.
Carefully, cut a slit on one side of fish steak to create a pocket.
In a bowl, add 1 tablespoon of the oil and lemon juice and mix.
Coat the both sides of fish with oil mixture evenly.
In a small skillet, add the remaining oil and garlic over medium heat and cook until heated. Add the spinach and cook for about 2-3 minutes or until wilted. Remove from the heat.
Stuff the fish pocket with spinach, followed by the feta cheese. Grill the fish pocket for about 8 minutes.
Flip and cook for about 5-6 minutes or until desired doneness of fish.
Cut the fish pocket into 2 equal sized pieces and serve.

**Nutrition:** Calories 296, Fat 17 g, Carbs 2.5 g, Protein 32.5 g

### 608. Tilapia in Herb Sauce

**Prep Time:** 15 minutes  
**Servings:** 4  

**Cook Time:** 14 minutes

**Ingredients:**
- 2 (14-ounce) cans diced tomatoes with basil and garlic, undrained
- 1/3 cup fresh parsley, chopped and divided
- ¼ teaspoon dried oregano
- ½ teaspoon red pepper flakes, crushed
- 4 (6-ounce) tilapia fillets
- 2 tablespoons fresh lemon juice
- 2/3 cup feta cheese, crumbled

**Prep:** Preheat the oven to 400 degrees F.
In a shallow baking dish, add the tomatoes, ¼ cup of the parsley, oregano and red pepper flakes and mix until well combined.
Arrange the tilapia fillets over the tomato mixture in a single layer and drizzle with the lemon juice.
Place some tomato mixture over the tilapia fillets and sprinkle with the feta cheese evenly. Bake for about 12-14 minutes.
Serve hot with the garnishing of remaining parsley.

### 609. Tomato Olive Fish Fillets

**Prep Time:** 10 minutes  
**Servings:** 4  

**Cook Time:** 8 minutes

**Ingredients:**
- 2 lbs halibut fish fillets
- 2 oregano sprigs
- 2 rosemary sprigs
- 2 tbsp fresh lime juice
- 1 cup olives, pitted
- 28 oz can tomatoes, diced
- 1 tbsp garlic, minced
- 1 onion, chopped
- 2 tbsp olive oil

**Prep:** Add oil into the inner pot of instant pot and set the pot on sauté mode. Add onion and sauté for 3 minutes. Add garlic and sauté for a minute. Add lime juice, olives, herb sprigs, and tomatoes and stir well. Seal pot with lid and cook on high for 3 minutes. Once done, release pressure using quick release. Remove lid. Add fish fillets and seal pot again with lid and cook on high for 2 minutes. Once done, release pressure using quick release.

**Nutrition:** Calories 333, Fat 19.1 g, Carbs 31.8 g, Protein 13.4 g

### 610. Tuna with Olives

**Prep Time:** 15 minutes  
**Servings:** 4  

**Cook Time:** 14 minutes

**Ingredients:**
- 4 (6-ounce) (1-inch thick) tuna steaks
- 2 tablespoons extra-virgin olive oil, divided
- Salt and ground black pepper, as required
- 2 garlic cloves, minced
- 1 cup fresh tomatoes, chopped
- 1 cup dry white wine
- 2/3 cup green olives, pitted and sliced
- ¼ cup capers, drained
- 2 tablespoons fresh thyme, chopped
- 1½ tablespoons fresh lemon zest, grated
- 2 tablespoons fresh lemon juice
- 3 tablespoons fresh parsley, chopped

**Prep:** Preheat the grill to high heat. Grease the grill grate.
Coat the tuna steaks with 1 tablespoon of the oil and sprinkle with salt and black pepper. Set aside for about 5 minutes.

For sauce: in a small skillet, heat the remaining oil over medium heat and sauté the garlic for about 1 minute. Add the tomatoes and cook for about 2 minutes. Stir in the wine and bring to a boil. Add the remaining ingredients except the parsley and cook, uncovered for about 5 minutes. Stir in the parsley, salt and black pepper and remove from the heat.
Meanwhile, grill the tuna steaks over direct heat for about 1-2 minutes per side.
Serve the tuna steaks hot with the topping of sauce.

**Nutrition:** Calories 468, Fat 20.4 g, Carbs 7.3 g, Protein 52.1 g

## 611. Butter Shrimp

**Prep Time:** 10 minutes  
**Servings:** 3  
**Cook Time:** 30 minutes

**Ingredients:**
- ½ oz. Parmigiano Reggiano, grated
- 2 tbsp. Almond Flour
- ½ tsp. Baking Powder
- ¼ tsp. Curry Powder
- 1 tbsp. Water
- 1 large Egg
- medium Shrimps
- 3 tbsp. Coconut Oil

**Creamy Butter Sauce**
- 2 tbsp. Unsalted Butter
- ½ small Onion, diced
- 1 clove Garlic, finely chopped
- small Thai Chilies, sliced
- 2 tbsp. Curry Leaves
- Salt and Pepper to Taste
- 1/8 tsp. Sesame Seeds

**Prep:** Remove the shells of the shrimps but leave the tail part if you'd like.
In a bowl, add grated Parmigiano Reggiano, almond flour, baking powder and curry powder. Mix well.
Cut the surface of the shrimps and devein. Clean into the mixture, add in 1 egg and water. Mix well until smooth.
Preheat a pan on medium heat. Add in coconut oil. Once the oil is hot, coat the shrimps with the batter and pan-fry the shrimps. Wait until the shrimps turn golden and remove them from the pan. Put on a cooling rack. Pan-fry extra batter if any left.
Preheat a pan to medium-low heat. Add in unsalted butter. Once the butter has melted, add in chopped onion.
Wait until the onion turns translucent and then add in finely chopped garlic, sliced Thai chilies, and curry leaves. Stir-fry everything until fragrant. Add in the battered shrimp and coat with the sauce.
Garnish with sesame seeds and serve.

**Nutrition:** 570 Calories, 52 g Fat, 3 g Carbs, 14 g Protein

## 612. Creamy Fish Gratin

**Prep Time:** 5 minutes  
**Servings:** 6  
**Cook Time:** 1 hour

**Ingredients:**
- 1 cup heavy cream
- 2 salmon fillets, cubed
- 2 cod fillets, cubed
- 2 sea bass fillets, cubed
- 1 celery stalk, sliced
- Salt and pepper to taste
- ½ cup grated Parmesan
- ½ cup feta cheese, crumbled

**Prep:** Combine the cream with the fish fillets and celery in a deep-dish baking pan. Add salt and pepper to taste then top with the Parmesan and feta cheese. Cook in the preheated oven at 350 °F for 20 minutes.
Serve the gratin right away.

**Nutrition:** Calories: 301, Fat: 16.1 g, Carbs: 1.3 g, Protein: 36.9 g

## 613. Fish Stew

**Prep Time:** 5 minutes  
**Servings:** 4  
**Cook Time:** 30 minutes

**Ingredients:**
- 1 tablespoon olive oil
- 1 chopped onion or leek
- 2 chopped stalks celery
- 2 chopped carrots
- 1 clove minced garlic
- 1 tablespoon parsley
- 1 bay leaf
- 1 clove
- 1/8 teaspoon kelp or dulse (seaweed)
- ¼ teaspoon salt
- Fish—leftover, cooked, diced
- 2–3 cups vegetable broth

**Prep:** Add all of ingredients and simmer on the stove for 20 minutes.

**Nutrition:** Calories: 342; Fat: 15 g; Carbs: 8 g; Protein: 10 g

### 614. Greek Roasted Fish

**Prep Time:** 5 minutes  
**Servings:** 4  
**Cook Time:** 30 minutes

**Ingredients:**
- 4 salmon fillets
- 1 tablespoon chopped oregano
- 1 teaspoon dried basil
- 1 zucchini, sliced
- 1 red onion, sliced
- 1 carrot, sliced
- 1 lemon, sliced
- 2 tablespoons extra virgin olive oil
- Salt and pepper to taste

**Prep:** Add all the ingredients in a deep dish baking pan.
Season with salt and pepper and cook in the preheated oven at 350 °F for 20 minutes.

**Nutrition:** Calories: 328; Fat: 13 g; Protein: 38 g; Carbs: 8 g

### 615. Grilled Salmon with Pineapple Salsa

**Prep Time:** 5 minutes  
**Servings:** 4  
**Cook Time:** 30 minutes

**Ingredients:**
- 4 salmon fillets
- Salt and pepper to taste
- 2 tablespoons Cajun seasoning
- A fresh pineapple, peeled and diced
- 1 cup cherry tomatoes, quartered
- 2 tablespoons chopped cilantro
- chopped parsley
- 1 teaspoon dried mint
- 2 tablespoons lemon juice
- 2 tablespoons extra virgin olive oil
- 1 teaspoon honey
- Salt and pepper to taste

**Prep:** Add salt, pepper and Cajun seasoning to the fish.
Heat a grill pan over medium flame. Cook fish on the grill on each side for 3-4 minutes.
For the salsa, mix the pineapple, tomatoes, cilantro, parsley, mint, lemon juice and honey in a bowl. Season with salt and pepper.
Serve the grilled salmon with the pineapple salsa.

**Nutrition:** Calories: 332; Fat: 12 g; Protein: 34 g

### 616. Seafood Corn Chowder

**Prep Time:** 10 minutes  
**Servings:** 4  
**Cook Time:** 12 minutes

**Ingredients:**
- 1 tablespoon butter
- 1 cup onion
- 1/3 cup celery
- ½ cup green bell pepper
- ½ cup red bell pepper
- 1 tablespoon white flour
- 14 ounces chicken broth
- 2 cups cream
- 6 ounces evaporated milk
- 10 ounces surimi imitation crab chunks
- 2 cups frozen corn kernels
- ½ teaspoon black pepper
- ½ teaspoon paprika

**Prep:** Place a suitably-sized saucepan over medium heat and add butter to melt. Toss in green and red peppers, onion, and celery, then sauté for 5 minutes. Stir in flour and whisk well for 2 minutes.
Pour in chicken broth and stir until it boils. Add evaporated milk, corn, surimi crab, paprika, black pepper, and creamer.
Cook for 5 minutes.

**Nutrition:** 175 Calories, 8 g Protein, 7 g Fat

### 617. Tuna Tapas and Avocado

**Prep Time:** 10 minutes  
**Servings:** 4  
**Cook Time:** 10 minutes

**Ingredients:**
- 12 oz. can Solid tuna packed in water
- 3 + more for garnish Green onions
- ½ Red bell pepper
- Garlic, salt and black pepper as desired
- 1 tbsp. Mayonnaise
- 1 dash Balsamic vinegar
- 2 Ripe avocados

**Prep:** Drain the tuna thoroughly. Remove the pit and slice the avocados into halves.
Chop the bell pepper, and thinly slice the onions. Whisk the vinegar, red pepper, onions, salt, pepper, mayonnaise, and tuna.
Load the avocado halves with the tuna.
Top it off with a portion of green onions and black pepper before serve.

### 618. Avocados Stuffed with Salmon

**Prep Time:** 5 minutes
**Servings:** 2
**Cook Time:** 5 minutes

**Ingredients:**
- Avocado (pitted and halved): 1
- Olive oil: 2 tablespoons
- Lemon juice: 1
- Smoked salmon (flaked): 2 ounces
- Goat cheese (crumbled): 1 ounce
- Salt and black pepper

**Prep:** Combine the salmon with lemon juice, oil, cheese, salt, and pepper in your food processor and pulsate well.
Divide this mixture into avocado halves and serve.

**Nutrition:** Calories: 300; Fat: 15 g; Carbs: 8 g; Protein: 16 g

### 619. Tuna Cobbler

**Prep Time:** 15 minutes
**Servings:** 4
**Cook Time:** 25 minutes

**Ingredients:**
- Water, cold (1/3 cup)
- Tuna, canned, drained (10 ounces)
- Sweet pickle relish (2 tablespoons)
- Mixed vegetables, frozen (1 ½ cups)
- Soup, cream of chicken, condensed (10 ¾ ounces)
- Pimientos, sliced, drained (2 ounces)
- Lemon juice (1 teaspoon)
- Paprika

**Prep:** Preheat the air fryer at 375 degrees F.
Mist cooking spray into a round casserole (1 ½ quarts).
Mix the frozen vegetables with soup, lemon juice, relish, pimientos, and tuna in a saucepan. Cook for 8 minutes over medium heat.
Fill the casserole with the tuna mixture.
Mix the biscuit mix with cold water to form a soft dough. Beat for half a minute before dropping by four spoonsful into the casserole. Dust the dish with paprika before air-frying for twenty to twenty-five minutes.

**Nutrition:** Calories 320; Fat 10 g; Protein 20 g; Carbs 30 g

### 620. Herbed Roasted Cod

**Prep Time:** 10 Minutes
**Servings:** 4
**Cook Time:** 45 minutes

**Ingredients:**
- 4 cod fillets
- 4 parsley sprigs
- 2 cilantro sprigs
- 2 basil sprigs
- 1 lemon, sliced
- Salt and pepper to taste
- 2 tablespoons olive oil

**Prep:** Season the cod with salt and pepper.
Place the parsley, cilantro, basil and lemon slices at the bottom of a deep dish baking pan.
Place the cod over the herbs and cook in the preheated oven at 350 °F for 15 minutes.
Serve the cod warm and fresh with your favorite side dish.

**Nutrition:** Calories: 192 Fat: 8.1 g Protein: 28.6 g Carbs: 0.1 g

### 621. Lemony Parmesan Salmon

**Prep Time:** 10 minutes
**Servings:** 4
**Cook Time:** 25 minutes

**Ingredients:**
- Butter, melted (2 tablespoons)

- Green onions, sliced thinly (2 tablespoons)
- Breadcrumbs, white, fresh (3/4 cup)
- Thyme leaves, dried (1/4 teaspoon)
- Salmon fillet, 1 ¼-pound (1 piece)
- Salt (1/4 teaspoon)
- Parmesan cheese, grated (1/4 cup)
- Lemon peel, grated (2 teaspoons)

**Prep:** Preheat the oven at 350 degrees F.
Mist cooking spray onto a baking pan (shallow). Fill with pat-dried salmon. Brush salmon with butter (1 tablespoon) before sprinkling with salt.
Combine the breadcrumbs with onions, thyme, lemon peel, cheese, and remaining butter (1 tablespoon).
Cover salmon with the breadcrumb mixture. Air-fry for fifteen to twenty-five minutes.

**Nutrition:** Calories 290; Fat 10 g; Protein 30 g

## 622. Tuna Melts

**Prep Time: 15 minutes**  
**Servings: 8**

**Cook Time: 20 minutes**

**Ingredients:**
- Salt (1/8 teaspoon)
- Onion, chopped (1/3 cup)
- Biscuits, refrigerated, flaky layers (16 1/3 ounces)
- Tuna, water packed, drained (10 ounces)
- Mayonnaise (1/3 cup)
- Pepper (1/8 teaspoon)
- Cheddar cheese, shredded (4 ounces)
- Tomato, chopped
- Sour cream
- Lettuce, shredded

**Prep:** Preheat the air fryer at 325 degrees F.
Mist cooking spray onto a cookie sheet.
Mix tuna with mayonnaise, pepper, salt, and onion.
Separate dough so you have 8 biscuits; press each into 5-inch rounds.
Arrange 4 biscuit rounds on the sheet. Fill at the center with tuna mixture before topping with cheese. Cover with the remaining biscuit rounds and press to seal.
Air-fry for fifteen to twenty minutes. Slice each sandwich into halves. Serve each piece topped with lettuce, tomato, and sour cream.

**Nutrition:** Calories 320; Fat 10 g; Protein 10 g; Carbs 20 g

# BEEF AND LAMB

### 623. Lamb with Egg

**Prep time:** 20 minutes  
**Servings:** 6  

**Cook time:** 1 hour

**Ingredients:**
- 12 lamb ribs
- Olive oil
- 5 eggs
- 2 lemons cut in wedges
- Salt and pepper
- 1 minced onion
- 1 cup of red wine
- Nutmeg
- 4 tbsp of mashed lard
- 6 ripe tomatoes
- Minced Parsley

**Prep:** Wash the tomatoes, gut, peel and dry them.
In a large pan, sizzle the lard with the minced onion. Put in the ribs, add salt and pepper. Pour in the wine and add the chopped tomato pulp. Cook on low heat.
On the side, beat the eggs with a whip, season with grated and parsley.
When the ribs are perfectly cooked, add the eggs. Mix carefully and frequently with a wooden spoon and avoid overcooking the eggs.
Serve with some lemon wedges on the side.

**Nutrition:** Calories 424, Carbs 6.5 g, Protein 41.5 g, Fat 23.7 g

### 624. Veal Roast with Lemon

**Prep time:** 10 minutes  
**Servings:** 6  

**Cook time:** 1 hour

**Ingredients:**
- 35 oz of veal loin
- 1 1/4 cup of sliced bacon

**For marinate:**
- 2 tbsp of olive oil
- Juice of 2 lemons
- 1 onion

- 2 bay leaves

**For cooking:**
- 2 tbsp of butter
- ½ cup of white wine

**For dressing:**
- Juice of 2 lemons

- Sage leaves
- 2 tbsp of olive oil
- 1 cup of broth
- 1 tbsp of flour

- Salt and pepper
- Ground hot pepper

**Prep:** Wrap the loin into the bacon strips. Place it in a casserole and drizzle on the lemon juice, oil, infuse with the bay leaves, onion slices and sage leaves.
Add salt and pepper and leave to rest for few hours.
Remove the meat from the marinading and place it in a casserole, sizzle with butter and oil. Pour in the white wine, broth and let it cook with a lid on.
In a bowl, whip the lemon juice, hot pepper, flour and the leftovers from the roast. Slice the meat and put onto a serving dish. Season with the sauce and serve.

**Nutrition:** Calories 327, Carbs 20.4 g, Protein 25.7 g, Fat 15.1 g

### 625. Flattened Meat Loaf

**Prep time:** 15 minutes  
**Servings:** 6  

**Cook time:** 20 minutes

**Ingredients:**
- 1 cup of minced mortadella
- 28 oz of veal meat mince
- 4 tbsp of breadcrumbs
- 3/4 cup of grated parmesan
- 2 eggs
- Butter
- 1 garlic clove
- Minced Parsley
- Nutmeg
- Salt and pepper

**Prep:** prepare the mixture with: eggs, parmesan, mortadella, veal, garlic, parsley and some of the breadcrumbs, grated nutmeg, salt and pepper. Roll the mixture and shape into a flattened circle. Coat the meat in the remaining breadcrumbs.
In a large pan, melt the butter; lay the meat and let it cook on low heat 5 minutes for each side.

**Nutrition:** Calories 465, Carbs 11.8 g, Protein 36.3 g, Fat 28.5 g

### 626. Sweet and Sour Meatballs with Almonds

**Prep time:** 25 minutes  
**Servings:** 4  

**Cook time:** 20 minutes

**Ingredients:**
- 14 oz of minced veal pulp
- 3 tbsp of grated pecorino
- Breadcrumbs
- ½ cup of vinegar
- 1 egg
- 1 cup of toasted almonds
- 1 tbsp of sugar
- 1 sprig of parsley
- Extra virgin olive oil
- Salt and pepper

**Prep:** combine the meat with the minced parsley, egg, salt, pepper, pecorino and breadcrumbs, to reach an even and thick mixture. Roll the meatballs and fry them in hot oil; strain and lay them onto some paper towel. Combine well the vinegar with the sugar. Put the meat again into the pan and let it marinate for few minutes; cover in almons and serve the meatballs warm or at room temperature.

**Nutrition:** Calories 302.6, Carbs 9.6 g, Protein 14.3 g, Fat 21.6 g

### 627. Pizzaiola Slices (Slices in Tomato Salsa)

**Prep time:** 5 minutes  
**Servings:** 4  

**Cook time:** 15 minutes

**Ingredients:**
- 6 canned tomatoes
- 3 garlic cloves
- Parsley
- 4 beef ribs
- Olive oil
- Oregano
- Salt and pepper

**Prep:** Sizzle the garlic in some olive oil, add the canned tomatoes and cook on high heat until the water evaporates. In a separate pan, fry the ribs in oil on very high heat. Pour the sauce on top and let marinate on low heat for about 5 minutes.

**Nutrition:** Calories 171.5, Carbs 2.5 g, Protein 16.3 g, Fat 15.6 g

### 628. Castrated Chops

**Prep time:** 10 minutes  
**Servings:** 6  
**Cook time:** 30 minutes

**Ingredients:**
- 6 castrated chops
- 2 garlic cloves
- Extra virgin olive oil
- Coarse Salt
- Rosemary sprigs
- Pepper

**Prep:** mince the garlic, coarse salt and rosemary.
Grill the ribs and flip them frequently. Cook thoroughly.
Before serving, add the minced seasoning and some oil.
Serve with some lemon wedges on the side.

**Nutrition:** Calories 405, Carbs 2.5 g, Protein 32.5 g, Fat 28.1 g

### 629. Lamb Ribs

**Prep time:** 20 minutes  
**Servings:** 6  
**Cook time:** 30 minutes

**Ingredients:**
- 12 lamb ribs
- 3 eggs
- Flour
- 2 wedged lemons
- Salt and pepper
- Lard
- Breadcrumbs

**Prep:** In a bowl, beat the eggs with a whisk and add some salt and pepper.
Coat the ribs in flour and then into the eggs and lastly into the breadcrumbs.
Sizzle the lard in a pan, put in the ribs, flip them to cook evenly.
Serve with some lemon wedges on the side.

**Nutrition:** Calories 718, Carbs 21.4 g, Protein 51.3 g, Fat 53.7 g

### 630. Veal Meatballs with Chocolate

**Prep time:** 20 minutes  
**Servings:** 4  
**Cook time:** 15 minutes

**Ingredients:**
- 14 oz of veal mince
- 1 1/2 cup of skinned almonds
- 2 eggs
- Cinnamon
- 1 cup of hard crumbled bread
- milk
- Salt
- Marsala liquor
- Extra virgin olive oil
- 3/4 cup unsweetened cacao powder
- 1 cup of sugar

**Prep:** Mix the minced meat with some tbsp of sugar, the minced almonds, some cinnamon, the eggs, crumbled bread soaked in milk and a pinch of salt and squeezed. Combine well and then pour in 2 tbsp of Marsala; roll the meatballs and fry them into plenty of hot oil. When they are ready, drain and place them onto some paper towel. In a pan pour the sugar, cacao and a little water; let the ingredients melt on low heat until you reach a cream. Add the meatballs and roll them for few minutes.

**Nutrition:** Calories 718, Carbs 21.4 g, Protein 51.3 g, Fat 53.7 g

### 631. Beef Filet with Ham

**Prep time:** 20 minutes  
**Servings:** 6  
**Cook time:** 30 minutes

**Ingredients:**
- 15 oz of beef filet
- 4 tbsp of grated parmesan
- Salt and pepper
- 3/4 cup of sliced ham
- 3 tbsp of olive oil
- ¼ cup of butter

**Prep:** Open the filet and stuff it with the ham slices and the cheese; roll them and secure with some string.
Heat the oil and butter in a pan, gently lay the filet, sprinkle some salt and pepper. Flip it a few times and let it cook.
Slice the filet and serve.

**Nutrition:** Calories 364, Carbs 0.4 g, Protein 41.3 g, Fat 20.4 g

### 632. Lamb Mince

Prep time: 15 minutes  
Servings: 6  
Cook time: 2 hours e 20 minutes

**Ingredients:**
- 35 oz of chopped lamb
- 2 sliced onions
- 3 sage leaves
- 3 pressed garlic cloves
- 1 sprig of rosemary
- Salt and pepper
- 6 ripe tomatoes
- ½ minced red hot pepper
- 1 chopped celery stick

**Prep:** In a pan, sizzle the lamb with garlic, rosemary and sage.
In a separate pot pour about 1 gallon of water, add in the celery, tomatoes (previously peeled and drained), onion and hot pepper. Let the ingredients boil for a while. Then add the lamb, salt and pepper and let it cook for a couple of hors.

**Nutrition:** Calories 494, Carbs 9.6 g, Protein 48.6 g, Fat 23.9 g

### 633. Beef Mince

Prep time: 20 minutes  
Servings: 6  
Cook time: 2 hours 20 minutes

**Ingredients:**
- 35 oz beef pulp
- 1 cup of red whine
- Salt and pepper
- 1 chopped onion
- 1 cup of olive oil
- 2 tbsp of tomato concentrate

**Prep:** Cut the meat in pieces or in cubes not too small.
In a big pan, sizzle the chopped onion in some oil; put in the meat when the onion has browned, add salt and pepper, mix some more and let marinate.
Now take down the heat to the minimum, add the tomato concentrate, pour a cup of hot water, cover with a lid and keep cooking for an hour.
Adjust the salt to taste and then serve.

**Nutrition:** Calories 524.6, Carbs 9.4 g, Protein 44.2 g, Fat 28.4 g

### 634. Veal Mince with Peas

Prep time: 15 minutes  
Servings: 6  
Cook time: 1 hour

**Ingredients:**
- 35 oz of veal cut into pieces
- 14 oz of shelled peas
- 8 oz of minced carrots
- 1 minced onion
- 5 tbsp of butter
- Olive Oil
- Parsley
- Salt and pepper

**Prep:** Place the meat in a casserole with oil and butter; let sizzle on high heat and then leave it aside. In the same ingredients, on a low heat, add the onion and carrot and deglaze with the wine. Combine the peas, let them absorb the flavor and then add the meat, pour in salted water and let cook until both the meat and peas are fully cooked.
Five minutes before turning off the heat sprinkle plenty of parsley.

**Nutrition:** Calories 524.6, Carbs 9.4 g, Protein 44.2 g, Fat 28.4 g

## 635. Stew with Milk

**Prep time:** 15 minutes  
**Servings:** 6  
**Cook time:** 2 hours 20 minutes

**Ingredients:**
- *42 oz of beef pulp*
- *33 oz of milk*
- *1 chopped carrot*
- *1 chopped celery stick*
- *1 chopped onion*
- *Salt*
- *2 1/2 tbsp di butter*
- *1 shot of rum*
- *10 oz of pickled onions*
- *¼ cup of tomato sauce*

**Prep:** In casserole put the meat, cover with milk and rum, chopped vegetables (withhold the onions) and tomato sauce. Adjust the salt to taste and let marinate for some hours. Place the casserole on low heat for 2 hours.
Move the meat in another pan with the hot butter. Pour in the sauce, add the onions and keep cooking until the latter are fully cooked.
Serve the stew still hot and slice it, with a side of the pickled onions and the gravy.

**Nutrition:** Calories 553, Carbs 13.4 g, Protein 58.9 g, Fat 25.6 g

## 636. Stuffed Lamb Leg

**Prep time:** 1 hour  
**Servings:** 4  
**Cook time:** 1 hour e 15 minutes

**Ingredients:**
- *1 lamb leg*
- *3 garlic cloves*
- *1 cup of grated pecorino*
- *1 sprig of parsley*
- *1 sprig of mint*
- *Extra virgin olive oil*
- *Salt and pepper*

**Prep:** combine the pecorino with the minced garlic, parsley, mint, salt and pepper.
Make some cuts in the leg and distribute the mixture, let the meat marinate for 1 hour. Grease the lamb with oil and season with salt and pepper.
Put in a tray and then in the oven at 350°F for about 1 hour.

**Nutrition:** Calories 475, Carbs 14.2 g, Protein 36.1 g, Fat 27.5 g

## 637. Lamb with Potatoes

**Prep time:** 30 minutes  
**Servings:** 4  
**Cook time:** 1 hour e 30 minutes

**Ingredients:**
- *52 oz lamb in chunks*
- *21 oz of potatoes*
- *4 ripe tomatoes*
- *1 onion*
- *1 bay leaf*
- *1 sprig of parsley*
- *½ cup white wine*
- *Extra virgin olive oil*
- *Salt and pepper*

**Prep:** Sizzle the lamb in a pan with the sliced onion, bay leaf and 5 tbsp of oil. When it becomes golden, deglaze with the wine and let it evaporate. Add the potatoes cut in cubes. Combine the tomatoes peeled and diced, minced parsley, salt and pepper. Cover with a drizzle of water and let cook on low heat for about 1 hour.

**Nutrition:** Calories 681, Carbs 38.7 g, Protein 41.8 g, Fat 41.5 g

## 638. Baked Lamb

**Prep time:** 20 minutes  
**Servings:** 4  
**Cook time:** 1 hour e 30 minutes

**Ingredients:**
- *52 oz of lamb chunks*
- *35 oz of potatoes*
- *1 onion*

- ½ cup of white wine
- 14 oz of canned tomatoes
- 1 rosemary sprig
- ½ cup of olive oil
- Salt and pepper

**Prep:** Wedge the onion and put it in a oven tray with some oil. Add the lamb, diced potatoes, chopped tomatoes, rosemary, salt and pepper. Mix everything well.
Pour some whine and bake at 375°F, occasionally mixing.

**Nutrition:** Calories 711, Carbs 38.7 g, Protein 43.7 g, Fat 39.5 g

### 639. Lamb with Mint

**Prep time:** 40 minutes
**Servings:** 4
**Cook time:** 1 hour e 30 minutes

**Ingredients:**
- 1 lamb leg
- 1 cup of vinegar
- ½ cup of olive oil
- 1 cup of white wine
- ½ cup of mint leaves
- 1 tbsp of sugar
- Salt and pepper

**Prep:** Season the leg with salt and pepper and brush on some oil. Bake at 400°F in a preheated oven. While baking, turn the leg a few times and add on top some tbsp of wine.
While the meat is cooking, prepare the sauce: finely chop the mint and put it in a bowl, add the sugar, vinegar, 4 tbsp of water, salt and pepper. Mix well until the mixture is even.
Move the leg onto a serving dish and season with the gravy. Serve the mint sauce on the side.

**Nutrition:** Calories 378, Carbs 0.4 g, Protein 72.4 g, Fat 11.5 g

### 640. Lamb with Eggs

**Prep time:** 30 minutes
**Servings:** 4
**Cook time:** 1 hour e 20 minutes

**Ingredients:**
- 52 oz of lamb chunks
- 3 eggs
- ½ cup of olive oil
- 2 lemons
- Salt and pepper

**Prep:** Wash the lamb with some water and the juice of 1 lemon. Dry it and move it to a casserole with some oil. Let sizzle on a low heat and stir it. When the meat has browned, season with salt and pepper and add 1 cup of hot water. Cover with a lid and cook for about 1 hour.
When it has finished cooking, pour in the beaten eggs and juice the other lemon, add a pinch of salt.

**Nutrition:** Calories 764, Carbs 2.4 g, Protein 76.7 g, Fat 62.5 g

### 641. Roasted Veal coated in Breadcrumbs

**Prep time:** 10 minutes
**Servings:** 4
**Cook time:** 5 minutes

**Ingredients:**
- 4 veal cutlets
- Olive oil
- Breadcrumbs
- Oregano
- Salt and pepper

**Prep:** Beat the cutlets and spread some oil on both sides. Coat the in a mixture of breadcrumbs, oregano, salt and pepper, cook on a hot grill.

**Nutrition:** Calories 365, Carbs 26.3 g, Protein 30.3 g, Fat 15 g

## 642. Veal Rolls with Sauce

**Prep time:** 30 minutes  
**Servings:** 4  
**Cook time:** 40 minutes

**Ingredients:**
- 12 veal cutlets
- 1 cup thick salami slices
- 3 hardboiled eggs
- 1 egg
- 1 cup of breadcrumbs
- 50 g of grated pecorino
- 1 cup of caciocavallo
- 1 sprig of parsley
- 1 garlic clove
- 16 oz tomato salsa
- 1 cup of olive oil
- Salt and pepper

**Prep:** In a bowl pour in the breadcrumbs, pecorino, minced parsley, salami, caciocavallo in small pieces, garlic, beaten egg and 2 tbsp of oil, salt and pepper. Combine well everything and spread the mixture on the meat slices. Pour some oil and season with a pinch of salt.
Place a wedge of hardboiled egg in the middle and wrap around it the meat to form the rolls. Tie the rolls with some cooking string and sizzle in a pan with 5 tbsp of oil.
On the side, boil the tomato sauce, dip the rolls and keep cooking for 30 minutes.

**Nutrition:** Calories 375, Carbs 27.6 g, Protein 42.1 g, Fat 29.9 g

## 643. Baked Castrate

**Prep time:** 20 minutes  
**Servings:** 4  
**Cook time:** 1 hour e 30 minutes

**Ingredients:**
- 52 oz of castrate chunks
- 1 onion
- 1 lemon
- Oregano
- Extra virgin olive oil
- Salt and pepper

**Prep:** Soak the castrate in water and lemon cut in wedges for about 30 minutes.
Move the meat to a greased tray. Add the sliced onion, ½ a cup of oil, plenty of oregano, salt and pepper and mix well.
Bake at 350°F and occasionally flip the meat.

**Nutrition:** Calories 685, Carbs 18.4 g, Protein 37.7 g, Fat 25.7 g

## 644. Veal Cutlet with Pecorino

**Prep time:** 15 minutes  
**Servings:** 4  
**Cook time:** 5 minutes

**Ingredients:**
- 4 veal slices
- 2 eggs
- Vinegar
- ½ cup of grated pecorino
- 1 garlic clove
- 1 sprig of parsley
- Extra virgin olive oil
- Salt and pepper
- breadcrumbs

**Prep:** Marinate the meat for few minutes in a oil and vinegar mixture.
Coat the slices in the cheese, then into the beaten eggs and lastly in the breadcrumbs with minced garlic and parsley.
Fry in hot oil.

**Nutrition:** Calories 641, Carbs 41.5 g, Protein 40.7 g, Fat 35.8 g

## 645. Veal Rolls with Raisins and Pine Nuts

**Prep time:** 30 minutes  
**Servings:** 4  
**Cook time:** 40 minutes

**Ingredients:**
- 12 veal slices
- 1 1/2 cup of breadcrumbs
- ½ cup of grated pecorino
- ½ cup of raisins
- 2 tbsp of pine nuts
- 1 onion
- ½ cup of white wine
- 1 sprig of parsley
- Extra virgin olive oil

- *Salt and pepper*

**Prep:** In a bowl mix the breadcrumbs, pecorino, raisins, pine nuts and minced parsley, salt, pepper and a drizzle of oil. Combine well the ingredients and scoop on each meat slice. Roll them and secure with a toothpick.
Let the onion reduce in a pan with 5 tbsp of oil. Add the rolls, sizzle and flip them occasionally.
Deglaze with the wine. Add 2 tbsp of water and keep cooking for 10 minutes on low heat.

**Nutrition:** Calories 383, Carbs 26.8 g, Protein 42.6 g, Fat 31.7 g

## 646. Lard Meatballs

**Prep time: 15 minutes**  
**Servings: 6**  
**Cook time: 15 minutes**

**Ingredients:**
- 21 oz of ground beef
- 9 oz of breadcrumbs
- 1 egg
- 1 1/4 cup of grated parmesan
- ¼ cup of butter
- 1 garlic clove
- ¾ cup of lard
- 1 sprig of parsley
- Extra virgin olive oil
- Salt and pepper
- 1 cup di butter

**Prep:** make a mixture of eggs, parmesan, breadcrumbs, lard, half of the parsley, salt and meat.
Mince the lard with the leftover parsley, pepper and garlic. Wet your hands and roll the meatballs adding some minced lard in the middle, then slightly flatten them. Fry the meatballs in oil and butter on medium heat and flip them until you reach the perfect cooking. They will be ready when golden on the outside.

**Nutrition:** Calories 458, Carbs 16.1 g, Protein 18.3 g, Fat 38.3 g

## 647. Veal with Capers

**Prep time: 15 minutes**  
**Servings: 6**  
**Cook time: 20 minutes**

**Ingredients:**
- 31 oz of veal slices
- 3/4 cup of butter
- Olive oil
- Flour
- 5 tbsp of capers
- Parsley
- 1/4 cup of vinegar
- ½ cup of water
- Salt and pepper

**Prep:** Coat the meat in the flour and place it in a pan with hot butter and oil. Add the capers and water, salt, parsley and pepper; cook for few minutes and stir. Pour the vinegar and let cook for another minute.

**Nutrition:** Calories 271, Carbs 10.6 g, Protein 25.2 g, Fat 14.7 g

## 648. Baked Skewer Rolls

**Prep time: 15 minutes**  
**Servings: 4**  
**Cook time: 30 minutes**

**Ingredients:**
- 12 veal slices of
- 1 cup of breadcrumbs
- 50 g of grated pecorino
- 1 cup of caciocavallo
- 1 garlic clove
- 1 sprig of parsley
- 1 onion
- Bay leaves
- Extra virgin olive oil
- Salt and pepper

**Prep:** In a bowl mix the breadcrumbs with pecorino, minced garlic and parsley, finely chopped caciocavallo, salt, pepper and a drizzle of oil. Pour the mixture onto the meat lightly greased and with a dash of salt. Roll each slice to form a roll.
Skewer the rolls and alternate the meat to onion chunks and bay leaves.
Drizzle some oil on and lay them in an oven tray lined with parchment paper. Bake at 350°F for 30 minutes.

**Nutrition:** Calories 362, Carbs 26.8 g, Protein 42.6 g, Fat 22.3 g

## 649. Silverside with Tomato

**Prep time:** 20 minutes  
**Servings:** 4  
**Cook time:** 2 hours

**Ingredients:**
- 28 oz of beef silverside
- 2 onions
- 1 carrot
- 2 celery sticks
- 1 sprig of parsley
- ½ cup of white
- 2 tomatoes
- Extra virgin olive oil
- Salt and pepper

**Prep:** Slice the onions and let them reduce on a pan with 5 tbsp of oil and 1 tbsp of water. Combine the meat tied with some string and sizzle it, flipping it occasionally. When it is golden, pour in some oil and let deglaze. Cover halfway up with hot water, add the peeled tomatoes diced, the carrot, celery and parsley. Add salt and pepper and cook on low heat for 1 hour and 30 minutes. When it has finished cooking remove the meat and let it cool down.
If needed keep cooking the gravy to allow it to thicken.
Slice the meat and place it in the casserole with the gravy.

**Nutrition:** Calories 311, Carbs 17.1 g, Protein 44.5 g, Fat 22.6 g

## 650. Ground Beef and Brussels Sprouts

**Prep Time:** 20 minutes  
**Serving:** 4  
**Cook Time:** 36 minutes

**Ingredients:**
- 6 oz. ground beef
- 2 garlic cloves, crushed
- ½ cup grated sweet potato
- 1 cup grated Brussels sprouts
- 1 egg, boiled

**Prep:** In a medium saucepan, cook olive oil over medium heat. Gently sauté the ½ onion and garlic until the onion is soft and translucent. Add in the beef and the sweet potato and cook until the meat is fully cooked.
Stir in the Brussels sprouts and cook for about 5 minutes more. Season well and serve topped with a boiled egg.

**Nutrition:** 314 Calories, 15 g Fat, 6 g Protein

## 651. Italian Mini Meatballs

**Prep Time:** 13 minutes  
**Serving:** 6  
**Cook Time:** 20 minutes

**Ingredients:**
- 1 lb. ground beef
- 1 onion, grated
- 1 egg, lightly whisked
- 1 tsp. garlic powder
- 1 tsp. dried basil, oregano, parsley

**Prep:** Combine ground beef, onion, egg, parsley, garlic powder, basil and oregano. Mix very well with hands. Roll tablespoonfuls of the meat mixture into balls.
Place meatballs on a lined baking tray. Bake 20 minutes or until brown.

**Nutrition:** 275 Calories, 9 g Fat, 1 g Protein

## 652. Beef & Tapioca Stew

**Prep Time:** 20 minutes  
**Servings:** 8  
**Cook Time:** 1¾ hours

**Ingredients:**
- 1 tablespoon olive oil
- 2 pounds boneless beef chuck roast, cut into ¾-inch cubes
- 1 (14½-ounce) can diced tomatoes with juice
- ¼ cup quick-cooking tapioca
- 1 tablespoon honey
- 2 teaspoons ground cinnamon
- ¼ teaspoon garlic powder
- Ground black pepper, as required
- ¼ cup red wine vinegar
- 2 cups beef broth
- 3 cups sweet potato, peeled and cubed
- 2 medium onions, cut into thin wedges
- 2 cups prunes, pitted

**Prep:** In a Dutch oven, heat 1 tablespoon of oil over medium-high heat and sear the beef cubes in 2 batches for bout 4-5 minutes or until browned. Drain off the grease from the pan.
Stir in the tomatoes, tapioca, honey, cinnamon, garlic powder, black pepper, vinegar and broth and bring to a boil. Reduce the heat to low and simmer, covered for about 1 hour, stirring occasionally.
Stir in the onions and sweet potato and simmer, covered for about 20-30 minutes. Stir in the prunes and cook for about 3-5 minutes.

**Nutrition:** Calories 675, Fat 34. 1 g, Carbs 59.6 g, Protein 34.1 g

## 653. Beef, Artichoke & Mushroom Stew

**Prep Time:** 20 minutes  
**Servings:** 6  
**Cook Time:** 2¼ hours

**Ingredients:**

**For Beef Marinade:**
- 1 onion, chopped
- 1 garlic clove, crushed
- 2 tablespoons fresh thyme, hopped
- ½ cup dry red wine

**For Stew:**
- 2 tablespoons olive oil
- 2 tablespoons all-purpose flour
- ½ cup water
- ½ cup dry red wine

- 2 tablespoons tomato puree
- 2 tablespoons olive oil
- 1 teaspoon cayenne pepper

- 12 ounces jar artichoke hearts, drained and cut into small chunks
- 4 ounces button mushrooms, sliced

- Pinch of salt and ground black pepper
- 1½ pounds beef stew meat, cut into large chunks

- Salt and ground black pepper, as required

**Prep:** For marinade: in a large bowl, add all the ingredients except the beef and mix well.
Add the beef and coat with the marinade generously. Refrigerate to marinate overnight.
Remove the beef from bowl, reserving the marinade.
In a large pan, heat the oil and sear the beef in 2 batches for about 5 minutes or until browned.
With a slotted spoon, transfer the beef into a bowl.
In the same pan, add the reserved marinade, flour, water and wine and stir to combine. Stir in the cooked beef and bring to a boil. Reduce the heat to low and simmer, covered for about 2 hours, stirring occasionally. Stir in the artichoke hearts and mushrooms and simmer for about 30 minutes. Stir in the salt and black pepper and bring to a boil over high heat.
Remove from the heat ad serve hot.

**Nutrition:** Calories 367, Fat 16.6 g, Carbs 9.6 g, Protein 36.7 g

## 654. Ground Lamb Koftas

**Prep Time:** 15 minutes  
**Servings:** 6  
**Cook Time:** 10 minutes

**Ingredients:**

**For Lamb Koftas:**
- 1-pound ground lamb
- 2 tablespoons plain Greek yogurt
- 2 tablespoons onion, grated
- 2 teaspoons garlic, minced

**For Yogurt Sauce:**
- ½ cup fat-free plain Greek yogurt
- ¼ cup roasted red bell pepper, chopped
- 2 teaspoons garlic, minced

- 2 tablespoons fresh cilantro, minced
- 1 teaspoon ground coriander
- 1 teaspoon ground cumin
- 1 teaspoon ground turmeric

- 1 teaspoon ground coriander
- 1 teaspoon ground cumin
- ½ teaspoon red pepper flakes, crushed

- Salt and ground black pepper, as required
- 1 tablespoon olive oil

- Salt, as required

**Prep:** For Koftas: in a large bowl, add all the ingredients except lamb and mix until well combined.
Make 12 equal sized oblong patties.
In a large nonstick skillet, heat oil over medium-high heat and cook the patties for about 10 minutes or until browned completely, flipping occasionally.
For yogurt sauce: in a bowl, add all the ingredients and mix until well combined.
Serve the Koftas alongside the yogurt sauce.

**Nutrition:** Calories 189, Fat 8.4 g, Carbs 3.8 g, Protein 23.1 g

## 655. Lamb Chops with Veggies

**Prep Time:** 20 minutes  
**Servings:** 4  
**Cook Time:** 27 minutes

### Ingredients:
- 8 (4-ounce) lamb loin chops
- ½ cup fresh basil leaves
- ½ cup fresh mint leaves
- 1 tablespoon fresh rosemary leaves
- 2 garlic cloves
- 3 tablespoons olive oil
- 2 zucchinis, sliced
- 1 red bell pepper, seeded and cut into large chucks
- 1 eggplant, sliced
- 1¾ ounces feta cheese, crumbled
- 8 ounces cherry tomatoes

**Prep:** Preheat the oven to 390 degrees F.
In a food processor, add the fresh herbs, garlic and 2 tablespoons of the oil and pulse until smooth.
Transfer the herb mixture into a bowl. Add the lamb chops and coat with the herb mixture evenly.
Refrigerate to marinate for about 2-3 hours.
In the bottom of a large baking sheet, place the zucchini, bell pepper and eggplant slices and drizzle with the remaining oil. Arrange the lamb chops on top in a single layer. Bake for about 20 minutes.
Remove from the oven and transfer the chops onto a platter. With a piece of foil, cover the chops to keep warm.
Now, place the cherry tomatoes into the baking sheet with veggies and top with the feta cheese.
Bake for about 5 minutes.
Serve the chops alongside the vegetables.

**Nutrition:** Calories 619, Fat 23.6 g, Carbs 17.1 g, Protein 69.2 g

## 656. Lamb Shanks with Veggies

**Prep Time:** 25 minutes  
**Servings:** 4  
**Cook Time:** 3 hours 25 minutes

### Ingredients:
- 1 tablespoon vegetable oil
- 4 (½-pound) lamb shanks
- 2 cups green olives, pitted
- 3 carrots, peeled and cut into ½-inch pieces
- 1 large celery root, peeled and cut into ½-inch pieces
- 1 large onion, minced
- 1 garlic clove, minced
- 2 tablespoons fresh ginger, grated
- 1 cup red wine
- 4 plum tomatoes, peeled, seeded and chopped
- 2 tablespoons lemon rind, grated
- 1 bay leaf
- ¼ teaspoon ground cinnamon
- ¼ teaspoon ground coriander
- ¼ teaspoon ground cumin
- ½ teaspoon red pepper flakes
- 3 cups low-sodium chicken broth
- Salt and ground black pepper, as required
- ¼ cup parsley leaves, minced
- ¼ cup cilantro leaves, minced

**Prep:** In a large, heavy-bottomed pan, heat the oil over medium heat and sear the shanks for about 5 minutes per side. With a slotted spoon, transfer the shanks onto a plate and set aside.
In the same pan, add the olives, carrots, celery, onion, garlic and ginger over medium heat and cook for about 5 minutes. Stir frequently.
With a slotted spoon, transfer the vegetables onto a plate and set aside.
In the same pan, add the wine over high heat and cook for about 5 minutes, scraping up the brown bits. Add the shanks, vegetables, tomatoes, lemon rind, bay leaf and spices and stir to combine. Reduce the heat to medium-low and simmer, covered partially for about 3 hours.
Stir I the salt and black pepper and remove from the heat.
Serve immediately with the garnishing of parsley and cilantro.

**Nutrition:** Calories 554, Fat 24.9 g, Carbs 35.5 g, Protein 37.7 g

## 657. Leg of Lamb with Potatoes

**Prep Time:** 20 minutes  
**Servings:** 8  
**Cook Time:** 1¼ hours

### Ingredients:

**For Lamb & Potatoes:**
- 1 (4-pound) bone in leg of lamb, fat trimmed
- Salt and ground black pepper, as required
- 5 garlic cloves, sliced
- 8 medium potatoes, peeled and cut into wedges
- 1 medium onion, peeled and cut into wedges
- 1 teaspoon garlic powder

- 1 teaspoon paprika

**For Spice Mixture:**
- ½ cup olive oil
- ¼ cup fresh lemon juice
- 5 garlic cloves, peeled
- 2 cups water
- 2 tablespoons dried mint
- 2 tablespoons dried oregano
- 1 tablespoon paprika
- ½ tablespoon ground nutmeg

**Prep:** Remove the leg of lamb from the refrigerator and set aside in room temperature for about 1 hour before cooking.
For spice mixture: in a food processor, add all the ingredients and pulse until smooth.
Transfer the spice mixture into a bowl and set aside.
Preheat the broiler of the oven.
With paper towels, pat dry the leg of lamb completely. With a knife, make a few slits on both sides the leg of lamb and season with salt and black pepper. Place the leg of lamb onto a wire rack and arrange the rack onto the top oven rack.
Broil for about 5-7 minutes per side. Remove from the oven and transfer the leg of lamb onto a platter to cool slightly.
Then, set the oven temperature to 375 degrees F. Arrange a rack in the middle of the oven. Place a wire rack into a large roasting pan. Carefully, insert the garlic slices in the slits of leg of lamb and rub with spice mixture generously.
In a bowl, add the potato, onion, garlic powder, paprika and a little salt and toss to coat well. Place 2 cups of water into the bottom of the prepared roasting pan.
Place the leg of lamb in the middle of the prepared roasting pan and arrange the potato and onion wedges around the lamb. With a large piece of foil, cover the roasting pan. Roast for about 1 hour.
Remove the foil and roast for about 10-15 minutes more. Remove from the oven and place the leg of lamb onto a cutting board for at least 20 minutes before carving.
Cut into desired sized slices and serve alongside potatoes.

**Nutrition:** Calories 700, Fat 29.9 g, Carbs 37.9 g, Protein 68.1 g

## 658. Steak with Hummus

**Prep Time:** 15 minutes  
**Servings:** 6  
**Cook Time:** 17 minutes

**Ingredients:**
- ¼ cup fresh oregano leaves, chopped
- 1½ tablespoons garlic, minced
- 1 tablespoon fresh lemon peel, grated
- ½ teaspoon red pepper flakes, crushed
- Salt and ground black pepper, as required
- 1 pound boneless beef top sirloin steak
- 1½ cups prepared hummus
- 1/3 cup feta cheese, crumbled

**Prep:** Preheat the grill to medium-high heat. Grease the grill grate.
In a bowl, add the garlic, lemon peel, oregano, red pepper flakes, salt and pepper and mix well.
Rub the garlic mixture evenly over the stick.
Grill, covered for about 12 minutes, flipping occasionally.
Transfer the steak to a cutting board for 5 minutes.
With a knife, cut the steak into desired sized slices. Divide the steaks and hummus onto serving plates and serve with the topping of the feta cheese.

**Nutrition:** Calories 280, Fat 12.8 g, Carbs 12.2 g, Protein 29.6 g

## 659. Steak with Yogurt Sauce

**Prep Time:** 15 minutes  
**Servings:** 6  
**Cook Time:** 15 minutes

**Ingredients:**

**For Steak:**
- 3 garlic cloves, minced
- 2 tablespoons fresh rosemary, chopped

**For Sauce:**
- 1½ cups plain Greek yogurt
- 1 cucumber, peeled, seeded and chopped finely
- Salt and ground black pepper, as required
- 2 pounds flank steak, trimmed
- 1 cup fresh parsley, chopped
- 1 garlic clove, minced
- 1 teaspoon fresh lemon zest, grated finely
- 1/8 teaspoon cayenne pepper
- Salt and ground black pepper, as required

**Prep:** Preheat the grill to medium heat. Grease the grill grate.

For steak: in a large bowl, add all the ingredients except steak and mix well. Add the steak and cost with mixture generously. Set aside for about 15 minutes.

Grill the steak for about 12-15 minutes, flipping after every 3-4 minutes. Transfer the steak onto a cutting board for about 5 minutes.

Meanwhile, for sauce: in a bowl, add all the ingredients and mix well.

With a knife, cut the steak into desired sized slices and serve with the topping of the yogurt sauce.

**Nutrition:** Calories 354, Fat 13.7 g, Carbs 8.1 g, Protein 46.3 g

### 660. Bacon Cheeseburger Casserole

**Prep Time:** 10 minutes  
**Servings:** 6  
**Cook Time:** 43 minutes

**Ingredients:**
- 1 lb. Ground Beef (80/20)
- 3 slices Bacon
- 1/2 cup Almond Flour
- 265g Cauliflower, riced (~3 cups chopped)
- 1 tbsp. Psyllium Husk Powder
- 1/2 tsp. Garlic Powder
- 1/2 tsp. Onion Powder
- 2 tbsp. Reduced Sugar Ketchup
- 1 tbsp. Dijon Mustard
- 2 tbsp. Mayonnaise
- 3 large Eggs
- 4 oz. Cheddar Cheese
- Salt and Pepper to Taste

**Prep:** Pre-heat oven to 350F. Rice cauliflower in the food processor. Add dry ingredients and mix them.

Process bacon and ground beef in the food processor until crumbly and slightly pasty. Cook over medium, seasoning with salt and pepper.

Shred the cheese while the meat is cooking. Once the meat isready, combine all ingredients in a large bowl and add 2 oz. of cheddar cheese. Add eggs, mayonnaise, ketchup, and mustard to the mixture. Using a fork, mix everything well.

Press mixture into a baking sheet lined with parchment paper. Then, top with the other half of the cheddar cheese.

Place on top rack and bake for 30 minutes. Remove from oven and let cool for 10 minutes.

Slice, and serve with additional toppings.

**Nutrition:** 478 Calories, 35 g Fat, 6 g Carbs, 32 g Protein

### 661. Balsamic Beef and Mushrooms Mix

**Prep Time:** 5 minutes  
**Servings:** 4  
**Cook Time:** 8 hours

**Ingredients:**
- 2 pounds' beef, cut into strips
- ¼ cup balsamic vinegar
- 2 cups beef stock
- tablespoon ginger, grated
- Juice of ½ lemon
- 1 cup brown mushrooms, sliced
- A pinch of salt and black pepper
- 1 teaspoon ground cinnamon

**Prep:** Mix all the ingredients in your slow cooker, cover and cook on low for 8 hours.

Divide everything between plates and serve.

**Nutrition:** Calories 446, Fat 14 g, Carbs 2.9 g, Protein 70,8 g

### 662. Cheesy Bacon Burger

**Prep Time:** 10 minutes  
**Servings:** 2  
**Cook Time:** 20 minutes

**Ingredients:**
- 8 oz. Ground Beef
- 2 slices Bacon, pre-cooked
- 1 oz. Mozzarella Cheese
- 2 oz. Cheddar Cheese
- 1 tsp. Salt
- ½ tsp. Pepper
- 1 tsp. Cajun Seasoning
- 1 tbsp. Butter

**Prep:** Season ground beef with all of the spices and mix lightly.

Prepare the cheese by cubing 1 oz. Mozzarella, and sliced 2 oz. of Cheddar.

Form patties with the ground beef and place mozzarella cheese inside, enclosing the cheese with the beef.

Heat 1 tbsp. butter per burger in a skillet, and wait until bubbling. Add burger to the skillet. Cover with a cloche and let cook for 3 minutes. Flip the burger and place cheddar cheese on top. Place cloche back on top and let cook for about 1-2 minutes more.

Chop the bacon slice in half and place on top of the burger.

**Nutrition:** 614 Calories, 51 g Fat, 5 g Carbs, 33 g Protein

## 663. Sesame Beef

**Prep Time:** 10 minutes
**Servings:** 4

**Cook Time:** 40 minutes

**Ingredients:**
- medium Daikon Radish
- 1 lb. Ribeye Steak, sliced into ¼" strips
- 1 tbsp. Coconut Flour
- ½ tsp. Guar Gum
- 1 tbsp. Coconut Oil
- 4 tbsp. Soy Sauce
- 1 tsp. Sesame Oil
- 1 tsp. Oyster Sauce
- 1 tbsp. + 1 tsp. Rice Vinegar
- 1 tsp. Sriracha or Sambal Olek and ½ tsp. Red Pepper Flakes
- 1 tbsp. Toasted Sesame Seeds
- ½ medium Red Pepper, sliced into thin strips
- ½ medium Jalapeno Pepper, sliced into thin rings
- 1 medium Green Onion, chopped
- 1 clove Garlic, minced
- 1 tsp. Ginger, minced
- 7 drops Liquid Stevia
- Oil for frying

**Prep:** Begin by preparing the daikon noodles: using a spiralizer, slice the daikon radish.
Soak the daikon noodles in a bowl of cold water for 20 minutes.
Chop rib-eye steak into small strips (1/4 in thickness). Place the rib eye steak in a bowl and pour the coconut flour and guar gum over the meat to coat all the pieces. This flour will act as light bread rings, green onion into small pieces, and mince the garlic and ginger.
Prepare thevegetables: slice red pepper into thin strips, and jalapeno into thin rings.
In a large skillet, heat coconut oil over medium heat. Once hot, add ginger, garlic, and red pepper strips. Fry for 2 minutes.
Add the oyster sauce, soy sauce, rice vinegar, sesame oil, stevia, and sriracha. Whisk to combine and let cool for 1 minutes.
Add sesame seeds and red pepper flakes to the sauce mixture and stir.
While vegetables are cooking, heat cooking oil in a large pot over high heat. Add beef strips. Turn the meat in the pan once to allow both sides to cook evenly. Fry for 2-3 minutes on each side.
Remove the beef from the oil and place on paper towels to absorb some of the oil.
Next, drop the cooked crispy beef into the wok pan containing the sauce and stir to combine. Cook for an additional 2 minutes to develop the flavors of the meat and sauce together.
Drain the noodles and divide them on each serving plate.
Top each plate with a portion of the sesame beef. Garnish with green onion and jalapeno slices.

**Nutrition:** 412 calories, 33 g Fat, 5 g Carbs, 25 g Protein

## 664. Stuffed Meatballs

**Prep Time:** 10 minutes
**Servings:** 4

**Cook Time:** 40 minutes

**Ingredients:**
- 1/2 lb. Ground Beef (80/20)
- 1 tsp. Oregano
- 1/2 tsp. Italian Seasoning
- 1 tsp. Minced Garlic
- 1/2 tsp. Onion powder
- 2 tbsp. Tomato Paste
- 2 tbsp. Flaxseed Meal
- 2 large Eggs
- 1/2 cup Olives, sliced
- 1/2 cup Mozzarella Cheese
- 1 tsp. Worcestershire Sauce reached.
- Salt and Pepper to Taste

**Prep:** In a mixing bowl, add the ground beef, oregano, Italian seasoning, and garlic and onion powder. Mix well using your hands.
Add eggs, tomato paste, flaxseed, and Worcestershire to the meat and mix again.
Finally, slice the olives into small pieces and add to the meat along with the shredded mozzarella cheese. Mix everything.
Preheat the oven to 400 °F and then start to form the meatballs. You end up with about 20 meatballs in total. Lay these on a foil-covered cookie sheet. Bake the meatballs for 20 minutes.

**Nutrition:** 594 Calories, 48 g Fat, 8 g Carbs, 38 g Protein

## 665. Greek Style Mini Burger Pies

**Prep Time:** 15 minutes
**Servings:** 6

**Cook Time:** 40 minutes

**Ingredients:**

**Burger mixture:**
- Onion, large, chopped (1 piece)
- Red bell peppers, roasted, diced (1/2 cup)
- Ground lamb, 80% lean (1 pound)
- Red pepper flakes (1/4 teaspoon)
- Feta cheese, crumbled (2 ounces)

**Baking mixture:**
- Milk (1/2 cup)
- Biscuit mix, classic (1/2 cup)
- Eggs (2 pieces)

**Prep:** Preheat oven at 350 degrees F.
Grease 12 muffin cups using cooking spray.
Cook the onion and meat in a skillet heated on medium-high. Once lamb is browned and cooked through, drain and let cool for five minutes. Stir together with feta cheese, roasted red peppers, and red pepper flakes.
Whisk the baking mixture ingredients together. Fill each muffin cup with baking mixture (1 tablespoon).
Air-fry for twenty-five to thirty minutes. Let cool before serving.

**Nutrition:** Calories 270; Fat 10 g; Protein 10 g; Carbs 10 g

### 666. Lamb and Potatoes Stew

**Prep Time:** 10 minutes  
**Servings:** 4  
**Cook Time:** 1 hour and 20 minutes

**Ingredients:**
- 2 pounds lamb shoulder, boneless and cubed
- Salt and black pepper to the taste
- 1 yellow onion, chopped
- 3 tbsps. olive oil
- 3 tomatoes, grated
- 2 cups chicken stock
- 2 and ½ pounds gold potatoes, cubed
- ¾ cup green olives, pitted and sliced
- 1 tbsp. cilantro, chopped

**Prep:** Heat up a pot with the oil over medium-high heat, add the lamb, and brown for 5 minutes on each side. Add the onion and sauté for 5 minutes more. Add the rest of the ingredients, bring to a simmer, and cook over medium heat and cook for 1 hour and 10 minutes.
Divide the stew into bowls and serve.

**Nutrition:** Calories 411, Fat: 17.4 g, Carbs: 25.5 g, Protein: 34.3 g

### 667. Mouth-watering Beef Pie

**Prep Time:** 15 minutes  
**Servings:** 8  
**Cook Time:** 45 minutes

**Ingredients:**
- 3/4-pound beef; ground
- 1/2 onion; chopped.
- 1 pie crust
- 3 tablespoons taco seasoning
- 1 teaspoon baking soda
- Mango salsa for serving
- 1/2 red bell pepper; chopped.
- A handful cilantro; chopped.
- 8 eggs
- 1 teaspoon coconut oil
- Salt and black pepper to taste

**Prep:**
Heat up a pan, add oil, beef, cook until it browns and mixes with salt, pepper and taco seasoning.
Stir again, transfer to a bowl and leave aside for now.
Heat up the pan again over medium heat with cooking juices from the meat, add onion and pepper; stir and cook for 4 minutes. Add eggs, baking soda and some salt and stir well. Add cilantro; stir again and take off heat.
Spread beef mix in pie crust, add veggies mix and spread over meat, heat oven at 350 degrees F and bake for 45 minutes.
Leave the pie to cool, slice, divide between plates and serve with mango salsa on top.

**Nutrition:** Calories: 198; Fat: 11 g; Carbs: 12 g; Protein: 12 g

### 668. Lamb with Vegetables

**Prep Time:** 20 minutes  
**Servings:** 4  
**Cook Time:** 27 minutes

**Ingredients:**
- 8 (4-ounce) lamb loin chops
- ½ cup fresh basil leaves
- ½ cup fresh mint leaves
- 1 tablespoon fresh rosemary leaves
- 2 garlic cloves
- 3 tablespoons olive oil
- 2 zucchinis, sliced
- 1 red bell pepper, seeded and cut into large chucks
- 1 eggplant, sliced
- 1¾ ounces feta cheese, crumbled
- 8 ounces cherry tomatoes

**Prep:** Preheat the oven to 390 degrees F.

In a food processor, add the garlic, fresh herbs, and 2 tablespoons of the oil and pulse until smooth.
Transfer the herb mixture into a large bowl. Add the lamb chops and coat with the herb mixture evenly.
Refrigerate to marinate for about 2-3 hours.
In the bottom of a large baking sheet, place the zucchini, bell pepper and eggplant slices and drizzle with the remaining oil. Arrange the lamb chops on top in a single layer.
Bake for about 20 minutes.
Remove from the oven and transfer the chops onto a platter.
With a piece of foil, cover the chops to keep warm.
Now, place the cherry tomatoes into the baking sheet with veggies and top with the feta cheese.
Bake for about 5-7 minutes or until the cheese just starts to become golden brown.
Serve the chops alongside the vegetables.

**Nutrition:** Calories 619, Fat 23.6 g, Carbs 17.1 g, Protein 69.2 g

## 669. Beef Tartar

**Prep Time:** 10 minutes                                                                                           **Servings:** 1

### Ingredients:
- 1 shallot, chopped
- 4 ounces beef fillet
- 5 small cucumbers
- 1 egg yolk
- 2 teaspoons mustard
- 1 tablespoon parsley
- 1 parsley spring

**Direction:** Incorporate meat with shallot, egg yolk, salt, pepper, mustard, cucumbers and parsley.
Stir well and arrange on a platter.
Garnish with the chopped parsley spring and serve.

**Nutrition:** 210 Calories, 3 g Fat, 8 g Protein

# POULTRY

## 670. Rabbit with Mushrooms

**Prep time:** 10 minutes
**Servings:** 6

**Cook time:** 1 hour e 10 minutes

**Ingredients:**
- 1 rabbit
- 1 minced celery stick
- 1 minced onion
- 1 minced carrot
- 2 rosemary sprigs
- 1 1/4 cup of ham in one slice cut into dices
- Salt
- 4 tbsp of dried mushrooms
- Sage leaves
- 4 tbsp of olive oil
- 1 cup of white wine
- 2 tbsp of butter

**Prep:** Wash the rabbit and cut in in pieces.
Sizzle the oil in a casserole, put in the rabbit pieces and sprinkle some minced sage and rosemary.
Adjust salt to taste and turn the meat several times to cook evenly.
Separately sizzle the butter and chopped vegetables. Add the ham and mushrooms (previously soaked). Mix and let marinate for about 10 minutes in a covered casserole.
Pout the gravy on the rabbit and add the wine and let it deglaze, add some water to allow to finish cooking.

**Nutrition:** Calories 388, Carbs 7.2 g, Protein 31.4 g, Fat 18.1 g

## 671. Baked Rabbit

**Prep time:** 20 minutes
**Servings:** 6

**Cook time:** 1 hour e 20 minutes

**Ingredients:**
- 1 rabbit
- 1 cup of white wine
- Coarse Salt
- 1 1/4 cup of lard
- 1 sprig of wild fennel
- 2 garlic cloves
- Pepper
- Juice of 2 lemons

**Prep:** Clean the rabbit and remove the head.

Stuff with the liver, lard, fennel, pepper, garlic cloves and coarse salt. With a needle and thread sew the intestine, fold the legs and tie them to the body; put it in a casserole. Add some pieces of lard, wet with half of the wine and put in a preheated oven at 350°F and let cook for about one hour. Flip every half an hour. Pour on the lemon juice and white wine a few minutes before removing the rabbit and finishing the cooking.
Serve hot and cut in pieces.

**Nutrition:** Calories 562, Carbs 7.9 g, Protein 44.6 g, Fat 29.2 g

### 672. Chicken with Peppers

**Prep time: 15 minutes**  **Cook time: 35 minutes**
**Servings: 6**

**Ingredients:**
- 1 chicken
- 4 bell peppers
- Una onion
- 1/4 cup di butter
- ½ cup of white wine
- 4 ripe tomatoes
- 1 garlic clove
- Salt and pepper
- 2 1/2 tbsp of lard

**Prep:** Clean the peppers by removing the stem, seeds, and the white insides; cut the pulp into slices or cubes. Clean well chicken: torch to remove the fuzz and cut it into pieces.
In a large pan, sizzle the pieces of chicken with a little butter e oil; turn them some times, add the peppers, minced garlic and onion, tomatoes, salt and pepper, mix some more. Put the lid on and cook on low heat. Pour some wine occasionally in small quantities. Serve the chicken straight out from the oven.

**Nutrition:** Calories 375.6, Carbs 12.4 g, Protein 39.6 g, Fat 15.6 g

### 673. Chicken with Vinegar

**Prep time: 20 minutes**  **Cook time: 1 hour**
**Servings: 6**

**Ingredients:**
- 1 chicken
- 2 cups of vinegar
- Salt and pepper
- Juniper berries
- 1 sliced lemon
- 3 garlic cloves
- ½ cup of olive oil
- 3 sage leaves
- 2 rosemary sprigs

**Prep:** Torch the chicken to remove the fuzz, open it and wash it carefully. Dry it with a cloth and put it into a big and toll casserole. Mince the garlic, sage and rosemary, then add the chicken. Add 1 tbsp of juniper berries, lemon slices, adjust the salt and pepper to taste, pour the vinegar and some warm water. Let marinate for at least 3 hours.
Put the chicken in a casserole with hot oil, cover with a lid and let cook for 1 hour on low heat.

**Nutrition:** Calories 205, Carbs 8.4 g, Protein 30.7 g, Fat 5.2 g

### 674. Snipe in a Pan

**Prep time: 15 minutes**  **Cook time: 45 minutes**
**Servings: 4**

**Ingredients:**
- 8 snipes tender and cleaned
- 17 oz of tomatoes
- Salt and pepper
- 3 garlic cloves
- ½ cup of extra virgin olive oil

**Prep:** In a pan, heat up the oil and garlic, add the snipes and sizzle on low heat, stir often to combine the flavors. When the snipes are evenly golden, add the chopped tomatoes, a dust of pepper and salt and keep cooking with a lid on for half an hour, adding some warm water if needed.

### 675. Cacciatora Chicken

**Prep time: 20 minutes**  **Cook time: 50 minutes**
**Servings: 6**

**Ingredients:**
- 1 chicken
- ½ cup of oil
- 1 tbsp of lard
- 8 oz of onion
- 17 oz of tomatoes
- 1 rosemary sprig
- ½ bay leaf
- Salt
- Pepper

**Prep:** Cut the chicken in 10 pieces, wash and dry it. In a casserole add oil, the onion, rosemary, chicken, butter, salt, bay and pepper, sizzle on high heat and stir frequently. Let the chicken brown and then add the tomatoes peeled and drained, stir often and lower the heat and cover with a lid; cook from half an hour. Serve the chicken hot with its gravy.

**Nutrition:** Calories 520, Carbs 8.2 g, Protein 47.6 g, Fat 30.6 g

### 676. Turkey with Ham and Cheese

**Prep time:** 15 minutes  
**Servings:** 6  
**Cook time:** 30 minutes

**Ingredients:**
- 28 oz of turkey breast
- 3/4 cup of ham slices
- Salt and pepper
- Breadcrumbs
- 2 eggs
- 2 tbsp di butter
- 1 1/4 cup of string cheese slices
- 3 tbsp of olive oil

**Prep:** Cut the turkey, beat the slices and coat them in the beaten egg with added pepper and salt, then move into the breadcrumbs. Fry the slices in a pan with hot oil and butter.
Cover with a slice of ham and one of cheese; put in a preheated oven at 350°F, leaving it to bake until the cheese melts.

**Nutrition:** Calories 253, Carbs 2.4 g, Protein 29.3 g, Fat 16.5 g

### 677. Chicken Mince

**Prep time:** 15 minutes  
**Servings:** 5  
**Cook time:** 1 hour

**Ingredients:**
- 26 oz of boneless chicken meat
- Rosemary
- 2 garlic cloves
- Pepper
- Olive oil
- 8 oz of mustard
- Salt

**Prep:** Cut the chicken in pieces then into a pan, pour the oil, add the mustard, stir occasionally to coat all the pieces, sprinkle plenty of rosemary, pepper and salt. Cook for about half an hour in a preheated oven.

**Nutrition:** Calories 420.4, Carbs 5.2 g, Protein 36.6 g, Fat 27.2 g

### 678. Duck Ham

**Prep time:** 20 minutes  
**Servings:** 4

**Ingredients:**
- 2 goose legs
- Coarse Salt
- minced duck skin
- Salt and pepper
- Cloves

**Prep:** Vertically open the duck legs, remove the bone, flatten and cover in coarse salt and let marinate for at least 4 days.
Mash and mince the duck skin, mix it with pepper, salt, minced cloves; stuff the legs with the mixture. Sew the flaps with needle and cotton thread, dry and let age in a fresh and dry place. The aging period requires a few months to work properly.

### 679. Goose with Salt

**Prep time:** 1 hour e 40 minutes  
**Servings:** 6  
**Cook time:** 1 hour e 15 minutes

**Ingredients:**
- 1 goose
- 6 sage leaves
- Coarse salt

- *1 rosemary sprig*
- *1 tbsp of Brandy*
- *1 garlic clove*

**Prep:** mince together the rosemary, sage and oil.
Clean the goose carefully, dry it and stuff with the minced herbs and brandy.
Tightly tie the string on the meat, move the goose to a tray lined with coarse salt. Cover in more salt, and put the tray in the oven at 350°F for 1.30 hour.
Remove the salt layer, cut the thread and cut the goose, serve hot.

**Nutrition:** Calories 680, Carbs 10.1 g, Protein 67.6 g, Fat 21.3 g

### 680. Guinea Fowl Hen with Bacon

**Prep time: 10 minutes**  
**Servings: 6**

**Cook time: 1 hour**

**Ingredients:**
- *2 small guinea fowl hens*
- *1 chopped onion*
- *3 garlic cloves*
- *Lard and olive oil*
- *12 bacon slices*
- *2 bay leaves*
- *4 sage leaves*
- *2 cups of tomato sauce*
- *2 rosemary sprigs*
- *1 cup of broth*
- *Salt and pepper*

**Prep:** clean inside and out the hens, wash them under running water. Cut them into pieces, wrap into the bacon strips, stab with toothpicks and put in a pan with hot oil, butter and chopped onion.
Add the sage and bay leaves and rosemary, broth and garlic wedges. Adjust salt and pepper to taste. Cook for at least 1 hour

**Nutrition:** Calories 887, Carbs 19.3 g, Protein 76.3 g, Fat 44.7 g

### 681. Goose with Sauce

**Prep time: 15 minutes**  
**Servings: 4**

**Cook time: 1 hour e 30 minutes**

**Ingredients:**
- *1 goose cleaned and chopped*
- *42 oz of tomato sauce*
- *1 onion*
- *Extra virgin olive oil*
- *1 garlic clove*
- *1 sprig of parsley*
- *1 lemon*
- *Marsala*
- *sugar*
- *Salt*
- *Hot pepper*

**Prep:** Mince the onion, garlic and parsley and sizzle in a casserole with 5 tbsp of oil. Add the goose. Pour in ½ cup of Marsala and let deglaze. Pour in the tomato soup, a handful of salt, a pinch of sugar, ground hot pepper. Mix and cook for about 1 hour e 30 minutes.

**Nutrition:** Calories 448, Carbs 4.7 g, Protein 56.4 g, Fat 21.2 g

### 682. Rabbit with Sauce

**Prep time: 15 minutes**  
**Servings: 4**

**Cook time: 1 hour**

**Ingredients:**
- *1 rabbit cut into pieces*
- *1 onion*
- *42 oz of tomato sauce*
- *1 rosemary sprig*
- *1 garlic clove*
- *White wine*
- *1 lemon*
- *Olive oil*
- *Sugar*
- *Salt and pepper*

**Prep:** reduce the onion in a pan, garlic and rosemary in a pan with 5 tbsp of oil. Add the rabbit and sizzle it, turn it in the seasoning. Pour ½ cup of wine and let deglaze it; then pour the tomato sauce. Add salt and pepper and a pinch of sugar. Mix and cook for 1 hour.

**Nutrition:** Calories 351, Carbs 6.5 g, Protein 33.4 g, Fat 16.5 g

## 683. Sweet and Sour Rabbit

**Prep time:** 30 minutes  
**Servings:** 4  
**Cook time:** 1 hour

**Ingredients:**
- 1 rabbit cut into pieces
- 1 bay leaf
- 1 onion
- 1 celery stick
- 1 lemon
- 17 oz ripe tomatoes
- 1 cup of green olives
- 1 tbsp of capers
- 1 tbsp of raisins
- 1 tbsp of pine nuts
- Oregano
- Extra virgin olive oil
- 1 cup of vinegar
- ½ tbsp of sugar
- Salt and pepper

**Prep:** put the rabbit in a pan with ½ cup of oil, the bay and sizzled onion and celery. Let the rabbit sizzle turning it often and add occasionally 1 tbsp of hot water.
Pour the vinegar with the sugar and let it evaporate slowly. Add the minced tomatoes, olives, capers, raisins, pine nuts, pepper, a pinch of oregano, and let cook on medium heat.

**Nutrition:** Calories 433, Carbs 2.3 g, Protein 51.7 g, Fat 22.4 g

## 684. Rabbit Stew

**Prep time:** 20 minutes  
**Servings:** 4  
**Cook time:** 1 hour

**Ingredients:**
- 1 rabbit cut in pieces
- 1 bay leaf
- 1 onion
- 1 garlic clove
- 14 oz of canned tomatoes
- Oregano
- 1 ½ of olive oil
- Vinegar
- 4 basil leaves
- Salt and pepper

**Prep:** Blend the garlic with the basil, salt, minced tomatoes, half of the oil to reach a smooth sauce.
In a pan sizzle the rabbit with the remaining oil, bay and minced garlic. When the rabbit has become golden pour the vinegar and let evaporate. Add the prepared sauce, a dash of salt and pepper and oregano and keep cooking on medium heat for 30 minutes.

**Nutrition:** Calories 363, Carbs 6.2 g, Protein 34.4 g, Fat 20.1 g

## 685. Portuguese Style Rabbit

**Prep time:** 20 minutes  
**Servings:** 4  
**Cook time:** 70 minutes

**Ingredients:**
- 52 oz of rabbit pieces
- 1 onion
- 1 garlic clove
- 1 bay leaf
- 1 tbsp of tomato concentrate
- 9 oz of canned tomatoes
- Marsala
- 1 sprig of parsley
- Extra virgin olive oil
- Salt and pepper

**Prep:** put the rabbit in a bowl, pour the Marsala and let marinate for 30 minutes. Put the rabbit and sizzle it ½ cup of oil.
In another pan, let reduce the onion with 5 tbsp of oil, pressed garlic, bay and chopped parsley. Add the rabbit and let the flavors combine for few minutes. Pour ½ cup of Marsala and let evaporate. Add the tomato concentrate melted ½ cup of water, the minced tomatoes, salt and pepper, and cook on low heat for 40 minutes.

**Nutrition:** Calories 387, Carbs 7.1 g, Protein 37.9 g, Fat 21.3 g

## 686. Rabbit with Almonds

**Prep time:** 15 minutes  
**Servings:** 4  
**Cook time:** 45 minutes

**Ingredients:**
- 1 rabbit in pieces
- 2 bay leaves
- ½ cup of skinned almonds

- ½ cup of vinegar
- 1 rosemary sprig
- 6 tbsp of olive oil
- 2 garlic cloves
- 1 lemon
- Salt and pepper

**Prep:** soak the rabbit in water and lemon cut in quarters for few minutes.
Heat up 2 tbsp of oil in a casserole and sizzle the rabbit, add the vinegar and let it evaporate. Add the minced garlic, bay and ½ cup of water.
Add the minced toasted almonds, the rosemary and cook on medium heat for about 20 minutes.

**Nutrition:** Calories 429, Carbs 7.2 g, Protein 31.2 g, Fat 16.8 g

### 687. Broiled Chicken

**Prep time:** 15 minutes  
**Servings:** 4  
**Cook time:** 20 minutes

**Ingredients:**
- 2 deboned chickens
- Rosemary
- Oregano
- Sage
- Parsley
- Extra virgin olive oil
- Salt and pepper

**Prep:** Beat the chickens so they are as beat up as possible.
Put on a hot grill and occasionally brush an emulsion of oil, parsley, sage, oregano, minced rosemary, salt and pepper.
When the chicken has browned on one side, turn and add more seasoning.

**Nutrition:** Calories 341, Carbs 18.7 g, Protein 22 g, Fat 18.7 g

### 688. Baked Chicken with Pecorino

**Prep time:** 30 minutes  
**Servings:** 6  
**Cook time:** 2 hours e 30 minutes

**Ingredients:**
- 1 chicken
- 1 onion
- 1 carrot
- 1 celery stick
- 1 sprig of parsley
- 1 bay leaf
- 1 clove
- ½ cup of grated pecorino
- 1 tazza di breadcrumbs
- 2 lemons
- Oregano
- Extra virgin olive oil
- Salt and pepper

**Prep:** In a dish add the carrot, celery, parsley, onion, clove, bay and pepper. Cover everything with 0.7 gallons of cold water and bring to a boil. Dip the chicken and cook for 2 hours.
When the chicken is fully cooked, finely cut it, dip in into an emulsion of oil, sage, oregano, salt and pepper.
Coat the chicken in breadcrumbs and pecorino and lay it into a tray greased with oil. Bake at 375°F for 45 minutes.

**Nutrition:** Calories 517, Carbs 6.2 g, Protein 44.1 g, Fat 31.6 g

### 689. Chicken with Potatoes

**Prep time:** 30 minutes  
**Servings:** 6  
**Cook time:** 1 hour e 30 minutes

**Ingredients:**
- 1 chicken in pieces
- 35 oz of potatoes
- 9 oz canned tomatoes
- 1 onion
- 2 rosemary sprigs
- ½ cup of white wine
- 1 bay leaf
- Extra virgin olive oil
- Salt and pepper

**Prep:** Put the chicken in a greased tray and add minced onion, potato wedges, bay, and tomatoes.
Dust salt and pepper, add the rosemary and wine. Bake in the oven at 400°F and turn the chicken occasionally.

**Nutrition:** Calories 567, Carbs 37 g, Protein 38.7 g, Fat 20.8 g

### 690. Chicken in Salt Crust

**Prep time:** 40 minutes  
**Servings:** 6  
**Cook time:** 1 hour

**Ingredients:**
- 1 chicken
- 6 lbs of marine salt
- 1 rosemary sprig
- 1 bay leaf
- 1 sprig of parsley
- pepper

**Prep:** Stuff the chicken with a rosemary sprig, bay and minced parsley and then tie it with string. Dust some pepper and put aside.
In a bowl pour the salt, rosemary and 11 oz of water. Knead until you reach an even dough. Spread half of the dough in a tray and forming a thick an even layer. Pour in the chicken and cover with the remained salt.
Bake in a preheated oven at 375°F for about 1 hour.

**Nutrition:** Calories 157, Carbs 1.3 g, Protein 23.6 g, Fat 5.2 g

### 691. Chicken with Vinegar (2nd version)

**Prep time:** 30 minutes  
**Servings:** 4  
**Cook time:** 1 hour

**Ingredients:**
- 1 chicken in pieces
- ½ cup of vinegar
- 1 cup of broth
- 2 lemons
- Bay
- Extra virgin olive oil
- Salt and pepper

**Prep:** Brush the chicken with ½ lemon dipped in salt. Wash and dry well.
In a pan sizzle 2 tbsp of oil and stir occasionally. Pour the vinegar and let it evaporate.
Pour in the broth, lemon juice and 4 tbsp of oil. Cover in salt, pepper, bay and cook with a lid on for 45 minutes.

**Nutrition:** Calories 331, Carbs 3.5 g, Protein 28.6 g, Fat 20.3 g

### 692. Sweet and Sour Chicken

**Prep time:** 20 minutes  
**Servings:** 4  
**Cook time:** 25 minutes

**Ingredients:**
- 24 oz of chicken breast
- 2 garlic cloves
- 17 oz of canned tomatoes
- 1 sprig of parsley
- ½ tbsp of sugar
- Oregano
- ½ cup of vinegar
- 1 cup of skinned almonds
- Extra virgin olive oil
- Salt and pepper

**Prep:** Brown the minced garlic and parsley in a pan with 5 tbsp of oil. Add the diced tomatoes, oregano, salt and pepper, and cook for 10 minutes.
Cut the chicken in strips and sizzle it in a pan with 4 tbsp of oil, add the sauce and let it marinate for 5 minutes. Pour in the vinegar with sugar and keep on the heat for 2 minutes, sprinkle the minced toasted almonds and serve cold.

**Nutrition:** Calories 889, Carbs 77.8 g, Protein 44.1 g, Fat 55.7 g

### 693. Chicken Pot Pie

**Prep time:** 30 minutes  
**Servings:** 4  
**Cook time:** 1 hour e 45 minutes

**Ingredients:**
- 1 chicken in pieces
- 1 ripe tomato
- 1 potato
- 1 onion
- 1 carrot
- 1 celery stick
- 1 sprig of parsley
- 1 bay leaf
- 1 cup di grated pecorino
- 3 eggs
- Extra virgin olive oil
- Salt and pepper

**Prep:** Boil the chicken in a pot full of water with the carrot, the potato, tomato, celery, onion, parsley, bay, salt and pepper. When it has finished cooking, drain it and move into a pan with 2 tbsp of oil and ½ cup of broth and let it marinate for few minutes. Add the beaten eggs and pecorino and let it thicken on medium heat.

## 694. Chicken Stew with Potatoes

**Prep time: 30 minutes**
**Servings: 4**

**Cook time: 1 hour e 20 minutes**

**Ingredients:**
- 35 oz di chicken in pieces
- 24 oz of tomato sauce
- 35 oz of potatoes
- 1 onion
- ½ cup of white wine
- 1 cup of olive oil
- 1 lemon
- 1 sprig of basil
- Salt and pepper

**Prep:** brush the chicken with a lemon dipped into salt.
Dice the potatoes and let them brown in a pan with half of the oil.
In a separate pan pout the remaining oil, onion and chicken, when it becomes golden, pour in the wine and let it evaporate. Add the basil, potatoes, adjust the salt and pepper to taste and keep cooking for 50 minutes.

## 695. Quail in a Pan

**Prep time: 10 minutes**
**Servings: 4**

**Cook time: 40 minutes**

**Ingredients:**
- 8 cleaned quails
- Salt and pepper
- 1 bay leave
- 5 tbsp of olive oil
- ½ cup of white wine

**Prep:** Wash and dry the quails; sizzle with the bay and hot oil in the pan. Pour the white wine and deglaze. Adjust pepper and salt to taste, pour a little water and let it cook for 20 minutes on low heat.

## 696. Chicken & Veggie Kabobs

**Prep Time: 20 minutes**
**Servings: 8**

**Cook Time: 10 minutes**

**Ingredients:**
- ¼ cup white vinegar
- ¼ cup fresh lemon juice
- ¼ cup olive oil
- 2 garlic cloves, minced
- ½ teaspoon dried thyme, crushed
- ½ teaspoon dried oregano, crushed
- 1 teaspoon ground cumin
- Salt and ground black pepper, as required
- 2 pounds skinless, boneless chicken breast, cubed into ½-inch size
- 1 large orange bell pepper, seeded and cubed into 1-inch size
- 1 large green bell pepper, seeded and cubed into 1-inch size
- 16 fresh mushrooms
- 16 cherry tomatoes
- 1 large red onion, quartered and separated into pieces

**Prep:** In a large bowl, add the vinegar, lemon juice, oil, garlic, dried herbs, cumin, salt and black pepper and mix until well combined. Add the chicken cubes and coat with mixture generously. Refrigerate, covered to marinate for about 2-4 hours.
Preheat the outdoor grill to medium-high heat. Grease the grill grate.
Remove the chicken from the bowl and discard the excess marinade. Thread the chicken and vegetables onto pre-soaked wooden skewers respectively. Grill for about 10 minutes, flipping occasionally.

**Nutrition:** Calories 232, Fat 10.7 g, Carbs 7.1 g, Protein 27.4 g

## 697. Chicken with Caper Sauce

**Prep Time: 20 minutes**
**Servings: 5**

**Cook Time: 18 minutes**

**Ingredients:**
**For Chicken:**
- 2 eggs

- Salt and ground black pepper, as required
- 1 cup dry breadcrumbs

**For Capers Sauce:**
- 3 tablespoons capers
- ½ cup dry white wine
- 2 tablespoons olive oil
- 3 tablespoons fresh lemon juice
- Salt and ground black pepper, as required
- 1½ pounds skinless, boneless chicken breast halves, pounded into ¾-inch thickness and cut into pieces
- 2 tablespoons fresh parsley, chopped

**Prep:** For chicken: in a shallow dish, add the eggs, salt and black pepper and beat until well combined.
In another shallow dish, place breadcrumbs.
Dip the chicken pieces in egg mixture then coat with the breadcrumbs evenly.
In a large skillet, heat the oil over medium heat and cook the chicken pieces for about 7 minutes per side. With a slotted spoon, transfer the chicken pieces onto a paper towel-lined plate. With a piece of the foil, cover the chicken pieces to keep them warm. In the same skillet, add all the sauce ingredients except parsley and cook for about 2-3 minutes, stirring continuously. Stir in the parsley and remove from heat.
Serve the chicken pieces with the topping of capers sauce.

**Nutrition:** Calories 352, Fat 13.5 g, Carbs 16.9 g, Protein 35.7 g

## 698. Chicken, Dried Fruit & Olives Casserole

**Prep Time:** 20 minutes
**Servings:** 4

**Cook Time:** 50 minutes

**Ingredients:**
- 6 ounces dried apricots, quartered
- 6 ounces dried prunes, quartered
- 4 ounces green olives, pitted
- 2 ounces capers
- 2 garlic cloves, crushed
- 2 tablespoons fresh oregano, minced
- Salt and ground black pepper, as required
- 1 bay leaf
- 2/3 cup red wine vinegar
- ¼ cup olive oil
- 4 (6-ounce) chicken breasts
- 3 tablespoons brown sugar
- ¾ cup white wine

**Prep:** For marinade: in a large baking dish, add the apricots, prunes, olives, capers, garlic, oregano, salt, black pepper, bay leaf, vinegar and oil and mix until well combined. Add the chicken breasts and coat with the marinade generously. Refrigerate, covered overnight. Remove from the refrigerator and set aside in the room temperature for at least 1 hour before cooking.
Preheat the oven to 325 degrees F.
Remove the chicken breasts from the bowl and arrange in a baking dish in a single layer. Spread the marinade over the chicken breasts evenly and sprinkle with the brown sugar. Place the white wine around the chicken breasts. Bake for about 50 minutes.
Serve the chicken breasts with the topping of pan sauce.

**Nutrition:** Calories 559, Fat 22.5 g, Carbs 44.4 g, Protein 40.4 g

## 699. Grilled Chicken Breasts

**Prep Time:** 15 minutes
**Servings:** 4

**Cook Time:** 12 minutes

**Ingredients:**
- 4 (4-ounce) boneless, skinless chicken breast halves
- 3 garlic cloves, chopped finely
- 3 tablespoons fresh parsley, chopped
- 3 tablespoons olive oil
- 3 tablespoons lemon juice
- 1 teaspoon paprika
- ½ teaspoon dried oregano
- Salt and ground black pepper, as required

**Prep:** With a fork, pierce chicken breasts several times
In a large bowl, add all the ingredients except the chicken breasts and mix until well combined. Add the chicken breasts and coat with the marinade generously.
Refrigerate to marinate for about 2-3 hours.
Preheat the grill to medium-high heat. Grease the grill grate.
Remove chicken from marinade and grill for about 5-6 minutes per side.

**Nutrition:** Calories 315, Fat 19.1, Carbs 1.6 g, Protein 33.2 g

## 700. Bbq Chicken Pizza

**Prep Time:** 10 minutes  
**Cook Time:** 1 hour 10 minutes  
**Servings:** 4

**Ingredients:**

**Dairy-Free Pizza Crust**
- 6 Eggs
- 6 tbsp. Parmesan Cheese
- 3 tbsp. Psyllium Husk Powder
- 1 ½ tsp. Italian Seasoning Salt and Pepper to Taste

**Toppings**
- 4 oz. Cheddar Cheese
- 6 oz. Rotisserie Chicken, shredded
- 1 tbsp. Mayonnaise
- 4 tbsp. BBQ Sauce
- 4 tbsp. Rao's Tomato Sauce

**Prep:** Pre-heat oven to 425°F and shred cheese. Set aside.
Using an immersion blender, combine all the ingredients for the crust until well mixed.
Spread dough using a silicone spatula.
Once the crust is evenly distributed, place it in the oven and bake on the top rack for 10 minutes. Flip the pizza over.
Top with your favorite toppings and then bake for an additional 3 minutes in the oven.

**Nutrition:** 357 Calories, 25 g Fat, 9 g Carbs, 25 g Protein

## 701. Chicken Broccoli Salad with Avocado Dressing

**Prep Time:** 5 minutes  
**Cook Time:** 40 minutes  
**Servings:** 6

**Ingredients:**
- 2 chicken breasts
- pound broccoli, cut into florets
- 1 avocado, peeled and pitted
- ½ lemon, juiced
- garlic cloves
- ¼ teaspoon chili powder
- ¼ teaspoon cumin powder
- Salt and pepper to taste

**Prep:** Cook the chicken in a large pot of salty water.
Drain and cut the chicken into small cubes. Place in a salad bowl. Add the broccoli and mix well.
Combine the avocado, lemon juice, garlic, chili powder, cumin powder, salt and pepper in a blender. Pulse until smooth. Spoon the dressing over the salad and mix well.

**Nutrition:** Calories: 195; Fat: 11 g; Protein: 14 g; Carbs: 3 g

## 702. Chicken Stew

**Prep Time:** 5 minutes  
**Cook Time:** 45 minutes  
**Servings:** 6

**Ingredients:**
- 2 tablespoons extra virgin olive oil
- 6 chicken thighs
- sweet onion, chopped
- garlic cloves, minced
- red bell peppers, cored and diced
- 2 carrots, diced
- 1 rosemary sprig
- 1 thyme sprig
- tomatoes, peeled and diced
- ½ cup tomato juice
- ¼ cup dry white wine
- 1 cup chicken stock
- 1 bay leaf
- Salt and pepper to taste

**Prep:** Heat the oil in a heavy saucepan. Cook chicken on all sides until golden.
Stir in the onion and garlic and cook for 2 minutes.
Stir in the rest of the ingredients and season with salt and pepper. Cook on low heat for 30 minutes.

**Nutrition:** Calories: 363; Fat: 14 g; Protein: 42 g; Carbs: 9 g

## 703. Coconut Curry Chicken Tenders

**Prep Time:** 5 minutes  
**Cook Time:** 40 minutes  
**Servings:** 6

**Ingredients:**
- 24 oz. Chicken Thighs, deboned with skin on (~5 thighs)
- 1 Egg

- 1/2 cup Pork Rinds, crumbled (~1 1/2 oz.)
- 1/2 cup Unsweetened Shredded Coconut
- 2 tsp. Curry Powder
- 1/2 tsp. Coriander
- 1/4 tsp. Garlic Powder
- 1/4 tsp. Onion Powder
- Salt and Pepper to Taste
- Sweet and Spicy Mango Dipping Sauce

**Prep**: Pre-heat oven to 400F. Get a cookie sheet with a wire rack ready. In a shallow bowl or plate with lips, beat an egg.
In a plastic bag, place pork rinds, coconut, and spices.
Debone chicken thighs with kitchen shears. Make sure that you leave the skin on the chicken thighs.
Cut the chicken thighs into strips (or tenders), lengthwise. This should get around 4 chicken tenders per thigh.
Dip half of the chicken into an egg and place it into the bag. Seal and shake to coat. Place chicken on wire rack. Repeat step 4 with the other half of the chicken.
Bake on the top rack in the oven for 15 minutes. Remove from the oven, flip each chicken tender, and bake for 20 minutes more.
While the chicken is cooking, prepare the sauce by mixing all of the ingredients. Set aside until the chicken is finished.
Remove the chicken from the oven and serve immediately.

**Nutrition**: 494 Calories, 34 g Fat, 1 g Carbs, 24 g Protein

## 704. Garlic Chicken Balls

**Prep Time: 15 minutes**
**Servings: 4**

**Cook Time: 10 minutes**

**Ingredients:**
- 2 cups ground chicken
- teaspoon minced garlic
- 1 teaspoon dried dill
- 1/3 carrot, grated
- 1 egg, beaten
- 1 tablespoon olive oil
- ¼ cup coconut flakes
- ½ teaspoon salt

**Prep**: In the mixing bowl mix up together ground chicken, minced garlic, dried dill, carrot, egg, and salt.
Stir the chicken mixture with the help of the fingertips until homogenous.
Then make medium balls from the mixture.
Coat every chicken ball in coconut flakes.
Heat up olive oil in the skillet. Add chicken balls and cook them for 3 minutes from each side. The cooked chicken balls will have a golden-brown color.

**Nutrition**: Calories 200; Fat 11.5 g; Carbs 1.7 g; Protein 21.9 g

## 705. Garlicky Tomato Chicken Casserole

**Prep Time: 5 minutes**
**Servings: 4**

**Cook Time: 50 minutes**

**Ingredients:**
- 4 chicken breasts
- 2 tomatoes, sliced
- can diced tomatoes
- garlic cloves, chopped
- 1 shallot, chopped
- 1 bay leaf
- 1 thyme sprig
- ½ cup dry white wine
- ½ cup chicken stock
- Salt and pepper to taste

**Prep**: Combine the chicken and the remaining ingredients in a dish baking pan.
Adjust with salt and pepper and cover the pot with an aluminum foil.
Cook in the preheated oven at 330 °F for 40 minutes.

**Nutrition**: Calories: 313; Fat: 8 g, Protein: 47 g, Carbs: 6 g

## 706. Herbed Roasted Chicken Breasts

**Prep Time: 5 minutes**
**Servings: 4**

**Cook Time: 50 minutes**

**Ingredients:**
- 2 tablespoons extra virgin olive oil
- 2 tablespoons chopped parsley
- 2 tablespoons chopped cilantro
- teaspoon dried oregano
- 1 teaspoon dried basil
- tablespoons lemon juice
- Salt and pepper to taste
- chicken breasts

**Prep**: Combine the oil, parsley, cilantro, oregano, basil, lemon juice, salt and pepper in a bowl.

Spread this mixture over the chicken and rub it well into the meat.
Place in a dish baking pan and cover with aluminum foil.
Cook in the preheated oven at 350F for 20 minutes then remove the foil and cook for 25 additional minutes.
Serve the chicken warm and fresh with your favorite side dish.

**Nutrition:** Calories: 330; Fat: 15 g; Protein: 40.7 g; Carbs: 1 g

## 707. Glazed Chicken

**Prep Time:** 10 minutes  **Cook Time:** 50 minutes
**Servings:** 3

**Ingredients:**
- 2 medium Chicken Thighs, bone-in skin-on
- 1 tsp. Ground Ginger
- Salt and Pepper to Taste
- 1/4 cup Peanuts
- 1/2 medium Green Pepper
- 2 large Spring Onions
- 4 red Bird's Eye Chilies, deseeded

**The Sauce**
- 1 tbsp. Soy Sauce
- 2 tsp. Rice Wine Vinegar
- 2 tbsp. Chili Garlic Paste
- 1 tbsp. Reduced Sugar Ketchup
- 2 tsp. Sesame Oil
- 1/2 tsp. Maple Extract
- 10 drops Liquid Stevia

**Prep:** Debone chicken using kitchen shears. Cut chicken into bite-sized pieces. Season with salt, pepper, and ground ginger.
Heat a pan over medium heat and once hot, add chicken. Let the chicken cook for about 10 minutes.
Chop up and prep vegetables and chilies. Set aside.
Prepare the sauce by combining all ingredient and mixing well.
Once the chicken is browned, mix everything together and let it cook for a few minutes more. Add vegetables and peanuts to the pan and let cook for about 3-4 minutes.
Add the sauce to the pan and let it simmer to reduce slightly.

**Nutrition:** 362 Calories, 24 g Fat, 2 g Carbs, 23 g Protein

## 708. Paprika Moussaka

**Prep Time:** 15 minutes  **Cook Time:** 45 minutes
**Servings:** 3

**Ingredients:**
- A eggplant, trimmed
- 1 cup ground chicken
- 1/3 cup white onion, diced
- 2 oz. Cheddar cheese, shredded
- 1 potato, sliced
- 1 teaspoon olive oil
- 1 teaspoon salt
- ½ cup milk
- 1 tablespoon butter
- 1 tablespoon ground paprika
- 1 tablespoon Italian seasoning
- 1 teaspoon tomato paste

**Prep:** Slice the eggplant lengthwise and sprinkle with salt.
Pour olive oil in the skillet and add sliced potato. Roast potato for 2 minutes from each side. Then transfer it in the plate.
Put eggplant in the skillet and roast it for 2 minutes from each side too.
Pour milk in the pan and bring it to boil. Add tomato paste, Italian seasoning, paprika, butter, and Cheddar cheese.
Then mix up together onion with ground chicken.
Arrange the sliced potato in the casserole in one layer.
Then add ½ part of all sliced eggplants. Spread the eggplants with ½ part of chicken mixture. Then add remaining eggplants. Pour the milk mixture over the eggplants.
Bake moussaka for 30 minutes at 355 °F.

**Nutrition:** Calories 387, Fat 21.2 g, Carbs 26.3 g, Protein 25.4 g

## 709. Low-Carb Chicken Curry

**Prep Time:** 10 minutes  **Cook Time:** 30 minutes
**Servings:** 3

**Ingredients:**
- 2 tbsp. Coconut Oil
- 5 inch Ginger
- 1 medium Green Chili
- 2 small Shallots
- 2 cloves Garlic
- 2 tsp. Turmeric Powder
- 1 stalk Lemongrass
- 1/2 cup Coconut Milk
- 1/2 cup Water

- 6 small Chicken Drumsticks (~21 oz. bone-in)
- 1/2 tsp. Salt
- 1 tbsp. Cilantro, chopped

**Prep**: Bruise the stalk lemongrass.
In a blender, add ginger, green chili, shallots, and cloves garlic.
In a pre-heated pot over medium heat, melt coconut oil. Once hot, add in the pounded ingredients and sauté.
After 3 minutes, add in 2 turmeric powder and the smashed lemongrass and sauté once again.
Add in chicken and mix well with the sautéed ingredients.
Once the chicken is coated, pour in coconut milk and water.
Add in salt and cover the pot. Let cook for about 20 minutes.
Sprinkle chopped cilantro over the top and serve.

**Nutrition**: 493 Calories, 35 g Protein, 8 g Carbs, 35 g Protein

### 710. Marinated Chicken Breasts

**Prep Time:** 5 minutes
**Servings:** 4

**Cook Time:** 2 hours

**Ingredients:**
- 4 chicken breasts
- Salt and pepper to taste
- lemon, juiced
- 1 rosemary sprig
- 1 thyme sprig
- garlic cloves, crushed
- sage leaves
- tablespoons extra virgin olive oil
- ½ cup buttermilk

**Prep:** Boil the chicken with salt and pepper and place it in a resealable bag.
Add remaining ingredients and seal bag.
Refrigerate for at least 1 hour.
After 1 hour, heat a roasting pan over medium heat, then place the chicken on the grill.
Cook on each side for 8 minutes.

**Nutrition:** Calories: 371; Fat: 21 g; Protein: 46 g; Carbs: 2 g

### 711. Roasted Turkey Legs

**Prep Time:** 10 minutes
**Servings:** 4

**Cook Time:** 1 hour 40 minutes

**Ingredients:**
- 2 medium Turkey Legs
- 2 tsp. Salt
- 1/2 tsp. Pepper
- 1/4 tsp. Cayenne Pepper
- 1/2 tsp. Onion Powder
- 1/2 tsp. Garlic Powder
- 1/2 tsp. Dried Thyme
- 1/2 tsp. Ancho Chili Powder
- tsp. Liquid Smoke
- 1 tsp. Worcestershire
- 2 tbsp. oil

**Prep:** Mix all dry spices in a small bowl. Then, add wet ingredients and mix them together into a rub.
Dry the turkey legs completely with paper towels. Then, rub the turkey leg with dressing.
Pre-heat oven to 350°F. Bring the oil to medium-high heat in a cast-iron skillet. Once the oil starts to smoke, add turkey legs into the pan and sear on each side for 2 minutes.
Place in the oven at 350F for 60 minutes.
Remove turkey from the oven and let rest for a few minutes.

**Nutrition:** 382 Calories, 25 g Fat, 0.8 g Carbs, 44 g Protein

### 712. Bacon Wings

**Prep Time:** 15 minutes
**Servings:** 12

**Cook Time:** 1 hour 15 minutes

**Ingredients:**
- Bacon strips (12 pieces)
- Paprika (1 teaspoon)
- Black pepper (1 tablespoon)
- Oregano (1 teaspoon)
- Chicken wings (12 pieces)
- Kosher salt (1 tablespoon)
- Brown sugar (1 tablespoon)
- Chili powder (1 teaspoon)
- Celery sticks
- Blue cheese dressing

**Prep:** Preheat the air fryer at 325 degrees Fahrenheit.

Mix sugar, salt, chili powder, oregano, pepper, and paprika. Coat chicken wings with this dry rub.
Wrap a bacon strip around each wing. Arrange wrapped wings in the air fryer basket.
Cook for thirty minutes on each side in the air fryer. Let cool for five minutes.
Serve and enjoy with celery and blue cheese.

### 713. Buffalo Chicken Sliders

**Prep Time:** 10 minutes  
**Servings:** 12  
**Cook Time:** 15 minutes

**Ingredients:**
- Chicken breasts (2 lb., cooked, shredded)
- Wing sauce (1 cup)
- Ranch dressing mix (1 pack)
- Blue cheese dressing (1/4 cup, low fat)
- Lettuce (for topping)
- Buns (12, slider)

**Prep:** Add the chicken breasts (shredded, cooked) in a large bowl along with the ranch dressing and wing sauce. Stir well to incorporate, then place a piece of lettuce onto each slider roll.
Top off using the chicken mixture.
Drizzle blue cheese dressing over chicken then top off using top buns of slider rolls.

**Nutrition:** Calories: 300; Fat: 14 g; Cholesterol: 25 mg

### 714. Chicken Omelet

**Prep Time:** 5 minutes  
**Servings:** 1  
**Cook Time:** 15 minutes

**Ingredients:**
- 2 bacon slices; cooked and crumbled
- 2 eggs
- 1 tablespoon homemade mayonnaise
- 1 tomato; chopped.
- 1-ounce rotisserie chicken; shredded
- 1 teaspoon mustard
- 1 small avocado; pitted, peeled and chopped.
- Salt and black pepper

**Prep:** In a bowl, mix eggs with some salt and pepper and whisk gently.
Heat up a pan over medium heat; spray with cooking oil, add eggs and cook for 5 minutes. Add avocado, tomato, chicken, bacon, mayonnaise and mustard on one half of the omelet.
Fold omelet, cover pan and cook for another 5 minutes.

**Nutrition:** Calories: 400; Fat: 32 g; Carbs: 4 g; Protein: 25 g

### 715. Chicken Salad (2nd version)

**Prep Time:** 30 minutes  
**Servings:** 4  
**Cook Time:** 45 minutes

**Ingredients:**
- 1 ½ pounds chicken breast, skinless, boneless
- 1 tbsp. dill, chopped
- Zest of 2 lemons, grated

**For the barley:**
- 2 and ½ cups chicken stock
- 1 cup barley
- 1 tsp. oregano, dried
- Zest of 1 lemon, grated
- Juice of 2 lemons
- 3 tbsps. olive oil
- 1 tbsp. oregano, chopped
- Juice of 1 lemon
- ¼ cup olive oil
- 2 red leaf lettuce heads, chopped
- 1 red onion, sliced
- 3 tbsps. parsley, chopped
- A pinch of salt and black pepper
- 1 pint of cherry tomatoes, sliced
- 2 avocados, peeled, pitted and sliced

**Prep:** Put the chicken breasts in a bowl, add the dill, zest of 2 lemons, juice of 2 lemons, 3 tbsps. Oil, 1 tbsp. oregano, parsley, salt and pepper, toss, cover the bowl and leave aside for 30 minutes.
Heat up your grill over medium-high heat, add the chicken, cook for 6 minutes on each side, cool down, slice, and put in a bowl.
Put the stock in a pot, add the barley, salt, and pepper. Bring to a simmer over medium heat, cook for 45 minutes, then drain and put in the same bowl with the chicken. Add the dried oregano, zest of 1 lemon, juice of 1 lemon, ¼ cup oil, the lettuce, onion, tomatoes, and the avocados, toss and serve.

**Nutrition:** Calories 342, Fat: 17.4 g, Carbs: 27.7 g, Protein: 26.4 g

## 716. Chicken Skillet

**Prep Time:** 10 minutes  
**Servings:** 6  
**Cook Time:** 35 minutes

**Ingredients:**
- 6 chicken thighs, bone-in and skin-on
- Juice of 2 lemons
- 1 tsp. oregano, dried
- 1 red onion, chopped
- Salt and black pepper to the taste
- 1 tsp. garlic powder
- 2 garlic cloves, minced
- 2 tbsps. olive oil
- 2 ½ cups chicken stock
- 1 cup white rice
- 1 tbsp. oregano, chopped
- 1 cup green olives, pitted and sliced
- 1/3 cup parsley, chopped
- ½ cup feta cheese, crumbled

**Prep:** Heat up a pan with the oil over medium heat, add the chicken thighs skin side down, cook for 4 minutes on each side and transfer to a plate. Add the garlic and the onion to the pan, stir and sauté for 5 minutes.
Add the rice, salt, pepper, the stock, oregano, and lemon juice, stir, cook for 1-2 minutes more, and take off the heat. Add the chicken to the pan, introduce the pan in the oven and bake at 375F for 25 minutes.
Add the cheese, olives, and the parsley, divide the whole mix between plates.

**Nutrition:** Calories 435, Fat: 18.5 g, Carbs: 27.8 g, Protein: 25.6 g

## 717. Turkish Marinated Chicken

**Prep Time:** 10 Minutes  
**Servings:** 4  
**Cook Time:** 15 minutes

**Ingredients:**
- 4-6 chicken breasts, boneless, skinless

**For the marinade:**
- 1 tablespoon dried oregano
- 1 tablespoon garlic, minced
- 1 tablespoon red wine vinegar
- 1 teaspoon dried thyme
- 1/2 cup lemon juice, freshly squeezed
- 1/2 cup olive oil

**Prep:** If there are any visible fat on the chicken, trim them off. Cut each breast into 5-6 pieces 1-inch thick crosswise strips. Put them in a Ziploc bag with tight lid.
Whisk the marinade ingredients together until combined. Pour into the bag with the chicken, seal, and shake the bag or the container to coat the chicken. Marinade for 8 hours or more in the refrigerator.
When marinated, remove the chicken from the fridge, let thaw to room temperature, and drain; discard the marinade. Thread the chicken strips into skewers, about 6 pieces on each skewer, the meat folded over to it would not spin around on the skewers.
Mist the grill with olive oil. Preheat the charcoal or gas grill to medium high.
Grill the skewers for about 12-15 minutes, turning once.

**Nutrition:** 360 Calories, 26 g Fat, 3 g Carbs, 30 g Protein

## 718. Chicken Stuffed Peppers

**Prep Time:** 10 minutes  
**Servings:** 6

**Ingredients:**
- 1 cup Greek yogurt
- 2 tbsps. mustard
- Salt and pepper to the taste
- 1 lb. rotisserie chicken meat, cubed
- 4 celery stalks, chopped
- 2 tbsps. balsamic vinegar
- 1 bunch scallions, sliced
- ¼ cup parsley, chopped
- 1 cucumber, sliced
- 3 red bell peppers, halved and deseeded
- 1 pint of cherry tomatoes, quartered

**Prep:** In a bowl, mix the chicken with the celery and the rest of the ingredients except the bell peppers and toss well.
Stuff the peppers halves with the chicken mix and serve.

## 719. High Protein Chicken Meatballs

**Prep Time:** 5 minutes  
**Servings:** 2  
**Cook Time:** 25 minutes

**Ingredients:**
- Chicken (1 lbs., lean, ground)
- Oats (3/4 cup, rolled)
- Onions (2, grated)

- *Allspice (2 tsp. ground)*
- *Salt and black pepper (dash)*

**Prep:** Heat a skillet over medium heat then grease using cooking spray.
Add in the onions, chicken, oats, allspice, and a dash of salt and black pepper in a large-sized bowl, stir well to incorporate.
Shape mixture into meatballs.
Place into the skillet (greased). Cook for roughly 5 minutes until golden brown on all sides.
Remove meatballs from heat then serve immediately.

**Nutrition:** Calories: 519; Protein: 57 g; Carbs: 32 g; Fat: 15 g

## 720. Mediterranean Chicken Bites

**Prep time:** 10 minutes  **Cook time:** 10 minutes
**Servings:** 4

**Ingredients:**
- *20 ounces canned pineapple slices*
- *A drizzle of olive oil*
- *3 cups chicken thighs*
- *A tablespoon of smoked paprika*

**Prep:** Situate pan over medium high heat, add pineapple slices, cook them for a few minutes on each side, transfer to a cutting board, cool them down and cut into medium cubes.
Heat another pan with a drizzle of oil over medium high heat, rub chicken pieces with paprika, add them to the pan and cook for 5 minutes on each side.
Arrange chicken cubes on a platter, add a pineapple piece on top of each and stick a toothpick in each.
Serve.

**Nutrition:** 120 Calories; 3g Fat; 2g Protein

# PORK

### 721. Baked Ham

**Prep time:** 20 minutes  
**Servings:** 6  
**Cook time:** 1 hour

**Ingredients:**
- *35 oz of fresh deboned ham*

**For the marinading:**
- *Olive oil*
- *2 sprigs of rosemary*
- *2 pressed garlic cloves*
- *2 cups of white wine*
- *Coarse salt*

**For cooking:**
- *2 rosemary sprigs*
- *2 garlic cloves*
- *Olive oil*

**Prep:** In a casserole, marinate the ham for some hours with rosemary, garlic, salt, oil and wine.
Then move it to a tray and season with oil, garlic and rosemary. Bake in a preheated oven at 350°F and bake for about 1 hour. When it is cooked take the ham out and slice it.

**Nutrition:** Calories 531, Carbs 8.2 g, Protein 66.4 g, Fat 11.8 g

### 722. Dried Sausage Stew

**Prep time:** 30 minutes  
**Servings:** 4  
**Cook time:** 1 hour 30 minutes

**Ingredients:**
- *8 dried sausages*
- *24 oz of potatoes*
- *Sugar*
- *1 sprig of wild fennel*
- *1 sprig of parsley*
- *Salt and pepper*
- *24 oz of tomato sauce*
- *1 onion*
- *Extra virgin olive oil*

**Prep:** Peel the potatoes, dice them and golden in a pan with hot oil.
Strain and keep warm. Add the sausage and let it absorb the flavor from the leftover gravy in the pan, stir for few minutes.
Wash and mince the fennel and onion, let them reduce in a pan with some oil. Pour the tomato sauce, a pinch of sugar, a pinch of salt and a dust of pepper. Cook on medium heat for 10 minutes. Then add the sausage, potatoes, cover and let cook for one hour on low heat.

### 723. Chops in Balsamic Vinegar

**Prep time:** 10 minutes  
**Servings:** 6  
**Cook time:** 15 minutes

**Ingredients:**
- 35 oz pork chop
- 2 tbsp of balsamic vinegar
- 3 tbsp of olive oil
- Salt
- 1/4 cup di butter
- Flour
- ¼ cup of broth

**Prep:** Coat the pork chops in the flour and sizzle them in a pan with hot oil and butter. Flip them to cook evenly. Adjust the salt to taste and put the chops into the vinegar, broth and let marinate.
Serve the pork chop in the gravy.

**Nutrition:** Calories 426, Carbs 12.3 g, Protein 47.4 g, Fat 26.1 g

### 724. Pork and Ricotta Meat Loaf

**Prep time:** 15 minutes  
**Servings:** 6  
**Cook time:** 1 hour

**Ingredients:**
- 16 oz of minced pork pulp
- 2 hardboiled eggs
- Salt and pepper
- 6 pickles
- 1 egg
- 9 oz of ricotta
- 4 tbsp of grated parmesan
- 3 pistachios
- 4 tbsp di butter
- 1 cup of meat broth
- Milk if needed

**Prep:** Mix the ricotta with the meat, then add the egg, salt and pepper. Place the hardboiled eggs, pistachios, pickles in the mixture and form into a loaf. Wrap in a cloth and tie both the ends with a cotton string.
Melt the butter in a casserole and put in the meat loaf. Pour in the broth, cover with a lid and let it cook on low heat. To prevent the meat loaf from drying too much add a little milk at a time.
After about 1 hour the meat loaf will be thoroughly cooked. Remove the cloth and let it cool down before serving.

**Nutrition:** Calories 467, Carbs 13.8 g, Protein 38.3 g, Fat 28.4 g

### 725. Pork Chop Stew

**Prep time:** 15 minutes  
**Servings:** 4  
**Cook time:** 2 hours 30 minutes

**Ingredients:**
- 35 oz of pork chops
- 24 oz of potatoes
- Sugar
- 1 cup of olive oil
- Salt and pepper
- ½ cup of white wine
- 1 onion

**Prep:** Heat up the oil in a pan, add the peeled and diced potatoes, fry for few minutes and flip often for added flavor. When the potatoes are golden, strain and put them on the side. To the same pan add the pork chops and onion to cook together. Deglaze with wine, then pour in the sauce. Add the salt, a pinch of sugar for sweetness and some pepper, then let cook on low heat for some hours, mix occasionally. Add in the potatoes halfway through and allow to finish cooking.

**Nutrition:** Calories 350.6, Carbs 24.3 g, Protein 21.3 g, Fat 14.2 g

### 726.  Stuffed Pork Ribs

**Prep time:** 20 minutes  
**Servings:** 4  
**Cook time:** 50 minutes

**Ingredients:**
- 4 thick pork ribs with the bone
- 8 oz of sausage
- 3 tbsp of breadcrumbs
- 2 tbsp of grated pecorino
- 1 egg
- 1 sprig of parsley
- 1 onion
- ½ cup of red
- 4 tbsp of olive oil
- Salt and pepper

**Prep:** Slice the ribs to open in half.
In a bowl, mix the skinned sausages with pecorino, breadcrumbs, minced parsley, beaten egg, salt and pepper. Distribute the mixture inside the ribs, close the opening and close with a toothpick.
Mince the onion and let it reduce in a pan with a drizzle of oil. Add the ribs and cook them flipping halfway through. When they have browned add salt and pepper. Deglaze with the wine. Add ½ cup of hot water and keep cooking for another 30 minutes.

**Nutrition:** Calories 917, Carbs 29.6 g, Protein 58.2 g, Fat 53.7 g

### 727.  Pork Ribs with Wine

**Prep time:** 5 minutes  
**Servings:** 4  
**Cook time:** 25 minutes

**Ingredients:**
- 4 ribs
- ½ cup of red
- 5 tbsp of olive oil
- Salt and pepper

**Prep:** Heat the oil in a pan and cook the ribs on low heat. Deglaze with the wine, add salt and pepper and pour in 3 tbsp of water. Keep cooking for another 5 minutes.

**Nutrition:** Calories 578, Carbs 21.2 g, Protein 31.7 g, Fat 22.1 g

### 728.  Pork Cutlet

**Prep time:** 5 minutes  
**Servings:** 2  
**Cook time:** 7 minutes

**Ingredients:**
- 4 slices of pork loin
- 2 eggs
- 1 garlic clove
- ½ cup of grated pecorino
- 1 sprig of parsley
- 1 cup di breadcrumbs
- Extra virgin olive oil
- Salt and pepper

**Prep:** Mix the breadcrumbs with minced garlic and parsley, pecorino, salt and pepper.
Coat the meat in the beaten eggs and then move into the breadcrumbs.
Fry the cutlets into hot oil and enjoy.

**Nutrition:** Calories 879, Carbs 71 g, Protein 61.2 g, Fat 82.8 g

### 729.  Homemade Pork Buns

**Prep Time:** 20 minutes  
**Servings:** 8  
**Cook Time:** 25 minutes

**Ingredients:**
- Green onions, sliced thinly (3 pieces)
- Egg, beaten (1 piece)
- Pulled pork, diced, w/ barbecue sauce (1 cup)
- Buttermilk biscuits, refrigerated (16 1/3 ounces)
- Soy sauce (1 teaspoon)

**Prep:** Preheat the air fryer at 325 degrees F.
Use parchment paper to line your baking sheet. Combine pork with green onions.
Separate and press the dough to form 8 four-inch rounds. Fill each biscuit round's center with two tablespoons of pork mixture. Cover with the dough edges and seal by pinching. Arrange the buns on the sheet and brush with a mixture of soy sauce and egg.
Cook in the air fryer for twenty to twenty-five minutes.

### 730. Prosciutto e Faggioli

**Prep Time:** 10 minutes  
**Servings:** 4  

**Cook Time:** 15 minutes

**Ingredients:**
- 12 oz pasta, cooked and drained
- Pepper and salt to taste
- 3 tbsp snipped fresh chives
- 3 cups arugula or watercress leaves, loosely packed
- ½ cup chicken broth, warm
- 1 tbsp Herbed garlic butter
- ½ cup shredded pecorino Toscano
- 4 oz prosciutto, cut into bite sizes
- 2 cups cherry tomatoes, halved
- 1 can of 19oz white kidney beans, rinsed and drained

**Prep:** Heat over medium low fire herbed garlic butter, cheese, prosciutto, tomatoes and beans in a big saucepan for 2 minutes.
Once mixture is simmering, stir constantly to melt cheese while gradually stirring in the broth.
Once cheese is fully melted and incorporated, add chives, arugula, pepper and salt.
Turn off the fire and toss in the cooked pasta. Serve and enjoy.

**Nutrition:** Calories: 452; Carbs: 57.9 g; Protein: 30.64 g; Fat: 11.7 g

### 731. Oregano Pork Mix

**Prep Time:** 5 minutes  
**Servings:** 4  

**Cook Time:** 7 hours and 6 minutes

**Ingredients:**
- 2 pounds' pork roast
- 7 ounces' tomato paste
- yellow onion, chopped
- 1 cup beef stock
- tablespoons ground cumin
- tablespoons olive oil
- 2 tablespoons fresh oregano, chopped
- 1 tablespoon garlic, minced
- ½ cup fresh thyme, chopped

**Prep:** Heat up a sauté pan with the oil over medium-high heat, add the roast, brown it for 3 minutes on each side and then transfer to your slow cooker. Add the rest of the ingredients, toss a bit, cover and cook on low for 7 hours.
Slice the roast, divide it between plates and serve.

### 732. Pork Chops with Capers

**Prep time:** 15 minutes  
**Servings:** 4  

**Cook time:** 25 minutes

**Ingredients:**
- 4 pork chops
- 2 garlic cloves
- Pepper to taste
- Salt to taste
- Breadcrumbs
- Olive Oil
- Chopped parsley to taste
- 3 oz of capers

**Prep:** Wash and dry the ribs and sprinkle with breadcrumbs. Take a baking pan and grease it with oil, lay the ribs and put a piece of garlic on top of each one, parsley, pepper, salt and capers. Sprinkle with a little oil and bake for about 20 minutes in an oven, already hot at 350 degrees F.
Serve the ribs hot and steaming.

**Nutrition:** Calories 504.3, Carbs 31.4 g, Protein 44.2 g, Fat 20.3 g

### 733. Pork Loins

**Prep time:** 10 minutes  
**Servings:** 4  

**Cook time:** 45 minutes

**Ingredients:**

- 2 lb of pork loins
- 2 garlic cloves
- 8 sage leaves
- ½ glass dry white wine
- ¼ cup of lard
- Salt and pepper to taste

**Prep:** Flatten the loins, place a clove of garlic and a sage leaf on top, roll up and secure using a toothpick. Heat the lard in a frying pan, place the roulades and brown over high heat on both sides, for even and homogeneous cooking. Lower the heat, add a little wine and water, salt and pepper to taste and leave to cook for about 30 minutes, until the meat is tender.

**Nutrition:** Calories 165.3, Carbs 1.3 g, Protein 22.3 g, Fat 9.4 g

## 734. Sausages with Tomato

**Prep time: 15 minutes**  
**Servings: 6**  
**Cooking time: 40 minutes**

**Ingredients:**
- 12 sausages
- 4 oz of tomato paste
- ½ glass dry white wine
- Olive oil
- ¼ cup of lard
- Salt to taste

**Prep:** Prick the sausages with a fork, place over medium heat in a pan with oil and lard. Turn occasionally and add a few tablespoons of water to prevent the fat from burning. Once browned, douse with white wine and allow to evaporate. Add the tomato paste, 1 cup of water and salt. Cook for about half an hour. With the sauce you could also season a first course.

**Nutrition:** Calories 720, Carbs 8.4 g, Protein 21.6 g, Fat 61.6 g

## 735. Sausages in Pan

**Prep time: 10 minutes**  
**Servings: 6**  
**Cooking time: 1 hour**

**Ingredients:**
- 12 sausages
- Salt to taste
- ½ glass of dry white wine
- 1 tablespoon of lard

**Prep:** Prick the sausages with a fork, place over high heat in a pan with the lard. Brown and turn every so often to cook evenly and uniformly. If the fat should start to burn, pour in a few drops of white wine. Once the sausages are golden brown, pour some water and finish cooking, about 1 hour. You could season a first course with this sauce.

## 736. Pork Stew

**Prep time: 30 minutes**  
**Servings: 6**  
**Cooking time: 1 hour and 50 minutes**

**Ingredients:**
- 1 lb. and 8 oz of pork meat in pieces
- 6 sausages
- 2 garlic cloves
- 1 onion
- 5 oz of pork rind
- 3 cups of tomato paste
- Sugar to taste
- ½ glass of red wine
- 1 bay leaf
- Salt and pepper to taste

**Prep:** Flame the pork rinds; scrape and wash thoroughly; blanch, drain and cut into strips. Prick the sausages with a fork and blanch in a little water with the peeled garlic, to be removed at the end of cooking, and oil. Add, as soon as it has wilted, the bay leaf and the pork meat, brown everything over a low heat, turning from time to time with a wooden spoon to even out the cooking. Deglaze with the wine and a pinch of sugar. Adjust the salt and cook for 40 minutes over medium heat. Then add the pork rinds and sausage and finish cooking for one hour.

**Nutrition:** Calories 248.6, Carbs 7.1 g, Protein 6.2 g, Fat 2.8 g

## 737. Braised Sausage

**Prep time: 10 minutes**  
**Servings: 4**  
**Cooking time: 30 minutes**

**Ingredients:**
- *1 lb. and 8 oz of sausages*

**Prep:** Roll the sausage into a spiral and thread with two wooden skewers in a cross shape. Place on the grill and cook for about half an hour over hot coals.

**Nutrition:** Calories 248.6, Carbs 1.2 g, Protein 16.2 g, Fat 0.4 g

## 738. Fried Sausage

**Prep time: 10 minutes**  
**Servings: 4**

**Cooking time: 30 minutes**

**Ingredients:**
- *1 lb. and 8 oz of sausages*

**Prep:** Roll the sausage on itself. Thread with wooden skewers and place on a pan. Prick the sausage in several places with a fork and cover everything with a little water. Cook over medium heat and allow the liquid to evaporate partially. Turn the sausage wheel over and leave for a few minutes. Now remove the liquid and fry the sausage in its own fat, turning when golden brown to even out the cooking.

**Nutrition:** Calories 314.6, Carbs 0.4 g, Protein 24.2 g, Fat 22.6 g

## 739. Sausage Ragout

**Prep time: 30 minutes**  
**Servings: 4**

**Cooking time: 1 hour and 30 minutes**

**Ingredients:**
- *1 onion*
- *7 oz of pork rind*
- *Olive oil to taste*
- *3 cups of tomato paste*
- *1 bay leaf*
- *Salt and pepper to taste*
- *8 pieces of sausages*

**Prep:** Flame the pork rinds and wash them carefully under running water. Blanch, drain and cut into pieces. Blanch the sausage in hot water for a few minutes, after piercing it with a fork. Pour some oil into a pan, add the peeled onion, bay leaf, a pinch of sugar and salt, pepper and the tomato puree. Simmer for about ten minutes. At this point, add the pork rinds and the drained sausage and continue cooking for an hour or so over medium heat.

**Nutrition:** Calories 155.6, Carbs 7.4 g, Protein 8.2 g, Fat 10.6 g

## 740. Grilled Pork Chops

**Prep time: 5 minutes**  
**Servings: 4**

**Cooking time: 7 minutes**

**Ingredients:**
- *4 pork ribs*
- *Salt and pepper to taste*
- *Olive oil*

**Prep:** Heat the grill thoroughly and lay the meat on it. Cook the ribs for a few minutes, turn, to make an even cooking, and finish cooking. Season with a little oil, pepper and salt and serve steaming hot.

**Nutrition:** Calories 276.3, Carbs 2.6 g, Protein 14.2 g, Fat 22.3 g

## 741. Pork Cutlets

**Prep time: 20 minutes**  
**Servings: 4**

**Cooking time: 5 minutes**

**Ingredients:**
- *4 slices of pork*
- *2 eggs*
- *2 oz grated pecorino cheese*
- *2/3 cup of breadcrumbs*
- *1 sprig of parsley*
- *1 garlic clove*
- *Salt and pepper to taste*
- *Olive oil to taste*

**Prep:** Mix the breadcrumbs with parsley, salt, pecorino cheese, minced garlic and pepper. Soak the meat in the beaten eggs for about twenty minutes. Drain and dip in seasoned bread. Fry the slices in hot oil and serve.

**Nutrition:** Calories 270.3, Carbs 6.6 g, Protein 22.6 g, Fat 17.3 g

### 742. Brown Sugar Smokies

**Prep time:** 10 minutes  
**Servings:** 12  
**Cook time:** 4 minutes

**Ingredients**
- 1-pound bacon
- (16 ounces) package little smokie sausages
- 1 cup brown sugar, or to taste

**Prep:** Preheat the oven to 350 ° F.
Cut the bacon in three and wrap each strip around a little sausage. Place sausages wrapped on wooden skewers, several to one place the kebabs on a baking sheet and sprinkle generously with brown sugar.
Bake until the bacon is crispy, and the brown sugar has melted.

**Nutrition:** 356 Calories 27.2g Fat 9g Protein

# VEGETABLES AND SALADS

## 743. Veggie Bowls

**Prep time:** 10 minutes
**Servings:** 4

**Cook time:** 5 minutes

**Ingredients:**
- 1 tablespoon olive oil
- 1 pound asparagus, trimmed and roughly chopped
- 3 cups kale, shredded
- 3 cups Brussels sprouts, shredded
- ½ cup hummus
- 1 avocado, peeled, pitted and sliced
- 4 eggs, soft boiled, peeled and sliced
- For the dressing:
- 2 tablespoons lemon juice
- 1 garlic clove, minced
- 2 teaspoons Dijon mustard
- 2 tablespoons olive oil
- Salt and black pepper to the taste

**Prep:** Heat up a pan with 2 tablespoons oil over medium-high heat, add the asparagus and sauté for 5 minutes stirring often. In a bowl, combine the other 2 tablespoons oil with the lemon juice, garlic, mustard, salt and pepper and whisk well. In a salad bowl, combine the asparagus with the kale, sprouts, hummus, avocado and the eggs and toss gently. Add the dressing, toss and serve for breakfast.

**Nutrition:** Calories 323, Fat 21 g, Carbs 24 g

## 744. Eggplants with Balsamic Vinegar

**Prep time:** 20 minutes
**Servings:** 6

**Cook time:** 30 minutes

**Ingredients:**
- 2 eggs
- Flour
- 2 tbsp di butter
- 21 oz of eggplants
- Salt
- 4 tbsp of olive oil
- Breadcrumbs
- 2 tbsp of balsamic vinegar

**Prep:** wash the eggplants, then remove the stem and bottom, slice and cover in salt to let the excess water drip. Dry them and coat into the flour, then into the beaten eggs and lastly in the breadcrumbs. Fry the eggplants in a pan with butter and oil. Dry the eggplants into some paper towel. Lay them onto a serving dish and drizzle on the balsamic vinegar.

**Nutrition:** Calories 292, Carbs 17.1 g, Protein 6.6 g, Fat 31.2 g

### 745. Asparagus with Ham

**Prep time:** 10 minutes  
**Servings:** 6  
**Cook time:** 15 minutes

**Ingredients:**
- 42 oz of asparagus
- salt
- 4 tbsp di grated parmesan
- 4 tbsp di butter
- 12 slices of ham

**Prep:** Clean the asparagus, trim the ends, tie them with a string and boil in hot water leaving them crunchy and keeping the tops out. Strain and divide them into groups of 2-3 pieces. Roll them into ham slices and leave out the tips.
Move them into a big dish with melted butter; sprinkle some grated parmesan, season with the remaining butter and put into a preheated oven at 350°F. the asparagus will be ready in less than 10 minutes.

**Nutrition:** Calories 301, Carbs 0.3 g, Protein 17.3 g, Fat 13 g

### 746. Boiled Broccoli

**Prep time:** 15 minutes  
**Servings:** 4  
**Cook time:** 20 minutes

**Ingredients:**
- 35 oz of broccoli
- 6 tbsp of extra virgin olive oil
- Salt, pepper
- 1 lemon

**Prep:** Clean the broccoli and keep the tops; wash and boil in a pot full of water with salt. Strain leaving the vegetables still crunchy and serve hot with a drizzle of oil, pepper and lemon juice.

**Nutrition:** Calories 32.6, Carbs 2.4 g, Protein 3.3 g, Fat 0.14 g

### 747. Broccoli with Tomato

**Prep time:** 15 minutes  
**Servings:** 4  
**Cook time:** 45 minutes

**Ingredients:**
- 1 cauliflower
- 1 cup of white wine
- ½ cup of olive oil
- 1 onion
- 1 sprig of parsley
- 1 tbsp of pine nuts
- Salt, pepper
- 1 1/2 cup of canned tomatoes
- Minced Parsley

**Prep:** Wash well the cauliflowers. Let the onion reduce in a pan with some oil, pine nuts and raisins, then add the minced tomatoes and let marinate for few minutes. Add a little hot water, salt and pepper, cover with a lid on low heat. Halfway through sprinkle the minced parsley and then pour in the wine.

**Nutrition:** Calories 34.2, Carbs 3.1 g, Protein 4.2 g, Fat 4.1 g

### 748. Asparagus au gratin

**Prep time:** 20 minutes  
**Servings:** 6  
**Cook time:** 30 minutes

**Ingredients:**
- 4 lbs of asparagus
- 1 1/4 cup of grated parmesan
- 1 ¼ cup of butter
- Salt

**Prep:** Clean the asparagus and tie them in bunches, trim the edges to make them even and cook them straight up without tilting. Dip into the water and boil. After about 20 minutes the asparagus will be ready. Release the bunches and dry them onto a cloth.

Grease an oven tray with butter, layer first the asparagus, season with melted butter and sprinkle some grated parmesan. Add another layer of asparagus, more melted butter and parmesan. Put the parmesan as the last layer as it will form a crust. Put in a preheated oven at 375°F, bake for 10 minutes and serve.

**Nutrition:** Calories 337, Carbs 2.6 g, Protein 17.7 g, Fat 27.1 g

## 749.   Onion and Bean Salad

**Prep time: 10 minutes**                                                                                                Servings: 4

**Ingredients:**
- 14 oz of beans
- 1 red onion
- Oregano
- 2 tbsp vinegar
- Extra virgin olive oil
- Salt and pepper

**Prep:** place the cooked beans in a bowl, season with a drizzle of oil, salt, vinegar, oregano and pepper. Add the onion cut into rings, mix well and let the taste develop for few minutes before serving.

**Nutrition:** Calories 124.3, Carbs 9 g, Protein 4.2 g, Fat 5.2 g

## 750.   Tomato and Onion Salad

**Prep time: 15 minutes**                                                                                                Servings: 4

**Ingredients:**
- 1 red onion
- 6 ripe tomatoes
- White Vinegar
- Extra virgin olive oil
- Salt and pepper

**Prep:** Wash and slice the tomatoes, peel the onion, wash and dry it and cut it into rings. Move everything into a pot with tomatoes. Season the salad with oil, 1 cup of vinegar and a dash of pepper and salt.

**Nutrition:** Calories 122.9, Carbs 2.6 g, Protein 1.9 g, Fat 10.2 g

## 751.   Tomato and Cucumber Salad

**Prep time: 20 minutes**                                                                                                Servings: 4

**Ingredients:**
- 1 cucumber
- 4 ripe tomatoes
- 1 red onion
- Oregano
- 2 tbsp of white vinegar
- ½ cup of extra virgin olive oil
- Salt and pepper

**Prep:** Wash and slice the tomatoes. Peel the onion, cut it into rings and move it into a bowl with the tomatoes. Season the salad with oil and vinegar, a dash of pepper and a pinch of salt.

**Nutrition:** Calories 124.3, Carbs 2.2 g, Protein 1.5 g, Fat 11.2 g

## 752.   Lettuce and Fennel Salad

**Prep time: 15 minutes**                                                                                                Servings: 4

**Ingredients:**
- 1 lettuce
- Vinegar or lemon
- 2 fennels
- Extra virgin olive oil
- Salt and pepper

**Prep:** Wash the lettuce; strain and chop. Wash the fennel and remove the outermost leaves, cut it into thin slices. Add all the ingredients into a bowl and season with salt, vinegar or lemon, pepper and a drizzle of oil.

**Nutrition:** Calories 243, Carbs 12.3 g, Protein 5.8 g, Fat 18.1 g

### 753.  Orange Salad

**Prep time: 20 minutes**      Servings: 4

**Ingredients:**
- 4 oranges
- Extra virgin olive oil
- Salt and pepper

**Prep:** peel the oranges and each wedge as well. Lay onto a serving dish. Pour some oil, pepper and salt, let the taste develop for few minutes and then serve.

**Nutrition:** Calories 234, Carbs 11.5 g, Protein 6 g, Fat 19.3 g

### 754.  Baked Cardoon

**Prep time: 20 minutes**      Cook time: 1 hour
**Servings: 6**

**Ingredients:**
- 2 cardoons
- 3 tbsp of flour
- 2 lemons
- 100 oz of water
- 1 1/4 cup of butter
- 1 1/4 cup of grated parmesan
- Salt

**Prep:** Remove the stringy bits of the cardoons, the cores and edges, cut into sticks and dip into water with lemon juice to prevent them from bruising.
In a pot, add the flour with the water and add lemon and salt. Pour the cardoon pieces when the water is boiling and let them simmer on low heat for 45 minutes, strain and dry them with a cloth.
Grease an oven tray, place one layer of cardoon pieces and add some pieces of butter, then sprinkle some grated parmesan. Keep alternating the layers and finish off with parmesan. Cook for 20 minutes and then cook au gratin.

**Nutrition:** Calories 261.6, Carbs 14.2 g, Protein 8.6 g, Fat 15.9 g

### 755.  Cardoons with Dressing

**Prep time: 30 minutes**      Cook time: 50 minutes
**Servings: 6**

**Ingredients:**
- 2 cardoons
- 1 1/4 cup of mashed lard
- Salt and pepper
- 1 lemon
- 1 cup of tomato sauce

**Prep:** Remove the stringy bits of the cardoons, the cores and edges, cut into sticks and dip into water with lemon juice to prevent them from bruising.
In a big casserole, sizzle the lard, add the cardoons in pieces, pour the tomato sauce, warm water, salt and pepper and let cook with a lid one for about one and a half hour.
Serve hot and steamy.

**Nutrition:** Calories 245.3, Carbs 7.1 g, Protein 12.6 g, Fat 17.1 g

### 756.  Fried Cauliflowers

**Prep time: 10 minutes**      Cook time: 10 minutes
**Servings: 6**

**Ingredients:**
- 35 oz of cauliflowers
- Salt
- Flour
- Lard

**Prep:** Clean the cauliflower and cook it into boiling water with salt. Halfway through remove the cauliflowers and cut them into pieces. Coat them in flour and fry into boiling lard.

**Nutrition:** Calories 615, Carbs 26.5 g, Protein 15.4 g, Fat 47.9 g

## 757. Fried Onion

**Prep time:** 15 minutes  
**Servings:** 6  
**Cook time:** 15 minutes

**Ingredients:**
- 10 oz di onion
- Salt
- 1 1/4 cup of mashed lard

**Prep:** In a pan sizzle the lard with the finely chopped onion. Add salt and mix until it is golden, then serve.

**Nutrition:** Calories 241, Carbs 17.6 g, Protein 3.2 g, Fat 18.2 g

## 758. Sweet and Sour Onions

**Prep time:** 5 minutes  
**Servings:** 6  
**Cook time:** 15 minutes

**Ingredients:**
- 10 oz of small, pressed onions
- Salt
- 1 tbsp of sugar
- 1 tbsp of balsamic vinegar
- 1 tbsp of butter
- 2 tbsp of olive oil

**Prep:** Wash the onions and dry them in a cloth.
Fry in a pan until they reduce. Add the butter and oil. Let it cook and brown on each side, pour the balsamic vinegar and let it dry out, add salt and dust some sugar. Cover with a lid and finish cooking. Add some drops of water if they start drying out too much. Serve the onions very hot and steamy with their gravy.

**Nutrition:** Calories 75.5, Carbs 17.9 g, Protein 0.8 g, Fat 0.2 g

## 759. Fennels with Sauce

**Prep time:** 5 minutes  
**Servings:** 6  
**Cook time:** 10 minutes

**Ingredients:**
- 3 fennels
- 3/4 cup of butter

**Sauce:**
- 1 ¾ cup of flour
- 6 yolks
- Salt
- Juice of 2 lemons
- 2 cups of broth

**Prep:** Clean the fennels, cut in quarters and boil in water.
Strain and let brown in a pan with melted butter.
Prepare the sauce: in a casserole pour the flour, yolks, broth and lemon juice and cook on a low heat.
Adjust the salt to taste and stir the sauce with a wooden spoon until it thickens.
Place the fennel in a serving dish, season with the sauce and serve.

**Nutrition:** Calories 43.2, Carbs 21.7 g, Protein 7.2 g, Fat 13.3 g

## 760. Fried Pumpkin Flowers (3rd Version)

**Prep time:** 15 minutes  
**Servings:** 6  
**Cook time:** 5 minutes

**Ingredients:**
- 35 oz of pumpkin flowers
- 16 oz of milk
- Salt
- 1 egg
- Lard and olive oil
- 3 tbsp of flour

**Prep:** Remove the pistils and trim the stems of the pumpkin flowers, wash and dry them.
Prepare the batter with flour, milk and eggs. Dust with some salt and dip in the batter, then into the hot oil to fry the flowers.

**Nutrition:** Calories 551.6, Carbs 42 g, Protein 7.6 g, Fat 40.2 g

### 761. Stuffed Mushrooms Porcini

**Prep time:** 10 minutes  
**Cook time:** 50 minutes  
**Servings:** 6

**Ingredients:**
- 12 porcini mushrooms
- Olive oil
- Salt and pepper
- Butter
- 1 cup of meat broth
- Toasted bread slices
- 12 butter curls
- lemon juice
- Breadcrumbs

**Prep:** Clean the mushrooms and remove the stems. Place them in a large greased tray. Season the mushrooms with some lemon drops, salt, pepper and a drizzle of oil. Bake in a preheated oven at 350°F for about 10 minutes.
Take out of the oven, add some broth, place a butter curl and sprinkle some breadcrumbs.
Put back into the oven and finish to cook.
Serve the mushrooms on to some toasted bread slices.

**Nutrition:** Calories 119, Carbs 21.5 g, Protein 6.8 g, Fat 17.4 g

### 762. Eggplants with Ham

**Prep time:** 40 minutes  
**Cook time:** 1 hour e 30 minutes  
**Servings:** 6

**Ingredients:**
- 6 eggplants
- ¼ cup of butter
- 16 oz of olive oil
- Salt and pepper
- 1 cup di diced ham
- 1 minced onion
- 4 ripe tomatoes

**Prep:** Clean the eggplants, remove the bottom and stem and slice them. Cover them in salt to release the bitter water inside. After few hours, strain and boil them into water with salt for few minutes. Strain and dry with a cloth.
Take a big pan and heat up the oil and butter, fry the onion, when it has browned add the ham and lastly the minced tomatoes.
Combine the eggplants, adjust salt and pepper to taste and let cook on low heat, flipping them often.

**Nutrition:** Calories 29, Carbs 0.5 g, Protein 6.1 g, Fat 1.6 g

### 763. Potatoes with Balsamic Vinegar

**Prep time:** 10 minutes  
**Cook time:** 15 minutes  
**Servings:** 6

**Ingredients:**
- 14 oz of potatoes
- 2 tbsp of balsamic vinegar
- Salt
- 4 tbsp of olive oil

**Prep:** Peel the potatoes, cut them in half lengthwise and open in half. Fry the potatoes in a pan with hot oil and flip them often to evenly cook them on both sides. Once they start to sizzle add the balsamic vinegar, adjust salt and pepper and finish cooking.

### 764. Potato Cream

**Prep time:** 25 minutes  
**Cook time:** 20 minutes  
**Servings:** 6

**Ingredients:**
- 35 oz of potatoes
- 2 minced garlic cloves
- Salt and pepper in grinders
- 1 tbsp of parsley
- 1 1/4 cup of mashed lard

**Prep:** Boil the potatoes in a pot full of water, strain, peel and mash them with a potato masher.
Add the mixture to a bowl and season with the sizzled garlic, parsley and lard.
Adjust salt and pepper to taste, mix carefully and use the mixture to spread on the bread slices.

**Nutrition:** Calories 264, Carbs 35.1 g, Protein 7 g, Fat 8.3 g

## 765. Mixed Peppers

**Prep time:** 15 minutes  
**Servings:** 6  

**Cook time:** 50 minutes

**Ingredients:**
- 35 oz of yellow, green and red peppers
- 2 bay leaves
- Salt and pepper
- 10 oz of onions
- 1 tbsp of sugar
- 2 garlic cloves
- 21 oz of softened and gutted tomatoes
- Extra virgin olive oil

**Prep:** Fry the peppers into hot oil. Peel and slice them. Pour the oil in a casserole, add the sliced garlic and onions, bay and let them brown on low heat mixing often with a wooden spoon.
Add the peppers, salt and pepper and leave to fry for about 10 minutes. Then add the sugar and tomatoes, let cook for some hours and if needed adjust salt and pepper to taste.

**Nutrition:** Calories 180.5, Carbs 18.9 g, Protein 4.2 g, Fat 11.2 g

## 766. Mixed Fried Vegetables

**Prep time:** 15 minutes  
**Servings:** 6  

**Cook time:** 30 minutes

**Ingredients:**
- 17 oz ripe tomatoes
- 3 sliced zucchini
- 3 tbsp of olive oil
- 1 diced pepper
- 6 small onions sliced in disks
- 1 diced eggplant
- Salt and pepper

**Prep:** take a big pan and fry in oil the onions, the eggplant and zucchini. Adjust salt and pepper to taste, cover with a lid and let cook on low heat.
After about 20 minutes add the chopped tomatoes, mix and finish cooking.

**Nutrition:** Calories 104, Carbs 8.1 g, Protein 3.2 g, Fat 6.3 g

## 767. Stuffed Tomatoes (3rd Version)

**Prep time:** 10 minutes  
**Servings:** 6  

**Cook time:** 1 hour

**Ingredients:**
- 6 ripe tomatoes
- 6 basil leaves
- 1 garlic clove
- 2 onions
- Salt and pepper
- 2 tbsp of parsley
- 16 oz of olive oil

**Prep:** Cut in half the tomatoes, remove the seeds and excess water. Mince the basil, garlic, onions, parsley and mix with pepper, salt and oil. Stuff the tomatoes with the mixture and bake in a preheated oven at 350°F for 1 hour.

**Nutrition:** Calories 202.4, Carbs 1.6 g, Protein 8.6 g, Fat 3.5 g

## 768. Potato Puree

**Prep time:** 20 minutes  
**Servings:** 6  

**Cook time:** 1 hour

**Ingredients:**
- 35 oz of potatoes
- Salt
- 1 cup of grated parmesan
- 4 tbsp of butter
- 16 oz of milk
- Nutmeg

**Prep:** Cook the potatoes in boiling salted water. Strain, peel and mash them with a potato masher while they are still hot.

Put the puree in a casserole on medium heat, add the butter, milk and keep mixing. When it starts to boil, remove from the heat and add the salt, parmesan, ground nutmeg and slowly add the warm milk in drops if needed.

**Nutrition:** Calories 285, Carbs 36.4 g, Protein 7.4 g, Fat 10.6 g

### 769. Meat Stuffed Zucchini

**Prep time:** 25 minutes  
**Servings:** 6  
**Cook time:** 1 hour

**Ingredients:**
- 12 zucchinis
- 1 chopped onion
- 1 minced celery stick
- 21 oz of crushed tomatoes
- 21 oz of meatball mixture
- 1 cup of milk
- 1 tbs of sugar
- 1 cup di raw minced ham
- 1 minced carrot
- Olive oil
- 1 cup of white wine
- Salt and pepper

**Prep:** Soften the zucchini in boiling water with salt for few minutes. Rinse them under running cold water, dry them with a cloth and gut them. Finely mince the inside of the zucchinis and add it to the meatball mixture. Stuff the zucchinis with the mixture. In a pot, fry in oil the onion, the celery, carrot and ham, add a little salt. Add the zucchinis and deglaze with wine. Add the tomato sauce, milk and sugar. Cook and add salt and pepper if needed.

**Nutrition:** Calories 143, Carbs 2.4 g, Protein 12.5 g, Fat 6.7 g

### 770. Battered Cauliflowers

**Prep time:** 15 minutes  
**Servings:** 6  
**Cook time:** 5 minutes

**Ingredients:**
- 18 pumpkin flowers
- 16 oz of milk
- Salt
- 1 egg
- Lard and olive oil
- 3 tbsp di flour

**Prep:** Clean the cauliflower and place it into boiling water with salt. Halfway through remove it and cut it into pieces.
Prepare the batter by mixing flour, milk and eggs.
Sprinkle with salt, dip them into the batter, then into the hot oil and fry them.
Serve hot.

**Nutrition:** Calories 531.2, Carbs 42 g, Protein 7.5 g, Fat 41.3 g

### 771. Battered Onion

**Prep time:** 15 minutes  
**Servings:** 6  
**Cook time:** 5 minutes

**Ingredients:**
- 17 oz of onions
- 16 oz of milk
- Salt
- 1 egg
- Lard and olive oil
- 3 tbsp of flour

**Prep:** Prepare the batter by mixing flour, milk and eggs.
Sprinkle the onions with salt, dip them into the batter, then into the hot oil to fry them.

**Nutrition:** Calories 511, Carbs 44 g, Protein 7.6 g, Fat 39.8 g

### 772. Potato Croquettes

**Prep time:** 45 minutes  
**Servings:** 6  
**Cook time:** 30 minutes

**Ingredients:**
- 1 1/2 cup of minced veal pulp
- Salt and pepper
- 2 eggs

- 35 oz of potatoes
- 1 minced garlic clove
- Breadcrumbs
- 3/4 cup of grated parmesan
- Butter e olive oil

**Prep:** Boil the potatoes in water with salt, strain peel and mash them. Add the cream in the minced meat, eggs and cheese. Adjust salt and pepper if needed and mix carefully with a wooden spoon. Divide the mixture into balls and lightly press them. Coat in breadcrumbs and fry in a pan with oil and butter. Flip them often to brown on each side. Drain onto some paper towel and serve hot.

**Nutrition:** Calories 445.2, Carbs 17.5 g, Protein 11.5 g, Fat 33.8 g

### 773. Cheesy Cauliflower Florets

**Prep Time:** 25 minutes  **Cook Time:** 16 minutes
**Serving:** 6

**Ingredients:**
- 1 small cauliflower, cut into florets
- 1 tbsp. garlic powder
- 1 tsp. paprika
- 4 tbsp. extra virgin olive oil
- 1/2 cup grated Parmesan cheese

**Prep:** Combine olive oil, paprika, salt, pepper and garlic powder. Throw in the cauliflower florets and position in a baking dish in single layer.
Bake in a preheated to 350 F oven for 20 minutes. Pull out from the oven, stir, and topped with Parmesan cheese. Bake for 5 minutes more.

**Nutrition:** 297 Calories, 13 g Fat, 6 g Protein

### 774. Bean Salad

**Prep Time:** 10 minutes  **Servings:** 4

**Ingredients:**
- 1 ½ cups cucumber, cubed
- 15 oz. canned garbanzo beans, drained and rinsed
- 3 oz. black olives, pitted and sliced
- 1 tomato, chopped
- ¼ cup red onion, chopped
- 5 cups salad greens
- A pinch of salt and black pepper
- ½ cup feta cheese, crumbled
- 3 tbsps. olive oil
- 1 tbsp. lemon juice
- ¼ cup parsley, chopped

**Prep:** In a salad bowl, combine the garbanzo beans with the cucumber, tomato, and the rest of the ingredients except the cheese and toss.
Divide the mix into small bowls, sprinkle the cheese on top, and serve.

**Nutrition:** Calories 268, Fat: 16 g, Carbs: 24 g, Protein: 9 g

### 775. Mushroom and Olives Steaks

**Prep Time:** 20 minutes  **Cook Time:** 9 minutes
**Serving:** 6

**Ingredients:**
- 1 lb. boneless beef sirloin steak
- 1 large onion, sliced
- 5-6 white mushrooms
- 1/2 cup green olives, coarsely chopped
- 1 cup parsley leaves, finely cut

**Prep:** Cook olive oil in a heavy bottomed pan at medium-high heat. Cook the steaks until well browned on each side then keep aside.
Gently sauté the onion in the same pan, for 3 minutes. Cook the mushrooms and olives until the mushrooms are done.
Return the steaks to the skillet, cover, and cook for 5-6 minutes. Stir in parsley and serve.

**Nutrition:** 281 Calories, 14 g Fat, 3 g Protein

### 776. Veggie Casserole

**Prep Time:** 25 minutes  **Cook Time:** 45 minutes
**Serving:** 4

**Ingredients:**
- 1 lb. okra, trimmed
- 3 tomatoes, cut into wedges
- 3 garlic cloves, chopped
- 1 cup fresh parsley leaves, finely cut

**Prep:** In a deep ovenproof baking dish, combine okra, sliced tomatoes, olive oil and garlic. Add in salt and black pepper to taste, and toss to combine. Bake in a prepared oven at 350 F for 45 minutes. Garnish with parsley and serve.

**Nutrition:** 302 Calories, 13 g Fat, 6 g Protein

## 777. Buffalo Cauliflower

**Prep Time:** 5 minutes
**Servings:** 1
**Cook Time:** 15 minutes

**Ingredients:**
- 1 Cauliflower
- 1 cup of panko breadcrumbs
- 1 tsp. salt
- 1 cup of cauliflower florets
- Buffalo coating
- 1/4 cup of Vegan Buffalo sauce
- 1/4 cup of melted vegan butter

**Prep:** Melt butter in microwave and whisk in buffalo sauce.
Dip each cauliflower floret into buffalo mixture, ensuring it gets coated well. Holdover a bowl till floret is done dripping.
Mix breadcrumbs with salt. Immerse dipped florets into breadcrumbs and place them into Air Fryer. Lock the air fryer lid. Set temperature to 350°F and set time to 15 minutes. When slightly browned, they are ready to eat.

**Nutrition:** Calories: 194; Fat: 17 g; Protein: 10 g

## 778. Cauliflower Curry

**Prep Time:** 5 minutes
**Servings:** 4
**Cook Time:** 5 hours

**Ingredients:**
- 1 cauliflower head, florets separated
- 2 carrots, sliced
- 1 red onion, chopped
- ¾ cup coconut milk
- garlic cloves, minced
- 2 tablespoons curry powder
- A pinch of salt and black pepper
- 1 tablespoon red pepper flakes
- 1 teaspoon garam masala

**Prep:** In your slow cooker, mix all the ingredients.
Cover, cook on high for 5 hours, divide into bowls and serve.

**Nutrition:** Calories 160, Fat 11.5 g, Carbs 14.7 g, Protein 3,6 g

## 779. Cucumber Bowl with Spices and Greek Yogurt

**Prep Time:** 10 minutes
**Servings:** 3
**Cook Time:** 20 minutes

**Ingredients:**
- 4 cucumbers
- ½ teaspoon chili pepper
- ¼ cup fresh parsley, chopped
- ¾ cup fresh dill, chopped
- 2 tablespoons lemon juice
- ½ teaspoon salt
- ½ teaspoon ground black pepper
- ¼ teaspoon sage
- ½ teaspoon dried oregano
- 1/3 cup Greek yogurt

**Prep:** Make the cucumber dressing: blend the dill and parsley until you get green mash.
Then combine together green mash with lemon juice, salt, ground black pepper, sage, dried oregano, Greek yogurt, and chili pepper. Churn the mixture well.
Chop the cucumbers roughly and combine them with cucumber dressing. Mix up well.
Refrigerate the cucumber for 20 minutes.

**Nutrition:** Calories 114; Fat 1.6 g; Carbs 23.2 g; Protein 7.6 g

## 780. Mediterranean Chickpea Salad

**Prep Time:** 5 minutes
**Servings:** 6
**Cook Time:** 20 minutes

**Ingredients:**
- 1 can chickpeas, drained
- 1 fennel bulb, sliced
- 1 red onion, sliced
- 1 teaspoon dried basil
- 1 teaspoon dried oregano
- 2 tablespoons chopped parsley
- garlic cloves, minced
- 2 tablespoons lemon juice
- 2 tablespoons extra virgin olive oil
- Salt and pepper to taste

**Prep:** Combine the chickpeas, fennel, red onion, herbs, garlic, lemon juice and oil in a salad bowl. Add salt and pepper and serve the salad fresh.

**Nutrition:** Calories: 200; Fat: 9 g; Protein: 4 g; Carbs: 28 g

## 781. Black Bean Stuffed Sweet Potatoes with Quinoa

**Prep Time:** 10 minutes
**Servings:** 8
**Cook Time:** 60 minutes

**Ingredients:**
- 4 sweet potatoes
- ½ onion, diced
- 1 garlic glove, crushed and diced
- ½ large bell pepper diced (about 2/3 cups)
- Handful of diced cilantro
- ½ cup cooked quinoa
- ½ cup black beans
- 1 tbsp olive oil
- 1 tbsp chili powder
- ½ tbsp cumin
- ½ tbsp paprika
- ½ tbsp oregano
- 2 tbsp lime juice
- 2 tbsp honey
- Sprinkle salt
- 1 cup shredded cheddar cheese
- Chopped spring onions, for garnish

**Prep:** Preheat oven to 400 °F.
Wash and scrub outside of potatoes. Poke with fork a few times and then place on parchment paper on cookie sheet. Bake for 40-45 minutes or until it is cooked.
While potatoes are baking, sauté onions, garlic, olive oil and spices in a pan on the stove until onions are translucent and soft.
In the last 10 minutes while the potatoes are cooking, in a large bowl combine the onion mixture with the beans, quinoa, honey, lime juice, cilantro and ½ cup cheese. Mix well.
When potatoes are cooked, remove from oven and let cool slightly. When cool to touch, cut in half (hot dog style) and scoop out most of the insides. Leave a thin ring of potato so that it will hold its shape. Fill with bean and quinoa mixture. Top with remaining cheddar cheese.
If making this a freezer meal, stop here. Individually wrap potato skins in plastic wrap and place on flat surface to freeze. Once frozen, place all potatoes in large zip lock container.
Return to oven for an additional 10 minutes or until cheese is melted.

**Nutrition:** Calories: 243; Carbs: 37.6 g; Protein: 8.5 g; Fat: 7.3 g

## 782. Bok Choy with Tofu Stir Fry

**Prep Time:** 15 minutes
**Servings:** 4
**Cook Time:** 15 minutes

**Ingredients:**
- Super-firm tofu: 1 lb. (drained and pressed)
- Coconut oil: one tablespoon
- Clove of garlic: 1 (minced)
- Baby bok Choy: 3 heads (chopped)
- Low-sodium vegetable broth;
- Maple syrup: 2 teaspoons
- Braggs liquid aminos
- Sambal oelek: 1 to 2 teaspoons (similar chili sauce)
- Scallion or green onion: 1 (chopped)
- Freshly grated ginger: 1 teaspoon
- Quinoa, for serving

**Prep:** With paper towels, pat the tofu dry and cut into tiny pieces of bite-size around 1/2 inch wide.
Heat coconut oil in a wide skillet over medium heat.
Remove tofu and stir-fry until painted softly.
Stir-fry for 1-2 minutes, before the Choy of the Bok starts to wilt.
When this occurs, you'll want to apply the vegetable broth and all the remaining ingredients to the skillet.
Hold the mixture stir-frying until all components are well coated, and the bulk of the liquid evaporates, around 5-6 min.
Serve over quinoa.

**Nutrition:** Calories: 263.7; Fat 4.2 g; Carbohydrate: 35.7 g

## 783. Chickpeas and Millet Stew

**Prep Time:** 10 minutes  
**Servings:** 4  

**Cook Time:** 1 hour and 5 minutes

**Ingredients:**
- 1 cup millet
- 2 tbsps. olive oil
- A pinch of salt and pepper
- 1 eggplant, cubed
- 1 yellow onion, chopped
- 14 oz. canned tomatoes, chopped
- 14 oz. canned chickpeas, drained and rinsed
- 3 garlic cloves, minced
- 2 tbsps. harissa paste
- 1 bunch cilantro, chopped
- 2 cups water

**Prep:** Put the water in a pan, bring to a simmer over medium heat, add the millet, simmer for 25 minutes, take off the heat, fluff with a fork and leave aside for now.
Heat up a pan with half of the oil over medium heat, add the eggplant, salt, and pepper. Stir and cook for 10 minutes and transfer to a bowl. Add the rest of the oil to the pan, heat up over medium heat again, add the onion and sauté for 10 minutes. Add the garlic, more salt and pepper, the harissa paste, chickpeas, tomatoes and return the eggplant, stir and cook over low heat for 15 minutes more.
Add the millet, toss, divide the mix into bowls, sprinkle the cilantro on top and serve.

**Nutrition:** Calories 671, Fat: 15.6 g, Carbs: 87.5 g, Protein: 27.1 g

## 784. Greek Baked Zucchini & Potatoes

**Prep Time:** 30 minutes  
**Servings:** 4  

**Cook Time:** 2 hours

**Ingredients:**
- 2 lb. Potatoes
- 4 large Zucchini
- 4 small Red onions
- 6 pureed Ripe tomatoes
- ½ cup Olive oil
- 2 tbsp. Freshly chopped parsley
- Black pepper & salt to taste

**Prep:** Thinly slice the zucchini, onions, and potatoes.
Set the oven to reach 400°F.
Chop and spread the onions, zucchini, and potatoes in a baking pan. Cover with pureed tomatoes, parsley, and olive oil. Sprinkle using the salt and pepper. Toss until evenly coated. Bake them for approximately one hour or until the veggies are moist and softened.
Cool them slightly and serve.

**Nutrition:** Calories 534, Fat: 28.3 g, Protein: 11.3 g

## 785. Green Beans & Feta

**Prep Time:** 10 minutes  
**Servings:** 8  

**Cook Time:** 15 minutes

**Ingredients:**
- 2 tbsp. Olive oil
- 1 lb. Freshly trimmed green beans
- 2 tbsp. Red onion
- 1 tbsp. Tarragon vinegar
- ½ tsp. Salt
- ¼ tsp. Pepper
- 1 clove Garlic
- ½ cup or 2 oz. Crumbled feta cheese

**Prep:** Add one inch of water into the pan and add the beans.
Finely chop the onion and garlic and add the rest of the fixings (omit the cheese) to simmer for eight to ten minutes with the lid off.
Drain. Scoop the beans into a Servings dish and add the cheese.
Toss and serve warm.

## 786. Herbed Garlic Black Beans

**Prep Time:** 10 Minutes  
**Servings:** 8  

**Cook Time:** 7 Hours

**Ingredients:**
- 3 cups dried black beans, rinsed and drained
- 2 onions, chopped
- 8 garlic cloves, minced
- 6 cups low-sodium vegetable broth
- ½ teaspoon salt
- 1 teaspoon dried basil leaves
- ½ teaspoon dried thyme leaves
- ½ teaspoon dried oregano leaves

**Prep:** In a 6-quart slow cooker, mix all the ingredients. Cover and cook on low for 7 to 9 hours, or until the beans have absorbed the liquid and are tender.
Remove and discard the bay leaf.

**Nutrition:** Calories: 250; Carbs: 47 g; Protein: 15g

## 787. Kale - Mediterranean-Style

**Prep Time:** 10 minutes  **Cook Time:** 15 minutes
**Servings:** 6

**Ingredients:**
- 12 cups Chopped kale
- 1 tbsp./as needed Olive oil
- 1 tbsp. Minced garlic
- Salt and black pepper as preferred
- 1 tsp. Soy sauce
- 2 tbsp. Lemon juice

**Prep:** Prepare a saucepan with a steamer insert. Pour in plenty of water to cover the bottom.
Put a lid on the pot and boil using the high-temperature setting.
Toss in the kale. Once it boils, time for 7-10 minutes. Drain.
Whisk the soy sauce, lemon juice, garlic, oil, black pepper, and salt. Toss in the steamed kale. Toss until coated and serve.

**Nutrition:** Calories 91, Fat: 3.2 g, Protein: 4.6 g

## 788. Maple Lemon Tempeh Cubes

**Prep Time:** 10 minutes  **Cook Time:** 30 minutes
**Servings:** 4

**Ingredients:**
- Tempeh: 1 packet
- Coconut oil: 2 teaspoons
- Lemon juice: 3 tablespoons
- Maple syrup; 2 teaspoons
- Low-sodium tamari: 2 teaspoons
- Water: 2 teaspoons
- Dried basil: 1/4 teaspoon
- Powdered garlic: 1/4 teaspoon
- Black pepper, to taste

**Prep:** Heat your oven to 400 ° F.
Cut your tempeh block into squares in bite form.
Heat coconut oil over medium to high heat in a non-stick skillet. When melted and heated, add the tempeh and cook on one side for 2-4 minutes, or until the tempeh turns down into a golden-brown color. Flip the tempeh bits, and cook for 2-4 minutes.
Mix the lemon juice, tamari, maple syrup, basil, water, garlic, and black pepper while the tempeh is browning.
Drop the mixture over tempeh, then swirl to cover the tempeh.
Sauté for 2-3 minutes, then turn the tempeh and sauté 1-2 minutes more.

**Nutrition:** Carbs: 22; Fats: 17 g; Protein: 21 g

## 789. Mediterranean Endive Boats

**Prep Time:** 10 minutes  **Cook Time:** 10 minutes
**Servings:** 8

**Ingredients:**
- 1/3 cup Chopped sun-dried tomatoes
- 0.66 cup Chickpeas
- 1 tbsp. Olive oil
- ¼ cup Crumbled feta
- 3 Chopped basil leaves
- 2 tbsp. Balsamic reduction

**Prep:** Rinse and drain the chickpeas. Combine the oil, with the drained chickpeas, and tomatoes.
Cut the base of the endive and pull the leaves apart. (It should make eight).
Arrange the leaves on the servings platter and add the chickpea mixture.
Garnish it with the crumbled feta and top it off with chopped basil and a spritz of balsamic reduction.

**Nutrition:** Calories 715, Fat: 30 g, Protein: 32 g

## 790. Mediterranean Potatoes

**Prep Time:** 15 minutes  **Cook Time:** 45-50 minutes
**Servings:** 4

**Ingredients:**

- 4-5 Medium potatoes
- 1 tbsp. Olive oil
- 1 tbsp. Butter, melted
- 6 tsp. Greek seasoning
- 1/8 tsp. Garlic seasoning

**Prep:** Set the oven temperature to 350°F.
Cube the potatoes and toss them into the dish with the rest of the fixings. Bake them for 30-40 minutes. Turn occasionally. Serve when the potatoes are browned to your liking.

**Nutrition:** Calories 207.8, Fat: 6.3 g, Protein: 3.8 g

### 791. Greek Eggplant Dish

**Prep Time:** 30 minutes  
**Servings:** 2  
**Cook Time:** 1 hour 15 minutes

**Ingredients:**
- 1 Eggplant
- 14.5 oz. can Diced tomatoes, drained
- 1 tbsp. Tomato paste
- 1 Medium onion
- 1 tbsp./to taste Minced garlic
- 1 tsp. Ground cinnamon
- Pepper & salt as desired
- 3 tbsp. Olive oil

**Prep:** Set the oven to reach 350°F.
Slice the eggplant - lengthwise - in half. Cut out the halves leaving about a one-inch shell. Set the flesh aside.
Arrange the shells on a baking pan. Lightly spritz the eggplant using oil and bake until softened (30 min.).
Chop the leftover eggplant into small pieces.
Prepare a skillet using the medium temperature setting with two tbsps. of oil. Dice and add the onion, garlic, and chopped eggplant to sauté for a few minutes.
Dump the tomato paste and tomatoes and simmer using the low-heat temperature setting.
Transfer the shells to the countertop, and spoon in the tomato/eggplant mixture. Sprinkle using cinnamon and bake for another 30 minutes.

**Nutrition:** Calories 314, Fat: 20.8 g, Protein: 5.3 g

### 792. Almond Kale

**Prep Time:** 7 minutes  
**Servings** 2  
**Cook Time:** 10 minutes

**Ingredients:**
- 2 cups kale, chopped
- 1 tablespoon butter
- 1 cup of water
- 1 tablespoon almond, chopped
- 1 teaspoon cumin seeds
- ½ teaspoon salt

**Prep:** Bring the water to boil. Add kale in the hot water and boil the greens for 3 minutes.
After this, drain the water.
Melt the butter in the skillet.
Add cumin seeds and roast them for 1 minute over the medium heat or until they start to give a smell. Add boiled kale and mix up.
After this, sprinkle the kale with salt and almonds. Mix up well.
Roast the kale for 2 minutes.

**Nutrition:** 105 Calories; 7.5 g Fat; 2.9 g Protein

### 793. Apples and Pomegranate Salad

**Prep Time:** 10 minutes  
**Servings:** 4

**Ingredients:**
- 3 big apples, cored and cubed
- 1 cup pomegranate seeds
- 3 cups baby arugula
- 1 cup walnuts, chopped
- 1 tablespoon olive oil
- 1 teaspoon white sesame seeds
- 2 tablespoons apple cider vinegar

**Prep:** Mix the apples with the arugula and the rest of the ingredients in a bowl.
Toss and serve cold.

**Nutrition:** 160 Calories, 4.3 g Fat, 10 g Protein

## 794. Arugula Salad

**Prep Time:** 5 minutes  **Servings:** 4

**Ingredients:**
- Arugula leaves (4 cups)
- Cherry tomatoes (1 cup)
- Pine nuts (.25 cup)
- Rice vinegar (1 tbsp.)
- Olive/grapeseed oil (2 tbsp.)
- Grated parmesan cheese (.25 cup)
- Black pepper & salt
- Large sliced avocado (1)

**Prep:** Peel and slice the avocado.
Rinse and dry the arugula leaves, grate the cheese, and slice the cherry tomatoes into halves.
Combine the arugula, pine nuts, tomatoes, oil, vinegar, salt, pepper, and cheese.
Toss the salad to mix and portion it onto plates with the avocado slices to serve.

**Nutrition:** 257 Calories, 23 g Fat, 6.1 g Protein

## 795. Balsamic Eggplant Mix

**Prep Time:** 10 minutes  **Cook Time:** 20 minutes
**Servings:** 6

**Ingredients:**
- 1/3 cup chicken stock
- 2 tablespoons balsamic vinegar
- 1 tablespoon lime juice
- 2 big eggplants
- 1 tablespoon rosemary
- ¼ cup cilantro
- 2 tablespoons olive oil

**Prep:** In a roasting pan, combine the eggplants with the stock, the vinegar and the rest of the ingredients, introduce the pan in the oven and bake at 390 °F for 20 minutes.
Divide the mix between plates.

**Nutrition:** 201 Calories, 4.5 g Fat, 3 g Protein

## 796. Bean Lettuce Wraps

**Prep Time:** 10 minutes  **Cook Time:** 10 minutes
**Servings** 4

**Ingredients:**
- 1 tablespoon extra-virgin olive oil
- ½ cup diced red onion
- ¾ cup chopped fresh tomatoes
- ¼ teaspoon freshly ground black pepper
- 1 (15-ounce) can cannellini beans
- ¼ cup curly parsley
- ½ cup Lemony Garlic Hummus
- 8 romaine lettuce leaves

**Prep:** Place a skillet over medium heat, and heat the oil. Add the onion and cook for 4 minutes, stirring occasionally. Add the tomatoes and pepper and cook for another 3 minutes. Add the beans and cook for 3 minutes, stirring. Remove from the heat, and stir in parsley.
Spread 1 tablespoon of hummus on each lettuce leaf.
Evenly distribute the bean mixture in the center of each leaf.
Fold one side of the lettuce leaf over the filling lengthwise, then fold over the other side to forma wrap.

**Nutrition:** 211 Calories; 8 g Fat; 10 g Protein

## 797. Cheese Beet Salad

**Prep Time:** 15 minutes  **Servings:** 4

**Ingredients:**
- 6 red beets
- 3 ounces feta cheese
- 2 tablespoons olive oil
- 2 tablespoons balsamic vinegar

**Prep:** Combine everything together and serve.

**Nutrition:** 230 Calories; 7.3 g Protein; 12 g Fat

### 798. Chickpea Salad

**Prep Time:** 15 minutes  **Servings:** 4

**Ingredients:**
- Cooked chickpeas (15 oz.)
- Diced Roma tomato (1)
- Diced green medium bell pepper (half of 1)
- Fresh parsley (1 tbsp.)
- Small white onion (1)
- Minced garlic (.5 tsp.)
- Lemon (1 juiced)

**Prep:** Chop the tomato, green pepper, and onion.
Mince the garlic.
Combine each of the other ingredients into a salad bowl and toss well.
Cover the salad to chill for at least 15 minutes in the fridge.

**Nutrition:** 163 Calories; 7 g Fats; 4 g Protein

### 799. Creamy Carrot Chowder

**Prep Time:** 11 minutes  **Cook Time:** 40 minutes
**Servings** 8

**Ingredients:**
- 8 fresh mint sprigs
- ½ cup 2% Greek Style Plain yogurt
- 1 tsp fresh ginger
- 2 cups chicken broth
- 1 lb. baby carrots
- 1/3 cup sliced shallots
- 2 tsp sesame oil

**Prep:** On medium fire, place a heavy bottom pot and heat oil. Sauté shallots until tender around minutes.
Add carrots and sauté for another 4 minutes.
Pour broth, cover and bring to a boil. Once soup is boiling, slow fi re to a simmer and cook carrots until tender around 22 minutes.
Add ginger and continue cooking while covered for another eight minutes.
Turn off fire and let it cool for 10 minutes.
Pour mixture into blender and puree. If needed, puree carrots in batches then return to pot.
Heat pureed carrots until heated through around 2 minutes.
Turn off fire and evenly pour into 8 serving bowls.

**Nutrition:** 47 Calories; 2.2 g Protein; 1.6 g Fat

### 800. Creamy Chicken Salad

**Prep time:** 10 minutes  **Servings:** 6

**Ingredients:**
- 20 ounces chicken meat
- ½ cup pecans, chopped
- 1 cup green grapes
- ½ cup celery, chopped
- 2 ounces canned mandarin oranges, drained

**For the creamy cucumber salad dressing:**
- 1 cup Greek yogurt cucumber, chopped garlic clove
- 1 teaspoon lemon juice

**Prep:** In a bowl, mix cucumber with salt, pepper to taste, lemon juice, garlic and yogurt and stir very well.
In a salad bowl, mix chicken meat with grapes, pecans, oranges and celery.
Add cucumber salad dressing, toss to coat and keep in the fridge until you serve it.

**Nutrition:** 200 Calories; 3g Fat; 8g Protein

### 801. Feta Tomato Salad

**Prep time:** 5 minutes  **Servings:** 4

**Ingredients:**
- Balsamic vinegar (2 tbsp.)
- Freshly minced basil (1.5 tsp.) or Dried (.5 tsp.)
- Salt (.5 tsp.)
- Coarsely chopped sweet onion (.5 cup)
- Olive oil (2 tbsp.)
- Cherry or grape tomatoes (1 lb.)
- Crumbled feta cheese (.25 cup.)

**Prep:** Whisk the salt, basil, and vinegar.
Toss the onion into the vinegar mixture for 5 minutes.
Slice the tomatoes into halves and stir in the tomatoes, feta cheese, and oil to serve.

**Nutrition:** 121 Calories; 9g Fats; 3g Protein

### 802. Braised Kale with Cherry Tomatoes

**Prep time: 7 minutes**  
**Servings 6**  
**Cook time: 32 minutes**

**Ingredients:**
- 1 lb. Kale
- 1 Cup Cherry Tomatoes, Halved
- 2 Teaspoons Olive Oil
- 4 Cloves Garlic, Sliced Thin
- ½ Cup Vegetable Stock
- ¼ Teaspoon Sea Salt, Fine
- 1 Tablespoon Lemon Juice, Fresh
- 1/8 Teaspoon Black Pepper

**Prep:** Preheat olive oil in a frying pan using medium heat, and add in your garlic. Sauté for 1 minute or 2 until lightly golden.
Mix your kale and vegetable stock with your garlic, adding it to your pan. Cover the pan and then turn the heat down to medium-low. Allow it to cook until kale wilts and part of vegetable stock should be dissolved.
Stir in tomatoes and cook without a lid until your kale is tender, and then remove it from heat.
Mix in salt, pepper and lemon juice before serving warm.

**Nutrition:** 70 Calories; 4g Protein; 0.5g Fat

### 803. Gorgonzola Sweet Potato Burgers

**Prep time: 10 minutes**  
**Servings 4**  
**Cook time: 15 minutes**

**Ingredients:**
- 1 large sweet potato (about 8 ounces)
- 2 tablespoons extra-virgin olive oil, divided
- 1 cup chopped onion (about ½ medium onion)
- 1 cup old-fashioned rolled oats
- 1 large egg
- 1 tablespoon balsamic vinegar
- 1 tablespoon dried oregano
- 1 garlic clove
- ¼ teaspoon kosher or sea salt
- ½ cup crumbled Gorgonzola

**Prep:** Prick sweet potato all over and microwave on high for 4 to 5 minutes. Cool slightly, then slice in half.
While the sweet potato is cooking, in a large skillet over medium-high heat, heat 1 tablespoon of oil and cook the onion.
Using a spoon, carefully scoop the sweet potato flesh out of the skin and put the flesh in a food processor. Blend onion, oats, egg, vinegar, oregano, garlic, and salt. Add the cheese and pulse four times to barely combine. With your hands, form the mixture into four (½-cup-size) burgers. Place the burgers on a plate, and press to flatten each to about ¾-inch thick.
Clean out the skillet with a paper towel, then heat the remaining 1 tablespoon of oil over medium-high heat until hot, for about 2 minutes. Add the burgers to the hot oil, then turn the heat down to medium. Cook the burgers for 5 minutes, flip with a spatula, then cook an additional 5 minutes.
Enjoy as is or serve on salad greens or whole-wheat rolls.

**Nutrition:** 223 Calories; 13g Fat; 7g Protein

### 804. Greek Stuffed Collard Greens

**Prep time: 10 minutes**  
**Servings 4**  
**Cook time: 20 minutes**

**Ingredients:**
- 1 (28-ounce) can low-sodium crushed tomatoes
- 8 collard green leaves
- 2 (10-ounce) bags frozen grain medley
- 2 tablespoons grated Parmesan cheese

**Prep:** Preheat the oven to 400°F (200°C). Pour the tomatoes into a baking pan and set aside.
Fill a large stockpot about three-quarters of the way with water and bring to a boil.
Add the collard greens and cook for 2 minutes. Drain in a colander. Put the greens on a clean towel or paper towels and blot dry.
To assemble the stuffed collards, lay one leaf flat on the counter vertically add about ½ cup of the lentils and rice mixture to the middle of the leaf, and spread it evenly along the middle of the leaf.

Fold one long side of the leaf over the rice filling, then fold over the other long side so it is slightly overlapping. Take the bottom end, where the stem was, and gently but firmly roll up until you have a slightly square package.
Carefully transfer the stuffed leaf to the baking pan, and place it seam-side down in the crushed tomatoes.
Repeat with the remaining leaves.
Sprinkle the leaves with the grated cheese, and cover the pan with aluminum foil.
Bake for 20 minutes, or until the collards are tender-firm.
Serve.

**Nutrition:** 205 Calories; 8g Fat; 6g Protein

## 805. Grilled Veggie and Hummus Wrap

**Prep time: 15 minutes**　　　　　　　　　　　　　　　　　　　　**Cook time: 10 minutes**
**Servings 6**

**Ingredients:**
- 1 large eggplant
- 1 large onion
- ½ cup extra-virgin olive oil
- 1 teaspoon salt
- 6 lavash wraps or large pita bread
- 1 cup Creamy Traditional Hummus

**Prep:** Preheat a large grill pan on medium heat.
Slice the eggplant and onion into circles. Rub vegetables with olive oil and sprinkle with salt.
Cook the vegetables on both sides, about 3 to 4 minutes each side.
To make the wrap, lay the lavash or pita flat. Spread about 2 tablespoons of hummus on the wrap.
Evenly divide the vegetables among the wraps, layering them along one side of the wrap. Gently fold over the side of the wrap with the vegetables, tucking them in and making a tight wrap.
Lay the wrap seam side-down and cut in half or thirds.

**Nutrition:** 362 Calories; 15g Protein; 26g Fat

## 806. Mediterranean Quiche

**Prep time: 7 minutes**　　　　　　　　　　　　　　　　　　　　**Cook time: 25 minutes**
**Servings 6**

**Ingredients:**
- ½ cup sundried tomatoes
- 2 cloves garlic, minced
- 1 onion, diced
- 2 tablespoons butter
- 1 prepared pie crust
- boiling water
- 1 red pepper, diced
- 2 cups spinach, fresh
- ¼ cup kalamata olives
- 1 teaspoon oregano
- 1 teaspoon parsley
- 1/3 cup feta cheese, crumbled
- 4 eggs, large
- 1 ¼ cup milk
- sea salt & black pepper to taste
- 1 cup cheddar cheese, shredded & divided

**Prep:** Add your tomatoes to boiling water and allow it to cook for 5 minutes before draining.
Chop the tomatoes before setting them to the side, and adjust the oven to 375 ° F (190 °C).
Spread the pie crust into a nine-inch pie pan, and heat the butter and add in your garlic and onion.
Cook for 3 minutes before adding in your red pepper, and then cook for another 3 minutes.
Add in your parsley and oregano before adding in your spinach and olives. Cook for about another 5 minutes.
Take it off heat, and then add in your feta cheese and tomatoes.
Spread your mixture into the prepared pie crust, and then beat the egg and milk. Season with salt and pepper and then add in half a cup of cheese.
Pour this mixture over your spinach, and then bake for 25 minutes. It should be golden.
Serve warm.

**Nutrition:** 417 Calories; 14.5g Protein; 13.3g Fat

## 807. Mediterranean Sweet Potato

**Prep time: 6 minutes**　　　　　　　　　　　　　　　　　　　　**Cook time: 25 minutes**
**Servings 4**

**Ingredients:**
- 4 sweet potatoes
- 15 ounce can chickpeas, rinsed & drained
- ½ tablespoon olive oil
- ½ teaspoon cumin
- ½ teaspoon coriander
- ½ teaspoon cinnamon
- 1 pinch sea salt, fine
- ½ teaspoon paprika

- ¼ cup hummus
- 1 tablespoon lemon juice, fresh
- 2-3 teaspoon dill, fresh
- 3 cloves garlic, minced
- unsweetened almond milk as needed

**Prep:** Set oven to 400 °F (200 °C), and then get out a baking sheet. Line it with foil.
Wash your sweet potatoes before halving them lengthwise.
Take your olive oil, cumin, chickpeas, coriander, sea salt and paprika on your baking sheet.
Rub the sweet potatoes with olive oil, placing them face down over the mixture. Roast for 20 to 25 minutes.
Mix your dill, lemon juice, hummus, garlic and a dash of almond milk.
Smash the insides of the sweet potato down.
Topping with chickpea mixture and sauce before serving.

**Nutrition:** 313 Calories; 8.6g Protein; 9g Fats

### 808. Mediterranean Veggie Bowl

**Prep time:** 10 minutes  
**Servings** 4  
**Cook time:** 20 minutes

**Ingredients:**
- 2 cups water
- 1 cup quinoa
- 1½ teaspoons salt, divided
- 1-pint (2 cups) cherry tomatoes
- 1 large bell pepper
- 1 large cucumber
- 1 cup Kalamata olives
- ½ cup freshly squeezed lemon juice
- 1 cup extra-virgin olive oil
- ½ teaspoon black pepper

**Prep:** Situate medium pot over medium heat, boil the water. Add the bulgur (or quinoa) and 1 teaspoon of salt.
Cover and cook for 15 minutes.
To arrange the veggies in your 4 bowls, visually divide each bowl into 5 sections.
Place the cooked bulgur in one section. Follow with the tomatoes, bell pepper, cucumbers, and olives.
Scourge lemon juice, olive oil, remaining ½ teaspoon salt, and black pepper.
Evenly spoon the dressing over the 4 bowls.
Serve immediately or cover and refrigerate for later.

**Nutrition:** 772 Calories; 6g Protein; 68g Fat

### 809. Melon Salad

**Prep time:** 20 Minutes  
**Size/ Portion:** 2 cups  
**Servings:** 6

**Ingredients:**
- ¼ teaspoon sea salt
- ¼ teaspoon black pepper
- 1 tablespoon balsamic vinegar
- 1 cantaloupe
- 12 watermelons
- 2 cups mozzarella balls, fresh
- 1/3 cup basil, fresh & torn
- 2 tablespoons olive oil

**Prep:** Spoon out balls of cantaloupe, then situate them in a colander over bowl.
Using melon baller to cut the watermelon as well.
Drain fruits for ten minutes, then chill the juice.
Wipe the bowl dry, and then place your fruit in it.
Mix in basil, oil, vinegar, mozzarella and tomatoes before seasoning and gently mix.
Serve.

**Nutrition:** 218 Calories; 10g Protein; 13g Fat

### 810. North African Peanut Stew over Cauliflower Rice

**Prep time:** 5 minutes  
**Servings** 4  
**Cook time:** 25 minutes

**Ingredients:**
- 1 cup frozen corn
- 2 tablespoons extra-virgin olive oil
- 1 cup chopped onion
- 2 medium Yukon Gold potatoes
- 1 large sweet potato
- 3 garlic cloves
- 1½ teaspoons ground cumin
- 1 teaspoon ground allspice
- 1 teaspoon freshly grated ginger root
- ½ teaspoon crushed red pepper
- ¼ teaspoon kosher or sea salt
- ½ cup water

- 1 (28-ounce) can diced tomatoes, undrained
- 1 (12-ounce) package frozen plain cauliflower rice
- 1 (15-ounce) can lentils, undrained
- 1/3 cup creamy peanut butter

**Prep:** Put the corn on the counter to partially thaw while making the stew.
In a large stockpot over medium-high heat, heat the oil and add the onion, potatoes, and sweet potatoes. Cook for 7 minutes.
Move the potatoes to the edges of the pot, and add the garlic, cumin, allspice, ginger, crushed red pepper, and salt. Cook for 1 minute, stirring constantly. Stir in the water and cook for 1 more minute, scraping up the crispy bits from the bottom of the pan.
Add the tomatoes with their juices to the stockpot. Cook for 15 minutes uncovered, stirring occasionally.
While the tomatoes are cooking, cook the cauliflower rice according to the package prep.
Into the tomato mixture, stir in the lentils, partially thawed corn, and peanut butter. Adjust to medium heat and cook for 1 to 2 minutes.
Serve over the cauliflower rice with hot peppers, peanuts, and fresh cilantro, if desired.

**Nutrition:** 467 Calories; 20g Fat; 21g Protein

### 811. Orange Celery Salad

**Prep time: 16 minutes**     **Servings 6**

**Ingredients:**
- 1 tablespoon lemon juice, fresh
- ¼ teaspoon sea salt, fine
- ¼ teaspoon black pepper
- 1 tablespoon olive brine
- 1 tablespoon olive oil
- ¼ cup red onion, sliced
- ½ cup green olives
- 2 oranges, peeled & sliced
- 3 celery stalks, sliced diagonally in ½ inch slices

**Prep:** Put your oranges, olives, onion and celery in a shallow bowl.
Stir oil, olive brine and lemon juice, pour this over your salad.
Season with salt and pepper before serving.

**Nutrition:** 65 Calories; 2g Protein; 0.2g Fat

### 812. Passion Fruit and Spicy Couscous

**Prep time: 15 minutes**     **Cook time: 15 minutes**
**Servings 4**

**Ingredients:**
- 1 pinch of salt
- 1 pinch of allspice
- 1 teaspoon of mixed spice
- 1 cup of boiling water
- 2 teaspoons of extra-virgin olive oil
- ½ cup of full-fat Greek yogurt
- ½ cup of honey
- 1 cup of couscous
- 1 teaspoon of orange zest
- 2 oranges, peeled and sliced
- 2 tablespoons of passion fruit pulp
- ½ cup of blueberries
- ½ cup of walnuts, roasted and unsalted
- 2 tablespoons of fresh mint

**Prep:** In a mixing bowl, combine the salt, allspice, mixed spice, honey, couscous, and boiling water.
Cover the bowl and allow to rest for 5 to 10 minutes, or until the water has been absorbed.
Using a fork, give the mixture a good stir, then add the diced walnuts.
In a separate bowl, combine the passion fruit, yogurt, and orange zest.
To serve, dish the couscous up into four bowls, add the yogurt mixture, and top with the sliced orange, blueberries, and mint leaves.

**Nutrition:** 100 Calories; 10.5g Fat; 2.1g Protein

### 813. Pistachio Arugula Salad

**Prep time: 20 minutes**     **Servings 6**
**Size/ Portion: 2 cups**

**Ingredients:**
- ¼ cup olive oil
- 6 cups kale, chopped rough
- 2 cups arugula
- ½ teaspoon smoked paprika
- 2 tablespoons lemon juice, fresh
- 1/3 cup pistachios, unsalted & shelled
- 6 tablespoons parmesan, grated

**Prep:** Get out a large bowl and combine your oil, lemon juice, kale and smoked paprika.
Massage it into the leaves for about 15 seconds. You then need to allow it to sit for 10 minutes.

Mix everything together before serving with grated cheese on top.

**Nutrition:** 150 Calories; 5g Protein; 12g Fat

## 814. Pork and Greens Salad

**Prep time:** 10 minutes
**Servings:** 4
**Cook time:** 15 minutes

**Ingredients:**
- 1-pound pork chops
- 8 ounces white mushrooms, sliced
- ½ cup Italian dressing
- 6 cups mixed salad greens
- 6 ounces jarred artichoke hearts, drained
- Salt and black pepper to the taste
- ½ cup basil, chopped
- 1 tablespoon olive oil

**Prep:** Heat a pan with the oil over medium-high heat, add the pork and brown for 5 minutes. Add the mushrooms, stir and sauté for 5 minutes more. Add the dressing, artichokes, salad greens, salt, pepper and the basil, cook for 4-5 minutes, divide everything into bowls. Serve.

**Nutrition:** 235 Calories; 6g Fat; 11g Protein

## 815. Roasted Brussels Sprouts And Pecans

**Prep time:** 9 minutes
**Serving;** 7
**Cook time:** 3 hours

**Ingredients:**
- 1 ½ pounds fresh Brussels sprouts
- 4 tablespoons olive oil
- 4 cloves of garlic, minced
- 3 tablespoons water
- Salt and pepper to taste
- ½ cup chopped pecans

**Prep:** Place all ingredients in the Instant Pot.
Combine all ingredients until well combined.
Close the lid and make sure that the steam release vent is set to "Venting."
Press the "Slow Cook" button and adjust the cook time to 3 hours.

**Nutrition:** 161 Calories; 4.1g Protein; 13g Fat

## 816. Rosemary Beets

**Prep time:** 10 minutes
**Servings:** 4
**Cook time:** 20 minutes

**Ingredients:**
- 4 medium beets
- 1/3 cup balsamic vinegar
- 1 teaspoon rosemary, chopped
- 1 garlic clove, minced
- ½ teaspoon Italian seasoning
- 1 tablespoon olive oil

**Prep:** Place pan with the oil over medium heat, add the beets and the rest of the ingredients, toss, and cook for 20 minutes. Divide the mix between plates and serve.

**Nutrition:** 165 Calories; 3.4g Fat; 2.3g Protein

## 817. Sautéed Garlic Spinach

**Prep time:** 5 minutes
**Servings** 4
**Cook time:** 10 minutes

**Ingredients:**
- ¼ cup extra-virgin olive oil
- 1 large onion, thinly sliced
- 3 cloves garlic, minced
- 6 (1-pound) bags of baby spinach, washed
- ½ teaspoon salt
- 1 lemon, cut into wedges

**Prep:** Cook the olive oil, onion, and garlic in a large skillet for 2 minutes over medium heat.
Add one bag of spinach and ½ teaspoon of salt. Cover the skillet and let the spinach wilt for 30 seconds. Repeat (omitting the salt), adding 1 bag of spinach at a time.

Once all the spinach has been added, remove the cover and cook for 3 minutes, letting some of the moisture evaporate. Serve with squeeze of lemon over the top.

**Nutrition:** 301 Calories; 17g Protein; 14g Fat

## 818. Spanish Green Beans

**Prep time: 10 minutes**
**Servings 4**

**Cook time: 20 minutes**

**Ingredients:**
- ¼ cup extra-virgin olive oil
- 1 large onion, chopped
- 4 cloves garlic, finely chopped
- 1-pound green beans
- 1½ teaspoons salt, divided
- 1 (15-ounce) can diced tomatoes
- ½ teaspoon freshly ground black pepper

**Prep:** Position large pot over medium heat, cook olive oil, onion, and garlic.
Cut the green beans into 2-inch pieces.
Add the green beans and 1 teaspoon of salt to the pot and toss everything together and cook for 3 minutes.
Add the diced tomatoes, remaining ½ teaspoon of salt, and black pepper to the pot.
Continue to cook for another 12 minutes, stirring occasionally.

**Nutrition:** 200 Calories; 4g Protein; 14g Fat

## 819. Spicy Green Beans Mix

**Prep time: 5 minutes**
**Servings: 4**

**Cook time: 15 minutes**

**Ingredients:**
- 4 teaspoons olive oil
- 1 garlic clove, minced
- ½ teaspoon hot paprika
- ¾ cup veggie stock
- 1 yellow onion, sliced
- 1-pound green beans
- ½ cup goat cheese, shredded
- 2 teaspoon balsamic vinegar

**Prep:** Put pan with the oil over medium heat, add the garlic, stir and cook for 1 minute.
Add the green beans and the rest of the ingredients. Toss.
Cook everything for 15 minutes more.
Divide between plates and serve.

**Nutrition:** 188 Calories; 4g Fat; 4.4g Protein

## 820. Quinoa Salad

**Prep time: 10 minutes**
**Servings 4**

**Cook time: 25 minutes**

**Ingredients**
**For vinaigrette:**
- 1 pinch of salt
- 1 pinch of black pepper
- ½ teaspoon of dried thyme
- ½ teaspoon of dried oregano
- ¼ cup of extra-virgin olive oil
- 1 tablespoon of honey
- juice of 1 lemon
- 1 clove of garlic, minced
- 2 tablespoons of fresh basil, diced

**For salad:**
- 1 ½ cups of cooked quinoa
- 4 cups of mixed leafy greens
- ½ cup of kalamata olives, halved and pitted
- ¼ cup of sun-dried tomatoes, diced
- ½ cup of almonds, raw, unsalted and diced

**Prep:** Combine all the vinaigrette ingredients together, either by hand or using a blender or food processor.
Set the vinaigrette aside in the refrigerator. In a large salad bowl, combine the salad ingredients.
Drizzle the vinaigrette over the salad and serve.

**Nutrition:** 201 Calories; 13g Fat; 4g Protein

## 821. Stewed Okra

**Prep time: 5 minutes**
**Servings 4**

**Cook time: 25 minutes**

**Ingredients:**
- ¼ cup extra-virgin olive oil
- 1 large onion, chopped
- 4 cloves garlic, finely chopped
- 1 teaspoon salt
- 1 pound fresh or frozen okra, cleaned
- 1 (15-ounce) can plain tomato sauce
- 2 cups water
- ½ cup fresh cilantro, finely chopped
- ½ teaspoon freshly ground black pepper

**Prep:** Situate pot over medium heat, stir and cook the olive oil, onion, garlic, and salt for 1 minute.
Stir in the okra and cook for 3 minutes.
Add the tomato sauce, water, cilantro, and black pepper; stir, cover, and let cook for 15 minutes, stirring occasionally.
Serve warm.

**Nutrition:** 201 Calories; 4g Protein; 14g Fat

## 822. Tomato Tabbouleh

**Prep time: 6 minutes**  
**Servings 4**  
**Cook time: 30 minutes**

**Ingredients:**
- 8 beefsteak tomatoes
- ½ cup water
- 3 tablespoons olive oil, divided
- ½ cup whole wheat couscous, uncooked
- 1 ½ cups parsley, fresh & minced
- 2 scallions chopped
- 1/3 cup mint, fresh & minced
- sea salt & black pepper to taste
- 1 lemon
- 4 teaspoons honey, raw
- 1/3 cup almonds, chopped

**Prep:** Set oven to 400 °F (200 °C). Take your tomato and slice the top off each one before scooping the flesh out. Put the tops flesh and seeds in a mixing bowl.
Get out a baking dish before adding in a tablespoon of oil to grease it. Place your tomatoes in the dish, and then cover your dish with foil.
Now you will make your couscous while your tomatoes cook. Bring the water to a boil using a saucepan and then add the couscous in and cover. Remove it from heat, and allow it to sit for 5 minutes. Fluff it with a fork.
Chop your tomato flesh and tops up, and then drain the excess water using a colander. Measure a cup of your chopped tomatoes and place them back in the mixing bowl. Mix with mint scallions, pepper, salt and parsley.
Zest lemon, and then half the lemon. Squeeze the lemon juice in, and mix well.
Add your tomato mix to the couscous.
Carefully remove your tomatoes from the oven and then divide your tabbouleh among your tomatoes. Cover the pan with foil and then put it in the oven. Cook for another 8 to 10 minutes.
Drizzle with honey and top with almonds before serving.

**Nutrition:** 314 Calories; 8g Protein; 15g Fat

## 823. Zucchini Lasagna

**Prep time: 13 minutes**  
**Servings 4**  
**Cook time: 45 minutes**

**Ingredients:**
- 2 zucchinis, trimmed
- 1 cup Mozzarella, shredded
- ½ cup tomato sauce
- 1 onion, chopped
- 1 tablespoon olive oil
- ½ cup potato, boiled, mashed
- 1 teaspoon Italian seasonings
- ¼ cup tomato sauce
- 1 teaspoon butter, softened

**Prep:** Heat up olive oil in the skillet. Add onion and roast it until light brown.
Meanwhile, slice the zucchini lengthwise.
Grease the casserole mold with butter from inside. Put ½ part of sliced zucchini in the casserole mold to get the layer.
Then add the layer of cooked onion and a ½ cup of Mozzarella cheese.
After this, make the layer from the remaining zucchini. Top the vegetables with a layer of mashed potatoes and Mozzarella.
Pour the tomato sauce over the cheese and cover the surface of the mold with foil. Secure the edges.
Bake the lasagna for 30 minutes at 365F (185°C).
Then discard the foil and cook lasagna for 10 minutes more.
Serve.

**Nutrition:** 103 Calories; 6.3g Fat; 4.1g Protein

## 824. Zucchini-Eggplant Gratin

**Prep time:** 10 minutes  
**Servings** 6  
**Cook time:** 20 minutes

**Ingredients:**
- 1 large eggplant
- 2 large zucchinis
- ¼ teaspoon black pepper
- ¼ teaspoon kosher or sea salt
- 3 tablespoons extra-virgin olive oil
- 1 tablespoon all-purpose flour
- ¾ cup 2% milk
- 1/3 cup Parmesan cheese
- 1 cup chopped tomato
- 1 cup diced or shredded fresh mozzarella
- ¼ cup fresh basil leaves

**Prep:** Preheat the oven to 425°F.
Mix eggplant, zucchini, pepper, and salt.
Situate skillet over medium-high heat, heat 1 tablespoon of oil. Add half the veggie mixture to the skillet. Stir a few times, then cover and cook for 5 minutes, stirring occasionally. Pour the cooked veggies into a baking dish. Situate skillet back on the heat, add 1 tablespoon of oil, and repeat with the remaining veggies. Add the veggies to the baking dish.
While the vegetables are cooking, heat the milk in the microwave for 1 minute. Set aside.
Place a medium saucepan over medium heat. Add the remaining tablespoon of oil and flour, and whisk together for about 1 minute Slowly pour the warm milk into the oil mixture, whisking the entire time. Add Parmesan cheese, and whisk until melted. Pour the cheese sauce over the vegetables in the baking dish and mix well.
Gently mix in the tomatoes and mozzarella cheese. Roast in the oven for 10 minutes, or until the gratin is almost set and not runny. Garnish with the fresh basil leaves and the remaining 2 tablespoons of Parmesan cheese before serving.

**Nutrition:** 207 Calories; 14g Fat; 11g Protein

## 825. Wrapped Plums

**Prep time:** 5 minutes  
**Servings:** 8

**Ingredients:**
- 2 ounces prosciutto, cut into 16 pieces
- 4 plums, quartered
- 1 tablespoon chives, chopped
- A pinch of red pepper flakes, crushed

**Prep:** Wrap each plum quarter in a prosciutto slice, arrange them all on a platter, sprinkle the chives and pepper flakes all over.

**Nutrition:** Calories 30, Fat 1, Carbs 4, Protein 2

## 826. Tomato Salad

**Prep time:** 15 minutes  
**Servings:** 4

**Ingredients:**
- 8 tomatoes
- ½ cup olive oil
- Oregano to taste
- 2 tablespoons white vinegar
- Salt and pepper to taste

**Prep:** Wash and dry the tomatoes, cut them into wedges and place them in a salad bowl. Pour the oil into a bowl and add: vinegar, pepper, oregano, a pinch of salt, beat everything with a fork. Pour over the tomatoes and mix carefully.

## 827. Turkish Salad

**Prep time:** 30 minutes  
**Servings:** 4  
**Cook time:** 40 minutes

**Ingredients:**
- 2 onions
- 2 peppers
- 1 sprig of parsley
- 3 garlic cloves
- 1 eggplant
- Oregano to taste
- White vinegar
- Olive oil
- Salt and pepper to taste

**Prep:** Wash and dry the peppers; grill, peel and cut into fillets. Rinse the eggplants and remove the stalks. Peel the onions. Slice the vegetables and cook on a hot grill. Once cooked, transfer everything to a serving dish. Season with chopped parsley and garlic and finally a drizzle of oil, oregano, pepper, salt and vinegar.

## 828. Braised Artichokes

**Prep time:** 30 minutes  
**Cook time:** 20 minutes  
**Servings:** 4

**Ingredients:**
- 8 artichokes
- 2 garlic cloves
- Salt and pepper
- Olive oil
- 1 sprig of mint
- 1 sprig of parsley

**Prep:** Wash the artichokes properly and cut off the stalks; turn upside down and tap lightly on a flat surface to enlarge the leaves. Prepare a chopped mixture of: mint, garlic and parsley. Soften with oil and sprinkle with pepper. Salt the artichokes and distribute inside them a little of the previously prepared seasoning, then put them on the grill and roast for 20 minutes. When cooked, remove the outer leaves from the artichokes and serve.

## 829. Fried Artichokes

**Prep time:** 20 minutes  
**Cook time:** 10 minutes  
**Servings:** 4

**Ingredients:**
- 6 artichokes
- Flour to taste
- Salt to taste
- Olive oil
- 1 lemon

**Prep:** Peel the artichokes and remove the outer leaves, cut the artichoke into quarters. Blanch for 5 minutes in salted water acidified with lemon juice; drain and dry with kitchen paper. Finally, fry in plenty of boiling oil; serve immediately. You could pass the artichokes in a layer of flour before frying.

**Nutrition:** Calories 211.6 kcal, Carbs 11.2 g, Protein 6.9 g, Fat 14.2 g

## 830. Artichokes in a Pan

**Prep time:** 15 minutes  
**Cook time:** 30 minutes  
**Servings:** 4

**Ingredients:**
- 8 artichokes
- 1 bunch of parsley
- 2 garlic cloves
- Salt and pepper
- 2 lemons
- Olive oil

**Prep:** Wash the artichokes and remove the outer leaves, beat them lightly on a flat surface and place them, standing upright, in a pan. Sprinkle over the chopped parsley and garlic. Sprinkle with pepper, abundant, and salt, and drizzle with a little oil. Finally pour a little water on the bottom of the casserole and cook for about half an hour.

**Nutrition:** Calories 66.3 kcal, Carbs 3.6 g, Protein 1.6 g, Fat 4.3 g

## 831. Artichokes in a Pan with Lemon

**Prep time:** 40 minutes  
**Cook time:** 30 minutes  
**Servings:** 4

**Ingredients:**
- 8 artichokes
- 1 bunch of parsley
- 2 garlic cloves
- Salt and pepper
- 2 lemons
- Olive oil

**Prep:** Peel the artichokes, cut them in half and remove any hay. Reduce to wedges and plunge into water acidified with the juice of a lemon. Finely chop the parsley and garlic and brown in a pan with oil. Add artichokes drained in part and let them flavor for 5 minutes, always stirring carefully. Season with salt and pepper, cover with a little water acidified with the leftover lemon juice. Cook, covered, for about 20 minutes.

**Nutrition:** Calories 68.3 kcal, Carbs 4.6 g, Protein 6.6 g, Fat 5.3 g

### 832. Fried Thistles

**Prep time:** 30 minutes  
**Servings:** 4  
**Cook time:** 50 minutes

**Ingredients:**
- 3 lb. thistles
- Flour
- 1 lemon
- 3 eggs
- Breadcrumbs
- Olive oil
- Salt and pepper to taste

**Prep:** Clean the cardoons, eliminating the filaments and the harder parts. Cut them into small pieces and soak them in water acidified with lemon juice for about 20 minutes. Drain and boil in abundant salted water for about 40 minutes. Drain and dry with kitchen paper, flour the vegetables and dip them in beaten eggs with a pinch of salt and a pinch of pepper. Finally, dip in breadcrumbs and fry in hot oil.

### 833. Thistles in Batter

**Prep time:** 30 minutes  
**Servings:** 4  
**Cook time:** 50 minutes

**Ingredients:**
- 3 lb. thistles
- 2 cup flour
- 1 lemon
- Salt to taste
- Olive oil

**Prep:** Clean the cardoons and remove the hardest parts and filaments. Cut into pieces and soak in water acidified with lemon juice for about 20 minutes. Drain the vegetables and boil in salted water for half an hour. Drain and pat the cardoons dry with kitchen paper. Prepare a batter with the flour and 2 cups of water; dip the pieces and then put them in plenty of hot oil. When the cardoons are golden brown, remove them from the oil using a slotted spoon to drain off the excess grease and place them on sheets of absorbent paper; season with salt and serve hot.

### 834. Fried Cauliflower

**Prep time:** 10 minutes  
**Servings:** 4  
**Cook time:** 20 minutes

**Ingredients:**
- 1 Cauliflower
- Flour to taste
- Olive oil
- Salt to taste

**Prep:** Thoroughly clean the cauliflower, cut into florets and boil in plenty of boiling salted water. Drain "al dente" and leave to cool. Sift the flour into a large bowl and pour in 2 cups of warm water, season with a pinch of salt. Dip in hot oil. Drain and dry on sheets of paper towels and serve the cauliflower hot.

### 835. Boiled Cauliflower

**Prep time:** 10 minutes  
**Servings:** 4  
**Cook time:** 20 minutes

**Ingredients:**
- 1 Cauliflower
- 1 lemon
- Olive oil
- Salt and pepper to taste

**Prep:** Clean the cardoons, eliminating the filaments and the harder parts; then cut them into small pieces and soak them in water acidified with lemon juice for about 20 minutes. Drain and boil in abundant salted water for about 40 minutes. Drain and dry with kitchen paper, flour the vegetables and dip them in beaten eggs with a pinch of salt and a pinch of pepper. Finally, dip in breadcrumbs and fry in hot oil.

### 836. Baked Onions

**Prep time:** 30 minutes  
**Servings:** 4  
**Cook time:** 50 minutes

**Ingredients:**

- 1 lb. onions
- Olive oil
- Salt and pepper to taste

**Prep:** Peel the onions, wash and boil for about 10 minutes in plenty of salted water. Drain and transfer to a pan greased with oil. Drizzle with a little more oil and sprinkle with pepper. Bake at 350 degrees F for 40 minutes.

## 837. Boiled Onions

**Prep time:** 30 minutes  
**Servings:** 4  
**Cook time:** 40 minutes

**Ingredients:**
- 2 lbs. of onions
- oregano
- Vinegar
- Olive oil
- Salt and pepper to taste

**Prep:** Peel the spring onions, rinse and leave in plenty of boiling salted water for about 40 minutes. Once tender, drain and let cool, season with a drizzle of oil, oregano, pepper and vinegar. Serve the boiled onions.

**Nutrition:** Calories 42.6, Carbs 9.5 g, Protein 2.6 g, Fat 0.4 g

## 838. Mint Beans

**Prep time:** 15 minutes  
**Servings:** 4  
**Cook time:** 1 hour 30 minutes

**Ingredients:**
- 1 lb. shelled beans
- 1 celery rib
- 1 onion
- 1 bay leaf
- 1 bunch of mint
- Vinegar to taste
- Salt, pepper and olive oil to taste

**Prep:** Boil the beans in water with the bay leaf, celery and onion. add salt towards the end of cooking. Drain and season with a drizzle of oil, pepper, mint and vinegar. leave to infuse for at least an hour and then serve.

**Nutrition:** Calories 687.5, Carbs 42.6 g, Protein 34.5 g, Fat 32.6 g

## 839. Stewed Beans

**Prep time:** 20 minutes  
**Servings:** 4  
**Cook time:** 3 hour

**Ingredients:**
- 1 lb. dried beans
- 1 celery rib
- 1 onion
- 1 bay leaf
- 1 lb. tomatoes
- 1 sprig of parsley
- Salt, pepper and olive oil to taste

**Prep:** Let the beans soak for about 12 hours in cold water. Drain and boil with half an onion, celery and bay leaf. Add salt towards the end of cooking. Wilt chopped onion in a pan with a little oil. Add the tomatoes, peeled and chopped with the fingers. Leave to gain flavor for a few minutes. Add the chopped parsley to the beans and their sauce; adjust salt and pepper and cook for 20 minutes over medium heat.

**Nutrition:** Calories 153.1, Carbs 20.4 g, Protein 6.5 g, Fat 4.2 g

## 840. Broad Beans with Onion

**Prep time:** 40 minutes  
**Servings:** 6  
**Cook time:** 20 minutes

**Ingredients:**
- 3 lb. fresh broad beans
- 1 onion
- Olive oil
- Salt and pepper to taste

**Prep:** Shell the broad beans, boil in salted water for 10 minutes. Drain, peel and keep warm. Chop onion finely and brown in a pan with hot oil. Once wilted, add the broad beans. Season with salt and sprinkle with black pepper. Let everything season for 5 minutes, stirring thoroughly with a wooden spoon. Serve as a side dish piping hot.

### 841. Broad Beans and Bacon

**Prep time:** 10 minutes  
**Servings:** 4  
**Cook time:** 25 minutes

**Ingredients:**
- 1 lb. and 6 oz dried beans
- 1/2 onion
- Olive oil
- 4 oz of bacon
- Salt, pepper to taste

**Prep:** Blanch fava beans in salted water for 5 minutes. Wilt the chopped onion, in a pan with boiling oil. Add the diced onion and brown everything for a few minutes, stirring often to even out the cooking. with a wooden spoon. Add the broad beans, season with plenty of pepper and leave to gain flavor for 10 minutes over medium heat.

**Nutrition:** Calories 153.1, Carbs 20.4 g, Protein 6.5 g, Fat 4.2 g

### 842. Mint Broad Beans

**Prep time:** 10 minutes  
**Servings:** 4

**Ingredients:**
- 1 lb. and 6 oz of dried beans
- 1 sprig of fresh mint
- Olive oil
- Vinegar to taste
- Salt, pepper to taste

**Prep:** Put the beans in a salad bowl. finely chop the mint and soften with a dash of oil and vinegar. Add a pinch of salt, sprinkle with pepper and mix everything together thoroughly. Drizzle the beans with the previously prepared dressing and leave to season for about 30 minutes before serving.

**Nutrition:** Calories 286.3, Carbs 2.9 g, Protein 12.6 g, Fat 24.2 g

### 843. Fresh Stewed Broad Beans

**Prep time:** 10 minutes  
**Servings:** 4  
**Cook time:** 25 minutes

**Ingredients:**
- 1 lb. and 6 oz of dried beans
- 1/2 onion
- 9 oz of tomatoes
- 1 sprig of parsley
- Salt, pepper and olive oil to taste

**Prep:** Fry the sliced onion in the oil. then add the broad beans and the tomato chopped up with your fingers and leave to flavor for a few minutes. Adjust salt and pepper, sprinkle with chopped parsley and cook for 20 minutes.

**Nutrition:** Calories 476.3, Carbs 40.2 g, Protein 30.3 g, Fat 22.1 g

### 844. Battered Pumpkin Flowers

**Prep time:** 15 minutes  
**Servings:** 4  
**Cook time:** 5 minutes

**Ingredients:**
- 20 pumpkin flowers
- 1 cup and 2 oz flour
- Olive oil
- Salt, pepper to taste

**Prep:** Clean the zucchini flowers, removing the pistils. Wash, drain and dry with kitchen paper. Sift the flour into a bowl and add enough water to make a fairly soft, but not too runny, batter. Season with salt and pepper. Dip the zucchini flowers in the previously prepared mixture, taking them from the stem. Fry in hot oil. Let excess oil drain off by placing squash blossoms on blotting paper, then serve.

**Nutrition:** Calories 245.9, Carbs 27.5 g, Protein 8.3 g, Fat 10.1 g

### 845. Cutlet Mushrooms

**Prep time:** 15 minutes  
**Servings:** 4  
**Cook time:** 7 minutes

**Ingredients:**
- 2 lb. and 3 oz of mushrooms
- 1 cup of breadcrumbs
- 3 eggs
- 1 sprig of parsley
- Salt, pepper and olive oil to taste

**Prep:** Clean the mushrooms with a damp cloth; remove the stalks and dip the caps in the eggs, beaten, with salt and pepper. Drain and coat in breadcrumbs and chopped parsley. Finally, fry the mushrooms in a frying pan in hot oil; serve.

**Nutrition:** Calories 92.6, Carbs 4.2 g, Protein 3.6 g, Fat 7.5 g

## 846. Grilled Mushrooms

**Prep time: 10 minutes**  **Cook time: 6 minutes**
**Servings: 4**

**Ingredients:**
- 8 big mushroom caps
- 2 garlic cloves
- Olive oil
- 1 sprig of parsley
- Salt, pepper to taste

**Prep:** Thoroughly clean the mushrooms with a damp cloth and brush each mushroom with oil. Cook on a hot grill, turning halfway through cooking. Now, transfer the mushrooms to a large serving platter. Chop the garlic with the parsley. Add 5 tablespoons of oil, a pinch of salt and pepper. Finally, pour the dressing over the mushrooms and serve.

**Nutrition:** Calories 156.3, Carbs 9.6 g, Protein 12.6 g, Fat 4.3 g

# SAUCES, SALSAS AND DRESSINGS

### 847. Anchovy Sauce

**Prep time:** 15 minutes  
**Servings:** 6  
**Cook time:** 5 minutes

**Ingredients:**
- 12 salted anchovies
- 6 tbsp of olive oil

**Prep:** Filet the anchovies and place them under running water. Heat up some oil in a pan and add the anchovies after drying on a cloth. Mash the anchovies with a fork and keep on low heat. In few minutes the sauce will be ready.
Use on boiled fish or meat, hardboiled eggs, fresh salads.

### 848. Garlic Sauce

**Prep time:** 10 minutes  
**Servings:** 6

**Ingredients:**
- 6 garlic cloves
- 1 tbsp of breadcrumbs
- ¼ cup of vinegar

**Prep:** Wet the breadcrumbs with vinegar, then mash in a mortar together with the garlic. When the consistency is smooth add the remaining vinegar. As an option add some oil, a pinch of salt and pepper. Pair the sauce with fish, meat or boiled vegetables.

### 849. Garlic Sauce for Fish

**Prep time:** 10 minutes  
**Servings:** 6

**Ingredients:**
- 20 g di onion
- 1 tbsp of rosemary
- 5 garlic cloves
- 4 tbsp of vinegar
- ¼ cup of water
- 4 tbsp of olive oil
- salt

**Prep:** Mince the onion, rosemary and garlic. Mix well with vinegar, water, oil, salt. Serve as a starter before fish dishes.

### 850. Walnut Cream

**Prep time:** 10 minutes     **Servings:** 6

**Ingredients:**
- 17 oz of walnuts
- 2 tbsp of grated parmesan
- 1 garlic clove
- 2 tbsp of breadcrumbs
- ½ cup of milk
- 5 tbsp of extra virgin olive oil

**Prep:** Boil the walnuts for 5 minutes and wet the breadcrumbs with the milk. Mash the walnuts with the garlic, add the breadcrumbs, mash and add the grated cheese, keep mashing and lastly add the salt. Mix by adding a drizzle of oil to reach a smooth consistency. Add some hot cooking water to dress the pasta.

### 851. Spinach Cream

**Prep time:** 10 minutes     **Cook time:** 40 minutes
**Servings:** 6

**Ingredients:**
- 35 oz of spinach
- 50 g di butter
- 1/4 cup of flour
- 16 oz of milk cream
- salt

**Prep:** Wash the spinach and boil them. Squeeze the excess water and put in a casserole with butter and salt, leave to sizzle. Add the flour a little at a time, mix well on low heat for 30 minutes. Pair the spinach cream with boiled meat, eggs or other dishes.

### 852. Mushroom Sauce

**Prep time:** 10 minutes     **Cook time:** 1 hour e 10 minutes
**Servings:** 6

**Ingredients:**
- 10 oz of fresh mushrooms
- 3 zucchinis
- 2 eggplants
- 1 cup of olive oil
- 2 minced garlic cloves
- 2 tbsp of parsley
- 2 tbsp of oregano
- Salt and pepper

**Prep:** Clean and wash well the fresh mushrooms and let them dry on a cloth. Remove the stems from the base of the eggplants and slice finely. Cut the mushrooms in pieces and the zucchinis into disks. Fry in a pan with some oil the garlic and parsley for few minutes. Add vegetables, oregano, salt and pepper, cover and let cook for about one hour. Use this sauce to season pasta or meat dishes.

### 853. Mushrooms Dressing

**Prep time:** 15 minutes     **Cook time:** 40 minutes
**Servings:** 6

**Ingredients:**
- 17 oz of fresh porcini mushrooms
- 1 garlic clove
- 1 tbsp di rosemary
- 4 tomatoes
- 1 tbsp of butter
- 2 tbsp of olive oil
- Salt and pepper

**Prep:** Clean, wash and cut into pieces the fresh mushrooms. Peel the tomatoes and gut them. Crush the garlic and rosemary and let them sizzle. When the garlic had browned add the mushrooms and let cook for 15 minutes. If the mushrooms should stick to the bottom, add some water. Roughly chop the tomatoes and add them to the mushrooms and salt and pepper. Let cook for 20 minutes. Serve as a side dressing for boiled meat or grills.

### 854. Genovese Pesto

**Prep time:** 10 minutes     **Servings:** 6

**Ingredients:**
- 1 garlic clove
- 2 tbsp di grated parmesan
- 2 tbsp of grated aged pecorino
- 1 tbsp of pine nuts
- 6 tbsp of olive oil
- coarse salt
- ½ cup of basil

**Prep:** Wash and dry the basil leaves. Add to a mortar the garlic and salt, then crush. Put in the basil, pine nuts and cheese. Lastly the oil one drop at the time. Use this pesto to season pasta.

### 855. Genovese Sauce

**Prep time: 10 minutes**  **Servings: 6**

**Ingredients:**
- 3 tbsp of parsley
- 1 tbsp of pine nuts
- 1 garlic clove
- 1 cooked egg yolk
- breadcrumbs
- 1 tbsp of white vinegar
- ½ lemon juiced
- 10 olives with no pit
- 1 tbsp of capers
- 2 salted anchovies
- 5 tbsp olive oil
- salt

**Prep:** Wet the breadcrumbs in vinegar. Rinse the anchovies under running water and filet. Crush all the ingredients in a mortar then add 1 tbsp of vinegar and half cup of oil. Side this sauce with boiled meat.

### 856. Dark Sauce

**Prep time: 10 minutes**  **Cook time: 5 minutes**
**Servings: 6**

**Ingredients:**
- ¾ cup of butter
- Nutmeg
- 33 oz of meat broth
- Salt and pepper
- 1 cup of flour
- 1 clove
- Bay leaf
- Mixed spices
- Onion

**Prep:** on a low heat cook the flour and butter, gently keep mix. When it has browned add the a little minced onion, clove, parsley and after few minutes the hot broth a little at a time.

### 857. Béchamel Sauce

**Prep time: 10 minutes**  **Cook time: 5 minutes**
**Servings: 6**

**Ingredients:**
- ½ cup pf flour
- 16 oz of milk
- ½ cup of butter
- A pinch of salt
- pepper
- nutmeg

**Prep:** in a pan melt the butter, add the flour and dilute with hot milk. Add a pinch of pepper and nutmeg, mix and bring to a boil. Let cook for 3 minutes. This sauce has many uses but can be paired with jacket eggs.

### 858. Tomato Sauce

**Prep time: 10 minutes**  **Cook time: 50 minutes**
**Servings: 6**

**Ingredients:**
- 21 oz of tomatoes
- 1 celery stick
- 1 carrot
- 1 onion
- 1 garlic clove
- 1 tbsp di parsley
- 5 tbsp of olive oil
- 1 tbsp of sugar
- salt

**Prep:** Cut the tomato in pieces as well as the celery, carrot and onion. Boil everything on medium heat. After 20 minutes, mash the vegetables and put the sauce on high heat add in half a cup of oil, 1 tsp of sugar and salt. Mix everything and cook until the sauce thickens. Use as a pasta seasoning.

### 859. Hot Sauce

**Prep time: 15 minutes**  **Servings: 6**

**Ingredients:**
- 2 anchovies
- 1 tsp of minced parsley
- ½ garlic clove
- 2 tbsp of pine nuts
- 1 tbsp of capers
- 2 tbsp breadcrumbs wetted with vinegar
- 5 tbsp olive oil
- 4 tbsp of vinegar
- salt

**Prep:** wash the anchovy filets under running water. Crush in a mortar the garlic, parsley, pine nuts, capers and breadcrumbs. Sift the cream and dilute with vinegar, oil and salt. Use this sauce on Cappon magro, salsify, bean sprouts, cauliflower and fish dishes.

## 860. Sauce for Boiled Dishes

**Prep time:** 5 minutes  **Cook time:** 15 minutes
**Servings:** 6

**Ingredients:**
- 3 hardboiled yolks
- 3 tbsp of vinegar
- 2 tsp of mustard
- ½ cup of capers
- Marjoram
- Parsley
- 2 anchovies canned
- 1 cup of oil
- Salt
- 5 tbsp of olives
- 2 garlic cloves

**Prep:** boil the eggs in water for around 7 minutes. Keep under running water to cool them down. Peel and mince the egg whites, mash the yolks.
Turn on the heat under the oil and butter.
When the oil is sizzling add some dry white wine, marjoram, minced parsley, olives and capers. After few minutes, turn off the heat and dip the anchovies in pieces. Add the crushed yolks.

## 861. Green Sauce with Pine Nuts

**Prep time:** 15 minutes  **Servings:** 6

**Ingredients:**
- ½ cup of pine nuts
- 2 basil bunches
- 1 garlic clove
- 1 anchovy
- 8 tbsp of olive oil
- salt

**Prep:** remove and filet the anchovy. Mash the basil leaves, anchovy filet, pine nuts and garlic in a mortar. Add the oil one drop at a time and some warm water. Adjust the salt if needed when the sauce is ready. Use it to season the cappon magro and boiled cauliflowers.

## 862. Green Sauce with Capers

**Prep time:** 10 minutes  **Servings:** 6

**Ingredients:**
- 2 tbsp of capers
- Olive oil
- Pepper
- 2 tbsp of broth
- 1 tbsp of vinegar
- 1 tsp of mustard
- Parsley
- Salt

**Prep:** Remove the stems and leaves of the parsley and blend with all the other ingredients, withhold the capers.
Taste to adjust salt and vinegar if needed. Add the broth if the sauce is too thick.
Soak the capers in a bowl of water and then combine them in.
Use this sauce as a side for meat and fish.

## 863. Sweet and Sour Sauce

**Prep time:** 10 minutes  **Cook time:** 25 minutes
**Servings:** 6

**Ingredients:**
- 3 ripe tomatoes
- 1 onion
- ½ celery stick
- 1 garlic clove
- 1 cup of olive oil
- 1 zucchini
- ½ cup of vinegar
- 1 tsp of ground mustard
- 2 tbsp of sugar
- salt

**Prep:** Boil the tomato, onion, zucchini and celery. In a pan fry in some oil the garlic and then sift the other ingredients. Add the cream to the pan with the garlic. Add the sugar, vinegar and mustard, let cook for 20 minutes mixing frequently. Serve cold, perfect if paired to boiled meat.

## 864. Red Sauce for Boiled Meat

**Prep time: 10 minutes**
**Servings: 6**
**Cook time: 30 minutes**

**Ingredients:**
- 4 ripe tomatoes
- 1 onion
- 6 garlic cloves
- 1 celery stick
- 1 zucchini
- 1 cup of olive oil
- salt
- pepper

**Prep:** In a pot, boil the onion, 3 pressed garlic cloves, the tomato, celery and zucchini, then sift.
In a pan fry another 3 garlic cloves and the other boiled vegetables. Add the remaining oil and let cook on low heat for 20 minutes. In the end add salt and pepper to taste. Serve this sauce with boiled meat.

## 865.  Snail Sauce

**Prep time: 5 days and 20 minutes**
**Servings: 6**
**Cook time: 2 hours**

**Ingredients:**
- 60 snails
- 1 1/2 cup of bran
- 1 cup of vinegar
- 2 tbsp of bacon
- 1 tbsp of tomato sauce
- ½ onion
- 1 small carrot
- 1 sprig of parsley
- 1 garlic clove
- 3 sage leaves
- 1 sprig of rosemary
- 10g di butter
- Olive oil
- ½ cup of white wine
- salt

**Prep:** purge the snails in 4 inches of bran for 5 days. Boil the water and pour in 1 cup of vinegar. When the water starts to boil, add the snails and simmer for 30 minutes. Then strain the snails and shell them with a toothpick.
Mince the bacon, onion, garlic, sage leaves, rosemary, carrot and parsley and sizzle in oil and butter.
Mince the snails and put them into the tomato sauce, lastly add the fried ingredients, stir and cook for one hour.

## 866.  Lean Sauce

**Prep time: 30 minutes**
**Servings: 6**
**Cook time: 40 minutes**

**Ingredients:**
- 6 ripe tomatoes
- ¼ cup of pine nuts
- 1 onion
- 2 garlic cloves
- 1 ¾ cups of butter
- ½ cup of fresh mushrooms
- 2 anchovies
- 2 tbsp of olive oil
- 1 tbsp di flour
- 1 rosemary sprig

**Prep:** Mince the onion, garlic, anchovy and peel and gut the tomatoes.
Clean the mushrooms and cut in pieces.
Fry the pine nuts in the butter, then add the minced garlic, rosemary, onion and salt.
When the fried mixture is ready add the mushrooms and tomato pulp. Let cook on low heat for 20 minutes. Crush the pine nuts with the flour, dilute the anchovy filets and add to the sauce. Mix and dilute with water needed. Use the sauce to season pasta.

## 867.  Chicken Ragù

**Prep time: 10 minutes**
**Servings: 6**
**Cook time: 2 hours**

**Ingredients:**
- 1 boneless chicken cut in pieces
- 2 cups of olive oil
- 1 herb sprig (bay and parsley)
- 2 finely chopped onions
- 33 oz of tomato sauce
- salt

**Prep:** In a pan, fry the onion with the herbs and some oil. Add the chicken pieces and mix. Pour the wine and let it evaporate. Add the tomato sauce, salt and pepper and keep cooking for a couple of hours on low heat.

## 868.  Herb Sauce

**Prep time: 10 minutes**
**Servings: 6**
**Cook time: 5 minutes**

**Ingredients:**
- 4 carrots
- 3 celery sticks
- 6 basil leaves
- 10 sage leaves
- 2 tbsp of minced parsley
- 1 tsp of rosemary
- 1 1/2 cup of coarse salt

**Prep:** After mincing the vegetables put them in a mason jar with a sealed lid, cover in salt and close for a couple of days. Then open and mix the seasoning for meat and fish grills.

## 869. Apple Sauce

**Prep time: 10 minutes**  **Servings: 6**

**Ingredients:**
- 17 oz of apples (peeled and finely chopped)
- 1 cup of olive oil
- 1 tbsp of saffron pistils
- salt

**Prep:** In a pot, fry in the oil and saffron with a pinch of salt. Add the apples and mix some more and finish cooking. Serve hot with meat dishes.

## 870. Pepper Sauce

**Prep time: 10 minutes**  **Cook time: 1 hour**
**Servings: 6**

**Ingredients:**
- 35 oz of sweet peppers
- 1 1/4 cup of sugar
- 1 tbsp of white wine vinegar
- salt

**Prep:** After washing and cleaning the peppers, blitz them in a blender. In a pan, add the pepper cream, sugar, vinegar and salt. Mix some more and cover with a lid, cook on low heat.

## 871. Cod Sauce

**Prep time: 20 minutes**  **Cook time: 40 minutes**
**Servings: 6**

**Ingredients:**
- 17 oz of cod in pieces
- 2 cups of olive oil
- 1 minced onion
- ½ cup of white wine
- 1 minced garlic clove
- ½ bay leaf
- Thyme
- ½ hot pepper
- 6 canned tomatoes
- Juice of 1 lemon
- Salt and pepper

**Prep:** In a casserole, fry the onion in the oil. When it goldens, add the cod and keep mixing. Add the wine, garlic, thyme, bay and hot pepper and wait for the wine to evaporate. Pour the diced tomatoes, salt and pepper. add the lemon juice and finish cooking.

## 872. Onion Sauce

**Prep time: 5 minutes**  **Cook time: 30 minutes**
**Servings: 6**

**Ingredients:**
- 35 oz of ripe tomatoes
- 35 oz of onions
- 2 cups of wine vinegar
- 1 tbsp of coarse salt

**Prep:** After slicing the onions and tomatoes, layer them in a bowl and cover in salt, leave overnight. Strain the water and pour everything into a pot. Add the vinegar and bring to a boil, mix often.

## 873. Tomato and Guanciale Sauce

**Prep time: 5 minutes**  **Cook time: 15 minutes**
**Servings: 6**

**Ingredients:**
- 35 oz of ripe tomatoes
- 1 pressed garlic clove
- 8 oz of guanciale
- 2 tbsp of grated pecorino
- 1 onion
- Salt
- Olive oil

**Prep:** In a pan, fry in the oil the diced tomatoes and add the garlic. Add the guanciale cubes and a finely chopped onion. Mix some more, add the salt and cook for 15 minutes. Add the grated pecorino. Ideal sauce to side pasta dishes.

## 874. Parsley Sauce

**Prep time:** 10 minutes     **Servings:** 6

**Ingredients:**
- ½ cup of parsley
- ¼ cup of olive oil
- ½ tsp of saffron pistils
- salt

**Prep:** In bowl pour the oil, salt and saffron. Mince the parsley and add it in. mix carefully until the consistency is smooth. Side with fish dishes.

## 875. Egg Sauce

**Prep time:** 5 minutes     **Cook time:** 5 minutes
**Servings:** 6

**Ingredients:**
- 10 egg yolks
- ½ cup of white wine vinegar
- Ground cinnamon
- salt

**Prep:** In a bowl, beat the eggs with vinegar, add the salt and cinnamon. Move the mixture to a pan and let it slightly reduce on low heat.

## 876. Anchovy and Capers Sauce

**Prep time:** 10 minutes     **Servings:** 6

**Ingredients:**
- 2 garlic cloves
- 1 tbsp of pickled capers
- 1 onion
- 2 salted anchovies
- ¼ cup of olive oil
- ½ cup of water
- ¼ cup of breadcrumbs

**Prep:** In a bowl, after mincing the garlic, capers, onion and anchovies, add the oil and mix to reach a smoot consistency.

## 877. Garlic Pesto

**Prep time:** 5 minutes     **Servings:** 6

**Ingredients:**
- ½ cup of basil
- ½ cup of rosemary
- sage leaves
- 1 1/4 cup di coarse salt
- 5 garlic cloves

**Prep:** mince the garlic cloves with basil and rosemary. Crush the salt with a rolling pin on the side. Add the ingredients together. Use to season meat before cooking. Save in sealed lid jars.

## 878. Tomato Salsa

**Prep time:** 15 minutes     **Cook time:** 45 minutes
**Servings:** 6 people

**Ingredients:**
- Ground Salicylic acid
- Salt
- Ripe tomatoes

**Prep:** Cut the tomatoes in half and let them dry in the sun on a tray for some days. Sift to reach a cram consistency. Sprinkle the salicylic acid (1 g for 2 lbs of pulp) and a lot of fine salt. Mix with a wooden spoon and let reduce into a firm sauce, then sift. Pour into glass jars and cover with a lid.

## 879. Mayonnaise

**Prep time: 10 minutes**  **Servings: 6**

**Ingredients:**
- 16 oz of oil
- Salt
- Lemon juice
- 3 egg yolks

**Prep:** In a bowl add the salt, some lemon drops and the yolks. Beat with a whisk in the same direction. After few minutes pour the oil and keep beating. When the mayonnaise thickened add salt and lemon to taste.
Optionally add a tbsp of mustard.

## 880. Marinading

**Prep time: 2 minutes**  **Servings: 6**

**Ingredients:**
- 3 tbsp of olive oil
- 4 garlic cloves
- 33 oz of vinegar
- 2 chopped onions
- Salt
- 3 pepper grains
- Hot pepper

**Prep:** in hot oil, fry the onion, add the vinegar and let marinate. Add the pepper grains, hot pepper and garlic cloves. Use the sauce to marinate fish.

## 881. Beef Ragù

**Prep time: 20 minutes**  **Cook time: 3 hours e 30 minutes**
**Servings: 6**

**Ingredients:**
- 1 cup of guanciale
- 17 oz ground beef meat
- Una celery stick
- 1 carrot
- 1 onion
- 1/4 cup of butter
- Salt and pepper
- 10 oz of tomatoes

**Prep:** mince the celery, carrot and onion. Boil them in a pot with some butter. Crush the guanciale and add it in. add the beef and let cook on low heat for at least one hour. Add the sifted ripe tomatoes and boil for few hours. Serve very hot and use to season the pasta.

## 882. Raw Sauce

**Prep time: 5 minutes**  **Servings: 6**

**Ingredients:**
- 2 hardboiled eggs
- Salt
- 3 egg yolks
- Extra virgin olive oil
- 2 tbsp of balsamic vinegar
- 2 tbsp of capers

**Prep:** Beat the yolks with a whip. Pour the vinegar and keep mixing. Add the minced capers lots of oil, salt and minced hardboiled eggs. Mix until the consistency it thick. Add according to taste the ground mustard or hot sauce.

## 883. Carrot Sauce

**Prep time: 5 minutes**  **Cook time: 10 minutes**
**Servings: 6**

**Ingredients:**

- 16 oz of olive oil
- 2 tbsp of tomato concentrate
- 3 tbsp of vinegar
- 2 tbsp of parsley
- 17 oz of carrots
- Salt
- 1 tbsp of capers

**Prep:** Clean the carrots and fry them in a pan with oil and salt.
After few minutes, add the tomato concentrate, vinegar and keep mixing. At the end, turn off the heat and allow to cool down, sift and pour the sauce into a bowl.
Add the minced capers and parsley, mix some more and serve cool to side boiled dishes or meat.

## 884. Red Sauce with Balsamic Vinegar

**Prep time:** 20 minutes
**Servings:** 6

**Cook time:** 1 hour e 15 minutes

**Ingredients:**
- 1 onion
- 1 celery stick
- Olive oil
- 1 tbsp of balsamic vinegar
- 35 oz of ripe tomatoes
- 3 basil leaves
- 1 tbsp of parsley
- Salt and pepper

**Prep:** Peel and drain the tomatoes.
In a casserole, simmer on low heat the minced tomatoes, onion, celery, basil and parsley. Sift everything and then put back on the heat with oil, adjust salt and pepper to taste. And before turning off the heat add the balsamic vinegar and mix.
Serve warm or cold.

## 885. Boar Sauce

**Prep time:** 30 minutes
**Servings:** 6

**Cook time:** 4 hours e 15 minutes

**Ingredients:**
- 2 tbsp olive oil
- 1 onion
- 17 oz minced boar meat
- 1 cup f meat broth
- 1 tbsp of tomato sauce
- 1 cup of red wine
- 2 juniper berries
- ½ celery stick
- Salt and pepper

**Prep:** Ina pan fry with some oil the onion and celery. Add the mashed juniper berries, boar meat, pour in the wine and deglaze.
Add the broth and tomato sauce and let cook for at least 1 hour, adjust salt and pepper to taste and boil for some hours.

## 886. Grape Sauce

**Prep time:** 2 minutes
**Servings:** 6

**Cook time:** 1 hour e 10 minutes

**Ingredients:**
- 8 oz of flour
- 50 oz of grape must

**Prep:** Filter and boil the grape must in a pan and skim it. After one hour keep mixing with a wooden spoon and add in the flour a little at a time. After few minutes turn off the heat and pour the mixture in small bowls and allow to cool.

# DESSERTS

## 887. Apple Fritters

**Prep time:** 15 minutes  
**Servings:** 6  
**Cook time:** 20 minutes

**Ingredients:**
- 4 apples
- 9 oz of sugar
- 14 oz of flour
- Milk
- 3 eggs
- 2 tbsp of oil
- Salt

**Prep:** Wash, peel and remove the core from the apples. Slice each apple into 8 slices.
On the side prepare the batter: add in a bowl the sugar, flour, oil and eggs. Combine well and pout the needed milk to reach a smooth but not liquid consistency.
Put the slices in the batter and fry into a pan with hot oil.

**Nutrition:** Calories 561, Carbs 57.9 g, Protein 4.6 g, Fat 33.9 g

## 888. Amaretti (Cookies)

**Prep time:** 35 minutes  
**Cook time:** 20 minutes

**Ingredients:**
- 1 1/2 cup of sweet almonds
- 1 1/2 cup of bitter almonds
- 14 oz of confectioner sugar
- 2 egg whites

**Prep:** Boil the almonds to peel them, dry them in the oven and mince them.
Add the egg whites and sugar, whip until the consistency is soft.
Roll out with a rolling pin the pastry and cut out many disks, using the rim of a cup.
Bake the amaretti in a preheated oven at 338°F for 15 minutes. Remove from the oven, let cool and serve.

**Nutrition:** Calories 42.4, Carbs 6.1 g, Protein 1.6 g, Fat 1.7 g

### 889. Long Dessert

**Prep time: 15 minutes**  **Cook time: 45 minutes**

**Ingredients:**
- *35 oz of flour*
- *Peel of 2 lemons*
- *5 eggs and 1 yolk*
- *Salt*
- *Baking powder*
- *2 ¼ cups of sugar*
- *14 tbsp of butter*
- *1 cup of milk*

**Prep:** On a chopping board pour the flour and make a well, pour. Int the softened butter, baking powder, lemon zest, sugar, eggs and a pinch of salt.
Knead until the dough is soft, pack it as if it was a loaf of bread. First cooking, slice the top vertically and rest under a cloth for one hour. Brush the top with the egg yolk and sprinkle some sugar. Put in a preheated oven at 350°F, for half an hour.

### 890. Family Cookies

**Prep time: 20 minutes**  **Cook time: 15 minutes**

**Ingredients:**
- *4 ½ cups of flour*
- *¼ cup of vanilla flavored sugar*
- *1 cup of butter*
- *1 cup of confectioner sugar*
- *1 cup of milk*
- *2 tsp og ground ammonia*
- *Salt*

**Prep:** On a chopping board pour the flour and make a well, add the ammonia a pinch of salt, milk, sugar, butter and vanilla flavored sugar. Mix well to reach a firm and smooth dough. Roll out with a rolling pin in a thick layer.
Cut the dough in strips and then in chucks; place on a tray lined with flour and bake at 350°F for 15 minutes.

### 891. Ring Cookies

**Prep time: 10 minutes**  **Cook time: 30 minutes**

**Ingredients:**
- *17 oz of flour*
- *21 oz of sugar*
- *15 egg yolks*
- *Zest of 2 lemons*
- *Flour*
- *Butter*

**Prep:** In a big bowl, whisk the sugar and yolks, add in slowly the flour and the lemon zest.
Stretch the dough to form a snake shape about 5 inch long and roll the ends of each piece. Grease a pan with butter, sprinkle some flour, place the cookies and bake at 350°F for about 30 minutes.

### 892. Baked Doughnuts

**Prep time: 30 minutes**  **Cook time: 15 minutes**

**Ingredients:**
- *35 oz of flour*
- *Milk*
- *3 eggs*
- *Lard*
- *1 1/2 cup of sugar*
- *Half pack of baking powder*
- *1 egg white*
- *Nutmeg*
- *One small cup of aniseed*

**Prep:** On a chopping board pour the flour and make a well, pour the ingredients and lastly the milk. Knead to reach a smooth and firm dough. Stretch the dough to form a snake shape about 5 inch long and roll the ends of each piece. Fry in lard first then bake at 350°F.

### 893. Lemon Pudding

**Prep time: 30 minutes**  **Cook time: 25 minutes**

**Ingredients:**
- *Juice of 6 lemons*
- *6 eggs*
- *3 shots of Alchermes*
- *3 ½ cups of sugar*

**Prep:** Combine the sugar and lemon juice in a bowl overnight.
Whisk the eggs with a whip, add the marinated sugar and the liquor. Keep mixing.
In a stamp pour some sugar and melt on low heat to caramelize it and coat the sides.
Pour the mixture and bake for 25 minutes on medium heat.
Remove the stamp from the oven, let it cool and put the pudding in the fridge for some hors before serving.

**Nutrition:** Calories 181, Carbs 29.1 g, Protein 4.2 g, Fat 5.3 g

## 894. Breadcrumbs Dessert

**Prep time:** 20 minutes  
**Servings:** 6  
**Cook time:** 2 hours

**Ingredients:**
- 33 oz of milk
- 1/2 tsp of baking soda
- 3 eggs
- Butter
- Zest of 1 lemon
- ¾ cup of butter
- 10 oz of sugar
- Breadcrumbs

**Prep:** Beat the eggs and sugar with a whisk.
In a pan, melt the butter, turn off the heat and add the milk, lemon zest, soda and mix with a wooden spoon.
Add the whisked eggs and mix to reach a smooth mixture. Grease a pan and sprinkle breadcrumbs, the pour the batter. Bake the tray at 350°F for 2 hours until a golden crust forms.

## 895. Batter Dessert

**Prep time:** 10 minutes  
**Cook time:** 15 minutes

**Ingredients:**
- 9 oz of white flour
- 9 oz of yellow flour
- Salt
- sugar
- Extra virgin olive oil

**Prep:** In a bowl, mix the flour, the n 3-4 cups of warm water, add salt and mix to create the batter.
On the stove, heat a pan and scoop the batter, flip and cook evenly on both sides.
When it is ready, marinate in a serving plate and drizzle oil and sugar.
Serve hot or warm.

## 896. Milk Dessert

**Prep time:** 5 minutes  
**Cook time:** 20 minutes

**Ingredients:**
- 33 oz of whole milk
- Lemon juice
- lard
- 8 oz of breadcrumbs

**Prep:** Boil the milk with the breadcrumbs and lemon juice. Grease a pan with lard and pour the batter. Bake at 350°F for about 20 minutes.
Serve sliced and warm.

## 897. Ricotta and Coffee Dessert

**Prep time:** 20 minutes

**Ingredients:**
- 17 oz of ricotta
- 1 cup of chopped dark chocolate
- 4 tbsp of toasted almonds
- Coffee
- 1 ¾ cup of sugar
- One pack of vanilla extract
- Rum
- 3/4 cup of diced citron rolled in sugar
- 8 oz of savoiardi biscuits

**Prep:** Mix the ricotta and sugar in a bowl, add all the other ingredients.

Cover the sides of a mold with the savoiardi, soak them in the rum and coffee, pour the mixture and cover with other biscuits. Put in the fridge for some hours before serving. Take a few minutes of the fridge before enjoying.

**Nutrition:** Calories 238, Carbs 35.4 g, Protein 5.2 g, Fat 6.5 g

### 898. Carnival Dessert

**Prep time: 20 minutes**                                           **Cook time: 20 minutes**

**Ingredients:**
- 17 oz of flour
- Salt
- 5 eggs
- Lard
- Sugar

**Prep:** On a chopping board pour the flour and make a well, add the eggs, a pinch of lard, a pinch of salt and knead for a soft and firm dough.
Let rise in a bowl covered by a cloth in a warm place for at least 2 hours.
Roll out the dough to forma snake shape the size of a finger; cut out some chunks.
In a pan fry the lard and pour the chunks. Then strain and place on a paper towel, sprinkle some sugar.

**Nutrition:** Calories 620.4, Carbs 36.5 g, Protein 6.6 g, Fat 45.9 g

### 899. Doughnut

**Prep time: 15 minutes**                                           **Cook time: 45 minutes**

**Ingredients:**
- 9 oz of flour
- 9 oz of butter
- 10 eggs
- 9 oz of sugar
- 2 lemons
- Ground sugar
- Caramelized sugar
- 10 egg yolks

**Prep:** Ground the zest and put aside.
On a chopping board pour the flour and make a well, pour the eggs, softened butter, sugar, yolks and then the lemon juice. Knead well for a smooth and firm dough.
Grease a mold and pour in the mixture, bake in a preheated oven at 338°F for 45 minutes, then brush on the caramelized sugar and lemon zest. Cool down and serve sliced.

**Nutrition:** Calories 514.2, Carbs 52.1 g, Protein 14.2 g, Fat 24.3 g

### 900. Crunchy Almond Bar

**Prep time: 10 minutes**                                           **Cook time: 30 minutes**

**Ingredients:**
- 10 oz of almonds
- 4 tbsp of butter
- Oil
- 2 ¾ cups of sugar

**Prep:** Melt the butter in a casserole, add the almonds and sugar. Mix with a wooden spoon until the sugar has melted and caramelizes. Grease a surface and pour the mixture with a greased spatula.
When it cools down, cut into squares.
Remove from the surface, put the chunks in a serving dish and enjoy.

**Nutrition:** Calories 420, Carbs 45.6 g, Protein 8.5 g, Fat 25.6 g

### 901. Easter Cake

**Prep time: 40 minutes**                                           **Cook time: 1 hour**

**Ingredients:**
- 66 oz of flour
- 2 packs of vanilla extract
- 10 eggs
- Zest of 3 lemons
- raisins
- 35 oz of risen dough

- *42 oz of sugar*
- *Salt*
- *Brewer's yeast*
- *1 1/2 cup of lard*

**Prep:** On a chopping board pour the flour and make a well, add the risen dough and all the other ingredients. Knead to reach a mixture smooth and soft. Form into a dome. Cover with a cloth and let rise for few hours.
Brush the top with the beaten eggs and slice a cross, bake at 350°F for 1 hour

## 902.  Puff Pastry

**Prep time: 10 minutes**  **Cook time: 20 minutes**

**Ingredients:**
- *1 cup of flour*
- *8 oz of butter*
- *4 tbsp of vanilla flavored sugar*
- *10 gr of potato starch*
- *3 eggs*
- *4 egg yolks*
- *12 1/2 tbsp of sugar*
- *Ground ammonia*

**Prep:** Whisk the eggs with sugar in a bowl, add the softened butter and keep kneading.
Add the flour and combine well.
Grease a tray and pour in some flour, sprinkle the ammonia and bake 350°F for 20 minutes.

**Nutrition:** Calories 440, Carbs 54.7 g, Protein 5.6 g, Fat 19.8 g

## 903.  Dried Fruit Cake

**Prep time: 30 minutes**  **Cook time: 30 minutes**

**Ingredients:**
- *14 oz o flour*
- *3 minced walnuts*
- *4 tbsp olive oil*
- *1 1/2 cup of sugar*
- *1 pack of baking soda*
- *1 cup of red wine*
- *1 tbsp of minced almonds*
- *1 tbsp of pine nuts*
- *1 beaten yolk*
- *Salt*

**Prep:** On a chopping board pour the flour and make a well, add the wine, baking powder, oil and sugar and gently knead.
Grease a mold and put in the dough, sprinkle on the minced walnuts, pine nuts and almonds.
Brush on an egg yolk. Bake at 350°F, for at least half an hour.
Serve warm.

**Nutrition:** Calories 447, Carbs 63.6 g, Protein 5.9 g, Fat 18.6 g

## 904.  Sweet Salami

**Prep time: 30 minutes**  **Cook time: 5 minutes**

**Ingredients:**
- *17 oz of dried biscuits*
- *1 egg*
- *2 tbsp of butter*
- *2 1/2 tbsp of cacao powder*
- *17 oz of sugar*
- *1 shot of bitter almond liquor*

**Prep:** Crush the biscuits.
Soften the butter next to a hot spot and pour it in the casserole, add the cacao, egg, crushed biscuits, sugar, liquor, lay on an aluminum foil. Roll the mixture as a salami and harden in the fridge.
Take out of the foil and serve cold.

**Nutrition:** Calories 525, Carbs 74.4 g, Protein 5.2 g, Fat 21.8 g

## 905.  Almond and Liquor Cake

**Prep time: 5 minutes**  **Cook time: 50 minutes**

**Ingredients:**
- *9 oz of flour*
- *9 oz of butter*
- *9 oz of sugar*

- *8 oz of peeled almonds*
- *1 cup of liquor*
- *2 yolks*
- *½ pack of vanilla flavored sugar*

**Prep:** Mince the almonds. Lay on a chopping bord the flour and make a well, add sugar, melted butter, yolks and liquor, minced almonds, knead for some minutes.
Pour the dough in a greased pan, bake at 350°F for 50 minutes.

**Nutrition:** Calories 590.5, Carbs 54.2 g, Protein 15.4 g, Fat 32.6 g

### 906. Raisin and Rum Cake

**Prep time: 30 minutes**                                                                 **Cook time: 50 minutes**

**Ingredients:**
- *10 oz of flour*
- *4 tbsp of raisins soaked in rum*
- *1 shot of rum*
- *1 ½ cup of butter*
- *5 eggs*
- *Salt*
- *10 oz of sugar*

**Prep:** In a big bowl, beat the yolks and sugar with a whisk. Mix well and add the raisins, beaten egg whites into soft peaks and mix well.
Grease a pan and pour the mixture in a preheated oven at 350°F, for 50 minutes.
Serve cold.

**Nutrition:** Calories 610, Carbs 85.6 g, Protein 15.6 g, Fat 24.5 g

### 907. Almond Cake

**Prep time: 20 minutes**                                                                 **Cook time: 40 minutes**

**Ingredients:**
- *14 oz of sugar*
- *3/4 cup of butter*
- *5 egg yolks*
- *10 oz of flour*
- *11 oz of almonds*
- *Butter*
- *Milk*
- *1 pack of baking powder*

**Prep:** Toast the almonds into boiling water, to remove the skin and dry with a cloth.
Beat the yolks and sugar in a bowl with a whisk add the softened butter, baking powder and mix, lastly add the almonds and baking soda. Miz with a wooden spoon for a smooth consistency (if needed add some drops of milk).
Pour the mixture in a greased cake mold and bake at 350°F for 40 minutes, until golden.
Serve warm or cold.

**Nutrition:** Calories 451, Carbs 36.6 g, Protein 7.8 g, Fat 29.7 g

### 908. Prune Cake

**Prep time: 25 minutes**                                                                 **Cook time: 1 hour**

**Ingredients:**
- *14 oz of flour*
- *1 1/2 cup of sugar*
- *2 eggs*
- *1 ¾ cups of butter*
- *1 pack of baking powder*
- *1 ¾ cups of prunes with no pit*
- *Crushed dry biscuits*

**Prep:** Arrange the flour open on a cutting board and make a well; add the softened butter, then the eggs, sugar and yeast and knead.
Roll out the mixture with a rolling pin, divide into two parts, with the first, line the bottom of the greased pan; arrange the chopped plums and the crushed biscuits; cover with the other half of the dough, meet the edges.
Bake in a preheated oven at 350 ° F for one hour.
Serve warm or cold, cut into wedges.

**Nutrition:** Calories 436, Carbs 52 g, Protein 8.9 g, Fat 20.7 g

### 909. Italian Style Pumpkin Pie

**Prep time:** 10 minutes  
**Cook time:** 50 minutes

**Ingredients:**
- 35 oz baked pumpkin
- 1 1/2 cup of sugar
- 3 eggs
- 8 oz r di flour
- Salt
- Cinnamon
- 1 shot of grappa
- 1 pack of baking powder
- 9 oz of crushed amaretti
- 3 tbsp of liquid cream

**Prep:** Clean the peel of the pumpkin, sift the pulp, soak with flour and very little salt.
In a bowl, whisk the egg yolks, add the sugar, cinnamon, pour the liquid cream, then the yeast and finally the pumpkin flour mixture. Also add the shot of grappa and the crushed amaretti. Knead carefully, add the beaten egg whites and continue to mix. Grease the walls of a low and wide pan, sprinkle with a little flour, pour the mixture and put in a preheated oven at 350 ° F for half an hour. Remove from the oven as soon as the cake is golden and dry.
Serve warm or cold cut into wedges.

**Nutrition:** Calories 510, Carbs 33.7 g, Protein 8.6 g, Fat 33.8 g

### 910. Cherry Soup

**Prep time:** 30 minutes  
**Cook time:** 30 minutes

**Ingredients:**
- 35 oz of cherries
- Half lemon peeled
- Sponge cake slices
- 2 1/2 tbsp of sugar
- ½ cup of sugar (to sprinkle on)
- 9 oz of dark chocolate
- 1/4 cup of butter

**Prep:** Remove the bone from the cherries, cook them in a saucepan with the sugar, a cup of water and the lemon zest. After half an hour the cherries will be cooked.
In a bowl, line the walls with slices of sponge cake, soaked in syrup, then alternate the layers of cherries with slices of sponge cake, like this until the end.
In a separate saucepan, melt the sugar in very little water; add the chocolate and melt. Remove from the heat and add the butter, mix and finally pour over the last layer of sponge cake. Refrigerate for 2-3 hours before serving.

**Nutrition:** Calories 190, Carbs 34.5 g, Protein 5.2 g, Fat 6.8 g

### 911. Apple and Berries Ambrosia

**Prep Time:** 15 minutes  
**Serving:** 4

**Ingredients:**
- 2 cups unsweetened coconut milk, chilled
- 2 tablespoons raw honey
- An apple, peeled, cored, and chopped
- 2 cups fresh raspberries
- 2 cups fresh blueberries

**Prep:** Spoon the chilled milk in a large bowl, then mix in the honey. Stir to mix well.
Then mix in the remaining ingredients. Stir to coat the fruits well and serve immediately.

**Nutrition:** 386 Calories, 21.1 g Fat, 4.2 g Protein

### 912. Baked Ricotta & Pears

**Prep Time:** 15 minutes  
**Servings:** 4  
**Cook Time:** 30 minutes

**Ingredients:**
- ¼ cup White whole wheat flour
- 1 tbsp. Sugar
- ¼ tsp. Nutmeg
- Ricotta cheese (1 cup)
- 16 oz. container whole-milk
- 2 Large eggs
- 1 Diced pear
- 2 tbsp. Water
- 1 tsp. Vanilla extract
- 1 tbsp. Honey
- Also Needed: 4 - 6 oz. ramekins

**Prep:** Warm the oven to 400°F.
Lightly spritz the ramekins with a cooking oil spray.
Whisk the flour, nutmeg, sugar, vanilla, eggs, and ricotta together in a large mixing container.
Spoon the fixings into the dishes. Bake them for 20 to 25 minutes or until they're firm and set. Transfer them to the countertop and wait for them to cool.
In a saucepan, using the medium temperature setting, toss the pear into the water for about ten minutes until its slightly softened. Take the pan from the burner and stir in the honey.
Serve the ricotta ramekins with the warm pear when it's ready.

**Nutrition:** Calories 312, Protein: 17 g, Fat: 17 g

## 913. Banana Cinnamon Fritters

**Prep Time:** 15 minutes  **Cook Time:** 6 minutes
**Serving:** 4

**Ingredients:**
- 1 cup self-rising flour
- 1 egg, beaten
- 3/4 cup sparkling water
- 2 tsp. ground cinnamon
- 2-3 bananas, cut diagonally into 4 pieces each

**Prep:** Sift flour and cinnamon into a bowl and make a well in the center. Add egg and enough sparkling water to mix to a smooth batter.
Heat sunflower oil in a saucepan, enough to cover the base by 1-2 inch, so when a little batter dropped into the oil sizzles and rises to the surface. Dip banana pieces into the batter, then fry for 2-3 minutes or until golden. Pull out with a slotted spoon and drain on paper towels.

**Nutrition:** 209 Calories, 10 g Fat, 2 g Protein

## 914. Caramel Popcorn

**Prep Time:** 30 minutes  **Cook Time:** 1 hour
**Servings:** 20

**Ingredients:**
- 2 cups brown sugar
- 1/2 cup of corn syrup
- 1/2 teaspoon baking powder
- 1 teaspoon vanilla extract
- 5 cups of popcorn
- 1 cup of butter
- 1 tsp. salt

**Prep:** Preheat the oven to 250° F. Put the popcorn in a large bowl.
Melt butter in a pan over medium heat. Stir in brown sugar, salt, and corn syrup. Bring to a boil, and cook (without stirring) for 4 minutes. Then remove from heat and stir in the vanilla. Pour in a thin layer on the popcorn and stir well.
Place in two large shallow baking tins and bake in the preheated oven, stirring every 15 minutes for an hour. Remove from the oven and let cool completely before breaking into pieces.

**Nutrition:** 253 Calories, 32.8 g Carbs, 14 g Fat

## 915. Creamy Peach Smoothie

**Prep Time:** 15 minutes  **Servings:** 2

**Ingredients:**
- 2 cups packed frozen peaches, partially thawed
- ½ ripe avocado
- ½ cup plain or Greek yogurt
- 2 tablespoons flax meal
- 1 tablespoon honey
- 1 teaspoon orange extract
- 1 teaspoon extract

**Prep:** Place all the ingredients in a blender and blend until completely mixed and smooth.
Divide the mixture into two bowls and serve immediately.

**Nutrition:** Calories: 212 Fat: 13.1 g Protein: 6 g Carbs: 22.5 g

## 916. Blueberry Smoothie

**Prep Time:** 5 minutes

**Servings:** 1

**Ingredients:**
- 1 cup unsweetened almond milk
- ¼ cup frozen blueberries
- 2 tablespoons unsweetened almond butter
- 1 tablespoon extra-virgin olive oil
- 1 tablespoon ground flaxseed or chia seeds
- 1 to 2 teaspoons maple syrup
- ½ teaspoon extract
- ¼ teaspoon ground cinnamon

**Prep:** Blend all the ingredients in a blender until smooth and creamy.

**Nutrition:** Calories: 459 Fat: 40.1 g Protein: 8.9 g Carbs: 20 g

## 917. Red Quinoa Peach Porridge

**Prep Time:** 10 minutes
**Servings:** 1

**Cook Time:** 30 minutes

**Ingredients:**
- ¼ cup old fashioned rolled oats
- ¼ cup red quinoa
- ½ cup milk
- 1 ½ cups water
- 2 peaches, peeled and sliced

**Prep:** On a small saucepan, place the peaches and quinoa. Add water and cook for 30 minutes. Add the oatmeal and milk last and cook until the oats become tender. Stir occasionally to avoid the porridge from sticking on the bottom of the pan.

**Nutrition:** Calories: 456.6; Carbs: 77.3 g; Protein: 16.6 g; Fat: 9 g

## 918. Walnuts Yogurt Dip

**Prep time:** 5 minutes

**Servings:** 8

**Ingredients:**
- 3 garlic cloves, minced
- 2 cups Greek yogurt
- ¼ cup dill, chopped
- 1 tablespoon chives, chopped
- ¼ cup walnuts, chopped
- Salt and black pepper to taste

**Prep:** In a bowl, mix the garlic with the yogurt and the rest of the ingredients, and whisk well. Divide into small cups and serve as a party dip.

**Nutrition:** Calories 200, Fat 6.5 g, Carbs 15.5 g, Protein 8.4 g

## 919. Yogurt Dip

**Prep time:** 10 minutes

**Servings:** 6

**Ingredients:**
- 2 cups Greek yogurt
- 2 tablespoons pistachios, toasted and chopped
- A pinch of salt and white pepper
- 2 tablespoons mint, chopped
- 1 tablespoon kalamata olives, pitted and chopped
- ¼ cup za'atar spice
- ¼ cup pomegranate seeds
- 1/3 cup olive oil

**Prep:** In a bowl, combine the yogurt with the rest of the ingredients, and whisk well. Divide into cups and serve with pita chips on the side.

**Nutrition:** Calories 294, Fat 18g, Carbs 21g, Protein 10g

## 920. Apples and Plum Cake

**Prep time:** 10 minutes
**Servings:** 4

**Cook time:** 40 minutes

**Ingredients:**
- 7 oz. almond flour
- 1 egg, whisked
- 5 tbsps. stevia
- 2 oz. warm almond milk
- 3 pounds plums, pitted and cut into quarters

- 2 apples, cored and chopped
- Zest of 1 lemon, grated
- 1 tsp. baking powder

**Prep:** In a bowl, mix all ingredients and whisk well.
Grease a cake pan with the oil, pour cake mix inside, place in the oven, and bake at 350°F for fourty minutes.
Cool, slice, and serve.

**Nutrition:** Calories 209, Fat: 6.4g, Carbs: 8g, Protein: 6.6g

## 921. Banana Shake Bowls

**Prep time: 5 minutes**      **Servings: 4**

**Ingredients:**
- 4 medium bananas, peeled
- 1 avocado, peeled, pitted and mashed
- ¾ cup almond milk
- ½ tsp. vanilla extract

**Prep:** In a blender, combine all ingredients, pulse, divide into bowls and keep in the fridge until serving.

**Nutrition:** Calories 185, Fat: 4.3g, Carbs: 6g, Protein: 6.45g

## 922. Blackberry and Apples Cobbler

**Prep time: 10 minutes**      **Cook time: 30 minutes**
**Servings: 6**

**Ingredients:**
- ¾ cup stevia
- 6 cups blackberries
- ¼ cup apples, cored and cubed
- ¼ tsp. baking powder
- 1 tbsp. lime juice
- ½ cup almond flour
- ½ cup water and ½ tbsp. avocado oil
- Cooking spray

**Prep:** In a bowl, mix berries with lemon juice and half of the stevia, sprinkle with flour, whisk and pour into a baking dish greased with cooking spray.
In another bowl, mix flour with baking powder, the rest of the stevia, oil and water, and mix everything together with your hands.
Spread over the berries, place in the oven at 375°F and bake for 30 minutes.
Serve warm.

**Nutrition:** Calories 221, Fat: 6.3g, Carbs: 6g, Protein: 9g

## 923. Black Tea Cake

**Prep time: 10 minutes**      **Cook time: 35 minutes**
**Servings: 8**

**Ingredients:**
- 6 tbsps. black tea powder
- 2 cups almond milk, warmed up
- 1 cup avocado oil
- 2 cups stevia
- 3 eggs
- 2 tsps. vanilla extract
- ½ cups almond flour
- 1 tsp. baking soda
- 3 tsps. baking powder

**Prep:** In a bowl, combine all ingredients and whisk well.
Pour everything into a cake pan lined with baking paper, place in the oven at 350°F and bake for 35 minutes.
Allow the cake to cool, cut into slice and serve.

**Nutrition:** Calories 200, Fat: 6.4g, Carbs: 6.5g, Protein: 5.4g

## 924. Cherry Cream

**Prep time: 2 hours**      **Servings: 4**

**Ingredients:**
- 2 cups cherries, pitted and chopped
- 1 cup almond milk
- ½ cup whipping cream
- 2 eggs, whisked
- 1/3 cup stevia
- 1 tsp. lemon juice
- ½ tsp. vanilla extract

**Prep:** In your food processor, combine all ingredients, pulse well, divide into cups and keep in the fridge for 2 hours before servings.

**Nutrition:** Calories 200, Fat: 4.5g, Carbs: 5.6g, Protein: 3.4g

## 925. Cocoa Brownies

**Prep time:** 10 minutes  **Cook time:** 20 minutes
**Servings:** 8

**Ingredients:**
- 30 oz. canned lentils, rinsed and drained
- 1 tbsp. honey
- 1 banana, peeled and chopped
- ½ tsp. baking soda
- 4 tbsps. almond butter
- 2 tbsps. cocoa powder
- Cooking spray

**Prep:** In your food processor, combine all ingredients (except the cooking spray) and pulse well.
Pour everything into a pan greased with cooking spray, spread evenly, introduce in the oven at 375°F and bake for 20 minutes. Cut the brownies and serve cold.

**Nutrition:** Calories 200, Fat: 4.5g, Carbs: 8.7g, Protein: 4.3g

## 926. Cold Lemon Squares

**Prep time:** 30 minutes  **Servings:** 4

**Ingredients:**
- 1 cup avocado oil + a drizzle
- 2 bananas, peeled and chopped
- 1 tbsp. honey
- ¼ cup lemon juice
- A pinch of lemon zest, grated

**Prep:** In a food processor, combine all ingredients, pulse well and spread on the bottom of a pan greased with a drizzle of oil. Introduce in the fridge for 30 minutes, slice into squares and serve.

**Nutrition:** Calories 136, Fat: 11.2g, Carbs: 7g, Protein: 1.1g

## 927. Glazed Mediterranean Puffy Fig

**Prep time:** 5 minutes  **Cook time:** 25 minutes
**Servings:** 8

**Ingredients:**
- 2 sheets (from 1 pack of 4 sheets) puff pastry
- 20 figs or dry figs (dry or fresh)
- 8 oz. mascarpone cheese
- 2 tbsps. butter
- ½ cup (or 8 tbsps.) honey
- ½ tsp. cinnamon
- ½ tsp. nutmeg
- ¼ tsp. salt
- 4 mint leaves, for garnish

**Prep:** Preheat the oven 400°F.
Slice the puff pastry into triangle and place into a nonstick baking sheet; bake for about 15-20 minutes or until golden brown. When bakes, remove from the oven and allow to cool.
If using dry figs, rehydrate for 1 hour and then cut into half. Put the butter into a nonstick pan over medium flame or heat. Add the figs; cook for about 3 to 5 minutes. Add the honey, salt, cinnamon, and nutmeg; cook, stirring, for about 3 minutes. Remove the skillet from hat and allow to cool for about 5 to 10 minutes.
Place a baked pastry slice in a serving plate, top with 1 tbsp. of cheese, some figs, and then drizzle with the glaze. Repeat the topping, if desired. Garnish with the mint leaves and serve.

**Nutrition:** Calories 486, Fat: 22.8g, Carbs: 67.4g, Protein: 7.9g

## 928. Figs Pie

**Prep time:** 10 minutes  **Cook time:** 1 hour
**Servings:** 8

**Ingredients:**
- ½ cup stevia
- 6 figs, cut into quarters
- ½ tsp. vanilla extract

- 1 cup almond flour
- 4 eggs, whisked

**Prep:** Spread the figs on the bottom of a spring form pan lined with baking paper.
In a bowl, combine the other ingredients, whisk, and pour over the figs.
Bake at 375°F for 1 hour, flip the pie upside down when it's done and serve.

**Nutrition:** Calories 200, Fat: 4.4g, Carbs: 7.6g, Protein: 8g

## 929. Greek Cheesecake

**Prep time:** 1 hour, 20 minutes  
**Cook time:** 30 minutes  
**Servings:** 8-10

**Ingredients:**
- 4 eggs
- 250g whole-wheat digestive cookies
- 125g butter, melted
- ½ tsp. cinnamon
- ½ cup sugar
- ½ cup honey
- 1 tsp. vanilla extract
- 1 tsp. lemon zest
- 1 kg ricotta cheese

**For topping:**
- 750g black cherries, pitted
- 2 leaves gelatin
- 300g sugar

**Prep:** Process the digestive biscuits in a food processor until crumbled. Add the butter and cinnamon, process again until the mixture is like wet sand in texture. Press the mixture into a 20-cm spring-form tin, pressing some of the mixture up the sides of the tin to make a ridge. Refrigerate until ready to use.
Preheat the oven to 375°F.
With an electric mixer, beat the cheese and sugar together until creamy. One by one, add in the eggs, the lemon zest, the vanilla extract, and honey. Pour the cheese mixture over the refrigerated biscuit base.
Place the spring-form tin in the oven and with the oven door ajar, bake for 30 minutes or until firm. Remove the cake from the oven and let cool.
Meanwhile prepare the cherries. Place the gelatin leaves in a bowl with cold water, soak until soft. Put the sugar and the pitted cherries into a frying pan, heat over high flame or hear; stew for about 6 minutes or until the cherries release their juices. Add in the softened gelatins; stir well until well mixed. Remove the pan from the heat and let cool for a bit. When slightly cool, pour over the cooled cheesecake.
Refrigerate until the cherry topping set. Serve cold.

**Nutrition:** Calories 561, Fat: 19.9g, Carbs: 80.5g, Protein: 18.8g

## 930. Almond Rice Dessert

**Prep time:** 10 minutes  
**Cook time:** 20 minutes  
**Servings:** 4

**Ingredients:**
- 1 cup white rice
- 2 cups almond milk
- 1 cup almonds, chopped
- ½ cup stevia
- 1 tbsp. cinnamon powder
- ½ cup pomegranate seeds

**Prep:** In a pot, stir the rice with stevia and milk, bring to a simmer, and cook for 20 minutes.
Add the rest of the ingredients, whisk, divide into bowls, and serve.

**Nutrition:** Calories 234, Fat: 9.5g, Carbs: 12.4g, Protein: 6.5g

## 931. Apple Couscous Pudding

**Prep time:** 10 minutes  
**Cook time:** 25 minutes  
**Servings:** 4

**Ingredients:**
- ½ cup couscous
- ½ cups milk
- ¼ cup apple, cored and chopped
- 2 tbsps. stevia
- ½ tsp. rose water
- 1 tbsp. orange zest, grated

**Prep:** Heat a skillet with the milk over medium heat, add the rest of the ingredients, whisk, simmer for 25 minutes, divide into bowls and serve.

**Nutrition:** Calories 151, Fat: 3.9g, Carbs: 7.5g, Protein: 4g

## 932. Banana Cinnamon Cupcakes

**Prep time:** 10 minutes  
**Servings:** 4  
**Cook time:** 20 minutes

**Ingredients:**
- 4 tbsps. avocado oil
- 4 eggs
- ½ cup orange juice
- 2 tsps. cinnamon powder
- 1 tsp. vanilla extract
- 2 bananas, peeled and chopped
- ¾ cup almond flour
- ½ tsp. baking powder
- Cooking spray

**Prep:** In a bowl, add all ingredients except the cooking spray, whisk well, pour in a cupcake pan greased with the cooking spray, introduce in the oven at 350°F and bake for 20 minutes.
Cool the cupcakes and serve.

**Nutrition:** Calories 142, Fat: 5.8g, Carbs: 5.7g, Protein: 1.6g

## 933. Bananas Foster

**Prep time:** 5 minutes  
**Servings:** 4  
**Cook time:** 5 minutes

**Ingredients**
- 2/3 cup dark brown sugar
- 1/2 teaspoons vanilla extract
- 1/2 teaspoon of ground cinnamon
- 2 bananas, peeled and cut lengthwise and broad
- 1/4 cup chopped nuts, butter
- 3 ½ tbsp. rum

**Prep:** Melt the butter in a deep-frying pan over medium heat. Stir in sugar, rum, vanilla, and cinnamon.
When the mixture starts to bubble, place the bananas and nuts in the pan. Bake until the bananas are hot, 1 to 2 minutes.

**Nutrition:** 534 Calories 23.8g Fat 4.6g Protein

## 934. Berries Stew

**Prep time:** 10 minutes  
**Servings:** 4  
**Cook time:** 10 minutes

**Ingredients:**
- 2 cups blueberries
- 3 tbsps. stevia
- ½ cups pure apple juice
- 1 tsp. vanilla extract

**Prep:** In a pan, combine all ingredients, bring to a simmer and cook over medium-low heat for 10 minutes.
Divide into cups and serve cold.

**Nutrition:** Calories 192, Fat: 5.4g, Carbs: 9.4g, Protein: 4.5g

## 935. Cardamom Almond Cream

**Prep time:** 30 minutes  
**Servings:** 4

**Ingredients:**
- Juice of 1 lime
- ½ cup stevia
- ½ cups water
- 2 cups almond milk
- ½ cup honey
- 3 Tsps. cardamom, ground
- 1 tsp. rose water
- 1 tsp. vanilla extract

**Prep:** In a blender, combine all ingredients, pulse well, divide into cups and put in the fridge for 30 minutes before servings.

**Nutrition:** Calories 283, Fat: 11.8g, Carbs: 4.7g, Protein: 7.1g

## 936. Chia and Berries Smoothie Bowl

**Prep time:** 5 minutes  
**Servings:** 2

**Ingredients:**
- ½ cup almond milk
- 1 cup blackberries
- ¼ cup strawberries, chopped

- 1 ½ tbsps. chia seeds
- 1 tsp. cinnamon powder

**Prep:** In a blender, combine all ingredients, pulse well, divide into small bowls and serve cold.

**Nutrition:** Calories 182, Fat: 3.4g, Carbs: 8.4g, Protein: 3g

### 937. Chocolate Covered Strawberries

**Prep time:** 15 minutes  
**Servings:** 24  
**Cook time:** 4 minutes

**Ingredients:**
- 16 ounces milk chocolate chips
- 2 tablespoons shortening
- 1-pound fresh strawberries with leaves

**Prep:** In a bain-marie, melt chocolate and shortening, occasionally stirring until smooth. Pierce the tops of the strawberries with toothpicks and immerse them in the chocolate mixture.
Turn the strawberries and put the toothpick in Styrofoam so that the chocolate cools.

**Nutrition:** 115 Calories, 7.3g Fat, 12.7g Carbs

### 938. Chocolate Ganache

**Prep time:** 10 minutes  
**Servings:** 16  
**Cook time:** 3 minutes

**Ingredients:**
- 9 ounces bittersweet chocolate, chopped
- 1 cup heavy cream
- dark rum (optional)

**Prep:** Put the chocolate in a medium bowl. Heat the cream in a small saucepan over medium heat.
Bring to a boil. When the cream has reached a boiling point, pour the chopped chocolate over it and beat until smooth.
Stir the rum if desired.
Begin in the middle of the cake and work outside. For a fluffy icing or chocolate filling, let it cool until thick and beat with a whisk until light and fluffy.

**Nutrition:** 142 Calories, 10.8g Fat, 1.4g Protein

### 939. Cinnamon Chickpeas Cookies

**Prep time:** 10 minutes  
**Servings:** 12  
**Cook time:** 20 minutes

**Ingredients:**
- 1 cup canned chickpeas, drained, rinsed, and mashed
- cups almond flour
- 1 tsp. cinnamon powder
- 1 tsp. baking powder
- 1 cup avocado oil
- ½ cup stevia
- 1 egg, whisked
- 2 Tsps. almond extract
- 1 cup raisins
- 1 cup coconut, unsweetened and shredded

**Prep:** In a bowl, combine the chickpeas with the flour, cinnamon, and the other ingredients, and whisk well until you obtain a dough.
Scoop the dough on a baking sheet lined with baking paper, introduce them in the oven at 350F and bake for 20 minutes.
Let them cool for a few minutes and serve.

**Nutrition:** Calories 200, Fat: 4.5g, Carbs: 9.5g, Protein: 2.4g

### 940. Cocoa Sweet Cherry Cream

**Prep time:** 2 hours  
**Servings:** 4

**Ingredients:**
- ½ cup cocoa powder
- ¾ cup red cherry jam
- ¼ cup stevia

- 2 cups water
- 1 lb. cherries, pitted and halved

**Prep:** In a blender, combine all ingredients, pulse well, divide into cups and put in the fridge for 2 hours before serving.

**Nutrition:** Calories 162, Fat: 3.4g, Carbs: 5g, Protein: 1g

## 941. Cranberries and Pears Pie

**Prep time:** 10 minutes  
**Servings:** 4  
**Cook time:** 40 minutes

**Ingredients:**
- 2 cup cranberries
- 3 cups pears, cubed
- A drizzle of olive oil
- 1 cup stevia
- 1/3 cup almond flour
- 1 cup rolled oats
- ¼ avocado oil

**Prep:** In a bowl, add all ingredients except the olive oil and the oats, and stir well.
Grease a cake pan with a drizzle of olive oil, pour the pears mix inside, sprinkle the oats all over and bake at 350°F for 40 minutes. Let it cool and serve.

**Nutrition:** Calories 172, Fat: 3.4g, Carbs: 11.5g, Protein: 4.5g

## 942. Creamy Mint Strawberry Mix

**Prep time:** 10 minutes  
**Servings:** 6  
**Cook time:** 30 minutes

**Ingredients:**
- Cooking spray
- ¼ cup stevia
- ½ cup almond flour
- 1 tsp. baking powder
- 1 cup almond milk
- 1 egg, whisked
- 2 cups strawberries, sliced
- 1 tbsp. mint, chopped
- 1 tsp. lime zest, grated
- ½ cup whipping cream

**Prep:** In a bowl, add all ingredients except the cooking spray and whisk well.
Grease 6 ramekins with the cooking spray, pour the mix inside, put in the oven and bake at 350°F for 30 minutes. Cool down and serve.

**Nutrition:** Calories 200, Fat: 6.3g, Carbs: 6.5g, Protein: 8g

## 943. Dessert Cheese Pie

**Prep time:** 16 minutes  
**Servings:** 12  
**Cook time:** 18 minutes

**Ingredients:**
- 1 cup all-purpose flour
- A package of cream cheese
- 8 oz. whipped cream topping
- 1 (4-oz) package of instant chocolate pudding
- 1/2 cup butter, white sugar
- ¾ cup sugar

**Prep:** Preheat the oven to 350 ° F.
In a large bowl, mix butter, flour and 1/4 cup sugar until the mixture looks like coarse breadcrumbs. Push the mixture into the bottom of a 9 x 13-inch baking dish. Bake in the preheated oven for 18 minutes or until lightly browned, then cool to room temperature.
In a large bowl, beat cream cheese and 1/2 cup sugar until smooth. Stir in half of the whipped topping. Spread the mixture over the cooled crust.
Garnish with the remaining whipped cream. Cool in the fridge.

**Nutrition:** 376 Calories, 23g Fat, 3.6g Protein

## 944. Frosty Strawberry Dessert

**Prep time:** 5 minutes  
**Servings:** 16  
**Cook time:** 21 minutes

**Ingredients:**
- 1 cup flour
- 1 cup whipped cream
- 1/2 cup chopped walnuts
- ½ cup butter
- 2 cups of sliced strawberries
- 3 tablespoons lemon juice
- 1/4 cup brown sugar

**Prep:** Preheat the oven to 350 °F.
Mix the flour, brown sugar, nuts, and melted butter in a bowl. Spread on a baking sheet and bake for 20 minutes in the preheated oven. Remove from the oven and let cool completely.
Mix the strawberries in the lemon juice and stir in the whipped cream until it is absorbed.
Crumble the walnut mixture and spread 2/3 evenly over the bottom of a 9-inch by 13-inch dish. Place the strawberry mixture on the crumbs and sprinkle the rest of the crumbs. Place in the freezer for two hours. Take them out of the freezer a few minutes before serving to facilitate cutting.

**Nutrition:** 184 Calories, 9.2g Fat, 2.2g Protein

## 945. Greek Almond Rounds Shortbread

**Prep time:** 45 minutes, plus 1hr chilling  
**Servings:** 8  
**Cook time:** 12 minutes

**Ingredients:**
- ½ cups butter, softened
- 1 cup blanched almonds, lightly toasted and finely ground
- 2 cup powdered sugar
- 1 egg yolks
- 3 tbsps. brandy or orange juice
- 2 tbsps. rose flower water, (optional)
- 1 Tsps. vanilla
- ½ cups cake flour
- Powdered sugar

**Prep:** Using an electric mixer, beat the butter on MEDIUM or HIGH speed for about 30 seconds in a large sized bowl. Add the 1 cup powdered sugar; beat until the mixture is light in color and fluffy, occasionally scraping the bowl as needed.
Beat in the yolks, vanilla, and the brandy until combined.
With a wooden spoon, stir in the flour and almonds until well incorporated. Cover and refrigerate for about 1 hour or until chilled and the dough is easy to handle.
Preheat the oven to 325°F.
Shape the dough into 1-inch balls. Place the balls 2 inches apart init an ungreased cookie sheet. Dip a glass in the additional powdered sugar and use it to flatten each ball into ¼ -inch thickness, dipping the bottom of the glass every time you flatten a ball into cookies.
Place the cookie sheet into the preheated oven; bake for about 12-14 minutes or until the cookies are set.
When the cookies are baked, transfer them on wire racks. While they are still warm, brush with the rose water, if desired. Sprinkle with more powdered sugar. Let cool completely on the wire racks.
Notes: If using rose water, make sure that you use the edible kind. To store, layer the cookies with waxed paper between each cookie and keep on airtight containers. Close the container tightly and store at room temperature for up to 3 days or freeze for up to 3 months.

**Nutrition:** Calories 62, Fat: 4g, Carbs: 5.7g, Protein: 0.9g

## 946. Ice Cream Sandwich Dessert

**Prep time:** 20 minutes  
**Servings:** 12

**Ingredients:**
- 22 ice cream sandwiches
- Frozen whipped topping in 16 oz. container, thawed
- Jar (12 oz.) Caramel ice cream
- 1/2 cups of salted peanuts

**Prep:** Cut a sandwich in two. Place a whole sandwich and a half sandwich on a short side of a 9 x 13-inch baking dish. Repeat this until the bottom is covered, alternate the full sandwich, and the half sandwich.
Spread half of the whipped topping. Pour the caramel over it. Sprinkle with half the peanuts. Repeat the layers with the rest of the ice cream sandwiches, whipped cream, and peanuts.
Cover and freeze. Remove from the freezer 20 minutes before serving. Cut into squares.

**Nutrition:** 559 Calories, 28.8g Fat, 10g Protein

## 947. Green Tea and Vanilla Cream

**Prep time:** 2 hours  
**Servings:** 4

**Ingredients:**
- 14 oz. almond milk, hot
- 2 tbsps. green tea powder
- 14 oz. heavy cream
- 3 tbsps. stevia
- 1 tsp. vanilla extract
- 1 tsp. gelatin powder

**Prep:** In a bowl, combine all ingredients, whisk well, cool down, divide into cups, and keep in the fridge for 2 hours before servings.

**Nutrition:** Calories 120, Fat: 3g, Carbs: 7g, Protein: 4g

## 948. Hazelnut-Orange Olive Oil Cookies

**Prep time:** 30 minutes, plus 1-hour firming  
**Cook time:** 20 minutes  
**Servings:** 6 dozen cookies

**Ingredients:**
- 5 oz. (1 1/8 cups) whole-wheat flour
- 5 oz. (1 1/8 cups) unbleached all-purpose flour
- ¾ cup plus 2 tbsps. granulated sugar
- 2 large eggs
- 2 cups toasted and skinned hazelnuts
- 1 tsp. of baking powder
- ¼ tsp. table salt
- ½ cup olive oil, extra-virgin
- 1 tsp. vanilla extract
- Finely grated zest of oranges (about 1 ½ packed tbsp.)

**Prep:** In a food processor, put the hazelnuts and process until finely ground. In a medium bowl, add the ground hazelnuts, baking powder, flours, and salt and combine until blended. With an hand mixer fitted with a paddle attachment, beat the eggs, oil, sugar, orange zest, and vanilla on LOW speed for about 15 seconds or until the sugar is moistened. Increase the speed to HIGH; mix for 15 minutes more or until well combined, the sugar will be dissolved at this point. Add the hazelnut mixture; mix on LOW speed for about 30 to 60 seconds or until the dough has just pulled together.
Divide the dough into 2 portions. Pile one of the dough's on a piece of parchment paper. With the aid of the parchment paper, shape the dough into a 2-inch diameter 11-inch long log. Wrap the parchment around the log, twisting the ends to secure it. Repeat the process with the remaining dough. Refrigerate and chill for about 1 hour or until firm.
Position the oven racks in the lower thirds and the upper position in the oven; preheat the oven to 350F. Line 4 pieces cookie sheets with nonstick baking liners or parchment paper.
Unwrap the logs. Cut the logs into ¼ -inch thick slices. Set them 1-inch apart from each other on the prepared sheets. Place 2 baking sheets in the oven; bake the cookies for about 10 minutes, swapping and rotating the sheets halfway through the baking. Let the cookies cool completely on racks.

**Nutrition:** Calories 60, Fat: 4g, Carbs: 6g

## 949. Mediterranean Stuffed Custard Pancakes

**Prep time:** 60 minutes  
**Cook time:** 20 minutes  
**Servings:** 10

**Ingredients:**
**For the batter:**
- 2 cups flour
- ½ cup whole-wheat flour
- 2 cups milk
- 1 cup water
- 1 tsp. yeast
- 1 tsp. baking powder
- 1 tsp. sugar

**For the custard:**
- 2 cups whole milk
- 2 cups fat-free milk or 2 % milk
- 1 cup heavy cream
- 2 tbsps. sugar
- ½ cup cornstarch
- ½ cup water
- 7 pieces medium-sized white bread, crust removed
- 1 tbsp. rose water
- 1 tbsp. orange blossom water

**For the topping:**
- 1 cup pistachio
- 1 tbsp. honey or simple syrup

**Prep:**

**For the custard:** In a medium-sized pot, pour in the milks, heavy cream, cornstarch, and sugar; heat the mixture, stirring.

Cut the bread into pieces and add into the pot; stir until the mixture starts to thicken. Add the orange and rose water; stir until the custard is very thick. Remove from the heat and then pour into a bowl; let cool for 1 hour, stirring every 15 minutes. Cover with saran wrap and then refrigerate to completely cool.

**For the batter:** Mix all the batter ingredients in a mixing bowl, stirring until well combined; let sit for 20 minutes. Over medium-low flame or heat, heat a nonstick pan. Pour ¼ cup-worth of the batter to make a 3-inch diameter pancake; cook for about 30 seconds or until the top of the batter is bubbly and no longer wet and the bottom is golden brown. Transfer into a dish to cool. Repeat the process with the remaining batter.

**To assemble:** Take out the bowl of custard from the refrigerator. Transfer the chilled custard into a piping bag.
Fold a pancake together, pinching the edges to make a pocket. Pipe the custard into the pancake pocket, filling it. Repeat the process with the remaining pancakes and custard. Top each filled pocket with the ground pistachio. Refrigerate until ready to serve. To serve, transfer the custard-filled pancakes into a serving plate, drizzle with honey or simple syrup.

**Nutrition:** Calories 450, Fat: 19g, Carbs: 60g, Protein: 13g

## 950. Orange-Glazed Apricots and Ouzo Whipped Cream

**Prep time:** 20 minutes, plus 30 minutes chilling  
**Cook time:** 10 minutes  
**Servings:** 4

**Ingredients:**
- 3 cups quartered apricots
- 1 tbsp. olive oil spread
- Chopped almonds

**For the ouzo whipped cream:**
- 1 tsp. sugar
- 1 tsp. ouzo liqueur (anise-flavored)
- ½ cup whipping cream

**For the sauce:**
- 2 tbsps. sugar
- 2 tbsps. honey
- ¼ cup orange juice

**Prep:**

**For the syrup:** Mix the syrup ingredients inside a saucepan. Bring to a boil, and stir until honey and sugar are dissolved and reduce the heat. Simmer the mixture, without cover, for 10 minutes and set aside.

**For the ouzo whipped cream:** In a medium-sized chilled bowl, beat the ouzo whipped cream ingredients using electric mixer on medium speed until soft peaks form with the tips curled. Cover and refrigerate for about 30 minutes to chill.

**For the grilled fruit:** Toss the olive oil and the apricots in a mixing bowl. Transfer the fruits into a foil pan or grill pan. If using charcoal grill, put pan with apricots on the uncovered grill rack over medium coals; grill for about 10-12 minutes, stirring occasionally, until the fruits are heated through.
Divide the apricots between 4 pieces dessert plates and drizzle with the honey syrup. Sprinkle with the almonds.
Serve with the ouzo whipped cream.

**Nutrition:** Calories 267, Fat: 15g, Carbs: 36g, Protein: 2g

## 951. Poached Cherries

**Prep time:** 10 minutes  
**Cook time:** 10 minutes  
**Servings:** 5 (½ cup each)

**Ingredients:**
- 1 lb. fresh and sweet cherries, rinsed, pitted
- Orange zest
- Lemon zest
- 2/3 cup sugar
- 15 peppercorns
- ¼ vanilla bean, split but not scraped
- ¾ cups water

**Prep:** In a saucepan, mix the water, citrus zest, sugar, peppercorns, and vanilla bean; bring to a boil, stirring until the sugar is dissolved. Add the cherries; simmer for about 10 minutes until the cherries are soft, but not falling apart. Skim any foam from the surface and let the poached cherries cool. Refrigerate with the poaching liquid. Before Servings, strain the cherries.

**Nutrition:** Calories 170, Fat: 1g, Carbs: 42g

## 952. Strawberries Cream

**Prep time:** 10 minutes  
**Cook time:** 20 minutes  
**Servings:** 4

**Ingredients:**
- ½ cup stevia
- 2 pounds strawberries, chopped
- 1 cup almond milk
- Zest of 1 lemon, grated
- ½ cup heavy cream
- 1 egg yolks, whisked

**Prep:** Heat up a pan with the milk over medium-high heat, add all other ingredients, whisk well, simmer for 20 minutes, divide into cups and serve cold.

**Nutrition:** Calories 152, Fat: 4.4g, Carbs: 5.1g, Protein: 0.8g

## 953. Watermelon-Strawberry Rosewater Yogurt

**Prep time:** 20 minutes
**Servings:** 4

**Cook time:** 5 minutes

**Ingredients:**
- 500 g seedless watermelon, peeled, and cut into 5-mm pieces
- 3 tsps. rosewater
- 1 cup honey-flavored yogurt
- 1 cup thickened cream
- 2 tsps. gelatin powder
- 2 tbsps. caster sugar
- 10 strawberries, washed, hulled, and cut into 5-mm pieces
- 1 tbsp. hot water
- Honey, to serve
- Vegetable oil, to grease

**Prep:** Brush 4 pieces of 125 ml sprinkle molds with vegetable oil to grease.
Put the yogurt into a large-sized heat-safe bowl.
Place the sugar and the cream into a small-sized saucepan and heat over medium heat; stir until the sugar is heated through and the sugar is dissolved.
Place the hot water into a small-sized heat-safe bowl. Sprinkle the gelatin over the hot water. Place the bowl into a small-sized saucepan. Add enough boiling water to fill the saucepan about ¾ deep on the side of the bowl. With a fork, whisk the mixture until the gelatin is dissolved.
Add the gelatin mixture and the cream mixture into the yogurt, whisking until well combined. Strain the mixture through a fine sieve. Pour the strained mixture into the prepared molds. Cover each mold with a plastic wrap. Refrigerate for 6 hours until set.
In a medium bowl, combine the strawberry, watermelon, and rosewater.
Turn the panna cottas into servings bowl. Spoon the strawberry-watermelon over each panna cotta. Drizzle with honey and serve.
Notes: For a different version, you can omit the rosewater, strawberries, and the honey. Combine the watermelon with 1/3 cup of fresh passion fruit pulp, and spoon over the panna cottas.

**Nutrition:** Calories 364.96, Fat: 26g, Carbs: 26g, Protein: 7g

## 954. Key Lime Pie

**Prep time:** 8 minutes
**Servings:** 8

**Cook time:** 9 minutes

**Ingredients:**
- (9-inch) prepared graham cracker crust
- 2 cups of sweetened condensed milk
- 1/2 cup sour cream
- 3/4 cup lime juice
- 1 tablespoon grated lime zest

**Prep:** Preheat the oven to 350 °F.
Combine the condensed milk, sour cream, lime juice, and lime zest in a medium bowl. Mix well and pour into the graham cracker crust.
Bake in the preheated oven for 5 to 8 minutes until small bubbles burst on the surface of the cake.
Cool the cake well before serving. Decorate with lime slices and whipped cream if desired.

**Nutrition:** 553 Calories, 20.5g Fat, 10.9g Protein

## 955. Lemon Cream

**Prep time:** 1 hour
**Servings:** 6

**Cook time:** 10 minutes

**Ingredients:**
- 2 eggs, whisked
- ¼ cup stevia
- 10 tbsps. avocado oil
- 1 cup heavy cream
- Juice of 2 lemons
- Zest of 2 lemons, grated

**Prep:** In a pan, combine all ingredients, whisk well and cook for ten minutes. Divide into cups, and keep in the fridge for 1 hour before serving.

**Nutrition:** Calories 200, Fat: 8.5g, Carbs: 8.6g, Protein: 4.5g

## 956. Mandarin Cream

**Prep time: 20 minutes**  **Servings: 8**

**Ingredients:**
- 2 mandarins, peeled and cut into segments
- Juice of 2 mandarins
- 2 tbsps. stevia
- 4 eggs, whisked
- ¾ cup stevia
- ¾ cup almonds, ground

**Prep:** In a blender, combine all ingredients, whisk well, divide into cups and keep in the fridge for twenty minutes before serving.

**Nutrition:** Calories 106, Fat: 3.4g, Carbs: 2.4g, Protein: 4g

## 957. Minty Coconut Cream

**Prep time: 4 minutes**  **Servings: 2**

**Ingredients:**
- 1 banana, peeled
- 2 cups coconut flesh, shredded
- 3 tbsps. mint, chopped
- 1 and ½ cups coconut water
- 2 tbsps. stevia
- ½ avocado, pitted and peeled

**Prep:** In a blender, combine all ingredients, and pulse well. Divide into cups and serve cold.

**Nutrition:** Calories 193, Fat: 5.4g, Carbs: 7.6g, Protein: 3g

## 958. Orange Cake

**Prep time: 20 minutes**  **Cook time: 60 minutes**
**Servings: 8**

**Ingredients:**
- 4 oranges
- 1/3 cup water
- ½ cup Erythritol
- ½ tsp. ground cinnamon
- 4 eggs, beaten
- 3 tbsps. stevia powder
- 10 oz. Phyllo pastry
- ½ tsp. baking powder
- ½ cup Plain yogurt
- 3 tbsps. olive oil

**Prep:** Squeeze the juice from 1 orange and pour it in the saucepan.
Add water, squeezed oranges, ground cinnamon, and Erythritol. Bring the liquid to boil.
Simmer the liquid for 5 minutes over the medium heat. When the time is over, cool it.
Grease the baking mold with 1 tbsp. of olive oil. Chop the phyllo dough and place it in the baking mold.
Slice ½ of orange for decorating the cake. Slice it. Squeeze juice from remaining oranges.
Then mix up together, squeeze orange juice, Plain yogurt, baking powder, stevia powder, and eggs. Add remaining olive oil.
Mix up the mixture with the help of the hand mixer.
Pour the liquid over the chopped Phyllo dough. Stir to distribute evenly.
Top the cake with sliced orange and bake in the oven for 50 minutes at 370°F.
Pour the baked cake with cooled orange juice syrup. Leave it for 10 minutes to let the cake soaks the syrup.
Cut it into servings.

**Nutrition:** Calories 237, Fat: 4.4 g, Carbs: 36.9 g, Protein: 1.9 g

## 959. Papaya Cream

**Prep time: 10 minutes**  **Servings: 2**

**Ingredients:**
- 1 cup papaya, peeled and chopped
- 1 cup heavy cream
- 1 tbsp. stevia
- ½ tsp. vanilla extract

**Prep:** In a blender, combine the cream with the papaya and the other ingredients, pulse well, divide into cups and serve cold.

**Nutrition:** Calories 182, Fat: 3.1g, Carbs: 3.5g, Protein: 2g

## 960. Peach Sorbet

**Prep time: 2 hours**  
**Servings: 4**

**Cook time: 10 minutes**

### Ingredients:
- 2 cups apple juice
- 1 cup stevia
- 2 tbsps. lemon zest, grated
- 3 pounds peaches, pitted and quartered

**Prep:** Heat up a pan over medium heat, combine all ingredients and simmer for 10 minutes. Transfer to a blender, pulse, divide into cups and keep in the freezer for 2 hours before serving.

**Nutrition:** Calories 182, Fat: 5.4g, Carbs: 12g, Protein: 5.4g

## 961. Strawberry Phyllo Cups

**Prep time: 25 minutes**  
**Servings: 12**

**Cook time: 8 minutes**

### Ingredients:
- 8 sheets (14 x 9-inch) frozen phyllo dough, thawed
- Nonstick cooking spray
- 4 tsps. sugar

**For the lemon cheesecake filling:**
- 8 ounce cream cheese, softened
- 2 tbsps. lemon curd
- 1/3 cup sugar

**For the strawberry-honey filling:**
- 3 oz. cream cheese, softened
- ½ cup whipping cream
- ½ tsp. vanilla
- 2 tbsps. honey
- Fresh strawberries, sliced

**For the macadamia espresso coconut filling:**
- 8 ounce cream cheese, softened
- 1/3 cup sugar
- ½ cup whipping cream
- 1 tsp. espresso powder, instant
- ½ cup toasted coconut
- ¼ cup macadamia nuts, finely chopped

**Prep:**

**For the phyllo cups:** Preheat the oven to 350°F.
Lightly grease 12 pieces of 2 ½-inch muffin cups with the cooking spray; set aside.
Lay out 1 phyllo sheet, lightly grease with the cooking spray, sprinkle with some sugar, and then top with another 1 phyllo sheet. Repeat the process until 4 phyllo sheets are stacked, lightly greasing with the cooking spray, sprinkling with the sugar in the process. Repeat the procedure to make 2 stacks of 4-pieces phyllo sheets. Cut each stack lengthwise into halves. Then cut crosswise into thirds, making 12 rectangles.
Press 1 rectangle into each greased muffin cup, pleating the phyllo to form a cup, as necessary. Put the muffin cups in the oven and bake for about 8 minutes or until the phyllo cups are golden. When baked, remove the muffin tins from the oven and let cool in the pan for about 5 minutes. Remove the phyllo cups from the muffin tins and let cool completely. Fill each cup with desire filling. They can be filled for up to 1 hour before Servings.

**For the lemon cheesecake filling:** Put the cream cheese and the sugar into a bowl; beat until the mixture is smooth. Beat in the lemon curd until mixed. Spoon the mixture into phyllo cups. If desired, garnish with lemon peel twists.

**For the strawberry-honey filling:** Put the cream cheese in a bowl; beat until smooth. Beat in the vanilla and the honey. Add in the whipping cream; beat until stiff peaks form. Spoon the mixture into phyllo cups. Top with sliced strawberries. Drizzle with more honey, if desired.

**For the macadamia espresso coconut filling:** Put the cream cheese, sugar, and the espresso powder in a bowl; beat. Add in the whipping cream until stiff peaks form. Stir in the nuts and toasted coconut. Spoon the mixture into phyllo cups. If desired, garnish with additional toasted coconut and nuts.

**Nutrition:** Calories 161, Fat: 8g, Carbs: 20g, Protein: 3g

### 962. Pumpkin Cream

**Prep time:** 5 minutes  
**Servings:** 2  
**Cook time:** 5 minutes

**Ingredients:**
- 2 cups canned pumpkin flesh
- 2 tbsps. stevia
- 1 tsp. vanilla extract
- 2 tbsps. water
- A pinch of pumpkin spice

**Prep:** In a pan, combine the pumpkin flesh with the other ingredients, simmer for 5 minutes, divide into cups and serve cold.

**Nutrition:** Calories 192, Fat: 3.4g, Carbs: 7.6g, Protein: 3.5g

### 963. Apples and Rhubarb Cream

**Prep time:** 10 minutes  
**Servings:** 6

**Ingredients:**
- 3 cups rhubarb, chopped
- ½ cups stevia
- 2 eggs, whisked
- ½ tsp. nutmeg, ground
- 1 tbsp. avocado oil
- 1/3 cup almond milk

**Prep:** In a blender, combine all ingredients, pulse well, divide into cups and serve cold.

**Nutrition:** Calories 200, Fat: 5.2g, Carbs: 7.6g, Protein: 2.5g

### 964. Strawberry Rhubarb Crunch

**Prep time:** 15 minutes  
**Servings:** 18  
**Cook time:** 45 minutes

**Ingredients:**
- 4 and 1/2 tablespoons all-purpose flour (divided)
- 3 cups of fresh strawberries, sliced
- 3 cups of rhubarb, cut into cubes
- 1/2 cup flour
- 1 cup butter
- 1 cup of white sugar
- 1 cup of brown sugar
- 2 cups oats

**Prep:** Preheat the oven to 375°F.
Combine white sugar, 3 tablespoons flour, strawberries and rhubarb in a large bowl. Place the mixture in a 9 x 13-inch baking dish.
Mix 1 1/2 cups of flour, brown sugar, butter, and oats until a crumbly texture is obtained. You may want to use a blender for this.
Crumble the mixture of rhubarb and strawberry.
Bake in the preheated oven for 45 minutes or until crispy and light brown.

**Nutrition:** 253 Calories, 10.8g Fat, 2.3g Protein

### 965. Ricotta Ramekins

**Prep time:** 10 minutes  
**Servings:** 4  
**Cook time:** 1 hour

**Ingredients:**
- 6 eggs, whisked
- ½ pounds ricotta cheese, soft
- ½ pound stevia
- 1 tsp. vanilla extract
- ½ tsp. baking powder
- Cooking spray

**Prep:** In a bowl, add and stir well all ingredients (except the cooking spray).
Grease 4 ramekins with the cooking spray, pour the ricotta cream in each and bake at 360°F for 1 hour.
Serve cold.

**Nutrition:** Calories 180, Fat: 5.3g, Carbs: 11.5g, Protein: 4g

### 966. Strawberry Angel Dessert

**Prep time:** 15 minutes  
**Servings:** 18

**Ingredients :**
- angel cake (10 inches)
- packages of softened cream cheese

- container (8 oz.) of frozen fluff, thawed
- 1 liter of fresh strawberries, sliced
- 1 jar of strawberry icing
- 1 cup sugar

**Prep:** Crumble the cake in a 9 x 13-inch dish.
Beat the cream cheese and 1 cup sugar in a medium bowl until the mixture is light and fluffy. Stir in the whipped topping. Crush the cake with your hands, and spread the cream cheese mixture over the cake.
Add the strawberries over the layer of cream cheese.
Bake for 45 minutes at the preheated oven to 375°F.
Cool until ready to serve.

**Nutrition:** 261 Calories, 11g Fat, 3.2g Protein

## 967. Vanilla Cake

**Prep time:** 10 minutes
**Servings:** 10

**Cook time:** 25 minutes

**Ingredients:**
- 3 cups almond flour
- 3 tsps. baking powder
- 1 cup olive oil
- 1 and ½ cup almond milk
- 1 and 2/3 cup stevia
- 2 cups water
- 1 tbsp. lime juice
- 2 Tsps. vanilla extract
- Cooking spray

**Prep:** In a bowl, add and whisk well all ingredients except the cooking spray.
Pour the mix into a cake pan greased with cooking spray, put in the oven, and bake at 370°F for 25 minutes.
Let it cool, cut and serve.

**Nutrition:** Calories 201, Fat: 8g, Carbs: 5.5g, Protein: 4.5g

## 968. Watermelon Cream

**Prep time:** 15 minutes

**Servings:** 2

**Ingredients:**
- 1 lb. watermelon, peeled and chopped
- 1 tsp. vanilla extract
- 1 cup heavy cream
- 1 tsp. lime juice
- 2 tbsps. stevia

**Prep:** In a blender, combine all ingredients, pulse well, divide into cups and keep in the fridge for 15 minutes before Servings.

**Nutrition:** Calories 122, Fat: 5.7g, Carbs: 5.3g, Protein: 0.4g

## 969. Lemon Curd Filled Almond-Lemon Cake

**Prep time:** 30 minutes
**Servings:** 8 (1 wedge)

**Cook time:** 35 minutes

**Ingredients:**
- 4 large egg yolks
- 4 large egg whites
- 2 tsps. matzo cake meal
- 2 cups fresh raspberries
- ¼ tsp. of salt
- ¼ cup matzo cake meal
- ¼ cup blanched almonds, ground
- ½ tsp. grated lemon rind
- tsp. lemon juice, fresh
- 1 cup sugar
- 1 cup Lemon Curd
- 1 ½ tsps. water
- Cooking spray

**Prep:** Preheat the oven to 350F.
Coat a 9-inch spring-form pan with the cooking spray. Dust the pan with the 2 tsps. Of matzo cake meal.
Place the yolks into a large-sized bowl; beat with a mixer at high speed for about 2 minutes. Gradually add the sugar and beat the mixture until pale and thick, about 1 minute. Add the ¼ cup matzo cake meal, water, lemon rind, lemon juice, and salt; beat until the mixture is just blended. Fold in the almonds.
Place the egg whites into a large-sized bowl. With clean, dry beaters, beat the egg whites using a mixer at high speed until stiff peaks form. Gently stir in ¼ of the egg whites into the yolk mixture; gently fold in the remaining of the egg whites. Spoon the batter into prepared spring-form pan.
Bake for about 35 minutes at 350F or until the cake is set and brown; remove the pan from the oven, place in a wire rack, and let cool for 10 minutes. Run a knife around the edge of the cake, remove the cake from the pan, place in the wire rack and let cool completely. The cake will sink as it cools.

Spread about 1 cup of lemon curd in the center of the cake. Top with the raspberries. Cut the cake into 8 wedges with a serrated knife. Serve immediately.

**Nutrition:** Calories 238, Fat: 6.6g, Protein: 5.9g, Carbs: 41.4g

## 970. Mascarpone and Ricotta Stuffed Dates

**Prep time:** 20 minutes  
**Servings:** 5  
**Cook time:** 10 minutes

**Ingredients:**
- 125 g fresh ricotta
- 125 g mascarpone
- 2 tsps. finely grated orange rind
- 30 pieces fresh dates
- ¼ cup dry roasted hazelnuts, coarsely chopped, for sprinkling
- ¼ cup icing sugar mixture

**For the syrup:**
- 1/3 cup Frangelico liqueur
- ½ cup water
- 1 cup caster sugar

**Prep:** With an electric beater, beat the mascarpone, icing sugar, ricotta, and orange rind into a large-sized bowl until the mixture is smooth.
With a knife, cut a slit in each date. Remove the stones and discard. Spoon 1 heaped tsp. of the ricotta mixture into each date.

**To make the syrup:** Add sugar and water into a medium-sized saucepan. Heat over low heat: cook for about 2 to 3 minutes, stirring until the sugar is dissolved. Increase the heat to high and bring the mixture to a boil. Cook for 5 minutes without stirring or until the syrup is slightly thick. Stir the Frangelico liqueur. Remove from saucepan from the heat, set aside for 30 minutes to cool. Put the dates into a servings platter. Pour the syrup over the dates. Sprinkle with hazelnuts and then serve.

**Nutrition:** Calories 115.92, Fat: 3.5g, Carbs: 26g, Protein: 1.5g

## 971. Mediterranean Biscuits

**Prep time:** 25 minutes  
**Servings:** 3  
**Cook time:** 1 hour

**Ingredients:**
- 2 eggs
- 1 cup whole-wheat flour
- 1 cup all-purpose flour
- ¾ cup parmesan cheese, grated
- 2 Tsps. baking powder
- 3 tbsps. sugar
- ¼ cup sun-dried tomato, finely chopped
- ¼ cup Kalamata olive, finely chopped
- 1/3 cup olive oil
- ½ tsp. salt
- ½ tsp. black pepper, cracked
- 1 tsp. dried oregano
- 1 tsp. dried basil

**Prep:** Into a large-sized bowl, beat the eggs and the sugar together. Pour in the olive; beat until smooth.
In another bowl, add the flours, pepper, salt, baking powder, oregano, and basil. Stir the flour mix into the egg mixture, stirring until blended.
Stir in the cheese, tomatoes, and olives; stirring until thoroughly combined.
Divide the dough into 2 portions: shape each into 10-inch long logs. Place the logs into a parchment-lined cookie sheet; flatten the log tops slightly.
Bake for about 30 minutes in a preheated 375°F oven.
Remove from the oven; let cool on the baking sheet for 3 minutes. Transfer the logs into a cutting board; slice each log into ½-inch diagonal slices using a serrated knife.
Place the biscotti slices on the baking sheet, return into the 325F oven, and bake for about 20 to 25 minutes until dry and firm. Flip the slices halfway through baking. Remove from the oven, transfer on a wire rack, and let cool.

**Nutrition:** Calories 731.6, Fat: 36.5g, Carbs: 77.8g, Protein: 23.3g

## 972. Mediterranean Bread Pudding

**Prep time:** 10 minutes (plus 6 hr. for chilling)  
**Servings:** 6  
**Cook time:** 20 minutes

**Ingredients:**
- ¼ of a lemon, juiced
- ½ cup sugar
- 8 white bread slices, edges removed, toasted, or more as needed
- 2 cups Lebanese cream
- ½ cup simple syrup
- ½ cup shredded coconut, toasted
- ½ cup pine nuts

**Prep:** Put the sugar, lemon juice, and water into a thick-bottomed pan. Place the pan on the stove and heat over high flame or heat; bring to a boil, continuously stirring. When boiling, let simmer for 5 minutes, continuously stirring, until the mixture is amber in color, being careful it does not burn and turn bitter.

Choose a metal pan according to your desired size. Immediately pour the caramel into the pan, swirling the pan to spread the caramel evenly.

In a single layer, arrange the toasted bread on top of the caramel layer. Generously pour the simple syrup over the bread and spread with the Lebanese cream. If you are using a small metal pan, repeat the layer of bread, drizzle of caramel, and cream. Generously sprinkle with the coconut and the pine nuts. Cover the pan and refrigerate for at least 6 hours or overnight. When chilled, slice into 6 portion and serve.

**Nutrition:** Calories 619, Fat: 10g, Carbs: 130g, Protein: 5g

## 973. Mediterranean Cheesecake

**Prep time:** 15 minutes  
**Servings:** 8  
**Cook time:** 20 minutes

**Ingredients:**
- 8 oz. cream cheese
- ¼ cup sour cream
- ½ cup condensed milk, sweetened
- 5 tbsps. sugar, divided
- 1 tbsp. vanilla
- 1 tbsp. orange blossom
- 1 tbsp. rose water
- 1 tbsp. orange zest
- 1 egg
- ½ cup butter
- cups phyllo dough or Kaddafi
- ½ cup toasted coconut
- ½ cup pistachios
- ½ cup simple syrup

**Prep:** Preheat the oven to 325 °F.

With a hand mixer, mix the condensed milk, cream cheese, and the sour cream in a large bowl until well blended.

Add the orange zest, orange blossom, rose water, vanilla, and sugar, blend for 1 minute. Add in the egg and blend for 30 seconds.

In another bowl, break the Kaddafi into pieces. Add 3 tbsps. Of the sugar, and the butter, mix until well combined.

Line the bottom and the sides of a cheesecake pan or a muffin tin with the Kaddafi mixture.

Pour the cheesecake mixture into the cheesecake pan or muffin tin, filling 80% of the container. Place into the oven and bake for 20 minutes. Remove from the oven and let completely cool before servings.

When completely cool, slice the cake into 8 portions, top with the syrup, pistachio and/or coconut, and glaze with more simple syrup. Serve.

**Nutrition:** Calories 742, Fat: 43g, Carbs: 78g, Protein: 12g

## 974. Grapes Stew

**Prep time:** 10 minutes  
**Servings:** 4  
**Cook time:** 10 minutes

**Ingredients:**
- 2/3 cup stevia
- 1 tbsp. olive oil
- 1/3 cup coconut water
- 1 tsp. vanilla extract
- 1 tsp. lemon zest, grated
- 2 cup red grapes, halved

**Prep:** Heat up a pan with the water over medium heat, add and toss all other ingredients, simmer for 10 minutes, divide into cups and serve.

**Nutrition:** Calories 122, Fat: 3.7g, Carbs: 2.3g, Protein: 0.4g

## 975. Orange Cookies

**Prep time:** 30 minutes  
**Servings:** 6  
**Cook time:** 20 minutes

**Ingredients:**
- 4 eggs
- 3 oranges
- 1 cup of meal
- A pinch of baking soda
- 1 cup of sugar
- Salt to taste

**Prep:** Work the yolks with 3/4 cup of sugar, then add the flour and, very little, bicarbonate. Also add the grated rind of the oranges. Squeeze the citrus fruit then add to the mixture obtaining a fairly soft mixture. Finally, add the egg whites just beaten to stiff peaks with a pinch of salt and make round-shaped cookies. Sprinkle sugar and put in the oven, already hot at 350 degrees F, for 20 minutes or so.

**Nutrition:** Calories 450.3, Carbs 69.6 g, Protein 3.6 g, Fat 14.3 g

### 976. Pumpkin Cookies

**Prep time:** 45 minutes  
**Servings:** 10

**Cook time:** 15 minutes

**Ingredients:**
- 3 cups of meal
- 1 lemon
- 11 oz of pumpkin jam
- 2 sachets of yeast
- 9 eggs
- 2 cups of sugar

**Prep:** Sift the flour with the yeast, open a fountain and shell the eggs in the center, also add the sugar and grated lemon zest. Knead everything long and carefully until you get a solid and smooth mixture. Roll out into thin sheets and cut into discs. Put the pumpkin jam in the center of half of them and cover with the remaining halves. Seal edges with care and bake in preheated oven at 375 degrees F for 15 minutes.

**Nutrition:** Calories 1156.3 kcal, Carbs 169.6 g, Protein 20.6 g, Fat 36.6 g

### 977. Favette

**Prep time:** 1 hour  
**Servings:** 8

**Cook time:** 15 minutes

**Ingredients:**
- 2 cups of meal
- Butter to taste
- Cinnamon to taste
- 1 cup of sugar

**Prep:** Pour a little water into a saucepan and then add the sugar; scent with a pinch of cinnamon. Sieve the flour into a fountain and pour the mixture in the center, mix thoroughly obtaining a solid and smooth dough. Flatten the dough and divide into hazelnuts and each of them, give the shape of a bean. Put everything in a buttered baking dish and bake in the oven, already hot at 350 degrees for about ten minutes.

### 978. Sweetened Almonds

**Prep time:** 15 minutes

**Cook time:** 30 minutes

**Ingredients:**
- 1 lb. and 2 oz of peeled almonds
- 2 cups of sugar

**Prep:** Pour the sugar into a saucepan with a glass of water. Also add the almonds and cook over very low heat, until the mixture is golden brown and comes away from the sides of the saucepan, sizzling. Now, scoop out the almonds with a slotted spoon and spread them out on a marble surface greased with oil. Leave to cool and serve.

**Nutrition:** Calories 510.6, Carbs 53.6 g, Protein 10.6 g, Fats 17.3 g
dsewazzz

### 979. Pistachio Cookies

**Prep time:** 30 minutes  
**Servings:** 8

**Cook time:** 40 minutes

**Ingredients:**
- 9 oz of peeled pistachios
- 6 eggs
- 10 tablespoon of caster sugar
- 1 orange
- Salt and butter to taste
- 3 oz of potato starch

**Prep:** Finely chop the pistachios along with 2 tablespoons of sugar. Whip the egg yolks with the remaining sugar, slowly incorporate the starch continuing to mix carefully. Add the chopped pistachios and the grated orange zest and mix carefully. As soon as the mixture is smooth, gently stir in the egg whites previously beaten to stiff peaks together with a pinch of salt. Distribute the mixture into buttered moulds. Place in preheated oven at 325 degrees for 40 minutes.

### 980. Moscardini

**Prep time:** 50 minutes

**Cook time:** 15 minutes

**Ingredients:**
- 7 cups of meal
- 1 lemon
- 3 ½ cups of sugar

**Prep:** Sift the flour and mix with the sugar, grated lemon zest and a little water, obtaining a hard mixture. Flatten and divide into strings, then cut into small pieces. Blanch the cookies for a minute, dipping them with a perforated ladle in boiling water. Drain and allow to dry for a couple of days. At this point, place in oven, already hot at 375 degrees for 15 minutes.

### 981. Almond Nibbles

**Prep time: 40 minutes**  
**Servings: 10**  
**Cook time: 15 minutes**

**Ingredients:**
- 1 lb. 2 oz of peeled almonds
- 1 lemon
- 3 egg whites
- 2 cup of sugar
- 1 sachet of vanillin
- 1 teaspoon of honey

**Prep:** Grind the almonds in a food processor. Then add the vanillin, honey and grated lemon zest. Incorporate the lightly beaten egg whites and carefully blend everything together, obtaining a uniform mixture. Scoop out the mixture with a spoon and form small balls. Place in a baking dish with baking paper and bake at 350 degrees for 15 minutes.

### 982. Chocolate Almond Balls

**Prep time: 30 minutes**  
**Servings: 8**

**Ingredients:**
- 7 oz of peeled and toasted almonds
- 2 spoons of rum
- 3 tablespoons of bitter cocoa
- 1 ½ cups of sugar
- 1 sachet of vanillin

**Prep:** Chop the almonds, in a kitchen machine, with a little sugar; add the cocoa, rum and remaining sugar and blend everything. Obtain a homogeneous mixture and extract and divide into small quantities. Obtain small balls the size of an olive. Roll in sugar and place in a serving dish.

### 983. Marsala's Balls

**Prep time: 30 minutes**  
**Servings: 4**

**Ingredients:**
- 7 oz of peeled almonds
- Marsala to taste
- 8 tablespoons of bitter cocoa
- 1 ½ cups of sugar

**Prep:** Toast the almonds, then chop with the sugar in a mixer, soften the mixture with 3 tablespoons of Marsala. Take the mixture out of the mixer and form small balls. Roll in cocoa and place in paper ramekins. Serve after letting the treats rest for a couple of hours.

### 984. Orange Almond Balls

**Prep time: 30 minutes**  
**Servings: 8**

**Ingredients:**
- 8 oz of peeled and toasted almonds
- 1 cup orange liqueur
- 3 tablespoons of orange juice
- 1 ½ cups of sugar

**Prep:** Finely chop the almonds in a blender. Now, transfer to a bowl. Add 15 tablespoons of sugar, orange liqueur and the orange juice, now mix carefully obtaining a homogeneous dough. Cut into small balls and roll in the remaining sugar.

### 985. Easter Cake (2nd Version)

**Prep time: 45 minutes**  
**Servings: 6**

**Ingredients:**
- 1 lb. and 2 oz almond paste
- food colorants
- 9 oz of citron preserves

**Prep:** Roll out the almond paste and divide into two parts. Place one in a mold veiled with starch and fill with the preserves, then cover with the remaining pastry and carefully seal the edges. Leave to dry for 1 whole day. Now, draw the details as desired with the dye and allow to dry afterwards. Lay the whole on a tray and serve.

## 986. Ricotta Cheese Flan

**Prep time:** 20 minutes  
**Servings:** 4

**Cook time:** 45 minutes

**Ingredients:**
- 2 lb. of ricotta cheese
- 6 eggs
- 10 spoons of dark chocolate
- ½ cup of flour
- 1 sachet of vanillin
- Cinnamon to taste
- Salt to taste
- 1 cup of sugar
- Powdered sugar
- Butter and flour for the baking tray

**Prep:** Sift the ricotta cheese and mix it with the sugar, vanillin, the already sifted flour, a pinch of salt and the egg yolks. Add the chopped chocolate and the beaten egg whites and pour everything into a buttered and floured baking pan. Place the pan in a 350 degrees F oven and cook for about 45 minutes. Finally, take out of the oven and let cool. Sprinkle with powdered sugar before serving.

## 987. Almond Cake (2nd Version)

**Prep time:** 40 minutes  
**Servings:** 8

**Cook time:** 30 minutes

**Ingredients:**
- 9 oz of almonds
- 6 eggs
- 7 teaspoons of flour
- 1 cup of sugar
- 1 stick of butter
- Butter and flour for the mould

**Prep:** Whip the egg yolks together with the sugar. Add chopped almonds, soft butter and flour, mix everything thoroughly. Once the mixture is fairly homogeneous, incorporate the egg whites until stiff and pour everything into a floured and buttered baking dish. Bake at 350 degrees F for half an hour.

## 988. Hazelnut Cake

**Prep time:** 20 minutes  
**Servings:** 6

**Cook time:** 35 minutes

**Ingredients:**
- 1 cup and 2 oz of flour
- 3 eggs
- 7 oz of toasted hazelnuts
- 1 cup of sugar
- 1 stick of butter
- ½ cup of milk
- Salt to taste
- 1 sachet of yeast
- Butter and flour for the mould

**Prep:** Chop hazelnuts in a mixer along with 2 tablespoons of sugar.
Work and whisk the egg whites with a little salt. Beat the egg yolks with the butter and remaining sugar, obtaining a fairly whipped mixture. Pour in the milk, the flour already sifted with the yeast and finally the chopped hazelnuts. Mix everything thoroughly. Add, slowly, the egg whites. Pour the whole mixture into a pan already floured and buttered and finally put in a preheated oven at 350 degrees F for 30 minutes.

## 989. Sponge Cake

**Prep time:** 40 minutes  
**Servings:** 8

**Cook time:** 30 minutes

**Ingredients:**
- 20 tablespoons flour
- 6 eggs
- vanillin to taste
- 1 cup of sugar
- 1 pinch of baking powder
- Salt to taste

**Prep:** Beat the egg yolks with the sugar for a long time until eggnog is obtained. Then add a few tablespoons of egg whites whipped to stiff peaks with a pinch of salt and slowly pour in the sifted flour with the baking powder and flavorings, without stopping to mix vigorously and carefully with the whisk. Finally, carefully mix in the rest of the egg whites and pour everything into an already floured and buttered baking pan. Bake in the oven for 30 minutes at 350 degrees F.

### 990. St. Joseph's Beard

**Prep time:** 10 minutes  
**Servings:** 4  
**Cook time:** 5 minutes

**Ingredients:**
- 11 oz of pasta
- 2 oz of breadcrumbs
- 7 and 1/2 tablespoons of honey
- Salt to taste

**Prep:** Toast the breadcrumbs. Heat the honey in a bain-marie along with 2 tablespoons of water and keep warm. Boil the pasta in boiling water with very little salt. Drain al dente and mix with the honey. Then add the breadcrumbs and mix carefully and gently. Finally pour everything into a tray and serve.

### 991. Creamy Cinnamon Milk

**Prep time:** 5 minutes  
**Servings:** 8  
**Cook time:** 20 minutes

**Ingredients:**
- 1 US quart of milk
- 4 oz of baking starch
- Cinnamon to taste
- 1 cup of sugar

**Prep:** Steep the baking starch in a little cold milk. Then add the remaining milk and sugar and, while continuing to stir, let the cream thicken, over medium heat. Pour into a serving dish and allow to rest and cool in the refrigerator. Once completely cold sprinkle with cinnamon powder.

### 992. Chickpeas with Honey

**Prep time:** 5 minutes  
**Servings:** 4  
**Cook time:** 4 hours

**Ingredients:**
- 1 lb. and 2 oz of chickpeas
- 1 cup of honey
- Salt to taste
- 1 bay leaf

**Prep:** Soak the chickpeas for 24 hours. Rinse and boil, for 4 hours, in abundant water with a bay leaf and add a little salt at the end of cooking. Once the legumes are tender, drain and transfer to a serving dish. Drizzle with honey and serve.

### 993. Starch Cream

**Prep time:** 10 minutes  
**Servings:** 4  
**Cook time:** 20 minutes

**Ingredients:**
- 2 egg yolks
- 2 cups of milk
- 1 lemon
- 2 oz of baking starch
- 2 oz of sugar
- Salt to taste
- Dark chocolate flakes to taste
- 1 sachet of vanillin

**Prep:** Steep the starch in a little cold milk and add the sugar, the remaining milk, the whole lemon zest and the vanillin. Stirring continuously and carefully, let the cream thicken over medium heat. Distribute in small cups and leave to cool. Sprinkle with chocolate and serve.

### 994. Milk Cream

**Prep time:** 10 minutes  
**Servings:** 4  
**Cook time:** 20 minutes

**Ingredients:**
- 2 cups of milk
- 3 oz of baking starch
- 1 lemon
- ½ cup of sugar

**Prep:** Heat 3/4 cup milk with lemon zest and sugar. Strain and add to the remaining milk in which it will already be dissolved with the starch. Put everything on a gentle flame and let it thicken.

### 995. Ricotta Cream

**Prep time: 15 minutes**  **Servings: 4**

**Ingredients:**
- 1 lb. and 1 oz ricotta
- ½ cup of sugar
- Salt to taste
- ½ sachet of vanillin

**Prep:** Sift the ricotta and collect it in a saucepan. Add the sugar, a pinch of salt and the vanillin and mix thoroughly until you obtain a uniform and homogeneous cream.

### 996. Sweet Couscous

**Prep time: 45 minutes**  **Cook time: 1 hour 15 minutes**
**Servings: 4**

**Ingredients:**
- 11 oz of durum wheat semolina
- 1 orange
- 3 leaves of laurel
- 15 spoons of dark chocolate
- 4 oz of peeled pistachios
- Powdered sugar to taste
- 4 oz of peeled and toasted almonds
- Cinnamon to taste
- 4 oz of candied pumpkin cubes

**Prep:** Bind the semolina with a little water and let it dry. Steam in a couscous pot with the bay leaves and a chopped orange peel. When cooked, pour into a tray and leave to cool. Season with a few tablespoons of powdered sugar, the pumpkin cubes, chopped almonds, chopped chocolate and pistachios. Sprinkle a pinch of cinnamon.
Mix everything together carefully and let stand for a few minutes. Serve.

### 997. Chocolate Rice

**Prep time: 15 minutes**  **Cook time: 30 minutes**
**Servings: 6**

**Ingredients:**
- 21 tablespoons of rice
- 1 tablespoon of cinnamon
- Salt to taste
- 1 US quart and 2 cup of milk
- 1 cup of sugar
- ½ cup of dark chocolate
- 2 tablespoons of powdered sugar

**Prep:** Boil the rice in lightly salted, boiling milk for half an hour. When cooked, season with the sugar and melted chocolate. Mix everything together carefully and transfer the mixture to a large serving dish. Leave to cool, then sprinkle with a pinch of cinnamon and powdered sugar. Serve cold.

**Nutrition:** Calories 390.6, Carbs 83.6 g, Protein 7.6 g, Fats 2.1 g

### 998. Ricotta and Honey

**Prep time: 15 minutes**  **Servings: 4**

**Ingredients:**
- 1 lb 2 oz of ricotta
- 4 oz of diced pumpkin
- 5 tablespoons of honey
- Cinnamon to taste
- 5 tablespoons of flaky dark chocolate

**Prep:** Sift the ricotta and put it in a bowl; then add the honey and mix thoroughly. When the mixture is smooth, add pumpkin and chocolate.
Distribute the cream in small cups. Sprinkle the portions with a sprinkling of cinnamon and serve.

**Nutrition:** Calories 198.6, Carbs 25.1 g, Protein 4.2 g, Fats 8.3 g

### 999. Battered Eggs in Marsala

**Prep time:** 20 minutes  
**Servings:** 4

**Ingredients:**
- 4 yolks
- 8 tablespoons of Marsala
- 4 tablespoons of sugar

**Prep:** Place yolks in four cups and beat each with 1 tablespoon sugar, working long and vigorously until frothy and puffy. When the cream takes on a lemon-yellow color, add 2 tablespoons of Marsala for each cup. Pour slowly while continuing to stir vigorously for a few more minutes.

### 1000. Cream Cannoli

**Prep time:** 5 minutes  
**Cook time:** 10 minutes  
**Servings:** 4

**Ingredients:**
- 4 cannoli peels
- 7 oz of fondant
- 1 cup of whipped cream
- 10 tablespoons dark chocolate

**Prep:** Finely break up the chocolate and transfer to a pan in a bain-marie with the fondant. Melt, stirring carefully, over low heat and, when the mixture is fluid enough, dip the cannoli peels to cover the surface completely.
Place to drip on a grating and, once the glaze has hardened, fill with whipped cream and refrigerate to rest.

**Nutrition:** Calories 207.6 kcal, Carbs 16.4 g, Protein 5.3 g, Fats 12.5 g

### 1001. Angel Hair

**Prep time:** 20 minutes  
**Cook time:** 15 minutes  
**Servings:** 4

**Ingredients:**
- 4 eggs
- Cinnamon to taste
- Salt to taste
- 2 oz of toasted almonds
- 2 oz of toasted hazelnuts
- ½ cup of honey
- Olive oil

**Prep:** Beat the eggs in a bowl with a little pinch of salt. Pour the mixture, a little at a time, into a small pan greased with oil and prepare small thin omelets. Let cool and cut into strips.
Place in a serving dish and pour over honey melted in a bain-marie. Sprinkle the mixture with a pinch of cinnamon and chopped almonds and hazelnuts, then serve.

### 1002. Ricotta Fritters

**Prep time:** 20 minutes  
**Cook time:** 5 minutes  
**Servings:** 8

**Ingredients:**
- 1 lb and 2 oz of ricotta
- 2 yolks
- 1 cup of sugar
- Cinnamon to taste
- 1 orange
- Olive oil
- Flour to taste

**Prep:** Pass the ricotta through a sieve and pour in the flour, half the sugar, grated orange zest and egg yolks. Cover and let rest for a few hours.
Take the mixture by spoonful and fry in plenty of hot oil. Once the fritters are golden, drain and place in absorbent paper to lose the excess grease.
Finally, sprinkle with sugar and cinnamon and serve.

### 1003. Sweet Fried Ricotta

**Prep time: 10 minutes**  
**Servings: 4**

**Cook time: 5 minutes**

**Ingredients:**
- 1 lb and 4 oz of ricotta
- sugar to taste
- Cinnamon to taste
- Olive oil to taste
- Flour to taste

**Prep:** Slice the dry ricotta, flour it and fry a little at a time in a pan with a drizzle of hot oil. Drain and place in a serving dish. Sprinkle sugar and cinnamon to taste. Serve cold or warm.

### 1004. Coffee Granita

**Prep time: 5 minutes**  
**Servings: 4**

**Cook time: 10 minutes**

**Ingredients:**
- 1 cup of coffee
- 1 cup of sugar
- ½ US quart of water

**Prep:** Prepare a syrup with water and the sugar. Let simmer for a few minutes, let cool and stir in the coffee.
Once the mixture is fairly smooth, strain and place in the freezer to solidify, stir often, to make the ice cream grainy.

### 1005. Yellow Melon Granita

**Prep time: 15 minutes**  
**Servings: 4**

**Cook time: 10 minutes**

**Ingredients:**
- 1 lb. and 2 oz yellow melon pulp
- 1 lemon
- 5 tablespoons sugar
- 1 1/4 water

**Prep:** Pass the pulp through a sieve, then dissolve the sugar in the water brought to a boil. Let simmer for a few minutes, turn off the heat and let cool.
Combine the lemon juice and add the fruit puree. Place the mixture in a container in the freezer to solidify for about 8 hours. Stir occasionally with a spatula.

# Conversion Tables

## Volume

| Imperial | Metric | Imperial | Metric |
|---|---|---|---|
| 1 tbsp | 15ml | 1 pint | 570 ml |
| 2 fl oz | 55 ml | 1 ¼ pints | 725 ml |
| 3 fl oz | 75 ml | 1 ¾ pints | 1 liter |
| 5 fl oz (¼ pint) | 150 ml | 2 pints | 1.2 liters |
| 10 fl oz (½ pint) | 275 ml | 2½ pints | 1.5 liters |
| | | 4 pints | 2.25 liters |

## Weight

| Imperial | Metric | Imperial | Metric | Imperial | Metric |
|---|---|---|---|---|---|
| ½ oz | 10 g | 4 oz | 110 g | 10 oz | 275 g |
| ¾ oz | 20 g | 4½ oz | 125 g | 12 oz | 350 g |
| 1 oz | 25 g | 5 oz | 150 g | 1 lb. | 450 g |
| 1½ oz | 40 g | 6 oz | 175 g | 1 lb. 8 oz | 700 g |
| 2 oz | 50 g | 7 oz | 200 g | 2 lb. | 900 g |
| 2½ oz | 60 g | 8 oz | 225 g | 3 lb. | 1.35 kg |
| 3 oz | 75 g | 9 oz | 250 g | | |

## Metric cups conversion

| Cups | Imperial | Metric |
| --- | --- | --- |
| 1 cup flour | 5oz | 150g |
| 1 cup caster or granulated sugar | 8oz | 225g |
| 1 cup soft brown sugar | 6oz | 175g |
| 1 cup soft butter/margarine | 8oz | 225g |
| 1 cup sultanas/raisins | 7oz | 200g |
| 1 cup currants | 5oz | 150g |
| 1 cup ground almonds | 4oz | 110g |
| 1 cup oats | 4oz | 110g |
| 1 cup golden syrup/honey | 12oz | 350g |
| 1 cup uncooked rice | 7oz | 200g |
| 1 cup grated cheese | 4oz | 110g |
| 1 stick butter | 4oz | 110g |
| ¼ cup liquid (water, milk, oil etc.) | 4 tablespoons | 60ml |
| ½ cup liquid (water, milk, oil etc.) | ¼ pint | 125ml |
| 1 cup liquid (water, milk, oil etc.) | ½ pint | 250ml |

**Oven temperatures**

| Gas Mark | Fahrenheit | Celsius | Gas Mark | Fahrenheit | Celsius |
|---|---|---|---|---|---|
| 1/4 | 225 | 110 | 4 | 350 | 180 |
| 1/2 | 250 | 130 | 5 | 375 | 190 |
| 1 | 275 | 140 | 6 | 400 | 200 |
| 2 | 300 | 150 | 7 | 425 | 220 |
| 3 | 325 | 170 | 8 | 450 | 230 |
|  |  |  | 9 | 475 | 240 |

# 30-DAY MEAL PLAN

| Day | Breakfast | Lunch | Dinner |
| --- | --- | --- | --- |
| 1 | Baked Omelet Mix | Mint Avocado Chilled Soup | Chicken with Caper Sauce |
| 2 | Banana Oats | Cannellini Bean Lettuce Wraps | Cheesy Bacon Burger |
| 3 | Strawberry and Rhubarb Smoothie | Farfalle with Fresh Tomatoes | Chicken Breast in Balsamic Vinegar |
| 4 | Sun-dried Tomatoes Oatmeal | Rice with Pesto | Beef, Artichoke & Mushroom Stew |
| 5 | Avocado Muffins | Greek Lima Beans Soup | Coconut Curry Chicken Tenders |
| 6 | Watermelon "Pizza" | Gluten-Free Spanish Rice | Pork Ribs with Wine |
| 7 | Cheesy Yogurt | Greek Baked Zucchini & Potatoes | Bbq Chicken Pizza |
| 8 | Cauliflower Fritters | Chickpeas Soup | Codfish with Shrimp |
| 9 | Berry Oats | Mantis Shrimp Soup | 5 Minute Pizza |
| 10 | Walnuts Yogurt Mix | Cabbage Stew | Bacon Wings |
| 11 | Tahini Pine Nuts Toast | Broth Passatelli | Sword Fish Cutlets |
| 12 | Blueberries Quinoa | Chicken Salad | Lamb with Mint |
| 13 | Raspberries and Yogurt Smoothie | Baked Gnocchi with Ragù and Mozzarella | Cod in Tomato Sauce |
| 14 | Cottage Cheese and Berries Omelet | Green Beans & Feta | Chicken with Peppers |
| 15 | Salmon Frittata | Kale - Mediterranean-Style | Pork and Ricotta Meat Loaf |
| 16 | Olive Paste and Avocado on Toasted Rye Bread | Mediterranean Endive Boats | Sesame Beef |
| 17 | Homemade Muesli | Herb Risotto | Grilled Tuna |
| 18 | Raisin Quinoa Breakfast | Mediterranean Potatoes | Herbed Roasted Chicken Breasts |
| 19 | Banana Cinnamon Fritters | Greek Eggplant Dish | Seafood Stew |
| 20 | Scramble Eggs with Tomatoes | Whole Wheat Pasta with Tuna | Feta Tomato Salad |

| | | | |
|---|---|---|---|
| 21 | Avocado Toast | Ground Beef and Brussels Sprouts | Mediterranean Chickpea Salad |
| 22 | Veggie Quiche | Spaghetti with Artichokes | Italian Mini Meatballs |
| 23 | Ham Muffins | Buffalo Chicken Sliders | Legume Soup |
| 24 | Fruit Bulgur Breakfast Bowls | Vegan Olive Pasta | Salmon Kebabs |
| 25 | Eggs in a Squash | Rice and Bean Soup | Turkish Salad |
| 26 | Avocado and Apple Smoothie | Spaghetti with Anchovies | Tilapia in Herb Sauce |
| 27 | Bacon and Brie Omelet Wedges | Pork Loins | Black Bean Stuffed Sweet Potatoes with Quinoa |
| 28 | Coconut Porridge | Tagliatelle with Mushroom Ragù | Orange Celery Salad |
| 29 | Oats with Raspberries | Lemony Parmesan Salmon | Lamb with Egg |
| 30 | Hearty Pear and Mango Smoothie | Gorgonzola Sweet Potato Burgers | Asparagus Soup |

# INDEX:

| | | | |
|---|---|---|---|
| 5 Minute Pizza | 80 | Au Gratin Scallops | 61 |
| 5-Minute Tomato & Cucumber Toast | 64 | Avocado and Apple Smoothie | 83 |
| Almond and Liquor Cake | 271 | Avocado and Chickpea Sandwiches | 65 |
| Almond Cake | 272 | Avocado Chickpea Pizza | 86 |
| Almond Cake (2nd version) | 294 | Avocado Muffins | 84 |
| Almond Kale | 242 | Avocado Spread | 87 |
| Almond Nibbles | 293 | Avocado Toast | 83 |
| Almond Pesto Pasta | 111 | Avocado, Roasted Mushroom and Feta Spaghetti | 142 |
| Almond Rice Dessert | 278 | Avocados Stuffed with Salmon | 188 |
| Amaretti (Cookies) | 267 | Bacon and Brie Omelet Wedges | 92 |
| Anchovies Au Gratin | 52 | Bacon and Lemon spiced Muffins | 69 |
| Anchovy and Capers Sauce | 264 | Bacon Cheeseburger Casserole | 202 |
| Anchovy and Zucchini Fritters | 62 | Bacon Wings | 218 |
| Anchovy Dumplings | 45 | Baked Apples | 13 |
| Anchovy Sauce | 258 | Baked Bream Fish | 174 |
| Angel Hair | 297 | Baked Cardoon | 232 |
| Apple and Berries Ambrosia | 273 | Baked Castrate | 196 |
| Apple Couscous Pudding | 278 | Baked Chicken with Pecorino | 211 |
| Apple Fritters | 267 | Baked Dentex with Olives | 171 |
| Apple Sauce | 263 | Baked Doughnuts | 268 |
| Apples and Plum Cake | 275 | Baked Eggs in Avocado | 69 |
| Apples and Pomegranate Salad | 242 | Baked Gnocchi with Ragù and Mozzarella | 122 |
| Apples and Rhubarb Cream | 288 | Baked Gray Mullet | 164 |
| Arancini with Ricotta | 40 | Baked Ham | 222 |
| Artichoke Dip | 15 | Baked Lamb | 194 |
| Artichoke Dip with Mozzarella | 14 | Baked Omelet Mix | 87 |
| Artichoke Frittata | 90 | Baked Onions | 254 |
| Artichoke Pie | 58 | Baked Rabbit | 206 |
| Artichoke Tart | 49 | Baked Ricotta & Pears | 273 |
| Artichokes and Cheese Omelet | 89 | Baked Shrimp | 173 |
| Artichokes in a Pan | 253 | Baked Skewer Rolls | 197 |
| Artichokes in a Pan with Lemon | 253 | Baked Tagliatelle | 134 |
| Arugula Salad | 243 | Balsamic Beef and Mushrooms Mix | 202 |
| Asparagus au gratin | 230 | Balsamic Eggplant Mix | 243 |
| Asparagus Frittata | 69 | Balsamic Vinegar Risotto | 140 |
| Asparagus Pie | 57 | Banana and Quinoa Casserole | 86 |
| Asparagus Soup | 131 | Banana Cinnamon Cupcakes | 279 |
| Asparagus with Ham | 230 | Banana Cinnamon Fritters | 274 |
| Au gratin Lobster | 168 | Banana Oats | 82 |
| Au Gratin Mackerel | 172 | Banana Shake Bowls | 276 |
| Au Gratin Mussels | 53 | | |

| | |
|---|---|
| Bananas Foster | 279 |
| Barley and Chicken Soup | 144 |
| Barley and Endive Soup | 138 |
| Barley Porridge | 91 |
| Barley Risotto | 155 |
| Batter Dessert | 269 |
| Battered Cauliflowers | 236 |
| Battered Eggs in Marsala | 297 |
| Battered Onion | 236 |
| Battered Pumpkin Flowers | 256 |
| Battered Sea Anemones | 44 |
| Bbq Chicken Pizza | 215 |
| Bean Lettuce Wraps | 70 |
| Bean Salad | 237 |
| Beans Soup | 142 |
| Béchamel Sauce | 260 |
| Beef & Tapioca Stew | 198 |
| Beef Filet with Ham | 192 |
| Beef Mince | 193 |
| Beef Ragù | 265 |
| Beef Sage Soup | 153 |
| Beef Tartar | 205 |
| Beef with Broccoli and Cauliflower Rice | 155 |
| Beef, Artichoke & Mushroom Stew | 199 |
| Beet and Ricotta Pie | 48 |
| Beet Pie | 57 |
| Beet Soup | 132 |
| Beetroot and Carrot Soup | 155 |
| Beetroot Chips | 14 |
| Bell Pepper Muffins | 14 |
| Bell Pepper Roast | 46 |
| Bell Pepper Soup | 151 |
| Berries Stew | 279 |
| Berry Oats | 84 |
| Berry Oats (2nd version) | 94 |
| Black Bean Stuffed Sweet Potatoes with Quinoa | 239 |
| Black Olives with Orange | 62 |
| Black Tea Cake | 276 |
| Blackberry and Apples Cobbler | 276 |
| Blueberries Quinoa | 95 |
| Blueberry Smoothie | 275 |
| Blueberry, Hazelnut, and Lemon Grain Salad | 95 |
| Boar Sauce | 266 |
| Boiled Broccoli | 230 |
| Boiled Cauliflower | 254 |
| Boiled Onions | 255 |
| Bok Choy with Tofu Stir Fry | 239 |
| Borage Fritters | 43 |
| Boscaiola Style Spelt | 101 |
| Braised Artichokes | 253 |
| Braised Kale with Cherry Tomatoes | 245 |
| Braised Sausage | 226 |
| Bread Balls | 73 |
| Bread with Potatoes | 74 |
| Bread with Scamorza, Capers and Anchovies | 76 |
| Bread with Walnuts | 74 |
| Breadcrumbs Dessert | 269 |
| Breaded Grilled Squid | 169 |
| Breaded Prickly Pears' Peels Cutlets | 41 |
| Bream Fish in Salt Crust | 175 |
| Bream with Potatoes | 175 |
| Broad Beans and Bacon | 256 |
| Broad Beans with Onion | 255 |
| Broccoli Focaccia | 72 |
| Broccoli Pesto Spaghetti | 144 |
| Broccoli Soup | 112 |
| Broccoli with Tomato | 230 |
| Broiled Chicken | 211 |
| Broth Passatelli | 103 |
| Brown Rice Salad | 95 |
| Brown Sugar Smokies | 228 |
| Bruschetta Hummus Platter | 27 |
| Bruschetta with Sausage | 52 |
| Bucatini with Eggs and Asparagus | 125 |
| Bucatini with Hot Peppers | 125 |
| Bucatini with Leaf Broccoli | 124 |
| Bucatini with Tomato and Ricotta | 124 |
| Buffalo Cauliflower | 238 |
| Buffalo Chicken Sliders | 219 |
| Butter Shrimp | 186 |
| Butternut Squash Fries | 33 |
| Cabbage Stew | 110 |
| Cabbage Tortelli | 136 |
| Cacciatora Chicken | 207 |
| Calzone with Ham and Cheese | 76 |
| Cannellini Bean Lettuce Wraps | 243 |

| | |
|---|---:|
| Cannelloni | 136 |
| Cappelletti with Ricotta and Herbs | 114 |
| Cappon Magro | 54 |
| Caramel Popcorn | 274 |
| Cardamom Almond Cream | 279 |
| Cardoons with Dressing | 232 |
| Carnival Dessert | 270 |
| Carrot Sauce | 265 |
| Castrated Chops | 192 |
| Cauliflower Breakfast Porridge | 99 |
| Cauliflower Croquettes | 42 |
| Cauliflower Curry | 238 |
| Cauliflower Focaccia | 71 |
| Cauliflower Fritters | 88 |
| Cauliflower Rice and Chipotle Chicken | 146 |
| Cheese Beet Salad | 243 |
| Cheese Pie | 77 |
| Cheesy Bacon Burger | 202 |
| Cheesy Broccoli Soup | 153 |
| Cheesy Cauliflower Florets | 237 |
| Cheesy Olives Bread | 94 |
| Cheesy Yogurt | 87 |
| Cheesy Yogurt | 94 |
| Cherry Cream | 276 |
| Cherry Soup | 273 |
| Chestnut Flour Trofie | 120 |
| Chestnut, Ricotta and Spelt Soup | 108 |
| Chia and Berries Smoothie Bowl | 279 |
| Chicken & Veggie Kabobs | 213 |
| Chicken and Rice Soup | 156 |
| Chicken Breast in Balsamic Vinegar | 52 |
| Chicken Breast Soup | 144 |
| Chicken Broccoli Salad with Avocado Dressing | 215 |
| Chicken in Salt Crust | 212 |
| Chicken Mince | 208 |
| Chicken Omelet | 219 |
| Chicken Parmesan Wraps | 38 |
| Chicken Pasta | 147 |
| Chicken Pastry Rolls | 61 |
| Chicken Pot Pie | 212 |
| Chicken Ragù | 262 |
| Chicken Rolls | 64 |
| Chicken Salad | 51 |
| Chicken Salad (2nd version) | 219 |
| Chicken Skillet | 220 |
| Chicken Stew | 215 |
| Chicken Stew with Potatoes | 213 |
| Chicken Stuffed Peppers | 220 |
| Chicken Wild Rice Soup | 152 |
| Chicken with Caper Sauce | 213 |
| Chicken with Peppers | 207 |
| Chicken with Potatoes | 211 |
| Chicken with Vinegar | 207 |
| Chicken with Vinegar (2nd version) | 212 |
| Chicken, Dried Fruit & Olives Casserole | 214 |
| Chickpea and Broccoli Soup | 126 |
| Chickpea Flat Bread | 49 |
| Chickpea Focaccia | 78 |
| Chickpea Fritters | 54 |
| Chickpea Salad | 244 |
| Chickpeas and Millet Stew | 240 |
| Chickpeas Soup | 141 |
| Chickpeas Soup (2nd version) | 156 |
| Chickpeas with Honey | 295 |
| Chicory and Potatoes Soup | 132 |
| Chicory Soup | 109 |
| Chili Chicken Wings | 15 |
| Chili Oregano Baked Cheese | 67 |
| Chocolate Almond Balls | 293 |
| Chocolate Covered Strawberries | 280 |
| Chocolate Ganache | 280 |
| Chocolate Rice | 296 |
| Chops in Balsamic Vinegar | 223 |
| Chunky Nuts Mix | 15 |
| Cinnamon Chickpeas Cookies | 280 |
| Classic Apple Oats | 39 |
| Classic Minestrone | 153 |
| Clementine & Pistachio Ricotta | 37 |
| Cocoa Brownies | 277 |
| Cocoa Sweet Cherry Cream | 280 |
| Coconut Clam Chowder | 178 |
| Coconut Curry Chicken Tenders | 215 |
| Coconut Porridge | 93 |
| Cod Balls | 177 |
| Cod in Tomato Sauce | 178 |
| Cod Sauce | 263 |

| | |
|---|---|
| Cod with Dressing | 164 |
| Cod with Olives and Potatoes | 168 |
| Cod with Potatoes | 164 |
| Codfish with Shrimp | 180 |
| Coffee Granita | 298 |
| Cold Lemon Squares | 277 |
| Cold Spaghetti | 106 |
| Cool Tomato and Dill Frittata | 91 |
| Corn and Shrimp Salad | 94 |
| Corn Focaccia | 75 |
| Cottage Cheese and Berries Omelet | 65 |
| Courgette Risotto | 144 |
| Couscous Salad | 92 |
| Crab Soup | 139 |
| Crabs in Dressing | 173 |
| Cranberries and Pears Pie | 281 |
| Cream Cannoli | 297 |
| Creamy Carrot Chowder | 244 |
| Creamy Chicken Salad | 244 |
| Creamy Chicken Soup | 145 |
| Creamy Cinnamon Milk | 295 |
| Creamy Fish Gratin | 186 |
| Creamy Fish Stew | 179 |
| Creamy Mint Strawberry Mix | 281 |
| Creamy Peach Smoothie | 274 |
| Creamy Penne | 145 |
| Crispy Garlic Oven Potatoes | 30 |
| Crumbled Feta and Scallions | 93 |
| Crunchy Almond Bar | 270 |
| Cucumber Bowl with Spices and Greek Yogurt | 238 |
| Cucumber Chunks with Avocado | 16 |
| Cucumber Tomato Okra Salsa | 16 |
| Cutlet Mushrooms | 256 |
| Dark Sauce | 260 |
| Date and Fig Smoothie | 17 |
| Date Wraps | 37 |
| Dessert Cheese Pie | 281 |
| Dill Salmon Salad Wraps | 38 |
| Dogtooth Violet with Sausage | 134 |
| Doughnut | 270 |
| Dried Fig Tapenade | 33 |
| Dried Fruit Cake | 271 |
| Dried Sausage Stew | 222 |
| Duck Ham | 208 |
| Easter Cake | 270 |
| Easter Cake (2nd version) | 293 |
| Eel Fritta | 163 |
| Eel with Grapes | 163 |
| Egg Bake | 68 |
| Egg Sauce | 264 |
| Egg White Scramble with Cherry Tomatoes & Spinach | 65 |
| Eggplant Bites | 18 |
| Eggplant Caponata | 17 |
| Eggplant Caviar | 30 |
| Eggplant Dip | 16 |
| Eggplant Pie | 50 |
| Eggplant Rolls | 51 |
| Eggplant Salad | 90 |
| Eggplants with Balsamic Vinegar | 229 |
| Eggplants with Ham | 234 |
| Eggs in a Squash | 91 |
| Eggs with Zucchini Noodles | 82 |
| Endive Bites | 18 |
| Endives, Fennel and Orange Salad | 95 |
| Falafel | 36 |
| Family Cookies | 268 |
| Family Pizza | 80 |
| Farfalle Pasta with Capers | 113 |
| Farfalle Pasta with Peas | 113 |
| Farfalle with Fresh Tomatoes | 156 |
| Favette | 292 |
| Fennel Wild Risotto | 145 |
| Fennels with Sauce | 233 |
| Feta - Avocado & Mashed Chickpea Toast | 66 |
| Feta & Quinoa Egg Muffins | 66 |
| Feta Cheese Baked in Foil | 66 |
| Feta Frittata | 67 |
| Feta Tomato Salad | 244 |
| Feta Tomato Sea Bass | 180 |
| Fettuccine with Eggplant and Green Beans | 115 |
| Fig and Prosciutto Pita Bread Pizza | 81 |
| Fig with Yogurt and Honey | 35 |
| Fig-Pecan Bites | 18 |
| Figs Pie | 277 |
| Fish Soup | 157 |
| Fish Stew | 186 |

| | |
|---|---|
| Fish Stuffed Grenadine | 56 |
| Flattened Meat Loaf | 191 |
| Flavorful Mac & Cheese | 159 |
| Focaccia Dough | 71 |
| Focaccia with Anchovies; Black Olives and Cheese | 78 |
| Focaccia with Broccoli and Sausage | 75 |
| Focaccia with Olives and Oregano | 79 |
| Focaccia with Onion, Tomatoes and Olives | 76 |
| Focaccia with Potatoes and Onion | 79 |
| Focaccia with Sage | 55 |
| Focaccia with Tomatoes, Peppers and Anchovies | 79 |
| Focaccia with Tuna and Black Olives | 75 |
| Focaccia with Tuna and Peppers | 80 |
| Fresh Stewed Broad Beans | 256 |
| Fried Artichokes | 253 |
| Fried Black Olives | 44 |
| Fried Cauliflower | 254 |
| Fried Cauliflowers | 232 |
| Fried Cod | 165 |
| Fried Cod (2nd version) | 174 |
| Fried Damselfish | 172 |
| Fried Frogs | 166 |
| Fried Milk | 43 |
| Fried Onion | 233 |
| Fried Paniccia | 56 |
| Fried Pumpkin Flowers | 43 |
| Fried Pumpkin Flowers (2nd version) | 60 |
| Fried Pumpkin Flowers (3rd version) | 233 |
| Fried Rice with Spinach, Peppers & Artichokes | 157 |
| Fried Ricotta | 42 |
| Fried Sandeel Fish | 170 |
| Fried Sausage | 227 |
| Fried Sea Scallops | 176 |
| Fried Shrimp | 173 |
| Fried Skewers | 47 |
| Fried Squid | 169 |
| Fried Squid and Shrimp | 172 |
| Fried Thistles | 254 |
| Fried Veggie Starter | 53 |
| Friselle | 48 |
| Fritters with Ham and Cheese | 47 |
| Frogs in Oil | 166 |
| Frosty Strawberry Dessert | 281 |
| Frozen Blueberry Yogurt | 19 |
| Fruit Bulgur Breakfast Bowls | 99 |
| Fusilli with Meatalls | 130 |
| Garbanzo Bean Salad | 90 |
| Garlic Bean Dip | 19 |
| Garlic Chicken Balls | 216 |
| Garlic Pesto | 264 |
| Garlic Prawn and Pea Risotto | 160 |
| Garlic Sauce | 258 |
| Garlic Sauce for Fish | 258 |
| Garlic Soup | 141 |
| Garlicky Clams | 180 |
| Garlicky Shrimp | 181 |
| Garlicky Tomato Chicken Casserole | 216 |
| Garlic-Lemon Hummus | 28 |
| Genovese Pesto | 259 |
| Genovese Sauce | 260 |
| Glazed Chicken | 217 |
| Glazed Mediterranean Puffy Fig | 277 |
| Gluten-Free Spanish Rice | 158 |
| Goose with Salt | 208 |
| Goose with Sauce | 209 |
| Gorgonzola Sweet Potato Burgers | 245 |
| Grape Sauce | 266 |
| Grapes Stew | 291 |
| Greek Almond Rounds Shortbread | 282 |
| Greek Baked Zucchini & Potatoes | 240 |
| Greek Cheesecake | 278 |
| Greek Chicken Pasta | 149 |
| Greek Eggplant Dish | 242 |
| Greek Fava | 35 |
| Greek Lima Beans Soup | 157 |
| Greek Pasta Salad | 161 |
| Greek Roasted Fish | 187 |
| Greek Salad Wraps | 38 |
| Greek Shrimp Saganaki | 35 |
| Greek Stuffed Collard Greens | 245 |
| Greek Style Mini Burger Pies | 203 |
| Greek Style Nachos | 19 |
| Greek Style Quesadillas | 67 |
| Greek Yogurt with Walnuts and Honey | 96 |
| Green Beans & Feta | 240 |

| | |
|---|---:|
| Green Beans Soup | 109 |
| Green Olive Tapenade | 31 |
| Green Olives with Garlic and Parsley | 45 |
| Green Risotto with Porcini Mushrooms | 105 |
| Green Sauce with Capers | 261 |
| Green Sauce with Pine Nuts | 261 |
| Green Tea and Vanilla Cream | 283 |
| Grilled Chicken Breasts | 214 |
| Grilled Dentex | 171 |
| Grilled Lobster | 168 |
| Grilled Mushrooms | 257 |
| Grilled Pork Chops | 227 |
| Grilled Salmon with Pineapple Salsa | 187 |
| Grilled Shrimp | 173 |
| Grilled Tempeh Sticks | 19 |
| Grilled Tuna | 167 |
| Grilled Veggie and Hummus Wrap | 246 |
| Ground Beef and Brussels Sprouts | 198 |
| Ground Lamb Koftas | 199 |
| Ground Pork and Tomatoes Soup | 158 |
| Grouper in Dressing | 170 |
| Guinea Fowl Hen with Bacon | 209 |
| Halibut Soup | 143 |
| Ham in Balsamic Vinegar | 64 |
| Ham Muffins | 86 |
| Hazelnut Cake | 294 |
| Hazelnut-Orange Olive Oil Cookies | 283 |
| Healthy Carrot & Shrimp | 181 |
| Hearty Pear and Mango Smoothie | 90 |
| Herb Polenta | 150 |
| Herb Risotto | 147 |
| Herb Sauce | 262 |
| Herbed Garlic Black Beans | 240 |
| Herbed Roasted Chicken Breasts | 216 |
| Herbed Roasted Cod | 188 |
| Herbed Wild Rice | 158 |
| Herring in Oil | 171 |
| High Protein Chicken Meatballs | 220 |
| Homemade Chicken Broth | 146 |
| Homemade Muesli | 96 |
| Homemade Pork Buns | 224 |
| Homemade Salsa | 20 |
| Homemade Vegetable Broth | 146 |
| Honey Garlic Shrimp | 181 |
| Hot Asparagus | 60 |
| Hot Focaccia with Fennel Seeds | 77 |
| Hot Pepper Dip with Cheese | 14 |
| Hot Sauce | 260 |
| Hummus | 30 |
| Hummus and Olive Pita Bread | 34 |
| Hummus and Tomato Breakfast Pittas | 96 |
| Hummus, Feta & Bell Pepper Crackers | 36 |
| Ice Cream Sandwich Dessert | 282 |
| Israeli Pasta | 160 |
| Italian Chicken Pasta | 149 |
| Italian Mac & Cheese | 159 |
| Italian Mini Meatballs | 198 |
| Italian Potatoes | 22 |
| Italian Roasted Vegetables | 27 |
| Italian Style Potato Fries | 20 |
| Italian Style Pumpkin Pie | 273 |
| Jalapeno Bacon Cheddar Soup | 146 |
| Jalapeno Chickpea Hummus | 20 |
| Kale - Mediterranean-Style | 241 |
| Kale Wraps with Apple and Chicken | 21 |
| Key Lime Pie | 285 |
| Lamb and Potatoes Stew | 204 |
| Lamb Chops with Veggies | 200 |
| Lamb Mince | 193 |
| Lamb Ribs | 192 |
| Lamb Shanks with Veggies | 200 |
| Lamb with Egg | 190 |
| Lamb with Eggs | 195 |
| Lamb with Mint | 195 |
| Lamb with Potatoes | 194 |
| Lamb with Vegetables | 204 |
| Lard Meatballs | 197 |
| Layered Dip | 21 |
| Lean Sauce | 262 |
| Leek, Potato, and Carrot Soup | 152 |
| Leeks and Eggs Muffins | 89 |
| Leg of Lamb with Potatoes | 200 |
| Legume Soup | 110 |
| Lemon Cauliflower Florets | 21 |
| Lemon Clams | 184 |
| Lemon Cream | 285 |

| | |
|---|---:|
| Lemon Mushroom Rice | 161 |
| Lemon Pudding | 268 |
| Lemon Curd Filled Almond-Lemon Cake | 289 |
| Lemon-Pepper Cucumbers | 36 |
| Lemony Orzo | 29 |
| Lemony Parmesan Salmon | 188 |
| Lentil Soup | 108 |
| Lettuce and Fennel Salad | 231 |
| Lettuce Fritters | 50 |
| Light Garlic Hummus | 21 |
| Linguine with Squid | 117 |
| Long Dessert | 268 |
| Low-Carb Chicken Curry | 217 |
| Mac & Cheese | 159 |
| Macaroni with Artichokes and Clams | 133 |
| Macaroni with Pork Ragù and Vegetables | 111 |
| Macaroni with Sausage and Ricotta | 125 |
| Macaroni with Sausage and Tomato Sauce | 125 |
| Macaroni, Bacon and Mozzarella | 133 |
| Maltagliati with Beans and Chestnuts | 139 |
| Mandarin Cream | 286 |
| Mantis Shrimp Soup | 141 |
| Maple Lemon Tempeh Cubes | 241 |
| Marinading | 265 |
| Marinate Anchovies | 13 |
| Marinated and Fried Anchovies | 167 |
| Marinated Chicken Breasts | 218 |
| Marinated Eels | 48 |
| Marinated Olives | 32 |
| Marinated Shrimp | 43 |
| Marsala's Balls | 293 |
| Mascarpone and Ricotta Stuffed Dates | 290 |
| Mayonnaise | 265 |
| Meat Dumplings | 45 |
| Meat Stuffed Zucchini | 236 |
| Meat Tortelloni with Parmesan and Truffle Sauce | 107 |
| Mediterranean Baked Salmon | 177 |
| Mediterranean Biscuits | 290 |
| Mediterranean Bread Pudding | 290 |
| Mediterranean Burrito | 67 |
| Mediterranean Cheesecake | 291 |
| Mediterranean Chicken Bites | 221 |
| Mediterranean Chickpea Salad | 238 |
| Mediterranean Crostini | 27 |
| Mediterranean Eggs | 68 |
| Mediterranean Endive Boats | 241 |
| Mediterranean Fish Fillets | 181 |
| Mediterranean Fish Tacos | 179 |
| Mediterranean Lentil Soup | 154 |
| Mediterranean Lentils and Rice | 161 |
| Mediterranean Nachos | 17 |
| Mediterranean Nachos with Hummus | 33 |
| Mediterranean Potatoes | 241 |
| Mediterranean Quiche | 246 |
| Mediterranean Stuffed Custard Pancakes | 283 |
| Mediterranean Sweet Potato | 246 |
| Mediterranean Trail Mix | 28 |
| Mediterranean Veggie Bowl | 247 |
| Melon Salad | 247 |
| Menola Fish with Onion | 175 |
| Milk Cream | 295 |
| Milk Dessert | 269 |
| Mini Frittatas | 83 |
| Mint Avocado Chilled Soup | 155 |
| Mint Beans | 255 |
| Mint Broad Beans | 256 |
| Mint Labneh | 32 |
| Minty Coconut Cream | 286 |
| Mixed Fried Vegetables | 235 |
| Mixed Grill | 174 |
| Mixed Peppers | 235 |
| Mortadella Mousse | 51 |
| Moscardini | 292 |
| Mouth-watering Beef Pie | 204 |
| Mushroom and Olives Steaks | 237 |
| Mushroom Pie | 59 |
| Mushroom Pie (2nd version) | 77 |
| Mushroom Sauce | 259 |
| Mushroom Soup | 158 |
| Mushroom Tagliatelle | 106 |
| Mushrooms Dressing | 259 |
| Mussels with Pepper | 171 |
| Mussels with Tomatoes & Wine | 182 |
| North African Peanut Stew over Cauliflower Rice | 247 |
| Oats with Raspberries | 100 |
| Olive Paste and Avocado on Rye Bread | 65 |

| | |
|---|---|
| Olives and Mozzarella Pie | 78 |
| Olives with wild Fennel | 44 |
| Onion and Bean Salad | 231 |
| Onion Focaccia | 55 |
| Onion Pie | 58 |
| Onion Sauce | 263 |
| Onion Soup | 138 |
| Orange Almond Balls | 293 |
| Orange Cake | 286 |
| Orange Celery Salad | 248 |
| Orange Cookies | 291 |
| Orange Salad | 232 |
| Orange-Glazed Apricots and Ouzo Whipped Cream | 284 |
| Oregano Pork Mix | 225 |
| Oven Backed Pasta with Cauliflower | 126 |
| Oven Sturgeon | 167 |
| Palermitana style Potato Croquettes | 42 |
| Panelle | 45 |
| Paniccia | 56 |
| Panzanella | 73 |
| Papaya Cream | 286 |
| Paprika Moussaka | 217 |
| Parmigiana Cod | 164 |
| Parsley Cheese Balls | 22 |
| Parsley Sauce | 264 |
| Passion Fruit and Spicy Couscous | 248 |
| Pasta and Potato Soup | 108 |
| Pasta with Bacon and Vegetables | 131 |
| Pasta with Beans and Sausages | 127 |
| Pasta with Cauliflowers | 127 |
| Pasta with Chickpeas | 104 |
| Pasta with Eggplant and Ricotta | 123 |
| Pasta with Fresh Pecorino and Ragù | 123 |
| Pasta with Lentils | 127 |
| Pasta with Mushrooms | 115 |
| Pasta with Olive Pesto | 124 |
| Pasta with Onion Sauce | 131 |
| Pasta with Peas | 103 |
| Pasta with Pecorino and Eggs | 127 |
| Pasta with Peppers and Tomatoes | 112 |
| Pasta with Potatoes and Zucchinis | 129 |
| Pasta with Pumpkin | 103 |
| Pasta with Royal Agaric Mushrooms, and Walnuts | 115 |
| Pasta with Sardines | 126 |
| Pasta with Scallion Sauce | 134 |
| Pasta with Sword Fish Ragù | 111 |
| Pasta with Tomato and Eggplant | 112 |
| Pasta with Vegetables | 147 |
| Peach Sorbet | 287 |
| Peanut Butter Yogurt Dip | 22 |
| Peas Soup | 138 |
| Pecorino Pasta with Sausage and Fresh Tomato | 150 |
| Penne with Basil | 122 |
| Penne with Hot Salami | 122 |
| Penne with Potatoes and Eggs | 129 |
| Penne with Ricotta and Cherry Tomatoes | 102 |
| Penne with Sausage and Olives | 128 |
| Pepper Sauce | 263 |
| Pesto Chicken Pasta | 149 |
| Pesto Fish Fillet | 182 |
| Pesto Pasta and Shrimps | 150 |
| Pesto Ravioli with Potatoes | 116 |
| Pesto Silk Blankets | 113 |
| Phyllo Bites with Cheddar | 15 |
| Pickled Turnips | 32 |
| Pie with Liver and Onions | 79 |
| Pistachio Arugula Salad | 248 |
| Pistachio Cookies | 292 |
| Pizza Genovese | 56 |
| Pizza with Cheese | 74 |
| Poached Cherries | 284 |
| Polenta | 139 |
| Polenta with Cauliflower | 139 |
| Polenta with Figs | 140 |
| Porcini Mushroom Mixed Starter | 62 |
| Pork and Greens Salad | 249 |
| Pork and Ricotta Meat Loaf | 223 |
| Pork Chop Stew | 223 |
| Pork Chops with Capers | 225 |
| Pork Cutlet | 224 |
| Pork Cutlets | 227 |
| Pork Loins | 225 |
| Pork Meat Soup | 138 |
| Pork Ribs with Wine | 224 |
| Pork Stew | 226 |

| Portuguese Style Rabbit | 210 |
| --- | --- |
| Potato and Bacon Rolls | 63 |
| Potato and Broccoli Soup | 131 |
| Potato Arancini | 40 |
| Potato Cream | 234 |
| Potato Croquettes | 236 |
| Potato Hash | 89 |
| Potato Pie | 78 |
| Potato Puree | 235 |
| Potato Soup | 110 |
| Potato Soup (2nd version) | 154 |
| Potato Spread | 16 |
| Potatoes with Balsamic Vinegar | 234 |
| Potatoes with Parmesan | 22 |
| Prosciutto e Faggioli | 225 |
| Prune Cake | 272 |
| Puff Pastry | 271 |
| Puff Pastry Roll with Roasted Vegetables | 29 |
| Pumpkin and Beans Soup | 108 |
| Pumpkin Cappelletti | 114 |
| Pumpkin Cookies | 292 |
| Pumpkin Cream | 288 |
| Pumpkin Pie | 59 |
| Pumpkin Pie Parfait | 68 |
| Pumpkin Rice | 120 |
| Puttanesca Linguine | 118 |
| Puttanesca Style Bucatini | 150 |
| Quail in a Pan | 213 |
| Quinoa & Dried Apricots and Figs | 39 |
| Quinoa and Eggs Pan | 85 |
| Quinoa and Eggs Salad | 89 |
| Quinoa Buffalo Bites | 69 |
| Quinoa Chicken Salad | 93 |
| Quinoa Muffins | 84 |
| Quinoa Salad | 250 |
| Rabbit Stew | 210 |
| Rabbit with Almonds | 210 |
| Rabbit with Mushrooms | 206 |
| Rabbit with Sauce | 209 |
| Radish Bread Bites | 23 |
| Raisin and Rum Cake | 272 |
| Raisin Quinoa Breakfast | 97 |
| Raspberries and Yogurt Smoothie | 97 |

| Ravioli with Artichoke Stuffing | 116 |
| --- | --- |
| Ravioli with Potato, Leek and Zucchini | 117 |
| Ravioli with Seafood | 117 |
| Raw Sauce | 265 |
| Raw Tomato Sauce & Brie on Linguine | 151 |
| Red Hot Pepper Bruschetta | 74 |
| Red Quinoa Peach Porridge | 275 |
| Red Sauce for Boiled Meat | 261 |
| Red Sauce with Balsamic Vinegar | 266 |
| Red Wine Risotto | 151 |
| Rice and Bean Soup | 104 |
| Rice Balls in Broth | 129 |
| Rice Burgers | 23 |
| Rice Grenadine | 55 |
| Rice with Dried Mushrooms and Anchovy Flavor | 121 |
| Rice with Eggs | 141 |
| Rice with Fennel and Ricotta | 130 |
| Rice with Milk and Chestnuts | 120 |
| Rice with Pesto | 121 |
| Rice, Tomatoes and Porcini Mushrooms | 121 |
| Ricotta and Coffee Dessert | 269 |
| Ricotta and Honey | 296 |
| Ricotta Cheese Flan | 294 |
| Ricotta Cream | 296 |
| Ricotta Croquettes | 44 |
| Ricotta Fritters | 297 |
| Ricotta Gnocchi | 102 |
| Ricotta Ramekins | 288 |
| Ricotta Toast with Strawberries | 99 |
| Rigatoni with Beans and Mushrooms | 129 |
| Rigatoni with Peppers | 104 |
| Ring Cookies | 268 |
| Risotto with Apples | 123 |
| Risotto with Red Radish | 124 |
| Risotto with Zucchini and Squid | 104 |
| Roast Asparagus | 34 |
| Roasted Baby Potatoes | 18 |
| Roasted Baby Potatoes (2nd version) | 35 |
| Roasted Brussels Sprouts And Pecans | 249 |
| Roasted Chickpeas | 23 |
| Roasted Mantis Shrimp | 170 |
| Roasted Pepper Pasta | 148 |
| Roasted Squid | 166 |

| | |
|---|---|
| Roasted Tomatoes | 46 |
| Roasted Turkey Legs | 218 |
| Roasted Veal coated in Breadcrumbs | 195 |
| Rolled Focaccia with Sausage and Ricotta | 72 |
| Rolled Pizza with Potatoes | 75 |
| Rosemary Beets | 249 |
| Rustic Pizza with Mozzarella | 73 |
| Saffron Mussels | 53 |
| Saffron Risotto | 122 |
| Salad's Spaghetti | 128 |
| Salmon Frittata | 178 |
| Salmon Kebabs | 178 |
| Salmon Stew | 180 |
| Salmon with Broccoli | 182 |
| Salmon with Potatoes | 183 |
| Salsa Fish Fillets | 183 |
| Salted Anchovies | 39 |
| Salty Almonds | 24 |
| Sardine Balls with Sauce | 177 |
| Sauce for Boiled Dishes | 261 |
| Sausage Ragout | 227 |
| Sausages in Pan | 226 |
| Sausages with Tomato | 226 |
| Sauté Catfish | 165 |
| Sautéed Garlic Spinach | 249 |
| Savory Mediterranean Popcorn | 28 |
| Scamorza Crunchy Bites | 60 |
| Scramble Eggs with Tomatoes | 100 |
| Scrambled Eggs | 85 |
| Sea Appetizer | 60 |
| Sea Bream Baked in Foil | 165 |
| Sea Salad (2nd Version) | 49 |
| Sea Urchins | 46 |
| Seafood Corn Chowder | 187 |
| Seafood Stew | 183 |
| Seasoned Bresaola | 61 |
| Seasoned Olives | 40 |
| Seasoned Squid | 168 |
| Serrano-Wrapped Plums | 37 |
| Sesame Beef | 203 |
| Shrimp Scampi | 183 |
| Shrimp with Alfredo Sauce | 179 |
| Shrimp with Mint | 172 |
| Shrimp Zoodles | 184 |
| Sicilian Style Mussels Au Gratin | 42 |
| Silverside with Tomato | 198 |
| Skordalia | 31 |
| Slow-cooked Peppers Frittata | 83 |
| Small Focaccias with Anchovies | 72 |
| Small Pizzas with Onion and Anchovy | 76 |
| Snail Sauce | 262 |
| Snipe in a Pan | 207 |
| Sour Whitebait | 53 |
| Spaghetti allo Scoglio | 102 |
| Spaghetti Flan | 119 |
| Spaghetti Primavera | 128 |
| Spaghetti Squash | 160 |
| Spaghetti with Anchovies | 140 |
| Spaghetti with Anchovies and Capers | 118 |
| Spaghetti with Artichokes | 112 |
| Spaghetti with Bacon | 121 |
| Spaghetti with Clams | 107 |
| Spaghetti with Crab Sauce | 133 |
| Spaghetti with Dried Tomatoes | 128 |
| Spaghetti with Eggplant | 140 |
| Spaghetti with Mustard and Capers Dressing | 162 |
| Spaghetti with Squid | 118 |
| Spaghetti with Squid and Mushrooms | 106 |
| Spaghetti with Squid Ink | 105 |
| Spaghetti with Tuna Sauce | 105 |
| Spaghetti with Walnuts and Asparagus | 105 |
| Spanish Green Beans | 250 |
| Spelt and Mushroom Soup | 108 |
| Spelt Pie | 59 |
| Spiced Chickpeas Bowls | 86 |
| Spicy Fettuccine | 132 |
| Spicy Gnocchi | 132 |
| Spicy Green Beans Mix | 250 |
| Spinach and Egg Breakfast Wraps | 100 |
| Spinach Cream | 259 |
| Spinach Pesto Pasta | 149 |
| Spinach Soup | 142 |
| Sponge Cake | 294 |
| Squash and Turmeric Soup | 152 |
| Squid in Dressing | 169 |
| St. Joseph's Beard | 295 |

| | | | |
|---|---|---|---|
| Starch Cream | 295 | Sweet-and-sour Crunchy Bites | 51 |
| Steak with Hummus | 201 | Sweetened Almonds | 292 |
| Steak with Yogurt Sauce | 201 | Sword Fish Carpaccio | 41 |
| Stew with Milk | 194 | Sword Fish Cutlets | 170 |
| Stewed Beans | 255 | Sword Fish in Dressing | 176 |
| Stewed Mussels & Scallops | 184 | Sword Fish Rolls | 174 |
| Stewed Okra | 250 | Sword Fish with Oil | 176 |
| Stracciatella | 106 | Sword Fish with Olives, Capers and Mint | 176 |
| Strawberries Cream | 284 | Tagliatelle au gratin with Asparagus | 118 |
| Strawberry and Rhubarb Smoothie | 92 | Tagliatelle Pie | 135 |
| Strawberry Angel Dessert | 288 | Tagliatelle with 3 Flours | 116 |
| Strawberry Phyllo Cups | 287 | Tagliatelle with Aged Ricotta | 111 |
| Strawberry Popsicle | 24 | Tagliatelle with Bean Cream | 135 |
| Strawberry Rhubarb Crunch | 288 | Tagliatelle with Boar | 102 |
| Stuffed Anchovies | 52 | Tagliatelle with Chickpeas and Dried Peppers | 130 |
| Stuffed Celery | 32 | Tagliatelle with Chickpeas and Potatoes | 119 |
| Stuffed Dried Tomatoes | 46 | Tagliatelle with Frog Sauce | 133 |
| Stuffed Lamb Leg | 194 | Tagliatelle with Mushroom Ragù | 134 |
| Stuffed Macaroni | 114 | Tagliatelle with Pesto | 115 |
| Stuffed Meatballs | 203 | Tagliatelle with Tomato and Parsley | 135 |
| Stuffed Mushrooms Porcini | 234 | Tagliatelle with Walnut Sauce | 136 |
| Stuffed Pita Breads | 97 | Tahini Pine Nuts Toast | 98 |
| Stuffed Pork Ribs | 224 | Tangerine and Pomegranate Fruit Salad | 98 |
| Stuffed Sardines | 166 | Thistle Pie | 58 |
| Stuffed Squid | 169 | Thistles in Batter | 254 |
| Stuffed Sweet Potato | 87 | Tilapia in Herb Sauce | 185 |
| Stuffed Swordfish | 184 | Tomato & Basil Bruschetta | 36 |
| Stuffed Tomatoes | 50 | Tomato and Cucumber Salad | 231 |
| Stuffed Tomatoes (2nd version) | 85 | Tomato and Eggplant Focaccia | 73 |
| Stuffed Tomatoes (3rd version) | 235 | Tomato and Guanciale Sauce | 263 |
| Sun-dried Tomatoes Oatmeal | 97 | Tomato and Onion Salad | 231 |
| Sweet and Sour Chicken | 212 | Tomato Appetizer | 57 |
| Sweet and Sour Dogfish | 175 | Tomato Finger Sandwich | 24 |
| Sweet and Sour Meatballs with Almonds | 191 | Tomato Olive Fish Fillets | 185 |
| Sweet and Sour Onions | 233 | Tomato Salad | 252 |
| Sweet and Sour Rabbit | 210 | Tomato Salsa | 264 |
| Sweet and Sour Sauce | 261 | Tomato Sauce | 260 |
| Sweet Couscous | 296 | Tomato Tabbouleh | 251 |
| Sweet Fried Ricotta | 298 | Tomato, Arugula and Feta Spaghetti | 142 |
| Sweet Potato Chips | 33 | Tomatoes and Anchovy Fritters | 63 |
| Sweet Potato Fries | 24 | Tomatoes Oatmeal | 84 |
| Sweet Potato Tart | 97 | Tortelli with Apple Filling | 137 |
| Sweet Salami | 271 | Tortelloni with Ricotta and Parsley | 137 |

| | |
|---|---|
| Tortiglioni with Peppers and Guanciale | 119 |
| Traditional Mediterranean Hummus | 25 |
| Truffle Cannelloni | 101 |
| Tuna Bottarga | 40 |
| Tuna Carpaccio | 41 |
| Tuna Cobbler | 188 |
| Tuna Melts | 189 |
| Tuna Risotto | 143 |
| Tuna Roll | 63 |
| Tuna Salad | 88 |
| Tuna Salad in Lettuce Cups | 25 |
| Tuna Starter | 61 |
| Tuna Tapas and Avocado | 187 |
| Tuna Whole Wheat Pasta | 143 |
| Tuna with Olives | 185 |
| Turkey Meatball and Ditalini Soup | 154 |
| Turkey with Ham and Cheese | 208 |
| Turkish Marinated Chicken | 220 |
| Turkish Salad | 252 |
| Turkish-Spiced Nuts | 28 |
| Turmeric Crunchy Chickpeas | 29 |
| Tzatziki | 25 |
| Vanilla Cake | 289 |
| Veal Cutlet with Pecorino | 196 |
| Veal Meatballs with Chocolate | 192 |
| Veal Mince with Peas | 193 |
| Veal Roast with Lemon | 190 |
| Veal Rolls with Raisins and Pine Nuts | 196 |
| Veal Rolls with Sauce | 196 |
| Veal with Capers | 197 |
| Vegan Olive Pasta | 148 |
| Vegetable Chicken Wraps | 34 |
| Vegetable Tagliatelle | 130 |
| Vegetable Timbale | 47 |
| Veggie Bowls | 229 |
| Veggie Casserole | 237 |
| Veggie Fritters | 62 |
| Veggie Quiche | 88 |
| Vermicelli with Clams | 107 |
| Walnut and Freekeh Pilaf | 26 |
| Walnut and Red Pepper Spread | 31 |
| Walnut Cream | 259 |
| Walnut-Feta Yogurt Dip | 37 |
| Walnuts Yogurt Dip | 275 |
| Walnuts Yogurt Mix | 99 |
| Watermelon "Pizza" | 85 |
| Watermelon Cream | 289 |
| Watermelon-Strawberry Rosewater Yogurt | 285 |
| Wheat Berry Burgers | 25 |
| Whitebait Flat Bread | 55 |
| Whole Wheat Pasta with Tuna | 148 |
| Whole-Grain Lavash Chips | 26 |
| Wrapped Plums | 252 |
| Yellow Melon Granita | 298 |
| Yogurt Dip | 275 |
| Zaatar Fries | 34 |
| Zucchini and Egg Soup | 110 |
| Zucchini and Eggplant Fritters | 63 |
| Zucchini and Potato Soup | 109 |
| Zucchini and Pumpkin Flowers Soup | 126 |
| Zucchini Chips | 26 |
| Zucchini Lasagna | 251 |
| Zucchini Noodles | 143 |
| Zucchini Pie | 49 |
| Zucchini-Eggplant Gratin | 252 |

Made in the USA
Columbia, SC
09 February 2022